SAUDI BUSINESS
AND LABOR LAW

SAUDI BUSINESS AND LABOR LAW

Its interpretation and application

Second Edition

Alison Lerrick, AB Barnard College, JD Harvard Law School, PhD Princeton University

Q. Javed Mian, BA, LLB University of Punjab, LLM University of Miami

Graham & Trotman

A member of the Kluwer Academic Publishers Group

First published in 1982

Second Edition
Published in 1987 by

Graham & Trotman Ltd.   Kluwer Inc
Sterling House   101 Philip Drive
66 Wilton Road   Assinippi Park
London SW1V 1DE   Norwell, MA 02061 USA

© A. Lerrick and Q.J. Mian 1987

Lerrick, A.
  Saudi business and Labor Law: its
  interpretation and application——2nd ed.
  1. Commercial law——Saudi Arabia
  I. Title II. Mian, Q.J.
  345.3'8067   [LAW]

ISBN 0–86010–573–3

LCCCN 86–670–1767

Typeset in Great Britain by Eastern Press, London and Reading
Printed and bound in Great Britain by The Alden Press, Oxford

Contents

CONTENTS

CHAPTER 6   THE DIYAH   330

APPENDICES 1–51

It should be noted that the following appendices are translated from the Arabic texts. In all cases, the Arabic original is the governing text.

CONTENTS

Authors' Preface

The second edition of this work is an entirely revised and updated version of the first edition. It reflects various developments in Saudi regulatory law that have occurred since the original publication date. Most notably, the chapter on Arbitration is completely new in view of the issue of the 1983 Arbitration Regulations and the 1985 Implementing Rules thereunder. In addition, the chapter on the Limited Liability Company has been substantially developed in order to provide detailed guidelines for practitioners. The chapter on Judicial Organization has been revised to reflect recent developments and, in particular, to include references to the new Civil Rights Rules relating to enforcement of private rights. Finally, a substantial number (56) of appendixes containing administrative and regulatory materials have been added to the revised edition for the reference and convenience of readers.

An index of all the regulatory acts cited in the book has also been prepared for their convenience.

The reader will note that the second edition contains an increased number of references to Islamic law materials. Such materials are fundamental and integral to Saudi law. Nonetheless, this work concentrates on the various regulatory or administrative acts applicable to business transactions.[1]

Similarly, the reader should be aware that references to judicial decisions are given for the purpose of gaining insight into the functioning of the Saudi legal system, since such decisions do not constitute "case law" as understood in common law systems. Furthermore, since judicial decisions are not generally published, various opinions of administrative or judicial authorities have been used to supplement black letter regulatory materials. For this reason, it is at times difficult to express a decisive opinion on certain legal points.

The authors request the reader's indulgence with regard to their use of both the Gregorian and hijrah calendars in the various citations. In order to orient those persons unfamiliar with the hijrah calendar, let it be stated that the hijrah calendar is a lunar, rather than a solar calendar.

Finally, the reader's attention is called to the fact that, although this work is oriented to the needs of the practising lawyer, it speaks as of its

---

[1] For an understanding of the sources of Saudi regulatory law, the reader is referred generally to the Council of Ministers Regulations, translated in Appendix 1.

date and changes in the Saudi legal system, as in any other legal system, may occur suddenly. Consequently the advice of local counsel should be sought with respect to specific issues.

Alison Lerrick
Q. Javed Mian
June 1986

Foreword

This book on "Saudi Business and Labor Law—Its Interpretation and Application" is another valuable addition to the material available on the laws and regulations of Saudi Arabia. As the book covers in detail some of the aspects of the laws and regulations of special relevance to commercial and business activities, I consider it to be an extremely useful reference source, both to businessmen as well as to practising lawyers.

During my past experience as Secretary-General of the Foreign Capital Investment Committee and at present, I have observed that foreign companies are eager to benefit from the business opportunities in the Kingdom, but many of these companies lack knowledge of the rules and procedures relating to their business activities. This lack of knowledge results in many difficulties for these companies and inconvenience to government authorities, and therefore it is essential that foreign companies and businessmen familiarize themselves with the procedures and rules before undertaking business activities in the Kingdom.

This book provides answers to most of the legal questions that businessmen face every day in the Kingdom. It is a book written by practising lawyers with years of practical experience and knowledge of the legal system of the Kingdom and covers such important areas as the Companies Regulations, the Labor Regulations, Agency Regulations and related aspects, taxation, licensing, registration and other commercial regulations; and of the judicial system and its different methods of solving disputes in the business community. Therefore the book covers broadly most of the legal topics and issues of interest to businessmen with in-depth coverage of those areas and aspects of greater importance.

The areas of in-depth discussion are the employment contract and entitlements, termination, and labor disputes under the labor law; issues and definitions relating to the different types of commercial agency and the basis of their operation and limitations; all relevant aspects of the formation, registration and functioning of the limited liability company which is the form suitable for foreign investors and joint venture projects; the arbitration procedure involving disputes with the public sector, the procedure involving disputes in the private sector and the manner of the enforcement of arbitration awards; and finally a very detailed discussion of the judicial organization and its functioning.

This is a brief outline of the more important aspects and issues of the laws and regulations of Saudi Arabia in relation to Saudi business, covered in the book. They are all subjects about which persons or companies involved in business activities should have a sound understanding, and I therefore commend this book to the business community.

Mubarak Al-Khafrah
former Secretary General
Foreign Capital Investment Committee
Ministry of Industry and Electricity

Tables of Legislation

REGULATIONS

TABLES OF LEGISLATION

ROYAL LEGISLATION

RESOLUTIONS, DECISIONS, CIRCULARS, LETTERS

Council of Ministers

RULES

DECISIONS

AGREEMENTS AND CONVENTIONS

Chapter 1
AGENCY

I. The Agent

This chapter deals with the two regulatory forms of "agency", "commercial agency", governed by the Commercial Agencies Regulations,[1] and "services agency", governed by the Regulations Governing the Relationship between the Foreign Contractor and its Saudi Agent ["Services Agents Regulations"],[2] the latter of which apply solely to public sector contracts. Both the commercial agent and the services agent are creatures of regulation. Although called agents, they are, generally, independent contractors. The same agent may act as both commercial and services agent for the same "principal". However, in view of practical considerations and registration procedures, the parties will in such cases enter into separate agreements covering these different aspects of their relationship.

A. BROKER OR INTERMEDIARY DISTINGUISHED

The only regulatory definition of a "broker" is found in the Commercial Court Regulations, which define a "broker" as a person who "acts as an intermediary between a buyer and a seller to conclude a sale for a fee."[3] Brokers and intermediaries, with respect to the public sector, are subject to a different legal treatment from the regulatory agents. Brokerage is

---

[1] Royal Decree No. 11 (1962), *as amended by* Royal Decrees Nos. M/5 (11/6/1389), M/8 (30/3/1393), & M/32 (10/8/1400).

[2] Royal Decree No. M/2 (1978).

[3] High Order No. 32, art. 30 (1931) (repealed in part). The rights, duties, and fees of brokers are governed by established usage and custom. *Id.* art. 31. Since a broker is defined as an "intermediary" and since brokers and intermediaries are subject to the same legal rules, the term "brokerage" will at times be employed in this chapter in preference to the more literal translation of the Arabic word "wisātah" ("mediation") as being more expressive of the meaning in English.

prohibited with respect to government contracts, while the prohibition of agency is as a rule limited to arms contracts.[4] The main prohibition of brokerage in the public sector is contained in article 2 of the Tenders and Auctions Regulations ["Old Tender Regulations"], which prohibits brokerage in contracts "for the sale of materials that are usually sold to the Government alone, such as locomotives, railroad cars, telephones, arms, and ammunition, whether or not the contract is concluded by means of tender offer."[5]

The prohibition of brokerage provided in article 2 was officially interpreted by the Deputy Minister of Finance and National Economy, who explained that

> the prohibition of brokerage in contracting for the procurement of materials mentioned in article 2 . . . means that it is prohibited for the Government to purchase materials through an intermediary, that is, no party whatsoever may act as intermediary between the producer of such materials and the Government. In other words, the contract for the sale of such materials must be concluded between the Government and the producer thereof. . . . Only companies producing the material subject to tender, whether public or restricted, may submit bids. If any other person submits a bid, such bid will be deemed null.[6]

Therefore, the prohibition of brokerage seemed restricted to contracts for the procurement of materials. However, this interpretation proved too narrow; the prohibition was subsequently reinterpreted to cover any kind of work to be executed coming within the purview of the Old Tender Regulations.[7] The policy concern underlying the prohibition of brokerage has been expressed as the Government's desire to check price increases. Council of Ministers Resolution No. 208 provides

> [a]s the Government of the Kingdom of Saudi Arabia has embarked on the implementation of an ambitious development program aimed at furthering the status and prosperity of its people, international companies have been invited from friendly countries to participate in

---

[4] *See generally* pp. 3–4 *infra.*

[5] Royal Decree No. M/6, art. 2 (1966) (provisions inconsistent with present tender regulations repealed 1977) (but making an exception for brokered bids approved by President of Council of Ministers in the public interest).

[6] Deputy Minister of Fin. & Nat'l Econ. Letter No. 5262/12 (2/5/1387). It may be noted, however, that government purchases of goods or materials may be made through authorized representatives of producers or manufacturers.

[7] *See, e.g.,* Minister of Fin. & Nat'l Econ. Circular No. 9818/4/1 (7/8/1388) (all contracts to which Old Tender Regulations apply must include contractor's representation that no commission was paid to any broker or intermediary for the purpose of securing the contract) (if proved otherwise, the government authority client may deduct an amount equivalent to such commission from payments to the contractor).

the implementation of this program as the Government believes in international cooperation and the growth of friendly relations between populations by means of the furtherance of mutual interests.

The Kingdom of Saudi Arabia has recently noticed that the costs of its program have increased constantly and appreciably exceeding all limits and inconsistent with international and domestic inflation, despite the intensive efforts of the Government to create a proper climate for its citizens together with operating companies with an aim to achieve productive and fruitful work.

This has recently obliged the Government to cancel tenders of projects which are vital to the interests and welfare of the people of this country. An investigation into the reasons resulting in this state of affairs indicates the following

.   .   .   .

> A number of middlemen have convinced some companies that they can provide them with work in the country by means of their personal influence, regardless of the costs of the items [quoted by such companies].

.   .   .   .

Therefore, the Government of Saudi Arabia wishes to announce that it will not allow these or similar things to obstruct the development march of the country or to divert it, and while it has been working actively to fulfill its obligations to its people, it affirms its continuous determination to preserve their wealth and savings.

Consequently, the Council of Ministers has adopted the following resolution

.   .   .   .

Fifth: Companies are prohibited from seeking the help of brokers and intermediaries, but are allowed to seek the assistance of Saudi businessmen as agents in accordance with rules that will be issued by the Council of Ministers to regulate the relationship between the foreign contractor and its Saudi agent.[8]

It will be noted that, even though Resolution No. 208 and other applicable regulatory rules distinguish between brokers and agents, services agents are expressly prohibited from carrying out brokerage activities. Article 10 of the Services Agents Regulations provides that "the purpose of agency may not be resorting to the utilization of influence or mediation."

Until 1975, the use of commercial agents, as contrasted with brokers and intermediaries, was not prohibited with respect to the sale of arms and military equipment to the Saudi Government. In that year, Council of Ministers Resolution No. 1275 was issued prohibiting the payment of

---

[8] Resolution No. 208 (9/3/1397).

3

commissions on such sales to commercial agents and representatives in addition to brokers and intermediaries. It provides

(i) [n]o firm holding a contract with the Saudi Government for the supply of arms or [military] equipment required by the Saudi Government may pay any sum as a commission to any agent, intermediary, sales representative, or broker. [This prohibition] shall apply regardless of the nationality of the firm or the nationality of the intermediary, sales agent, representative or broker and whether the contract was concluded directly between the Saudi Government and the firm or through a third-party state. No recognition is accorded to any commission agreement previously concluded by any such firm with any party, and such agreement shall have no validity vis-à-vis the Saudi Government.

(ii) If among the foreign firms mentioned in paragraph (i) there are any that are obligated under commission agreements that they have made, they shall stop payment of the commissions due after having been warned by this Resolution and deduct the amounts of the commission from the total value of the contract in favor of the Saudi Government.[9]

This rule is reiterated in the Regulations for the Procurement of Government Purchases and Execution of its Projects and Works ["Tender Regulations"].[10] Article 3(k) provides that "arms shall be procured by means of direct agreement with the producing companies." In addition, article 4 of the Services Agents Regulations provides that "agency is not permitted in armament contracts and services related thereto."[11]

In summary, the use of brokers, intermediaries, or other middlemen is prohibited with respect to all public sector contracts, whether supply or service contracts. This prohibition applies to any subcontractors, suppliers, consultants, agents, employees, and other parties with respect to any government contract, whether such parties are involved in such contracts directly or indirectly and regardless of their nationality. However, it will be noted that no such prohibition exists with respect to the private sector of the Kingdom.

B. FOREIGN AGENT OR CONSULTANT

While the preceding rules of Saudi law are clear, certain ambiguities exist with respect to the territorial scope of the ban on brokerage and/or

[9] Resolution No. 1275 (Sept. 17, 1975).

[10] Royal Decree No. M/14 (1977).

[11] However, the use of a services agent with respect to contracts for the construction, installation, or maintenance of military equipment or certain defense executory projects may be required or permitted, as determined by the Ministry of Defense and Aviation on a case-by-case basis.

agency. For example, a problem may arise if a nonSaudi natural or juristic person located outside the Kingdom and acting as an intermediary, broker, promoter, representative, consultant, or agent has entered into an agreement, in consideration of a certain compensation, with a foreign contractor having obtained or seeking to obtain a contract with the Saudi Government or one of its agencies or instrumentalities. Such a person or entity may have agreed to assist the contractor in obtaining projects in the Kingdom, directly or indirectly, including by the mere provision of introductions which may eventually result in the contractor's obtaining Saudi public sector contracts. In such a case, the parties may have entered into their agreement outside the Kingdom, arranged for compensation to be paid outside the Kingdom, and provided that their agreement and the services to be performed thereunder, whether inside or outside Saudi Arabia, will be governed by the laws of a jurisdiction other than Saudi Arabia. Typically, the services to be performed will be among the services generally performed by and restricted by Saudi law to Saudi commercial or services agents. It has been maintained that such agreements are "private agreements" between the parties outside the scope of Saudi law and beyond the reach of Saudi jurisdiction. However, the position of Saudi authorities is that any matters relating to Saudi government contracts are subject generally to Saudi law and that regulatory provisions relating to agents, brokers, and intermediaries are applicable to any such intermediaries, whether inside or outside Saudi Arabia. It may also be observed that article 1 of the Services Agents Regulations provides that the Regulations apply to any "foreign contractor" entering into a contract with the Saudi Government and makes no territorial limitation on their scope. In addition, article 2 makes the Regulations applicable to all "contracts" entered into between a foreign contractor and the Saudi Government. Consequently, both the foreign contractor and the "contract" are subject to the Regulations. Therefore, any agents, brokers, intermediaries, promoters, representatives, or consultants, wherever located, are also subject to the relevant regulatory restrictions. Notably, article 3 of the Services Agents Regulations prohibits the contractor from appointing a nonSaudi as its agent. Furthermore, neither article 2 of the Old Tender Regulations nor Council of Ministers Resolutions No. 1275 and No. 208 contemplate any exception for foreign brokers or brokerage agreements entered into outside the Kingdom. Therefore the prohibitions expressed therein may also be viewed as extraterritorial in scope. Thus, any payment of a commission or fee to a promoter, representative, agent, or consultant other than a Saudi agent within the meaning of Saudi regulations constitutes a violation of Saudi law and the public policy against burdening public sector contracts with payments to middlemen.[12] However, a distinction must be drawn

---

[12] Payments to brokers or intermediaries are also unlawful under art. 10 of the Services Agents Regs.

between illusory services purported to be provided by "agents" or other intermediaries and legitimate professional services. There is no prohibition of the provision of such services by a nonSaudi natural or juristic person located outside the Kingdom with respect to Saudi public sector projects.[13] However, in all cases, regardless of the language the parties choose to describe their relationship and activities, their agreement will be interpreted according to its substance and the actual intent of the parties, and a Saudi court will distinguish genuine professional services from other services which resemble brokerage or services required to be performed by agents in Saudi Arabia.[14]

C. SPONSOR

Sponsorship is a legal relationship supplementing various other relationships generally arising out of employment or business transactions. Generally speaking, nonSaudi natural persons not entitled to national treatment may not enter the Kingdom unless they have a local sponsor. The Arabic word "kafīl", which is translated as "sponsor" in this specific context, means generally a "guarantor" or "surety".[15] A sponsor obtains entry visas for sponsored persons. Conversely, the person, whether natural or juristic, under whose name an entry visa is issued to a foreigner is considered that person's sponsor. The responsibilities and duties of a sponsor, in addition to established general practice, will also depend on the nature of the relationship between the parties. Likewise, the responsibilities and duties of a sponsor vis-à-vis third parties, including the Government, are determined to a great extent by the facts of each individual case. The following are the basic sponsorship situations in Saudi Arabia.

Employment

In order to work in the Kingdom, nonSaudi persons must be under the sponsorship of their actual employers. The sponsoring employer, however, is not required to be a Saudi natural or juristic person but may be a foreign person or entity duly licensed or permitted to carry on activities in Saudi

---

[13] If such professional services are to be provided in whole or in part in Saudi Arabia, the consultant must obtain the requisite permission from the Ministry of Commerce and/or other competent authorities.

[14] Since any agreement providing for services in violation of Saudi law will be unenforceable in Saudi Arabia, a foreign judgment or award enforcing an agreement between a contractor and an intermediary will not be enforced by Saudi authorities, regardless of whether either party has performed thereunder. Even assuming that the agreement is not illegal on its face, any claim for payment in consideration of acts contrary to law or public policy will be unenforceable under Saudi law.

[15] See generally Residence Regs., High Royal Approval No. 17I2/25/1337, art. 5(d)(1371) (sponsor guarantees sponsored person's undertakings, obligations, and reexit).

Arabia. Regardless of the form of license or permission, such a person or entity may sponsor expatriate employees required for its business purposes.[16] In addition, Saudi and nonSaudi natural persons of certain statuses are also permitted to apply for and obtain entry visas for domestic servants and to sponsor such persons.

Personal relationships

Saudi natural persons and certain categories of nonSaudi natural persons legally present in the Kingdom may obtain visit visas for and sponsor nonSaudi visitors. However, the policy of the Ministry of the Interior is somewhat restrictive with respect to granting such visas requested by nonSaudi natural persons. Such visas are generally granted only with respect to family members, such as a spouse, children, or parents.

Business relationships

In the case where a business relationship or opportunity is proposed or under study, persons representing a foreign entity may need to visit the Kingdom to perform business analyses, market evaluations, feasibility studies, to establish contacts, and to carry on negotiations. In the case of the formation and/or establishment of a new entity in Saudi Arabia and/or the obtaining of a license or other relevant approval, procedures generally take some time. Until the foreign entity is registered or licensed or the company under formation may legally conduct business on its own, the representatives of the foreign entity, when visiting Saudi Arabia, must be under the sponsorship of a Saudi person or another entity registered or licensed in Saudi Arabia. The sponsor is often a Saudi company or a sole proprietorship which may be a future partner, services or commercial agent, customer or client. Upon registration or obtention of the relevant license, a foreign entity will not need a sponsor and may itself sponsor its, directors and employees, and visiting businessmen.

A commercial agent or distributor normally sponsors the technical staff of the foreign sellers it represents who are required to come to Saudi Arabia periodically to render technical services to the agent or distributor or to customers. An agent or distributor may also sponsor other representatives of such foreign sellers. Similarly, a services agent usually sponsors the staff of a foreign contractor it represents during the period of tendering for and negotiating public sector contracts until such time as the contract is signed and the contractor obtains a temporary license to execute the project. At this point, the contractor itself is permitted to sponsor its officers, representatives, and employees.

---

[16] However, the number of expatriate employees permitted to be imported may be limited by governmental authorities according to the entity's business needs. *See, e.g.,* p. 41 and note 111, *infra.*

"Sponsorship agreement" distinguished

Certain foreign entities unfamiliar with Saudi law enter into "sponsorship agreements" with Saudi business enterprises under the misapprehension that such arrangements will afford them a legal presence in the Kingdom in order to carry out business activities in the private or public sector without the need to obtain governmental authorization. Such entities then proceed to bid for and perform contracts, generally in the name of their sponsors, in disregard of the fact that they are carrying on business in violation of Saudi law. Such a contractual "business sponsorship" will not normally afford a foreign enterprise a legal presence in the Kingdom. Business enterprises are generally required to be licensed and/or registered.[17] The fact that such "sponsorship agreements" are not required to be submitted to, approved by, or registered with any governmental authority will not rectify the foreign company's legal situation.[18] The general principle of Saudi law is that nonSaudis may not operate in the private sector without having obtained commercial registration, after fulfilling the procedures applicable to the investment of foreign capital.[19] NonSaudi professionals are required to obtain the appropriate license before operating within the Kingdom.

II. Commercial Agent

A. DIRECT SALES

Saudi law permits a seller located outside Saudi Arabia to make direct sales to purchasers within Saudi Arabia, both in the public and private

---

[17] Art. 228 of the Companies Regs., Royal Decree No. M/6 (1965), *as amended by* Royal Decrees Nos. M/5 (12/3/1387), M/23 (28/6/1402) & M/46 (4/7/1405) provides

[f]oreign companies may not establish branches, agencies or offices to represent them, nor may they issue securities or offer them for subscription or sale within the Kingdom except with permission from the Minister of Commerce and Industry. Such branches, agencies, or offices shall be subject to the regulations in force within the Kingdom applicable to the particular activity in which they engage.

If such branch, agency or office conducts business before fulfilling the requirements specified in these or other regulations, the persons who may have conducted such business shall be held personally and jointly responsible therefor.

[18] Furthermore, certification of such an agreement by a Saudi Chamber of Commerce is without legal effect with respect to such fundamental defect. Certification or other attestation only attests to the genuineness of signatures, inasmuch as business enterprises registered or licensed in Saudi Arabia are required to belong to a Chamber of Commerce and signatures of their authorized representatives are kept on file in order to be compared with signatures of such persons on documents presented to the Chamber of Commerce. If the signature is genuine, the Chamber of Commerce will certify the document without regard for its substance.

[19] *See generally* pp. 62–69 *infra.* For public sector projects *see* pp. 58–59 *infra.*

sectors, without imposing on such a seller any requirement of having local representation.[20] In contrast, Fonco[21] may not open a sales office in the Kingdom or send a representative there to solicit orders. Furthermore, Saudi law does not permit a foreign seller to perform customs clearance of its goods, whether in its own name or in the name of the customer, or to transport or store them in the Kingdom. Even though Fonco, if the sales agreement requires it to fulfill certain warranties or provide technical services, may send technical or advisory personnel to Saudi Arabia under the sponsorship of a customer, it may do so only on a temporary or periodical basis. If performed on a permanent or stable basis or on a large scale, the provision of technical services in the Kingdom is subject to governmental licensing. This rule applies regardless of the manner of payment of the services fee and whether or not the fee is included in the price of the goods.

The disadvantages to a Fonco desiring to make more than an occasional direct sale to the Kingdom are obvious. Consequently, if Fonco wishes to take full advantage of the Saudi market, its sole option is to contract for representation by a local Saudi commercial agent or distributor.

B. DEFINITIONS

This section addresses the more significant terminology in the area of Saudi commercial agency law.

1. Trade/commerce

The Arabic adjective used to describe both commercial, as contrasted with professional,[22] activity and trade is "tijārī". The Commercial Court

[20] The view expressed by some commentators that goods may not be sold to Saudi Arabia except through a local agent or distributor is incorrect. *See, e.g.*, Ministry of Commerce Model Commercial Agency or Distribution Agreement, art. 10 (covering direct sales) (translated in Appendix 2). Nonetheless, foreign sellers are subject to Saudi legal constraints relating to the identity of the seller and the nature of the goods. *See, e.g.*, Boycott of Israel Regs., Royal Decree No. 28 (1962), *as amended by* Royal Decree No. M/8 (26/5/1404); Arms & Ammunition Regs., Royal Decree No. M/8 (1981). Sales to the public sector are regulated by the Tender Regs., their implementing rules, and other applicable regulatory law. With respect to goods and materials required by public sector customers for which Saudi agents or distributors exist, the general policy is to procure such items from such Saudi agents or distributors. Other goods and materials are normally procured directly from the manufacturer or other seller.
[21] "Fonco" is an entity organized under the laws of a jurisdiction other than Saudi Arabia, not having its main office in the Kingdom, and, as a rule, not having any Saudi equity participation. Any Fonco having such Saudi participation is outside the scope of this chapter. *See also* note 24 *infra*.
[22] Saudi law recognizes the liberal professions as generally defined by civilized nations. For certain applicable regulations, see p. 69 n. 36 *infra*.

Regulations provide the following nonexclusive definition of "commercial activities"

(*a*) any purchase of goods or produce, such as foodstuffs and the like, for resale or after manufacture or processing;

(*b*) any contract or commitment to supply items or services relating to commission trade or land or sea transport or relating to commercial premises and offices and auction rooms;

(*c*) any activities relating to drafts of any kind, money-changing, and brokerage;

(*d*) all contracts and undertakings entered into by traders, retailers, brokers, money-changers, and the various categories of agents, and all contracts for the construction of buildings and the like if the contractor undertakes to supply the required materials and tools;

(*e*) any operation relating to the construction, repair, sale, or purchase locally and abroad of commercial or noncommercial sailing vessels, or any act relating to the chartering or leasing of the same, or the sale or purchase of machinery, tools, and fittings thereof, the wages of their workmen and salaries of the crew and servants; any loan or borrowing made against the vessel or its cargo and all insurance policies relating thereto and contracts relating to maritime commerce.[23]

It is apparent that the preceding list includes activities commonly regarded as trade and/or commerce. With respect to Saudi nationals and Saucos,[24] it is irrelevant, from a legal standpoint, to distinguish between

---

[23] High Order No. 32, art. 2. It will be noted that, under the definition of art. 2, some isolated acts are deemed "commercial", while other acts are required to be performed on a repetitive and organized basis in order to receive that qualification. *Cf.* Commercial Register Regs., Royal Order No. 21/1/4470, art. 13 (1955) (defining a "person engaged in commercial activities" for purposes of such regulations as "any person making a career of the purchase of personal property for the purpose of resale or leasing or contractors of any nature, brokers, commission agents, commercial agents and intermediaries of any nature, money-changers, importers, exporters, persons engaged in banking activities and sea, land, or air transportation, and generally any person engaged in the practice of a commercial activity or who is deemed a person engaged in commercial activities by virtue of the provisions of regulations of the Kingdom"); Ministry of Fin. Resolution No. 340, art. 10 (May 8, 1951) (Income Tax Regs. Implementing Rules) (defining same as any person engaged in commercial activities or making a career thereof in accordance with Commercial Court Regs.).

[24] Nationals of other states treated as Saudi nationals in the relevant respects, whether by virtue of international agreements or otherwise, will be included in the term "Saudi national". For purposes of discussion, all Saudi nationals are assumed to be males. "Sauco" is a company wholly owned by Saudi natural or juristic persons, formed under the laws of Saudi Arabia, and having its main office in the Kingdom. Both a sole proprietorship, which is the legal form under which Saudi individuals engage in commercial activities and which is not a company under Saudi law, and any entity other than a Sauco entitled to national treatment in the relevant respects, whether by virtue of international agreement or otherwise, will be regarded as a Sauco for purposes of this work.

the two terms, since Saudi law permits any such persons, on compliance with the necessary formalities, to engage in both trade and other forms of commerce. In contrast, although nonSaudi natural persons and Foncos having complied with the necessary formalities are permitted to carry on certain commercial activities in the Kingdom,[25] Saudi law generally bars such persons and any Mixco[26] in which they participate from engaging in trade.[27] It thus becomes of interest to identify that subclass of commercial activities which Saudi law regards as "trade".[28] Although no comprehensive official definition has issued, "trade" under Saudi law may be defined generally as the buying for resale, selling, or bartering of goods, including certain isolated transactions,[29] without adding significant value thereto or converting them into another form or part of another object by the application of technology, materials, and/or labor. In contrast, trade excludes, *inter alia*, the production, manufacturing, and processing of goods, services such as, by way of example, the transportation of persons and of goods, and activities such as construction, installation, maintenance, assembling and operation.[30] Nonetheless, Saudi regulatory law reserves certain commercial nontrade activities to Saudi nationals and Saucos. Such

[25] In all cases, in order to engage in permitted commercial activities, nonSaudis must establish a legal commercial presence in the Kingdom.

[26] "Mixco" is a company owned by both Saudi and nonSaudi natural or juristic persons regardless of their respective percentages of equity participation, formed under the laws of Saudi Arabia, and having its main office in the Kingdom.

[27] Thus, even though the nationals of Bahrain, Kuwait, and Qatar are treated as Saudi nationals for purposes of Saudi tax law (*see* Royal Decrees Nos. 10236 & 10237 (11/17/1956), Royal Decree No. 800 (8/16/1956), Royal Decree No. 4899 (12/19/1957)), they are barred from engaging in other than retail trade and from acting as importers and commercial agents; Deputy Prime Minister Letter No. 5/M/1539, para. 2 (17/1/1398). *But see* Council of Ministers Resolution No. 3 (1/1/1398) (making exception for limited number of foreigners with respect to activities potentially or actually including trade).

[28] Alternatively, the distinction between those activities generally restricted to Saudis and the activities not so restricted may be conceptualized as drawn between "purely commercial operations" and "commercial-industrial operations". *See, e.g.*, Statement of Dr. Soliman al-Solaim, Minister of Commerce, *Imports by Foreign Companies* [hereinafter *cited as* Solaim Statement], Saudi Econ. Survey, Jan. 27, 1982, at 4, col. 1 ("purely commercial operations" such as importation, wholesale trade, and commercial agency restricted to Saudis distinguishable from "commercial-industrial activities" serving economic development plans).

[29] For example, goods entering the Kingdom for the purpose of exhibitions, fairs, or other demonstrations are generally required to be reexported and may not be sold locally in the absence of special permission.

[30] The Commercial Court Regulations specifically exclude from the scope of commercial activities the sale of agricultural produce by a landowner or farmer, the sale of any real property, and the purchase of any real or personal property for personal use, as opposed to sale or rental. Since commercial activities as set forth in those regulations are broader than trade, exclusion of the preceding activities from the sphere of commercial activities necessarily excludes them from the scope of their subclass, trade. Commercial Court Regs., art. 3 (applicable to local produce). *See also* Commercial Agencies Regs. Implementing Rules, Minister of Commerce Resolution No. 1897, art. 8(8) (24/5/1401) (commercial agency applicable to agricultural produce).

activities include the transportation of persons by motor vehicle[31] and the act of importing.[32] In the absence of an authoritative definition, the meaning given to the term "trade" in Saudi Arabia may be most easily derived from the study of practical illustrations.

(a) Fonco or Mixco enters into a contract to construct and install a television station in the Kingdom. The contractor is also required by the client to supply[33] ten videotape sets for the sole purpose of providing

[31] *See, e.g.,* Rules of Procedures and Conditions of Granting Licenses to Engage in the Activity of Car Rental, Minister of Communications Resolution No. 33, art. 2(1)–(2) (4/2/1404) (applicant must be Saudi national or 100% Saudi-owned company); Rules of Procedures and Conditions of Granting Licenses to Engage in the Activity of Transporting Passengers in Hired Cars and Buses between the Cities of the Kingdom and Other States, Minister of Communications Resolution No. 51, arts. 2(1), (5) (notified 1/3/1404) (same).

[32] In private letter rulings and public statements, the Ministry of Commerce has expressed its position that the "importing" of goods and raw materials for public and private sector projects is prohibited to Foncos having a presence in the Kingdom and also to Mixcos in their own name. *Cf.* Ministry of Commerce Model Commercial Agency or Distribution Agreement (reciting that importing is prohibited to nonSaudis) (translated in Appendix 2). The prohibition of importing applies whether the goods are to be imported pursuant to a supply contract, a supply and installation contract, or as part of construction, operation, or maintenance contract. The Minister of Commerce has interpreted the term "supply" as appearing in certain public sector contracts as "the provision of [materials] at the project site and not the importing thereof." *See, e.g.,* Solaim Statement, at 4, col. 2. There is therefore a clear distinction between "supply" (tawrîd), as construed to mean "provision", and "importing" (istîrâd). Thus, one Fonco which obtained a government contract for the "supply" of materials was refused a temporary license by the Ministry of Commerce on the grounds that such license could not be granted for "importing" and that the government purchaser could directly import its requirements. This result obtained because the granting of such a licence would result in Fonco's being present in the Kingdom. Hence, its provision of such materials would involve "importing", as contrasted with the "export" of such items from abroad by a foreign seller not present in the Kingdom. It will be noted that, even though Fonco is not permitted to "import", there is no restriction on its "export" from outside the Kingdom pursuant to supply contracts which may or may not be signed in Saudi Arabia by Fonco's representatives. In contrast, if Fonco is performing a public sector executory contract or Mixco is performing executory works in either the public or private sector, neither Fonco nor Mixco may import in its own name materials required for its works except for any used equipment owned by Fonco outside the Kingdom. *See* Council of Ministers Resolution No. 124, para. 2 (29/5/1403) (requiring government contractors to purchase tools and equipment in the Kingdom) (prohibiting importing of other than used tools and equipment belonging to foreign contractor) (translated in Appendix 3). Nonetheless, the fact that Fonco is performing a government contract will not prevent Fonco's office outside the Kingdom, as a foreign manufacturer or seller of goods, from "exporting" items to the Kingdom as required by local customers. In the case of a Mixco, it may also be noted that the activity of "importing" is not among those activities which may be authorized under a foreign capital investment license or included in the objectives clause of its articles of association, as approved by the Ministry of Commerce. For foreign capital investment license, *see generally* pp. 66–68 *infra.* However, Mixco is entitled to import through its Saudi partner for the purpose of its activities, *see* Solaim Statement, at 4, col. 2, subject to the general rule that all contractors in the public sector are required to use locally produced goods, *see generally* pp. 80–81 *infra,* and, if not available, to procure such goods locally. Only if the goods are not available on the domestic market may they be imported through local commercial agents, distributors, or other Saudi importers.

[33] *See also* note 32 *supra.*

recreation to its workmen. The sets are not integrated into the machinery and equipment required for the execution of the project but do become the property of the customer. The customer is not invoiced separately for the sets, whose price is included in the project price. The contractor realizes a profit on the sale of such sets. Nonetheless, the sale for profit of the sets is not considered a prohibited engaging in trade, since the sale is incidental to the prime activity of construction and installation and represents a minor portion of the contractor's total profit relating to the project.

(b) Fonco or Mixco, or Fonco associated with Sauco as joint adventurers, obtains a contract for the construction of a factory producing precast building materials. During the course of construction, material or equipment is purchased which proves to be in excess of need; or, some of the material purchased happens, by a justifiable mistake of the contractor, to be contrary to specifications; or, certain machinery, material, or equipment is to be replaced due to a change in the requirements of the customer; or, such items are no longer required for completion of the factory. In any of the preceding situations, the sale of the materials, machinery, or equipment will not be considered trade prohibited to Fonco or Mixco, since such sale was not originally intended and is incidental to the commercial activity permitted to Fonco or Mixco.

(c) Mixco owns a factory producing precast building materials. During the course of operation of the factory, material or equipment is purchased which proves to be in excess of need; or, some of the material purchased happens, by a justifiable mistake of the factory, to be contrary to specifications; or, certain machinery, materials, or equipment is to be replaced due to the requirements of the business; or, such items are no longer required by the business; or the factory itself is to be sold as part of the process of liquidating Mixco or for other business reasons. In any of the preceding situations, the sale of the materials, machinery, or equipment will not be considered trade prohibited to Mixco, since such sale was not originally intended and is incidental to Mixco's permitted activities.

(d) Fonco or Mixco obtains a turnkey project for the construction of a hospital, to be fully equipped and ready for patients within two days of the delivery date. No part of such project is considered to come under the umbrella of "trade". However, if there are two separate contracts, one for construction, installation, and decoration, and the other for the sale and supply of the required materials, goods, and equipment, the latter activity will be deemed engaging in prohibited trade.

(e) X is a nonSaudi working in Saudi Arabia. He purchases an automobile, stereo equipment, a washing machine, and other items for his personal use. X is permitted to sell any or all of these items to a willing purchaser at any time, whether or not prior to his definitive departure from the Kingdom, and make a profit on any such sale. However, if X habitually engages in the purchase and resale for profit of any such items, he will be deemed to be engaging in prohibited trade.

(f) Fonco or Mixco has obtained a project for the construction of a building, road, bridge, power station, or the like, or is executing a services contract for the provision, for example, of life support services, or is performing an operation and/or maintenance contract. If the relevant contract requires Fonco or Mixco to provide certain materials and/or goods, whether or not altered by the application of skill or labor, the provision of such materials and/or goods will not be deemed prohibited trade since it will be incidental to the contractor's main activity and will normally represent only a relatively minor portion of the total contract.

2. Commercial agent

Prior to the 1980 amendments to the Commercial Agencies Regulations, Saudi regulatory law did not provide a precise definition of a "commercial agent",[34] but merely stated the rule that a commercial agent must be a Saudi natural or wholly-owned juristic person. Article 1 of the 1962 Regulations provides

> [n]onSaudis, whether in their capacity as natural or juristic persons, shall not be permitted to act as commercial agents in the Kingdom of Saudi Arabia, and Saudi companies acting as commercial agents shall have completely Saudi capital and the members of their boards of directors and the persons entitled to sign in their names shall be Saudi.

This rule of law has not been modified.[35] However, it was not until 1980 that a definition of the commercial agent was expressed, albeit indirectly, by regulation. The 1980 amendments make the Commercial Agencies Regulations and the amendments thereto applicable to "any person who contracts with a producer or its substitute in its country to undertake

---

[34] *But see* Commercial Court Regs., art. 18 (defining "commission agent").

[35] *See also* Commercial Agencies Regs. Implementing Rules, art. 9(4) (requiring among supporting documents for registration of agency or distribution agreement a statement that applicant's capital is wholly Saudi and that persons entitled to sign on behalf of, direct, or manage such enterprise are of Saudi nationality). Consequently, a Fonco may not enter into a general or exclusive agreement to manage a Sauco commercial agent, whether or not such Sauco is its agent. Nor may such Sauco grant a power of attorney for the same purpose in favor of a nonSaudi natural or juristic person. This rule also applies generally to all Saucos, which may not name a nonSaudi as general manager or in a capacity in which he has broad authority to manage the Sauco. The Ministry of the Interior has also taken the position that nonSaudis are prohibited from signing documents relating to immigration, visas, and the like and has also warned that Saudis giving powers in this regard to nonSaudis are subject to severe penalties. Furthermore, as a matter of practice, the Ministry of Justice has ceased to allow any such powers of attorney to be notarized and registered. *Cf.* Minister of Justice Circular No. 156/12/t (16/11/1399) (prohibiting general powers of attorney by Saudis in favor of foreigners).

commercial activities whether [such person] is an agent or a distributor whatsoever the form of agency or distributorship"[36] and thereby functionally define the "commercial agent". This proposition is further clarified by article 1 of the 1981 Commercial Agencies Regulations Implementing Rules, which defines a "commercial agent" for purposes of the application of the Commercial Agencies Regulations and the amendments thereto as

> any person who contracts with a producer or its legal substitute in its country to undertake commercial activities whether [such person] is an agent or a distributor whatsoever the form of agency or distributorship in return for a profit or a commission or benefits whatever their nature including agencies of maritime or air or land transportation and any agencies issued by resolution of the Minister of Commerce.[37]

Consequently, it will be noted that a "commercial agent" under Saudi law includes various types of sales representatives, distributors, and dealers.[38]

3. Scope of commercial agency

In addition to the sale and supply of goods, a commercial agent is normally required by the principal to perform certain activities related thereto. Thus, since a foreign seller is barred from undertaking customs clearance, transportation, or warehousing in Saudi Arabia, the commercial agent will as a rule perform these services for the seller, unless the seller prefers to have these activities performed by another Saudi entity licensed and/or registered to carry out such activities. After-sales service, if any, must be rendered by the agent,[39] who may, however, be assisted by technical personnel seconded to it by the principal.

If a sale or supply agreement executed between Fonco and the Saudi Government also includes, as a package transaction, the provision of services requiring Fonco to be present in the Kingdom such as consultancy, supervision, execution, operation, or maintenance, the seller must appoint a Saudi services agent. The commercial agent, provided that such activity is within its registered objectives, may perform this role according to the

---

[36] Royal Decree No. M/32, para. 2(1) (1980). *Cf. id.* para. 3 (making para. 2 applicable to importers, even if not agents or distributors). Agencies for "commercial services" are also subject to the Regulations and their implementing rules. Minister of Commerce Resolution No. 50 (24/7/1402).

[37] Commercial Agencies Regs. Implementing Rules, art. 1. For judicial construction of art. 1, *see, e.g.,* 596 F.Supp. 697 (E.D.Pa. 1984).

[38] In view of the regulatory definitions, the term "commercial agent" as employed in this chapter also applies to a distributor, dealer, sales representative, and, in some cases, an importer.

[39] *See* Royal Decree No. M/32, para. 2(2) (1980). However, in the case of direct sales made by the principal, the agent's obligation to provide such services will depend upon the terms of its agreement with the seller.

terms of a separate services agency agreement. Saudi law does not prohibit the same agent from acting both as services and commercial agent with respect to the same project and/or for the same principal. However, its activity as services agent will be subject to the Services Agents Regulations.[40] Furthermore, in the case of public sector tender offers which are not extended to foreign entities or other sales which may require a local distribution system, the commercial agent will submit bids, negotiate and enter into contracts, or otherwise sell, the principal's goods. In the case of private sector tender offers, a foreign seller may negotiate and enter into contracts and submit bids in its own name, provided that such foreign seller is not deemed to have a local presence or to be engaged in trading activities within the Kingdom. However, a foreign seller's ability to make such sales may depend on the desires of the private sector client, who may or may not prefer to deal with local agents, and upon the terms of the foreign seller's agency agreement, if any.

4. Registration

In order to act as a commercial agent, a Saudi enterprise must be registered with respect to such activity in the Commercial Register.[41] Additionally, each commercial agency agreement must be registered in the register maintained at the Ministry of Commerce.[42] A person acting as an agent without due registration of the agreement is subject to regulatory penalties.[43]

C. THE COMMERCIAL AGENCY AGREEMENT

In 1983, the Ministry of Commerce issued its second Model Commercial Agency or Distribution Agreement ["Model Agreement"].[44] The parties,

---

[40] Commercial Agencies Regs. Implementing Rules, art. 1.

[41] *See* Commercial Register Regs., art. 5.

[42] Commercial Agencies Regs., art. 3; Commercial Agencies Regs. Implementing Rules, arts. 6, 12. For registration procedures, application, and supporting documents, *see id.* arts. 6–9. Registration of the agreement is the responsibility of the agent or distributor. *See also id.* art. 10 (conditioning registrability of agreement on its having been entered into in seller's country and its inclusion of adequate description of rights and obligations of parties to one another and to consumers with respect to maintenance and spare parts).

[43] *See* Commercial Agencies Regs., art. 4, *as amended by* Royal Decree No. M/32 (1980). *See also* Commercial Register Regs., art. 14 (providing minor penalties for failure to obtain commercial registration).

[44] The 1983 Model Agreement replaced the 1981 model agreement issued by the Ministry of Commerce. Both agreements were issued under para. 2(4) of Royal Decree No. M/32, which provides

[t]he Ministry of Commerce shall prepare model agreements for the guidance of agents and distributors. They shall include all the basic particulars of the agreement such as the parties to the agreement, its place, duration and territory, the method of its

within the general confines of Saudi law and public policy, may expand upon, clarify, and supplement the basic provisions of the Model Agreement to a certain extent, either in the agreement itself or in a separate document.[45] In case of any conflict between the provisions of the agency agreement and another understanding between the parties, the provisions of the agency agreement, which is required to be registered, will prevail. This section discusses various issues relating to the agency or distribution arrangement ["agency agreement"] and provisions which the parties may desire to include in their understandings for their mutual benefit and protection.

1. Effective Marketing

Sales plan

In order to achieve the maximum benefit from the Saudi market potential, the agency agreement may set a minimum sales goal to be achieved by the agent.[46] For that purpose, the parties may draw up a sales or purchase plan to be revised periodically on the basis of sales achieved during prior periods and on current market conditions. However, any such revised plan may not require a sales level exceeding the figure or percentage set by the parties in their original agreement, unless both parties so agree. Such a plan, including its periodic revisions, may be made a part of the original agency agreement. The agreement may also provide that, if the minimum sales level is not achieved by the agent, the principal will have the right to terminate the agency agreement, with or without notice, as provided in the agreement.[47] The agreement may also include a "best efforts" clause. However, in view of the lack of an objective standard, such a clause may prove of small utility in the case of a disagreement between the parties. In addition, the agreement may permit the principal to make efforts to promote and increase sales by any lawful means, including direct sales from abroad to purchasers in the agency territory.[48] The agreement may also require the principal to send shipments, including any spare parts

renewal and termination, the mutual obligations of the parties and their obligations to the consumer particularly with respect to the assurance of maintenance and spare parts.

For translation of Model Agreement, see Appendix 2.

[45] *See* Commercial Agencies Regs. Implementing Rules, art. 11 (agreement required to include certain terms) (also permitting inclusion of other terms not inconsistent with effective regulations).

[46] The principal may, for this purpose, prefer to structure its arrangement as a distributorship. Since the distributor's own funds will be committed, a greater market penetration may result than in the case of an agency relationship.

[47] *But see* pp. 29–33 *infra* (relating to termination).

[48] *See also* Model Agreement, art. 10(a) (contemplating payment of a commission to the agent with respect to direct sales).

and components, promptly, to maintain sufficient stock in the Kingdom, and to provide technical advice and promotional materials as required by the agent for the purpose of market development. The principal may also be obligated to maintain certain quality levels with respect to the goods and to keep its prices competitive.[49]

Marketing assistance

The agreement may also provide that the principal will have the right to second a certain number of its employees to the agent in Saudi Arabia and that the agent will utilize the technical or professional services of such personnel to assist it in the effective marketing of the goods. The agent may be obligated to sponsor such personnel and obtain entry visas and work permits for them at the request of the principal. Since the principal has no legal presence in Saudi Arabia, any such seconded personnel will have the status of employees of the agent.[50] In addition, the agent may be obligated to follow certain instructions of the principal with respect to specified aspects of marketing. In the case that the agent fails to comply with such instructions, reasonable financial penalties may be imposed upon the agent if so provided in the agreement.[51] If not so provided, any actual deduction made by the principal may not exceed the amount of actual loss sustained by the principal as a result of the agent's noncompliance, if it is to be upheld in Saudi court. Conversely, the principal may be obligated to

---

[49] *Cf. id.* art. 10(b) (requiring principal to maintain quality standards, respect quantities and delivery dates). In all cases, the goods must conform to the standard specifications approved by the Saudi Arabian Standards Organization. *See id.* art. 7. *See also* Regs. for Combating Commercial Fraud, Royal Decree No. M/11, art. 3 (29/5/1404) (March 1, 1984); Regs. for Combating Commercial Fraud Implementing Rules, Minister of Commerce Resolution No. 1327/3/1, arts. 2–3 (1/6/1405) (Feb. 20, 1985) (specifying cases when nonconforming goods are to be deemed fraudulent or spoiled).

[50] Personnel seconded by a foreign seller to a commercial agent must have the legal status of workmen of the agent and work under its name and control. They should be paid by the agent. However, Saudi law does not prohibit a foreign seller from reimbursing its agent for costs associated with such employees. Legally speaking, the seconded employees should not sign, in the name of the foreign seller, direct order contracts with Saudi customers because such employees are legally present in the Kingdom as workmen of the agent and not of the foreign seller. If such employees sign direct order contracts in the name of the foreign seller and to which the agent is not a party, the latter may be deemed not only to be carrying on business illegally in Saudi Arabia but also to have a permanent establishment in the Kingdom giving rise to Saudi tax liability. *See* pp. 36–38 *infra.*

[51] Saudi law, generally, recognizes and enforces penalty clauses. *See, e.g.,* Majlis Kibār al-'Ulamā Decision No. 25 (21/8/1394), implemented by Minister of Justice Resolution No. 3314/95 (23/5/1395) (reasonable penalty clauses in contracts valid and enforceable) (available in the Institute of Public Administration library); Minister of Justice Circular No. 60/12/th (26/3/1395) (same) (*cited* in MINISTRY OF JUSTICE, REGULATIONS, RULES, CIRCULARS). *Cf.* Tender Regs., art. 9 (providing for percentage penalties with respect to government contracts). However, clauses providing for excessive penalties giving rise to an implication of consequential or liquidated damages will not be enforced.

dispatch to the agent qualified personnel thoroughly conversant with the products and experienced in marketing.[52] The parties may agree in advance on the actual number of persons in specified categories to be sent to assist the agent. The agent may require such personnel to work under its supervision and control. The parties may also agree upon certain financial penalties to be imposed on the principal for failure to fulfill such obligation. However, as in the case of penalties to be imposed on the agent, such penalties must be reasonable and may not be related to consequential or liquidated damages.

Basic and related services

The parties can further ensure the effectiveness of the marketing operations by drawing up a detailed list of services required from each party. The agent or distributor is required by regulation to provide spare parts and maintenance and to fulfill any warranties made with respect to the goods.[53] The agent may also be contractually obligated to perform any or all of the following functions, without limitation, and also any services related thereto: warehousing, transportation, and delivery; clearance of shipments from ports and through customs; preparation and submission of tenders; preparation and submission of reports to the principal in the areas of market evaluation, sales direction, customer development, analysis of prices of comparable products and services, together with agent's recommendations; and submission of reports on the activities of competitors.[54] The principal may in addition contract for the performance of other services which are not normally required from commercial agents in the course of business. The extent of ancillary services to be performed will also depend on the nature and volume of the goods sold and the business planning and strategy of the parties. The principal may agree to provide the agent with technical data, to assist it with regard to business strategies and negotiations with customers, and to advise it on bookkeeping methods and the like.

2. Eligibility of the agent

A commercial agent must be registered at the Ministry of Commerce as a business concern whose permitted activities include agency or distributorship. The principal is subject to no legal duty to ascertain the eligibility of

---

[52] *Cf.* Model Agreement, art. 9 (entitling agent to make use of services and technical expertise of principal when required by circumstances).

[53] Royal Decree No. M/32, para. 2(2) (1980); Commercial Agencies Regs. Implementing Rules, art. 3. *See also* Model Agreement, art. 6 (obligating principal to agent for provision of maintenance and spare parts at reasonable prices).

[54] *Cf.* Model Agreement, art. 9 (obligating agent to provide premises, staff, and storage, carry out promotion and marketing, open new distribution centers as required, provide local services).

the agent. However, it should do so for purposes of establishing its own good faith and avoiding the practical and legal difficulties which may result in the event that the agent is discovered to be acting without due permission. The agent's registration is checked by obtaining an extract of its commercial registration certificate from the Commercial Register.[55]

The agency agreement should not fail to include the agent's representation that it is authorized by law and qualified to act as an agent for the purpose of the agreement. Furthermore, the inaccuracy of this representation should be expressly made a ground for termination of the agreement by the principal. If not specifically so provided, in the event that the agent proves to be ineligible, it may have available to it the possibility of curing the defect by fulfilling the relevant legal requirements. However, if for any reason the agent has been barred from acting as an agent or blacklisted or its commercial registration has been cancelled, the agreement will be *per se* invalid. The agreement should also provide that the agent's inability, by reason of its ineligibility, to perform its obligations at any time will be a valid cause for termination of the agreement by the principal. The principal may provide for the recovery of damages in the case that such incapacity is attributable to the agent's negligent or intentional acts or omissions. In case the agent is incapacitated or disqualified from continuing to act as agent by the authorities, the agreement will be terminated by force of law as of the date of such decision.[56] In this event, the agent should be required immediately to inform the principal of its disqualification. Both should arrange to wind up their relationship within a minimal time.[57] Otherwise, either or both of the parties may be liable for doing business illegally, and may be subject to regulatory penalties.[58]

3. Governmental authorizations

The agent is required by law to register the agency agreement within three months of its effective date.[59] While the principal is not responsible for the agent's failure to register the agreement,[60] the failure of the agent

[55] Commercial Register Regs., art. 11. For commercial registration certificate of a company, see Appendix 4.

[56] *Cf.* Model Agreement, art. 11 (providing for termination in event of impossibility or loss of capacity of either party).

[57] This time may be defined as the time necessary to make arrangements with respect to shipments in transit, customer orders in the process of fulfillment, and the like. The time allowable will vary according to the facts of each case.

[58] Such penalties are in principle applicable solely to the agent. *See* Commercial Agencies Regs., art. 4, *as amended by* Royal Decree No. M/32 (1980). However, the principal may be penalized by having the entry of its goods into the Kingdom prohibited or being otherwise barred from doing business with Saudi Arabia.

[59] Commercial Agencies Regs. Implementing Rules, art. 6.

[60] It may be noted that an unregistered agreement is not *per se* invalid or unenforceable. However, failure to register the agreement may deprive the agent of the protection afforded

to fulfill this requirement may create practical business difficulties for the principal.[61] Additionally, the agent should agree, during the duration of the effectiveness of the agreement, to seek, obtain, and be in possession of all official approvals, licenses, registrations, and permits required by virtue of any applicable law or necessary for the effective operation of the business. The agent should also agree to hold the principal harmless for any failure to comply with the preceding obligation.

4. Exclusivity

Saudi law permits both exclusive and nonexclusive agency agreements and distributorships with respect to product and to territory. An agent may be given exclusive rights with respect to certain merchandise of the principal and nonexclusive rights relating to other merchandise of the same principal in territories defined in the agreement. Furthermore, in the case of a nonexclusive arrangement, the granting of exclusivity at a future date may be made conditional on the agent's having attained a specified level of sales. However, nonexclusive arrangements relating to the same products within a single territory are not favorably regarded by the Ministry of Commerce. In the case of an exclusive agreement, the principal must expressly reserve the right to ship the goods directly to customers within the territory if it is to retain such right. It is advisable in all cases that the duration of each agency be clearly defined. In general, it is practical to enter into a series of agreements for relatively short time periods, subject to renewal by the parties.

5. Subagents

Article 1 of the Commercial Agencies Regulations Implementing Rules permits an agent to contract with subagents within the agreement territory but provides that the agent will remain liable for the obligations to customers imposed by regulation. Depending on the nature of the goods and the parties' marketing strategy, the parties are free to agree as to whether or not any subagents will be appointed. This matter should be covered in the agreement and, if the agent is to be given the right to appoint subagents, the relevant clause should be extremely comprehensive

by art. 16 of the Model Agreement, pursuant to which the Ministry of Commerce, in the event of a dispute between the parties, will refrain from registering an agency agreement between the principal and a new agent covering the same items and territory until issuance of a final arbitral award or judgment resolving the dispute. It may also be noted that failure to register would constitute a breach by the agent of its obligation under art. 18 of the Model Agreement, giving rise, at least in theory, to a claim by the principal under art. 14 thereof.

[61] *See, e.g.*, Minister of Fin. & Nat'l Econ. Circular No. 1653/1402 (24/3/1402) (instructing ministries and government departments, organizations, and agencies not to contract with agents not having certificates attesting to the registration of the relevant agency).

and should specify whether or not any such appointments will be subject to the principal's prior approval. Particular attention should be given to the agent's rights with respect to trademarks and other trade designations, which should be registered in Saudi Arabia.[62] In the case of a distribution agreement, the principal may also desire to include a title retention clause in the agreement. As distinguished from the appointment of subagents, Saudi law does not address the issue of the assignment of the agency agreement by the agent. Therefore, the parties should cover this matter in the agreement.

6. Noncompetition

An agent is not prohibited by regulation from dealing in an unlimited number of products. Furthermore, Saudi law does not expressly bar the agent from dealing in products of a mutually competitive nature. The protection available to the principal will be based on the principle of the enforceability of any relevant contractual obligations and equity or general rules prohibiting unfair trade practices.[63] It is preferable to supplement such general rules by an express contractual provision in order to obtain greater protection. Thus, the principal may wish to include a noncompetition clause in the agreement. Such clause may provide that the agent is not presently involved in the business of handling products of a competitive nature and that it will refrain from dealing in any manner in products which may be of a competitive nature and/or which may affect the sale of the principal's products covered by the agency agreement. The agent, its parent, affiliates, and any entities in which the agent has a majority share or management control may also be prohibited from engaging, directly or indirectly, in such competitive activities as selling, promoting, importing, manufacturing, assembling, or processing products similar to or competitive with the principal's products which are subjects of the agency agreement, not only during the term of the agreement but also for a certain period after its termination. No maximum time limitation is prescribed by law for the preclusion of the agent from competitive activities. However, the period must be reasonable and based on principles of fairness. It may also be noted that, unless the agreement specifically provides that customer lists and similar items will be the sole property of the principal on termination, they will become the property of the agent.

7. Payments

Saudi law does not specify either minimum or maximum amounts with respect to the agent's commission or provide restrictions relating to the

---

[62] *Cf.* Model Agreement, art. 9 (giving agent right to use trademarks).
[63] *See, e.g.*, Commercial Court Regs., art. 5; *cf.* Model Agreement, art. 8 (imposing good faith duty on parties).

basis of such commission, the method of its computation,[64] or the means and timing of payment. Since no exchange controls are in effect in Saudi Arabia, payments from the customer may be made directly to the principal located outside of Saudi Arabia. The agent's commission may be remitted by the principal to the account of the agent whether inside or outside of the Kingdom. If the principal receives payments directly from customers and delays in payment of the agent's commission, the principal may be contractually made liable for a reasonable delay penalty. Alternatively, the agent may receive payments and deduct its commission before remitting such amounts to the principal. Saudi law does not expressly restrict the assignment of the proceeds of the agency agreement to any person, whether Saudi or nonSaudi, and whether inside or outside the Kingdom.

8. Financing

In the case of an agent, the amount or extent of credit to be extended by the principal should be specified in the agreement together with any bank guarantees the agent will furnish to the principal with respect thereto. In the case of a distributorship, the amount of the initial payments to be made by the distributor, any bank guarantees, and the scheduling of future payments should be specified. The agreement may provide that if the distributor, on receipt of payments from customers or at the scheduled times, delays in making the relevant payments to the principal, it may be made subject to a delay penalty expressed as a reasonable percentage of overdue amounts.[65] The parties should also determine which party will bear the costs of any bid or performance bonds relating to public or private sector supply contracts. Generally, payments to the principal are made by means of irrevocable and confirmed letter of credit. The parties are permitted to provide for International Chamber of Commerce documentary credits to be utilized provided that no related aspect is inconsistent with Saudi law.

9. Independent contractor

In Saudi Arabia, a regulatory "agent" is not automatically empowered to bind its principal vis-à-vis third parties or to sign or enter into agreements on behalf of the principal unless the principal has specifically so authorized the agent. However, the incidence of ambiguous situations is high. In the

---

[64] However, since payment of interest is prohibited, a clause in the agreement providing for interest payments will be unenforceable. Nonetheless, the existence of such a provision will not render the entire agreement null and void. Parties should consequently take the illegality of interest into account when negotiating the agreement.

[65] It may be noted that, practically speaking, it is not possible to perfect a security interest in the agent's accounts receivable from customers. Therefore, it may be advisable for the principal to obtain promissory notes from the agent with a view to protecting its position.

absence of a regulatory delimitation of an agent's authority, it is advisable to provide in the agency agreement that the agent is an independent contractor. Such clause should also provide that the agent will not make any commitments or agreements with third parties on behalf of or for the account of the principal or have the power to bind the principal in any way except as specifically provided in the agreement or as the principal may, from time to time, authorize the agent in writing.

10. Confidentiality

Unless the purpose of the parties is to conceal certain illegal aspects of their agreement, they may lawfully include a confidentiality clause therein. Such a clause may be made applicable to patents,[66] knowhow, technical data, or any other confidential information relating to the principal's business, including its merchandising or selling activities, the names of its customers, and financial positions of which the agent obtains knowledge or possession or pieces together from scattered bits of data to which it has access in the course of business. The clause may prohibit the agent from revealing such information in any manner to any person, inside or outside Saudi Arabia, except to governmental or judicial authorities in compliance with applicable law. The agent may also be obligated to use its best efforts to protect the principal's trade secrets and information and to incorporate this obligation into any agreements with subagents. The agent may be held liable, contractually, for any loss incurred. Although it is recommended to require the agent to include a confidentiality provision in the employment contracts of its employees, and, if relevant, of employees of subagents, the recovery of damages from an employee has its practical limitations. If, despite the reasonable care and precautions of the agent, one of such employees reveals any confidential information, the agent, in practice, may be held liable.

11. Changing laws

Changing circumstances in the Kingdom, especially in the sphere of business, may result in the issuing of new regulations or in the modification

---

[66] In the absence of any regulatory means of protecting patents, a customary method of publishing cautionary notices to the public is used, which does not afford extensive legal protection. In a recent case, the Commission for Settlement of Commercial Disputes held that the plaintiff was entitled to an order enjoining the defendant against further infringement of its patent in Saudi Arabia and, reasoning that registration is merely a form of giving notice, rejected the defense that such patent was not registered in the Kingdom. Damages, however, were not awarded as being incapable of being determined by the Commission. Labels may be protected by the Regulations for the Combat of Commercial Fraud, Royal Decree No. M/11, art. 3 (1984). *See* Regulations for Combating of Commercial Fraud Implementing Rules, Minister of Commerce Resolution No. 1327/3/1, arts. 2–3 (1985). *Cf.* Saudi Arabian Standards Organization, Labelling of Prepackaged Foods, art. 3/4 (1973) (prohibiting use of misleading labels) (translated in Appendix 5).

of existing regulations, rules, decrees, orders, and formal procedures. It is thus imperative to cover in the agency agreement the eventuality of an unfavorable alteration of the legal *status quo*. The parties may therefore agree that, if any part of the agreement is found to be invalid under the law existing at the time the agreement was entered into[67] or is subsequently rendered invalid by any applicable rule of Saudi law, either or both parties may cancel the entire agreement. The clause may also be made applicable to changes in the laws of another legal system to which the principal is subject. The right of the parties to terminate the agreement pursuant to such clause may be made unilateral and/or contingent on whether the laws of the country of the principal or of the agent have resulted in the illegality of the agreement. The provision for such termination may include, if the parties so desire, a commitment to try to enter into a new agreement on terms to be renegotiated. It may also provide for arbitration under Saudi law to resolve any disagreements arising out of the negotiation of any new terms necessitated by the change in the law.[68] In the alternative, the parties may provide in the agreement that any provisions that may be rendered illegal or void by force of law will be severable and that the remainder of the agreement will remain in full force and effect. If the parties make no provision in the original agreement for changes in the legal situation, the resolution of the question of whether the agreement remains valid and the illegal term drops out or the entire agreement is rendered unenforceable will vary according to the nature of the new legal rule and the facts of each case.

12. Legal structure of parties

In selecting an agent and in drafting the agency agreement, the principal should take into account the legal structure of the agent. If the agent is a natural person, it will do business in the form of a sole proprietorship, an entity which has no juristic personality. In this case, the agent's liability is unlimited. However, the existence of a sole proprietorship may be terminated at the sole discretion of the owner. A sole proprietorship is neither a company subject to the Companies Regulations nor a continuing entity but ends on the death of its owner.[69] An executor, appointed to liquidate the sole proprietorship, will distribute its capital and assets among the owner's heirs in accordance with the rules of Islamic law. No distribution can be made to the heirs until all creditors have been paid in full or satisfied, and certain amounts allocated and paid in accordance with

---

[67] The problem of invalidity under present law typically arises where the parties contract without knowledge of certain applicable rules of law.

[68] *Cf.* Model Agreement, art. 17.

[69] *Cf. id.* art. 11 (agreement terminates on death, incapacity, or bankruptcy of either party).

the decedent's will, if any, subject to Islamic law rules relating to bequests. In contrast, if the agent is a limited liability company, the liability of the partners is limited to the extent of their respective capital contributions.[70] Therefore, the selection of an agent with a structure permitting it to limit its liability may subject the principal to greater risk and financial exposure than in the case where the agent is operating in the form of a sole proprietorship. However, the advantage of choosing such an agent is that it can be an entity of infinite duration. The existence of a limited liability company does not end upon the death of any partner unless so provided in the articles of association.[71] Furthermore, if the agent is a company, the parties may provide in the agency agreement that the agent will not amend certain provisions in its articles of association without notice to or prior approval of the principal. The scope of any such provision should be clearly specified in the agency agreement. The agreement may also provide that the agent will furnish the principal with certain guarantees if any such change will result in increasing the financial exposure of the principal. Additionally, certain amendments of the agent's articles of association may be made an event of default in the agency agreement entitling the principal to terminate such agreement.

Similarly, the agent may wish to include in the agreement a provision ensuring that any alteration in the legal structure of the principal will have no adverse effect on the agency relationship. Problems have been known to arise in this regard. For example, assume that X, a nonSaudi manufacturer of refrigerators under the trade name L, has an exclusive Saudi agent A for the sale of such refrigerators. X then proceeds to obtain a majority interest in, or to merge with Y, a nonSaudi manufacturer of refrigerators under the trade name M which has an exclusive Saudi agent B for the sale of such refrigerators. Depending upon the understanding of X and Y, the name of Y may be changed to X in whole or in part. Since X and Y both have Saudi agents, the question arises as to whether A or B is the exclusive agent of the manufacturer previously doing business as the name of Y. The problem will be further complicated if the trade name of the refrigerators now being produced by the entity formerly called Y is changed from M to L. The result will be that B will lose the right to sell refrigerators in Saudi Arabia not only because its principal, Y, is no longer the same entity, but also because refrigerators bearing the trade name M, subject of its agency agreement, are no longer in production. Further complications may ensue if the refrigerators being manufactured by former Y bear both the trade names M and L. Consequently the agent will wish to protect its rights.

---

[70] Companies Regs., art. 157.
[71] *Id.* art. 178.

13. Bribery and unauthorized payments

Persons offering or making unauthorized payments, directly or indirectly, to public officials are subject to prosecution, fines, and imprisonment under the Regulations for Combating Bribery.[72] This rule applies whether the payment was made in consideration of a specific act or omission, or merely in the expectation that the public official will generally use his influence.[73] In addition, the Old Tender Regulations provide administrative sanctions with respect to acts of bribery. Article 82 provides

> [i]f the supplier or contractor is proved to have personally or through an intermediary, directly or indirectly, offered or attempted to offer a bribe to any government official or employee connected with the work forming the subject of the contract, its contract shall be immediately cancelled and the deposit forfeited in full, in addition to the striking of its name from the list of suppliers and contractors and the taking of the necessary action for its prosecution.

Article 110(e) provides that a government customer will have the right to withdraw work from any contractor who "gives, promises, or offers any present, loan, or gratuity to any government official or employee connected with the work subject of the contract." Acts performed outside Saudi Arabia are also within the scope of both of these regulations. The problem of unauthorized payments is complicated by the fact that the definition of a public official is both broad and amorphous. The antibribery regulations define public officials as

(a) permanent or temporary servants of the Government, government departments or public entities;

(b) arbitrators or experts appointed by the Government or a commission with judicial jurisdiction;

(c) doctors and midwives with respect to certificates they issue;

(d) any individual entrusted with a task of a government committee or any other administrative authority;

(e) officials of corporations or companies performing an obligation in public facilities.[74]

Furthermore, certain payments made to juristic persons not appearing to have any connection with public officials may, in fact, come within the

---

[72] Royal Decree No. 15 (1962), *as amended by* Royal Decrees Nos. M/35 (13/10/1388) & M/51 (17/7/1402) (translated in Appendix 6).

[73] *Id.* arts. 1, 5–6. It should be noted that a "bribe" need not be a tangible payment but may also be a promise. *Id.* art. 1. *Cf.* Civil Service Regs., Royal Decree No. 49, art. 12(c) (1397) (barring civil servants from accepting, *inter alia*, any payment unlawful under antibribery regulations).

[74] Regs. for Combating Bribery, art. 9.

scope of the antibribery regulations. The general rule is that civil servants are barred from actively pursuing commercial activities extrinsic to their official work.[75] However, their passive holding of interests as partner in a limited liability company or as partner with limited liability in a limited partnership, or shares in a corporation is permissible.[76] Thus, where certain payments are made to a commercial entity making distributions out of its profits to persons including a public official, such payments may be deemed "bribes" within the reach of the antibribery regulations. If the agent has made such a payment, its principal may be held liable.[77] The parties should therefore not fail to include an extremely comprehensive representation and covenant in the agency agreement that the agent has not made or promised to make any payment to a public official as defined by applicable Saudi law. Such clause should also provide that neither party shall make or promise to make any payment, whether in cash or kind or in the form of any other benefits or privileges, as a commission or otherwise, directly or indirectly, to any government official, government company director, officer, or employee, or any other person in a position to influence a government purchase or claiming to be in such a position. Such clause should also provide that any kind of commission, fee, or other payment, regardless of its form, will be paid only if not prohibited by Saudi law or the laws of any other jurisdiction as the parties may specify. Furthermore, the parties should expressly represent that they are aware of the Saudi regulations governing bribery, agency, and government purchases, and of any other relevant regulations, rules, and administrative orders, and will comply with them. The parties should also agree to hold one another harmless against the consequences of any violation of this provision on their respective parts. As a matter of practice, it is also recommended to require the agent to open a separate account to be used solely for the purposes of the agency arrangement and to provide that the agent only will have the right to operate such account. The parties may also agree on specific methods of payments and accounting techniques to be used with respect to their transactions in order to assure their mutual protection. Finally, it should be noted that acts of bribery made with respect to persons not deemed public officials, although outside the scope of the antibribery regulations, are nonetheless crimes punishable by Saudi law.

---

[75] Civil Service Regs., art. 13(a); Civil Service Regs. Implementing Rules, Civil Service Board Resolution No. 1, art. 13/1 (1977); cf. [Government] Employees Rules, Civil Service Board Resolution No. 3, art. 7 (1977).

[76] Civil Service Regs. Implementing Rules, art. 13/2(b). However, the Ministry of Commerce will no longer approve the participation of civil servants in a limited liability company.

[77] See Regs. for Combating Bribery, art. 6 (accessories, participants, and instigators liable for bribery crimes).

14. Termination

Manner of termination

The consequences of the termination of the agency agreement are determined by interpreting the terms of the agreement in the light of the facts of each case.[78] Therefore, the parties should not fail to include a termination clause in their agreement. In the absence of such a provision, if either party terminates the agreement, the question whether the termination was or was not legally justified will be decided by the appropriate judicial or arbitral authorities. Such decision will be based on the letter and spirit of the agreement and the intention of the parties as expressed therein. Even though evidence is admissible to supplement or, in theory, to contradict the language of the agreement, contractual provisions relating to termination should be specific. For example, if the parties have not expressly provided that the agent's failure to achieve a certain sales volume will be a valid ground for termination by the principal, the mere ground of low sales may not be considered sufficient justification for termination of the agency agreement. Similarly, if the agreement provides that the agent shall not claim compensation of any sort against the principal in the case of termination of the agreement under certain specified conditions, the agent will retain the right to claim compensation in any situation not fitting squarely within the contractual preclusion. Unless otherwise provided in the agreement, noncompliance with any required termination notice will render the termination improper. If the court finds that the termination was unjustified, it may order the terminating party to pay the actual expenses incurred by the other party in the implementation and performance of the agreement, as well as any damages actually sustained by the party who was injured. If the agreement provides that either party will have the right to terminate the agreement with or without cause, and the actual termination is without cause, the court may nonetheless order the terminating party to reimburse the other party for any actual expenses that it incurred in the implementation and performance of the agreement.

The Model Agreement includes various clauses governing termination and the rights of the parties relating thereto. Article 5 provides that the term of the agreement will be automatically renewable unless one party gives the other party a minimum of three months' prior written notice. Thus, the period of the agency should be clearly defined with respect to all territories and products. In practice, it is advisable to select a relatively

---

[78] No provision of regulatory law defines or addresses the validity or invalidity of grounds for termination of agency agreements.

short period, to be renewable subject to the consent of the parties. In the case of proper notice, it is apparent from the plain language of article 5 of the Model Agreement that a party need not justify its nonrenewal or base it on a "valid cause". In addition, article 11 provides that the agreement shall end upon the occurrence of certain stated events, namely, the impossibility of performance, the death, loss of capacity, or declaration of bankruptcy of either party. The agreement may also be terminated under this article by one of the parties on the grounds of a substantial default in performance by the other party. However, the parties may also elaborate on the events specified in article 11 and set forth other "valid causes", whether acts or omissions, giving either party, or both, the right to terminate the agreement.

Compensation

Articles 13 to 15 of the Model Agreement apply to compensation upon termination or expiration of the agreement.[79] Article 13 entitles the agent to claim "appropriate compensation" for its efforts in promoting the products and developing customers which have actually resulted in an evident business success,[80] in the event that the principal "refuses" to renew or continue the agreement,[81] if its efforts would result in an advantage to a subsequent agent for the products. Since regulatory law provides no guidance as to the computation of compensation under this article, the parties should keep article 13 in mind during the stage of negotiating the terms of their agreement.[82] Article 15 obligates either of

[79] In addition, arts. 12 and 14 give the parties a contractual right to claim compensation for damages suffered as a result of the other party's breach of the agreement and thus reaffirm this general rule of Saudi contract law. However, art. 12 also expressly gives the agent the right to claim damages for the principal's breach of its obligations according to commercial usage, which is not provided in art. 14, applying to the principal's right to claim compensation from the agent. Nonetheless, since art. 8 obligates both parties to perform the agreement in accordance with commercial usage, any failure to do so by the agent would be a contractual breach coming within the scope of art. 14. In all cases, the recovery of consequential damages is not permitted.

[80] The parties may provide a definition of "evident success" in the agreement.

[81] One of the concerns motivating the preparation of the Model Agreement was the Ministry of Commerce's desire to protect agents against the arbitrary termination of their agreements.

[82] The practical effect of art. 13 has been a reduction in the percentage of the commission or markup of the agent or distributor. For example, if the principal formerly would have agreed to a 4.5% commission, it will now go no higher than 1%. The agent, however, should be entitled to a commission consistent with normal business usage. Alternatively, the principal may resort to the expedient of including the potential amount of art. 13 compensation in the cost of the goods. The agent should resist such a practice. Furthermore, in certain cases, the principal may insist on providing in the agreement that the agent shall not engage in any promotional activities or incur any promotional expenses except after prior written approval by the principal, or that the agent's promotional activities will be carried out solely according

the parties to compensate the other for actual loss sustained by such other party as a result of termination of the agreement by the former at an "inappropriate time", taking into account the nonterminating party's efforts and tangible and intangible resources placed at the service of the agency prior to termination.[83]

Disputes

Article 16 provides that, should the parties be unable to resolve their disputes by amicable means, such disputes will be brought before the Commission for the Settlement of Commercial Disputes or a Saudi arbitration committee.[84] In addition, it provides that, in this case, pending the issuance of a final judgment or award, no agreement with a new agent covering the same products or services in the agency territory may be registered. The nonregistrability of an agreement with a new agent is not expressly provided in either the Commercial Agencies Regulations or their Implementing Rules. Consequently, there is a question whether article 16 expresses an obligatory rule or whether it is merely a contractual covenant to which the parties are free not to agree and which would not be binding upon the Ministry of Commerce. In practice, however, it has been found that the Ministry of Commerce generally refuses to register agreements not including such a clause, since article 16 expresses the Ministry's policy of protecting agents against arbitrary termination.[85]

to promotion plans provided by the principal. The agent, during negotiations, may object to such a clause on the grounds that it may adversely affect its potential sales level. Such a provision is justifiable if the nature of the products is such that they are sold on a direct order basis and do not require a local distribution system and promotional activities. In some instances, the parties may agree in advance on the method of computation of art. 13 compensation. For example, they may agree that the agent's compensation for its promotional activities will amount to a certain percentage of its gross sales during a specified period, such as the year prior to the termination date.

[83] It may be noted that arts. 12–14 entitle the aggrieved party to "claim compensation", whereas a wrongfully terminating party is obligated by art. 15 to compensate the other party for loss sustained. Consequently, there is a divergence of opinion in the Saudi legal community relating to the proper interpretation of art. 15. The majority view is that, despite the obligatory language of art. 15, the termination of the agreement for a "valid cause" will preclude the terminated party from claiming damages for loss incurred as a result of such termination. However, it should be noted that art. 15, which addresses compensation for improper termination, does not bear upon an agent's or distributor's right to claim compensation for its efforts under art. 13.

[84] See generally pp. 150–68 & 222-24 infra.

[85] See also Minister of Commerce Affirms (Necessity of) Resolving Dispute(s) Amicably or Judicially, al-Riyadh, March 5, 1985, at 11, col. 1 (affirming that new agency may not be registered pending resolution of dispute); Changes in Law said Significant, Saudi Gazette, April 27, 1985 (nonregistrability of new agency applicable regardless of whether former agent was registered with Ministry) (suggesting possibility of providing bank guarantee to allow registration pending resolution of dispute).

Pending the outcome of litigation or arbitration, the principal may as a rule continue to make direct sales to customers within the Kingdom.[86] However, even though neither the Commission for the Settlement of Commercial Disputes nor the Ministry of Commerce has the power to grant specific performance or compel either party to continue with the other, either has discretion, on request of a terminated agent on a showing of good cause or hardship, to order the Customs Department to block the entry of the principal's goods into the Kingdom.

Issues relating to the goods

In the event of termination and, in particular, a disputed termination pending the outcome of which a new agency may not be registered, the most important practical consideration is the maintenance of market flow and the provision of goods and services to customers.[87] To forestall any interruptions in the flow, the parties may agree in advance that, in the case of termination, the agent will return to the principal any of the latter's products, merchandise, and materials which the agent may have in its possession at that time or to surrender such goods to another person designated by the principal. In the case of distributorships, the principal may retain the option to buy back the goods. Both distribution and agency agreements may also include detailed provisions covering the settlement of accounts, payments, refunds, and dispositions relating to any goods in transit. The ownership and constructive possession of goods in the Kingdom by a foreign principal during a reasonable transitional period between agents is not prohibited or considered to be engaging in trade. However, the foreign principal may not perform local marketing activities except by means of appointing a new agent.

In cases where the principal is financing the sales of its goods by means of a credit arrangement with the agent, in which case it will normally have received appropriate financial guarantees from the agent, the agreement should provide that

(a) In the event of termination, the agent will permit and help the principal to repossess its products, merchandise, and materials, in settlement of the credit balance and any other outstanding debts. This clause may be made expressly applicable to all products, merchandise and materials of which the agent has custody or possession, whether direct or indirect, actual or constructive.

---

[86] But see pp. 8–9 *supra*.

[87] *Cf.* Royal Decree No. M/32, para. 2(2) (1980); Commercial Agencies Regs. Implementing Rules, art. 3 (requiring agent to provide spare parts and maintenance and fulfill warranties for one year after termination or until appointment of a new agent, whichever occurs first).

(b) Orders already received and undertaken by the agent may be taken over by the principal itself or by any other agent whom it may appoint. All goods in transit may be considered as imported for the principal's account and may be transferred to any other entity designated by the principal.

(c) After the principal has taken constructive possession of any goods and materials from the agents, any amounts outstanding on the credit balance or any other debts may be settled directly by the agent in cash and/or by the principal's enforcement of any guarantees that the agent has established in its favor.

(d) If the principal already has title to the goods, either by virtue of a title retention clause or otherwise, the principal may take possession of the goods until they are transferred to the new agent, or the principal may appoint a Sauco as trustee for this purpose.

In case of the agent's failure to fulfill any relevant obligation upon termination, the principal may have the right to enforce any bank guarantees given by the agent to the principal, depending upon the terms of any such guarantees.

D. TAXATION

1. Direct sales

The profits of a foreign seller not directly carrying on any activity within Saudi Arabia and shipping its goods F.O.B. or C.I.F. Saudi port of entry are not subject to Saudi tax. Director-General of the Department of Zakāt and Income Tax ["DZIT"] Circular No. 2, applicable to profits arising out of direct supply contracts, provides

[i]n accordance with Articles I, II, and III of the Income Tax Regulations, Royal Decree No. 3321 of 1370 H, as amended by Royal Decree No. 576 of 1376 H, providing that income is subject to tax if it arises from a local source in the Kingdom, as a result of carrying out work within the Kingdom, or work performed both inside and outside the Kingdom.

And pursuant to the order of H.E. the Minister of Finance and National Economy in his Letter No. 906/4/1 dated 15/1/1389 H, stating the extent to which income tax is due on profits with respect to contracts concluded between government authorities and producing and exporting companies, together with the execution of certain works in the Kingdom.

.　　.　　.　　.

And in order to facilitate the application of the principles and rules provided in the Regulations and in the said letters, the following shall be observed

(a) Profits from supply operations only and supply and delivery operations in the Kingdom are exempt from income tax, whether the contracts therefor are entered into outside or inside the Kingdom, since the company or establishment in such case is not carrying out any work provided in the contract inside Saudi territory. The Regulations provide that tax shall be imposed on the profits of a company carrying out its work within the Kingdom.

(b) The net profit on contracts which include supply, installation and operation or maintenance are subject to tax. The company or establishment having contracted to perform such works shall submit to the Department of Zakāt and Income Tax accounts or works in which shall be set forth in detail the value of imported materials and any other expenses, in order to assess tax on its works inside the Kingdom and to collect the same at the times specified in the Regulations.

(c) In explaining the meaning of the term "carrying out" in paragraph (a), the following shall be observed

First: The signing of a contract inside the Kingdom by the representative of a company or establishment together with its obligation to supply materials and deliver them in Riyadh,[88] for example, or in any other place inside the Kingdom, is considered carrying out commercial activity inside the Kingdom and consequently subject to income tax, since the mere operation of transportation from the port of entry to the place of delivery inside is considered to be carrying out work inside the Kingdom. The contracting company or establishment shall submit accounts of its works in the Kingdom in which shall be set forth the value of imported materials, the costs of freight and transportation inside and outside the country, the costs of insurance and any other expenses. Tax shall be paid on the net profits of its works inside the Kingdom at the times specified in the Regulations.

Second: Those contracts entered into by representatives of the company [with] importers and which are usually signed abroad and do not include an obligation to transport the goods inside the Kingdom are not considered carrying out a commercial activity in the Kingdom and consequently are not subject to tax. The sale is usually on a C.I.F. or F.O.B. basis (delivery on board at loading port or delivery at port of entry), so that the manufacturing or exporting company does not carry out any work inside the Kingdom.

---

[88] Riyadh figures in the circular merely as an example of a nonseaport city within the Kingdom to which goods shipped by sea would have to be transported. However, if goods are shipped to Riyadh by air, Riyadh would be the port of entry. It should be noted that the seller's tax liability will not be altered if the contract is signed outside the Kingdom.

To apply the principles and rules set forth above, the following shall be observed

1. The exemption of "supply operations only", and the operations of "supply and delivery" in the Kingdom mentioned in paragraph (a) is conditioned on the contract's not including any work considered to be carrying out an activity inside the Kingdom as defined in paragraphs (b) and (c). If such condition is not satisfied, the operation will be subject to tax.
2. It is necessary that the contract be reviewed and its contents and particulars be studied in detail. General information or description of the operation made by either contracting party shall not be sufficient, whether the party be the government authority or the company or establishment contracting therewith.[89]

The criterion established by Circular No. 2 and other Saudi tax law applicable to direct supplies is the performance of commercial activities within the Kingdom. The method by which customers pay for the goods will not affect the seller's tax liability. Thus, they may make payments either directly to the foreign seller or to its commercial agent, if any, to be transferred to the principal. Furthermore, it is immaterial, from a tax standpoint, whether the agent deducts its commissions before transferring such payments or whether the principal makes separate payments of the commission to the agent. Finally, it should be noted that the mere retention of title to goods located in the Kingdom by a foreign seller does not constitute engaging in commercial activity within the Kingdom or subject such a seller not otherwise engaged in local commercial activity to Saudi tax.

In contrast, if a supply contract also requires the supplier to provide, directly or indirectly, certain services within the Kingdom such as delivery of the goods to the site, storage, maintenance, training of related personnel, and the like,[90] the supplier's total profits with respect to such contract may be subject to tax.[91] This rule applies to both public and private sector supply contracts. Apportionment between the value of the goods sold and the services rendered in the Kingdom is in many cases not accepted by the DZIT. Therefore, if a seller is to provide any services in Saudi Arabia, it is

---

[89] Circular No. 2 (13/5/1389). *Cf.* Director-Gen'l of DZIT Circular No. 788/1 (5/2/1404) (citing Minister of Fin. & Nat'l Econ. Letter No. 4/195 (20/1/1404)) (reaffirming that supply contracts F.O.B. or C.I.F. loading port or Saudi port of entry are not subject to tax) (delivery operations connected with supply considered engaging in commercial activity if delivery performed inside the cities of the Kingdom, hence supply operation connected with such delivery subject to tax) (translated in Appendix 7).

[90] Whether the seller is allowed to engage directly in any such local activities is a different question, *see generally* pp. 8–9 *supra*, and is irrelevant to its tax liability.

[91] For applicable tax rates, see p. 76 *infra*.

advisable to enter into two separate agreements, respectively for the sale of the goods F.O.B. or C.I.F. Saudi port of entry and for the relevant services. Preferably, the two agreements will be signed, with respect to the foreign seller, by two different entities.

With respect to any supply contracts including the provision of services in Saudi Arabia, the seller is required to file a Saudi tax return[92] no later than fourteen and a half months from the date of signature of the contract, *i.e.* the date at which point the taxpayer's financial year will be deemed to commence.[93] Failure to file a return will expose the taxpayer to arbitrary assessment of its taxable profits by the DZIT in the amount of fifteen percent of the total value of the contract. If the supply contract is on a F.O.B. or C.I.F. Saudi port basis and does not provide for services to be rendered in Saudi Arabia, no tax return is required to be filed. However, if a public sector contract is involved, the purchaser is required to withhold certain payments until production by the supplier of a certificate from the DZIT evidencing its payment of its tax liabilities.[94] Consequently, a supplier, even in the case of a pure supply contract, is advised to request the DZIT to issue a letter stating that the relevant contract is not subject to Saudi tax. In addition, purchasers in the private sector are to notify the DZIT of any such sale and purchase transaction and may withhold amounts up to the maximum potential tax liability of a foreign seller on its deemed profits generated by such transaction from payments to such a seller until it produces a tax clearance certificate from the DZIT.

2. Commercial agent or distributor

The tax status of a foreign seller is not *per se* altered by the sole fact that it may have appointed a local agent or distributor. Such representation will not cause such a seller to be considered to be carrying on commercial activities locally or to have a permanent establishment in the Kingdom for purposes of Saudi tax law, which has adopted the following analysis

II. Corporate Tax:

Upon reviewing articles X and XIII of the Income Tax Regulations, it has been found that the legislator has adopted a clear criterion, *i.e.* performing work within Saudi Arabia or both within and outside Saudi Arabia. This means that taxation is conditioned on the place of performance of work

---

[92] For standard tax return form, see Appendix 8.

[93] If the taxpayer desires a different financial year, it must obtain permission from the DZIT within 12 months of signature of the contract.

[94] Tender Regs., art. 8(b).

III. When a foreign enterprise is considered to have performed its work inside Saudi Arabia: The Income Tax Regulations have imposed tax on foreign companies which perform their work in Saudi Arabia only or those which perform their work both inside and outside Saudi Arabia simultaneously. This means that profits are subject to tax if the foreign enterprise has a permanent establishment in the Kingdom. But a permanent establishment is not restricted to a fixed place where it practises all or part of the enterprise's activity.

Guided by [concepts of the Economic Commission of the United Nations] we hereby describe some cases covered by a permanent establishment and under which a foreign enterprise is subject to tax, also cases which are not covered by a permanent establishment and thus the foreign enterprise is not subject to tax.

A permanent establishment includes

(1) Administration office, factory, workshop, mine, quarry, or any other place of extracting natural resources, or buildings or construction site or assembly plant.

(2) (a) The installation of a person by the foreign enterprise in Saudi Arabia who has the authority to negotiate and sign contracts on behalf of the enterprise;

(b) Or has a stock of commodities in the Kingdom owned by the foreign enterprise from which he regularly supplies orders on behalf of the foreign enterprise.

(3) The existence of equipment, machinery, supplies or tools, or other assets owned by the foreign enterprise and leased to an individual or juristic person in Saudi Arabia although such lease may have been arranged outside Saudi Arabia.

(4) Insurance of various types on persons and personal or real property in Saudi Arabia even if contracts are concluded abroad.

A permanent establishment does not include the following, hence no taxation

(1) Utilization of special facilities for the purpose of storing or exhibiting commodities or goods owned by the foreign enterprise and only for this sole purpose.

(2) Maintaining a stock of commodities owned by the foreign enterprise for the purpose of storing or exhibiting only.

(3) Maintaining a business office for direct advertisement or promotion for the foreign enterprise or to give information to conduct scientific research or similar preparatory or auxiliary activities.

(4) The conducting of scientific studies or statistical work or similar activities by a foreign enterprise for the Government or any of its agencies or for any other public or private enterprise or any natural or juristic person in the Kingdom.

(5) Undertaking commercial activities through a broker or an agent

for a commission or any other independent agent, any of whom are working within his own field.[95]

Thus, whether or not provided by agreement that the agent will have the legal status of an independent contractor,[96] it will not be considered a permanent establishment of a foreign seller whose products it sells or for whose account it solicits orders. The rationale underlying this result is that the products in Saudi Arabia are sold by the agent and not by the principal. This is the rule, whether or not the principal retains title to the products until payment therefor is received in full. In appointing a commercial agent or distributor, in structuring the relationship between the parties, and in drafting the agency or distribution agreement, a foreign seller should keep in mind both the tax advantages it may receive by reason of such appointment and the tax liabilities it may incur as a result of poor structuring or draftsmanship. First, it should be noted that with respect to any direct supply contracts in its own name, if any services are to be provided to customers by the principal within the Kingdom, the principal's tax liability will not change by virtue of the sole appointment of a commercial agent. If, however, it is the agent that will render such services,[97] the principal will have a basis for maintaining that it has no tax liability with respect to any such supply/services contracts in the event of a challenge by the DZIT. The language of the contract in this regard should clearly provide that the principal will not itself directly render any services within the Kingdom and that its Saudi agent or another Sauco will render any such required services. Alternatively, such a contract may be signed by the agent instead of the principal itself. Second, particular care should be taken with respect to the structuring of the services to be provided by the principal to the agent as expressed in the parties' agreement. It is essential in all cases, from a tax viewpoint, that the principal should not be deemed to be carrying on commercial activities within the Kingdom. Thus, all shipments to the agent should be made F.O.B. or C.I.F. Saudi port.

E. LOCAL PRESENCE

A foreign seller's involvement with Saudi Arabia, relationship with its agent or distributor, or commitments to local customers may be such as to necessitate its establishing a presence in the Kingdom. A couple of the vehicles available to Fonco are described in this section.

---

[95] Minutes of Meeting, Ministry of Fin. Committee on Taxation (6/1/1394), *approved by* Acting Minister of State of Fin. & Nat'l Econ. Letter No. 4/9976 (20/5/1394).

[96] *See generally* pp. 23–24 *supra*.

[97] *See also* Royal Decree No. M/32, para. 2(2) (1980); Commercial Agencies Regs. Implementing Rules, art. 3; Model Agreement, art. 6 (requiring agent to provide maintenance and fulfill warranties with respect to products subjects of the agency).

1. Commercial alternative: services company

If the nature of the products being sold or to be sold in the Kingdom requires after-sales service, such as repairs, replacements, maintenance, and the like, such servicing will be performed by the technical personnel of the commercial agent.[98] However, where the scale of actual or projected after-sales service is vast and likely to generate significant profits, the principal may wish to form a limited liability company[99] to perform this type of activity with the participation of the agent and/or other participants.[100] Such a company's permitted activities need not be restricted to after-sales servicing of the principal's products but may also extend to operation, maintenance, installation, and the like, provided that any such activity has received due governmental approvals. Furthermore, such activities may also be performed with respect to products other than the principal's which the company has the technical capabilities to handle.[101] Since contributions to the capital of the company may be made in kind,[102] the principal will be able to contribute such items as equipment, machinery, raw material, or spare parts required for the company's activities toward its share in the capital. Since the principal normally possesses relevant knowhow, experience, and technology, certain provisions of the company's articles of association or bylaws may permit the principal's suggestions to be given proper weight even in the case where it is a minority participant in the company. Certain other provisions in the articles of association or bylaws may enable the company to achieve the desired level of operational stability. The efforts of the Saudi participant(s) will be invaluable in respect of various local aspects of the business.

Tax benefits

One of the major advantages to be derived by the principal from its participation in such a company is the five-year tax holiday afforded to the profit shares of nonSaudi participants[103] in such a service company having a minimum of twenty-five percent Saudi equity participation,[104] provided that

---

[98] See generally p. 15 supra.

[99] Unless permission is obtained to open a local branch, which permission is rarely granted, the limited liability company is the form generally available to Fonco. See p. 63 infra.

[100] The governmental permissions required for and the licensing and registration procedures applicable to the formation of such a company are set forth at length in Chap. 2.

[101] If, however, a Saudi agent has been appointed with respect to such other products, after-sales services will generally be performed by it.

[102] See Companies Regs., art. 3.

[103] Saudi participants remain liable for zakāt. However, their zakāt liability, if not diminished by virtue of the formation of such a company, will not be increased thereby, except in proportion to the increase in their net worth.

[104] Foreign Capital Investment Regs., Royal Decree No. M/4, art. 7(b) (1979). See generally pp. 73–75 infra.

Saudi participants are entitled to a minimum of twenty-five percent of such a company's profits.[105] Furthermore, in the event that the company applies for and obtains a license to carry out such activities as assembling certain parts, manufacturing components, packaging, processing, and the like, it will be licensed as an "industrial" rather than a "contracting" venture.[106] In this case, the applicable tax holiday will be ten years as from the date of commencement of production.[107]

2. Technical alternative: technical and scientific consulting office ["technical office"]

The activities of a technical office are confined to providing technical and scientific services, including advisory and consulting services, to the commercial agents, and other purchasers of the principal's products. The technical office may also render these services to end-users of the products. Furthermore, it may carry out market studies relating to such products and prepare reports for submission to the principal's offices outside the Kingdom. The activities of a technical office may not be commercial or generate profits, whether directly or indirectly. Another category of activities open to a technical office is that of services relating to the submission of bids in either the public or the private sector. Thus, in the case of bid submission by either the principal or its commercial agent, the technical office may provide technical assistance and/or advice and also explain any technical matters to the customer.[108] A technical office may participate in negotiations relating to bids for the purpose of explaining and clarifying technical points. In addition it may submit technical data, information reports, and feasibility studies to the principal, the agent and customers or consumers. The customer may seek technical advice and assistance directly from the technical office prior to the award of the contract to the principal or its commercial agent. In contrast, the technical office is prohibited from rendering services relating to goods produced or sold by third parties.

---

[105] It may be noted that profit-shares need not correspond to the participants' equity holdings. *See* Companies Regs., art. 171. *See generally* pp. 121–123 *infra*. However, an extreme disproportion may give rise to a presumption that the parties' arrangement is a sham transaction. Any disproportion between profit and equity ratios should therefore be supported in the articles of association by additional services required of the participant in whose favor such disproportion exists. If in favor of the Saudi participant, it may be supported by its obligation to provide local services, customer relations and development, promotional activities, logistical support, day-to-day administration of the company, and obtention of the required governmental permits, licenses, and approvals. If in favor of the nonSaudi participant, it may be supported by the provision of technology, knowhow, rights relating to its industrial property, or specialized operational or management services.

[106] *See* Minister of Indus. & Elec. Resolution No. 952, arts. 2, 5 (4/11/1400) (translated in Appendix 9).

[107] Foreign Capital Investment Regs., art. 7(b). *See generally* p. 73 *infra*.

[108] However, the technical office itself is not permitted to submit bids.

A technical office is licensed by the Ministry of Commerce under article 228 of the Companies Regulations and is specifically subject to Minister of Commerce Resolution No. 1532.[109] Although this requirement is not expressly set forth, the foreign seller must have a Saudi commercial agent in order to obtain a license.[110] The technical office and any branches it may eventually open are staffed by the technical personnel of the foreign seller seconded to the office.[111] Although it is permitted to possess any spare parts and equipment required for the provision of technical services, it is not permitted to import any such items, which will in general be imported by means of the agent. Furthermore, the technical office may not receive payments for the rendering of services to any person. Its books may show only expenditures. The office must thus be entirely funded by the foreign principal, either directly or through the principal's commercial agent in Saudi Arabia. A license is valid for one year and may be renewed annually. Along with the application for the renewal of its license, the

---

[109] Resolution No. 1532 (6/6/1395) (translated in Appendix 10). It may be noted that the policy of the Ministry of Commerce is restrictive with respect to licensing technical offices. The documents required to be submitted with the license application are: (a) a power of attorney in favor of either the future manager of the proposed office or a representative of the foreign principal; (b) a copy of the certificate of incorporation of the foreign principal in the country of its formation; (c) a description of the technical and scientific services which the office proposes to execute; (d) a resolution issued by the board of directors of the foreign principal authorizing the company to establish such an office in the Kingdom; (e) three letters of recommendation, two from customers located in the Kingdom and one from the principal's commercial agent or distributor. Persons writing the letters should state that they are in need of such technical services in connection with the goods of the foreign company. The documents mentioned under the headings (a), (b), and (d) *supra* must be notarized and attested by the Saudi consulate in the principal's country and translated into Arabic. Such translation should be certified or authenticated. *See* Minister of Commerce & Indus. Resolution No. 424 (26/2/1391). *See generally* Appendix 11 (requirements of Saudi consulate in United States). The application should also contain documentary evidence attesting to the capability, knowledge, experience, and knowhow of the applicant with respect to the technical and scientific services required by the customers or the commercial agent in connection with its products. No problem of convincing proof regarding the applicant's experience and knowhow will arise if the applicant is the manufacturer of the finished goods or of any major component part, or the assembler of the goods. Proof that the applicant is presently rendering or has rendered production management services in connection with the goods involved may also be sufficient to satisfy the requirement in certain cases. However, problems may arise if the applicant cannot prove either of the preceding facts or the required knowhow.

[110] *But see* requirement (e), note 109 *supra* (implicitly requiring foreign company to have Saudi commercial agent or distributor as condition precedent to obtaining license).

[111] As a rule, its license will permit the technical office to sponsor and employ only five nonSaudi nationals. There is no restriction on the number of "local employees", namely, Saudi nationals who may be employed by the office. A person who is already working in the Kingdom as an expatriate will be considered an expatriate even if hired by the technical office locally. Application for permission to increase the number of expatriate employees may be made to the Ministry of Commerce on the basis of the volume of work or the opening of new branches. In addition, the office may obtain visitor's visas for the personnel of the seller's foreign offices desiring to travel to the Kingdom.

technical office must submit a brief report describing its activities during the previous year. After the expiration of the initial year, the technical office may also apply for permission to establish additional branches if so desired.[112] The Ministry of Commerce will base its decision whether to allow the technical office to open new branches on the office's report on its activities of the prior year.

III. Services Agent

A. SCOPE OF SERVICES AGENTS REGULATIONS

1. Requirement of an agent

Until the Services Agents Regulations were issued in 1978, Fonco, as a foreign contractor, could contract with Saudi clients in the public sector to perform executory[113] projects or provide professional or consulting services without being required to have a Saudi agent. Foreign contractors were permitted to execute such projects solely on the basis of temporary licenses issued by the Ministry of Commerce. If they wished to appoint an agent to perform certain services, they could, of course, appoint a Saudi agent. Under present law, however, if Fonco as prime contractor has not appointed a Saudi services agent, it is barred from performing executory projects or undertaking consulting work in the public sector.[114] Article 3 of the Services Agents Regulations provides that a "foreign contractor who does not have a Saudi partner shall have a Saudi services agent. A foreign contractor may not appoint a nonSaudi as agent."[115] The sole exceptions provided in the Regulations to the requirement of appointing a services agent are contained in article 4, which provides that "agency is not permitted in armament contracts and services related thereto or in cases of direct dealings between the Government and foreign governments."[116] Except with respect to contracts within the scope of article 4, a foreign contractor is required to appoint a services agent as part of the process of tendering for public sector contracts

---

[112] The applicant will be required to prove demand for additional branches on the part of customers or consumers and its commercial agent.

[113] The term "executory" is used herein to describe contracts providing for the rendering of services, as distinguished from the supply of goods, and does not denote the time of performance of such contracts.

[114] The appointment of an agent, however, does not excuse Fonco from the requirement of obtaining a temporary license to execute any projects it may have obtained. *See generally* pp. 58–59 *infra*.

[115] *See also* note 127 *infra*.

[116] *See generally* pp. 3–4 *supra*.

subject to the Regulations.[117] Article 8 provides that a "foreign contractor shall submit with its bid a letter stating the agent and its address and confirmed by the agent."[118]

2. "Foreign contractor"

Article 1 sets forth the parties subject to the Regulations. It provides that a "Saudi agent and a foreign contractor who contracts with the Government of the Kingdom of Saudi Arabia shall be subject to the provisions of these Regulations. Individuals and companies undertaking executory or consulting works shall be considered as contractor[s]." The term "foreign contractor" appearing in the Regulations generally applies to all Foncos, including those licensed under the Foreign Capital Investment Regulations to open and operate branch offices in the Kingdom.[119] In contrast, any persons not fitting within the definition of a foreign contractor or its agent are not subject to the restrictions provided in the Regulations such as the ceiling on agents' fees or the number of foreign contractors for whom an agent may act. The Regulations do not apply to Mixcos as contractors.

Contractor

The term appearing in the Regulations translated as "contractor" is "muqāwil", which is the term commonly used for a contractor.[120] However, by virtue of article 1, the scope of the term "contractor" is expressly extended for purposes of the Regulations to include professionals and consultants, to whom the term does not apply in common usage.[121] In contrast, the

[117] In the case of the construction of a foreign embassy or diplomatic quarters, a question arises as to the proper qualification of the project. From the viewpoint of Saudi law, such a project is neither squarely within the "public sector" nor the "private sector." Therefore, it is unclear whether Fonco, as prime contractor, needs a temporary license and a services agent or not. This issue has been widely debated in Saudi legal and official circles.

[118] In practice, foreign contractors submit together with their bids a letter from the agent on its letterhead stating that it has agreed to act as agent for such contractor with respect to the tendered-for contract. See also Minister of Fin. & Nat'l Econ. Letter No. 4633/402, para. 1 (June 15, 1982); Director-Gen'l of DZIT Circular No. 9721/2, paras. 1-2 (Aug. 4, 1982) (only those fees paid to agents whose names and addresses, inter alia are specified in the foreign contractors' bids are deductible for Saudi tax purposes) (both translated in Appendix 12).

[119] See generally pp. 67–68 infra.

[120] Cf. Agency for Classification of Contractors, Ministry of Public Works & Housing, Contractor Classification Manual, pt. 3(2) (defining "contractor" as "any firm licensed to engage in construction and maintenance activities") (translated in Appendix 13); Minister of Indus. & Elec. Resolution No. 952, art. 6 (4/11/1400) (defining "contracting" as "the habitual execution of specified works for third parties for compensation" including civil construction and mechanical and electrical projects) (translated in Appendix 9).

[121] See also M. ABŪ AL-'AINAIN, MABĀDI' AL-QĀNŪN LI RIJĀL AL-A'MĀL FĪ AL-MAMLAKAH AL-ARABIYYAH AL-SU'ŪDIYYAH 342 (1981) (defining contract of muqāwalah (contracting) as "a contract concluded between a client and an independent contractor by virtue of which the contractor agrees to make a thing or to execute [certain] work in consideration of an amount of property") (distinguishing such a contract from an employment contract).

Regulations as presently interpreted and applied exclude from their scope a category of persons covered by the term "contractor", namely, subcontractors.[122] This result may be explained in various ways. It may, for example, be inferred from the fact that the Regulations consistently refer to the "contractor" and nowhere refer to subcontractors. Hence, the term "contractor" as employed therein would be strictly construed. In addition, it may be noted that article 1 provides that the Regulations are applicable to a foreign contractor "who contracts with" the Saudi Government. Hence, privity of contract could be viewed as required in order to give rise to the requirement of appointing a services agent.[123] Regardless of the reasoning, the result is that, for purposes of the Regulations, the term "contractor" should at present be interpreted to mean "prime contractor". It will be noted that the definition of a contractor implicit in article 1 is nonexclusive. The Regulations could, in theory, be applicable to persons having contracted with a public sector client with respect to other than executory or consulting works. For example, the term "muqāwalah" as employed in the Commercial Court Regulations is used, *inter alia*, to designate "contracting" for the supply of goods as well as for the provision of services.[124] However, the term "contractor" for purposes of the Services Agents Regulations does not extend to the mere supplier of goods. It may be observed that the Regulations, in practice, are not applied to that group. More important, Saudi regulations adhere to the common usage of "muqāwil", *i.e.* executory contractor. Thus, the Old Tender Regulations distinguish between the contractor, "muqāwil", and the supplier, "muta'ahhid."[125] To the extent that the drafters of article 1 intended to preserve this distinction, suppliers are clearly not subject to the Services Agents Regulations. It will also be noted that even though the present Tender Regulations as a rule subsume both contractors and suppliers under the global heading "muta'āqid", contracting party, in those few instances where they do differentiate linguistically between contractors and suppliers, the former term is clearly applicable to persons performing executory works.[126] Therefore, the

---

[122] *Cf.* Minister of Fin. & Nat'l Econ. Letter No. 4633/402, para. 2 (June 15, 1982) (directing DZIT to disallow deduction of agents' fees paid by subcontractors since such fees are not paid in accordance with regulations and are not obligatory) (translated in Appendix 12).

[123] This principle is not affected by any right of the public sector customer to approve the prime contractor's choice of subcontractor or the fact that the subcontractor may in some cases become a party to agreements between the customer and the prime contractor.

[124] *See* Commercial Court Regs., art. 2(b).

[125] *See, e.g.,* Old Tender Regs., arts. 75–77; *cf.* Minister of Fin. & Nat'l Econ. Memorandum No. 6238/12/2 (26/5/1387) (distinguishing between operations of contracting and supply). This distinction is regulatory, since the word "muta'ahhid" means generally "contractor", *i.e.* one who makes a contractual commitment. *Cf.* Commercial Court Regs., art. 2(b) (both terms applicable to supplying).

[126] *See, e.g.,* Tender Regs., art. 8(b) ("contractor's" entitlements to be paid according to progression of work); *cf.* Ministry of Fin. & Nat'l Econ. Circular No. 17/5374 (25/3/1398)

term "muqāwil", as appearing in the Services Agents Regulations, should be read to exclude any persons properly describable by the term "mutaʿahhid".

3. Saudi partner

Under article 3, if Fonco has a "Saudi partner", it need not appoint a services agent. If Fonco's business activities in Saudi Arabia are not of a professional or consulting nature, a "partner" for purposes of the Regulations may be a Saudi natural person, sole proprietorship, or juristic person as coparticipant with Fonco in a commercially registered company formed under the Companies Regulations and having its main office in Saudi Arabia. It will be noted that, although such Saudi participant is from a legal standpoint the partner of Fonco, this does not mean that Fonco has a "partner" for purposes of article 3. Rather, it will be the company in which Fonco participates that will tender for and execute projects. In such case, it will not be required to appoint a services agent because, as a Saudi company, it is not covered by the term "foreign contractor." However, if Fonco, even though a partner in such company, is to enter in its own name into a public sector contract, whether or not within the objectives of such company, it is required to appoint a services agent, since it retains its status of "foreign contractor" under the Services Agents Regulations.

Alternatively, the Saudi partner satisfying the requirement of article 3 may be Fonco's joint adventurer as provided in the Companies Regulations.[127] A "joint adventure" is defined as "a company of which third parties are not aware and which neither has a juristic personality nor is subject to publication formalities."[128] Joint adventures are not commercially registered. Nonetheless,

---

(differentiating between supply and handing over of executory work). *See also* Tender Regs. Implementing Rules, Minister of Fin. & Nat'l Econ. Resolution No. 17/2131, arts. 25, 28–29 (5/5/1397) (retaining old terminology); Ministry of Fin. & Nat'l Econ. Circular No. 17/11901 (12/7/1398) (same).

[127] *Cf.* Ministry of Commerce Legal Dep't Memorandum (21/4/1399) (approved by Deputy Minister of Commerce 23/4/1399) (foreign company executing contract jointly with Saudi partner may not have Saudi services agent), *cited in* S. YAḤYĀ, AL-WAJĪZ FI AL-NIZĀM AL-TIJĀRĪ AL-SUʿŪDĪ, 407 (4th ed. 1983).

[128] Companies Regs., art. 40. It will be observed that, although a joint adventure or, if one prefers, joint venture, is not infrequently regarded by persons unfamiliar with Saudi law as a mere contractual arrangement, it is a company subject to the Companies Regs., which generally define the forms which they provide as contracts. *See id.* art. 1. Thus, even though the contract establishing a joint adventure is not required to be acknowledged by a notary public, *see id.* art. 10, it is required to state certain particulars, *see id.* art. 43, in order to comply with Saudi regulations. Furthermore, a joint adventure has a financial year, and all adventurers are deemed creditors of the joint adventure with respect to their shares in the profits as of the time of determination of such shares at the end of the financial year. *See id.* arts. 26, 47. It may also be noted that, if the joint adventure contract is for an unspecified period, it is dissolved by force of law on the withdrawal, bankruptcy, or insolvency, *inter alia*, of any adventurer, unless the contract provides otherwise. *See id.* arts. 35, 47. The general advantage to operating under the form of a joint adventure is the fact that creditors will only have recourse against the adventurer with whom they dealt, provided that the existence of the joint adventure was not disclosed to any such third party. *Id.* art. 46.

joint adventurers are given the status of "partners" by the Companies Regulations, and this status is also respected by the Ministry of Commerce in its interpretation of the Services Agents Regulations.[129] Until now no comprehensive guidelines have officially been issued with respect to any required minimum Saudi participation in a joint adventure qualifying as a "partner" for purposes of article 3.[130]

If, in contrast, Fonco's activities in Saudi Arabia are professional or consulting activities, it will not have available to it the option of participating in a local commercially registered company. Thus, its only available "partner" for purposes of article 3 will be a Saudi consulting or professional office duly licensed to perform activities in the area of Fonco's specialization.

4. Subject contracts

Article 2 of the Services Agents Regulations provides that "[t]hese regulations shall apply to all contracts concluded between a foreign contractor and the Government of Saudi Arabia." The nature or subject of the contracts to which the Regulations apply is not elsewhere officially addressed. Nonetheless, the legal rule is that Fonco is required to appoint a services agent only with respect to executory or consulting contracts, as distinguished from supply contracts. This result is based on both legal and practical considerations. Notably, a foreign seller may only supply a public sector customer by direct sale from outside the Kingdom or by means of a Saudi commercial agent, distributor or importer.[131] In the former case, generally there will be no local services to be provided to the foreign seller, as opposed to the customer. Hence, the appointment of a services agent, whose role is to facilitate the activities of a contractor within the Kingdom,[132] will in most cases serve no useful function. In the latter case, the foreign principal will already have a local representative, which in general will be the party supplying the principal's products to the customer and responsible for assuring services as required by regulation and contract to the customer.

Those contracts to which the Regulations apply may require the provision of consulting services, the performance of executory works, or the performance of executory works together with the provision of goods, materials, and/or equipment relating to such works. This last category of mixed executory/supply contracts is to be distinguished from contracts for the sole supply of goods. Saudi law is, to a certain extent, flexible with respect to drawing lines

---

[129] Since Fonco is required to obtain a temporary license from the Ministry of Commerce in order to perform any public sector project it has obtained, a determination whether Fonco is required to have a services agent is made by that Ministry.

[130] Practically speaking, a 25% Saudi participation may be regarded as adequate, in view of other applicable regulatory rules.

[131] See generally pp. 8–9 supra.

[132] See generally pp. 52–53 infra.

between mixed executory and supply contracts. Nonetheless, it may not be stretched too far. The mere provision of certain after-sales services, periodical repairs and maintenance, technical advisory services on a temporary or periodical basis, any or all of which may be necessary and related to a sale and supply contract, will not transform such a contract into an executory contract to which the Regulations apply. Conversely, the sale or supply of goods, materials, and equipment required for and directly related to the main executory works contracted for will not transform an executory contract into a supply contract.[133]

Understanding the distinction between executory and supply contracts is essential if Fonco is not to fall foul of the Regulations. One context in which this distinction is of particular legal significance is that of the permissible amount of commissions payable to the agent in the case where the same Saudi entity is acting both as services agent and commercial agent for the same foreign contractor/principal with respect to the same project and customer. There is no restriction on the amount of commissions payable to a commercial agent, markup permitted to a distributor, or profit earnable by either. However, the regulatory maximum fee of five percent of the contract value[134] payable to a services agent applies not only to pure executory contracts but also to mixed executory contracts which include the supply of certain goods, materials, or equipment. Therefore, care should be taken in the structuring of the transaction if the project is of a mixed nature. If the contract involves both executory work and the provision of goods, whether a turnkey project or not, and it is not desirable or possible to split the contract into separate executory and supply contracts, it will be advisable to cover the supply portion under the services agency agreement in those cases where the contractor seeks to minimize its payouts. In such cases, the agent's commission will be limited to a maximum of five percent of the total contract price. However, if the subject contract is in substance a supply contract, whether or not providing for the rendering of after-sales services, the regulatory ceiling on commissions will be unavailable to Fonco, since such services are normally performed by a commercial agent and not a services agent. Conversely, if the foreign contractor is seeking to minimize its Saudi tax liability, it may endeavor to do so by covering the supply portion of its contract under the commercial agency agreement, provided that the goods are delivered F.O.B. or C.I.F. Saudi port and not to the site.[135]

---

[133] As a public sector contractor, Fonco will in all cases be required to procure goods and materials locally, where available at reasonable prices, and is barred from importing items except by means of a local Saudi agent or distributor, its Saudi "partner", if any, or a duly registered Saudi importer.

[134] See generally pp. 55–56 infra.

[135] See generally pp. 33–35 supra, pp. 60–61 infra.

B. THE AGENT

Article 5 of the Regulations provides that "the agent shall be of Saudi nationality, resid[e] in the Kingdom of Saudi Arabia, and hav[e] a commercial registration permitting it to be an agent." This general provision is subject to certain qualifications.

1. "Saudi nationality"

The agent is required to be Saudi.[136] Saudi nationals desiring to act as agents must either adopt the form of a sole proprietorship or professional office or participate in a company. If a company, the agent must be of wholly Saudi participation, despite the fact that, aside from joint adventures, mixed participation companies formed under the Companies Regulations and having their main offices in the Kingdom are deemed to have Saudi nationality.[137] A sole proprietorship, which has no juristic personality, has the nationality of its owner. Consequently, the phrase "of Saudi nationality residing in the Kingdom of Saudi Arabia" appearing in article 5 should be interpreted to mean "formed and registered or licensed under Saudi law, of wholly Saudi ownership and having its main office in the Kingdom."

2. "Commercial registration permitting it to be an agent"

Regardless of the form under which it is operating, a Saudi entity may not perform agency activities unless it is authorized to do so by the Ministry of Commerce or, in certain cases, by other competent authorities. Consequently, a joint adventure, which may not be registered or licensed, may not act as an agent, even if all members are of Saudi nationality.[138] The general rule is that commercial concerns of whatever nature must be commercially registered with the Ministry of Commerce.[139] In contrast, most professional or consulting offices, which are generally sole proprietorships, are licensed as professionals by, as opposed to commercially registered with, the Ministry of Commerce,[140]

---

[136] *See also* Services Agents Regs., art. 3 (providing both that a foreign contractor must have a Saudi agent and may not appoint a nonSaudi as agent).

[137] Companies Regs., art. 14.

[138] However, a duly registered or licensed member of a joint adventure may act as a services agent.

[139] *See* Commercial Register Regs., arts. 2–5. There are certain exceptions to the requirement of registration, including persons having no fixed place of business, such as itinerant plumbers, carpenters, and blacksmiths, and commercial endeavors having a capital not exceeding five thousand riyals, for which registration is optional.

[140] *See* Council of Ministers Resolution No. 66, art. 13 (6/4/1374) (approved by Royal Approval, High Office Letter No. 17/1/8117 (10/8/1374)) (authorizing Minister of Commerce to establish commercial register and to license both commercial enterprises and liberal professions). *Cf.* Council of Ministers Resolution No. 17, para. 4(b) (1982), *as amended by* Council of Ministers Resolution No. 80 (30/4/1405) (providing for registration of professional partnerships); Minister of Commerce Resolution No. 264, art. 9 (July 7, 1982) (relating to standard form articles of association for engineering consulting general partnerships).

and are not subject to the Commercial Register Regulations. Thus, the regulatory language requiring the agent to have a commercial registration should be interpreted to mean to have either a commercial registration certificate or a license. In either case, the document evidencing registration or licensing must include the activity of acting as an agent for foreign companies among the approved activities of the agent.

3. Professional services

Saudi law distinguishes between the liberal professions and commercial activities. The Regulations make this distinction in the area of services agency. Article 3, which requires foreign contractors to have Saudi services agents, also provides that "if the foreign contractor is performing consulting activities, its agent shall be a Saudi consulting office." Thus, an agent having a commercial registration certificate, rather than a professional license, may not act as agent for a foreign contractor with respect to consulting contracts with Saudi public sector customers. Conversely, consulting offices, which are not permitted to engage in commercial activities, may not act as agents for nonprofessional principals with respect to executory projects. Furthermore, a consulting office may not act as the agent of a professional whose profession is different from its own. For example, a Saudi engineering consulting office may not act as agent for a foreign financial management consulting firm.

However, the owner of a consulting office who is the Saudi license-holder may lawfully be a partner in a limited liability company, a limited partner in a limited partnership, or shareholder in a corporation, any of which is engaged in commercial activities, provided that he does so in his personal capacity as distinguished from acting in the name of the consulting office.[141] Furthermore, there is no restriction on any such person holding a majority interest in a commercial entity licensed to act as a commercial or services agent. Thus, the prohibition against consulting offices' engaging in commercial activities is, in fact, limited to activities performed by the consulting office in its own name. Despite this fact, any owner of a Saudi consulting office is subject to the constraints of article 9 of the Regulations. Article 9 provides

> a Saudi agent may not combine consulting agency and executory agency with respect to one project. However, a Saudi services agent may be an agent for a foreign contractor contracting for consulting works on a project and at the same time be an agent for a foreign contractor contracting for executory works on another project.

---

[141] In contrast, a professional consultant may not be a partner with unlimited liability in any of the commercial forms recognized by the Companies Regulations. Furthermore, a professional person may not establish a commercial sole proprietorship, whose owner is subject to unlimited liability.

Article 9 thus suggests that a Saudi consulting office may not act as services agent for a foreign consulting firm with respect to a certain project if a Saudi commercial entity in which the owner of the consulting office has an interest is the services agent of the contractor performing executory works with respect to such project.[142]

C. NONEXCLUSIVITY

Saudi law does not require exclusivity from either party to the services agency relationship. Article 6 of the Regulations provides that "[a] foreign contractor may have more than one Saudi agent in the case that it has diversified activities. A Saudi agent may be the agent for a number of foreign contractors not exceeding ten."

1. Multiple agents

There is no regulatory restriction on the number of Saudi services agents a foreign contractor may appoint with respect to its diversified activities. Furthermore, the article 6 "diversified activities" entitling the contractor to engage additional services agents may all relate to the same project. Thus, a foreign contractor may have more than one services agent, whether on a project-to-project basis, for a specified term either on an exclusive or nonexclusive basis, or simultaneously with respect to the contractor's various activities. For example, a foreign contractor may appoint one services agent with respect to the architectural portion of the contract, another with respect to infrastructure, planning, and design, and a third with respect to the portion of the contract relating to site supervision. If the foreign contractor is also involved in other projects, it may have different services agents for various activities, such as building construction, drilling of wells, installation of machinery, or construction of power stations. However, all portions of any government contract performed by Fonco as prime contractor must be covered under an agency.

2. Multiple contractors

A Saudi agent may not act as services agent for more than ten contractors at the same time. However, this limitation applies to registered or licensed business entities and not to the individuals participating in them. Thus, a Saudi consulting office whose owner holds, in his personal capacity, a majority

---

[142] No minimum or maximum percentages are set by law with respect to disqualifying ownership interests. *See also* Minister of Commerce Resolution No. 264, art. 16 (July 7, 1982) (prohibiting licensed engineering consultant from having direct or indirect interest in the commercial and contracting areas of the projects in which it is rendering engineering services).

interest in a commercial entity acting as agent for ten foreign commercial contractors, may lawfully act as agent for ten foreign consulting firms. Since the Regulations apply only to services agents and services agency agreements, any commercial agency agreements made between an agent and foreign principals are to be omitted from the count for purposes of article 6.

D. THE SERVICES AGENCY AGREEMENT

1. Requirement of agreement

Article 7 of the Regulations provides that "the relationship between the agent and the foreign contractor shall be regulated by an agency agreement defining the obligations of the parties." It is imperative that the rights and duties of the parties be clearly set forth in the agreement, not only to satisfy the requirement of article 7, but also because it is in accordance with the terms of that agreement that any eventual dispute arising between the parties with respect to the agency relationship will be resolved, to the extent that the parties' agreement is not contrary to Saudi law or public policy.[143]

2. Avoidance of ambiguity

The setting forth of the parties' respective obligations with specificity will also be of importance in the event of a government investigation of any acts deemed violative of the Regulations, or investigation or criminal prosecution under any other applicable law, including the antibribery regulations.[144] In case the obligations of the parties are not clearly defined in the agreement, the parties may have difficulties in accounting for certain payments made by the foreign contractor to the services agent or by the agent to a third party. In addition, the provisions of the agency agreement should be drafted with care to avoid any implication of an unlawful purpose or unlawful conduct of the parties. Unambiguity will be essential if such provisions, and in some cases the entire agreement, are to be valid and enforceable under Saudi law. In particular, the agreement should be drafted so as to give no implication that any of the services to be performed by the agent relate to brokerage or mediation. For example, the agreement may not provide that the agent will use its influence or relations to obtain projects or to obtain projects at a price above the market price or without submitting formal bids. A provision that the agent's fee will be a certain percentage of the contract value but, if the agent assists the contractor in obtaining contracts at prices higher than market rates or the price of the lowest bidder, an additional fee will be paid, is also

---

[143] *See generally* pp. 16–33 *supra* (certain aspects of discussion of commercial agency agreement also relevant to services agency agreement).

[144] *See generally* pp. 27–28 *supra*.

illegal and unenforceable. Furthermore, generally ambiguous language and contractual provisions casting doubt on the genuineness of the agent's services are likely to create problems. While a clause providing that the agent "shall assist the contractor in promoting its business" is valid, a clause providing that the agent will assist the contractor in improving rates or prices of contracts gives rise to an inference that the agent will be using its influence or contacts. In contrast, no problem is created by providing that the agent will assist the contractor in contract negotiations. The effect of an illegal or void provision on the agreement as a whole will depend on the nature of the clause at issue. Certain provisions, such as a clause providing for the use of a party's influence, may cause the entire agreement to become void, even if such agreement includes a severability clause. Other unenforceable provisions, such as a provision for the payment of interest, may simply drop out and will not contaminate the entire agreement.

3. Usual services

A services agent is generally required to render the following services: to provide information on local business conditions and opportunities; to assist in obtaining official classification of the contractor with the Agency for Classification of Contractors;[145] to assist the contractor in prequalifying with

[145] Classification rules are required to be observed by government customers subject to the Tender Regulations. *See, e.g.*, Ministry of Fin. & Nat'l Econ. Circular No. 17/7942 (3/5/1398) (interpreting art. 1(c) of Tender Regs.). Minister of Public Works and Housing Resolution No. 929 (Jan. 1, 1983) categorizes contractors with respect to their eligibility to obtain projects on the basis of project value as follows:

Contractor Category	5	4	3	2	1
Buildings	5	15	50	200	more than 200
Roads	10	30	100	300	,, ,, 300
Water & Sewage	10	30	100	300	,, ,, 300
Electrical	5	15	50	200	,, ,, 200
Mechanical	5	15	50	200	,, ,, 200
Industrial	10	30	100	300	,, ,, 300
Marine	10	30	100	300	,, ,, 300
Dams	5	15	50	100	,, ,, 100
Maintenance	2	10	30	100	,, ,, 100

(in millions of Saudi Riyals)

Classification is not made in certain areas, such as camp services and life support services. With respect to classification, no distinction is made in principle between Foncos, Mixcos, and Saucos. Contractors may bid only for projects whose value does not exceed the amount stated in the applicable category, provided that they have obtained a prequalification certificate. However, even though, for example, a building contractor in category 5 may not bid for a project in excess of five million riyals, it may obtain several projects, each not exceeding that value, at the same time. For classification forms and required supporting documentation, *see generally* Agency for Classification of Contractors, Ministry of Public Works & Housing, Contractor Classification Manual (translated in Appendix 13).

prospective clients in the public sector; to assist in the preparation and submission of bids; to give advice on local business practices and customs; to assist in arranging local financing; to sponsor the contractor's personnel and to assist the contractor in obtaining work permits and visas for its personnel and labor; to assist in securing payment from the customer; to assist in government relations; to provide logistical support; and to assist in obtaining any applicable licenses or other governmental authorizations.

In addition, either in the agency agreement or in separate agreements, the parties may agree that the agent will provide the foreign contractor with communication facilities, translation services, clerical staff, either fulltime or temporary, and office space or render any other services relating to the business of the foreign contractor.[146] The parties may agree to modify the nature and extent of the agent's services at different stages of the project or on the basis of changes in the contractor's business situation. In the case of an agency agreement on a contract basis, unless otherwise provided in the agreement, the agreement is deemed to commence as of the date of signature of the agreement and to end upon completion of the public sector contract.[147]

4. Notification

Unlike commercial agency agreements, services agency agreements are not subject to registration requirements.[148] However, at such time that Fonco applies to the Ministry of Commerce for a temporary license in order to execute its government contract,[149] a copy of the agency agreement must be submitted together with the license application. In addition, the Ministry of Commerce may require Fonco to submit a letter from its services agent confirming that it represents Fonco as agent for that specific contract. Even though Fonco has the right, subject to regulatory limitations, to have more than one services agent with respect to a given contract,[150] it is not required to notify either the Ministry of Commerce or its public sector client of all services agency agreements it has entered into with respect to such contract. Nonsubmission of the names of and copies of the agreements with any

[146] See generally pp. 56–58 infra.
[147] Completion of the contract in this context may be generally defined as the time of release of the performance guarantee. See generally Tender Regs., art. 8(b); Tender Regs. Implementing Rules, art. 24. In case the agency agreement is for a term and expires or is terminated by either party or is on a contract basis but is terminated prior to completion of such contract, the agreement should clearly specify the parties' respective rights and duties with respect to any period subsequent to termination.
[148] Although the Ministry of Commerce, after the issuance of the Services Agents Regs., had stated in unofficial communications that a separate register similar to the Commercial Agents and Distributors Register would be established for services agency agreements, in particular to enforce art. 6 of the Regs., limiting the number of contractors an agent may represent to ten, such a register has not yet been established.
[149] See generally pp. 58–59 infra.
[150] See generally p. 50 supra.

additional agents will not render such services agency agreements void or unenforceable. However, failure to submit any such agreements to the government client and to obtain its approval thereof prior to signing the government contract may expose Fonco to disallowance of fees paid pursuant to such agreements as tax deductions.

5. Assignment

There is a difference of opinion as to whether or not a services agency agreement may be assigned to another agent. The majority view is that the agency agreement may be assigned to another services agent if the parties so agree, provided that the assignee is a Saudi entity that qualifies under the Regulations. This view maintains that any such assignment is required to be notified to the Ministry of Commerce and the public sector client if they were originally notified of the agency relationship. In no case may the agreement be assigned to a Fonco or Mixco. In contrast, the agent may, for legitimate business reasons, assign any of its fees or the total proceeds of the agency agreement to a Fonco, Mixco, or Sauco.

E. THE AGENT'S FEES

1. Fees contrasted with share of profits

Article 8 of the Regulations provides that a "foreign contractor shall be obliged to pay the Saudi agent fees in consideration of the services it provides. Such fees shall be determined by agreement of the parties, provided that such fees shall not exceed five percent of the value of the contract which the foreign contractor is executing." Within the regulatory limit, article 8 allows the parties to determine the agent's fees by agreement. However, it does not contemplate either the gratuitous performance of agency services or payments made to agents in the absence of services actually rendered.[151] Additionally, article 8 suggests that payments to the services agent must take the form of "fees." The question then arises as to which forms of payments will and will not be considered as fees. The second sentence of article 8 contemplates the expression of fees as a percentage of the contract value. As a matter of practice, most fees are structured in this form. Alternatively, the parties may agree, in accordance with generally applicable legal rules and

---

[151] Under general rules of Islamic law, services must actually be performed in order to support compensation. Consequently, if the contractor demonstrates that no services were in fact performed by the agent, a Saudi court may not enforce its obligation to make fee payments as provided in the agency agreement. In this context, it may also be noted that the parties' agreement that the agent shall be paid a specified fee whether or not it performs any services is, in theory, void and unenforceable, as is a clause providing that the fee is payable without regard to the quality or extent of the agent's services.

business usage, that the agent's fees will be paid on a lump-sum basis. By the process of elimination, therefore, article 8 taken as a whole gives rise to the inference that a services agent is prohibited from sharing profits with the foreign contractor for which it is acting as agent if the relationship between the parties is based solely on an agency agreement. This inference is supported by the provisions of article 3, which requires a foreign contractor not having a Saudi partner to have a Saudi services agent. Consequently, the Regulations draw a distinction between the concepts of a "partner" and a "services agent" and contemplate a different legal treatment of each category. Furthermore, Saudi law applicable to a "partner" associates the sharing of profits with the sharing of the risks of doing business in participation and does not permit a "partner" to be entitled to guaranteed profits.[152] In contrast, the agent is entitled by regulation to fees in compensation for its services, as agreed by the parties, regardless of whether or not the contractor itself realizes a profit. Finally, the option of expressing "fees" as a percentage of the foreign contractor's profits is precluded by the ceiling placed on fees by article 8. Since the total amount of profits which will arise with respect to the contract cannot be known with certainty at the time of entering into the agency agreement, the agent's share of such profits, were its fees to be structured as a percentage thereof, could potentially exceed the regulatory ceiling of five percent of the contract value. Hence, the parties' agreement on fee payments would be capable at any time of being or becoming illegal and unenforceable. However, there is an opinion that the agent's fees may be structured as a percentage of the contractor's net profits not exceeding the regulatory limit if the nature of the agent's services may affect the amount of profits of the contractor.

2. Five percent of the value of the contract

The regulatory limit on agents' fees was established in order to curb brokerage, to check inflated prices, and to ensure that agents would not receive compensation incommensurate with services actually rendered. In view of the remedial purposes that it was designed to serve, the five percent ceiling is strictly enforced. The term "value of the contract" is interpreted to mean the value of a contract or the portion of a contract being performed by the foreign contractor. In computing the value of such contract or portion, any variation in value by reason of increase or reduction of the scope of work will be taken into account.[153] However, if any reduction is attributable to

---

[152] *See generally* p. 84 *infra.*

[153] *See generally* President of the Council of Ministers Circular No. 21909 (15/9/1403) (public sector project-owner has discretion to increase project value up to 10%) (reaffirming 20% reduction rate provided in art. 25 of Tender Regs. Implementing Rules) (translated in Appendix 14).

delay penalties imposed by the customer, the agent will be entitled to its fees as originally agreed unless otherwise provided in the agreement. In the case of contracts awarded on a cost-plus-fee basis, the "value of the contract" embraces the foreign contractor's portion of the total cost plus the total fee.

Since the five percent ceiling on services agency fees is associated with the total value of the contract, it does not vary on the basis of the number of services agents or foreign contractors. Thus, the total amount of fees payable by various contractors performing a "contract" in association, whether operating as a joint adventure or consortium, to their respective services agents may not exceed five percent of the contract value. Likewise, a sole contractor having several services agents with respect to the same contract may pay fees to each of its various agents in an aggregate amount not in excess of five percent of the value of such contract.

3. Method of payment

The parties are free to determine the timing, place, and manner of payment of the agent's fees in the agency agreement and are advised to do so in their mutual interest. Fees structured as a percentage of the value of the contract are normally paid prorated in proportion to the actual payments received by the foreign contractor from the customer. However, if payments by the customer are delayed or reduced by reason of delay or any other penalties, the agent will be entitled to receive fee payments as scheduled unless the parties have agreed otherwise. In practice, the parties frequently agree that the agent shall be entitled to fee payments in the relevant percentage of amounts actually received by the contractor from the customer and that payments to the agent shall be contingent on the contractor's actually having received such amounts. Particular attention may be given to the agent's rights with respect to payment of fees relating to the final payment by the customer.[154]

F. ADDITIONAL AGREEMENTS

In addition to the services agency agreement required by the Regulations, a foreign contractor may enter into agreements with its services agent with

---

[154] Such final payment may be delayed, *inter alia*, due to inability to fulfil administrative formalities. In one nonhypothetical case, on completion of the contract, the contractor could not claim its final payment since it was unable to submit the tax clearance certificate required to be submitted by the Tender Regulations due to its having differed with the DZIT with respect to its tax liability. The tax ruling was appealed. After more than three years from the date of its actual completion of the contract, the contractor submitted the required tax clearance certificate to the project-owner in order to obtain the final payment. However, the General Audit Board took the position that, according to Council of Ministers Resolution No. 968 of 16/9/1392, the contractor was required to claim such final payment within three hijrah years of completion of the contract and that its claim to such final payment was time-barred.

respect to other business matters. The fact that the agent is acting as agent of the foreign contractor with respect to its public sector contract(s) does not preclude the agent from dealing with the contractor on the same arms' length basis as any other third party. However, any attempt of the parties to avoid the constraints of the regulatory limit on fees payable to a services agent with respect to its agency services by covering any usual and customary agency services under more than one agreement, the total proceeds of which exceed the five percent limit, may not be enforceable. Furthermore, even though the agent may receive payments under various agreements with respect to the provision of services not customarily provided, or required to be provided, by services agents, in the case that total payments, including agency fees, to the agent exceed five percent of the value of the contract with respect to which the agent rendered such additional services, the parties' various transactions may be viewed as suspect unless such services are genuine nonagency services or of a specialized or professional nature.

1. Consulting agreement

The services agent may agree to provide the foreign contractor with consulting, professional, or other specialized services of which it may have need, either through the agent's own specialized staff or by procuring such services from third parties for compensation in addition to the agency fee. In order for such additional payments to be valid under Saudi law, the consulting agreement must require the agent to render genuine consulting services which are not normally considered services agency services and which are not included in the agency agreement. For example, payments pursuant to a "consulting agreement" requiring a services agent to render such customary agency services as assisting the foreign contractor in the preparation and submission of bids or providing local information and marketing advice will not withstand the scrutiny of Saudi judicial authorities. In contrast, legal services, accounting services, engineering services, and the like, are legitimate consulting services for which the agent may receive additional compensation. However, if any such genuine consulting services were already covered in the services agency agreement, excess payments under an additional agreement providing for the performance of those same services may be deemed illegal.

2. Other services

The parties may also enter into agreements for the provision by the agent of various services, provided that such services are neither services normally performed by services agents according to custom and business usage, nor included in or made in any way a part of the services agency agreement between the parties. Such agreements may include the provision of facilities, including, *inter alia*, office space, secretarial staff, transportation, living accommodations, or telecommunication facilities. The foreign contractor may procure its requirements through the agent or arrange for delivery or storage operations to be performed by the agent. These and other reasonable services or facilities will furnish valid justification for payments to the agent made in addition to its fees as provided in the agency agreement, provided that such services or facilities are actually needed and in fact provided.

3. Subcontracts

A foreign contractor is not barred from subcontracting portions of its public sector contract to a services agent appointed with respect to such contract, provided that the latter possesses the capabilities and capacity to perform the subcontract.

G. LICENSE

Fonco, having obtained a contract or contracts in the public sector, will, unless it has been permitted to open a branch,[155] require a license in order to perform such contract(s) in the Kingdom.

1. Temporary license

The requirement of obtaining a license for the specific purpose of performing a certain executory or consulting public sector contract or contracts applies to all foreign contractors engaged in such performance, whether operating independently or in the form of a joint adventure or consortium, whether or not any other members thereof are of Saudi nationality. It also applies to any foreign subcontractors, whether the prime contractor is a Fonco, Mixco, or Sauco.[156] The license application must be filed with the Ministry of Commerce within thirty days of the date of signature of the contract.[157] In the case of

---

[155] See generally pp. 63–64 infra.

[156] Minister of Commerce Resolution No. 680, para. 1 (9/11/1398) (translated in Appendix 15).

[157] Id. For application form, see Appendix 16. Certified true copies of the following documents, inter alia, must be attached to the license application: a certificate from a bank acceptable to the Saudi Arabian Monetary Agency attesting to the capability, reputation, and business dealings of the contractor; statement of projects executed outside Saudi Arabia in the same field, which should be certified by the Chamber of Commerce in the contractor's home country; completion certificates with respect to Saudi and nonSaudi projects performed by the contractor; copies of balance sheets and profit and loss statements for preceding two years certified by a recognized certified accountant; Minister of Commerce Resolution No. 940, art. 1 (29/12/1401). Copies of the government contract(s) with respect to which the license is applied for, the services agency agreement, if applicable, and the commercial registration certificate or license, whichever is applicable, of the agent are also required to be submitted, together with a power of attorney in favor of the contractor's manager or representative in the Kingdom. If such power was drawn up in a language other than Arabic, a translation certified by a Saudi licensed translation office must be attached. The rule is that

subcontractors, the application must be filed within thirty days of the date of signature of the subcontract. The temporary license is granted by the Ministry of Commerce under article 228 of the Companies Regulations.[158] It entitles Fonco to open an office in the Kingdom for the purpose of executing the contract(s) with respect to which the license was granted.[159] The duration of the license is limited to the duration of the contract(s) and any extensions thereof.[160]

A temporary license does not entitle the foreign contractor to benefit from those privileges reserved to entities licensed under the Foreign Capital Investment Regulations or to carry on activities in the private sector. However, it does entitle the foreign contractor, in its own name, to hire local employees, to obtain work visas for expatriate employees, and to import the workforce required for the execution of its public sector contract(s). It may also rent office space and dwellings, own motor vehicles, office equipment, and means of communication such as telephones and telexes. Its letterhead must bear the name of the foreign contractor, the number of the license issued by the Ministry of Commerce, and the complete address of the contractor's office in the Kingdom.

2. Supervision office

In addition to obtaining a temporary license, Fonco is permitted to apply to the Ministry of Commerce for a license to open a supervision office. Such an office is suitable for large Foncos executing several public sector projects or carrying out several kinds of activities in the Kingdom relating to its public sector contracts. The activities of a supervision office are restricted to the organization, follow up, and supervision of Fonco's activities, the liaison with its head office outside of the Kingdom, and the coordination of relations

---

all documents submitted to governmental authorities must be submitted in Arabic. *See, e.g.*, High Order No. 3/h/9574 (27/4/1401); High Order No. 30/h/15351 (20/6/1400); Council of Ministers Resolution No. 266 (21/2/1398) (providing fines for noncompliance) (translated in Appendix 17); Ministry of Fin. & Nat'l Econ. Circular No. 4/2877 (9/10/1403). *But see* High Order No. 3/9574 H (27/4/1401) (creating limited exception for common technical terms in international usage which may be included parenthetically in explanation of Arabic terms). In addition, most of the documents required to be submitted with the license application are, if executed or prepared outside of the Kingdom, required to be authenticated by the Saudi Embassy in such foreign country. For requisite formalities for authentication in the United States, see Appendix 11.

[158] *See generally* p. 8 & note 17 *supra*. Foreign companies contracting with corporations having State participation may also be licensed under art. 228 to perform such contracts in the Kingdom. *See* Legal Memorandum No. 422/q (11/5/1398) (approved by Minister of Commerce 12/5/1398), *cited in* S. YAHYĀ, *supra* note 127, at 404. Failure to obtain the required license will subject the contractor to the penalties provided in the Companies Regs.

[159] Minister of Commerce Resolution No. 680, para.1 (9/11/1398).

[160] *See* Minister of Commerce Circular No. 166/9/493 (29/7/1398), *cited in* Ministry of Fin. & Nat'l Econ. Circular No. 17/1788 (2/2/1399).

between Fonco and public sector customer(s).[161] The office is prohibited from engaging in any commercial activities, directly or indirectly, of its own.[162] Its number of employees is limited to that number permitted by the license issued by the Ministry of Commerce. The supervision office must be operated on a nonprofit basis and its books must show solely expenditures and no income. The license of the supervision office terminates automatically upon the end of Fonco's activities in the Kingdom.[163]

H. TAXATION

The general rule is that the profits of a foreign contractor generated under its public sector executory or consulting contracts performed in the Kingdom are subject to Saudi tax, whether the contractor is acting independently or in the form of a joint adventure.[164] Agency fees paid to a services agent within the limit of five percent of the contract value are deductible expenses, provided that the agency agreement was made prior to the obtention of the public sector contract and the agent's name was submitted with the contractor's bid in fulfillment of the regulatory requirements.[165] Similarly, other legitimate business expenses, including payments made to services agents in respect of other than customary agency services, provided that they are not made pursuant to additional "agency agreements", are deductible expense items.

However, the foreign contractor may reduce its tax liability by signing, where possible, two separate contracts with the customer. The first contract will provide for those services to be performed and/or goods to be sold or supplied from outside Saudi Arabia. Any such goods will be shipped F.O.B. or C.I.F. Saudi ports. The contractor's profits on such contract performed

---

[161] *See* Minister of Commerce Resolution No. 1502, art. 4 (8/3/1400).

[162] *Id.* art. 5.

[163] *Id.* art. 7.

[164] For applicable tax rates, see p. 76 *infra*.

[165] *See* Minister of Fin. & Nat'l Econ. Circular No. 4633/402, para. 1 (June 15, 1982); Director-Gen'l of DZIT Circular No. 9721/2, para. 2 (Aug. 4, 1982) (both translated in Appendix 12). A certificate from the public sector contracting party certifying that the contractor had specified the required particulars relating to the services agent in its tender is required to be submitted to the DZIT in order to claim the deduction of such agent's fees. *See id.* para. 1. Fees paid to an agent appointed by the contractor after it entered into a public sector contract, even if the relevant written agency agreement was made pursuant to an oral agreement predating the signature of the public sector contract, even if within the regulatory 5% limit, are not deductible by such contractor. *Id.* para. 3. However, there may be exceptions to the rule of deductibility. In one case involving a Fonco which, while executing a government contract, formed a Mixco with its services agent and continued to make fee payments pursuant to the agency agreement in addition to the agent's share in the profits as a partner, the DZIT disallowed the deduction of fees on the grounds that, since Fonco was not required by law to retain an agent, its discretionary expenditures on fees, even though within the limit of 5% of the contract value, were not a deductible expense with respect to calculating its tax liability.

outside Saudi Arabia will not in principle be subject to Saudi income tax. The second agreement will cover the services to be performed inside Saudi Arabia. Profits generated thereunder will be taxable. As a precaution against an unfavorable Saudi tax audit, the nature and value of the services provided in the former agreement should be clearly specified, and, where possible, such two contracts will be entered into by two separate entities.

In the alternative, the entire transaction may be covered under a single contract. In this case, the value of the goods and services to be performed should be divided into (i) services to be performed within the Kingdom and goods to be procured from the local market, and (ii) services to be performed and goods to be procured outside the Kingdom. For example, a foreign contractor may perform all the design work at its office outside Saudi Arabia. Profits generated by the latter services will not be subject to Saudi income tax, provided that the value of the portions performed respectively inside and outside Saudi Arabia is clearly and specifically set forth in the agreement. However, in order to avoid tax liability with respect to the entire agreement, it is recommended that the transaction be divided into two separate contracts signed by two different entities.

I. DISPUTES AND SANCTIONS

Article 11 of the Regulations provides that "[w]ithout prejudice to the provisions of other regulations, the Commission for the Settlement of Commercial Disputes shall have jurisdiction over any dispute that may arise out of the relationships [sic] between a foreign contractor and its Saudi agent." Alternatively, the parties may agree to resolve their disputes by arbitration under Saudi arbitration law.[166]

Article 12 provides

> if a foreign contractor commits any violation of the provisions of these Regulations, it shall be prohibited from operating in the Kingdom of Saudi Arabia. If a Saudi agent commits any violation of the provisions of these Regulations, its commercial registration shall be withdrawn and it shall be prohibited from being an agent.

---

[166] *See generally* pp. 151–56 *infra*.

Chapter 2

THE LIMITED LIABILITY COMPANY

Chapter 1 discusses how Fonco[1] can sell goods, directly or by means of a commercial agent, to purchasers in the Kingdom of Saudi Arabia and execute public sector contracts subject to the requirement of having a services agent or Saudi partner. However, in order to carry on certain commercial activities[2] relating to the public sector on a broader basis than that afforded by a temporary license and in the private sector generally, Fonco is required to establish an entity in the Kingdom.[3] To do so, it must obtain permission from the appropriate governmental authorities, which, in the majority of cases, will be both the Ministry of Industry and Electricity and the Ministry of Commerce.[4]

I. Foreign Capital Investment

A. FOREIGN CAPITAL INVESTMENT REGULATIONS ["FCIR"][5]

1. Applicability

As a rule, Fonco is subject to the Companies Regulations.[6] Article 227 provides that "[w]ithout prejudice to the provisions of the Foreign Capital

---

[1] For definition of "Fonco", see p. 9 n. 21 *supra*.

[2] Fonco is prohibited from engaging in trade, regardless of whether it has established a local identity. For discussion of "trade" and "commerce", see generally pp. 9–14 *supra*. Nonetheless, Saudi law reserves certain commercial activities to Saudi natural and wholly-owned juristic persons. *See generally* pp. 11–12 *supra*.

[3] A temporary license relates only to a specific contract or contracts and does not in principle afford Fonco an ongoing or permanent presence in the Kingdom. *See generally* p. 59 *supra*.

[4] It should be emphasized that Fonco is not permitted to operate within the Kingdom unless due authorization is obtained. With certain exceptions, private contractual arrangements purporting to allow Fonco to operate locally in association with a local entity will not afford Fonco a legal presence in the Kingdom.

[5] Royal Decree No. M/4 (1979).

[6] Royal Decree No. M/6 (1965), *as amended by* Royal Decrees No. M/5 (12/3/1387), No. M/23 (28/6/1402) and No. M/46 (4/7/1405).

Investment Regulations or to the special agreements concluded with certain companies, the provisions of these Regulations shall apply to foreign companies operating in the Kingdom."[7] Thus, with certain exceptions,[8] whether Fonco desires to open a local branch or to participate in the formation of a local company, it must first qualify under the FCIR, and obtain a license from the Ministry of Industry and Electricity.[9]

Company v. *branch*

With specific exceptions, the FCIR apply to the "investment" of "foreign capital" and do not specify whether such investment must be structured as a branch of Fonco or a company formed under local law. Essentially the same licensing procedures are applicable to both forms. However, Saudi policy regarding foreign capital investment strongly favors local participation. The official Industrial Policy Statement, for example, states that "[t]he Government welcomes foreign capital as well as foreign expertise and their participation in industrial development ventures *in cooperation with Saudi businessmen.*"[10] Hence, the policy of the Ministry of Industry and Electricity is extremely restrictive with respect to permitting foreign companies to open local branches.[11] In addition, a branch does not qualify for many of

[7] Although the Foreign Capital Investment Regulations as provided in art. 227 are the prior regulations, Royal Decree No. 35 (Feb. 25, 1964) (repealed 1979), the rule of that article applies to the present regulations.

[8] *See, e.g.*, Joint Economic Agreement among the Members of the Gulf Cooperation Council, art. 8 (approved by Royal Decree No. M/13 (Jan. 16, 1982)) (providing for freedom of economic activity) (not fully implemented in all areas); Unified Agreement for the Investment of Arab Capital among the Arab League States (approved by Royal Decree No. M/7 (11/4/1401)) ("Arab investors" guaranteed certain privileges) (further privileges available by qualifying under local law).

[9] A nonSaudi natural person is permitted to apply for a license under the FCIR. However, nonSaudi individual investors are outside the scope of this chapter.

[10] Industrial Policy Statement, para. x, DALĪL AL-ISTITHMAR AL-ṢINĀʿĪ 66 (6th ed. 1404) (emphasis added). Although the Statement applies specifically to industrial ventures, the policy expressed therein is also generally applicable to agricultural and contracting ventures. *Cf.* High Order No. 5/2023 (6/3/1404) (implementing Gulf Cooperation Council decision) (permitting citizens of Gulf states to engage in certain "economic activities" in Kingdom in participation with 25% Saudi capital for five-year period from date of decision).

[11] Similarly, although Saudi law does not prohibit several foreign investors from applying to form a local company without Saudi participation, any such application is subject to the same policy favoring Saudi participation, and an application to form a company with less than 25% Saudi participation is unlikely to be looked on favorably at the Ministry of Industry and Electricity. It should be noted that a minimum Saudi participation may also be required by other administrative authorities having the authority to license particular activities. *See, e.g.*, Minister of Communications Resolution No. 199, art. 3 (24/11/1397), *as amended by* Minister of Communications Resolution No. 176 (8/9/1403) (minimum of 51% Saudi participation required throughout period of license for transportation of goods by road).

the advantages available to locally formed mixed participation companies having specified levels of Saudi participation, in particular the tax holiday granted with respect to the profits of the nonSaudi participants in such companies.[12] Furthermore, even though a duly licensed and registered branch may carry on its activities in the private sector without being subject to any requirement of participation or association with Saudi entities or individuals, it is still required to appoint a services agent with respect to any public sector contracts it may seek to undertake.[13] Consequently, the overwhelming majority of foreign investment is structured in the form of companies organized under the Companies Regulations.

2. Substantive requirements for investment

Article 2 of the FCIR provides

[w]ithout prejudice to the provisions of other regulations in force, foreign capital investment shall be subject to the condition of obtaining a license issued by the Minister of Industry and Electricity on the basis of the recommendation of the foreign Capital Investment Committee when the two following conditions are fulfilled:
1. That it be invested in development ventures which for the purposes of the provisions of these Regulations do not include ventures for the extraction of petroleum and minerals.[14]
2. That it be accompanied by foreign technical expertise.

There are three basic criteria for the investment of capital by means of the obtention of a Foreign Capital Investment License ["License"], namely that the investment involve "foreign capital", that such capital be invested in development ventures, and that it be accompanied by foreign technology, knowhow, or expertise.

Foreign capital

In order to qualify as "foreign capital", capital sought to be invested must fit within the regulatory definition. Article 1 of the FCIR defines "foreign capital" as

[m]oney, securities, negotiable instruments, machines, equipment, spare parts, raw materials, products, means of transportation, and

---

[11] *See generally* pp. 73–75 *infra.*

[13] *See generally* pp. 42–43 *supra.*

[14] Mineral ventures, with certain exceptions, are subject to the Mining Regulations, Royal Decree No. M/21 (1392). *See also* Regs. for Commercial Companies Operating in the Field of Petroleum, Royal Decree No. M/1, art. 1 (1969) (license application to be submitted to Minister of Petroleum and Mineral Wealth).

intangible rights, such as patent rights, trademarks, and similar valuables, when they are owned by a natural person who is not a national of the Kingdom of Saudi Arabia or by a juristic person all of the participants of which are not nationals of the Kingdom of Saudi Arabia.

The regulatory definition is further elaborated in the FCIR Implementing Rules, which provide that the "foreign capital" referred to in Article 1 of the regulations includes, by way of example,

(a) Liquid wealth: such as money and securities—stocks, bonds, negotiable instruments—bills, drafts, and checks.

(b) Assets in kind: such as machinery, equipment, spare parts, raw materials, products, means of transportation, and other items in accordance with advanced development and modern technology.

(c) Intangible rights: such as patents and trademarks, provided that they are officially registered and duly acknowledged.[15]

"Development ventures"

Development ventures within the meaning of the FCIR are ventures coming within the framework of the relevant Development Plan of the Kingdom and as defined by resolution of the Minister of Industry and Electricity by virtue of his authority under article 3 of the FCIR. Since this article empowers the Minister to define "development ventures" generally, the categories established include not only industrial ventures, but also agricultural and contracting ventures,[16] all of which are consequently subject to the Ministry of Industry and Electricity licensing procedures. It should, however, be noted that the fact that a proposed venture fits within the formal definitional categories of Resolution No. 952 will not ensure that such a venture will obtain a License. The Foreign Capital Investment Committee ["FCIC"],[17] in accordance with whose proposals the Minister

---

[15] Minister of Indus. & Elec. Resolution No. 323/q/w/s, art. 1 (10/6/1399).

[16] *See generally* Minister of Indus. & Elec. Resolution No. 952 (4/11/1400) (relating to ventures considered development ventures in accordance with the FCIR) (translated in Appendix 9). Although Resolution No. 952 provides five categories, the categories as applied are "industrial", "agricultural" and "contracting."

[17] The FCIC is a special committee within the Ministry of Industry and Electricity constituted of:

The Deputy Minister of Industry and Electricity, or his designated representative as chairman;

A representative of the Ministry of Planning;

A representative of the Ministry of Finance and National Economy;

A representative of the Ministry of Agriculture and Water;

A representative of the Ministry of Petroleum and Mineral Wealth; and

A representative of the Ministry of Commerce.

See FCIR, art. 4.

issued Resolution No. 952,[18] may periodically recommend amendments to the definition of "development ventures" to be implemented by the Minister.[19] Practically speaking, since formal amendment is a lengthy process, the Ministry may begin to apply licensing policies on the basis of current market conditions or policy considerations and cease to grant Licenses with respect to certain activities figuring in the Resolution.[20] Such selective licensing policies are predicated on the underlying theory that Licenses are to be granted to foreign capital with respect to "development ventures", which, by definition, can only be in those areas requiring development. Hence, when a particular category has been sufficiently "developed" to be able to fill local demand, further licensing of ventures in that area cannot be justified inasmuch as such proposed ventures are no longer "development ventures" as a matter of fact.

3. Foreign Capital Investment License

Application

Fonco is required to submit a standard form application specific to the type of venture it contemplates to the Foreign Capital Investment Office in the Ministry of Industry and Electricity.[21] Data generally required include the capitalization and a description of the objectives of the proposed venture and, with respect to companies, as opposed to branches, the names of all partners, regardless of their nationalities, and the percentages of their respective proposed equity-holdings. With respect to Saudi participants, information other than their names and percentages of equity-holdings need not be included in the application. However, nonSaudi applicants must also submit, in addition to a copy of the draft articles of association of the company, if the proposed form is a company, documentary evidence

[18] The function of the FCIC is to: (1) propose ventures to be considered development ventures; (2) examine investment applications; (3) study complaints submitted by foreign investors or other interested parties or disputes arising from the application of the provisions of the FCIR, and forward its recommendations thereon to the competent authorities; (4) recommend penalties which it deems should be imposed on any enterprise violating the provisions of the FCIR; (5) consider draft implementing rules necessary to implement the FCIR; and (6) examine matters relating to the provisions of the FCIR referred to it by the Minister of Industry and Electricity. *Id.* art. 5. The draft implementing rules mentioned in subsection 5 were issued in 1979.

[19] *See* Minister of Indus. & Elec. Resolution No. 952, art. 8 (4/11/1400) (translated in Appendix 9).

[20] At present, *e.g.*, although the activities, *inter alia*, of civil construction, transportation of goods, and catering still figure in Resolution No. 952, obtention of a license in these areas has become exceedingly difficult, if not impossible.

[21] For standard form license applications for industrial and contracting ventures, *see generally* Appendices 18–19. Wholly Saudi-owned industrial enterprises capitalized by fixed assets, excluding land and buildings, of a minimum of one million riyals are also required to obtain a license from the Ministry.

demonstrating their experience and qualifications in the proposed areas of activity and their financial position. Additionally, nonSaudi applicants must undertake to render technical support and other necessary assistance to the proposed enterprise.[22]

The Foreign Capital Investment Office will register, study, and evaluate the application and submit the application together with its own findings to the FCIC.[23] The FCIC will issue a decision on the application, which becomes final after approval by the Minister of Industry and Electricity.[24] An applicant whose application was rejected may petition the Minister to reconsider such denial within sixty days from its notification of the rejection.[25] After reconsideration by the FCIC and a second denial, such denial may be appealed to the Board of Grievances.[26]

Terms and conditions

The License, when granted, is issued in the form of a Minister of Industry and Electricity Resolution.[27] It represents both the Ministry's recognition of Fonco's qualifications as an investor and its permission for Fonco to carry on specified business activities in the form proposed in its application. Both the License and the FCIR Implementing Rules require the participants or, in the case of a branch, the foreign investor to establish the enterprise in accordance with the data submitted to the Ministry of Industry and Electricity.[28] Any subsequent changes in the name, structure, address, amount of capital, or activities of the enterprise require the approval of the Ministry.[29] Approval of the Ministry will also be required if a company formed pursuant to a License desires to open a branch at a subsequent date.[30] In addition, the participants are barred from selling the business entity or the License or making an assignment of either in whole or in part except after approval from the Ministry. This restriction extends to any changes in the ownership or distribution of interests as approved in the License whether for consideration or gratuitously. With respect to

---

[22] For List of Required Documents to be attached to application to the FCIC as elaborating on the list provided on the final page of the standard form applications, see Appendix 20.

[23] *See* FCIR Implementing Rules, arts. 4–6.

[24] *See id.* art. 7.

[25] *Id.* art. 9.

[26] *See generally* pp. 238–43 *infra*.

[27] *See* FCIR, art. 2. For standard industrial and contracting Licenses, see Appendix 19.

[28] *See* standard Licenses, art. 3; FCIR Implementing Rules, art. 11.

[29] *See* standard Licenses, art. 3; FCIR Implementing Rules, art. 11.

[30] It may be noted that the Ministry no longer requires in all cases that the company's capital be increased in order to open new branches. However, a copy of the Ministry's approval must be submitted to the Commercial Register Office for the purpose of registration of any such branch. *See* Instructions Relating to the Amendment of Particulars of Companies and Sole Proprietorships, para. 3(a) (implementing Minister of Commerce Resolution No. 151(17/8/1403)) (translated in Appendix 22).

admission of new participants, if the proposed new participant is a foreign investor, it will be required to demonstrate its technical, business, and financial qualifications, experience and expertise. In addition, appropriate documents issued by the Saudi company authorizing or approving the admission of the new participant and the related amendments to the company's articles of association together with the proposed amended articles of association will be required to be submitted. If the new participant is Saudi, submission of the latter documents will suffice.[31]

Revocation

The License expressly provides that the Ministry may cancel the License if the owners of the enterprise violate any of its terms or if they do not take the measures necessary to implement it within six months from its date.[32] In addition, in the case of violation of the provisions of the FCIR, the Minister is empowered, *inter alia*, after due warning to the enterprise and its failure to comply with such warning and upon the recommendation of the FCIC, to revoke the License and liquidate the enterprise.[33] The resolution of the Minister imposing such penalties may be appealed to the Board of Grievances within thirty days from the date of official notification by registered letter to the parties. The Board of Grievance's decision is final.[34]

4. Exceptions

The FCIR do not apply to certain cases and activities. Article 9 provides

> [t]he provisions of these Regulations shall not apply to ventures in which foreign capital is invested in the following cases

---

[31] In all cases, changes in the equity participation require amendment of the articles of association of the company and compliance with the regulatory formalities of publication and registration. *See generally* pp. 87–90 and 104–06 *infra*.

[32] Article 10 of the FCIR Implementing Rules provides

> [p]arties licensed to invest foreign capital shall undertake the necessary measures to establish the venture within six months from the date of their notification of the license resolution issued to them. Otherwise, the Minister of Industry and Electricity shall have the right to cancel such license and to consider it nonexistent. The Chairman of the Investment Committee may permit, in case of necessity, an extension of this deadline for an appropriate period not to exceed another six months.

The "necessary measures" required to be taken within the specified period are, in the case of a company, the measures required toward the formation of the company, if the license was granted with respect to contracting activities. In the case of an industrial venture, the necessary measures may in addition involve the taking of relevant actions relating to the establishment of the venture such as applying for loans, renting real property, beginning construction of the plant, and the like.

[33] *See* FCIR, art. 10; FCIR Implementing Rules, art. 23.

[34] *See* FCIR, art. 10; FCIR Implementing Rules, art. 24.

(a) If they were validly existing prior to the effectiveness of these Regulations. However, the operations or the increase of the capital of such ventures shall be subject to the provisions hereof.

(b) If they were permitted to operate in the Kingdom by virtue of special decrees or agreements.[35]

In addition, activities within the sphere of consulting, or professional services,[36] banking activities,[37] and certain activities or forms licensed or permitted by the Minister of Commerce under article 228 of the Companies Regulations,[38] *inter alia*, are not subject to the FCIR.

B. PRIVILEGES ATTACHED TO SAUDI IDENTITY AND/OR PARTICIPATION

In the intent to stimulate national economic development and to attract nonSaudi knowhow and technical expertise, Saudi law affords certain economic privileges with respect to "investment" commitments in the development of the Kingdom. The availability of certain of these privileges may depend on the extent of Saudi participation in the local entity and/or the nature of its activities.

---

[35] Special agreements are those to which the Government, one of its agencies, or in some cases a corporate entity owned by the Government or one of its agencies in whole or in part is a party and which are designated as or deemed to be special agreements by the competent authorities.

[36] Professional activities are licensed by competent ministries. Certified accountants, legal consultants, and engineering consultants are licensed by the Ministry of Commerce. *See* Certified Accountants Regs., Royal Decree No. M/43, art. 1 (1394); Minister of Commerce Resolutions No. 1190 (Dec. 12, 1981) & No. 264 (July 7, 1982). *See also* Council of Ministers Resolution No. 17, para. 4(4)(b) (1982), *as amended by* Council of Ministers Resolution No. 80 (30/4/1405) (professional partnerships exempted from commercial registration and to be registered in special professional register at Ministry of Commerce). Medical practitioners are licensed by the Ministry of Health. However, a company seeking a license to open a private medical establishment from the regional General Health Administrations must be registered with the Ministry of Commerce. *See* Private Medical Establishments Regs. Implementing Rules, Minister of Health Resolution No. 5031/20, art. 1 (19/8/1403).

[37] Banks are licensed by the Minister of Fin. & Nat'l Economy. *See* Banks Control Regs., Royal Decree No. M/5, art. 3 (1966).

[38] Article 228, which also applies to branches licensed under the FCIR, provides that "[f]oreign companies may not establish branches, agencies, or offices to represent them, . . . except with permission from the Minister of Commerce and Industry." The Ministry of Commerce and Industry has been divided into the Ministry of Commerce and the Ministry of Industry and Electricity. No regulations have been issued governing the powers of either ministry under article 228. In practice, however, powers conferred by this article have been exercised by the Minister of Commerce. *See generally* Council of Ministers Resolution No. 66 (6/4/1374), *approved by* Royal Approval Letter No. 17/1/8117 (10/8/1374) (defining powers of Minister of Commerce) (available at the Institute of Public Administration library). For certain forms licensed by the Minister of Commerce under article 228, see generally pp. 40–42 and 59–60 *supra*.

1. General privileges available to licensed foreign capital[39]

Article 7 of the FCIR provides

> [f]oreign capital which has fulfilled the conditions provided in these
> Regulations shall benefit from the following privileges:
>
> (a) The privileges enjoyed by national capital under the Regulations
> for the Protection and Encouragement of National Industries
> with respect to industrial ventures only.
>
> (b) The exemption of industrial or agricultural venture(s) in which
> foreign capital is invested from income and companies tax for a
> period of ten years and exemption of other ventures from such
> taxes for a period of five years. Ventures enjoying exemption at
> the time these Regulations become effective shall benefit from
> the exemption provided in this paragraph. It is a condition to
> exemption that national capital shall own not less than twenty-
> five percent of the capital of the venture and that such percentage
> shall be maintained throughout the period of exemption. The
> period of exemption shall begin from the date of the
> commencement of production.
> The Council of Ministers may amend this paragraph.
>
> (c) Acquisition of the necessary real property in accordance with
> the Regulations for the Acquisition by nonSaudis of Real
> Property.

Enterprises violating the provisions of the FCIR are subject to withdrawal
of the privileges granted thereunder, in whole or in part, by resolution of
the Minister of Industry and Electricity upon the recommendation of the
FCIC.[40] Such decision is appealable to the Board of Grievances.[41]

Special privileges for industrial ventures[42]

By virtue of article 7, the privileges enjoyed by national capital under
the Regulations for the Protection and Encouragement of National

---

[39] The privileges discussed in this section are those generally applicable to foreign capital
"invested" under the FCIR. Privileges granted by virtue of other regulations, special
agreements, or international treaties or agreements are beyond the scope of this discussion.

[40] FCIR, art. 10.

[41] *Id.*

[42] Industrial ventures are defined as

> the process of conversion of raw materials to manufactured or semimanufactured
> materials or the conversion of semimanufactured materials to fully manufactured
> materials or the preparation of fully manufactured materials, filling and packing of the
> same.

Minister of Indus. & Elec. Resolution No. 952 (4/11/1400) (translated in Appendix 9).

Industries ["Protection Regulations"][43] are extended to foreign capital invested in industrial ventures. Article 2 of the Protection Regulations grants specified privileges and exemptions to "industrial establishments".[44] Neither the FCIR nor the Protection Regulations require Saudi participation in order for an industrial venture to be eligible for these privileges. Privileges under the Protection Regulations may also be available to industrial ventures authorized by special agreements, and which may not be required to qualify under the FCIR.[45]

The privileges granted by the Protection Regulations are:

— Exemptions from customs duties on machinery, equipment, tools, and spare parts imported for new industrial establishments, the expansion of existing industrial establishments, and the packing of production.[46]

— Exemptions from customs duties on primary raw and semimanufactured materials and packaging and filling items, provided that comparable goods in sufficient quantity are not available in the Kingdom.[47]
  The preceding exemptions are granted by resolution of the Minister of Industry and Electricity based on the recommendation of the Industrial Technical Office in the Ministry.[48]

— Nominal rental leases of state land necessary for the construction of factories and housing of workmen and employees. Such leases are granted by approval of the Minister of Industry and Electricity and may only be assigned with his approval.[49]

— Measures protecting local production including limiting or prohibiting the importation of similar foreign goods and imposing protective tariffs

---

[43] Royal Decree No. 50 (1962).

[44] An "industrial establishment" is defined by article 1 of the Protection Regulations as

> [a]ny place prepared and equipped for industrial exploitation to convert raw materials into manufactured or semimanufactured materials, or to convert semimanufactured materials into fully manufactured materials, or to prepare, pack, and wrap fully manufactured materials.

[45] *But see* Protection Regs., art. 9. (Regulations inapplicable to industrial establishment enjoying privileges and special conditions under special agreements except to extent such agreements are silent thereon.)

[46] *Id.* art. 4. Such exempted items may be used solely in the licensed factories and for the purpose for which the exemption was granted. *Id.* art. 10(b). Customs exemptions also are used to stimulate national agriculture. *See, e.g.,* Royal Decree No. M/59 (19/12/1403) (amending customs tariffs); Royal Decree No. M/9 (6/4/1393) (eliminating customs duties on certain agricultural tools and machinery).

[47] Protection Regs., art. 5.

[48] *Id.* arts. 4–5.

[49] *Id.* art. 6.

on similar foreign goods.[50] Protective measures are effected by resolution of the Council of Ministers.[51]

— Provision of various types of financial assistance by resolution of the Council of Ministers on the recommendation of the Minister of Industry and Electricity.[52]

— Exemption from export duties and other taxes on exports of local production by royal decree.[53]

Industrial loans[54]

Qualifying industrial ventures having a minimum Saudi participation of twenty-five percent are entitled to borrow at nominal charges from the Saudi Industrial Development Fund ["SIDF"]. SIDF's mission is the support and encouragement of national industrial development by

(i) offering interest-free medium or long-term loans to newly established industrial concerns within the Kingdom;

(ii) offering interest-free medium or long-term loans to existing private industrial concerns to enable them to expand their activities, replace their equipment, and introduce new modern technology;

(iii) offering, if needed and when possible, economic, technical, or administrative advice to industrial concerns within the Kingdom.[55]

[50] *Id.* art. 7.

[51] *See id.* Royal Decree No. M/9, para. 2 (6/4/1394), *as amended by* Royal Decree No. M/59 (19/12/1403) (Council of Ministers may by resolution amend customs tariffs for purpose of protection and encouragement of local industries and products based on proposal of Minister of Fin. & Nat'l Economy and Minister of Industry and Electricity). *See, e.g.*, Council of Ministers Resolution No. 50 (1/1/1406) (continuing 20% tariff on eggs); Royal Decree No. M/20 (20/12/1405) (Confirming Council of Ministers Resolution No. 223 (26/11/1405)) (extending 20% protective tariff on lubricating oil); Council of Ministers Resolution No. 292 (3/11/1403) (imposing 20% tariff on sulphuric acid based on proposals of the two ministries pursuant to request by Saudi Arabian Fertilizers Co.); Council of Ministers Resolution No. 22 (21/2/1403) (raising tariffs on aluminum items from 3% to 20%); Council of Ministers Resolution No. 2 (1402), *as amended by* Council of Ministers Resolution No. 84 (26/3/1403) (same with respect to dry batteries); Council of Ministers Resolution No. 4 (18/1/1399) (raising tariffs on biscuits and tents from 3% to 10%, on bottled drinking water to 20%).

[52] Protection Regs., art. 7(3); DALĪL AL-ISTITHMĀR AL-ṢINĀ·Ī 136 (6th ed. 1984).

[53] Protection Regs., art. 8.

[54] Financing for agricultural projects is provided by the Saudi Arabian Agricultural Bank. The Public Investment Fund finances government commercial projects.

[55] SIDF Regs., Royal Decree No. M/3, art. 2 (1974) (SIDF Charter). Art. 4(1) provides

[t]he Government industrial policy shall constitute the broad guidelines for the Fund activities regarding the support and encouragement of industry in the Kingdom. To achieve this goal, the Fund shall cooperate and coordinate with specialized government agencies and institutions.

Maximum funding is fifty percent of the cost of the project or its development.[56] This maximum amount is available to projects in which the Saudi participation is fifty percent or more. If the Saudi participation is less, the financing available is proportionately reduced.[57] Loans are not granted to cover working capital needs.[58] The term of SIDF loans may not exceed fifteen years.[59] Loans are secured by a security interest in the borrower's assets, generally its plant, machinery, and real property.[60]

Tax holiday

A ten-year tax holiday is available to industrial and agricultural ventures formed under Saudi law, having a minimum Saudi equity participation of twenty-five percent, and with respect to which Saudis are entitled to receive no less than twenty-five percent of the profits. A five-year tax holiday is available to the other companies licensed under the FCIR and formed under Saudi law, subject to the same equity participation and profit-entitlement ratios. The tax holiday may be calculated in Gregorian or hijrah years, according to the calendar selected by the parties in establishing the financial year of the company.[61] The tax holiday applies solely to the profits of the foreign capital. Saudi participants or participants of other nationalities treated as Saudi nationals[62] for tax purposes remain liable for payment of zakāt.[63]

Article 18 of the FCIR Implementing Rules provides

> [t]he period of the tax exemption afforded to ventures in which the investment of foreign capital is licensed shall begin as of the date of

---

[56] See id. art. 4(6), as amended by Royal Decree No. 71(14/12/1394). However, since SIDF loans are secured by a pledge of the borrower's hard assets, the available financing will also be contingent on the borrower's ability to pledge property acceptable as security to SIDF. SIDF also requires a minimum equity contribution of 25–30% of the total funding.

[57] See DALĪL AL IŜTITHMĀR AṬ-ṢINĀ'Ī 86 (6th ed. 1404). For standard SIDF loan application and loan agreement, see Appendix 23.

[58] See SIDF Regs., art. 4(7).

[59] Id. art. 4(8). Typically, the repayment schedule is seven to eight years, with a grace period of one and a half to three years.

[60] See id. art. 4(4). In addition, guarantees may be required with respect to limited liability companies. See also standard SIDF Pledge Agreement (reprinted in Appendix 21).

[61] Choice of the hijrah calendar will result in a reduction in the tax-exemption period.

[62] Nationals of Bahrain, Kuwait and Qatar are treated as Saudis for tax purposes. Royal Decrees Nos. 10236 & 10237 (1956); Royal Order No. 800 (Aug. 16, 1956); Royal Order No. 4899 (Dec. 19, 1957). Nationals of Gulf Cooperation Council states are treated as Saudi nationals for tax purposes. Minister of Fin. & Nat'l Econ. Resolution No. 3/719 (Jan. 1, 1985); Director-Gen'l of Dep't of Zakāt & Income Tax Circular No. 2896/1 (Feb. 1, 1985) (both translated in Appendix 24).

[63] Saudis pay zakāt in accordance with Islamic law. Royal Decree No. 17/2/28/577 (Oct. 19, 1956). See generally Royal Decree No. M/40 (2/7/1405) (providing for collection in entirety of zakāt).

commencement of production. With respect to other than industrial and agricultural ventures, the date of registration in the Commercial Register shall be considered the date of commencement of production.

Article 18 clarifies the date of applicability of the tax holiday as provided in article 7(b) of the FCIR, which defines such date solely as the date of commencement of production and does not define the date of applicability with respect to ventures licensed to carry out contracting activities. The most important consequence of both of these articles is that any contracts signed or works performed prior to the date of production or commercial registration, whichever is applicable, are subject to tax.[64] Even if no activities are carried out or profits generated prior to the beginning of the tax holiday, all profits generated under any contract signed prior to the applicable date will be subject to tax.[65] This rule also applies to contracts signed by any foreign contractor(s) or joint adventure, whether or not including any Saudi participant(s), subsequently assigned or subcontracted to a Mixco in which such foreign contractor(s) benefiting from the tax holiday participate(s). Such contracts are subject to tax.

The tax holiday is associated both with the exempted venture and with the identity of the participants. Article 20 of the FCIR Implementing Rules provides

> [t]he tax holiday afforded to the venture shall not be affected by the death of one of the foreign partners therein or the withdrawal of some of them or the admission of new partners as long as the venture remains validly existing and the share of the Saudi party is not less in all cases than twenty-five percent of the capital of the venture.

Thus, a new partner having qualified under the FCIR after the contract being performed by the company was signed is nonetheless entitled to a tax holiday, provided that the required level of Saudi participation is maintained. If, in contrast, the new partner had already been granted a tax holiday and has used up a portion thereof prior to joining the company, it will be entitled to tax exemption with respect to profits relating thereto within the limits of its original tax holiday and may not benefit from a

---

[64] Previously, the tax holiday was inapplicable only to contracts signed prior to obtention of the License. *See* Director-General of Dep't of Zakāt & Income Tax Circular No. 7 (1/12/1394). It should be noted that, even though certain Licences issued subsequent to the effectiveness of the FCIR and their implementing rules may contain a clause providing that the participants shall not be entitled to the tax exemption with respect to contracts signed and activities performed prior to licensing, the beginning of the tax holiday is governed by the present rule as stated in the FCIR and their implementing rules.

[65] The rationale of prior law underlying the inapplicability of the tax exemption in such cases is that the contract price had been established taking into account the tax payable by the contractor. *See* Minister of Fin. & Nat'l Econ. Letter No. 4502 (29/7/1394).

greater period of exemption by virtue of its new participation in such venture.

Article 21 of the FCIR Implementing Rules provides

> [t]he tax exemption is attached to the investment venture and not to its legal form or the identities of the investors, so that if the venture continues without changing its activities and completes the period of tax exemption it shall not be entitled on the occasion of a change in its legal form or all or some of the foreign investors to request a new tax exemption.

The tax holiday may not be extended or renewed on the basis of corporate restructurings or changes in participants in the venture. However, the tax holiday may also be viewed as associated with the identity of the participants in that they may not, by the expedient of dissolving a company having used up its tax holiday and applying to form a new company having the same or similar objectives, obtain a second tax holiday. Nonetheless, a foreign entity related to the foreign participants but having different activities may apply to form a new company and, provided that the technology or knowhow it is contributing is not derived from a parent company which also made that technology or knowhow available to the foreign participant with respect to whose enterprise the tax holiday has expired, obtain a tax holiday for the company it is forming. The tax holiday also applies to any gains realized from the liquidation of the company during the exemption period. Companies benefiting from tax holidays are nonetheless required to file annual tax returns.

Companies tax

In the absence of a tax holiday, the shares of nonSaudi participants, except for those nonSaudi participants treated as Saudis for tax purposes, in the profits of the company are subject to companies tax. This tax is also applicable to the profits of Fonco's local branch. Although in the case of a mixed participation company, the return is filed in the company's name, payments are made from the nonSaudi partners' share of the profits.[66] Companies' taxable profits are defined as

> 1. The net profit realized by any nonSaudi company operating in Saudi Arabia only, or operating inside and outside Saudi Arabia at the same time.
> 2. The total shares of nonSaudi partners in the net profits of Saudi companies.

[66] For Final Tax Return Form for nonSaudi Taxpayer, see Appendix 8.

3. The total shares of nonSaudi sleeping partners in the net profits of [Saudi] companies.[67]

The applicable tax rates are

Annual profits not exceeding S.R.100,000	25%
Annual profits in excess of S.R.100,000 but not exceeding S.R.500,000	35%
Annual profits exceeding S.R.500,000 but not exceeding S.R. 1 million	40%
Annual profits exceeding S.R.1 million	45%[68]

For example, if total annual net profits are S.R.1,500,000, tax is computed as follows

First S.R.100,000 × 25%	S.R. 25,000
Next S.R.400,000 × 35%	S.R.140,000
Next S.R.500,000 × 40%	S.R.200,000
Next S.R.500,000 × 45%	S.R.225,000
Total net profits S.R.1,500,000	Total Tax S.R.590,000

Ownership of real property

The general rule is that only Saudi natural persons and wholly-owned enterprises are entitled to own real property situated in Saudi Arabia.[69] Article 2 of the Regulations for the Acquisition by nonSaudis of Real Property in the Kingdom of Saudi Arabia ["Real Property Regulations"][70] provides that "a nonSaudi may not by any means other than inheritance acquire the right of ownership of or any other in rem right to real property located within the Kingdom of Saudi Arabia except for the cases provided in these Regulations." The exceptions to article 2[71] as provided in article 3

[67] Royal Decree No. 17/2/28/576 (Oct. 19, 1956), *as amended by* Royal Decree No. M/19 (Sept. 2, 1970). Under para. 1, only net profits relating to Saudi activities are taxable.

[68] Royal Decree No. M/19 (Sept. 2, 1970). These rates are not applicable to companies engaged in the production or sale of hydrocarbons.

[69] *But see* High Order No. 5/M 1539 (17/1/1398) (permitting ownership of real property by nationals of Kuwait, Qatar, United Arab Emirates); Joint Economic Agreement among the members of the Gulf Cooperation Council, art. 8.

[70] Royal Decree No. M/22 (1970).

[71] The exceptions are not stated to apply to article 1, which prohibits the acquisition by foreigners of real property within Makkah and Madinah by means other than inheritance, except if ownership is coupled with a waqf (charitable foundation) in accordance with Islamic law in favor of a specified Saudi beneficiary. *Cf.* Regs. for the Organization of Administrative Functions in the Shari'ah Court System, High Approval No. 109; art. 83 (1952) (permitting registration in name of foreigner of property to be dedicated as a waqf provided, *inter alia*, that such waqf be administered by a Saudi national, that beneficiaries be Saudi nationals or Muslims present in the Kingdom, and that proceeds not be transferred to foreigners outside the Kingdom).

include the ownership by diplomatic missions on the basis of reciprocity of their official seat or the residence of their ambassador, the ownership by international organizations of their official seat as provided by agreement,[72] the ownership of certain uncultivated land for agricultural purposes, and the ownership by a foreigner of real property for his residence or for utilization. Permission in these cases must be obtained from, respectively, the Minister of Foreign Affairs, the Minister of Agriculture and Water and the Minister of the Interior, and by means of royal approval based upon the proposal of the Minister of the Interior. In the context of foreign investment, article 3(c) provides

> foreign enterprises licensed to operate in the Kingdom of Saudi Arabia in accordance with the Foreign Capital Investment Regulations may acquire real property necessary to carry on their licensed activities as required by such activities, including real property necessary for the housing of the employees of such enterprises, provided that a license has been obtained from the Minister of Commerce and Industry.[73]

Although article 3(c) would appear to apply only to foreign companies, it is also applicable to Saudi companies with foreign participation.[74] In order to acquire real property,[75] such companies must apply to the Ministry of Industry and Electricity, which may authorize the transaction after consultation with the Ministry of the Interior.[76] Upon obtaining permission and acquiring real property, the purchaser must register the transaction with a notary public in order to perfect title.[77] Any unauthorized acquisition

---

[72] *But see* High Order No. 5/a/4391 (26/2/1402) (international organizations and agencies having their headquarters in Saudi Arabia are to be allocated real property for their use) (ownership remains in the state).

[73] The Ministry of Industry and Electricity is at present the ministry granting such license.

[74] Article 7(c) of the FCIR expressly subjects licensed foreign capital's right to acquire real property to the Real Property Regulations. It may also be noted that article 14 of the Companies Regulations provides

> [w]ith the exception of joint adventures, any company formed in accordance with these Regulations shall establish its head office in the Kingdom. It shall be deemed to have Saudi nationality, *but this shall not necessarily entail its enjoyment of such rights as may be restricted to Saudis* (emphasis added).

[75] The Regulations do not define "real property." However, in the context of construing the "diplomatic mission" exception, it was concluded that, since the Real Property Regs. do not define "real property", since land is real property, and since the Regulations permit diplomatic missions to own their seats without limiting such ownership to buildings, such missions may own their seats, both land and buildings; Council of Ministers Resolution No. 74 (29/1/1393).

[76] *See* High Order No. 12906 (5/5/1394); Council of Ministers Resolution No. 542 (April 23, 1974). In practice, the application process tends to be lengthy.

[77] Notaries public are prohibited from registering title deeds if the transferee is a nonSaudi prior to Ministry of Industry and Electricity authorization. *See* Real Property Regs., art. 5; *cf.* Notaries Public Regs., High Order No. 11083, art. 46 (1364) (transfers of real property to foreigners subject to Real Property Regs.) (referring to prior regulations) (applicable to present regulations) (translated in Appendix 25).

of real property, including an acquisition pending approval, is null and void.[78]

2. Preferential treatment in the public sector

In order to encourage local industry and wholly Saudi or mixed participation contractors, government ministries and agencies are required to give priority to local production and contractors. Article 1(d) of the Regulations for the Procurement of Government Purchases and Execution of its Projects and Works ["Tender Regulations"][79] provides

> Saudi individuals and enterprises permitted to operate in accordance with existing regulations and rules shall have priority in dealing with the Government. After them, enterprises formed of Saudis and nonSaudis shall have priority if the share of the former amounts to fifty percent or more of the capital of the enterprise.

Government purchases

Article 9 of the Tenders and Auctions Regulations of 1966[80] provides

> [m]inistries and independent agencies must devise the best methods to ensure procurement of their purchase requirements from locally manufactured goods and products. Locally manufactured goods and products even if made of foreign raw materials shall be preferred to similar foreign items if they approximate their specifications even if the formers' price exceeds the latters' by not more than ten percent and likewise if they are equal to them in price and inferior to them in specifications by not more than ten percent, provided that they serve the purpose. Leniency with local factories in determining the required supply period is permissible, provided that that is not inconsistent with the interest of the work.

---

[78] *See* Minister of Interior Circular No. 38/10536, para. 2 (23/8/1395); *but see id.* preamble (suggesting that knowledge of illegality required to render transaction void). In addition, the circular addresses attempts to circumvent the requirement of prior authorization by use of a Saudi person or entity which would purchase the real estate with the proceeds of a loan from a nonSaudi. In such case, the transaction is null and void, and both parties are subject to discretionary penalties imposed by the Minister of the Interior. *See id.* para. 3

[79] Royal Decree No. M/14 (1977).

[80] Royal Decree No. M/6 (1966) *as amended by* Council of Ministers Resolution No. 1044 (22/6/1396) (repealed in part 1977). The 1966 Regs. have been considered repealed in full. *See* Ministry of Fin. & Nat'l Econ. Circular No. 17/8636 (15/5/1397). However, another view strictly interprets the language of art. 14 of the Tender Regs., which provides that "these Regulations repeal whatsoever is inconsistent therewith." Consequently, those provisions of the Tenders and Auctions Regs. not inconsistent with the Tender Regs. would remain in effect.

Article 10 provides

[m]inistries and independent agencies may adopt the split-bid system, if they believe that it would make things easier for local factories, or if the quantities of the articles to be purchased are large. In this case, the advertisement shall state that bids shall be accepted for the quantity in whole or in part.

The Tender Regulations continue the prior policy of mandating preference of local industry and production. Article 1(e) provides

[m]anufactured goods and products of Saudi origin shall be preferred over similar foreign goods and products if they serve the purpose for which the tender was announced, even though their specifications are inferior to foreign goods and products.

.   .   .

No manufactured goods and products shall be considered of Saudi origin unless they are produced by an industrial enterprise licensed to operate inside the Kingdom and such enterprise has submitted a certificate from the Ministry of Industry and Electricity attesting that local raw materials or local labor have contributed a reasonable percentage to the production of such manufactured goods and products.[81]

Alternatively, government agencies may be ordered to fulfill certain requirements and obtain certain services locally.[82]

Specifications

Article 1(b) of the Tender Regulations Implementing Rules[83] provides that "in preparing specifications, administrative agencies shall be obliged to give priority to the products of national industries if they serve the desired purpose."[84] This rule was already expressed in Council of Ministers

[81] *Cf.* Ministry of Fin. & Nat'l Econ. Circular No. 17/1286 (24/1/1399) (omission of specified percentage from art. 1 of present Tender Regs. to be interpreted as giving authority to purchasing agency to buy local products serving its purpose within price limits established by Ministry of Industry and Electricity); Ministry of Fin. & Nat'l Econ. Letter No. 17/15830 (19/9/1399) (responding to query of Ministry of Health) (purchasing agency, within logical limits, balancing interests of public treasury and encouragement of national industry, has discretion to prefer local products comparing unfavorably in price or quality with foreign products in reasonable percentages, such as 10–20%); Joint Economic Agreement among the Members of the Gulf Cooperation Council, art. 3 (requiring minimum added value of 40% of final value in order for industrial products to qualify as products of national origin).

[82] *See, e.g.,* High Order No. 7/1550/M (19/5/1404) (relating to local advertising by government agencies and companies); High Order No. 7/471/M (7/3/1404) (reaffirming Council of Ministers Resolution No. 687 (25/11/1380)) (prohibiting government organs and public agencies from printing their materials outside the Kingdom) (to encourage local presses).

[83] Minister of Fin. & Nat'l Econ. Resolution No. 2131/17 (5/5/1397).

[84] It may be noted that art. 1(b) gives priority to products of "national" industries, whereas art. 9 of the Tenders and Auctions Regs. gives preference to "local" manufactured goods.

Resolution No. 1977, which provides that "[t]echnical departments in ministries and government agencies as well as consultants working for the Government are hereby required to give priority to the products of Saudi industry in their specifications as long as such products are satisfactory."[85] Article 7(b) provides that "it shall be stated in the price list whether the item to be supplied is manufactured or produced in the Kingdom or an Arab League state or another foreign country." In addition, article 6 of the Saudi Arabian Specifications and Standards Organization Regulations[86] provides that "ministries, independent departments and government agencies shall be bound by the obligatory national standard specifications in their purchases and works." Based upon this article, the Minister of Commerce issued Circular No. 1169[87] instructing competent authorities to comply therewith and at the time of entering into contracts with consulting companies to include in such contracts an obligation of consultants to apply national specifications and to be bound by them in their purchases.

"Buy-Saudi" lists

Council of Ministers Resolution No. 377 provides

(1) The Ministry of Industry and Electricity shall prepare every six months lists of locally manufactured goods suitable for government projects, having first ascertained the availability, quality, and fair price of such goods. These lists are to be circulated to all government departments.

(2) All government contracts shall contain a clause obligating contractors to purchase the locally manufactured goods in the lists prepared by the Ministry of Industry and Electricity. Such contractors are prohibited from importing goods similar to those in the lists.[88]

---

[85] Resolution No. 1977 (Nov. 17, 1976). *Cf.* Council of Ministers Resolution No. 590 (5/5/1393) (requiring government departments to stipulate in their specifications that Saudi marble be used except in "cases of extreme technical necessity" and provided that permission of Department of Public Works be obtained) (compliance therewith requested in Minister of Indus. & Elec. Resolution No. 1541 (17/2/1399)).

[86] Royal Decree No. M/10 (1392).

[87] Circular No. 1169 (7/4/1399).

[88] Resolution No. 377 (4/8/1978); *cf.* Council of Ministers Resolution No. 1291 (15/9/1394) (same). Standard licenses for contractors also include an obligation to use the locally manufactured products specified in the Ministry of Industry and Electricity lists based on Resolution No. 377. See Contracting License (translated in Appendix 19). For general restrictions on contractors' right to import, see generally pp. 11/12 and note 32 *supra*. Cf. Deputy President of Council of Ministers Circular No. 24851 (5/10/1397) (requiring government contracts to include clause prohibiting contractor from establishing a manufacturing unit, regardless of its size, without prior license from Ministry of Industry and Electricity) (also requiring use of goods manufactured locally). *See also* Consulting Company Undertaking (to purchase national products) (translated in Appendix 26).

In addition, public sector contractors are required to procure certain services from local firms.[89]

II. The Limited Liability Company

A. DEFINITION

With the uncommon exception of foreign investors licensed under the FCIR to open a Saudi branch, the license issued by the Ministry of Industry and Electricity will entitle the applicants to form a Saudi company in the form by Fonco and licensed by the Ministry. The general rule is that this form will be a limited liability company.

The Companies Regulations provide the following forms of companies: the general partnership; the limited partnership; the joint adventure; the corporation; the partnership limited by shares; the limited liability company; the company with variable capital; the cooperative company.[90] In addition, the validity of any other companies recognized by Islamic law is expressly reaffirmed in the Companies Regulations.[91] The Regulations are silent as to whether any of these forms is or is not available to nonSaudi participants.[92] However, after mutual consultation, it was agreed between the Ministry of Industry and Electricity and the Ministry of Commerce that mixed participation companies should take the form of limited liability companies, with the exception of banks, required to be corporations with the specified level of Saudi participation.[93] It was decided not to permit Foncos to be

[89] *See, e.g.*, Council of Ministers Resolution No. 124, para. 3 (29/5/1403) (requiring certain services to be procured from Saudi local enterprises) (translated in Appendix 3); Minister of Fin. & Nat'l Econ. Circular No. 3/1743, para. 1 (Nov. 24, 1985); Minister of Fin. & Nat'l Econ. Circular No. 5767/404, para. 1 (Aug. 6, 1984) (both translated in Appendix 27).

[90] Companies Regs., art. 2, *as amended by* Royal Decree No. M/23 (1982). With the exception of the joint adventure, all of these forms have juristic personalities. *Id.* art. 13. However, the company with variable capital is not a separate form of company but rather is a format permitting companies to increase and decrease their capital in accordance with the Companies Regulations and as provided in their articles of association and bylaws. *See id.* art. 181. Likewise, the cooperative company is not a separate form but a structure allowing a limited liability company or corporation to operate under the cooperative principles set forth in part 9 of the Regulations.

[91] *See id.* art. 2.

[92] *Cf.* standard license applications (giving applicants the possibility of selecting between various forms) (translated in Appendix 19).

[93] *See, e.g.*, Minister of Commerce Letter No. 3/9/sh/81/9/240 (14/7/1398) (concluding that all companies of mixed or foreign capital licensed under the FCIR should take the form of limited liability companies) (also referring to Ministry of Industry and Electricity's support of this position), *paraphrased in* A. al-Bakrī, al-Ta'sīs wa al-Idārah fi al-Sharikah Dhāt al-Mas'ūliyyah al Mahdūdah at 78–79 (1980–1981) (thesis in Institute of Public Administration Library); I. al-Rashīd, Sharikat Istithmār Ra's al-Māl al-Ajnabī al-Khaṣṣah wa Ashkāluha al-Qānūniyyah fi al-Mamlakah at 121, 128 (1979–1980) (thesis in Institute of Public Administration

admitted as general partners in either general or limited partnerships in order to protect both Saudi creditors and the Saudi general partners of any such proposed mixed partnerships against creditors' claims, in view of the fact that the assets of foreign partners are for the most part located outside of the Kingdom. In the event of insolvency of the partnership, creditors would therefore have difficulty in obtaining satisfaction of their claims out of assets of the nonSaudi partner(s) situated beyond the reach of Saudi judicial authorities, or would tend to seek satisfaction out of the assets more conveniently located in Saudi Arabia of the Saudi general partners.[94] Hence, the limited liability company, which is likened both to the French *société à responsabilité limitée* and the English private company, has emerged as the sole vehicle available for mixed participations and the most prevalent form of company in the Kingdom.

As a form of "company",[95] the limited liability company is subject to Islamic law,[96] general regulatory rules, the relevant general provisions of the Companies Regulations,[97] the provisions specific to the limited liability company,[98] and customary rules not inconsistent with the Companies Regulations.[99] Article 1 of the Regulations defines a "company" as "a contract under which two or more persons bind themselves to participate in a profit-seeking enterprise, each contributing a share consisting of property or work, for the purpose of dividing whatever profit or loss may arise from such enterprise." The constitutive elements of a company under article 1 may be analyzed as: contractual relationship; more than one participant;

Library). The continuing existence of the interministry agreement was orally affirmed in 1985 by a Ministry of Industry and Electricity competent official. *Cf.* Minister of Commerce Circular No. 3/9/sh/81/9/5893 (26/4/1398) (mixed participation companies must take form of limited liability company); Ministry of Commerce Legal Memorandum No. 458/11 (26/4/1402), *approved by* Minister of Commerce 27/4/1402 (1398 Circular has no retroactive effect on companies registered before its issuance), *cited in* S. YAHYĀ, AL-WAJĪZ FĪ AL-NIZĀM AL-TIJĀRĪ AL-SUʿŪDI 398 (4th ed. 1983) (hereinafter cited as YAHYĀ).

[94] *See* al-Bakri, *supra* note 93, at 79–80 (position explained by Mubarak al-Khafrah, then Secretary General of the FCIC). *See also* Council of Ministers Resolution No. 17, para. 4(3) (1982), *as amended by* Council of Ministers Resolution No. 80 (30/4/1405) (general partners required to be natural persons).

[95] The limited liability company is also commonly referred to as a "limited liability partnership." The Arabic word at issue, "sharikah", may be translated, *inter alia*, as company or partnership depending on the context. For example, the title of the governing regulations, employing the plural of the word, is generally translated as the "Companies Regulations." Since these regulations apply to various forms of association, including companies, partnerships, and corporations, the term "company" has been preferred to "partnership" in translation for the purpose of this work as being the more neutral of the two. In all cases, the structure of the entity rather than the translation of its designation will control.

[96] A discussion of the applicable rules of Islamic law is beyond the scope of this chapter.

[97] Companies Regs., art. 1–15, 216–226, 229–232, *as amended by* Royal Decree No. M/23 (1982). *See also* Commercial Court Regs., High Order No. 32 (1931) (repealed in part); Council of Ministers Resolution No. 17 (1982), *as amended by* Council of Ministers Resolution No. 80 (30/4/1405).

[98] Companies Regs., arts. 157–180.

[99] *Id.* art. 2, *as amended by* Royal Decree No. M/23 (1982).

enterprise for profit; contribution of capital; sharing of profit and loss. It may therefore be noted that

—The company, as a contract,[100] and the participants therein are subject to the general rules of contract law. Therefore, the capacity[101] and consent of the parties is required. The objectives of the enterprise must be both possible and lawful.[102] The parties are free to determine the terms of their contract provided that such terms are consistent with the Companies Regulations, Islamic law, other applicable regulatory law, public policy, and prevailing standards of morality.[103]

—Since the company is not only intended as a business form, but first and foremost is defined as a contract, with the exception of companies wholly-owned by the Government,[104] more than one participant is required.[105]

—The Companies Regulations do not expressly qualify the forms which they provide as "commercial" or "civil" companies.[106] They do, however, insist that the goals of such companies be profit-oriented.[107] Similarly, the Explanatory Memorandum to the Regulations refers to the agreement of the participants to carry on their activities for the purpose of "gain."[108] The profit sought by the parties must be "lawful."[109]

---

[100] The Explanatory Memorandum to the draft of the Companies Regulations, as subsequently issued, states that the intention of the regulations is the regulation of those companies established by means of contract.

[101] See generally pp. 85–86 infra.

[102] See, e.g., YAḤYĀ, at 124–26; A. AL-KHŪLĪ, DURŪS FĪ AL-QĀNŪN AL-TIJĀRĪ AL-SUʿŪDĪ 107–08 (1973). The term "possible" is distinguished from "lawful" in that the performance of fundamentally lawful activities may be prohibited to a company, such as the prohibition of a limited liability company's engaging in banking. See, e.g., YAHYA, at 125 n. 2.

[103] Cf. Companies Regs., art. 2, as amended by Royal Decree No. M/23 (1982).

[104] This exception has been justified on the grounds that government-owned companies are in fact owned by the Saudi general public. See also id. (Companies Regs. inapplicable to companies formed by the State or public juristic persons provided that such companies are established by a royal decree including their governing provisions) (also inapplicable to companies in whose formation the State or public juristic persons participate subject to same conditions).

[105] See also id. art. 15(3) (providing for dissolution of company upon transfer of all interests to one participant).

[106] It is generally acknowledged that a company will be deemed commercial if its activities are commercial, according to the principles set forth in arts. 1–3 of the Commercial Court Regs.

[107] Cf. Minister of Fin. Resolution No. 340, art. 4 (May 8, 1951) (Income Tax Regulations Implementing Rules) ("company" means any corporation, partnership, or association whether or not commercial provided material gain is its basic purpose).

[108] The participants' motivating purpose of realizing profit by means of making contributions is termed by Muslim jurists the "sabab", cause, of the contract, as distinguished from the shared business objectives of the partners to be carried out through the company. While there is a view that the cause inheres in the objectives, see, e.g., YAHYA, at 126, more traditional commentators affirm that the two concepts remain distinct. See, e.g., A. AL-KHŪLĪ, supra note 102, at 108 (also including the division of profit in the cause).

[109] See Commercial Court Regs., art. 11 (qualifying "profit" by "lawful") (requirement implicit in Companies Regs., art. 1).

—The participants' intention to share the risks of doing business is essential to the finding of the existence of a company and distinguishes this type of contract from joint ownership or utilization of property and from an employment agreement entitling the employee to receive a share in the company's profits.[110]

—Although not so provided in article 1, the contract of a company formed under the Companies Regulations, with the exception of joint adventures, must be expressed in writing. This requirement follows from the various provisions of the Regulations relating to notarization and publication of the articles of association of a company and commercial registration, together with their underlying purpose of giving notice to third parties.

Article 157 of the Companies Regulations defines the "limited liability company" as a "company formed by two or more participants responsible for the debts of the company to the extent of their shares in the capital and in which the number of participants does not exceed fifty." The two elements provided in article 157 which, in conjunction, distinguish the limited liability company from the other regulatory forms are the limitation of liability with respect to all participants and the limitation of the number of participants to fifty. This latter characteristic, together with the partners' rights of first refusal applicable to transfers of shares provided in article 165,[111] most notably distinguishes the limited liability company from the corporation, the only other regulatory form providing limited liability to all participants. In addition, the regulatory minimum capital of the limited liability company is significantly lower than that of the corporation[112] and may neither be raised by means of public subscription nor represented by negotiable certificates.[113] Finally, it may be noted that compliance with the provisions of articles 157 to 159 and 161 to 162 is essential to the validity of a limited liability company. Under article 163, violation of any of the

---

[110] It is also said to distinguish the company from a loan agreement entitling the lender to a share in the borrower's profit where the lender is exempted from sharing in the latter's losses. See, e.g., M. Barīrī, Qānūn al-Muʿāmalāt al-Tijāriyyah al-Sūʿūdī 133–34 (1402); M. Abū al-ʿAinain, Mabadiʾ al-Qānūn li Rijāl al-Aʿmāl fi al-Mamlakah al-ʿArabiyyah al-Suʿudiyyah 254 (1981). However, the general validity of such a loan transaction under Islamic law is open to question.

[111] See generally pp. 112–14 infra.

[112] The minimum capital of the limited liability company is S.R.500,000: Companies Regs., art. 158, as amended by Royal Decree No. M/23 (1982). The minimum capital of the corporation is S.R. 2 million if the shares are not to be offered for public subscription and S.R. 10 million if they are to be offered to the public. Id. art. 49, as amended by Royal Decree No. M/23.

[113] Id. art. 158. Partners and directors in a limited liability company and other persons offering shares or debt securities to the public for the account of the company with knowledge of such violation are subject to the penalties provided in art. 229 of the Regulations (maximum one-year prison sentence, S.R.20,000 fine, or both).

84

provisions of the aforementioned articles relating to the number of partners, amount of capital and treatment of capital shares, objectives, correct presentation of the articles of association, paying in and allotment of capital shares, and evaluation of contributions in kind, will cause the company to be deemed null and void as regards interested parties. However, the participants will not be permitted to invoke such invalidity against third parties. Various features of the limited liability company and legal rules applicable thereto are discussed in the following sections. The discussion is general in nature and applicable both to the wholly Saudi-owned and to the mixed participation limited liability company. Certain data relating exclusively to one or the other is also included where relevant.[114]

B. PARTNERS[115]

Although not expressly so provided in the Companies Regulations, the partners in a limited liability company may be natural[116] or juristic persons,[117] provided that their number is two or more.[118] However, public officials, minors under the guardianship of public officials, and students dispatched on study missions abroad for the account of the Government or its instrumentalities may not be partners in a limited liability company.[119]

---

[114] For purposes of discussion, the term "Saudi" will also apply to natural and juristic persons of other nationalities treated as Saudi nationals.

[115] Although the participants in a company are not generally referred to as "partners", this term will be employed in preference to such terms as "participant" or "associate", not only because the limited liability company may be structured and treated as a partnership for purposes of certain other legal systems, but also because it is the most prevalent translation of the Arabic term "sharīk". It will be noted that "partners" in a limited liability company are not agents of the company and do not have the power to bind the company without due authorization.

[116] If a natural person, the (Saudi) partner's name must include his three names, including his family name. Minister of Commerce Circular No. 221/1041 (16/3/1402), *cited in* YAHYĀ, at 388

[117] *See* Ministry of Commerce Legal Memorandum No. 583/M (24/6/1390) (juristic person may be partner in limited liability company provided it is duly authorized to engage in commercial activities (in its country of origin) and is represented by a natural person whose powers are defined in a letter issued by the board of directors of such juristic person), *cited in* YAHYĀ, at 388. In contrast, general partners must be natural persons: Council of Ministers Resolution No. 17, para. 4(3) (1982), *as amended by* Council of Ministers Resolution No. 80 (30/4/1405). However, certain entities may be subject to restrictions with respect to being partners in a limited liability company. *See, e.g.,* Banks Control Regs., art 10(2) (prohibiting banks from holding certain direct partnership interests).

[118] Companies Regs., art. 157.

[119] Minister of Commerce Circulars Nos. 222/9265/5632 (22/5/1401); 221/308 (23/1/1401); 221/2376 (9/5/1401) & 3/9/sh/6665 (13/6/1398), *cited in* YAHYĀ, at 387. *But see* Civil Servants Regs. Implementing Rules, Civil Service Board Resolution No. 1, art. 13/2 (27/7/1397) (permitting civil servants to own shares in limited liability companies). *See also* pp. 27–28 and n. 76, *supra*. However, a student may be a partner provided he submits a certificate from his school or institution attesting that he is currently enrolled and stating his scholastic year. Minister of Commerce Circular No. 3/9/sc/3250 (7/1/1398), *cited in* YAHYĀ, at 387.

Saudi law permits the formation of companies by closely related parties including spouses. The regulatory rules generally applicable to companies do not, in theory, prohibit a company formed by X and Y forming a limited liability company with the participation of another commercial company or partnership also wholly-owned by X and Y or with a sole proprietorship owned by X or Y. A limited liability company may also be formed by the following partners

(a) A sole proprietorship owned by X and a company owned by X and his minor children of whom X is the guardian or legal representative.

(b) A sole proprietorship owned by Y, who is the mother of minor children, and a company owned by the minor children and their guardian, X.

(c) A sole proprietorship owned by X and a company owned by X and any mental incompetents of whom X is the guardian or legal representative.

Notably, the preceding three arrangements presuppose the existence of a company between minors or incompetents and their parent, guardian, or legal representative.[120] The representation of minors, incompetents, and the like, and the consummation of transactions on their behalf are subject to Islamic law rules.[121] The preceding general principles are qualified, from a practical standpoint, with respect to mixed participation companies subject to the foreign investment licensing procedure. The policy of the FCIC is extremely restrictive with respect to granting licenses to nonSaudi natural persons.[122]

[120] However, minors, incompetents, and other persons lacking capacity may not be general partners with unlimited liability. It may be noted that the age of majority has been set at 18 hijrah years. *See* Consultative Council Resolution No. 114 (5/7/1374).

[121] Court approval of the participation of persons lacking capacity should be obtained. The Ministry of Commerce does not require a certificate embodying such approval to be submitted at any stage of the registration procedure. However, notaries public, by whom the company's articles of association are required to be notarized, *see generally* pp. 103–04 *infra*, may refuse to notarize the articles unless the appropriate certificate issued by a shari'ah court is produced. *See also* Minister of Justice Circular No. 50/2 (19/3/1393) (requiring final judgment for sale, purchase, or transfer of minors' rights); Minister of Justice Circular No. 213/1 (24/11/1391) (relating to fathers' sales or purchases on behalf of their minor sons) (both cited in MINISTRY OF JUSTICE, REGULATIONS, RULES, CIRCULARS).

[122] However, licenses may be obtained by nonSaudi individuals possessing specialized knowhow or outstanding qualifications in the area of business applied for and the readiness to invest "capital" within the definition of the FCIR.

C. AGREEMENTS AMONG THE PARTNERS

1. Articles of association[123]

Substantive requirements

The articles of association are the basic document required by regulation to constitute the limited liability company. Amended article 161 of the Companies Regulations provides

> [a] limited liability company shall be formed by virtue of articles of association signed by all of the partners. The said articles of association shall include the particulars which shall be determined by a resolution issued by the Minister of Commerce and Industry, provided they include the following particulars
>
> (1) The kind of company and its name, objective, and main office.[124]
> (2) The partners' names, addresses, occupations, and nationalities.
> (3) The names of the directors, whether or not they are partners, if they were named in the company's articles of association [sic].
> (4) The names of the members of the board of controllers, if any.
> (5) The amount of the capital and the amount of shares in cash and in kind, a detailed description of the shares in kind and the value thereof, and the names of the contributors in kind.
> (6) A statement of the partners that all the capital shares have been allotted and the value of such shares has been paid in full.

[123] The term "articles of association" is used throughout this chapter as being one of the two English terms for the company's constitutive document in common usage in the Kingdom, the other being "memorandum of association." The Arabic term used in the Companies Regulations is "contract." *Cf.*, Companies Regs. art. 1 (company is a "contract"). The Arabic term generally used to designate such contract, as appearing in the required publication of extracts of articles of association in Umm al-Qurā is literally translated as "contract of formation." The Ministry of Commerce standard form articles of association are designated simply as "contract", corresponding to the terminology of the Regulations.

[124] The name of a limited liability company may consist of the name of one or more partners and/or be derived from its objectives. *Id.* art. 160. However, the name of the company may not be a foreign name offensive to religion, customs, or traditions: Minister of Commerce Circular No. 3/3/1598 (11/5/1399), *cited in* YAHYĀ, at 390. Nor may the name include a foreign name unless such name is the name of a partner: Deputy Minister of Indus. & Elec. for Industrial Affairs Letter No. A/M/1168 (1/6/1401), *cited in id.* at 390–91. If the name resembles the name of another registered company, commercial registration will be refused, if the resemblance is such as to lead to confusion, deception, and misleading of the general public: Minister of Commerce Circular No. 9/s^c/1246 (11/10/1388), *cited in id.* at 391. A company's mark must be in the form of a symbol, an original logo, or distinctive design not contrary to public policy and morals and must be made a part of the company's official name. In all cases, such mark may not be in the form of a name the same as, or near to, or in contradiction with the company's official name: Minister of Commerce Circular No. 222/9136/957 (26/8/1401), *cited in id.* at 391. *See also* Minister of Commerce Circular No. 221/3056 (21/6/1401) (the word "Saudi" may not be added to the name of an enterprise in a context which would create misconceptions about the nature of the enterprise) (applicable to branches of foreign companies), *cited in id.* at 391.

(7) The method of distribution of the profits.

(8) The date of commencement and the date of expiration of the company.

(9) The form of notices to be directed by the company to the partners.

In implementation of article 161, the then Minister of Commerce and Industry issued Resolution No. 694, providing

Article 1: The articles of association of a limited liability company shall include the following particulars

1. The kind of company, its name, objectives, main office and branches.

2. The names of the partners, their places of residence, occupations, and nationalities, and the amount of their shares.

3. The date of commencement and expiration of the company.

4. The names of the directors, whether or not partners, their powers, term, and the manner of issuance of their resolutions in the case where there are several directors.[125]

5. The amount of capital, the value of the contributions, the amount of shares in cash and in kind, and a detailed description of the shares in kind, their value, and the names of the persons who contributed them.

6. A statement of the partners that all the capital shares have been allotted and the value of such shares has been paid in full.

7. The names of the members of the board of controllers, if any.

8. The majority required for the adoption of partners' resolutions.

9. The method of distribution of the profits.

10. The form of notices to be directed by the company to the partners.

11. The beginning and end of the financial year of the company.

Article 2: In addition to the particulars provided in the preceding article, the articles of association of a limited liability company in which the number of partners exceeds twenty shall include the following particulars

1. The number of members of the board of controllers, the term of their membership and the required quorum for the validity of the board meeting and the adoption of its resolutions.

2. The quorum required for the validity of the partners' general meeting and the adoption of its resolutions.

---

[125] However, directors need not be named in the articles of association but may be appointed in a separate document. *See* Companies Regs., art. 161(3) *as amended by* Royal Decree No. M/23 (1982), 167.

Article 3: The contents of this Resolution shall be published and the Companies Department in this Ministry shall have regard for the execution thereof.[126]

In addition, the articles of association are required to include the following provision: "The director(s) shall represent the company in its relations with third parties and before the courts and shall be entitled to appoint third parties as representatives with respect to legal proceedings and defence on behalf of the company."[127] The Ministry of Commerce has also issued model articles of association of a limited liability company.[128] These model articles were issued as guidelines and their utilization is not mandatory.

Practical considerations

In drafting the company's articles of association, certain considerations should be taken into account. First, it will be noted that the articles of association are the company's official constitutive document, and, by virtue of being signed before and notarized by a notary public,[129] who is a public official and member of the judiciary, the articles are given the force of proof in legal proceedings. Their contents must be given effect by the courts without submission of other evidence, and they may only be attacked on the grounds of illegality or falsification.[130] Consequently, in the case of a dispute between the partners or between the partners and third parties, the provisions of the articles of association will, in the absence of allegations and proof of illegality or falsification, prevail over any competing document, such as the company's bylaws, any other agreements among the partners, partners' resolutions, or board of directors' resolutions. The parties may therefore decide to seek additional protection by including in the articles of association certain aspects of the company's internal procedure which might otherwise be included in the company's bylaws[131] or certain items, such as a noncompetition clause or definition of the parties' respective rights relating to industrial property, which would ordinarily be included in the partners' agreement discussed in the following section. They are also free to provide that no partner shall be deemed an agent or representative of any other partner except as provided in the articles of association. In this

---

[126] Resolution No. 694 (22/6/1385).

[127] Commentary of Deputy Minister of Commerce on Ministry of Commerce Legal Department Memorandum of 14/6/1400, *cited in* YAḤYĀ, at 393.

[128] *See generally* Appendix 28.

[129] *See generally* pp. 103–04 *infra.*

[130] Judicial Regs., Royal Decree No. M/64, art. 96 (1975), *as amended by* Royal Decrees No. M/76 (14/10/1395), No. M/15 (3/4/1397), No. M/4 (1/3/1401), & No. M/3 (1/4/1404).

[131] In practice, limited liability companies do not ordinarily have separate bylaws distinct from their articles of association. "Bylaw" type provisions may be divided between the articles of association and the partners' agreement.

context, attention may be drawn to article 167 of the Regulations, which provides that the company shall be bound by the acts of the directors within the scope of their powers as provided in the articles of association and published. It should also be noted that, unless the parties expressly provide in the articles that the company will be dissolved upon the withdrawal, adjudged legal incapacity, insolvency, or bankruptcy of any partner, the company's existence will not be affected by the occurrence of any of these events unless all shares are transferred to a single partner as a result thereof.[132] Similarly, unless the articles of association prohibit the dissolution of the company before the end of its duration, the partners may decide to dissolve it by the applicable majority.[133] Ultimately, the decision whether or not to include certain items in the articles of association will be a matter of business judgment and strategy, depending on the circumstances and facts of each case and also upon the parties' desire to keep certain aspects of their relationship confidential. Although the articles of association are no longer required to be published in their entirety, they may be so published if the partners so desire. Furthermore, even if only an extract thereof is published, the complete articles of association may nonetheless have to be produced or submitted in various business or official contexts, such as to a lending institution or to certain government authorities. In the balance, the parties may prefer the safeguarding of the privacy of their understandings to the additional legal protection afforded by incorporating such understandings into the articles of association. Finally, the additional administrative and procedural burdens which the incorporation of certain provisions into the articles of association may entail should be taken into consideration. Any change in the articles will require the amendment thereof. Amendment involves not only the internal procedures of adopting the relevant partners' resolution but also the obtention of approval from the Ministry of Commerce and, with respect to information relating to the License, the Ministry of Industry and Electricity, if the company is of mixed participation, as well as fulfilment of the regulatory notarization, publication, and registration formalities with respect to each amendment. Such procedures are onerous, lengthy, and may deprive the parties of the desired level of flexibility in conducting their affairs. In view of the preceding considerations, the normal practice is to provide in the articles of association only those particulars required by the applicable regulatory rules and to incorporate the remainder of the parties' understandings into the partners' agreement.

[132] Companies Regs., art. 178.
[133] *Id.* art. 15(5). Such a provision, should the partners later wish to dissolve the company, may be removed by a pertinent amendment to the articles of association.

Liability for misrepresentation

The articles of association are intended not only to constitute the limited liability company and to define the basic rights and duties of the partners, but also to provide information to the general public and, in particular, to creditors on the company's financial and management structure. In the drafting of the articles of association, care should be taken, even if the statements made therein are technically accurate, not to omit information in the absence of which the statements included might be viewed as false or misleading so as to cause damage to third parties relying thereon.

Article 229(1) of the Regulations provides for penalties to be imposed with respect to intentional misrepresentations made in the articles of association.[134] In addition, the company or its directors may be held liable under general principles of law for damages to third parties. In order to recover damages, however, an aggrieved party must establish more than a mere false statement appearing in the articles of association. It must also prove actual reliance on the statement and a direct causal relationship between such reliance and the injury giving rise to the cause of action. The company is required to keep the particulars of its articles of association up to date in all respects, since they are intended to represent an accurate description of the essential facts relating to the company at all times and do not speak merely as of the date of their execution. The relationship between the company's liability for false statements and its duty to keep the information contained in its articles of association up to date by making timely relevant amendments to the articles is apparent. A statement, even if true at the time of publication of the original articles, may cease to become so and, if not amended, may give rise to claims of third parties who relied on the original statement.[135] The issue of whether an amendment was made in a timely fashion is a question of fact, depending on the circumstances of each case.

---

[134] Article 229 provides in part

> [w]ithout prejudice to the requirements of the Islamic sharīʿah, the following offenders shall be liable to imprisonment for a period of not less than three months and not more than one year and a fine of not less than five thousand and not more than twenty thousand Saudi riyals or to one of these penalties:
> (1) Anyone who wilfully inserts in the articles of association, bylaws, subscription documents or other documents of a company, or in the application for authorization to form the company, particulars which are false or contrary to the provisions of these Regulations, and anyone who signs or distributes such documents with knowledge thereof.

[135] *See also id.* art. 229(8), *as amended by* Royal Decree No. M/23 (1982) (imposing same penalties on company officials for noncompliance with obligatory regulatory rules) (applicable to failure to make appropriate amendments).

2. Partners' agreement

General considerations

The partners' agreement sets forth the understandings and intentions of the parties. It is normally entered into prior to the formation of the company for a term contemporaneous with the duration of the company to be formed. The execution of a partners' agreement is not required by regulation. However, it may serve a practical purpose, since it sets forth those details of the partners' relationship which are not required to be divulged to third parties. The agreement, if not in conflict with any rule of law or the provisions of the articles of association, is valid and enforceable as among the partners but may not be invoked against third parties. To ensure the validity and binding force of the partners' agreement, it should be adopted or ratified at the first general meeting of the partners held after the registration of the company. However, in case a conflict arises between the provisions of the articles of association and the partners' agreement, the provisions of the articles will prevail, since they are the regulatory and public document.

Specific provisions

The partners' agreement may define in detail the rights and obligations of each partner, as well as other business matters. Such agreement may cover, *inter alia*, the parties' respective liabilities for expenses incurred and obligations assumed prior to the formation of the company, personnel policies, methods of procurement, the conduct of ordinary and extra-ordinary business, and the like. The partners' agreement may also cover the division of obligations and responsibilities between the partners, directors and the general manager in addition to those issues covered in the articles of association. It may specify the extent of each partner's responsibility for obtaining guarantees, bonds, loans, and other financing, and any other services the individual partners may be required to render to the company. It may also include in detail procedures relating to the operation of bank accounts and specify persons authorized to sign checks, contracts, and other corporate documents. It should not fail to include, where applicable, a comprehensive treatment of the parties' rights with respect to trademarks, tradenames, copyrights, patents, and the like both during the existence of the company and in the event of its sale, merger, or dissolution. It may include certain partners' obligations to provide specialized, technical, or management services. It may place responsibility on a Saudi partner for obtaining all necessary governmental approvals and visas for expatriate employees and carrying out customs clearance and other facilitating activities for the company. It may include a confidentiality clause prohibiting partners from revealing business, financial, and/or technical information except to official authorities to the extent required by law. It may prohibit partners from acting as legal representatives of the company unless in possession of a valid power of attorney. It may cover any other relevant aspects of the partners' relationship and the company's activities. The agreement may also provide for dispute resolution by means of arbitration in accordance with Saudi law.[136]

Noncompetition/conflict of interest

The Industrial Policy Statement endorses the principle of "competition which serves the interests of local consumers."[137] However, there are no comprehensive regulatory rules protecting competition or prohibiting unfair competition, aside from provisions specific to trademark infringement and literary property rights. Article 5 of the Commercial Court Regulations provides generally

> [e]very businessman shall conduct himself in all his commercial activities according to religion and honor and shall not commit deceit, swindling, deception, fraud, misrepresentation, duplicity or anything contrary to religion and honor in any way whatsoever. If he does so, he shall merit a deterring penalty in accordance with the penalty provisions included in these Regulations.[138]

On the basis of article 5 and general rules of Islamic law mandating fair dealing, honesty, and good faith in transactions with third parties, an injured party may recover damages on proof of unfair dealing and actual harm sustained as a result of any such unfair competition.[139] In contrast, Saudi regulations are silent on the issue of competition between a partner and the company in which he is a participant and between partners and directors in such a company. It is therefore advisable for partners to cover the issue contractually in order to supplement and reinforce the generally applicable rules of law. A noncompetition clause is an indispensable provision, whether incorporated into the articles of association or the partners' agreement. Such a clause should prohibit the partners and their related parties from engaging in or holding an interest in any entity engaged in any activity competitive with the activities of the limited liability

---

[136] An arbitration clause may also be included in the articles of association. *See generally* pp. 160–61 *infra*.

[137] DALĪL AL-ISTITHMĀR AL-ṢINĀʻĪ 63 (6th ed. 1404).

[138] Art. 147 of the Commercial Court Regs. provides for a prison sentence of 10 days to 3 months or a minimal fine for violations of art. 5. *See also* p. 24 and note 66 *supra*.

[139] *See, e.g.*, M. BARĪRĪ, *supra* note 110, at 109–11.

company to be formed or any company in which it may acquire an interest without the consent of the other partners. This prohibition may also be extended to directors of the company, who may also be prohibited from sitting on the boards of directors of competitors. Such clause may also provide that any partner having knowledge of a business opportunity within the scope of the objectives of the company will bring it to the notice of the management, and that, if for any reason the company is not willing to utilize such opportunity, the partner having discovered the opportunity will have the right to undertake the activities for its own account. In addition, it may be provided that, if it is the nonSaudi partner who undertakes any such activities in the public sector, it will enter into an exclusive or nonexclusive agency agreement with the Saudi partner. Or, if it is the Saudi partner who undertakes such activities, it may be obligated to subcontract or assign certain portions of such contract to the nonSaudi partner.[140] Finally, it may be provided that, if the company acquires knowledge of any business opportunity that it does not wish to utilize, the company may offer the opportunity to its individual partners. Nonetheless, it may be noted, that, even in the absence of a noncompetition clause, Saudi law under certain circumstances may afford ample protection to the company against competition from its participants. For example, in one nonhypothetical fact situation illustrating the official position with respect to competition between a partner and a company in which it participates, a foreign corporation and a Saudi entity entered into an agreement specifying several areas of business to be undertaken at present and in the future in different phases. They formed a limited liability company for the purpose of undertaking electrical works. After the formation of the company, the foreign corporation independently obtained a project for electrical work in the public sector. When the foreign corporation applied for a License, the License was denied on the grounds that it was already a partner in the limited liability company having the same objectives.

D. OBJECTIVES

1. Permissible activities

Article 159 of the Companies Regulations provides that "the objective of a limited liability company may not be the undertaking of operations of insurance or savings or banks."[141] The prohibition of banking operations is

---

[140] *See generally* pp. 50–51.

[141] The Companies Regs. do not define the term "bank." However, art. 159 may be interpreted in the light of the provisions of the Banks Control Regulations. Art. 1 defines a "bank" as "any natural or juristic person basically engaged in any banking activity in the

clearly intended to ensure the soundness of the financial community and to protect the general public, in that the limited liability company, in view of the relatively small number of its participants and its relatively low capitalization, is not a suitable vehicle for a bank.[142] Islamic law generally prohibits insurance, which it assimilates to the illegal activity of speculation.[143] However, the practical necessity of obtaining insurance protection is recognized in the Kingdom.[144] In addition, any other activities which are prohibited by law or in conflict with public policy or morality

Kingdom." "Banking activities" are defined by that article as

> [a]ccepting time or demand deposits; opening current accounts; opening credits; issuing letters of guarantee; paying and collecting checks, drafts, pay orders, or other papers of value; discounting [promissory] notes, bills of exchange and other commercial papers; and [making] foreign exchange transactions as well as other banking transactions.

Cf. Commission for the Settlement of Commercial Disputes, Jeddah, Decision No. 507–1405 (17/11/1405) (since lending is among most important banking transactions loans by company to its partners including debit current accounts violated article 159) (subjecting directors to imprisonment and fines and requiring partners to restitute borrowed amounts).

[142] *See also* Minister of Commerce Resolution No. 948, art. 1 (1/1/1402) (prohibiting companies other than banks incorporated under the Banks Control Regs. from engaging in the business of mediation/brokerage for speculation in gold and silver in domestic and foreign markets); *cf.* Minister of Commerce Circular No. 3/3/1900 (11/6/1399) (prohibiting activity of mediation in circulation of financial instruments until issuance of regulation of such activity), *cited in* YAHYĀ, at 389; Minister of Commerce Circular No. 3/3/2143 (9/6/1399) relating to money-changing *cited in id.* at 389.

[143] The prohibition of speculative activities is strictly enforced. For example, one company was obliged to publish an apology to its customers for suspending a contest it had promoted and later suspended in compliance with the fatwā (legal opinion) of Sheikh Abd al-Aziz bn Baz, General President of the Directorate of Theological Studies, Legal Opinions, Missionary Activity, and Guidance, affirming the illegality of all forms of lotteries. It should be noted that the majority of Muslim jurists believe that, with the exclusion of life insurance, which is strictly prohibited, a general insurance enterprise based on cooperative principles is permissible. *See, e.g.* Royal Decree No. M/5 (17/4/1405) (8/1/1985) (authorizing formation of National Cooperative Insurance Company); Council of Ministers Resolution No. 292 (22/12/1404) (17/9/1984) (Council of Ministers to study possibility of authorizing formation of other cooperative insurance companies). However, due to the legal rule that only a limited liability company or a corporation may be structured on cooperative principles, the only business form available in principle to an insurance business is a corporation.

[144] *See, e.g.*, Council of Ministers Resolution No. 124, para. 3 (29/5/1403) (requiring public sector contractors to obtain insurance from local firms); Commercial Agencies Regs. Implementing Rules, Minister of Commerce Resolution No. 1897, art. 3(4) (24/5/1401) (requiring agents to maintain in their place of business documents evidencing *inter alia* insurance paid on imported goods); Minister of Communications Resolution No. 54, para. 3 (24/3/1403) (amending art. 169 of Ports, Harbors, and Lighthouses Implementing Rules, Minister of Communications Resolution No. 181 (9/10/1395)) (requiring submission of copies of insurance policies); Commercial Court Regs., ch. 11. (governing marine insurance); Minister of Fin. & Nat'l Econ. Resolution No. 679/11 (9/3/1392) (regulating deductible expenses of Saudi branches of foreign life insurance companies, computation of taxable profits of branches of general insurance companies). However, commercial registration to carry on insurance activities may not be obtained. Consequently, offshore insurance companies are obliged to operate by means of a registered Saudi agent whose objectives include the representation of nonSaudi companies.

may not be undertaken by the company.

Certain qualifications may be made with respect to certain activities. For example, Saudi holding companies are required to hold controlling interests, a criterion established at fifty-one percent of the equity, in companies in which they have holdings.[145] Although all limited liability companies are subject to article 159 and other general prohibitions, the scope of activities permitted to the company will also depend upon whether it is wholly Saudi-owned or of mixed participation. Mixed participation companies are prohibited from engaging in trade under applicable regulatory rules.[146] In addition, certain other commercial activities may be restricted to wholly Saudi-owned entities by regulatory act.[147] In the case of an industrial enterprise, in order to obtain commercial registration, its objectives must conform to the objectives licensed by the industrial licensing authority, in the case of a wholly Saudi-owned company, or by the FCIC in the case of a mixed participation company.[148]

2. Commercial/professional distinction

Both wholly Saudi and mixed participation companies are subject to the rule that commercial and professional activities may not be combined within the sphere of objectives of a single enterprise. It may be noted that the Ministry of Commerce distinguishes between management consulting, which it regards as professional activity, and operational management services, which it regards as commercial activity.[149] Nonetheless, a

---

[145] Ministry of Commerce Legal Memorandum No. 682/11 (15/7/1401), *cited in* YAHYĀ, at 396.

[146] *See generally* pp. 11–12 *supra. Cf.* Minister of Commerce Circular No. 3/9/sh/136/9/846 (21/8/1398) (requiring mixed participation industrial company licensed under FCIR to acknowledge when obtaining commercial registration that it "is registered by virtue of an industrial license and is not entitled to engage in trade except for the sale of its production"), *cited in* YAHYĀ, at 390.

[147] *See, e.g.,* Minister of Communications Resolution No. 9, para. 3(1) (5/2/1406); Rules of Procedures and Conditions of Granting Licenses to Engage in the Activity of Transporting Passengers in Hired Cars and Buses between the Cities of the Kingdom and Other States, Minister of Communications Resolution No. 51, art. 2 (1/3/1404) (license-holder must be Saudi individual or 100% Saudi-owned company whose capital must remain wholly Saudi-owned throughout period of license); Rules of Procedures and Conditions of Granting Licenses to Engage in the Activity of Car Rental, Minister of Communications Resolution No. 33, art. 2 (4/2/1404) (same with respect to car rental licenses).

[148] *See* Minister of Commerce Circular No. 3/9/sh/136/9/1244 (4/11/1394), *cited in* YAHYĀ, at 388. The same rule applies to nonindustrial mixed participation companies required to obtain commercial registration.

[149] *Cf.* Minister of Commerce Circulars Nos. 3/3/822 (23/6/1398) & 221/3835 (8/8/1401) (dividing "computer services" into "commercial activities" requiring commercial registration such as sale and leasing of hardware and spare parts, maintenance, and renting of computer time, all of which may be included in objectives of a commercial company, and "consulting services", such as programming, processing, *i.e.* software-related activities, which are licensed as activities of liberal professions), *cited in* YAHYĀ, at 389–90. For liberal professions recognized by the Ministry of Commerce, see MINISTRY OF COMMERCE, DALĪL AL-MIHAN AL

commercial enterprise may carry on a minor amount of professional activities in connection with its commercial objectives, provided that such activities are necessary and incidental or directly related to its primary commercial activities. However, practically speaking, it is difficult to obtain FCIC approval of applicants' objectives specifying the carrying on of professional activities even in conjunction with their commercial objectives.[150]

3. Drafting of objectives clause

The objectives clause in the company's articles of association should be narrowly drawn and specify the activities to be carried on with precision.[151] In contrast to the practice in certain other jurisdictions, the objectives clause may not provide generally that the objectives of the company shall be to engage in any lawful business activity or that the company shall be permitted to carry on all lawful business activities except for those expressly excluded in such clauses.[152] The objectives clauses of limited liability companies, and in particular those of mixed participation companies, tend to be short. By way of illustration, a selection of the complete texts of actual objectives clauses of mixed participation companies is presented as follows

— Undertaking works of transportation of merchandise by land.[153]

HURRAH 11 (1983) (enumerating, *inter alia*, as liberal professions: engineering consultancy, civil engineering, electrical and mechanical engineering, petroleum engineering, refrigeration engineering, chemical engineering, geological and hydrogeological engineering, surveying, industrial engineering, decor engineering, architecture, soil testing, water and agricultural consultancy, legal consultancy, administration and management consultancy, economic consultancy, translating, certified accounting and auditing, safety and security consultancy).

[150] The FCIC formerly approved objectives clauses submitted by applicants involving the provision of certain professional services, for example, such activities as "design and construction" of bridges, buildings, or the like. Due, however, to abuse on the part of certain companies, which operated under such clauses in a manner inconsistent with the interpretation of the clauses by the FCIC and proceeded to obtain contracts for pure design, the FCIC has adopted a restrictive policy with respect to approving such terms as "design", "manage", "supervise", and the like in applicants' proposed objectives clauses. Nonetheless, approval of the word "design" is not impossible to obtain. *See, e.g.*, Objectives Clause, Umm al-Qurā, March 6, 1984, at 23, col. 1 (approved objectives of mixed participation company including "analysis", "design", "installation", "operation", "maintenance", "preparation of operational programs", and "training" with respect to fire detection, warning systems, and fire-extinction equipment).

[151] *See, e.g.*, Minister of Commerce Circulars Nos. 221/16 (7/1/1400), 3/9/sh/100/9/b/4426 (16/2/1398), & 3/9/sh/100/9/b/4278 (5/4/1396) (if objectives of company include executory works, maintenance works, or other commercial activities, the kind and sphere of activity must be specified), *cited in* YAḤYĀ, at 388.

[152] In the case of a mixed participation company, it should be kept in mind that the draft articles of association are submitted to the FCIC together with the License application and must conform to the activities for which the License is to be granted.

[153] Umm al-Qurā, 3/11/1404, at 24, col. 1.

— Undertaking contracting works for construction of ports, jetties and marine constructions, dams, bridges, buildings, and water systems.[154]

— Undertaking works of installation, isolation, painting, and maintenance of pipes, steel structures and electromechanical equipment for petrochemical plants.[155]

— Production of agricultural greenhouses.[156]

— Undertaking works of installation, repair, and maintenance of valve generators for oil, gas, water, and chemicals pipes and training for such works.[157]

— Undertaking works of digging, deepening, and scraping of canals, passages, and water tunnels for ports.[158]

— Undertaking contracting works for the installation and maintenance of airconditioning, ventilation, and fire-fighting equipment.[159]

— Undertaking works of management, operation, and maintenance of water and sewage treatment plants and water and wells purification plants and related systems.[160]

— Undertaking works of construction, installation, operation, and maintenance of telecommunications sets and training.[161]

— Undertaking works of cathodic protection and installation, maintenance, and repair of related equipment.[162]

— Production of cement processing chemicals.[163]

— Undertaking contracting works for building construction.[164]

— Undertaking management works for civil, mechanical, and electrical projects in the Kingdom of Saudi Arabia.[165]

[154] *Id.* at 23, col. 1.
[155] *Id.* 10/8/1404, at 9, col. 1.
[156] *Id.* 10/11/1404, Supp., at 1, col. 1.
[157] *Id.* 2/9/1404, at 10, col. 2.
[158] *Id.* 14/8/1404, at 3, col. 1.
[159] *Id.* at 4, col. ?
[160] *Id.* at 5, col. 1.
[161] *Id.* 23/9/1404, at 14, col. 1.
[162] *Id.* 26/1/1404, Supp., at 1, col. 1.
[163] *Id.* 19/5/1403, at 13, col. 1.
[164] *Id.* 8/8/1403, at 14, col. 1.
[165] *Id.* 28/4/1403, at 12, col. 1.

— The object of the company is undertaking cleaning works for all kinds of constructions and buildings.[166]

— The objectives for which the company was formed are the undertaking of executing electrical and mechanical contracting works and related [ ] in the following fields; electrical power generating stations, electrical transformers and substations, laying of electrical cables and electrical power distribution systems including 23 kV and the outside and inside keyboards.[167]

E. CAPITAL

1. Nature of capital

Article 3 of the Companies Regulations provides

> [a] partner's contribution may be a specified sum of money (contribution in cash) and may be a capital asset (contribution in kind). It may also, except in the case where the provisions of these Regulations imply otherwise, be work. However, a partner's contribution may not be his reputation or influence.
>
> Only contributions in cash and contributions in kind shall form the company's capital. Such capital may not be altered except in accordance with the provisions of these Regulations and with such terms in the company's articles of association or bylaws as are not inconsistent therewith.

Article 3 is a general provision applicable to all forms of companies. It identifies the elements that may constitute a company's "capital." These are personal property, whether tangible or intangible, and real property. With respect to nonSaudi partners, it will be noted that the definition of capital by article 3 is less specific than the definition of "foreign capital" as provided in the FCIR and their implementing rules. However, since the FCIC is empowered to determine which types of "foreign capital" it will license on a case-by-case basis, practically speaking, foreign capital as licensed may ultimately prove to be narrower in scope than capital as defined in the FCIR and the Companies Regulations. Only property of a present and certain financial value may qualify as capital of a limited liability company. This principle is derived from article 162 of the Companies Regulations, which requires the capital of a limited liability

---

[166] *Id.* 16/3/1404, Supp., at 1, col. 2.
[167] *Id.* 23/10/1403, at 5, col. 1.

company to be paid in full.[168] Therefore, for example, even though the FCIR Implementing Rules include various forms of negotiable instruments within their definition of capital[169] and article 4 of the Companies Regulations contemplates contributions of claims against third parties,[170] neither promissory notes or other debt instruments nor claims against third parties, accounts receivable, and the like may be contributed as capital of a limited liability company. It will also be noted that article 3 as applied excludes not only reputation and influence from the capital of the company[171] but also such items as good will and creditworthiness, which may not constitute a contribution to capital or entitle a participant to a share in the equity, any rights attached thereto, or the relevant portion of the company's assets upon liquidation.

2. Paying-in of capital

The Companies Regulations leave the participants in a limited liability company free to determine the amount of the company's capital, provided that it exceeds the regulatory minimum of five hundred thousand Saudi riyals.[172] However, a higher capitalization may be required for certain activities.[173] In addition, as a matter of practice, if the FCIC determines

---

[168] Cf. Companies Regs., art. 161(6) (requiring articles of association of limited liability company to include partners' statement that all capital shares have been paid in full) with id. arts. 22(3), 39(2) (extract of articles of association of general and limited partnerships must specify contributions partners have undertaken to make).

[169] See p. 64–65 supra.

[170] Article 4 provides

> [if] the contribution of a partner is a right of ownership or usufruct or any other in rem right, the partner shall be responsible in accordance with the legal consequences of a bill of sale for guaranteeing the contribution in the case of loss or claim for recovery or the appearance of a defect or deficiency therein.

> If such contribution merely consists of a usufruct of property, the legal consequences of a lease shall apply to the said matters.

> If the contribution of a partner is claims it holds against third parties, its liability to the company shall only be discharged after collection of such claims.

It should be noted that the provisions of article 4 are general and apply to the limited liability company only within the legal framework applicable to that form.

[171] Cf. Minister of Commerce Circular No. 3/9/sh/1722/10/845 (21/7/1398) (affirming that reputation may not be considered a contribution to capital), cited in Yahyā, at 392.

[172] See Companies Regs., art. 158, as amended by Royal Decree No. M/23 (1982). This minimum does not apply to companies formed prior to the effectiveness of the 1982 amendment to article 158. If such companies wish to increase their capital, they are not required to attain the present minimum capitalization level. See also id. art. 2, as amended by Royal Decree No. M/23 (Council of Ministers may by resolution amend minimum and maximum capital limits of companies subject to the Regulations).

[173] See, e.g., Minister of Defence & Aviation Resolution No. 1/1/4/8/10, art. 3(3) (29/6/1400) (setting minimum capital of tourism and travel agencies at S.R. 1 million).

that the amount of capital as stated in the prospective partners' application for a License is, although in excess of the regulatory minimum, insufficient for the purposes of their proposed activities, it may require the applicants to increase their proposed capital or reduce their proposed activities correspondingly. Noncompliance may result in delaying the issuance of the License for an unspecified period of time or in denial of the License.

Whatever its amount, the capital of a limited liability company, whether in cash or in kind or both, with certain exceptions[174] must be paid in full. Article 162 provides that "the company shall not be definitively formed until all of the shares in cash and the shares in kind have been allotted to all the partners and paid in full."[175] As a result of this rule, ventures requiring a large amount of capital may encounter difficulties with the limited liability company, since, not only must its capital as a rule be paid in full, but also capital may not be raised by public subscription.[176] However, Saudi law does not place restrictions on the amount of indebtedness limited liability companies may incur. Therefore, in case the paid-in capital is not sufficient for the company's needs, it may freely borrow the required funds inside or outside Saudi Arabia.[177]

Contributions in cash must be deposited in the account of the company under formation at one of the banks approved by the Minister of Commerce.[178] The deposit of funds should be made prior to notarization of the articles of association by a notary public, since the articles include the partners' representation that the capital has been paid in full. The Ministry of Commerce requires a certificate of the deposit of funds issued by such bank to be submitted at the time of commercial registration of the company. Capital in kind is deemed contributed upon the signing of the articles of association before the notary public and the notarization of

---

[174] See, e.g., Minister of Indus. & Elec. & Minister of Commerce Resolution No. 1184 (29/12/1397) (as exception to rule of art. 162, partners in limited liability companies formed by Saudi Basic Industries Corporation ["SABIC"] or in which it participates are permitted to pay in less than the full amount of such companies' authorized capital, provided that such companies' articles of association or other basic document states such companies' capital and the amount which shall be paid initially and the companies' board of directors defines the manner and dates of payment of the balance in payments corresponding to the actual needs of such companies), cited in YAHYĀ, at 397; Extract of Articles of Association, Umm al-Qurā, July 26, 1985, at 18, cols.1–2 (less than 10% of capital paid in).

[175] Cf. Companies Regs., art. 12 (requiring amount of authorized and paid-in capital to be stated on all documents issued by company).

[176] Id. art. 158, as amended by Royal Decree No. M/23 (1982).

[177] However, interest payments with respect to loans made by lenders outside Saudi Arabia, whether or not banks, are taxable to the lender. See Minister of Fin. & Nat'l Econ. Letter No. 17/5209 (22/3/1399) (implementing legal opinion of Ministry reaching that conclusion). Note also that in order to qualify for SIDF loans, the participants are required to contribute a minimum of 25–30% of the financing as equity, resulting in an initial debt to equity ratio of approximately 3:1.

[178] Companies Regs., art. 162.

the articles. Contributions in kind are evaluated at current local market value at the time of contribution, regardless of their price or value at the time of acquisition, and must be appraised by a local appraiser, who in practice is generally a registered auditor. The partners are jointly liable without limitation to third parties for damages sustained by reason of the incorrect evaluation of contributions in kind.[179] Third party claims are subject to a three-year limitation period running from the date of publication of the articles of association.[180] The same rule applies with respect to increases of capital involving capital in kind. In this case, the relevant date is the date of publication of the relevant amendment to the articles of association. In addition, any person, whether or not a partner, who maliciously overestimates the value of capital in kind is subject to imprisonment for a term of three months to one year or a fine of five thousand to twenty thousand Saudi riyals or both.[181] Finally, if a violation of the provisions of article 162 has resulted in the invalidity of the company under article 163, the partners who caused such invalidity together with the directors are jointly liable to the other partners and to third parties for damages resulting from such invalidity.[182] However, a representation in the articles of association that all partners agree to the evaluation and accept it as correct and a covenant not to sue one another in the case of invalidity of the company on the grounds of incorrect evaluation will effectively preclude any partner from successfully raising a claim for damages.

3. Release of capital

Article 162 provides that the bank in which contributions in cash have been deposited may release the funds only upon presentation of "the documents evidencing publication of the company in the manner provided in article 164." At such time, the funds in the blocked capital account may be remitted to the authorized representatives of the company or transferred to an operating account opened in its name. No portion of the funds is required to be maintained in any account. However, they must be accounted for in the company's annual balance sheet, a copy of which is required to be submitted to the Ministry of Commerce together with other financial statements no later than six months from the close of every financial year.[183] Capital may not be used to make personal loans to partners.[184]

[179] Id.
[180] Id.
[181] Id. art. 229(3).
[182] Id. art. 163.
[183] Id. art. 175, as amended by Royal Decree No. M/23 (1982).
[184] See, e.g., Ministry of Commerce Legal Memorandum No. 283/11 (3/4/1400) (prohibiting partners from withdrawing company funds in the form of loans accounted for in partners'

F. FORMATION OF THE COMPANY

1. Ministry of Commerce approval of articles of association

The initial step in the formation of a limited liability company is the submission of the proposed articles of association to the Ministry of Commerce.[185] If any participants in the company under formation are nonSaudi and subject to the FCIR, the articles of association may not be submitted to the Ministry of Commerce until the License(s) has/have been granted to the foreign participant(s) by the Minister of Industry and Electricity.[186]

2. Notarization of articles of association

Article 10 of the Companies Regulations provides

> [w]ith the exception of a joint adventure, the company's articles of association and any amendment thereto shall be recorded in writing before a notary public. Otherwise, such articles of association or amendment shall not be effective vis-à-vis third parties.
>
> The partners may not invoke against third parties the ineffectiveness of the articles of association or any amendment thereto not notarized in the preceding manner, but third parties may invoke it against them.
>
> The directors or the board of directors of the company shall be jointly responsible for damages for any harm sustained by the company or the partners or third parties by reason of failure to notarize the articles of association or any amendment thereto.

After obtaining Ministry of Commerce approval, the articles of association must be signed by the partners or their authorized representatives[187] before

debt accounts) (such acts subject to penalties under art. 229 or exposing company to judicial dissolution under art. 15(7)), *cited in* YAḤYĀ, at 395, Legal Memorandum No. 859/11 (12/11/1400) (directors' resolution authorizing loans to partners invalid by force of law since inconsistent both with purpose of having capital available for company's stability and with concept of its juristic personality and also leading to difficulty with respect to realization of company's objectives). (Ministry may direct withdrawal of resolution and restitution of funds within specified period) (same penalties for noncompliance and possibility of dissolution applicable), *cited in id.* at 396; case cited note 141 *supra*.

[185] This requirement is not expressly provided in the Companies Regulations.

[186] It should be noted that art. 10 of the FCIR Implementing Rules requires licensed foreign investors to take measures toward formation of the company within six months of the granting of the License, unless an extension is obtained. A License provides that the Minister of Indus. and Elect. has the right to revoke it for noncompliance. *See generally* p. 68 and note 32 *supra*.

[187] In practice, the notary public may not accept a power of attorney by two or more partners in favor of the same representative for the purpose of signing the articles of association.

a notary public.[188] The articles are not sworn, and no affidavits need be submitted by partners or directors. The limited liability company is deemed formed at this point, and its articles of association are valid and binding as among the partners. The date of formation is significant because it commences the time period for completion of the publication and registration formalities. Even though article 161 provides that a limited liability company is "formed by virtue of articles of association signed by all partners" and article 162 provides that the company shall only be deemed formed after all shares have been allotted and paid in full, these provisions should not be interpreted as meaning that the company is "formed" if the partners merely sign the articles of association and/or pay in their contributions to capital. Article 161(6) requires the articles of association to include the partners' declaration that all capital shares have been allotted and paid in full. This declaration is not given legal effect until notarized by a notary public. Hence, it is at this point that the company is "formed" and acquires its juristic personality.[189] Delayed or future effectiveness of the articles of association is not permitted. Unnotarized articles of association, even if signed by all partners, are not a legal document constitutive of the company. However, under article 10, the ineffectiveness of the articles of association may be used against the partners by third parties even though it may not be used by the partners to avoid their obligations to third parties.

3. Publication and commercial registration

Even though the company is technically formed upon notarization of its articles of association, its existence may not be invoked vis-à-vis third parties until publication of an extract of the articles in Umm al-Qurā, the official journal. Article 11 of the Regulations provides

> [w]ith the exception of a joint adventure, the directors or members of the board of directors [of the company] shall publish the articles of association of the company and any amendments thereto in accordance with the provisions of these Regulations.
>
> If the articles are not published in the above mentioned manner, they shall not be effective vis-à-vis third parties.
>
> If nonpublication is limited to one or more of the particulars required to be published, only such particulars shall be ineffective vis-à-vis third parties.

[188] Notaries public are expressly empowered to notarize contracts such as articles of association. *See* Notaries Public Regs., art. 8(d) (translated in Appendix 25).

[189] However, such juristic personality may not be invoked against third parties until publication: Companies Regs., art. 13.

The directors or the members of the board of directors of the company shall be jointly responsible in damages for the harm sustained by the company or the partners or third parties by reason of nonpublication.

However, only an extract of the articles of association is required to be published. Amended article 164 provides

[t]he directors of the company shall, within thirty days from its formation, apply at the company's expense for the publication of an extract[190] of its articles of association in the official journal. The aforementioned extract shall include the provisions of the articles relating to the particulars stated in article 161. The directors shall likewise apply in the same aforementioned time limit for the registration of the company in the Companies Register in the General Companies Directorate and shall also register the company in the Commercial Register in accordance with the provisions of the Commercial Register Regulations. The aforementioned provisions shall apply to any amendment to the company's articles of association.[191]

The time limit for applying for the publication and registration is the thirty-day period from the date of notarization of the articles of association.[192] Publication formalities precede registration, since a receipt of payment of the publication fee is required to be submitted at the time of commercial registration together with the notarized articles of association.[193] However, since publication of the extract may take as long as a few

[190] Note that the 1403 Government Security Press Arabic edition of amended article 164 contains a typographical error, substituting "two addenda" for "extract."

[191] Obtaining commercial registration is also specifically made an obligation of the partners by the terms of the License, where foreign investors are involved. Commercial registration is a general legal requirement to which almost all commercial concerns, including individuals doing business in the form of sole proprietorships, are subject. *See* Commercial Register Regs., Royal Order No. 21/1/4470, arts. 2–3 (1955). Individuals whose capital does not exceed S.R.5,000 are not required to register but may do so if they wish; Council of Ministers Resolution No. 155 (15/3/1385). Registration fees are as follows

Company	S.R. 100
Branch of company	S.R. 50
Sole proprietorship	S.R. 50
Amendment	S.R. 20

[192] In the case of a branch licensed by the Minister of Indus. and Elect., the time period for applying for commercial registration is 30 days from the date of the License.

[193] *See* Minister of Commerce Circular No. 3/9/sh/81/9/5321 (6/6/1397) (receipt indicating payment of publication fees sufficient if submitted at time of commercial registration provided an undertaking is made to submit sufficient number of copies of Umm al-Qurā establishing publication) (otherwise articles of association in deemed state of non-publication and ineffective vis-à-vis third parties resulting in joint liability in damages for actual injury to company, partners and third parties for noncompliance with art. 11), *cited in* YAHYA, at 398.

months, commercial registration, as a matter of fact, will generally be obtained before actual publication takes place. Registration in the Companies Register precedes registration in the Commercial Register. Both are maintained at the Ministry of Commerce. Commercial registration is the final procedural step in the formation of the company. A commercial registration certificate is *prima facie* evidence of due execution, notarization, and registration of the articles of association.[194] It also demonstrates compliance with and performance of all conditions and acts required to have been performed prior to the formation of the company.[195]

G. JURISTIC PERSONALITY

A limited liability company has a juristic personality distinct from the personalities of its partners, whether these are natural or juristic persons. With the exception of joint adventures, the Companies Regulations do not espouse the view that the forms it provides are aggregates of their individual participants.[196] It has been alleged that Islamic law does not recognize the concept of the juristic person.[197] Such a view has been generally rejected as incorrect. Even though early Muslim jurists did not apply this concept to partnerships, this fact has been explained by the social and economic conditions of their time, when partnerships were generally comprised of a limited number of individuals.[198] In contrast, the concept of the juristic personality is well established under Islamic law with respect to such institutions as the public treasury, the waqf (charitable

---

[194] Extracts of commercial registration certificates may be obtained from the Ministry of Commerce.

[195] For translation of standard Commercial Registration Certificate of a company, *see* Appendix 4. It should be noted that, even though duly formed and registered, the company may in addition, before commencing its activities, be required to obtain licenses from a ministry having authority to regulate its sphere of activities. *See, e.g.,* Private Medical Establishments Regs. Implementing Rules, Minister of Health Resolution No. 5031/20 (19/8/1403) (specifying various licenses and licensing procedures); Minister of Defense & Aviation Resolution No. 1/1/4/8/10, art. 3 (29/6/1400) (requiring license for travel and tourism agencies and air transport); Rules of Procedures and Conditions for Granting Licenses to Transport Goods and Materials for Remuneration by Road, Minister of Communications Resolution No. 199, art. 1 (24/11/1397), *as amended by* Minister of Communications Resolution No. 176 (8/9/1403) (same with respect to land transport).

[196] In contrast, a distinction is made between limited liability companies on the one hand and general and limited partnerships and partnerships limited by shares on the other hand for tax, though not zakāt, purposes. The partners in the latter group are treated as individuals, whereas tax is levied on the total shares of nonSaudis in limited liability companies. Director-Gen'l of Dep't of Zakāt & Income Tax Circular No. 10989/2 (May 5, 1980).

[197] *See, e.g.,* J. SCHACHT, AN INTRODUCTION TO ISLAMIC LAW 125 (1964).

[198] *See, e.g.,* M. AL-MŪSĀ, SHARIKAT AL-ASHKHĀS BAIN AL-SHARĪ·AH WA AL-QĀNŪN 114 (published M.A. thesis at Imām Muhammad bn Su·ūd University 1401) (also observing, at 117, that neither the Qurān nor sunnah prohibits attributing a juristic personality to partnerships).

trust), schools, orphanages, hospitals, and mosques, all of which are recognized as having capacity to hold and exercise rights and be liable for obligations independently from their administrators.[199]

On its formation, a limited liability company acquires a juristic personality. Article 13 of the Companies Regulations provides that "[w]ith the exception of a joint adventure, a company shall from the time of its formation be considered a juristic person. However, such personality may not be invoked vis-à-vis third parties except after completion of the publication formalities." Thus, even though the company's juristic personality is deemed to arise at the time its articles of association are notarized, such personality does not obtain against third parties until the publication procedure is completed.

A limited liability company is a continuing legal entity which is not dissolved by the withdrawal, adjudged legal incapacity, or declaration of bankruptcy or insolvency of one of the partners, unless its articles of association provide otherwise.[200] It will not acquire a new juristic personality upon conversion into another form[201] and will retain its juristic personality. It is also retained during the process of liquidation to the extent required for winding up the business and until liquidation is completed.[202]

H. NATIONALITY

Article 14 of the Companies Regulations provides

> [w]ith the exception of a joint adventure, every company formed in accordance with the provision of these Regulations shall establish its main office in the Kingdom. Such company shall be deemed of Saudi nationality, but such nationality shall not necessarily entail the company's enjoyment of the rights restricted to Saudis.[203]

There is a difference of opinion as to whether the criterion of the nationality of a Saudi company is its formation under the Companies Regulations or the location of its *siège* within the Kingdom. Although it has been suggested that a company formed under the laws of another jurisdiction but having its main office in the Kingdom may have Saudi

---

[199] *See, e.g., id.* at 116 and citations nn. 1–4; 1 A. AUDAH, AL-TASHRĪʿ AL-JINĀʾĪ 292. *Cf.* Minister of Fin. Resolution No. 340, art. 10 (May 8, 1951) (waqf deemed to have juristic personality for tax purposes).

[200] Companies Regs., art. 178.

[201] *Id.* art. 211.

[202] *Id.* art. 216.

[203] Certain rights are restricted to Saudi natural persons, sole proprietorships, or wholly-owned juristic persons. Others are made contingent on specified levels of Saudi participation. *See generally* pp. 11–12, 96 *supra.*

nationality,[204] the better view is that both criteria must be satisfied in order for a company to possess Saudi nationality.[205] Alternatively, article 14 may be interpreted to mean that formation of a company under Saudi law is the criterion determinative of its nationality and that any company so formed is required to establish its main office in the Kingdom. Any change in the nationality of a Saudi limited liability company must be effected by unanimity of the partners.[206]

I. CREDITORS' RIGHTS

1. Creditors of company

The liability of partners, whether natural or juristic persons, to creditors of the company is limited to their contributions to the company's capital.[207] However, there are certain exceptions to the limitation of liability. If the company has been formed by means of conversion from a general or limited partnership, the partners will remain liable for the debts of the prior partnership unless relieved of liability by creditors' consent.[208] In addition, the joint liability of the partners to third parties is unlimited with respect to misevaluations of any contributions in kind to capital.[209] It may be noted that creditors of the company are specifically given the right to recover from any individual partners the amount of any distributions of "fictitious" profits made by the company to such partner.[210] However, partners may not be held personally liable for the debts, other liabilities, or obligations of the company, in the absence of their personal guarantee or an agreement imposing individual liability upon them. A creditor may not prevail on a claim against a partner or the company based solely on the fact that the status, reputation, or financial position of such partner was a factor having caused him to deal with the company.

2. Creditors of partners

The personal creditors of a partner may not satisfy their claims out of the company's assets. However, there is an opinion that an exception to

[204] *See, e.g.,* M. AL-JABR, AL-QĀNŪN AL-TIJĀRĪ AL-SUʿŪDĪ 178 (1981); A. AL-KHŪLĪ, *supra* note 102, at 138.

[205] *See, e.g.,* M. BARĪRĪ, *supra* note 110, at 141 (company formed under foreign law would not be formed in manner consistent with Saudi law, hence could not have Saudi nationality despite location of its main office in the Kingdom).

[206] Companies Regs., art. 173.

[207] *See id.* art. 157. Creditors of the company may satisfy their claims to the extent of the company's assets. *But see* Ministry of Commerce, Powers & Duties of Liquidators, art. 19 (suggesting liability of partners if company's assets are insufficient to satisfy creditors' claims on liquidation) (translated in Appendix 29).

[208] Companies Regs., art. 212. Consent is presumed if no creditor has objected to the conversion within 30 days from the date of notification thereof by registered letter: *Id.*

[209] *Id.* art. 162.

[210] *Id.* art. 8.

this rule may exist if a partner has contributed certain property with the intent to evade creditors.[211] In contrast, creditors may satisfy their claims out of a partner's share in the company's profits. Article 6 of the Companies Regulations provides

> [t]he personal creditor of a partner may not seek satisfaction of his claim out of his debtor's share in the company's capital. However, he may seek satisfaction of his claim out of such debtor's share in the profits in accordance with the company's balance sheet.

A court may assign a partner's share in the profits to his personal creditors.[212] In this case, such creditors are not entitled to interfere with the management of the company, to exercise voting rights, or to demand the sale or other disposition of the company's property. Under article 6, on dissolution of the company, creditors' rights with respect to their debtor partners' profit shares transfer automatically to such debtors' shares in the liquidation surplus. However, in the case of insolvency or liquidation of the company, the creditors of the company will have priority over the personal creditors of any partner, whether or not such latter creditors have been assigned such partner's share in the profits.

J. OWNERSHIP OF SHARES

The capital of a limited liability company must be divided into shares. The shares must be of equal value and the same class and are not divisible.[213]

1. Joint ownership

Article 158 of the Companies Regulations provides

> [i]f several persons own a share, the company may suspend the exercise of the rights attached thereto until the owners of the share select one of their number to be considered the sole owner thereof vis-à-vis the company. The company may set a time limit for the performance of such selection and, if not [performed], it shall be entitled after the expiration of the appointed time to sell the share for the account of its owners. In this case, the share shall be offered to the partners and then to third parties.

As is apparent from the provisions of article 158, joint ownership of a share is permissible, provided that the joint owners appoint one of their

---

[211] *See, e.g.*, M. Abū al-ʿAinain, *supra* note 110, at 263.
[212] A partner may also voluntarily assign its right to receive profit distributions to creditors.
[213] Companies Regs., art. 158, *as amended by* Royal Decree No. M/23 (1982).

number to be the "owner" of such share vis-à-vis the company. One of the principal purposes of requiring such an appointment is to assure the smooth administrative functioning of the company. If there is a period during which the rights attached to any jointly owned shares are not suspended, any joint owners not already partners in the company may be considered *de facto* partners with respect to such shares. This position may be remedied by taking immediate steps to suspend the exercise of the rights attached to such shares. However, the joint owners will not be divested of any rights attached to the shares, most notably the right to receive profit distributions, whether arising prior to or during the period of suspension. Such rights may only be suspended until such time as the joint owners select a "sole owner" to act as their representative vis-à-vis the company. The joint owners remain liable for the obligations attached to the jointly owned shares to the extent of their respective interests therein, unless they agree otherwise.

2. Share register

A limited liability company is required to keep a register in which the names of the partners and data relating to their equity participations are recorded. Article 166 of the Regulations provides

> [t]he company shall maintain a register designating the names of the partners and the number of shares each of them owns and the transactions affecting such shares. A transfer of ownership shall be valid vis-à-vis the company or third parties only upon entry of the cause of the transfer of ownership in the said register.

Article 166 is supplemented by Minister of Commerce Resolution No. 1214,[214] which provides

> *Article 1.* The statements in the register of the partners in limited liability companies provided for in article 166 of the said Companies Regulations shall include the following
> 1. The name, profession, nationality, address, and number and date of the identity card or passport of the partner.
> 2. The number and value of the shares owned by the partners in the company's capital.
> 3. The number of shares and the value thereof which are transferred, together with a statement of the kind of transfer (sale or purchase or inheritance or gift and the like).
> 4. The names of the transferor and the transferee and the signatures of both.

---

[214] Resolution No. 1214 (29/1/1400).

5. The date of the transfer of the shares.

6. The total shareholdings of the partners after making the transfer and the value thereof.

Article 2. The pages of the abovementioned register of partners shall be serially numbered. No page shall be torn off and no statement therein shall be removed or changed.

Before completing the commercial registration procedures, the director or representative of the company is required to sign a standard form undertaking to carry out the measures provided in Resolution No. 1214.[215]

No transfer of title, assignment, or any other transaction relating to the company's capital shares is effective until the date of entry in the share register. However if such an assignment or disposition is required to be notarized and published under article 164, it will not be effective vis-à-vis third parties until the publication formalities are completed.[216] Furthermore, any transaction requiring the approval of the Ministry of Industry and Electricity and/or the Ministry of Commerce cannot be executed until the relevant approvals are obtained. The register may be introduced in evidence to prove ownership of shares in case of dispute.

K. ASSIGNMENT OF SHARES

1. Mixed participation company

If a company has been formed pursuant to a Foreign Capital Investment License, Ministry of Industry and Electricity approval of any assignments, including transfers of shares between existing partners, must be obtained.[217] A standard License contains a clause barring the participants from selling or assigning the company or the License in whole or in part without prior consent of the Ministry.[218] If the proposed transferee of the shares is not Saudi, it will be required to demonstrate its qualifications to the FCIC and comply with the licensing procedures generally applicable to foreign investors. However, in contrast to transactions involving the sale or

---

[215] Minister of Commerce Circular No. 222/981/4078 (24/6/1400), *cited* in YAḤYĀ, at 394.

[216] Companies Regs., arts. 10–11.

[217] In addition, there may be restrictions on transfer of shares imposed by other authorities. *See, e.g.*, Minister of Communications Resolution No. 54, para. 2(5) (Jan. 8, 1983) (prohibiting Saudis holding shares in a marine vessel to dispose of same in favor of nonSaudis).

[218] *See* Standard Licenses (translated in Appendix 19). Furthermore, if an industrial company has obtained a SIDF loan, it will be obligated to obtain SIDF prior written consent to changes in its participants by the terms of the SIDF standard loan agreement (translated in Appendix 23).

assignment of shares in the company, certain rights attached to such shares may be assigned for a specific period, subject to the terms of the company's articles of association and/or any other agreements among the partners. The partners' right to make such assignments need not be stated in the company's articles of association or bylaws and is not subject to publication formalities.

2. Rights of first refusal

Even though shares in a limited liability company are transferable to third parties, all assignments of shares to third parties are subject to article 165, which guarantees to the participants rights of first refusal with respect to shares offered to third parties for value or to be assigned gratuitously. Article 165 provides

> [a] partner may assign its share to another partner or to a third party in accordance with the provisions of the company's articles of association. Nonetheless, if a partner wishes to assign its share to a third party for consideration, it shall notify the remaining partners through the director(s) of the company of the terms of the assignment. In this case, every partner may demand the recovery of the share at its actual price. If thirty days from the date of notification have elapsed without any of the partners having exercised its right of recovery, the owner of the share shall have the right to dispose of it, with due regard to the provisions of the second paragraph of article 157.
>
> If more than one partner exercises its right of recovery and the assignment involves a number of shares, such shares shall be divided among the [partners] having demanded recovery in proportion to the share of each of them in the capital.
>
> If the assignment relates to a single share, such share shall be awarded to the partners who have demanded recovery with due regard to the provisions of the second paragraph of article 158.
>
> If the assignment of the share is to be made without consideration, the partner demanding recovery shall pay its value according to the last [appraisal] made by the company. The right of recovery provided in this article shall not apply to the transfer of ownership of shares by inheritance or bequest.

The partners rights of first refusal apply in principle to all transfers of ownership of shares, except for transfers by inheritance or bequest. If the transfer by assignment, inheritance, including sales under article 158, or bequest, results in joint ownership of shares, the new owners will be required to select one of their number as "sole owner" in compliance with article 158.

The partners may, within the parameters of article 165, supplement or refine its provisions by means of an appropriate clause in the company's articles of association. Notably, they may narrow the scope of applicability of such rights of first refusal by expressly providing that such rights will not apply to assignments to certain specified related parties such as wholly-owned subsidiaries or entities controlled by, controlling, or under common control with any partner and the like. One actual clause, for example, provides in part that "every partner shall have the right to transfer its shares to a wholly-owned or affiliated company after it has signed an undertaking that the transferee will perform all its duties as partner in a satisfactory manner."[219] Another clause provides

> [w]ithin the limits of the terms provided in these articles, shares may be transferred from a partner to another or from a partner to an "affiliate" provided that the company shall be notified of such a transfer in order to register it in the share register maintained for that purpose. The term "affiliate" of a partner used in this article means any company or association or other juristic person controlling or controlled by or under the common control with such partner. The ownership of all of the shares of any company or association or other juristic person shall be considered control within the meaning of this article . . . Notwithstanding the [preceding], the partners may not agree to any sale of shares which would result in more than 75% of the company's shares becoming owned by nonSaudi persons or organizations of any kind during any period in which the company is enjoying a tax exemption granted by the Government of the Kingdom of Saudi Arabia.[220]

Another such clause provides that first refusal rights will not apply to transfers to companies in which any of the partners holds at least a fifty-one percent interest.[221]

Alternatively, the partners may impose in the articles of association greater restrictions on transferability of shares than those provided in article 165, whether with respect to copartners or to third parties. One such clause, for example, provides that the partners may only sell their shares in whole or in part "in the case of necessity or due to the existence of legal excuse."[222]

In the case of an assignment for value, if the other partners do exercise their first refusal rights, they are entitled to purchase the shares at their "actual price." The actual price may be the price offered by a third party

---

[219] Umm al-Qurā, 19/5/1403, at 13, col. 2.
[220] Id., Feb. 11, 1983, at 12, col. 2.
[221] Id., Dec. 20, 1983, at 2, col. 2.
[222] Id., Aug. 26, 1983, at 8, col. 2.

purchaser or may be established where appropriate by means of an auditor's appraisal. The normal practice is to provide in the articles of association and bylaws that the actual value of shares will be determined by auditors at the close of every financial year and that such value will remain effective until revaluation at the close of the following financial year. Such auditor's report or evaluation should be confirmed at the annual general meeting of the partners. One actual clause covers the issue by providing that "the actual value of the shares means the value agreed between the assignor partner and the assignee partner. In the case of failure to agree, the value shall be that determined by the auditor of the company's accounts in the last balance sheet according to accounting principles."[223]

Another more complex treatment of appraisal provides

> [i]f the partners disagree on the actual value of the shares offered for sale, the determination of the value shall be made by means of the company's certified accountant in addition to two certified accountants chosen by the partners.
>
> The examiners' assessment of the value after examination of the company's accounts and documents of record and the last balance sheet confirmed by the partners, provided that not more than three months shall have elapsed from that balance sheet as of the date of appraisal, shall be binding on the partners. Otherwise, a provisional balance sheet shall be prepared for that purpose. If it occurs for any reason that the assessment by the examiners is unjust or impossible to perform, the partners shall have recourse to arbitration . . . [224]

3. Admission of new partners

In case the partners do not exercise their first refusal rights, the assignor partner's right to transfer its shares to third parties remains subject to the provisions of article 157, limiting the number of partners to fifty. Assuming that that limit is not exceeded, the transferee of such shares may be admitted as a partner of the company. Such admission is consequently to be effected in accordance with the provisions of the company's articles of association and bylaws. The articles of association may condition the admission of new partners on the approval of the existing partners, whether by unanimity or a specified majority. Such admission may also be conditioned on the proposed new partners' agreement to become parties to the partners' agreement, if any, or to any other agreements previously entered into among the partners and/or to assume the obligations of the withdrawing partner(s). The admission of any such new partners will

---

[223] *Id.*, 2/3/1404, at 17, col. 2.
[224] *Id.*, Dec. 20, 1983, at 2, col. 2.

require amending the company's articles of association to include the name and shareholdings of the new partner(s). In addition, amendment may be required to incorporate any new understandings of the parties. Such amendment will be effective with respect to the partners as of the date of notarization of the amendment and will be effective with respect to third parties upon publication.

L. PLEDGE OF SHARES

No provision of the Companies Regulations is specifically applicable to the pledge of shares of a limited liability company.[225] The pledge to a lender or other creditor[226] is recognized under Islamic law and permitted by the Qurān, sunnah, and consensus.[227] A pledge is defined generally as property made a security for a debt, so that the debt may be satisfied from such property, in whole or in part, if the debtor is unable to repay it.[228] Property which may be sold may be pledged.[229] According to the Ḥanbalī school, the debt must be in existence as of the time the pledge is made.[230] Saudi regulations expressly give priority to a pledgee of real or personal property over other creditors both in the context of bankruptcy of the debtor[231] and attachment of property pledged to another creditor of the debtor.[232] However, with the exception of certain items such as ships[233] and trademarks,[234] no regulatory registration procedure is provided for pledges

---

[225] *Cf.*, *id.*, 5/8/1403, at 3, col. 1 (clause empowering directors, subject to approval of partners' general meeting, to pledge shares) (approved by Ministry of Commerce).

[226] If the lender is a bank subject to the Banks Control Regulations, it is permitted to acquire a direct interest in a company within two years or such longer period as agreed with the Saudi Arabian Monetary Agency: Banks Control Regs., art. 10(2).

[227] *See*, *e.g.*, 4 M. IBN QUDĀMĀ & SH. IBN QUDĀMĀ, AL-MUGHNĪ WA AL-SHARH AL-KABĪR ʿALĀ MATN AL-MUQNIʿ 366 (Beirut 1983).

[228] *See*, *e.g.*, *id.*; 3 M. AL-BAHŪTĪ, KASHSHĀF AL-QINĀʿ ʿAN MATN AL-IQNĀʿ 320–21 (Riyadh).

[229] *See*, *e.g.*, 4 IBN QUDĀMĀ, *supra* note 227, at 368, 387.

[230] *See*, *e.g.*, *id.* at 368 (rejecting validity of pledge securing future indebtedness) (comparing pledge to testimony). *See also* 2 M. AL-ḤAHŪTĪ, SHARḤ MUNTAHĀ AL-IRĀDAT 230–31 (Dār al-Fikr) (conditions of pledge include its execution; its contemporaneity with the debt; the pledgor's legal capacity to sell or donate; the pledgor's ownership of the pledged property (though acknowledging pledgeability of borrowed or rented property with the owner's consent); that its kind and description be known; that the debt be obligatory). Third parties may also pledge their property to secure the debt of another.

[231] *See* Commercial Court Regs., art. 121.

[232] *See id.* art. 581.

[233] *See* Vessels Pledge Regs., *approved by* High Office Letter No. 9/3/8469 (1/9/1374); *cf.* Commercial Court Regs., arts. 249 (relating to pledges in the context of charter parties), 300, 304, 307 (relating to pledges in context of marine borrowing agreements). Registration of pledges may also be made with respect to aircraft.

[234] *See* Trademarks Regs., Royal Decree No. M/5, art. 36 (1984); Trademarks Regs. Implementing Rules, Minister of Commerce Resolution No. 94, art. 25 (May 6, 1984) (pledges of trademarks to be registered with Trademarks Office in Ministry of Commerce and published in Umm al-Qurā).

other than registration with a notary public.

In the absence of specific applicable regulatory provisions, the validity and enforceability of pledges are governed by general legal rules. One of the most important of these rules is that, according to the Ḥanbalī school, a pledge is effective on possession,[235] provided that such possession was effected with the pledgor's consent.[236] Possession may be taken by the pledgee, his authorized representative, or in some cases a trustee. However, the pledgee's representative may not be the pledgor himself.[237] Continuous possession is also required.[238] Until such time as due possession of the pledged property is taken, the pledgor may dispose of it by sale or gift or pledge it to another creditor, even if the pledgor had already consented to the pledgee's taking of possession. Any disposition which would render a sale of such property invalid will also invalidate the pledge.[239] The traditional possession of personal property is actual physical possession.[240] Possession of real property is traditionally effected by the pledgor's allowing the pledgee unobstructed access to and enjoyment of such real property.[241] However, a pledge of real property is presently made by means of execution of a mortgage[242] registered with the relevant notary public, who will also make an annotation on the original title deed, thus giving notice to third parties.[243]

In the case of a pledge of stock of a corporation represented by share certificates, it is apparent that the requirement of actual possession may be satisfied. A problem arises, however, with respect to shares in a limited liability company. Various issues are involved with respect to the validity of

---

[235] See, e.g., 4 IBN QUDĀMA, supra note 227, at 368–69, 387; 3 M. AL-BAHŪTĪ, supra note 228, at 323, 330–31. But see Pres. of the Judiciary Circular No. 7595 (2/11/1380) (regarding the differing views on the requirement of possession) (cited in MINISTRY OF JUSTICE, REGULATIONS, RULES, CIRCULARS).

[236] See, e.g., 3 M. AL-BAHŪTĪ, supra note 228, at 331.

[237] See, e.g., id.

[238] See, e.g., 4 IBN QUDĀMA, supra note 227, at 387.

[239] See, e.g., 3 M. AL-BAHŪTĪ, supra note 228, at 331–32.

[240] See, e.g., 4 IBN QUDĀMA, supra note 227, at 371.

[241] See, e.g., id. at 372; 3 M. AL-BAHŪTĪ, supra note 228, at 331.

[242] The term "mortgage" is used in this context as being the English language term generally used with respect to security interests in real property. The same Arabic term "rahn" (pledge) applies to a security interest in either real or personal property.

[243] See generally Minister of Justice Circular No. 14/12/t (12/10/1396). It should be noted that mortgage registration may not be available to certain lenders. Notaries public have been instructed not to register mortgages of real property in favor of banks or institutional lenders assumed to be lending at interest. See Supreme Judicial Council Resolution No. 291 (Oct. 1401). Cf. Attributions of Sharī·ah Jurisprudence Responsibilities Regs., High Approval No. 109, art. 182 (24/1/1372) (prohibiting notaries from registering transactions contrary to sharī·ah). It will also be noted that, in the case of nonSaudis permitted to own real property directly or indirectly by virtue of the FCIR and relevant ministerial permissions, such ownership is limited to property necessary for their business activities. See generally pp. 76–78 supra.

a pledge of such shares. One group of lawyers takes the position that a pledge of shares in a limited liability company would be invalid *ab initio* as being equivalent to a pledge of a portion of the company's capital. Such a pledge would be invalid on the grounds that article 162 of the Companies Regulations requires the company's capital to be paid in full and the spirit of the Regulations would prohibit any charges or encumbrances on such capital. However it may be noted that a partner's shares give it no direct rights of disposition with respect to the company's capital and such partner's only claim to a share in such capital arises on liquidation of the company. Nonetheless, any conclusions on this point must be drawn in the light of article 6 of the Companies Regulations, which provides

> [t]he personal creditor of a partner may not seek satisfaction of his claim out of his debtor's share in the company's capital. However, he may seek satisfaction of his claim out of the said debtor's share in the profits in accordance with the company's balance sheet. If the company is dissolved, the creditor's right shall transfer to his debtor's share in the company's assets after payment of its debts.
>
> If a partner's [sic] share is represented by shares of stock, his personal creditor may, in addition to the rights referred to in the preceding paragraph, demand the sale of such shares in order to satisfy his claim out of the sale proceeds. However, the preceding provision shall not apply to shares of a cooperative company.

Article 6 does not refer to pledges given by a partner. However, the principle expressed therein that, with the exception of interests represented by shares of stock, a creditor may only satisfy its claim out of its debtor's share in the company's profits could be construed to apply in this context. In this case, a partner would only be able to assign its share in the company's profits. In the absence of an enforceable undertaking by the remaining partners not to retain profits in the company for liquidity purposes or the creation of additional reserves or to use them to increase the company's capital or for other reasons, the creditor may derive small benefit from such an assignment and may be forced to obtain a court order in order to receive its debtor's share in the profits. On liquidation of the company, such a creditor will come after the general creditors of the company and will rank with the other partners with respect to the liquidation surplus.

The second and more disputed issue relates to the feasibility of achieving a valid pledge of shares in a limited liability company, in view of the general requirement of possession of the shares by the pledgee. The shares of limited liability companies may not be represented by negotiable certificates.[244] In practice, certificates or documents evidencing ownership of shares are not issued by such companies. However, in principle, a company is not prohibited from issuing a nonnegotiable instrument evidencing a partner's ownership of its shares, in which case the pledgee would be able to achieve possession of the pledge in the same manner as possession of share certificates of a corporation.[245] This solution, which may satisfy the technical requirements for validity of the pledge, would nonetheless not serve the function of notice to purchasers or other creditors of the partner, since they would not be aware of the existence of such a nonnegotiable instrument and would not normally require its delivery as in the case of share certificates in a corporation, unless the issuance of such an instrument were provided in the company's articles of association. Similarly, it has been suggested that an annotation of the pledge could be made on the pledgor partner's counterpart of the company's articles of association, which could then be possessed by the pledgee. Notarization of the articles annotated to indicate the pledge, as well as of the pledge agreement, may significantly reinforce the validity of the pledge in the context of eventual judicial proceedings.[246] It may be noted, however, that a notary public, although competent to notarize and register such documents,[247] may in practice not do so. In this case, protection may be sought to be obtained by means of publication of the pledge in the official journal and/or local newspapers, similar to the practice of publication of cautionary notices with respect to patents employed in the absence of regulatory procedures. Finally, such solutions may be used in conjunction with an annotation in the company register. By analogy to the validity of constructive possession in the case of pledges of real property, ships, and trademarks, there is a view among Saudi lawyers that constructive possession would be sufficient to achieve a valid pledge of shares in a limited liability company. Even though no official public register exists for such purpose, advocates of this view maintain that an annotation of a pledge in the company's share register required by regulation[248] would adequately serve the function of notice to third parties and should be given

---

[244] Companies Regs., art. 158, *as amended by* Royal Decree No. M/23 (1982).

[245] However, there is a view that issuance even of a nonnegotiable instrument attesting to a partner's ownership of shares would subject the issuer to the penalties prescribed in art. 230 of the Regulations, subsection 2 of which applies to "any person who issues shares of stock or debentures or subscription receipts or provisional certificates or who offers them for circulation contrary to the provisions of these Regulations,"

[246] It may be noted that, even though a share pledge agreement may include an irrevocable power of attorney in favor of the pledgee authorizing it to sell the shares in event of default, Saudi law does not recognize irrevocable powers of attorney, which may be revoked at will and are revoked by the death or loss of capacity of the grantor.

[247] *See* Notaries Public Regs., arts. 8(e), 15 (relating to recording of pledges generally) (translated in Appendix 25).

[248] *See generally* pp. 110–11 *supra*.

the legal status of due registration of a pledge. However, even in this case, the importance of notarization of the pledge agreement should not be disregarded. Except in the case of voluntary compliance, enforcement of the pledge will be required to be made by court order, and the court may be reluctant to enforce such an unnotarized document, whether or not an annotation has been made in the share register.

In the event of enforcement of or voluntary compliance with the pledge, further issues arise. Even though it is generally believed that a pledge of shares to a creditor is not an "assignment" subject to the first refusal rights of other partners within the meaning of article 165 of the Companies Regulations,[249] the transfer of shares to a pledgee would be subject to such first refusal rights. Consequently, if the partners are contemplating pledging their shares, it is advisable to include in the articles of association, either originally or by amendment at the relevant time, a comprehensive provision defining the partners' rights to pledge their shares and specifying whether each or any such pledge will be subject to approval of the partners and, if so, stating the majority required for approval, and whether, in case of enforcement of the pledge, they will exercise or waive their first refusal rights[250] and, in the latter case, whether they agree to accept the pledgee as partner in the company. If the partners have not agreed in this manner to admit the pledgee as partner, they are entitled to refuse to do so. In this case, it has been suggested that the pledgee's only practical alternative may be to enter into an agreement with the pledgor for the purpose of utilizing the shares subject to the pledge. Under such an arrangement, which may be viewed as coming within the scope of article 6, the pledgor would retain its original status as "partner." The pledgee would have no direct rights with respect to the company and would not be entitled to participate in management or partners' meetings, even though it may be entitled to exercise certain rights indirectly through the pledgor/partner and may be entitled to profit distributions and to its proportionate share of the company's assets on liquidation.[251] Finally, it will be noted that if the company is of mixed participation, approval of the Ministry of Industry and Electricity will be required to be obtained with respect to any assignment of shares to the pledgee.[252] If such approval is withheld, as it would be likely to be if the pledgee is a foreign entity not possessing the necessary qualifications, direct or even indirect ownership of such shares by the

---

[249] See generally pp. 112–13 supra.

[250] If such agreement is deemed to "increase the partners' financial liabilities", any resolution to that effect must be made by unanimity. See Companies Regs., art. 173.

[251] The conditions of such an eventual arrangement, including the pledgor/partner's obligation to exercise its rights as a partner subject to the direction of the pledgee may be incorporated into the pledge agreement.

[252] See also note 217 supra.

pledgee could be construed as a violation of the terms of the License and expose the company to the risk of loss of its privileges or revocation of its License.[253] Consequently, even the utmost precautions with respect to the validity of the pledge may not prevent the transaction from finishing in an impasse. Therefore, it is recommended that a lender or other creditor of a partner, particularly in the case of a mixed participation company, seek to achieve a security interest in assets of such partner which may be taken into the possession, if not of the lender itself, of a third party trustee or authorized agent of the lender.

M. PROFIT- AND LOSS-SHARING

1. Requirement of sharing

Article 7 of the Companies Regulations, which is a general provision applying to relevant forms of companies, supplements the principle expressed in article 1 that the partners' mutual intent to share both the benefits and risks of doing business is an essential element of a company.[254] Article 7 provides

> [a]ll of the partners shall divide the profits and losses among themselves. If it is agreed to deprive any partner of profit or to exempt him from loss, such clause shall be null and void and the provisions of article 9 shall be applied in this case.
>
> However, it may be agreed to exempt a partner who only contributed his services from sharing in the loss, provided that a wage shall not have been allotted to him for his services.

The articles of association of a limited liability company are not in principle required to specify the shares of the partners in the profits and losses or the method of computation of such shares. Article 161(7) of the Regulations requires only that the method of profit distribution be specified. However, if the articles fail to "specify" the partners' shares in either the profits or the losses, as in the case where the articles deprive any partner of profits, such shares will be deemed to be proportional to the partners' shares in the capital, which are required to be specified in the articles of association. Article 9 provides

> [i]f the company's articles of association fail to specify a partner's share in the profits or the losses, such share shall be in proportion to his share in the capital.

[253] *See generally* pp. 68–70 *supra.*
[254] *See generally* pp. 82–84 *supra. Cf.* 2 SH. IBN QAYYIM AL-JAWZIYYAH, A‘LĀM AL-MUWAQQ‘ĪN ‘AN RABB AL-‘ĀLAMĪN 6 (Beirut) (partnership is based on justice between the partners) (to exclude a partner from receiving profits would be inequitable).

If the articles of association only specify a partner's share in the profit, his share in the loss shall be equal to his share in the profit. This shall also be the case if the articles of association specify only the share of the partner in the loss.[255]

It will be noted that the rule of article 9 applies only if either the shares in the profits or the losses are not specified or are invalid under article 7.

2. Disparity between capital shares and profit shares[256]

Article 171 of the Regulations provides that capital "shares confer equal rights in the net profits and equity upon liquidation unless the company's articles of association provide otherwise." It is apparent from the provisions of both article 171 and article 9 that partners' shares in the profits are not required by regulation to correspond to their shares in the capital. Although article 9 provides that, unless profit shares are "specified" in the articles of association, such shares will be proportional to the partners' respective capital shares, the articles of association need only state that the profit shares shall not or may not be proportional to the capital shares as determined by the partners in order to permit disparity between capital and profit shares. The actual numerical disparity is not required to be stated. There is no regulatory limit on the extent of permissible disparity between capital and profit shares. In practice, however, it may be noted that, in the case of a mixed participation company, the authorities do not look favorably upon an excessive disproportion of profits in favor of a nonSaudi partner in a limited liability company and, should the Saudi participants' profit entitlements fall below twenty-five percent of the total, the company may be subject to loss of its privileges or the License.

In view of the preceding discussion, the following clause may, in theory,[257] be included in the articles of association of a limited liability company

> The amount of the profits to be distributed among the partners at the end of each financial year may or may not correspond to the amount of their respective capital shares. The actual amounts of profits to which each partner shall be entitled shall be agreed upon by the partners once and for all or from time to time depending upon the business situation of the company and market considerations. Each

---

[255] Companies Regs., art. 9, *as amended by* Royal Decree No. M/23 (1982).

[256] It may be noted that the word "hissah" applies to shares in the capital, as contrasted with the word "nasib", which is used with respect to shares in profits and losses.

[257] In practice, the Ministry of Commerce may or may not approve such a clause. For "profits and losses" clause as proposed by the Ministry, *see* Ministry of Commerce Model Articles of Association (translated in Appendix 28).

and any of such agreement(s) shall be confirmed at the subsequent general meeting of the partners.

In theory, the following clause may also be included in the articles of association

> The net profits after setting aside the regulatory reserve shall be shared in proportion to and commensurate with the contribution of each partner to the capital of the company as well as the services and knowhow to be provided by each partner with respect to each project/contract undertaken by the company upon such specific terms and conditions of profit-sharing as shall be agreed to in writing by the partners prior to the execution of any project/contract by the company.
> On completion of each project/contract and after the fulfilment of all of the obligations of the company relating to such project/contract, the distribution of the net profits relating to such project/contract shall be in accordance with the specific profit-sharing agreement for such project/contract. The contribution to be borne by each partner with respect to the regulatory reserve shall be in accordance with the ratios of actual profit-sharing *or* (as agreed) according to the partner's respective interests in the capital. The net liquidation surplus upon the dissolution of the company shall be divided among the partners in proportion to their respective interests in the capital of the company.

For income tax purposes, under the preceding arrangement, the company may still be audited on the basis of its financial year as provided in its articles of association and bylaws.

It is also possible, in principle, to provide for alternative methods of profit allocations. The concept of guaranteeing a partner a fixed amount of profits is not permitted by Islamic law as being inconsistent with the principle of risk-sharing. However, the partners, by agreement, may structure the profit distributions for example, so that a certain partner will be entitled to receive an amount equal to X percent of all gross income during the first Y years of the company's duration on account of its share of the anticipated profits. However, since it is important in the case of a mixed participation company that the Saudi equity participation and profit-sharing should not be less than twenty-five percent, so that the nonSaudi partner(s) may continue to qualify for the tax holiday under the FCIR, any such structuring of profit allocations must take this consideration into account. Therefore, if the alternative profit allocation is made with respect to a Saudi partner, it should be provided that such partner's share of profits will be X percent of the gross income or twenty-five percent of the net profit whichever is *greater*. In such case, it should further be provided that in the event of any loss such partner will restitute to the company an amount equivalent to its respective share in such loss. In all cases, the validity of such an arrangement will be conditional on the genuineness of the reasons for the arrangement and its not being found to be a sham transaction in the light of the underlying factual circumstances.

3. Regulatory reserve

Article 176 of the Regulations provides that "[e]very company shall set aside every year at least ten percent of its net profits to form a reserve fund. The partners may resolve to discontinue such setting aside when the reserve amounts to one-half of the capital." Not more than ten percent of the company's net profits is required to be set aside as a reserve by regulation.[258] However, the partners' or directors' right to create additional reserves is generally, and should be, provided in the company's articles of association.[259] The partners' right to call an extraordinary partners' meeting in order to create additional reserves may also be provided in the articles of association.

The purpose of the regulatory reserve is to assure the company's financial stability and to protect its creditors. Failure to set aside the percentage required by article 176 may be prosecuted by the Ministry of Commerce.[260] However, reserve funds, in the same manner as the company's capital, may be used to carry on the day-to-day business of the company, provided they are accounted for in the company's books and annual balance sheet. Reserve funds may also be used to generate income by various means as permitted by applicable law. If funds are used to acquire capital assets, any appreciation in the value of such assets may be distributed among the partners. Conversely, any deficit arising from depreciation in value of such assets must be restituted to the reserve. Finally, reserve funds may be used to increase the company's capital. There is a difference of opinion as to whether such funds may only be incorporated into capital when they attain the regulatory level of fifty percent of the capital or whether they may be so incorporated at an earlier stage.[261] The result is indifferent with respect

---

[258] In the case of limited liability companies formed by SABIC or in which it participates, the required reserve may be reduced to 4% of net profits and may be discontinued when it amounts to one-fifth of the company's paid-in capital, as an exception to the rule of art. 176: Minister of Indus. & Elec. & Minister of Commerce Resolution No. 1184 (29/12/1397), *cited* in YAḤYĀ, at 397.

[259] Such right is also provided in the Ministry of Commerce Model Articles of Association. *See* Appendix 28.

[260] *Cf.* Minister of Commerce Circular No. 222/9136/269 (16/7/1401) (instructing companies' auditors to include in their reports all of companies' violations of Companies Regs. and in particular violations relating to setting aside of reserve), *cited in* YAḤYĀ, at 397.

[261] It should be noted that the Ministry of Commerce currently discourages the use of reserves to increase capital, even if they have attained the 50% level required by regulation, and may object to a clause in a company's proposed articles of association which would permit capital to be increased by way of incorporation of reserves.

to the purpose of protection of the company's creditors. However, by converting reserve funds to capital at any stage, contributions to the reserve fund will be required to be made *ab initio*, until reserves amount to fifty percent of the capital as augmented. Contributions to the reserve fund are subject to companies tax on the shares of any nonSaudi partners not enjoying a tax holiday and to zakāt on the shares of Saudi partners in the financial year that such profits arose. Losses may not be carried forward to reduce contributions to the regulatory reserve.

4. Distributions

The method of distribution of profits, as distinguished from the method of profit computation and the ratios of profit allocations, must be stated in the company's articles of association.[262] It may be provided, for example, that profits will be distributed at the time and place determined by the partners or that the time and manner of distribution will be determined by partners' resolution at the partners' annual general meeting. Alternatively, the articles of association may give the directors of the company the power to determine the time and manner of profit distribution. Distributions may be made solely out of net profits after deduction of the regulatory reserve and any other reserves the company may have duly created. Article 8 of the Regulations provides

> [w]ithout prejudice to the provisions of articles 106 and 205, dividends may be distributed to the partners only out of net profits. If fictitious profits are distributed to the partners, the creditors of the company may demand from each partner even if in good faith the restitution of such of those profits as he received. A partner shall not be liable for the restitution of the actual profits he has received, even if the company sustains losses in subsequent years.[263]

Directors of the company are subject to imprisonment for a term of three months to one year or a fine of five thousand to twenty thousand riyals or both for receiving or distributing "fictitious" profits.[264]

Net profits for purposes of the Regulations are the net profits derived from the totality of the operations of the company, as distinct from the operations of its partners, whether inside or outside Saudi Arabia, during the relevant financial year. The net profits, with respect to the year in which they arose and whether or not actually distributed, are subject to Saudi tax on the shares of nonSaudi partners not enjoying a tax holiday.

---

[262] Companies Regs., art. 161(7).
[263] In addition, it will be noted that lenders such as SIDF may place restrictions on distributions of profits. *See, e.g.,* standard SIDF Loan Agreement (reprinted in Appendix 23).
[264] Companies Regs., art. 229(5).

Saudi partners are liable for zakāt with respect to their profit shares.[265] Losses may neither be carried forward nor back for purposes of reducing tax liability. However, the company's articles of association may permit the partners or the directors to determine the amounts of actual distributions to be made or to set aside a certain portion of profits annually to be used to increase the company's capital or for other purposes.

If the profits are not actually distributed and remain in the company, the partners, in theory, have the status of creditors of the company with respect to their shares of such undistributed profits, which may be deemed loans made by the partners to the company. However, other creditors of the company will have priority generally over such partners in contexts such as liquidation. Therefore, partners may prefer to receive actual distributions. Actual distributions to partners are not subject to a further tax on distribution.

N. AGREEMENTS BETWEEN PARTNERS AND COMPANY

Agreements for the provision of specialized services may be entered into between one or more partners and the limited liability company. Whether or not such agreements must be authorized by resolution of the partners or directors will depend on the provisions of the company's articles of association and/or any other agreements among the partners. The fees payable with respect to such services may be computed on a flat fee basis or structured as a percentage of gross income or net profits. However, if such fees are payable to a nonSaudi partner, the total amount to which nonSaudi partners are entitled, including both profit-entitlements with respect to their equity participations and fee payments, should not exceed seventy-five percent of the company's net profits if the tax holidays of any such partners are to be maintained.

1. Technical services agreement

The limited liability company may enter into a technical services agreement with any of its partners. If such partner is nonSaudi, such an agreement is permissible even if not specifically authorized in its License, since such nonSaudi partner is a "related party" with respect to the company and is providing such services solely to the company and not to third parties, provided that such services are necessary and directly related to the company's objectives. The policy of the FCIC is to grant licenses only to foreign investors possessing experience and expertise in the applied-for area of activity and to encourage the transfer of such expertise or

---

[265] For tax rates, see p. 76 *supra*.

knowhow to Saudi companies. This policy does not preclude transfers by means of technical services agreements. Such agreements are not required to be approved by or registered with any governmental authority. However, under such an arrangement, the fee paid to the nonSaudi partner or its parent, subsidiaries, or affiliates with respect to services performed inside or outside the Kingdom will be subject to Saudi tax even if the nonSaudi partner is entitled to a tax holiday with respect to its share of the company's profits relating to its equity participation. For example, if either the nonSaudi partner or one of its related companies prepares certain designs or feasibility studies outside Saudi Arabia, the fee paid in consideration thereof will be taxable, even though such fees if paid to an unrelated third party not present in the Kingdom would not be subject to Saudi tax. Such fee payments are expenses generally deductible by the company.[266]

2. Management agreement

A nonSaudi partner may enter into an agreement to provide certain specific and specialized management services to the limited liability company in consideration of a fee. However, unlimited or extremely extensive management rights should not be given to such a partner on the basis of two policy considerations. First, the policy of Saudi authorities is that Saudi participants should assume an active role in the management of the day-to-day activities of the company in order to acquire experience and knowledge of the management, as well as the technical, aspects of the business. Second, if unlimited or overly broad management services are required from or rights given to a nonSaudi partner, the parties will expose themselves to the risk that their relationship may be deemed a sham arrangement by means of which the Saudi partner is merely acting as a front for the nonSaudi partner in return for a share in the profits. Such situations are actively sought to be discouraged.[267] Furthermore, an

---

[266] In order to avoid both any disallowances by the tax department of the local company's treatment of fee payments as deductible expenses and any tax liability of the partner rendering services with respect to such payments, it is advisable to indicate in the agreement that payments are made with respect to wages and other direct costs of technical staff and to furnish a detailed breakdown of hours worked and cost per hour. It is also advised that the foreign partner obtain a certificate from the auditors of any related entity outside the Kingdom providing the relevant services certifying that the fee paid to such entity does not include any element of profit or relate to overhead or other indirect expense items and represents the actual and fair market value of the services provided. In the absence of such a certificate, the risk of Saudi tax liability and disallowance of deductions, as mentioned above, will be substantially increased. *See also* Director-Gen'l of Dep't of Zakāt & Income Tax Circular No. 3 (Dec. 12, 1969) (relating to nondeductibility of indirect, including overhead, expenses) (translated in Appendix 30).

[267] *Cf.* Minister of Justice Circular No. 156/12/t (16/11/1399) (prohibiting Saudis from granting general powers of attorney to foreigners to prevent abuse by foreigners).

agreement granting extensive management powers to a nonSaudi partner may also conflict with the management provisions of the company's articles of association, in which case the latter will prevail. However, since such a management agreement is not required to be approved by or submitted to any governmental authority, the potential illegality of any such agreement may only come to light in the event of a dispute between the partners where one of the disputants initiates judicial or arbitral proceedings or seeks administrative redress. In such a case, if the agreement is found to conflict with public policy, it will be unenforceable and the party having sustained damage may be left without remedy.

Any management fees paid by the company to a nonSaudi partner or any of its related entities are subject to Saudi tax, even if such partner is entitled to a tax holiday with respect to its share of the company's profits. This is the rule whether such services are performed inside or outside Saudi Arabia and whether performed by the partner itself or its parent, subsidiaries, or affiliates, as contrasted with an unrelated party, which, if not present in the Kingdom, would not be subject to Saudi tax with respect thereto. For example, if one of such companies prepares personnel policies, production control plans, procurement policies, and the like, or performs any other services for the limited liability company, including any services which could not feasibly be performed in Saudi Arabia, the fee paid with respect thereto is taxable. The general rule that profits earned by entities having no presence in the Kingdom are not subject to Saudi tax does not apply in the case of management services provided by the parent or any subsidiaries or affiliates of a nonSaudi partner in a Saudi company. However, if such services are performed outside the Kingdom by third parties unrelated to the foreign partner and having no presence in Saudi Arabia, any fees paid in this regard will not be subject to Saudi tax. Management fees are expenses deductible by the limited liability company with regard to tax computation.[268]

3. Disproportionate profit share distinguished

As discussed above, any percentage of the company's profits paid to a nonSaudi partner as a fee for specialized services will be subject to Saudi tax, even though such partner's share of the profits of the company *qua* partner may simultaneously be tax-exempt by reason of a tax holiday. This result obtains not only because such services are provided pursuant to a separate agreement but also because "services" are not included within the definition of "foreign capital", as provided in the FCIR and their implementing rules, which may qualify for the regulatory tax holiday.

---

[268] *See generally* note 266 *supra.*

Consequently, even if payments for such services are not structured as a fee, regardless of the method of calculation, but rather as a percentage of the profits allocated, in the articles of association or otherwise, to the nonSaudi partner solely with respect to the provision of specified services, such payments are not tax-exempt. In contrast, the Companies Regulations permit a disproportion between partners' shares in the company's capital and their shares in its profits.[269] Such a disproportion may be justified on the grounds of additional obligations imposed upon or services required of a partner within the global framework of the various partners' rights and duties pursuant to the company's aritcles of association. In such a case, where no specific portion of the company's profits is apportioned to a nonSaudi partner with respect to specified services, such partner's entire share of profits, even though proportionately greater than its percentage of equity holding, will be exempt from tax during the period of its tax holiday, provided that at least twenty-five percent of the company's profits are allocated to Saudi participants and that no abuse of the principle of disproportion is made.

O. DIRECTORS

1. Appointment

Article 167 of the Companies Regulations provides

> [o]ne or more directors, who may or may not be partners, shall administer the company. The partners shall appoint the directors in the articles of association or in a separate document for a specified or unspecified period with or without remuneration.
>
> The articles of association may provide for the formation of a board of directors if there are several directors. In this case, the articles of association shall specify the manner of functioning of such board and the majority required for its resolutions. The company shall be bound by the acts of the directors which come within the scope of their powers as published in accordance with the provisions of article 164.[270]

---

[269] *See generally* pp. 121–23 *supra*.

[270] If the number of partners in the company exceeds 20, the articles of association must also provide for appointment of a board of controllers composed of a minimum of three partners. If the original number of partners was 20 or less and the admission of new partners causes the total number to exceed 20, a board of controllers must be appointed and the pertinent amendment made to the articles of association: Companies Regs., art. 170.

Directors must be natural persons. They may be partners,[271] employees of partners, or related or unrelated third parties.[272] In the case of a company duly formed between a father and his minor children, such father may also be the sole director of the company. Members of liberal professions may also act as directors of a limited liability company.[273] However, their role as directors should not extend beyond drawing policy guidelines for the company's affairs and should not involve any actual conducting of business matters. In contrast, public officials are prohibited from serving on companies' boards of directors except as government appointees.[274] Directors may be named in the articles of association. In this case, the articles of association will be required to be amended should the directors be changed.

If a board of directors is to be constituted, the manner of issuing its resolutions must be stated in the articles of association.[275] If the directors are not named in the articles of association, the partners may designate their representatives on the board by separate act. Approval or ratification of such designees by the other partners is not required, unless the articles of association so provide. In this case, the articles may also specify the manner of approval or ratification of the directors and any required majority in this regard. Partners are generally represented by a number of board members proportionate to their respective equity holdings. The articles of association may provide that partners will be represented in proportion to their shares and that, should ownership of shares change, board representation will change accordingly. Partners should reserve the

---

[271] However, a Saudi woman may not participate in the administration of companies, but must appoint a Saudi man as her representative. Minister of Commerce Circulars No. 3/3/2110 (6/6/1399), No. 3/3/737 (17/6/1398), No. 3/9/sh/1091/10/380 (18/7/1397), and No. 3/9Sᶜ/1673 (19/10/1396), *cited in* YAHYĀ, at 393.

[272] If a nonSaudi director is also to act as general manager of the company, he must be registered with the Ministry of Commerce. In this case, he should be on the sponsorship of the company and in possession of valid residence and work permits. *See* Instructions Relating to the Amendment of the Particulars of Companies and Sole Proprietorships, para. 4(1) (implementing Minister of Commerce Resolution No. 151 (17/8/1403) (translated in Appendix 22)). If a mixed participation company licensed under the FCIR desires to register a nonSaudi manager, whether or not such manager is also a director, it is sufficient at the time of the company's commercial registration for the authorized representative(s) of the company to submit an undertaking by the company to complete the required procedures relating to sponsorship and residence and work permits for such person within two months from registration. In the case where the company's undertaking is not fulfilled, the name of such person will be stricken from the company's commercial registration. *See* Minister of Commerce Circular No. 3/9/sh/136/9/6378 (24/5/1398), *cited in* YAHYĀ, at 393.

[273] Restrictions are imposed with respect to certain professions or persons. *See, e.g.*, Certified Accountants Regs., art. 22 (prohibiting certified accountants from acting as directors).

[274] Civil Servants Regs., Royal Decree No. M/49, art. 13 (1397).

[275] Minister of Commerce & Indus. Resolution No. 694, art. 1(4) (22/6/1385). *See* pp. 88–89 *supra*.

right to substitute at any time another designee for any board members named by them. However, regardless of the actual number of directors representing the respective partners, the combined voting power of the director(s) representing any partner will generally be proportionate to such partner's equity holding.

Directors should be appointed before notarization of the articles of association since the directors are made jointly liable for damages sustained by the company, the partners, or third parties resulting from failure to notarize the articles of association.[276] Furthermore, amended article 164 places the responsibility for carrying out the publication and commercial registration formalities upon the directors,[277] who are also jointly liable for damages sustained by the company, the partners, or third parties resulting from nonpublication of the articles of association.[278]

2. Powers

Under article 167, the company will be bound by acts of its directors within the scope of their powers as published. The Companies Regulations do not require that the powers of the directors be defined in the company's articles of association. However, Minister of Commerce and Industry Resolution No. 694 contains this requirement.[279] The clause defining their powers may be brief and general or set forth a detailed list of the acts within the scope of their powers. Such powers may be limited or extremely broad, whether or not specific acts are set forth. In all cases, directors must be given the power to represent the company in its relations with third parties and to appoint representatives with respect to legal proceedings relating to the company.[280] Directors may be given the "broadest powers" to direct the affairs of the company and establish its policies, to execute all contracts, and to buy and sell property. If the partners so desire, certain acts of the directors may be made subject to partners' prior approval, such as the opening of branches, the pledging of the company's property, making investment decisions, incurring indebtedness, or the creation of extraordinary reserves. The board of directors is typically given the power to appoint and determine the remuneration of the company's general manager.[281] Alternatively, one or more partners may be given the right to

---

[276] Companies Regs., art. 10. See p. 103 supra.

[277] See p. 105 supra.

[278] Companies Regs., art. 11. See p. 104–05 supra.

[279] Resolution No. 694, art. 1(4) (22/6/1385). See p. 88 supra.

[280] See p. 89 & note 127 supra.

[281] The general "manager" must be distinguished from the "director", even though the Arabic word "mudīr" is used for both. The manager is an employee of the company, generally appointed by and dismissed by the directors. A partner or a member of the board of directors may also be appointed as a general manager.

appoint the general manager or merely to nominate such manager to be confirmed by the board of directors. In actual articles of association approved by the Ministry of Commerce, the nonSaudi partners were given the right to name the general manager, provided that the Saudi partners would be entitled to have him removed if his performance was unsatisfactory.[282] Directors may also be given the right to delegate their powers and to vote by proxy at board meetings. In a limited liability company not having a board of controllers, a partner who is not a director retains the right to give advice to the directors and also to review the company's operations and inspect its books and documents at its main office within fifteen days of the date set for submission of the final annual accounts to the partners.[283] The powers of directors cease upon expiration of the company. However, they are required to continue to administer the company until liquidators are appointed and, until such time, are deemed liquidators with respect to third parties.[284]

3. Duties

In addition to their general duty to administer the company as provided in article 167, the Regulations impose certain specific duties upon the directors such as

— publication of the extract of the company's articles of association.[285]

— registration of the company in the Companies Register and the Commercial Register.

— publication and registration of any amendment to the articles of association.[286]

— convoking the annual general meeting or, if resolutions are to be adopted by means of voting by mail, sending all partners registered letters containing the proposed resolutions.[287]

— notifying other partners of a partner's decision to sell its shares and the terms of the sale, in order to permit such other partners to exercise their rights of first refusal.[288]

— preparation of the company's annual balance sheet, profit and loss statement, and a report on the operations and financial position of the company and the directors' proposals with respect to profit

---

[282] Umm al-Qurā, 2/3/1404, at 17, col. 3, 18, col. 1.

[283] Companies Regs., art. 171.

[284] *Id.* art. 217.

[285] *Id.* art. 164, *as amended by* Royal Decree No. M/23 (1982).

[286] *Id.*

[287] *Id.* arts. 172, 174, *as amended by* Royal Decree No. M/23 (1982).

[288] *Id.* art. 165.

distributions within four months of the closing date of every financial year, and, within two months of the date of preparation, submission of copies of the required documents together with copies of the auditor's reports[289] and the board of controllers' reports, if any, to the General Companies Directorate and to all partners.[290]

— convocation of the partners to a meeting, in the event that the company's losses amount to three-quarters of its capital in order to decide whether the company should continue or be dissolved.[291]

— maintaining the company register required by article 166.

— setting aside the reserve funds required by article 176.

Failure to carry out regulatory duties may result in prosecution under amended article 229(8) of the Regulations.[292]

4. Removal

Article 168 provides that "[d]irectors appointed in the articles of association or in a separate instrument may not be removed except with legal justification." According to article 168, directors, whether or not partners, whether or not appointed for a specific term, whether or not remunerated, and whether appointed by partners' resolution or designated by individual partners, may not be removed without a valid cause.[293] In practice, however, the articles of association of limited liability companies frequently entitle partners to remove and replace those directors they have appointed at any time, or permit partners holding a certain percentage of the company's shares to remove any director by way of resolution without mentioning that such removal shall require "legal justification". Even though mandatory regulatory rules may not be overridden by the parties' agreement,[294] the Ministry of Commerce's approval of such clauses may be

---

[289] A limited liability company is required to have one or more auditors. *Id.* art. 169.

[290] *Id.* art. 175.

[291] *Id.* art. 180.

[292] See, e.g., Commission for the Settlement of Commercial Disputes, Jeddah, Decision No. 120/98 (10/9/1398) (prosecution of director for failure to set aside reserve) (prosecutor demanded infliction of article 229 penalties) (summarized in YAḤYĀ, at 235 n. 2); Commission for the Settlement of Commercial Disputes, Jeddah, Decision No. 7/98 (15/1/1398) (prosecuting director under article 229(8) for failure duly to convoke annual general partners' meeting) (summarized in *id.* at 233 n. 1).

[293] *See also* YAḤYĀ, at 232 (drawing analogy to removal of directors of corporation); M. BARĪRĪ, *supra* note 110, at 282.

[294] *See* Companies Regs., art. 2, *as amended by* Royal Decree No. M/23 (1982).

taken into account.[295] Examples of "legal justification" would include a director's failure to carry out his duties as required by regulation, the company's articles of association or the instrument appointing him, violating the provisions of the Regulations or the articles of association, substantial errors in management, general incompetence as evidenced by the poor performance of the company or actual harm sustained by it, engaging in activities in competition with those of the company, as well as serious offenses, such as fraud, embezzlement, or issuing bad checks.

5. Liability

Article 168 provides

> [t]he directors shall be jointly liable in damages for the harm sustained by the company or the partners on third parties as a result of the violation of the provisions of these Regulations or the terms of the company's articles of association or as a result of their faults in the performance of their duties. Any provision to the contrary shall be considered nonexistent.
>
> Except in the cases of fraud and forgery, the agreement of the partners to relieve the directors of liability for their administration shall entail the extinction of the right vested in the company to bring an action in liability. In all cases, such action shall be barred after the expiration of one year from the date of such agreement.

In the case of nullity of the company under article 163, the initial directors of the company, together with those partners who caused such invalidity, are expressly made jointly liable to the remaining partners and to third parties.[296] Directors are also liable under articles 10 and 11 for failure to notarize the company's articles of association and to carry out the publication and registration formalities.

Under article 168, directors are expressly made liable for violations of the company's articles of association. Consequently, the inclusion of additional specified obligations of the directors in the articles of association will enable an aggrieved party to establish its right to damages more easily than if such party is required to prove that certain conduct of the director(s) was in fact a "fault" within the meaning of article 168. Article

---

[295] Similarly, it will be noted that the Ministry of Commerce Model Articles of Association include no provision restricting removal of directors to cases involving "legal justification." *See also* A. AL-KHŪLĪ, *supra* note 102, at 267 (commenting on ambiguity of article 168) (distinguishing between directors appointed in articles of association and in a separate instrument and between limited liability company and corporation) (concluding that director of limited liability company may be removed at any time, even if appointed in the articles of association, but that absence of legal justification could found such director's claim for damages).

[296] Companies Regs., art. 163.

168 provides that the partners' agreement to release the directors from liability will extinguish the company's right of action against such directors. The partners' release of directors from liability may be made in advance or on the occasion of the directors' acts or omissions and may be general or limited to specific acts, such as acts performed within the scope of their powers or the performance of certain duties, or may condition the release on the directors' good faith belief that they were acting in the best interests of the company. To ensure its binding effect on the company, a release of the director(s), unless included in the articles of association, should preferably take the form of a duly made partners' resolution. In addition, individual partners are free to waive their own claims against directors under article 168. Partners may not waive the company's right of action against directors with respect to fraud or forgery. It will be noted that any release by the partners will not affect the rights of third parties, who retain their right of action against the directors. However with the exception of fraud and forgery, the directors may be indemnified against any or all such claims, and insurance may also be procured with respect to certain claims against the directors or the company based on the acts of its directors, officers, or persons to whom they have duly delegated their powers. Competent authorities will in all cases retain the right to proceed against the directors for criminal offenses.

Article 168 provides a one-year limitation period for bringing actions against directors beginning on the date of the partners' agreement to relieve the directors of liability. A certain ambiguity is present in this clause, particularly in the case of a general agreement made in advance of the act at issue. Therefore, this provision has been interpreted to mean the one-year period beginning on the date of the directors' violation or fault.[297] Alternatively, the limitation period may be interpreted to apply to third-party claims against the company. In all noncriminal cases, actions against directors based on their performance of their duties are barred as of three years of publication of the notice of completion of liquidation of the company in the official journal.[298]

6. Penalties

Under amended article 229, directors are liable for prison sentences of three months to one year or a fine of five thousand to twenty thousand riyals or both for

— the wilful insertion of false information or information conflicting with the provisions of the Companies Regulations into company

[297] *See, e.g.*, A. AL-KHŪLĪ, *supra* note 102, at 267.
[298] Companies Regs., art. 226.

documents or the signature and distribution of the same with knowledge thereof;

— offering shares or debt securities for public subscription;

— receiving or distributing "fictitious" profits to partners or third parties;

— the wilful inclusion of false statements in the company's balance sheet or profit and loss statement or in reports prepared for the partners or the general meeting or the omission of material facts from such reports with the intent to conceal the company's financial position from the partners or third parties;

— the failure to comply with obligatory rules issued in regulations or resolutions[299];

— the failure to comply without reasonable cause with instructions issued by the Ministry of Commerce relating to the company's obligations, the review of its books and registers by Ministry representatives, or the submission of statements and information needed by the Ministry.

Under article 230, directors are liable for fines of between one thousand and five thousand riyals for

— violation of the provisions of article 12 (relating to particulars required to be stated on company documents);[300]

— issuing shares, debt securities, subscription receipts, or provisional certificates or offering the same for circulation contrary to the provisions of the Regulations;

— failure to submit the documents required by the Regulations to the General Companies Directorate;

— obstructing the work of an auditor.

The penalties provided in articles 229–230 are doubled as of the second offence.[301]

---

[299] *See* note 292 *supra.*

[300] *Cf.* Commission for the Settlement of Commercial Disputes, Jeddah, Decision No. 11/98 (5/2/1398) (company prosecuted and penalized for its officers' failure to state company name on its printed material).

[301] Companies Regs., art. 231.

P. PARTNERS' RESOLUTIONS

1. Subject matter of resolutions

The Companies Regulations provide for certain acts to be carried out by means of partners' resolution. Resolutions should be made *inter alia*

— to change the nationality of the company;[302]

— to increase the financial liabilities of the partners;[303]

— to discontinue contributions to the regulatory reserve when it has reached fifty percent of the capital;[304]

— to relieve directors of liability for their administration;[305]

— to approve the company's balance sheet and other financial statements after the close of each financial year;[306]

— to decide, in the event that the company's losses total three-quarters of its capital, whether to dissolve or continue the company;[307]

— to effect mergers or consolidations;[308]

— to decide whether to dissolve the company prior to its term;[309]

— to appoint and replace liquidators and determine their powers and remuneration, except in the case of judicial liquidation;[310]

— to authorize liquidators to sell the company's assets as a whole or contribute them to another company;[311]

— to approve the liquidators' annual financial reports and their final accounting.[312]

The partners are free to specify in the company's articles of association whether certain matters relating to the company's internal and external affairs are to be decided solely by means of partners' resolution or may be validly effected by the directors or the general manager. The right to carry out important acts, such as incurring indebtedness, issuing guarantees,

---

[302] *See id.* art. 173.
[303] *See id.*
[304] *See id.* art. 176.
[305] *See id.* art. 168.
[306] *See id.* arts. 174–175, *as amended by* Royal Decree No. M/23 (1982).
[307] *Id.* art. 180.
[308] *Id.* art. 214.
[309] *See id.* art. 15(5).
[310] *Id.* art. 218.
[311] *Id.* art. 220.
[312] *Id.* art. 223.

the purchase of significant property, the sale, leasing, and pledging of the company's property, the opening of branches, the determination of the remuneration of directors and high-level officers, the assignment of any of the company's rights or privileges, the entering into contracts above a certain value, and the like, is frequently explicitly reserved to the partners in the articles of association. However the power to carry out such acts may also be given to the company's directors in the articles of association.

2. Partners' meetings

Resolutions may be adopted either at ordinary or extraordinary partners' meetings, or, if there are not more than twenty partners, in writing. Article 172 provides

> [p]artners' resolutions shall be adopted at a general meeting. Nonetheless, in a company in which the number of partners does not exceed twenty, partners may express their opinions separately, and in this case, the director(s) of the company shall send each partner by registered letter the proposed resolutions so that the partner may vote thereon in writing.

Partners' meetings may be held at the company's main office or at such place as the partners may determine, as provided in the company's articles of association or otherwise agreed. Amended article 174 applies to the convocation of the partners' annual general meeting and extraordinary general meetings. It provides

> [t]he general meeting shall be called by the directors in the manner specified in the company's articles of association.[313] It shall be convened at least once a year within the six months following the close of the company's financial year. A general meeting may be called at any time at the request of the directors or the board of controllers or the auditor or a number of partners representing at least one-half of the capital.[314]

If a company does not hold a general meeting, any partner has the right to request the directors to call the partners to a meeting to deliberate on the financial statements and reports prepared by the directors and their proposals for profit distributions.[315]

---

[313] *Cf.* Minister of Commerce & Indus. Resolution No. 694 (22/6/1385).

[314] However, articles of association approved by the Ministry of Commerce have provided that partners collectively representing 24% of the capital may convoke a general meeting to deliberate on an urgent matter. *See* Umm al-Qurā, 2/3/1404, at 18, col. 1.

[315] Companies Regs., art. 175, *as amended by* Royal Decree No. M/23 (1982).

3. Voting

Voting rights are rights of the partners attached to their shares. All shares carry equal voting rights, and different classes of shares carrying different voting rights may not be created.[316] Article 171 provides

> [e]very partner shall have the right to participate in deliberations and in voting and shall be entitled to a number of votes equal to the number of shares he owns. An agreement otherwise is not permissible.
>
> Every partner may give a proxy in writing to another partner who is not a director to attend the partners' meetings and vote (on his behalf) unless the company's articles of association provide otherwise.

Consequently, proxy voting is permitted as between partners unless expressly prohibited in the articles of association. It may also be noted that article 158 permits the company to suspend the voting rights of shares owned by several persons until such time as the owners select one of their number to act as sole owner vis-à-vis the company.[317] In addition, it should be noted that article 171 prohibits depriving a partner of voting rights proportional to its interest in the capital but does not bar a partner from assigning such rights to another partner or third party for a specified period for valid reasons.

4. Majorities

Minister of Commerce and Industry Resolution No. 694 requires that the majority necessary for adoption of the partners' resolutions be specified in the company's articles of association.[318] If the company has more than twenty partners, the quorum required for the validity of partners' general meetings must also be provided therein.[319]

Ordinary resolutions

The regulatory rule is that partners' resolutions are valid only if adopted by partners representing at least one-half of the company's capital, unless the company's articles of association provide for a greater majority.[320] Therefore, article 172 permits the setting of a higher majority than that required by regulation either generally or with respect to particular matters and also permits, if so provided in the articles of association, such a higher

---

[316] It may be noted in this context that the shares of a limited liability company are not divisible. *Id.* art. 158.

[317] *See* p. 109 *supra*.

[318] Resolution No. 694, art. 1(8) (22/6/1385).

[319] *Id.* art. 2(2).

[320] Companies Regs., art. 172.

majority to apply even in the case where the required majority was not obtained at the first vote and resolutions adopted by a simple majority of those present would otherwise be valid. To do so, however, may in practice result in impeding the company's affairs and afford the possibility for misuse of such a requirement through its utilization for blocking tactics or other purposes which may not be in the best interests of the company. If the required majority does not obtain during the first deliberation or consultation, whether at a meeting or in writing, the partners must be summoned by registered letter to a meeting. Resolutions at such a meeting are valid if adopted by majority vote of those present, regardless of the amount of capital represented, unless the articles of association provide otherwise.[321]

Amendments to the articles of association

Depending on the nature of the amendment and the provisions of the articles of association, the relevant partners' resolution will be adopted by a supermajority, by an ordinary majority, or by unanimity. Article 173 of the Regulations provides

> [t]he nationality of the company may not be changed or the financial liabilities of the partners increased except by the agreement of all of the partners. In all but these two matters, the articles of association of the company may be amended by the agreement of a majority of the partners representing at least three-quarters of the capital unless the articles of association provide otherwise.

It is possible to require unanimity or a higher than the regulatory majority for amendments to the articles of association in cases other than a change in the company's nationality or an increase in the partners' financial liabilities; for example, with respect to mergers with other companies, transfer of the company's main office to another location within the Kingdom, increasing the regulatory reserve above the fifty percent limit set by article 176, creation of additional reserves, reduction of the company's capital, admission of new partners, or dissolution of the company. It is also possible, albeit inadvisable, to provide for a lower majority in such cases, provided it is not lower than votes representing one-half of the capital as provided in article 172. However, any resolution changing the company's nationality or increasing the financial liabilities of the partners will not be valid unless adopted by unanimity. The term "financial liabilities of the partners" appearing in article 173 has not been officially defined. However, it is established that loans made to the company are not deemed to

---

[321] *Id.*

increase the partners' financial liabilities.[322] The typical case involving an increase of the partners' financial liabilities would relate to increases in the company's capital. However, not all capital increases will involve increasing the financial liabilities of the partners, as in the case of admission of new participants or increase of capital by means of incorporation of reserves.[323] In contrast, such operations as conversion of the company into a form involving greater liability, such as a general partnership, would increase such liabilities. However, a reduction of the partners' rights, such as imposing greater limitations on the transferability of their shares, would not be deemed to increase their "financial liabilities".

Any amendment to the articles of association is subject to Ministry of Commerce approval and, in the case of amendments relating to the License of a mixed participation company, Ministry of Industry and Electricity approval. The same procedures of notarization, publication, and registration applicable to the original articles of association must also be carried out with respect to any amendments.[324]

5. Nullification of resolutions

Article 177 of the Regulations provides

> [w]ithout prejudice to the rights of good faith third parties, any resolution issued by the general meeting or the partners in violation of the provisions of these Regulations or of the terms of the company's articles of association shall be null and void. Nonetheless, only the partners who objected in writing to the resolution or who were unable to object to it after having knowledge thereof may demand its nullification. A nullified resolution shall be considered as nonexistent with respect to all partners. An action for nullification shall be barred after the expiration of one year from the date of the said resolution.

The general rule is that invalid resolutions are only invalid as among the partners and that the rights of third parties who relied on such resolutions

---

[322] Minutes of Committee in Companies Department (12/1/1400), *cited in* YAHYĀ, at 395.

[323] *But see* note 261 *supra*. It may be noted that in one case the FCIC took the position that the company's capital could be increased by a favorable vote of partners representing 75% of the capital. In the case of mixed participation companies, any increase in capital will require obtaining Minister of Indus. and Elect. (FCIC) approval. In contrast, permission to reduce capital is not easily obtainable and, should the FCIC deem such reduction appropriate or necessary under the particular circumstances, it may require that the company correspondingly reduce its activities and amend its objectives clause accordingly.

[324] Companies Regs., arts. 10–11, 164. *See also* Instructions Relating to the Amendment of the Particulars of Companies and Sole Proprietorships (implementing Minister of Commerce Resolution No. 151 (17/8/1403)) (giving commercial registration procedures and specifying documents to be submitted with respect to amendments involving changes in name, address, activities, capital, share distribution, opening of branches) (translated in Appendix 22).

in good faith are not affected by their nullity. However, an exception has been suggested with respect to invalid resolutions whose nullity resulted from a lack of capacity or a defect in consent of any partner, in which case the resolution would be nonexistent even with respect to third parties. If a partner endorsed such a resolution in good faith and later came to know that it was contrary to the Regulations or the company's articles of association, it may call for an extraordinary general meeting of the partners for the purpose of nullifying the resolution. If the other partners do not take appropriate measures to nullify the resolution, the objecting partner may seek nullification before the Commission for the Settlement of Commercial Disputes. Under article 177, a partner who duly objected to a resolution or was unable to object thereto may recover damages from the other partners for actual harm resulting to it from the adoption of such resolution. However, a partner who originally voted for a resolution may be unable to recover damages for any injury incurred prior to the date it became aware that the resolution was illegal or in violation of the company's articles of association or otherwise *ultra vires* and brought it to the notice of the other partners.

There is a divergence in views as to whether the one-year limitation period provided in article 177 applicable to actions for nullification begins to run on the date of the adoption of the resolution, or on the date of its effectiveness, or on the date the objecting partner had knowledge of it, or on the date it notified the other partners of its objection. The majority view, which strictly interprets the provisions of article 177, holds that such an action is barred one year from the date the resolution was adopted.

Q. DISSOLUTION

1. Provisions specific to limited liability companies

Article 178 of the Regulations provides that a "limited liability company shall not be dissolved by the withdrawal, adjudged legal incapacity, declaration of bankruptcy, or insolvency of a partner unless its articles of association provide otherwise." However, article 178 does not prohibit the partners from providing that the company will be dissolved upon the occurrence of any or all of the events stated therein. Even in the absence of such a provision in the articles of association, if such an event were seriously to affect the stability of the company and/or the conduct of its affairs, judicial dissolution might be available in a proper case.[325] It may be noted that article 178 does not include the death of a partner among the events which will not result in dissolution of the company. However, article

---

[325] *See generally* p. 145 *infra.*

178 is interpreted to include the death of a partner within its scope.[326] With respect to withdrawal of partners, the rule of article 178 is subject to the qualification that the withdrawal of one partner from a company having only two partners will result in its dissolution, if the shares of the withdrawing partner are transferred to the nonwithdrawing partner.[327]

Article 180 specifically requires the partners to determine by resolution whether the company should be dissolved in the case that its losses amount to three-quarters of its capital. It provides

> [i]f the losses of a limited liability company amount to three-quarters of the capital, the directors shall convoke the partners to a meeting to consider whether the company shall continue or be dissolved before the term specified in its articles of association.
>
> The partners' resolution in this respect shall not be valid unless adopted by the majority provided in article 173. In all cases, such resolution shall be published in the manner provided in article 164. If the directors fail to convoke the partners or if the partners are unable to adopt a resolution on the matter, any interested party may seek the dissolution of the company.

In addition, in the case that the losses of a company approach the amount of its capital, the General Companies Directorate may notify such company that its capital must be increased and that it must endeavor to procure business to cover its losses. If the company's position is not remedied, the matter may be brought before the Commission for the Settlement of Commercial Disputes and the dissolution of the company be requested on the grounds that the continuation of losses is a serious reason permitting dissolution.[328]

2. General provisions

Article 15 of the Regulations provides

> [w]ith due regard to the causes of dissolution specific to each kind of company, every company shall be dissolved for any of the following reasons:
>
> 1. The expiration of the term fixed for the company.
> 2. The realization of the objective for which the company was formed or the impossibility of the said objective.
> 3. The transfer of all interests or shares of stock to a single participant.

---

[326] *See, e.g.,* YAHYĀ, at 236; A AL-KHŪLĪ, *supra* note 102, at 269.
[327] Companies Regs., art. 15(3).
[328] Ministry of Commerce Legal Memorandum No. 283/11 (3/4/1400), *cited in* YAHYĀ, at 395–96.

4. The loss of all or the major part of the company's assets, so that the remainder cannot be effectively utilized.

5. The agreement of the partners to dissolve the company before the expiration of its term, unless the company's articles of association provide otherwise.

6. The merger of the company into another company.

7. The issuance of a decision to dissolve the company by the Commission for the Settlement of Commercial Disputes on the petition of an interested party, provided there are serious reasons justifying the same.

The regulatory grounds for dissolution may not be overridden by the parties' agreement.

Expiration of term

The company's existence terminates by force of law on the expiration of its duration as provided in its articles of association unless the partners duly amend the articles to extend such duration before the expiration date. It has been suggested that, unless the articles of association provide for a lesser majority, such decision of the partners would be required to be made by unanimity.[329] However, provided that such a resolution is adopted within the period of effectiveness of the articles of association, the majority specified to amend the articles of association may be sufficient in such a case, if such a resolution is viewed as an amendment to the "duration" clause of the articles. In contrast, a decision to extend the duration of the company after it has expired and the parties have ceased to be bound by the articles of association would in principle involve the formation of a new company. Hence, unanimous agreement of the parties would be required. If the partners agree to extend the company's duration prior to expiration of its term, creditors are not expressly given by regulation the right to object to such extension, in contrast to their right to object to a proposed merger.[330] Despite the absence of a regulatory provision giving creditors such a right, it has been suggested that creditors could nonetheless raise objections to the continuation of the company on the grounds of fraud or intent to cause prejudice to such creditors.[331] It may also be noted that, if the partners have decided to extend the duration of the company after the expiration of its term, in the case that any personal creditors of partners have been assigned such partners' shares in the company's profits under article 6 of the Regulations,[332] on dissolution of the company the creditors'

---

[329] *See* A. AL-KHŪLĪ, *supra* note 102, at 142.

[330] Companies Regs., art. 215.

[331] *See* A. AL-KHŪLĪ, *supra* note 102, at 143.

[332] *See generally* pp. 116–17 *supra*.

rights transfer to their debtors' shares in the company's liquidation surplus after payment of its debts. Consequently, not only creditors of the company but also personal creditors of partners could intervene in order to satisfy their claims from the assets of the company which has come to an end by force of law, and a court would not be precluded from accepting such claims.[333] If, however, no such creditors come forward, the partners have resolved to extend the duration of the company within a reasonable period from its expiration, and the company has continued its prior activities within its original objectives, has continued to function according to the rules applicable to nondissolved companies, and has made no indications of dissolution in its accounts and balance sheet, such company will be considered as continuing under its original form, provided that its articles of association were duly amended to reflect the extension of its term.

Transfer of all shares to one partner

The ownership of all shares by a single participant will result in the dissolution of the company under article 15(3) by virtue of the fundamental requirement expressed in articles 1 and 157 that a limited liability company must have a minimum of two participants.[334] Should all shares be transferred to one partner, article 179, by reference to article 147, makes such partner liable for the company's debts to the extent of the company's assets.

Loss of company's assets

The relevant assets may be either tangible assets or intangible property or rights, as in the case of loss of concession or licensing rights fundamental to the company's activities. However, in the case of loss of physical assets, where the parties have obtained insurance or are willing to make additional contributions to make up the deficit, the company will not be dissolved under article 15(4), since only those losses resulting in the company's inability to utilize effectively its remaining property or to continue to pursue effectively its objectives are covered by this subsection. Article 15(4) differs from article 180, in that no specific percentage of loss is set with respect to dissolution and the partners are not expressly permitted to decide to continue the company should the requisite amount of loss specified in article 15(4) be found to exist as a matter of fact. Therefore, there may be situations where the partners differ in opinion as to whether "the major part" of the company's property has in fact been lost. Unless such term has been defined in the articles of association or other instrument binding on all partners the parties may apply to the Commission for the

---

[333] It may be noted that by the mere fact of its duration having expired the company is deemed to enter into the stage of liquidation: Companies Regs., art. 216.

[334] *See generally* pp. 83–84 & note 104 *supra*.

Settlement of Commercial Disputes to appoint experts to make the requisite determination.[335]

Dissolution by Commission for the Settlement of Commercial Disputes[336]

The term "interested party" appearing in article 15(7) is generally interpreted to apply to partners. However, it has been suggested that such language is broad enough to extend to a company's creditors.[337] Creditors have generally the right to seek the judicial declaration of bankruptcy of a debtor whose debts exceed its assets and which is thereby unable to discharge its liability with respect to such debts.[338] Under article 15(7), only "serious reasons" are grounds for seeking judicial dissolution of the company. Where the petitioner is a partner, such reasons might include misuse of funds, fraud, or other wrongful acts. Dissolution be sought in such cases by an aggrieved party, who would also have the right to claim damages for any harm sustained as a result of such acts. In order for serious misunderstandings between the partners to justify judicial dissolution, they would have to be of such a nature as effectively to frustrate the company's ability to carry on its activities. In all cases, the Commission for the Settlement of Commercial Disputes has discretion to evaluate the desirability of dissolution of the company in the light of all of the circumstances. It may be noted that petitioning for dissolution under subsection 7 is also available to the Ministry of Commerce in certain cases as an alternative or cumulative sanction to proceeding under article 229.[339]

R. LIQUIDATION

The limited liability company is subject to the liquidation provisions of the Companies Regulations applicable generally to the forms it provides. The general rules may, however, be elaborated on or refined by the parties in the company's articles of association and/or bylaws, provided that any such provision does not conflict with mandatory rules of law. Article 15 provides that: "[u]pon dissolution, the company shall be liquidated in accordance with the provisions of Part Eleven of these Regulations to the extent that such provisions are not inconsistent with the terms of the

---

[335] *See, e.g.*, M. BARĪRĪ, *supra* n. 110, at 145.

[336] *See generally* pp. 222–24 *infra*.

[337] *See* M. BARĪRĪ, *supra* n. 110, at 148.

[338] *See* Commercial Court Regs., arts. 103, 108.

[339] *See, e.g.*, Ministry of Commerce Legal Memorandum No. 283/11 (3/4/1400) (dissolution may be sought on grounds of partners' appropriation of company funds for their personal use or for failure of company incurring losses to rectify its situation by increasing its capital or otherwise) (continuing loss deemed "serious reason" for purposes of art. 15(7)), *cited in* YAḤYĀ, at 395–96.

company's articles of association or bylaws." Immediately upon dissolution, by force of law the company enters into the stage of liquidation and the powers of its director(s) *qua* director(s) cease. Article 216 provides that the "company by the mere fact of its dissolution shall enter into the stage of liquidation and shall retain its juristic personality to the extent necessary for liquidation and until liquidation is completed." Article 217 provides that "the powers of the directors or the board of directors shall cease upon the dissolution of the company. However, they shall continue to administer the company and shall be deemed with respect to third parties as liquidators until the liquidator is appointed." All documents issued by a company under liquidation must bear a legend to the effect that such company is under liquidation.[340]

1. Appointment and powers of liquidators

Liquidation is required to be performed by duly appointed liquidators whose powers are set forth in the instrument of appointment.[341] Except in the case of judicial dissolution or invalidation of the company, the partners appoint the liquidators. Article 218 provides

> [o]ne or more liquidators, who may or may not be partners, shall effect the liquidation of the company. The partners or the general meeting shall appoint or [sic] replace the liquidators and determine their powers and remuneration. If the Commission for the Settlement of Commercial Disputes issued the decision to liquidate or invalidate the company, it shall appoint the liquidators and determine their powers and remuneration.

If there are two or more liquidators, they are required to act jointly unless the authority having appointed them authorizes them to act separately.[342] If the instrument appointing the liquidators has not placed restrictions on their powers, liquidators are given by regulation "the broadest powers" to realize the assets of the company. Such regulatory powers specifically include the power to sell the company's real and personal property privately or at public auction. However, unless so authorized by the authority having appointed them, liquidators may not sell the company's

---

[340] Companies Regs., art. 12. If such legend is not appended, the Company's liquidators are liable to third parties for damages resulting therefrom. *See* Ministry of Commerce, Powers & Duties of Liquidators, art. 4 (translated in Appendix 29).

[341] *See* Ministry of Commerce Powers & Duties of Liquidators (liquidator's powers may also be defined in articles of association) (if not restricted, liquidator will have power to carry out all acts required by Regulation) (translated in Appendix 29).

[342] Companies Regs., art. 219.

property in one lot or contribute it as a share in another company.[343] It may be noted that a company in the state of liquidation may merge with another company.[344] However, such a merger is not within the powers of liquidators, but is required to be effected, in the case of dissolution by the partners, by means of a partners' resolution adopted by the majority necessary for amending such company's articles of association.[345] Finally, liquidators are in all cases prohibited from commencing new operations unless such operations are necessary for the winding up of previous operations.[346] The company is bound by the acts of liquidators within the scope of their powers.[347] Nonetheless, the participants and instrumentalities of the company retain the prerogatives granted to them by the Companies Regulations and the company's articles of association to the extent that such prerogatives do not conflict with the liquidators'. In particular, the right of partners to inspect the company's records, as provided in the Regulations and the company's articles of association, is affirmed.[348]

2. Duties of liquidators

The basic duties of the liquidators are outlined in articles 220–223. The liquidators' initial duty is to publish the text of the decision appointing them and the limitations on their powers in the manner prescribed for publication of an amendment to the company's articles of association.[349] Within three months of beginning their operations, the liquidators are required to make an inventory, in conjunction with the company's auditor(s), of the company's assets and liabilities.[350] The liquidators are required to pay the company's debts if due and to set aside amounts necessary to pay future or contested debts.[351] Debts resulting from the

---

[343] *Id.* art. 220. The liquidation resolution may restrict the method of sale: *see* Ministry of Commerce Powers & Duties of Liquidators, art 5.

[344] Companies Regs., art. 213.

[345] *Id.* art. 214. Creditors of the company are given the right to object to mergers within 90 days of the publication of the merger resolution: *id.* art. 215.

[346] *Id.* art. 220.

[347] *Id.* art. 224.

[348] *Id.* art. 225.

[349] *Id.* art. 221. For Ministry of Commerce Model Liquidation Resolution, see Appendix 29.

[350] Companies Regs., art. 223. The directors of the company are required to submit to the liquidators the company's books, records, and documents and to furnish any clarifications or particulars that the liquidators may require: *id.* A report thereon must be approved by the partners and submitted to the Ministry of Commerce: *see* Ministry of Commerce, Powers & Duties of Liquidators, art. 2.

[351] Companies Regs., art. 222. If the liquidators do not pay the company's debts as they come due, partners or creditors of the company or other interested parties may petition for a judicial declaration of bankruptcy. *See* Commercial Court Regs., art. 108; Ministry of Commerce, Powers & Duties of Liquidators, art. 19.

liquidation are given priority by the Companies Regulations.[352] However, under the Labor Regulations, amounts to which workmen or their dependants are entitled are given the status of "first-class privileged debts". In the event of liquidation, such amounts are to be recorded as privileged debts, and the workmen are entitled to receive immediately the equivalent of one month's pay before payment of liquidation costs.[353] Tax claims are also given priority. A pledgee is entitled to satisfy the value of its claim out of the proceeds of the sale of pledged property. If such proceeds are less than the value of the debt, the pledgee must compete with the general mass of creditors for the balance. After settlement of the company's debts, the liquidators are required to distribute the value of the remaining assets among the partners in the manner specified in article 222. Article 222 provides

> [t]he liquidators shall after satisfaction of the debts . . . return to the partners the value of their shares in the capital and then distribute to them the surplus in accordance with the provisions of the company's articles of association. If the articles of association do not include provisions in this respect, the surplus shall be distributed to them in proportion to their shares in the capital. If the net assets of the company are not sufficient for payment of the partners' shares, the loss shall be distributed among them in accordance with the rate fixed for the division of losses.[354]

At the close of every financial year the liquidators are required to submit an annual balance sheet, profit and loss statement, and a report on the liquidation operations to the partners for approval in accordance with the company's articles of association.[355] On completion of liquidation, the liquidators are required to submit a final accounting to the partners. Liquidation is completed upon the partners' approval of the accounting.[356] Notice of completion of liquidation must be published by the liquidators in

---

[352] Companies Regs., art. 222.

[353] Labor Regs., Royal Decree No. M/21, art. 15 (1969), *as amended* by Royal Decree No. M/2 (7/2/1403). *Cf.* Ministry of Commerce, Powers & Duties of Liquidators, art. 11 (emphasizing importance of payment of debts to workmen). *See also id.* art. 18 (providing for special treatment of privileged debts).

[354] *Cf.* Companies Regs., art. 171 (shares confer equal rights to liquidation surplus unless articles of association provide otherwise); Ministry of Commerce, Powers & Duties of Liquidators, art. 12 (surplus or losses to be distributed according to ratios fixed for losses). Liquidation proceeds may not be distributed to the partners until completion of liquidation. *See id.* art. 18.

[355] A copy of such documents as approved must be submitted to the Ministry of Commerce within four months of the close of the financial year: Ministry of Commerce, Powers & Duties of Liquidators, art. 3.

[356] Companies Regs., art. 223. A copy of the report as approved must be submitted to the Ministry of Commerce. *See* Ministry of Commerce, Powers & Duties of Liquidators, art. 13. For Model Final Liquidation Account, see Appendix 29.

the same manner as amendments to the company's articles of association.[357]

3. Liability of liquidators

Liquidators are not personally liable for duly performed acts within the scope of their powers.[358] However, liquidators are jointly liable for damages sustained by the company, the partners, and third parties resulting from their *ultra vires* acts or faults committed in the performance of their operations.[359] A three-year limitation period, beginning from the date of publication of the notice of completion of liquidation, is applicable to actions brought against liquidators with respect to liquidation operations. The same limitation period applies to actions against the partners with respect to the operations of the company and against the directors or auditors with respect to acts performed in their respective functions.[360] Liquidators are subject to the regulatory penalties generally for failure to comply with regulations, rules, and Ministry of Commerce instructions and specifically for intentional misstatements in the financial statements and reports prepared by them or omission of material facts from such documents with the intent to conceal the financial position of the company from the partners or third parties.[361]

---

[357] Companies Regs., art. 223. For Form of Notice, see Ministry of Commerce Model Announcement of Completion of Liquidation (translated in Appendix 29).

[358] Companies Regs., art. 224.

[359] *Id.* art. 219. For example, liquidators are liable to third parties for failure to include the phrase "company under liquidation" in the company's documents. *See* Ministry of Commerce, Powers & Duties of Liquidators, art. 4.

[360] Companies Regs., art. 226.

[361] *Id.* art. 229(6), (8)–(9), *as amended by* Royal Decree No. M/23 (1982). *See also id.* art. 230(1) (imposing penalties for violations of article 12) (including failure to state on company's documents that company is under liquidation).

Chapter 3

ARBITRATION

During the last two decades, arbitration has become of increasing significance in Saudi Arabia as a means of resolving business disputes. In response to the phenomenon, Saudi Arabia issued its first Arbitration Regulations[1] in 1983 and the implementing rules thereunder in 1985.[2]

Prior to their issuance, Saudi law did not include a comprehensive regulation of arbitration.[3] Generally speaking, both conciliation and arbitration were regarded as valid means of resolving disputes within the private sector and, in certain cases, disputes between the Saudi Government and private parties. Nonetheless, courts were not legally required to give

---

[1] Royal Decree No. M/46 (1983). The Arbitration Regulations were published in Umm al-Qurā, the official journal, on June 3, 1983 and became effective 30 days as from that date. *See id.* art. 25.

[2] Arbitration Regulations Implementing Rules, Council of Ministers Resolution No. 7/2021/M(8/9/1405) (May 27, 1985) (the "Implementing Rules") (translated in Appendix 31). The Implementing Rules were published in Umm al-Qurā on June 28, 1985 and became effective as of that date. *Id.* art. 48.

[3] The procedural provisions of the Commercial Court Regulations, High Order No. 32 (1931), were applicable to commercial arbitration and conciliation proceedings. The arbitration provisions of these regulations were repealed simultaneous with the issuance of the Arbitration Regulations. *See* Royal Decree No. M/46, para. 2. In addition, the Chambers of Commerce and Industry were competent to resolve business disputes by arbitration if the parties so agreed. Chambers of Commerce & Indus. Regs., Royal Decree No. M/6, art. 5(h) (1400). The Chamber of Commerce Regulations Implementing Rules, Minister of Commerce Resolution No. 1871 (22/5/1401), state the procedures applicable to commercial arbitration proceedings before the Chambers of Commerce and Industry. If two Saudi parties belonging to the same Chamber of Commerce and Industry in the same locality agree to resolve a dispute by arbitration, they may submit a request for arbitration signed by both parties to the chairman of the board of directors of that Chamber. The rules provide for an arbitration committee of three members, one appointed by each party and the umpire appointed by the chairman of the board of directors: *Id.* art. 49. The umpire is responsible for setting the hearing date and notifying the other arbitrators and the parties of such date: *Id.* art. 50. Parties are entitled to be represented by counsel at the hearing: *Id.* art. 51. The award must be signed by the arbitrators and a copy thereof notified to the parties: *Id.* art. 53. If the two parties belong to different Chambers of Commerce and Industry, or if one of them is foreign, the Rules provide for the application of substantially the same procedures. *See id.* art. 54.

effect to parties' arbitration agreements or to renounce their jurisdiction to rehear a case in respect of which an arbitral award had issued. Arbitral awards were not automatically enforced.

I. Arbitration Regulations

A. ARBITRATION AGREEMENT

1. Scope

Article 1 of the Regulations provides that "arbitration may be agreed upon in a specific existing dispute. It may also be agreed in advance to arbitrate any dispute arising as a result of the execution of a specific contract." Article 1 therefore validates arbitration generally as a means of dispute resolution and does not limit arbitration to commercial matters.[4] It expressly recognizes the validity both of the submission, or agreement to resolve an actual dispute between the parties by means of arbitration, and of the agreement to refer or arbitration clause.[5] In view of the fact that Saudi arbitration clauses have historically tended to provide for arbitration of disputes arising out of the "interpretation" as well as the "execution" of a certain agreement,[6] the regulatory phrase "arising as a result of the execution of a specific contract" could be construed to exclude those issues relating to interpretation of the contract from the scope of a valid

---

[4] Thus, disputes relating to noncommercial property rights, civil debts or financial transactions, and the like may be resolved by arbitration.

[5] *Cf.* Rules of Procedure to be followed by Civil Rights Departments in claims of Private Rights, Minister of the Interior Resolution No. 20, art. 9(a)–(b) (2/1/1406) (enforcing arbitration agreements). The arbitration clause or agreement to settle future disputes by arbitration is not found in Islamic law texts. *See, e.g.,* S. SALEH, COMMERCIAL ARBITRATION IN THE ARAB MIDDLE EAST 21, 25, 48–49 (1984) (also suggesting that concept of arbitration clause contains elements irreconcilable with Islamic law, namely, an undertaking to execute in the future a revocable contract and an agreement to arbitrate before existence of a dispute, involving impermissible uncertainty and risk, but that clause is a valid obligation under principles of general contract law). Given the permissive character of article 1, the parties would remain free, in drafting an arbitration clause, to exclude certain matters from its scope to be adjudicated in the appropriate Saudi forum. However, in this case, in the event of ambiguity or difference of opinion between the parties as to whether a certain issue is within the scope of such clause, the determination would be required to be made by judicial ruling. It should also be noted that neither the Regulations nor the Implementing Rules address the issue of severability of the arbitration clause. However, the parties remain free to provide contractually for such severability, in order to preclude a party from resisting arbitration on the grounds of invalidity of the main contract.

[6] *See generally* section V *infra*.

arbitration clause.[7] However, it has been unofficially commented that the phrase employed in article 1 should be interpreted broadly so as to convey the meaning of "in the course of a specific contractual relationship." In contrast, article 1 does not contemplate an agreement to arbitrate future disputes not arising out of a specific contractual relationship. It should be noted that, even though an arbitration agreement or arbitration clause covered by article 1 and not in violation of the provisions of articles 2–3 constitutes a valid and binding obligation of the parties, its enforceability does not follow automatically from its validity but is subject to compliance with the procedural requirements of the Regulations.[8]

2. Exceptions

Subject matter

Article 2 of the Regulations refines the scope of arbitration as generally validated by article 1 by providing that "arbitration is not acceptable in matters where conciliation is not permitted."[9] Such matters, as clarified by the Implementing Rules,[10] are, generally speaking, criminal offenses, whether or not subject to the Quranic punishments, issues of public and administrative law and civil status, properly reserved to the State, and matters relating to inheritance, certain marital disputes and the like.

---

[7] *Cf.* Rice Contract, (*U.S.* v. *Iran*) Iran–United States Claims Tribunal (1982), *reprinted in part in* [1983] Y.B. Com. Arb. 313–14 (1983). Arbitrator Mosk, dissenting, observed

> [i]n Case 121, the so called "Rice Contract" provides: "any dispute arising from the execution of this agreement, if not settled amicably, shall be resolved through the Iranian legal authorities . . ." If "execution" means signing or validity, the clause may not cover disputes involving interpretation or performance of the agreement. If "execution" means performance, as suggested by the majority without discussion, then the clause does not necessarily cover questions concerning the validity or interpretation of the contract.

[8] *See generally* pp. 161–62 *infra*.

[9] Alternatively, the term "ṣulḥ", "conciliation", may be translated as "amicable settlement." However, in the context of article 16 of the Regulations, relating to the majority required for issuance of the award, the better translation of the term might be "amiable compositeur." Under Islamic law conciliation is generally permissible between Muslims with the exception of settlements purporting to permit prohibited matters or to prohibit the permissible. *See, e.g.*, 3 M. al-Bahūtī, Kashshāf al-Qinā· ·an Matn al-Iqnā· 390 (Riyadh). *Cf.* Governors and Administrative Councils Regs., Royal Will No. 11/1/1, art. 10 (1359) (governor may settle disputes with the agreement and consent of parties provided that prohibited matters are not permitted nor permitted matters prohibited). However, only a private right (ḥaqq ādamī) may be compromised; the "rights of God", such as issues relating to the Quranic punishments, expiation, or zakāt, may not be validly settled. *Cf.* 4 M. Ibn Qudāmā, al-Mughnī 369 (Cairo 1968) (settlement is permissible with respect to any thing for which a countervalue may be received, whether or not it can be sold, such as blood money in certain cases or defects in merchandise). *Cf.* 6 M. al-Bahūtī *supra*, at 309 (arbitration generally permissible).

[10] *See* Implementing Rules, art. 1.

Capacity

Prior to the issuance of the Arbitration Regulations, except for government entities not authorized by special permission to resort to arbitration,[11] any natural or juristic person, whether of Saudi or nonSaudi nationality, having legal capacity could enter into arbitration under Saudi law.[12] Article 2 reaffirms this principle in substance by providing that "the agreement to arbitrate is not valid unless [made] by a person of full capacity." Consequently, agreements entered into by, *inter alia*, minors, the insane, idiots, spendthrifts, the intoxicated, and bankrupts are void.[13] Conversely, agreements entered into by other persons are valid.

3. Public sector disputes

Council of Ministers Resolution No. 58[14]

Until 1963, the Saudi Government frequently provided for arbitration as a means of resolving disagreements between itself and private parties.[15] In that year, however, the Council of Ministers issued Resolution No. 58 prohibiting, *inter alia*, resorting to arbitration as a means of resolving disputes between the Saudi Government or its ministries, departments, or agencies[16] on the one hand, and individuals, companies, or private organizations on the other.

[11] Alternatively, the inability of government agencies to resolve their disputes by arbitration without authorization may be viewed as arising from a positive regulatory rule rather than any intrinsic defect in capacity, inasmuch as such agencies are permitted to enter into arbitration agreements in some cases.

[12] *See, e.g.*, Hejailan, *Saudi Arabia* [1979] Y.B. COM. ARB. 162, 167 (1979). Although no specific provision of Islamic or regulatory law expressly permitted juristic persons to enter into arbitration agreements, such capacity was considered to arise from their general capacity to contract, subject to any restrictions in applicable regulations or their corporate documents. For issue of recognition of juristic personality under Islamic law, see pp. 106–07 *supra*.

[13] *Cf.* Implementing Rules, art. 2 (requiring prior court approval of an arbitration agreement by the guardian of a minor or an endowment trustee). Additionally, persons in the stage of mortal illness are deprived of capacity to make certain dispositions. Hence, heirs or creditors may attack the validity of arbitration agreements. *See, e.g.*, S. SALEH, *supra* note 5, at 31.

[14] Resolution No. 58 (June 25, 1963).

[15] *See, e.g.*, Agreement between Saudi Arabia and Japan Petroleum Trading Co., Dec. 10, 1957, art. 55 (Gov't Press 2d ed. 1964) (disputes to be resolved finally by five-arbitrator panel sitting in Saudi Arabia); Agreement between Saudi Arabia and Pacific West Oil Corp., Feb. 20, 1949, art. 45 (Gov't Press 4th ed. 1964) (disputes to be finally resolved by three-arbitrator panel); Agreement between Saudi Arabia and Trans-Arabian Pipe Line Co., July 11, 1947, art. 23 (Gov't Press 2d ed. 1965) (providing for three-arbitrator panel sitting in Jeddah); Agreement between Saudi Arabia and Arabian American Oil Co., May 29, 1933, art. 31 (Gov't Press 2d ed. 1964) (providing for three-arbitrator panel). *See also* note 111, *infra* (Saudi Arabia held bound by International Chamber of Commerce arbitration clause).

[16] The term "agencies" found in the Resolution is uniformly construed to embrace ministries and government departments, and, in a proper case, government instrumentalities established in corporate form may be included. However, government corporations, even if not technically subject to Resolution No. 58, may voluntarily comply with its provisions.

Resolution No. 58 provides

1. No government agency shall conclude a contract with any individual, company, or private organization which includes a clause subjecting the government agency to any foreign court of law or any body having a judicial character.
2. No government agency shall accept arbitration as a means of settling disputes which may arise between it and any individual, company or private organization. This provision shall not, however, apply to exceptional cases wherein the State shall grant a concession and in doing so find the utmost advantage in including the arbitration clause in such concession.
3. The law applicable to disputes to which the State is a party shall be determined in accordance with the established general principles of private international law, the most important of which is the principle of application of the law of the place of performance. Government agencies may not choose any foreign law to govern their relationship with such individuals, companies, or private organizations.
4. The above provisions shall not apply to contracts actually concluded before the issuance of this Resolution.

Prior to issuance of the Arbitration Regulations, certain confusion was present among legal commentators as to the scope and nature of the prohibition of arbitration expressed in Resolution No. 58. Inasmuch as paragraphs 1 and 3 of the Resolution prohibit any Saudi government entity from submitting to the jurisdiction of any foreign court or from selecting nonSaudi law to govern its relationships with private parties, some commentators formed the opinion that the prohibition of arbitration applied only to arbitration held outside Saudi Arabia. Under this view, a Saudi government agency could lawfully enter into an arbitration agreement provided that the place of arbitration were within the Kingdom. This view was without merit, as is shown by article 3 of the Regulations. It may be noted that the literal language of the Resolution globally prohibits "arbitration as a means of settling disputes" and makes no qualification with respect to place.

Arbitration Regulations

Article 3 of the Regulations incorporates the prohibition of government entities entering into arbitration provided in Resolution No. 58 but enlarges the exception provided therein. It provides that "government agencies may not resort to arbitration to settle their disputes with third parties except after approval of the President of the Council of Ministers. This provision may be amended by resolution of the Council of Ministers."[17] Current law, therefore, contemplates approval of arbitration in a proper case and does not limit its permissibility to disputes between parties to "concessions." It will be noted that permission to arbitrate is granted by means of high order, as contrasted with Council of Ministers resolution as provided in prior drafts of article 3. This may be regarded as manifesting a favorable attitude toward arbitration as a means of resolving certain public sector disputes.

4. Enforceability

Prior law

Prior to the Arbitration Regulations, Saudi law did not expressly provide for the enforcement of arbitration agreements or clauses or the stay of judicial proceedings brought in violation of such agreements. The effectiveness of such agreements was therefore dependent upon the parties' respect for contractual obligations and the judiciary's view of the case, on a case-by-case basis. Neither the Commission for the Settlement of Commercial Disputes nor the sharī'ah courts were required to direct the parties to fulfill the terms of their agreement to arbitrate or to decline to take jurisdiction of the case. Indeed, in the absence of regulations on this issue, the courts could be deemed required to hear any cases within their jurisdiction.

If the parties were bound by a valid arbitration clause, the Commission for the Settlement of Commercial Disputes, which would normally be the forum for business-related litigation, was not barred from directing the parties to proceed to arbitration before hearing the case. The same rule could also be applied by Islamic law judges, who might urge litigants to proceed to conciliation or arbitration prior to rendering judgment. On the other hand, the judiciary might take jurisdiction over the case, despite the existence of a valid arbitration clause binding the parties, out of concern that the arbitrators would not properly apply the correct legal rules. This situation would, in particular, arise in a case where the parties agreed that the arbitration proceedings would be held outside Saudi Arabia. The taking of jurisdiction in such a case could be predicated upon the pleadings of a Muslim party that he distrusted arbitration performed outside the Kingdom by nonMuslims. This defense could be sustained even though the outside arbitrators were to be Muslim. However, the judiciary would be

---

[17] *Cf.* Implementing Rules, art. 8 (providing procedures for obtaining of President of Council of Ministers approval by government entities) (also permitting prior approval of arbitration clause in a specific contract). *See also* Minister of Fin. & Nat'l Econ. Letter No. 4307/403 (28/8/1403) (implementing article 3 of Regulations) (instructing administrative authorities not to include arbitration clauses in contracts without approval of President of Council of Ministers).

more inclined to uphold arbitration clauses where the arbitration proceedings were to be held within Saudi Arabia, since Saudi safeguards would be available to disputants within the Kingdom. This same defense was available to Saudi companies, even those with substantial foreign participation. In deciding whether to take jurisdiction of a case, the court would examine the language of the arbitration clause. If such clause provided that arbitration would be binding and enforceable on both parties, the court would be more likely not to take jurisdiction than in the absence of such language. In contrast, the court was not required to enforce contractual provisions stating that arbitration would be the exclusive means of resolving disputes between the parties,[18] even though it could take into consideration the principle of Islamic law that parties are bound by the terms of their agreements. However, as a matter of practice, most parties were said to comply with the terms of arbitration clauses for the reason that their business credibility within the community would be adversely affected by a refusal to execute the terms of their agreement.

Arbitration Regulations

Article 7 represents a significant departure from prior law. It provides that "if the disputing parties had agreed on arbitration before the dispute arose or if a decision approving the arbitration document has been issued in a specific dispute, the subject of the dispute may not be heard except in accordance with the provisions of these Regulations."[19] Consequently, if the appropriate judicial authority has duly approved the arbitration document, an agreement to arbitrate will be enforceable and may be submitted by a party seeking to stay judicial proceedings brought by another party with respect to the same dispute. Conversely, even if the parties have entered into a valid arbitration agreement, until judicial approval of the arbitration document, either party may commence judicial proceedings, and the court or judicial commission will not be required to decline jurisdiction under article 7. It should be noted that, although article 7 does not expressly condition the enforceability of an arbitration clause on judicial approval, the parties are nonetheless required under article 5 to deposit the "arbitration document."[20]

---

[18] *Cf.* Judicial Regs., Royal Decree No. M/64, art. 32 (1975), *as amended by* Royal Decrees No. M/6 (14/10/1395), No. M/15 (3/4/1397), No. M/4 (1/3/1401), & No. M/3 (1/4/1404) (sharī'ah courts have jurisdiction over all disputes except those excepted by regulation).

[19] The interpretation of article 7 is facilitated by consulting the prior draft of that article, which contained the phrase "by the courts or judicial commissions" following "heard." It may also be noted that the phrase "unless the parties agree otherwise", found at the end of the draft of article 7, does not appear in the article as issued.

[20] Arts. 5 and 6 provide for deposition and court approval of the arbitration document, or terms of reference. *See generally* pp. 161–62 *infra*.

B. ARBITRATORS

1. Qualifications

Article 4 of the Regulations provides that an "arbitrator shall be experienced, of good conduct and behavior and of full capacity."[21] Arbitrators must be Muslim but are not required to be Saudi nationals.[22] They may or may not be members of the liberal professions.[23] Public officials are permitted to act as arbitrators on approval of the government authority in which they hold office.[24] The word "experienced" as appearing in article 4 has not been officially interpreted. However, it may be noted that prior drafts of the Regulations contained the phrase "experienced in the subject of the dispute", which was interpreted to require the requisite level of technical or specialized expertise in the arbitrators with respect to the specific nature of the issue. In view of the omission of the words "in the subject of the dispute" from the Regulations as issued, it is considered that general experience is the quality required and that, should questions requiring technical knowledge arise, the arbitrator(s) will appoint experts accordingly.[25] The phrase "of good conduct and behavior" is elucidated by article 4 of the Implementing Rules, which disqualifies persons convicted of offenses against honor or discharged from public office pursuant to a disciplinary decision and adjudged bankrupts from acting as arbitrators. The Islamic law requirement of impartiality of arbitrators is included in article 4 of the Implementing Rules, which bars an arbitrator from having an interest in the dispute.

2. Number

Article 4 of the Regulations provides that "if there is more than one arbitrator, their number shall be uneven."[26] This rule formalizes prior practice, according to which, although no specific number of arbitrators was required by law,[27] parties tended to select panels of uneven number,

---

[21] The Implementing Rules provide for the preparation of a list of qualified arbitrators by agreement of the Minister of Justice, the Minister of Commerce, and the Chairman of the Board of Grievances to be notified to the courts, judicial commissions, and Chambers of Commerce and Industry. Parties are free to select arbitrators from such list or otherwise: Implementing Rules, art. 5.

[22] *Id.* art. 3.

[23] *Id.*

[24] *Id.*

[25] *See generally id.* art. 33 (relating to experts).

[26] *See also id.* art. 3 (if there is more than one arbitrator, the Chairman must be knowledgeable in sharīʿah rules, commercial regulations, practice and custom in the Kingdom).

[27] *See, e.g.,* Commercial Court Regs., arts. 493, 497 (permitting one or more arbitrators) (repealed 1983).

generally three, to issue awards by majority, in order to avoid a deadlock.[28] Within this general framework, the parties are free to select a mutually agreeable number, and, in case of judicial appointment, the agreed number will be respected.[29] Voting is governed by article 16, which provides that the arbitrators' decision shall be by majority voice[30] except in the case of amiable compositeur/conciliation, where unanimity is required.

3. Appointment

Party appointment

The Regulations do not provide procedures for party appointment of arbitrators. However, article 5, relating to deposition of the arbitration document with the judicial authority originally having jurisdiction over the dispute, indicates that the arbitrators will have been appointed prior to such deposition, inasmuch as the arbitration document must, *inter alia*, state the names of the arbitrators and include their acceptance of their mission.[31] Additionally, article 12 refers to formal notifications to be made by the parties to one another of the arbitrators they have respectively appointed. Consequently, where more than one arbitrator is to be appointed, the normal procedure will be for the parties to notify one another of their respective arbitrators and for the latter to consent to arbitrate the dispute. The appointment of the arbitrators should be deemed final upon deposition of the arbitration document with, and confirmation by, the appropriate judicial authority.[32]

Court appointment

Article 10 sets forth procedures for court appointment of arbitrators. It provides

> [i]f the parties fail to appoint the arbitrators or one of the parties fails to appoint the arbitrator or arbitrators he is unilaterally to choose or one or more of the arbitrators refuses to act or resigns or is prevented from undertaking the arbitration or is dismissed, and there is no

[28] *See generally* section V *infra*.

[29] *See* Arbitration Regs., art. 10.

[30] *Cf.* Implementing Rules, art. 41.

[31] *Cf. id.* art. 6 (arbitrator(s) to be appointed by agreement of the parties in the arbitration document).

[32] According to the Ḥanbalī school of Islamic law, the authority of an arbitrator is analogized to that of an agent and may be revoked at any time prior to the commencement of the issuance of the arbitral award. *See, e.g.,* 6 M. AL-BAHŪTĪ, *supra* note 9, at 309. Hence, judicial confirmation is required to render the arbitrator's authority irrevocable by one of the parties. *Cf.* Commercial Court Regs., art. 496 (party may not dismiss arbitrator after confirmation by court whether before or after award issues but is limited to objecting to award) (repealed 1983).

applicable provision [between]33 the parties, the authority originally [having jurisdiction]34 over the dispute shall appoint the requisite arbitrator(s) upon application of the party interested in expediting [the proceedings] in the presence of the other party or in his absence after summoning him to a session to be held for this purpose. The number of arbitrators appointed shall be equal or complementary to the number agreed between the parties. The decision in this respect shall be final.

4. Challenges and removal

Articles 11–12 apply to the disqualification of arbitrators. The parties are permitted to dismiss an arbitrator by mutual consent. In this case, the arbitrator is entitled to compensation if he has begun his duties and his actions were not the reason for his removal.35 Article 11 also provides that an arbitrator may not be disqualified "except for reasons occurring or appearing after deposition of the arbitration document." It will be noted that the determinative date is the date of deposition and not of court approval.

Article 12 provides

[t]he disqualification of an arbitrator may be requested for the same reasons as the disqualification of a judge. The request for disqualification shall be submitted to the authority originally having jurisdiction over the dispute within five days of the day of notification of the opposing party of appointment of the arbitrator or of the day of the appearance or occurrence of the reason for disqualification. The request for disqualification shall be decided after summoning the parties and the arbitrator whose disqualification is requested to a hearing held for this purpose.

5. Fees

The parties are free to determine the fees of the arbitrator(s) by mutual agreement. Article 22 provides

[t]he arbitrators' fees shall be determined by agreement of the parties. Unpaid amounts thereof shall be deposited with the authority originally having jurisdiction over the dispute within five days from the issuance of the decision approving the arbitration document and shall be paid within one week from the date of issuance of the execution order of the award.

33 The word "between" is found in a preliminary draft.
34 The words "having jurisdiction", absent from the text of art. 10 as published in the official journal, is found in a preliminary draft.
35 Arbitration Regs., art. 11.

Article 23 provides that, if the parties have not agreed on the arbitrators' fees, in the event of a dispute on this issue, the dispute will be decided by the authority originally having jurisdiction over the dispute. Such a decision is final.[36]

C. PLACE OF ARBITRATION

Arbitration Regulations

The Regulations do not explicitly distinguish between Saudi and foreign arbitrations. They also are silent on the issue of whether the arbitration proceedings must be held within Saudi Arabia in order for the parties to be able to obtain a stay of judicial proceedings or to obtain enforcement of the award under the Regulations. However, the general principle has been expressed that, if the arbitration proceedings are carried out in accordance with the procedural formalities provided in the Regulations and the Implementing Rules and Saudi law is applied in the proceedings, the parties would be permitted to hold the arbitration proceedings in a place of mutual convenience outside the Kingdom and to obtain an award enforceable under the Regulations. Such a view is supported by the fact that neither the Regulations nor the Implementing Rules expressly exclude arbitrations held outside the Kingdom from their scope.

Registered agreements

The parties' freedom to provide for a nonSaudi arbitration situs is restricted with respect to certain agreements required to be registered with the Ministry of Commerce. In 1979, the Ministry of Commerce issued a circular directing all branches of the Ministry and the Office of the Commercial Register in Riyadh not to approve or register any articles of association of Saudi companies containing a clause providing for the resolution of disputes between the partners or between the partners and the company by means of arbitration held outside of the Kingdom.[37] Moreover, in order to secure Ministry of Commerce approval, an arbitration clause included in the articles of association of companies should preferably provide that the place of arbitration will be within Saudi Arabia. Some companies have obtained Ministry of Commerce approval of a clause in their articles of association providing simply that disputes shall be resolved

---

[36] *See also* Implementing Rules, arts. 45–46 (if no party has prevailed on all claims, the authority having original jurisdiction may apportion the fees between them or require payment of all fees by one party) (assessment appealable to same authority within eight days of notification to party).

[37] Deputy Minister of Commerce Circular No. 3/9/sh/331/9/2903 (13/3/1399) (translated in Appendix 32).

by means of an arbitration agreement which the parties shall sign to that end."[38]

The 1979 circular does not by its terms apply to commercial agency agreements. However, practitioners take the view that an agency agreement may not provide for arbitration to be held outside of the Kingdom, because the Ministry of Commerce in practice applies the circular to all agreements submitted to it for registration. Commercial agency agreements are among those required to be submitted; if such agreements provide for foreign arbitration, registration will be denied.[39]

D. PROCEDURE

1. Judicial approval of arbitration document

Whether the parties are proceeding to arbitration on the basis of an arbitration clause or a submission agreement, an "arbitration document", or terms of reference, must be submitted for approval to the judicial authority having original jurisdiction over the dispute.[40] Article 5 provides

> [t]he parties to the dispute shall deposit the arbitration document with the authority originally having jurisdiction over the dispute. This document shall be signed by the parties or their official authorized representatives and by the arbitrators and shall state the subject of the dispute, the names of the parties, the names of the arbitrators, and their consent to hear the dispute. Copies of documents relating to the dispute shall be attached thereto.

The arbitration document is required to be in Arabic. It is not required to be notarized, authenticated, or witnessed, although any of these formalities may serve to forestall disputes relating to the authenticity of the document.[41] In addition to the mandatory items stated in article 5, the parties are free to include other terms. In particular, they should specify

---

[38] Articles of Association, Umm al-Qurā, Aug. 3, 1979.

[39] *Cf.* Ministry of Commerce Model Agency or Distribution Agreement, art. 16 (providing for arbitration by a "local" committee) (translated in Appendix 2); *Changes in law said significant*, Saudi Gazette, April 27, 1985. In practice, the Ministry of Commerce has also refused to accept services agency agreements containing clauses providing for nonSaudi arbitration when submitted with a nonSaudi contractor's application for a temporary license. *See generally* pp. 58–59 *supra.*

[40] For jurisdiction of the courts and other adjudicative bodies, see generally pp. 203–07, 222–27 *infra.*

[41] Although not specifically provided, the requirement of the use of Arabic is derived from the fact that only Arabic documents may be submitted to a court. *Cf.* Commercial Court Regs., art. 485 (written pleadings to be in Arabic). However, art. 493 of the Commercial Court Regs., requiring notarization of arbitration documents, has been repealed. Nonetheless, if the agreement containing the arbitration clause is subject to notarization, the clause must also be notarized.

the time period within which the arbitrators are to issue their award.[42] Article 6 provides that "the authority originally having jurisdiction over the dispute shall record the requests for arbitration submitted to it and shall issue a decision approving the arbitration document." The requirement of judicial approval is viewed as procedural and intended to avoid the eventuality of disputes between the parties as to the substance of their agreement. Hence, unless the provisions of the arbitration document are contrary to Saudi law or public policy, approval should not normally be withheld. The competent judicial authority is to issue its decision approving the arbitration document within fifteen days.[43]

Specific legal consequences flow from the issuance of the judicial approval decision. Most important, article 7 provides that, upon issuance of such a decision in the case of an arbitration agreement relating to a specific existing dispute, the authority having jurisdiction over the dispute may only hear the subject of the dispute in accordance with the provisions of the Regulations. However, the Regulations contain no formal procedures for obtaining a stay of judicial proceedings and do not address the case where one party commences a judicial action prior to submission of the request for arbitration. All fees as yet unpaid to the arbitrators are to be deposited with the authority having original jurisdiction within five days of approval of the arbitration document.[44] If the parties have not set a time limit for issuance of the award, the regulatory period will begin to run from the date of approval of the arbitration document.[45]

2. Time period for issuance of award

Article 9 of the Regulations provides

> [t]he award in the dispute shall be made on the date set in the arbitration document unless it is agreed to extend it. If the parties have not set a period for [issuance of] the award in the arbitration document, the arbitrators shall issue their award within ninety days of the date of issuance of the decision approving the arbitration document. Otherwise, any of the parties so desiring may refer the matter to the authority originally having jurisdiction over the dispute to decide whether to hear the subject or to extend the time limit for another period.

---

[42] If no time is set, the proceedings will be subject to the time provisions of art. 9.

[43] Implementing Rules, art. 7. Arbitrators and parties are to receive notice thereof within one week of the issuance of the decision. *Id.* art. 16.

[44] Arbitration Regs., art. 22.

[45] *Id.* art. 9.

Thus the parties are given the right to specify the period of arbitration in the initial document and also to extend it by mutual agreement. In addition, either party-determined or regulatory time limits may be extended under certain circumstances. If an arbitrator is appointed to replace a removed or resigning arbitrator, the period for issuance of the award is extended by thirty days.[46] In the event of the death of one of the parties, the arbitration continues, and the period is extended for thirty days, unless the arbitrators decide to extend it for a longer period.[47] Finally, article 15 provides that the arbitrators, by the same majority required to issue an award, may in a reasoned decision extend the time limit for rendering the award due to circumstances relating to the subject of the dispute.

3. Applicable law

The Arbitration Regulations are silent on the issue of the law applicable in the arbitration proceedings.[48] However, article 39 of the Implementing Rules requires awards to be issued in accordance with Islamic law and applicable regulations.

4. Rules of procedure and evidence

The Implementing Rules set forth the procedures to be followed in the arbitration proceedings. Article 39 provides that the arbitrators, in issuing awards, are not bound by regulatory procedures with the exception of those provided in the Regulations and the Implementing Rules. Article 36 generally requires the arbitrators to comply with Islamic litigation principles such as a party's right to confront the opposing party, to present its arguments, defenses and documents, and to examine documents relating to the case. Article 27 provides for the establishment of a record by the arbitral tribunal and specifies the formal requirements thereof.

Notices

All notices specified in the Regulations are required to be effected by the clerk of the judicial authority having original jurisdiction over the dispute.[49] Notices must be in Arabic and contain certain particulars.[50]

[46] Arbitration Regs., art. 14.
[47] *Id.* art. 13.
[48] *But see id.* art. 20 (conditioning enforcement order on absence of elements contrary to Islamic law).
[49] *Id.* art. 8; Implementing Rules, art. 9.
[50] Implementing Rules, art. 12. For the manner of service of notices, *see generally id.* arts. 11, 13–15.

Conduct of proceedings

Within five days of receipt of notification of the judicial decision approving the arbitration document, the arbitrators are to fix the date of the session and notify the parties thereof."[51] Sessions are public but may be held privately if the arbitrators so determine, either *sua sponte* or on a party's request.[52] The arbitrators are empowered to fix the time periods for the submission of the parties' oral and written arguments.[53] Parties are entitled to be represented by an attorney. However, the arbitrators may require a party's personal appearance if the circumstances so require.[54] The proceedings are directed by the chairman of the arbitral tribunal, who may question parties and witnesses on his own initiative or pursuant to the request of the other arbitrators or the parties.[55] The proceedings are required to be conducted in Arabic. Persons not speaking Arabic must be accompanied by an accredited interpreter.[56] The defendant is entitled to present his oral arguments last.[57] If, during the proceedings, an issue that is outside the arbitrators' competence arises, documents are attacked on the grounds of falsification or criminal proceedings are instigated with respect to the case, the arbitrators are required to stay the arbitration proceedings until a final judgment is rendered by the authority having jurisdiction over the matter.[58]

Evidence

Article 31 of the Implementing Rules subjects the admissibility and receipt of oral testimony to Islamic rules. Parties are permitted to introduce both oral and documentary evidence.[59] The arbitrators may, *sua sponte* or on a party's request, require parties to produce documentary evidence in their possession in certain cases.[60] Parties are entitled to request one or more adjournments for a reasonable period as determined by the arbitrators in order to produce documents.[61] The arbitrators are empowered to order independent investigations[62] and to conduct on-site inspections.[63] They are also authorized to appoint one or more experts to report on technical or

[51] *Id.* art. 10. The date may be extended for reasons of the parties. *See id.* art. 21.
[52] *Id.* art. 20.
[53] *Id.* art. 22.
[54] *Id.* art. 17.
[55] *See id.* arts. 23, 32.
[56] *Id.* art. 25.
[57] *Id.* art. 22.
[58] *Id.* art. 37.
[59] *Cf. id.* art. 31 (governing introduction of party witnesses).
[60] *See id.* art. 28.
[61] *Id.* art. 26.
[62] *Id.* art. 29.
[63] *Id.* art. 35.

other matters and to set such experts' fees and determine which party will bear them.[64] Parties may submit advisory reports on the issues.[65]

E. AWARD

When the case is ripe for decision, the arbitrators are to hold their deliberations in private.[66] A party is not permitted to submit oral explanations except in the presence of the opposing party, nor may the arbitrators receive memorials or documents from a party unless shown to the other party.[67] Interim settlements or other agreed-on statements of the parties may also be issued in the form of an award at any stage of the proceedings.[68]

1. Formal requirements

The award is required to be reasoned, in writing, and in Arabic. Article 17 of the Regulations provides

> [t]he award document shall include in particular the arbitration document, a summary of the oral statements and documents of the parties, the reasons and text of the award, the date of its issuance, and the signatures of the arbitrators. If one or more of them refuse to sign the award, that shall be stated in the award document.[69]

The arbitrators are permitted to correct technical errors on the face of the award.[70] Parties may request the arbitrators to clarify ambiguities in the original award by means of a supplementary explanatory award.[71]

2. Deposition and notification

Article 18 provides that "all awards issued by the arbitrators even if issued in an investigation procedure shall be deposited within five days with the authority originally having jurisdiction over the dispute and copies thereof shall be transmitted to the parties." This provision applies both to final awards and to interim awards or decisions, such as the appointment of experts by the arbitrators and the like.[72]

---

[64] *Id.* art. 33.
[65] *Id.* art. 34.
[66] *Id.* art. 38.
[67] *Id.* art. 40.
[68] *Id.* art. 24.
[69] *Cf. id.* art. 41 (requiring inclusion of additional data).
[70] *Id.* art. 42.
[71] *Id.* art. 43.
[72] *See also id.* art. 41 (providing for seven-day period from deposition of draft).

3. Objections and appeals

Limitation period

Article 18 of the Regulations permits the parties to submit their objections to the award to the authority with which the award was deposited within fifteen days from the date of their notification of the award. This rule also applies to explanatory awards[73] and to appeals from an award correcting the original award on the grounds that the arbitrators exceeded their authority.[74] Failing timely objection, the award becomes final.[75]

4. Judicial decision

Article 19 provides

> [i]f one or more of the parties submit(s) an objection to the arbitrators' award within the period provided in the preceding article, the authority originally having jurisdiction over the dispute shall hear the objection and decide either to reject it and issue an order for execution of the award or to accept the objection and make a decision thereon.

Neither the Regulations nor the Implementing Rules provide general grounds for objection. In addition to the grounds of illegality or violation of public policy, which would permit the judicial authority to refuse to enforce an award under article 20, the parties are not barred from raising objections based on lack of a valid arbitration clause or agreement, procedural defects or the arbitrators' lack of impartiality, abuse of their authority or exceeding their authority as stated in the judicially approved arbitration document.

F. JUDICIAL REVIEW AND ENFORCEMENT

1. Prior to Arbitration Regulations

Under prior law, domestic arbitral awards were not automatically enforceable, nor did they benefit from any expedited enforcement procedures. Without a court order, the executive arm of the Government will not enforce an arbitral award. If a party thus declined to comply

---

[73] *Id.* art. 43.

[74] *Id.* art. 42. The arbitrators' refusal to correct errors on the face of an award is non-appealable. *Id.*

[75] Although final, in the sense that objections are barred after the period has run, the award is not enforceable until a judicial enforcement order is issued. *See generally* pp. 166–67 *infra.*

voluntarily with the terms of an award, the party seeking execution could appeal to the regional governor, who would then refer the case to the appropriate judicial body for review.[76] In the case of commercial arbitrations, this body was generally the Commission for the Settlement of Commercial Disputes, which had the discretion either to determine from the face of the award whether it deviated from the provisions of the terms of reference and from applicable rules of law or to rehear the entire case on the merits, including full pleadings and receiving of evidence.[77] Under general principles of Islamic law, the Commission for the Settlement of Commercial Disputes could enforce awards resolving commercial disputes between private parties so long as such awards did not conflict with rules of Saudi law or public policy. An award, for example, providing for the payment of interest would not be enforced. Generally, such an illegal provision would be separable and would not render the rest of the award void. The Commission in deciding whether to enforce an award was entitled to take into account the fact that the arbitration clause engendering such award provided that the award would be final and binding on both parties. However, it was not required to uphold contractual agreements denying the parties the right to appeal the arbitral award, although it could in its discretion take the existence of such an ineffective agreement into consideration. However, the Commission was also free in these cases to reopen and hear the case on the merits. The same principle also applied to appeals taken to the Board of Grievances, where a government body had lawfully agreed on arbitration as a means of resolving disputes between itself and a private party. Consequently, it was said that arbitral awards had a persuasive value only. However, even though arbitral awards were not automatically enforceable, parties might opt for arbitration for the reason that judicial review of the award would take a substantially shorter time than the full litigation process. It was estimated that such review would be completed within six months, while a court action might continue for two or three years.

2. Arbitration Regulations

Arbitral awards become "final" and enforceable by the executive arm on issuance of an enforcement order by the appropriate judicial authority. Article 20 of the Regulations provides that "the arbitrators' award shall be enforceable when it becomes final by means of an order from the authority

---

[76] *See* Rules Governing New Powers of Regional Governors, Minister of the Interior Resolution, para. 2(1), Umm al-Qurā, 5/5/1395 (resolution unnumbered) (governors may hear any private right complaint).
[77] *See* Commercial Court Regs., art. 495 (court to confirm and execute awards in conformity with Islamic law and submission) (repealed 1983).

167

originally having jurisdiction over the dispute. Such order shall be issued upon the request of an interested party after ascertaining the absence of any legal bar to its execution."

In order to be enforceable, all awards are subject to the process of judicial review in order to ascertain whether the award is fully consistent with Saudi law and public policy. Upon issuance of the judicial enforcement order, the award is deemed to have the force of a judicial decision issued by the authority which issued the enforcement order.[78] Consequently, an award, although "final" under article 20, will be appealable to the extent that the decisions of the judicial authority issuing the enforcement order may be appealed.

II. International Agreements

A. ARAB LEAGUE ARBITRAL AWARDS

Saudi Arabia is a party to the Agreement on the Reciprocal Enforcement of Judgments among the Members of the League of Arab States.[79] Article 3 of the Agreement applies to the enforcement of arbitral awards rendered within the territories of member States in the other States parties to the Agreement. Under article 3, courts of the State where enforcement is sought are required to enforce such awards and are generally barred from reexamining the subject matter of the controversy underlying such awards.[80]

However, article 3 of the Agreement also provides certain exceptions permitting refusal to enforce an Arab League award, namely

    (a) If the laws of the State requested to enforce the award do not permit the settlement of the subject-matter of the dispute by way of arbitration.

---

[78] Arbitration Regs., art. 21. For text of legend to be inscribed on the original enforcement order delivered to the prevailing party, see Implementing Rules, art. 44.

[79] Agreement on the Reciprocal Enforcement of Judgments, *opened for signature* Nov. 10, 1952, 159 British & Foreign State Papers 616 (English translation). The Agreement does not apply to judgments rendered against the Governments of the States in which enforcement is sought or officials thereof in respect of their official duties. *Id.* art. 4. In addition, disputes arising with respect to Arab League "investments" may be settled by arbitration. *See* Unified Agreement on the Investment of Arab Capital among Arab League States Parties, arts. 25-27, *approved by* Royal Decree No. M/7 (11/4/1401). *See also* Agreement on Judicial Cooperation, April 4, 1983, art. 37 (signed by Arab League States in Riyadh) (relating to enforcement of arbitral awards).

[80] In view of the reference in art. 3 to art. 1 of the Agreement, providing for the enforcement of "final" judgments, an award whose enforcement is sought will be required to have the status of a final judgment in order to benefit from the Agreement. However, Arab League final judgments on arbitral awards rendered in other jurisdictions may also benefit from the provisions of the Agreement.

(b) If the arbitral award was not given pursuant to a valid stipulation or agreement for arbitration.

(c) If the arbitrators had no jurisdiction in accordance with the agreement or stipulation for arbitration or in accordance with the provisions of the law under which the arbitral award was made.

(d) If the parties were not properly notified.

(e) If the arbitral award includes anything contrary to public policy or the general principles of morality in the State where enforcement is sought. Such State is competent to decide the issue and to refrain from enforcing anything in the award which may be contrary to public policy or the general principles of morality.[81]

(f) If the arbitral award is not final in the State in which it was made.

The Board of Grievances is the authority in Saudi Arabia having jurisdiction to enforce foreign judgments, including judgments on arbitral awards.[82]

B. INTERNATIONAL CENTRE FOR THE SETTLEMENT OF INVESTMENT DISPUTES ["ICSID"]

1. Saudi reservation

Saudi Arabia is a party to the Washington Convention on the Settlement of Investment Disputes between States and Nationals of Other States (ICSID Convention),[83] providing for conciliation and arbitration as a means of binding resolution of investment disputes between states who are parties to the Convention ("Contracting States") or their constituent subdivisions or agencies on the one hand and nationals of other Contracting States. In its ratification instrument, the Kingdom "reserve[d] the right of not submitting all questions pertaining to oil and pertaining to acts of sovereignty to the International Centre for the Settlement of Commercial Disputes whether by way of conciliation or arbitration."[84] No official

---

[81] *Cf.* Agreement on the Reciprocal Enforcement of Judgments, art. 2(c) (also permitting nonenforcement of judgments repugnant to universal international rules).

[82] Board of Grievances Regs., Royal Decree No. M/51, art. 8(g) (1982). *See generally* pp. 235, 242 *infra.*

[83] Convention on the Settlement of Investment Disputes between States and Nationals of Other States ["ICSID Convention"], *entered into force* Oct. 14, 1966, 17 U.S.T. 1270, T.I.A.S. No. 6090, 575 U.N.T.S. 159.

[84] Saudi Ratification of ICSID Convention (deposited May 8, 1980) (entered into force in Saudi Arabia June 7, 1980). The reservation provides

AFTER reviewing the Convention on the Settlement of Investment Disputes between States and Nationals of Other States, emanating from the International Bank for Reconstruction and Development, which had been approved by the Council of Ministers

interpretation of the reservation has been made.[85] The phrase "acts of sovereignty" has been interpreted to refer to those discretionary executive actions which are not subject to judicial review, corresponding to the French concept of "actes de gouvernement."[86] In the absence of official guidance or an authoritative ruling on the issue, two constructions of the phrase 'pertaining to oil' have emerged within the Saudi legal community.

According to the majority view, questions pertaining to oil would relate solely to crude oil. Support for this view may be found in the Saudi tax law, which distinguishes for taxation purposes between companies engaged in the production of hydrocarbons and those engaged in all other activities.[87] Petrochemicals are not taxed at the higher rate applicable to hydrocarbons.[88]

by its Resolution No. (372) on 15/3/1394 A.H. and enacted by the Royal Decree No. (M/8) on 22/3/1394 and signed on 7/11/1399 A.H. corresponding to 28/9/1979 A.D.

AND AFTER scrutinizing the aforementioned Convention we have found it acceptable and have approved it in its entirety, be it confirmed (however) that the Kingdom reserves the right of not submitting all questions pertaining to oil and pertaining to acts of sovereignty to the International Centre for the Settlement of Investment Disputes whether by way of conciliation or arbitration.

WE HEREBY declare that we have ratified and concluded the Convention and we undertake, with the will of God, to carry out what is stipulated therein in all good faith.

Doc. ICSID/8-C, at 2–3 (1984). The Saudi reservation was made pursuant to art. 25(4) of the Convention, which provides

[a]ny Contracting State may, at the time of ratification, acceptance or approval of this Convention or at any time thereafter, notify the Centre of the class or classes of disputes which it would or would not consider submitting to the jurisdiction of the Centre.

It may be noted that the Saudi instrument is expressed as a reservation, rather than a notification as provided in article 25(4). The legal effectiveness of the Saudi ratification within Saudi Arabia has been questioned on the grounds that it was not published in Umm al-Qurā. Saudi law would require publication of such a legal instrument in order to serve the function of notice. Publication is said to be a prerequisite to the effective entry of any act into the Saudi legal system. *See, e.g.,* A. AL-ḤANFĀWĪ, SṢŪL AL-TASHRĪʿ FĪ AL-MAMLAKAH AL-ʿARABIYYAH AL SUʿŪDIYYAH 119 (undated). However, many Saudi legal acts which have not been published are nonetheless legally effective. Furthermore, many Saudi acts provide by their own terms that they shall not enter into effect until publication. The Saudi ratification of ICSID contains no such qualification. *See also* Royal Decree No. M/8 (23/3/1394) (approving signature of ICSID Convention).

[85] *See also* Delaume, *ICSID Arbitration and the Courts,* 77 AM. J. INT'L L. 784, 796 (finding the language of these declarations to be "broad"; interpretation of same within exclusive jurisdiction of ICSID) (1983). Pursuant to article 41 of the ICSID Convention, an Arbitral Tribunal would have jurisdiction to decide whether a given dispute were covered by the reservation.

[86] *Cf.* Board of Grievances Regs., Royal Decree No. M/51, art. 9 (1982) (no jurisdiction in Board over acts of sovereignty).

[87] *See* Royal Decree No. 7634 (12/26/1950) (imposing additional income tax on companies engaged in the *production* of petroleum or other hydrocarbons) (emphasis added). The tax rate on such companies is 85 percent of net operating income, as compared to a maximum rate of 45 percent of profits imposed on other companies. Royal Decree No. M/19 (9/2/1970).

[88] Additional support for this position may be derived from the fact that some Islamic law jurists would exclude minerals from the scope of private ownership, an exclusion inapplicable

The tax distinction is, of course, not dispositive of the interpretation of the ICSID reservation. Under the second view, the reservation not only encompasses questions pertaining to crude oil but extends to petrochemicals and related industries as well.[89] This theory holds that the domestic tax distinction will not be carried over into the context of international arbitration. Practically speaking, the exact scope of the reservation may not prove to be of extreme importance, in that ICSID has jurisdiction only over those legal disputes which the parties have consented in writing to submit to ICSID.[90] According to official sources, it is unlikely that the Saudi party would agree to such an arbitration clause in a contract relating to petrochemicals.[91] Furthermore, in order for ICSID to have jurisdiction over a dispute under the Convention the dispute must arise "directly" out of an investment.[92]

2. "Nationals" eligible for ICSID arbitration

With respect to jurisdiction *rationae personae*, article 25 of the Convention provides that ICSID's jurisdiction extends to disputes between a Contracting State, or one of its duly designated constituent subdivisions or agencies,

to chemicals. *See* A. Z. Yamani, Islamic Law and Contemporary Issues, Address delivered at Seminar on "Man and God" at the American University of Beirut, 23–24 (2/7/1967).

[89] *See also* Regs. for Commercial Companies Working in the Field of Petroleum, Royal Decree No. M/1, art. 1(c) (1969) (defining "hydrocarbons" to include crude oil, refined products, natural gas and its derivatives, and secondary products related to the production and manufacture of the preceding).

[90] *See* ICSID Convention, art. 25(1). However, in the case of submission of a dispute to ICSID which might appear covered by one of the relevant Saudi reservations, the Secretary-General would be unable to register the dispute if it were obviously oil-related and, in a borderline case, would request confirmation or clarification from the Saudi Government prior to registration. *See*, *e.g.*, Delaume, *supra* note 85, at 790 n. 21. Consequently, if the parties desire to refer to ICSID a dispute which could be construed to fall within the scope of the reservations, it is recommended to phrase the arbitration clause and/or the relevant consents to indicate that the dispute is intended to be within the jurisdiction of ICSID notwithstanding the Saudi reservation.

[91] Additionally, in the case of a constituent subdivision or agency, approval of the Government would also be required, unless the Government notifies ICSID that no such approval is required. ICSID Convention, art. 25(3).

[92] *Id.* art. 25(1). The term "investment" is not defined in the Convention or defined or interpreted by Saudi domestic legislative or administrative acts. That the term, as intended by the drafters, encompasses more than "those disputes arising out of host government undertakings pursuant to investment promotion laws" is suggested by the history of the Convention. *See*, *e.g.*, Broches, *The Convention on the Settlement of Investment Disputes between States and Nationals of Other States*, 136 Recueil des cours de l'Académie de droit international, 331, 362–63 & n. 21 (1972) (discussing drafters' solution of adopting flexible jurisdictional limits subject to parties' consent on a case-by-case basis). Thus, despite ICSID's adoption of a "modern notion of investment", *see* Delaume, *supra* note 85, at 795 & n. 40, extending to any significant contributions to the development of the Contracting State, provided the parties so agree, it should be noted that Saudi authorities have unofficially expressed the view that public sector contracts will not as a rule be considered to involve "investments" by the foreign party.

and a national of another Contracting State.[93] With respect to juristic persons, a "national" is defined as

> any juridical person which had the nationality of a Contracting State other than the State party to the dispute on the date on which the parties consented to submit such dispute to conciliation or arbitration and any juridical person which had the nationality of the Contracting State party to the dispute on that date and which, because of foreign control, the parties have agreed should be treated as a national of another Contracting State for the purposes of this Convention.[94]

The question whether a government party is a subdivision or agency of a Contracting State, in this case Saudi Arabia, should "normally not be difficult to determine",[95] since article 25(a) requires that Contracting States designate their constituent subdivisions or agencies to ICSID.[96] Such a notification will "presumably" be proof of their status as subdivision or agency.[97] With respect to the nationality of the private party, it has been suggested that the definition of article 25(2)(b) is broad enough to extend to arbitration between the Saudi Government or one of its subdivisions or agencies and "the typical foreign investment arrangement in the Kingdom—the joint venture company with majority Saudi financial interest."[98] According to this view, a Saudi limited liability company having entered into an investment agreement with the Saudi Government would also qualify for ICSID arbitration if the company's "management is substantially foreign-controlled."[99] This view is not supported by Saudi legal thought. The Saudi interpretation of "foreign control" gives the term the meaning of equity participation. Practically speaking, even in cases involving majority foreign participation, it is improbable that the Saudi Government will agree to treat a Saudi juristic person as the national of another State. In contrast, a foreign investor entering into a partnership agreement with a Saudi government agency may include, subject to authorization under article 3 of the Arbitration Regulations, in the partnership agreement a clause providing for ICSID arbitration in resolution of any disputes which may arise

---

[93] In addition, disputes in which one of the parties is neither a Contracting State nor a national of a Contracting State may be administered by ICSID in Additional Facility proceedings. *See* ICSID Additional Facility Rules, *approved* by the ICSID Administrative Council, Sept. 27, 1978, art. 2(a), (b), ICSID 12th Annual Report (1977/1978).

[94] ICSID Convention, art. 25(2)(b).

[95] Broches, *supra* note 92, at 354.

[96] As at the end of 1984, Saudi Arabia had not notified ICSID of any constituent subdivision or agency for purposes of ICSID proceedings. *See* DOC. ICSID/8–B.

[97] *See* Broches, *supra* note 92, at 354.

[98] *Saudi Arabia Accedes to International Arbitration*, MID. E. EXEC., REP. 8, 8–9 (Nov. 1979).

[99] *Into ICSID–with Reservations* MID. E. EXEC. REP., 13, 14 (June 1980).

between the partners.[100] Such an arbitration clause is permissible whether or not the foreign partner has management control over the Saudi partnership. For example, a nonSaudi company forming a partnership for investment purposes with Petromin could provide for ICSID arbitration. However, if the new subsidiary subsequently entered into a contract with Petromin or other government agency, any disputes arising out of the agreement would not qualify for ICSID arbitration.

C. OVERSEAS PRIVATE INVESTMENT CORPORATION ["OPIC"]

The Government of Saudi Arabia has agreed to settle by arbitration certain differences and claims relating to the Agreement on Guaranteed Private Investment[101] and guaranties of Saudi public sector contracts and investments to which it applies. Article 1 provides

[i]n order to increase participation by United States private enterprise in projects bringing new technology to Saudi Arabia, persons eligible under applicable United States legislation may be issued guaranties by the United States Government against loss due to specified risks relating to contracts or investments in Saudi Arabia which are approved by the Government of Saudi Arabia (hereinafter, "guaranties"). The Government of the United States of America agrees that a contract or investment shall be deemed approved for purposes of this Agreement only if entered into with the Government of Saudi Arabia, or an agency thereof, or otherwise approved in accordance with the applicable laws and regulations of Saudi Arabia.

If a contract or investment is concluded with the Government or one of its agencies, the Agreement applies automatically, and no provision as to its applicability need be included in the contract underlying the dispute. However, contracts to which a wholly-owned government corporation, which would not automatically fit within the definition of "agency", was a party could fall within the protection of the Agreement if approval were obtained by means of a Council of Ministers resolution, high order, or royal decree. With respect to guaranties issued in accordance with the Agreement, OPIC or any similar public agency of the United States which has made payments pursuant to the guaranties or has received assignments

---

[100] *See generally* pp. 153–55 *supra.*
[101] Feb. 27, 1975, United States–Saudi Arabia, 26 U.S.T. 459, T.I.A.S. No. 8045 (approved by Royal Decree No. M/22 (29/3/1395)); *cf.* Agreement on Legal Protection of Guaranteed Private Investments, Feb. 2, 1980, German Federal Republic, [1980] Bundesgesetzblatt II 693 (W. Ger.).

in connection therewith is recognized as succeeding to the rights of the guaranteed person or firm.[102]

Differences between the parties concerning interpretation of the Agreement are initially to be resolved by negotiations. Failing resolution of the controversy within three months of the request for negotiations, the difference shall be submitted at the request of either Government to an arbitral tribunal.[103] Any claim arising out of a guaranteed contract or investment against either Government which, in the opinion of the other, presents a question of public international law is likewise to be submitted to negotiations. If the claim has not been resolved "by mutual agreement" within three months of the request for negotiations by the Government presenting the claim, the claim, including the question of whether it presents a question of public international law, shall be submitted to an arbitral tribunal.[104] The arbitral tribunal shall consist of two arbitrators, one appointed by each Government, who shall designate a president, who must be a citizen of a third State, to be appointed by the parties.[105]

The arbitrators are required to base their decision on "the applicable principles and rules of public international law."[106] In all matters except for expenses and costs, the arbitrators are free to regulate their procedures.[107] The tribunal's decision is issued by majority vote and is final and binding.[108] It may be observed that arbitration proceedings held pursuant to the Agreement are, since destined to resolve disagreements between sovereign State parties, not in derogation of the Saudi municipal rule of law barring government agencies from entering into arbitration without prior authorization. Only the two Governments are permitted to request arbitration proceedings pursuant to the Agreement and to participate therein.[109] Consequently, the Agreement does not affect the right of Saudi government entities to submit to arbitration with respect to the contracts or investments underlying the guaranties.

III. Cases

A. ARBITRATION TO WHICH A SAUDI GOVERNMENT DEPARTMENT WAS A PARTY

In one dispute involving a foreign contractor and a government department, an arbitral award issued by an *ad hoc* arbitral committee was

[102] Agreement on Guaranteed Private Investment, art. 2.
[103] *Id.* art. 3(a).
[104] *Id.* art. 3(b).
[105] *Id.* art. 3(c)(i). If appointments are not made within the prescribed time limits, either Government may, in the absence of any other agreement, make the necessary appointment(s).
[106] *Id.* art. 3(c)(ii).
[107] *Id.* art. 3(c)(iv).
[108] *Id.* art. 3(c)(ii).
[109] *Id.*

implemented by the Ministry of Finance and National Economy after being approved by the King. The arbitration arose out of a dispute between the parties relating to a claim made by the company for additional costs incurred as a result of unforeseen circumstances, namely, unexpectedly hard soil and a change in customs tariffs. The underlying contract contained an arbitration clause. The arbitral committee applied both Saudi law and principles of natural justice in rendering its decision, and acted in accordance with generally accepted international procedure.[110]

B. PRIVATE PARTY ARBITRATION

Foreign Contractor v. *Saudi Corporation* involved an arbitral award made in 1980 by a sole arbitrator of Saudi nationality sitting in Riyadh. The case included 29 separate disputes between the contractor, who was constructing an office building in Riyadh, and its Saudi corporate owner having substantial government participation. The construction agreement had provided that all disputes were to be brought before the Board of Grievances. This being an improper forum for litigation between private parties, the parties agreed upon final and binding arbitration. After review by the Bureau of Experts in the Council of Ministers, the award was sent to the Office of the President of the Council of Ministers for enforcement.

C. INTERNATIONAL CHAMBER OF COMMERCE ["ICC"] ARBITRATION

Between May 1975 and September 1979, thirteen requests for arbitration arising out of disputes involving Saudi parties were filed with the ICC in Paris.[111] Of these, at least four were settled before an award was issued.[112] Twelve of the cases involved disputes having a substantial nexus with Saudi Arabia, and in all cases the arbitration proceedings were held outside of the Kingdom. Significantly, however, in one case settled in 1979, where both disputing parties were of Saudi nationality, the respondent sought to resist ICC arbitration on grounds of lack of jurisdiction since, under article 1 of its rules, the ICC's function was to resolve disputes of "international

---

[110] *See generally* Hejailan, *supra* note 12, at 169.

[111] No requests were filed prior to this period. Requests filed thereafter were not researched. *But see, e.g., Westland Helicopter Ltd.* v. *Arab Organization for Industrialization, United Arab Emirates, Saudi Arabia, Qatar, Egypt, Arab British Helicopter Co.,* 23 INT'L LEGAL MAT. 1071 (1984) (interim award) (as member and guarantor of obligations of supranational organization, Saudi Arabia was bound by arbitration clause executed thereby, subject to Swiss law).

[112] No information was available concerning the post-September 1979 status of five of the cases, one arbitration was pending in London in 1981.

character." Furthermore, it was argued that, under Saudi law, arbitration is only a voluntary means of settling disputes and may be conducted only if both parties agree to resort to arbitration as the means of settling their disputes. The respondent also maintained that the arbitral award would not be enforceable in Saudi Arabia.[113]

1. Awards

(a) In one 1979 award, the sole arbitrator sitting in London decided the claims of a European firm against Saudi natural persons for decorating work to be performed outside of the Kingdom. The arbitration was held despite the refusal of the Saudi parties to sign the terms of reference. Despite the parties' agreement on choice of law applicable to their contract, the sole arbitrator declined to apply the measure of damages under that law, on the grounds that the arbitration was governed by the procedural law of England. Hence, the measure of damages was to be governed by English law irrespective of the proper law of the underlying contract.

(b) Another 1979 award issued by a committee of three arbitrators sitting in Geneva resolved a dispute in favor of the Saudi applicant arising out of the breach by a European firm of its contract to construct a road in Saudi Arabia. Of the three arbitrators, one was Muslim of nonSaudi nationality; the other two were European. Swiss law was applied, and the arbitrators were also authorized to sit as amiable compositeur. Islamic law was not applied. The award was enforced in the country of its rendering.

(c) In 1979 proceedings held in Paris, the three arbitrators, of European nationalities, found in favor of the applicant, a European subcontractor, against the Saudi contractor. The respondent had argued that Saudi law should be applied under three theories: that the principal contract, of which the subcontract was a part, was entered into by the Saudi Government through one of its ministries; that the subcontract provided for the application of Saudi law; and that all events relating to the subcontract negotiations, performance, and termination had occurred in Saudi Arabia. The arbitrators, however, rejected these arguments and construed the terms of the contract in order to reach an equitable solution. The applicant was awarded damages, in an amount less than the full contract price. The Saudi party was aware that the award could most probably not have been enforced in Saudi Arabia, since none of the arbitrators was Muslim and the arbitrators had sat outside of the Kingdom applying nonSaudi law in the proceedings. However, it chose to pay the award.

---

[113] In 1979, arbitration proceedings in resolution of another dispute arising in Saudi Arabia between the two Saudi parties were commenced in London.

2. Choice of law

Saudi law was not applied in ICC arbitrations during the period through 1979. In one case settled in 1980 between a United States corporation and a Saudi company, the arbitration was scheduled to take place in London, to be conducted in the English language; in their initial determination the arbitrators had decided to apply English law. Again, in a case settled in 1978 involving allegedly defective raw material shipped to the Saudi applicant, the arbitrators determined the choice of law as a preliminary issue before the settlement was reached. Rejecting the contention that Saudi law should be applied, they found the proper law to be that of the State of the seller, which was also the place of shipment.

IV. History of Arbitration Clauses in Articles of Association of Saudi Limited Liability Companies

The following is a historical analysis of the crucial features of arbitration clauses found in articles of association between 1966 and 1980. Emphasis was placed on the place of arbitration and the choice of law.[114] The study did not focus on the number of arbitrators, since the overwhelming majority of arbitration clauses provided for constitution of an arbitration committee composed of three arbitrators, of whom two are selected by the disputing parties, and the umpire by the two arbitrators.

The conclusion, briefly stated, is that there were no significant structural variations between arbitration clauses found in articles of association of juristic entities of one hundred percent Saudi equity participation and those of companies formed with mixed Saudi and foreign capital. However, mixed companies, both on the basis of absolute number and percentage proportion, tended to provide for arbitration in their articles of association more than purely Saudi companies did, despite the fact that in terms of absolute number, more one hundred percent Saudi companies were formed in every year. In connection with this survey, it should be noted that, although a breakdown of Saudi/mixed companies was made, no further breakdown of the percentage of participation of mixed companies was made. Similarly, no analysis was made on the basis of stated capital of the companies surveyed. In addition, the majority of clauses predate the

---

[114] It should be noted that all of the clauses were published prior to the issuance of the Implementing Rules, which require the application of Islamic and Saudi regulatory law.

Ministry of Commerce Circular relating to the inclusion of nonSaudi arbitration clauses in companies articles of association.

The first arbitration clause is dated 1966.[115] It provides that "any dispute arising out of this agreement shall be settled by arbitration or by resort to authorities with jurisdiction in the Ministry of Commerce in the Kingdom of Saudi Arabia in accordance with Saudi commercial regulations and laws." The parties to the agreement were a Saudi natural person, a Lebanese natural person, and a Lebanese juristic person. This is the only disputes clause between private parties for that year.[116]

In 1967, another arbitration clause was found,[117] and in 1968, a third was found, providing for arbitration as a means of dispute resolution between seven Saudi partners.[118] In 1968, eleven articles of association between Saudi parties did not provide for arbitration: ten contained no disputes clause; one provided that the then Ministry of Commerce and Industry should settle the dispute; and two provided that the dispute should be settled in accordance with the Companies Regulations.

In 1969, two arbitration clauses were found. Both provided for arbitration as an alternative to litigation rather than as a substitute. One provided for the application of ICC rules of procedure.[119] In contrast, seven articles of association forming companies with solely Saudi partners contained no disputes clause. The only company formed with a nonSaudi partner provided that disputes should be resolved under Saudi law.

In 1970, the eight articles of association found contained two arbitration clauses. The first provided for a choice of arbitrators from among, in declining order of preference, the partners' agnates, their cognates, and people experienced in resolving disputes.[120] The other clause provided for final and binding arbitration, to be held in Jeddah.[121] Of the five other articles of association between solely Saudi partners, four contained no disputes clause, and one provided for the application of the Companies Regulations. The only articles of association concluded with a nonSaudi partner provided that disputes should be adjudicated in Saudi court.

The year 1971 revealed a preference for arbitration. Of the nine articles of association found, five contained arbitration clauses. Of the five, four clauses were contained in agreements between purely Saudi parties. Two

---

[115] Umm al-Qurā, Oct. 2, 1966.

[116] However, a second disputes clause providing for arbitration was published in articles of association between Petromin and a French company.

[117] Umm al-Qurā, May 5, 1967 (clause providing for disputes to be resolved by an arbitration committee to be held in Jeddah, for the Board of Grievances to appoint an umpire if the party-selected arbitrators failed to agree on his appointment, and for the arbitrators' decisions to be in accordance with justice).

[118] *Id.* April 12, 1968.

[119] *Id.* Feb. 21, 1969.

[120] *Id.* May 29, 1970.

[121] *Id.* Nov. 6, 1970.

provided for final arbitration without the right of appeal. One authorized the arbitrators to determine the applicable law and the arbitration procedures, and one provided for arbitration proceedings to be held in Paris according to ICC rules but required the arbitrators to apply Saudi law.[122] The remaining four articles of association contained no disputes clause.

In contrast, 1972 revealed only two arbitration clauses, one binding purely Saudi partners, and one in articles of association of a mixed company. Of the total of twenty other articles of association found, fourteen contained no disputes clause. Thirteen of these were between Saudis only. Of the three remaining articles of association of wholly-Saudi companies, one provided for submission of disputes to the then Ministry of Commerce and Industry, one to the Commission for the Settlement of Commercial Disputes, and one provided for the application of the Companies Regulations. Of the four articles of association of mixed companies, one had no disputes clause, two provided that disputes should be litigated in Saudi courts, and one provided that disputes should be resolved according to Saudi law.

In 1973, there were ten arbitration clauses found out of thirty-one articles of association. Of these, six were found in wholly-Saudi companies' articles of association. Five provided for final and binding arbitration.[123] Two provided for the decision to be rendered by a sole arbitrator.[124] Three addressed procedure: one provided for the application of ICC rules; one authorized the arbitrators to determine both the applicable procedure and the applicable law;[125] the other required the arbitrators to apply "the regulations and procedures of the Commission for the Settlement of Commercial Disputes in the Kingdom."[126] It did not, however, specify the place for the arbitration proceedings. The only clause that addressed the choice of place empowered the arbitrators to make that choice.[127] Of the remaining articles of association, sixteen contained no disputes clause. Three of these formed mixed companies. Of the five disputes clauses that did not provide for arbitration, three provided for adjudication in Saudi court or before the Commission for the Settlement of Commercial Disputes,

[122] *Id.* Dec. 17, 1971. This was the first clause found providing for arbitration to be held outside of Saudi Arabia.

[123] Interestingly, one such clause provided for "final" arbitration despite the fact that it also provided that "the parties may agree to attempt to resolve the(ir) disputes by means of arbitration *before* bringing them before (Saudi) courts" (emphasis added). *Id.* July 20, 1973.

[124] One clause provided for a final and nonreviewable award to be rendered by a sole arbitrator. *Id.* March 23, 1973.

[125] *Id.* Nov. 23, 1973 (mixed company formed by seven Saudi partners, four Lebanese partners).

[126] *Id.* July 6, 1973. This was also the first arbitration clause found providing for the allocation of costs (authorizing arbitrators to allot costs).

[127] *Id.* Sept. 23, 1973.

179

and two provided for the resolution of disputes according to Saudi law.

In 1974, thirteen arbitration clauses, of which six provided for final and binding arbitration, were found in thirty-eight articles of association. Four of them were in the articles of mixed companies.[128] Of these, two provided for the application of ICC rules of procedure and specified the place of the arbitration proceedings, respectively in Jeddah,[129] and in Geneva.[130] None of the clauses provided for choice of law, but two required the arbitrators to decide the disputes in accordance with the principles of justice. Of the articles of association which did not provide for arbitration, nineteen contained no disputes clause. Four of these were mixed companies', whereas only one mixed company provided for adjudication by the Commission for the Settlement of Commercial Disputes. In contrast, the articles of association of five wholly-owned Saudi companies provided for a Saudi forum.

In 1975, out of a total of ninety articles of association, thirty-seven contained arbitration clauses,[131] forty-eight contained no disputes clause, and five provided for adjudication before the Commission for the Settlement of Commercial Disputes. Of the arbitration clauses, sixteen provided for final and binding arbitration, and two provided for the exclusivity of the remedy of arbitration.

Choice of law: none of the clauses provided for the application of Saudi law; one provided for the application of Islamic law;[132] one empowered the arbitrators to choose the applicable law;[133] and seven required the award to conform to principles of justice or prevailing custom. Four provided for application of ICC rules of procedure.

Place of arbitration: two companies provided for arbitration in Saudi Arabia, and three provided for outside arbitration (two in London, one in Paris). Of those providing for arbitration in Saudi Arabia, one provided for application of ICC rules.[134] The correlation between the choice of a place of arbitration outside Saudi Arabia and the application of ICC rules was not perfect.

Of the total number of arbitration clauses, eighteen were found in the articles of association of companies with wholly Saudi equity participation.

---

[128] Five mixed companies did not have arbitration clauses. Of the 24 companies with 100 percent Saudi equity, 9 provided for arbitration. It may thus be seen that a greater percentage of mixed companies favor the inclusion of an arbitration clause; however, the percentage of wholly-Saudi companies providing for arbitration is nonetheless significant.

[129] Umm al-Qurā, Nov. 1, 1974 (also providing for the President of the ICC in Paris to select an umpire in case of stalemate).

[130] *Id.* June 7, 1974.

[131] *See generally* Section V *infra*.

[132] *See id.* clause No. 18.

[133] *See id.* clause No. 8.

[134] *See id.* clause No. 17.

Almost half of the absolute number of arbitration clauses were therefore found in the articles of association of Saudi companies. However, mixed companies showed a preference for arbitration. Of the thirty-six articles of association of mixed companies, nineteen, or more than half, provided for arbitration; thirteen contained no disputes clause; and four provided for adjudication before the Commission for the Settlement of Commercial Disputes. In contrast, of the articles of association of the fifty-four companies with one hundred percent Saudi participation, thirty-six, or exactly two-thirds, contained no disputes clause.

In 1976, out of a total of 202 articles of association published, 91 contained arbitration clauses, 95 contained no disputes clause, and 16 provided for adjudication in Saudi Arabia.

Place of arbitration: of the arbitration clauses, nine (four Saudi, five mixed companies) provided for arbitration to be held inside Saudi Arabia; twenty-two (five Saudi, seventeen mixed) provided for arbitration to be held in Europe. London (seven) and Geneva (eight) were the most popular choices.

Choice of law: only three arbitration clauses provided for application of Saudi law. Significantly, all three were found in the articles of association of mixed companies, two of which provided for arbitration to be held outside of the Kingdom. From this may be derived the principle that in the contemplation of Saudi lawyers, arbitrators within the Kingdom will automatically apply Saudi law. On the other hand, two arbitration clauses found in the articles of association of wholly-Saudi companies authorized the arbitrators to determine the applicable law. In addition, the first arbitration clause providing for a choice of foreign law was found in this year.[135] Four companies (two Saudi, two mixed) provided for application of Islamic law; sixteen companies (eight Saudi, eight mixed) provided for the application of principles of justice. The application of ICC rules of procedure was required by twenty seven arbitration clauses (three Saudi, twenty-four mixed).

Of the total number of arbitration clauses, thirty-seven were found in articles of association of one hundred percent Saudi companies, fifty-four in mixed companies'. Of the total of 148 one hundred percent Saudi companies formed, the articles of association of seventy contained no disputes clause, as compared to a total of eighty-four mixed companies, of which twenty-five of the articles of association contained no disputes clause. Thus, the proportion of no disputes clauses to arbitration clauses in one hundred percent Saudi articles of association remained roughly constant

---

[135] Umm al-Qurā, March 5, 1976 (providing for arbitrators to sit in Geneva and apply Swiss law).

from 1975 to 1976, while mixed companies showed an increasing preference for arbitration.

In 1977, out of a total of 286 articles of association, 108 contained arbitration clauses, 164 contained no disputes clause, and 14 provided for adjudication by the Commission for the Settlement of Commercial Disputes.

Place of arbitration: ten arbitration clauses provided for arbitration to be held inside Saudi Arabia, and twenty (four Saudi, sixteen mixed) for arbitration to be held abroad. Paris (eight) and London (eight) were the most popular choices.

Choice of law: Saudi law was chosen by six companies (two Saudi, four mixed); foreign law by two (mixed) companies; Islamic law by six companies (four Saudi, two mixed). Two Saudi arbitration clauses required the arbitral award not to conflict with Islamic law, and four arbitration clauses (two Saudi, two mixed) required the award not to conflict with Saudi law. Only four arbitration clauses (two Saudi, two mixed) provided for the application of principles of justice and prevailing custom. Four companies (two Saudi, two mixed) authorized the arbitrators to determine their own procedure; twenty-four companies (ten Saudi, fourteen mixed) provided for application of ICC rules of procedure.

Of the total number of arbitration clauses, thirty-eight were found in articles of association of one hundred percent Saudi companies, seventy in mixed companies'. Of the total of 158 one hundred percent Saudi companies, the articles of association of 114 contained no disputes clause, as compared to a total of 128 articles of association of mixed companies, of which 50 contained no disputes clause. The proportion of mixed companies not providing for dispute resolution is seen to increase in this year.

In 1978, out of a total of 332 articles of association, 136 contained arbitration clauses, 160 contained no disputes clause, and 36 provided for judicial resolution of disputes (two providing for submission of disputes to nonSaudi courts).

Place of arbitration: ten companies (six Saudi, four mixed) provided for arbitration to be held in Saudi Arabia; twenty-six (mixed) companies provided for arbitration to be held abroad.

Choice of law: this year shows a significant increase in both the absolute number and the percentage of companies providing for the application of Saudi law in the arbitration proceedings (twenty-six companies so providing, of which eighteen were of mixed participation). Additionally, two (mixed) companies provided for the application of Islamic law, six (mixed) companies required the award not to conflict with Saudi law, and six companies (four Saudi, two mixed) provided that the award should not conflict with Islamic law. Two (mixed) companies authorized the arbitrators to choose the applicable law, while twelve companies (six Saudi, six mixed) permitted the arbitrators to determine their procedure. No wholly-Saudi companies found provided for the application of ICC rules of procedure, whereas twenty-two mixed companies did so.

Of the total number of arbitration clauses, forty-eight were found in the articles of association of one hundred percent Saudi companies, eighty-eight in mixed companies'. Of the total of 164 articles of association of one hundred percent Saudi companies, 110 contained no disputes clause, as compared to a total of 168 articles of association of mixed companies, of which 50 contained no disputes clause. The percentage of mixed companies which did not provide for the mode of resolution of disputes declined significantly from the preceding year.

In 1979, out of a total of 645 articles of association, 246 contained arbitration clauses, 372 contained no disputes clause, and 27 provided for adjudication by the Commission for the Settlement of Commercial Disputes.

Due undoubtedly to the effect of Ministerial Resolution No. 3/9/SH/331/9/2903, only three articles of association provided for arbitration to be held outside of Saudi Arabia, whereas twenty-one provided for arbitration to be held inside the Kingdom. Increasingly, articles of association tended to provide for choice of law: forty-two articles of association (nine Saudi, thirty-three mixed) provided for application of Saudi law; twelve (three Saudi, nine mixed) provided for application of Islamic law; and eighteen (nine Saudi, nine mixed) provided for application of the principles of justice. Only six (mixed) companies provided for application of ICC rules of procedure. This decline in popularity of provision for ICC rules may be interpreted as a residual effect of the Ministerial Resolution, whose prohibition may have been viewed as broader than the literal language of the circular.

Of the total number of arbitration clauses, 96 were found in articles of association of one hundred percent Saudi companies, 150 in mixed companies'. Of the total of 387 articles of association of one hundred percent Saudi companies, 282 contained no disputes clause, as compared to a total of 258 articles of association of mixed companies, of which 90 contained no disputes clause.

In 1980, out of a total of 352 articles of association, 120 contained arbitration clauses, 182 contained no disputes clause, and 50 provided for adjudication by the Commission for the Settlement of Commercial Disputes.

No articles of association provided for arbitration to be held outside Saudi Arabia, whereas 36 companies (sixteen Saudi, twenty mixed) provided for arbitration to be held inside the Kingdom. Similarly, no choice of foreign law was found, whereas sixteen companies (eight Saudi, eight mixed) provided for choice of Saudi law, four (mixed) companies provided for application of Islamic law, and sixteen companies (ten Saudi, six mixed) provided for adherence to principles of justice. Four companies (two Saudi, two mixed) provided for application of ICC rules of procedure, while two (Saudi) companies provided for application of Saudi rules of procedure.

Of the total number of arbitration clauses, sixty-four were found in articles of association of one hundred percent Saudi companies, fixty-six in articles of association of mixed companies. Of the total of 226 articles of association of wholly-Saudi companies, 142 contained no disputes clause, as compared to a total of 126 articles of association of mixed companies, of which 40 contained no disputes clause.

V. Actual Arbitration Clauses in Articles of Association of Saudi Limited Liability Companies, 1970–1984

A. PUBLISHED ARBITRATION CLAUSES, 1983–1984

(1) Differences and disputes arising out of the application of this agreement or relating to the execution thereof shall be settled amicably between the partners. If not so settled, the dispute shall be referred to an arbitration board for final decision subject to the circulars regulating such procedures. Umm al-Qurā, 28/4/1404, at 22, col. 2.

(2) Differences and disputes arising from the application of this agreement or relating to the execution thereof shall be settled amicably between the partners. If not so settled, the dispute shall be brought before an arbitration board for final decision with regard for the instructions regulating such procedures. Umm al-Qurā, 28/4/1404, at 22, col. 2.

(3) 1 — In case any dispute occurs between the partners, such dispute shall first be resolved by amicable means. In case of failure of settlement attempts, the dispute shall be resolved by means of arbitration. The disputing parties shall choose the arbitrator or arbitrators in an arbitration agreement signed by each of them, and they shall fully specify therein the issues of the controversy.

2 — If the disputing parties do not agree on the choice of the arbitrator or arbitrators, any party may bring the matter to the Chairman of the Commission for the Settlement of Commercial Disputes, which has jurisdiction to decide the dispute, to appoint an arbitrator.

3 — The decision of the arbitrator or arbitrators shall be effective and nonappealable.

Umm al-Qurā, 23/10/1403, at 8, cols. 2–3.

(4) Any differences, disputes or complaints arising between the parties by reason of this agreement or related thereto shall be settled amicably as an initial stage. If it is impossible to reach an amicable settlement, the subject of the difference, dispute, or complaint shall be referred to an arbitration board for a final decision by arbitration pursuant to an arbitration agreement to be executed by the partners, unless the regulations in force in the Kingdom of Saudi Arabia require otherwise. Umm al-Qurā, 23/10/1403.

(5) In case a dispute arises between the partners relating to the interpretation or application of the provisions of this agreement, such dispute shall be referred to the Commission for the Settlement of Commercial Disputes in Jeddah, or any other commission substituting therefor, for decision in the dispute. Umm al-Qurā, 23/10/1403.

(6) Any dispute or difference arising between partners by reason of the execution of this agreement which cannot be settled amicably by means of negotiation shall be resolved by arbitration in Riyadh in the Kingdom of Saudi Arabia by a sole arbitrator approved by each partner; otherwise arbitration shall be carried out by three arbitrators, one of whom shall be selected by each partner.

If the arbitrators conclude that none of the provisions of this agreement are applicable to such dispute and it is not governed by the Saudi Companies Regulations, they shall decide the dispute in accordance with the principles of justice and equity according to shari‘ah rules. The arbitrators' award shall be made in both Arabic and English, shall be final and binding on parties and the arbitrators shall support their award by appropriate reasoning. The arbitrators shall assess the costs of the arbitration and also the costs of implementing any award which they shall make. Umm al-Qurā, 28/4/1403.

(7) The settlement of any dispute arising between the partners and their heirs or representatives relating to the execution of this agreement shall come within the jurisdiction of the oldest partner present. His decision in the dispute shall be final and binding on all the partners or their heirs. In the event of the death of any of the partners and the occurrence of any difference or dispute between the heirs, a committee shall be formed of three of the oldest members among them, provided that the most senior in age of all the heirs shall be selected, and their decision shall be final and binding on all. Umm al-Qurā, 1/8/1403.

B. ARBITRATION CLAUSES, 1980

(First two weeks)

(1) The parties have agreed that the disputes which shall arise between them in the course of the application of this agreement or the interpretation of its provisions shall be initially settled amicably. If an amicable solution has not been reached, the dispute shall be brought before an arbitration committee of three arbitrators. Each party to the dispute shall appoint an arbitrator and the two appointed arbitrators shall choose the third arbitrator. The arbitration committee shall issue its decisions by majority. With respect to legal issues, the provisions of this agreement shall be applied. In the absence of a provision in this agreement applicable to the dispute, the arbitration committee shall issue its decision in accordance with the rules of justice. The arbitral award shall be final and binding on the parties and not be subject to any appeal or protest. If one of the parties refuses or delays in the appointment of an arbitrator during a period of 30 days after the other party has appointed his arbitrator, the matter shall be brought before the Commission for the Settlement of Commercial Disputes in Jeddah. Umm al-Qurā, Jan. 1, 1980.

(2) The parties agree that if a dispute arises in the execution of the provisions of this agreement, may God not permit it, then it [shall be resolved] by means of arbitration in the Kingdom of Saudi Arabia. Umm al-Qurā, Jan. 1, 1980.

(3) In case a dispute arises between the partners relating to the interpretation or application of the provisions of this agreement, this dispute shall be brought to an arbitration committee to be held in Riyadh as long as the parties do not agree otherwise. If the parties agree on a sole arbitrator, then he shall decide the dispute, and if they fail to agree, each partner shall appoint an arbitrator within two weeks from the date of his notifying the other partners of the existence of a dispute and of his desire to resort to arbitration. If one of the partners fails to appoint his arbitrator during the aforementioned period, then he shall waive his right to appoint an arbitrator, and the other arbitrators shall decide the matter. If the number of arbitrators is uneven, they shall decide the dispute. If their number is even, then they shall choose an umpire. If the appointed arbitrators [cannot] agree on an umpire, then the umpire shall be appointed by the Commission for the Settlement of Commercial Disputes in Riyadh upon a request brought before it. The arbitration committee shall determine the procedures and rules which it shall follow in resolving the dispute. The arbitration committee shall also determine the applicable law and in all cases shall issue its decisions in accordance with the principles of justice. Umm al-Qurā, Jan. 1, 1980.

(4) Any disagreement or dispute arising between the partners relating to this agreement or its interpretation shall be resolved by arbitration. Each party shall appoint an arbitrator and the two arbitrators shall appoint a third arbitrator to be umpire. The decision of the arbitrators shall be binding on all of the parties whether it is issued by majority or unanimity of voices. Umm al-Qurā, Jan. 1, 1980.

(5) Same as No. 3 *supra*. Umm al-Qurā, Jan. 8, 1980.

(6) Each dispute which shall arise between the partners or between them and the heirs or representatives of one of them in the course of this agreement shall be resolved by means of an arbitration committee. In case they fail to resolve this dispute by amicable means, then the Commission for the Settlement of Commercial Disputes in the Minister of Commerce shall have jurisdiction to decide it. Umm al-Qurā, Jan. 8, 1980.

(7) In case of the arisal of any dispute between the partners with respect to the provisions of this agreement, the dispute shall initially be resolved amicably. In case of failure of attempts to reach an amicable solution, the dispute shall be resolved by means of arbitration. The two disputing parties shall choose an arbitrator or arbitrators in an arbitration agreement which each of them shall sign and in which they shall state fully the disputed issues. If the two disputing parties have not chosen the arbitrator or arbitrators during the 30 days following the date of the arbitration agreement, either party may bring the matter before His Excellency the President of the Commission for the Settlement of Commercial Disputes in Riyadh to appoint the arbitrator or arbitrators. The decision of the arbitrator or arbitrators shall be issued according to the laws in effect in the Kingdom of Saudi Arabia. This decision shall be effective and not subject to appeal. Umm al-Qurā, Jan. 8, 1980.

(8) If the two partners have failed to reach an amicable solution to a dispute arising out of the interpretation or application of these articles, they shall resort to arbitration . . . to resolve these disputes . . . . The arbitration committee shall be composed of three arbitrators . . . [and] the arbitration shall be held in the city of al-Khobar. The parties shall bear the costs of the arbitrators they have appointed, and the partnership shall bear the costs of the third arbitrator if this is necessary. The decision of the arbitration board shall be final and binding on the two parties and not subject to appeal or modification or review in any judicial court. Umm al-Qurā, Jan. 8, 1980.

(9) In the case of the arisal of disagreements or disputes between the partners or between the partners and the company, which shall arise out of

the interpretation of the articles of association or out of the activities of the company or in matters relating to the company and its shares and which cannot be resolved by amicable means, [they] shall be resolved by means of arbitration. The procedures for bringing the dispute to arbitration shall be the following: the party desiring arbitration shall notify the other party of his referring the dispute to arbitration and shall appoint the arbitrator he shall have chosen. The other party to the dispute shall then appoint his arbitrator within 45 days from his receipt of notification by the other party. The two arbitrators shall choose a third arbitrator or if one of the parties to the dispute has not undertaken or has refrained from the appointing of his arbitrator during the abovementioned period, the Chamber of Commerce in Riyadh or the Commission for the Settlement of Commercial Disputes may be requested to appoint the arbitrator of the dilatory party or to appoint the third arbitrator. The seat of the arbitration committee shall be in Riyadh. Umm al-Qurā, Jan. 11, 1980.

C. ARBITRATION CLAUSES, 1975 (totality of clauses)

(1) This agreement and the relations between one or more of the partners or the company with respect to that which has been established by reason of this contract shall be subject to the laws of the Kingdom of Saudi Arabia taking into consideration commercial custom and practice. If a dispute exists between the company and one or more of the partners with respect to this agreement, the dispute shall be brought for settlement by arbitration in London according to the rules of arbitration of the ICC, upon written notice which shall be delivered by hand or sent by registered mail from any party to the dispute to the other parties. The arbitration committee shall be composed of one arbitrator to be appointed by agreement of all the concerned parties. If the parties to the arbitration are unable to agree on one arbitrator within 30 days from the date of delivery or the mailing of the aforesaid notification, each party shall choose an arbitrator and notify the other parties of his name, and the arbitrators chosen shall appoint in this manner an umpire or more according to necessity so that the arbitration committee shall be formed of an uneven number of individuals. If agreement cannot be reached upon an umpire or umpires within 120 days from the date of delivery of the notification of the demand for arbitration or of its mailing by registered mail, then the umpires shall be appointed by means of the ICC. In case the arbitration committee is composed of more than one arbitrator, its decision shall be issued by a majority of the arbitrators including the umpires. In all cases the award shall be final and binding on all of the parties concerned. Umm al-Qurā, Jan. 31, 1975.

(2) In case of a dispute arising between the partners with respect to the interpretation or application of the provisions of this agreement, this dispute shall be resolved by arbitration by means of an arbitration committee composed of three individuals. Each of the disputing parties shall choose an arbitrator and these two shall choose a third arbitrator to be president of the committee. The committee shall issue its decisions according to the principles of justice and commercial custom and by majority voice, and its decisions shall be final and binding on the partners. Umm al-Qurā, March 21, 1975.

(3) The disputes which shall arise between the parties in the course of the application of this agreement or the interpretation of its provisions shall be settled initially by amicable means. If the dispute is not resolved amicably, it shall be brought before an arbitration committee composed of three arbitrators. Each party to the dispute shall appoint an arbitrator on his behalf, and the two appointed arbitrators shall agree on a third arbitrator. If one of the parties shall not have appointed his arbitrator in a period of 30 days after the other party shall have appointed his arbitrator, or if the two arbitrators cannot agree on the third arbitrator during a period of 30 days following the appointment of the second arbitrator, then the arbitrator of the party who did not appoint his arbitrator or the third arbitrator shall be appointed by the President of the ICC in Paris upon a demand by [the more diligent] party. The arbitration committee shall sit in Jeddah and shall issue its decisions during the 30 days from the date of appointment of the arbitrator. The decision of the arbitrators shall be final and binding on the parties. Umm al-Qurā, April 4, 1975.

(4) Any dispute which shall arise out of the interpretation or execution of this agreement [sic] the parties of the company shall appoint an arbitrator during one month from the arisal of the dispute. If they cannot agree on an individual and the dispute has not been settled, the subject of the dispute shall be brought before the Commission for the Settlement of Commercial Disputes in the Ministry of Commerce and Industry [sic] to issue a binding decision. Umm al-Qurā, April 11, 1975.

(5) Any dispute which shall arise between the partners or their heirs or their representatives with respect to the company or to its liquidation shall be brought to arbitration if an amicable solution has proved impossible. The arbitration committee shall be composed of a president and two members, and a judgment issuing from that committee shall be nonappealable and final. Umm al-Qurā, April 19, 1975.

(6) In case a dispute arises between the parties, irregardless whether [it is] with respect to the interpretation of the provisions of this agreement or its execution, it shall be resolved by means of arbitration. Each party shall

appoint an arbitrator, and the two appointed arbitrators shall choose a third arbitrator as umpire. The arbitrator shall resolve the dispute within one month from the third arbitrator's acceptance of the matter. The judgment of the arbitrators shall be final and not subject to any review or appeal. Umm al-Qurā, April 20, 1975.

(7) In case of any dispute arising between the partners relating to the interpretation of the principles of this agreement or its application, this dispute shall be resolved by means of a sole arbitrator to be agreed on by the parties. If they do not reach an agreement on one arbitrator, each party to the dispute shall appoint an arbitrator during the 14 days from the date of his notifying the other party of the existence of a dispute and of his desire to bring it to arbitration. If one of the parties fails to appoint an arbitrator in the designated period, his right to appoint an arbitrator shall be lost, and the other arbitrators shall decide the dispute. If their number is even, they shall choose an umpire, and if the appointed arbitrators fail to agree on an umpire, he shall be appointed by the Commission for the Settlement of Commercial Disputes in the place where the arbitration shall be held. The arbitration committee shall determine the procedures and rules which it shall follow in deciding the dispute, as in all cases, it shall issue its decisions in accordance with the principles of justice and prevailing custom. Um al-Qurā, May 9, 1975.

(8) In case of the occurrence of a dispute between the parties relating to the interpretation or the application of the principles of this agreement, that dispute shall be brought before an arbitration committee to be seated in Riyadh unless the parties agree otherwise. If the two parties agree on one arbitrator, then he shall decide the dispute. If they are unable to agree on an arbitrator, each party shall appoint one arbitrator within two weeks from the date of the notification of the aggrieved party of the existence of a dispute and of his desire to resort to arbitration. If one party fails to appoint an arbitrator within that period, the appointment shall be made by the President of the Chamber of Commerce in the city of Riyadh upon demand [of one of the parties] and a like procedure [shall be followed] in the matter of the appointment of an umpire if the two arbitrators are unable to agree on his appointment. The arbitration committee shall determine the procedures and rules which it shall follow in deciding the dispute, as it shall also determine the applicable law, and in all cases shall issue its decisions in accordance with the principles of justice. Umm al-Qurā, May 16, 1975.

(9) In case of the occurrence of a dispute between the partners which cannot be resolved amicably, the dispute shall be brought before an arbitration committee. Each partner shall choose an arbitrator, and the two

partners concerned shall choose a third arbitrator. The decision of the committee shall be by majority and binding on the parties. Umm al-Qurā, May 16, 1975.

(10) In case any dispute arises between the partners relating to the interpretation or the application of this agreement, this dispute shall be brought before an arbitration committee which shall sit in the city of Jeddah unless the parties agree otherwise. If the parties agree on one arbitrator, he shall decide the dispute. If they are unable to agree, each party to the dispute shall appoint one arbitrator during the two weeks from the date of the notification of the other parties of its existence [sic]. Umm al-Qurā, June 27, 1975.

(11) Any dispute arising between the partners or their successors in interest or their agents by reason of the company or its liquidation . . . shall be brought to arbitration if it cannot be resolved amicably. Umm al-Qurā, June 27, 1975.

(12) Same.

(13) Any dispute arising between the partners relating to the interpretation of the provisions of this agreement shall be resolved by means of a sole arbitrator on whom the parties shall agree. If they are unable to agree on one arbitrator, each party to the dispute shall appoint an arbitrator within 14 days from the date of his notifying the other parties of the existence of a dispute and his desire to bring it to arbitration. If one of the parties fails to appoint his arbitrator within that period, his right to appoint an arbitrator shall be waived, and the other arbitrators shall resolve the dispute. If the number of arbitrators is uneven, they shall decide the dispute. If their number is even, they shall appoint an umpire. If the arbitrators fail to agree on an umpire, the Commission for the Settlement of Commercial Disputes in the place where the arbitration shall be held shall appoint the umpire. The arbitration committee shall determine the procedures and principles which it shall follow in deciding the dispute and in all cases shall issue its decisions in accordance with the principles of justice and prevailing custom. Umm al-Qurā, July 4, 1975.

(14) In case a dispute occurs between the partners, it shall be resolved by means of arbitration. Each party shall choose an arbitrator, then the partners or the arbitrators shall choose umpires. The decision of the arbitration committee shall be by majority voice, and their opinion shall be final and not subject to any review, either ordinary or extraordinary. In case of failure to reach a result, the matter shall be brought before the Commission for the Settlement of Commercial Disputes for settlement. Umm al-Qurā, July 4, 1975.

(15) In case any dispute arises between the partners in the interpretation or execution of this agreement, it shall be resolved by agreement between them. If this proves difficult during a 30 day [period], either of them shall have the right to demand arbitration by means of a committee composed of three arbitrators. Each partner shall appoint one arbitrator, and the two arbitrators shall choose a third arbitrator. The decisions of the arbitration committee shall be issued by unanimity or by majority and shall be final and binding on the partners. Umm al-Qurā, July 11, 1975.

(16) In case a dispute arises between the partners in the interpretation or application of this agreement, and its amicable solution is impossible between them, the matter shall be brought to arbitration, and no other means [of resolution] shall be permissible. The decision shall be [made] by a sole arbitrator on whom they agree or by three arbitrators if they cannot agree on a sole arbitrator and shall be final and binding on the parties. Umm al-Qurā, July 11, 1975.

(17) In case a dispute arises between the company and one or more partners or between the partners relating to this agreement, the dispute shall be brought to arbitration in the city of Riyadh and the arbitration shall be conducted in the English language. The arbitration committee shall be composed of three arbitrators. These arbitrators shall be appointed according to the ICC rules. The arbitration committee's decision shall be final in all cases and binding on all of the parties concerned. Umm al-Qurā, July 25, 1975.

(18) In case of a dispute arising between the partners relating to the interpretation or the application of the provisions of this agreement, the dispute shall be resolved by arbitration by means of a committee composed of three arbitrators. Each party shall choose an arbitrator and the two arbitrators together shall choose the third arbitrator to be umpire between them and president of the arbitration committee. The arbitration committee shall determine the rules and procedures which it shall follow in deciding the dispute and in all cases shall issue its decisions in conformity with effective law and the principles of justice and the provisions of the noble sharī'ah. Umm al-Qurā, Aug. 1, 1975.

(19) In case a dispute arises between the partners in the interpretation of the provisions of this agreement or its application, and its amicable solution has been impossible, the matter shall be brought to arbitration and shall not be resolved by any other means. The decision of the sole arbitrator on whom the parties shall agree or the three arbitrators if they cannot agree on one arbitrator shall settle the dispute and be final and binding on the parties. Umm al-Qurā, Aug. 8, 1975.

(20) If a dispute arises between the partners in the course of the application of this agreement or the interpretation of its provisions, it shall initially be settled amicably and, if it has not been settled, the dispute shall be brought before an arbitration committee. Each disputing party shall choose his arbitrator, and if they are two, the two arbitrators shall choose a third to be their umpire. If the number of arbitrators is even, the two arbitrators shall choose a president of the committee. His voice shall be preponderant in case of equality of voices. The arbitration committee shall issue its decisions by majority and shall sit in the city of Jeddah, and its decisions shall be final and binding on all parties to the dispute. Umm al-Qurā, Aug. 15, 1975.

(21) All disputes or controversies arising out of the interpretation or application of this agreement shall be resolved by arbitration in the principal place of business of the company. Umm al-Qurā, Aug. 15, 1975.

(22) In case of a dispute arising between the partners, it shall be resolved by arbitration. Each party shall choose an arbitrator and the two arbitrators shall choose an umpire. The decision of the arbitrators shall be by majority and shall not be set aside. It is stipulated that the arbitrators shall issue their decisions within a maximum of one month from the date of their [appointment]. Their opinion shall be final. In the case of a disagreement, the matter shall be brought before the Commission for the Settlement of Commercial Disputes in Jeddah, whose opinion shall be effective. Umm al-Qurā, Aug. 22, 1975.

(23) The disputes arising out of this agreement shall be resolved finally in accordance with the rules of conciliation and arbitration of the ICC by means of one or more arbitrators who shall be appointed under these rules. Umm al-Qurā, Aug. 29, 1975.

(24) In case of a dispute arising between the partners in the interpretation or application of this agreement, the dispute shall be resolved by arbitrators. Each partner shall choose an arbitrator and these arbitrators shall choose an umpire. The decision of the arbitrators shall be binding on the partners if issued by absolute majority. Umm al-Qurā, Aug. 29, 1975.

(25) The disputes arising between the partners in the course of the application of this agreement or the interpretation of its provisions shall be initially settled by conciliation. If the matter is not resolved, the dispute shall be brought to an arbitration committee composed of three arbitrators. Each partner shall appoint an arbitrator and the two arbitrators shall agree on a third arbitrator. If one party fails to appoint an arbitrator during the 15-day period from the date the other party appointed his arbitrator or if the two arbitrators fail to agree on the third during the 20-day period after the appointment of the [second] arbitrator, then the President of the International Chamber of Commerce in Paris shall appoint [the arbitrator] upon the demand of the party desiring a speedy resolution. The decision of the arbitration committee shall be unanimous or by majority voice (the partners accept majority decision if it is not contrary to ICC rules) with respect to points relating to the subject matter or to the law or otherwise . . . The provisions of this agreement shall be applied and in the absence of a provision applicable to the dispute, the arbitration committee shall issue its decision according to the principles of justice. Umm al-Qurā, Sept. 5, 1975.

(26) This agreement and the relationship between the partners of the company established by reason of this agreement shall be subject to the laws of the Kingdom of Saudi Arabia and to commercial custom and practice. In case of a dispute arising between the partners out of the application of this agreement or the modification of its terms, it shall initially be settled amicably. If this fails, it shall be brought before an arbitration committee composed of three arbitrators, and the arbitration committee's decision shall be by majority and be final and binding on the parties. Umm al-Qurā, Sept. 12, 1975.

(27) Same. Umm al-Qurā, Sept. 19, 1975.

(28) In case a dispute arises relating to this agreement between the company and one or more of the partners or between the partners, the dispute shall be brought to arbitration upon written notice delivered [or sent] by mail or registered mail by any party to the other parties. The arbitration committee shall be composed of one arbitrator appointed by agreement of all of the parties concerned. In case the parties fail to agree on one arbitrator within 30 days from the date of delivery or mailing of notice, each party shall appoint an arbitrator and notify the other parties of his name and profession and domicile during the following 15 days. The appointed arbitrators shall appoint one or more umpires so that the number of arbitrators shall be uneven. If the arbitration committee is composed of more than one arbitrator, its decisions shall be by simple majority of the number of its members. In all cases, the decisions of the arbitration committee shall be final and binding on all parties. The arbitration shall in all cases be in accordance with the principles of justice and in conformity with commercial custom. Umm al-Qurā, Sept. 19, 1975.

(29) All disputes arising out of the interpretation or application of the provisions of this agreement which cannot be resolved by mutual agreement shall be settled by arbitration. The party desiring arbitration shall notify the other party in writing of the name and address of his arbitrator. In the ten days following the receipt of the preceding notification, the other party

shall inform the party desiring arbitration of the name and address of his arbitrator. The two arbitrators shall choose an umpire within the following ten days. The three arbitrators shall meet with all possible speed and issue their decision by majority voice. This decision shall be final and binding on all parties. The arbitrators shall be empowered to award costs and to allocate them between the parties as they see fit. Umm al-Qurā, Oct. 24, 1975.

(30) Any dispute occurring between the parties to this agreement concerning the interpretation, application or execution of the covenants and conditions of this agreement or with respect to any issue arising relating to their joint participation which cannot be resolved amicably shall be brought to arbitration by one of the parties . . . The two arbitrators shall appoint a third arbitrator, who shall not be of the same nationality as any of the parties, within 30 days [sic]. In case the arbitrators fail to agree on a third, he shall be appointed by the President of the International Chamber of Commerce in London . . . Arbitration shall be held in London. ICC rules shall be applied . . . In case one of the parties fails to appoint his arbitrator, the other party may transfer the case to the Commission for the Settlement of Commercial Disputes in Jeddah. Umm al-Qurā, Oct. 31, 1975.

(31) In case of a dispute arising between the partners, it shall be resolved by arbitration. Each partner shall choose an arbitrator, then the partners or the arbitrators shall choose an umpire. The decisions of the arbitration committee shall be by majority opinion, which shall be final and nonreviewable by ordinary or extraordinary means. Umm al-Qurā, Oct. 31, 1975.

(32) In case of a dispute between the parties to this agreement pertaining to the interpretation or execution of its provisions, the dispute shall be settled finally by arbitration according to the rules of conciliation and arbitration of the ICC in Paris, France. Umm al-Qurā, Oct. 31, 1975

(33) . . .
  (c) The arbitration committee shall sit in London.
  (d) The arbitration committee shall apply the rules of conciliation and arbitration of the ICC.
Umm al-Qurā, Nov. 14, 1975.

(34) All disputes occurring between the partners shall be initially resolved amicably. If resolution has proved impossible, the issue shall be brought to an arbitration committee composed of three arbitrators . . . Umm al-Qurā, Nov. 28, 1975.

(35) In case of a dispute arising between the partners, it shall be resolved by arbitration. Each party shall choose an arbitrator, then the partners or the arbitrators shall choose an umpire. The arbitration committee's decision shall be by majority and be final and nonreviewable by ordinary or extraordinary means. Umm al-Qurā, Nov. 28, 1975.

(36) In case of a dispute arising between the partners, it shall be resolved by a sole arbitrator agreed on by the parties. If they fail to agree on one arbitrator, each partner shall appoint an arbitrator during the 14 days following his notification of the other parties of his desire to arbitrate. If one party fails to appoint his arbitrator within that period, his right to appoint an arbitrator shall be waived, and the other arbitrators shall decide the dispute. If the number of arbitrators is uneven, they shall decide the dispute. If their number is even, they shall choose an umpire. If the arbitrators are unable to agree on an umpire, he shall be appointed by the Commission for the Settlement of Commercial Disputes in the place where the arbitration shall be held. The arbitration committee shall determine its procedures and rules of decision and in all cases shall issue its decisions according to the principles of justice and prevailing custom. Umm al-Qurā, Dec. 5, 1975.

(37) Disputes arising between the partners in the course of the application or interpretation of the provisions of this agreement shall be initially resolved amicably, and if not, the dispute shall be brought before an arbitration committee composed of one arbitrator representing each party. The two arbitrators shall choose a third. The decisions of the arbitration committee shall be issued by majority and shall be final and binding on all parties. Umm al-Qurā, Dec. 26, 1975.

D. ARBITRATION CLAUSES, 1970 (totality of clauses)

(1) In case a dispute occurs between the partners (may Allah not permit it) in the interpretation or execution of this agreement, one or more arbitrators shall be chosen from the members of kin on the male side or the female side or those [people] of experience in settling disputes. Umm al-Qurā, May 29, 1970.

(2) In case a dispute arises between the partners relating to the application of this agreement, the matter shall be brought before an arbitration committee which shall sit in Jeddah [unless the parties agree] otherwise. For this purpose, a sole arbitrator shall be appointed by agreement of the partners. In case the partners fail to agree within 14 days on the appointment of the sole arbitrator, each of the partners shall appoint an arbitrator within 14 days, and if one of the parties fails to

appoint an arbitrator within the 14 days, the other arbitrator actually appointed shall decide the dispute. The decision shall be final and binding on the partners. If the choice of the two arbitrators is completed, then they shall choose an umpire whose decision shall be final and binding on the partners. In case the two arbitrators fail to agree on the appointment of an umpire within 14 days, the umpire shall be appointed by the Commission for the Settlement of Commercial Disputes in Jeddah upon a demand brought to it by one of the partners. The arbitral decisions in all cases shall be in accordance with justice. Umm al-Qurā, Nov. 6, 1970.

Chapter 4
JUDICIAL ORGANIZATION

The Saudi Arabian judicial system is at present tripartite. The sharī'ah courts are courts of general jurisdiction.[1] However, certain specialized adjudicative bodies have subject-matter jurisdiction as provided in their enabling regulations or other applicable regulatory law. The integration of the specialized commissions into the sharī'ah court system is presently under study.[2] Finally, regardless of the subject-matter of the dispute, the Board of Grievances is made by regulation the administrative court having jurisdiction over cases to which the Government or any of its agencies or instrumentalities is a party.

I. Sharī'ah Courts

A. HISTORY

The sharī'ah courts were first formally organized in Saudi Arabia in 1927. In 1936, and again in 1952, comprehensive regulations, both entitled the Attributions of Sharī'ah Jurisprudence Responsibilities Regulations, were issued organizing the judiciary. The basic structure of the judicial system as defined by these regulations consisted, in ascending order, of summary

---

[1] For a historical treatment of the Saudi judicial system, see; S. Solaim, Constitutional and Judicial Organization in Saudi Arabia (1970) (unpublished Ph.D. dissertation at Johns Hopkins University); M. al-Rasheed, Criminal Procedure in Saudi Arabian Judicial Institutions (1973) (unpublished Ph.D. thesis at University of Durham).

[2] See generally Council of Ministers Resolution No. 167 (14/9/1401) (specialized labor and commercial courts to be created within sharī'ah system).

courts, courts of general original jurisdiction and an ultimate reviewing authority, the President of the Judiciary. An intermediate tier of two appellate courts was added in 1962. This structure persisted until 1970, when the Ministry of Justice took over the administrative functions of the Presidency of the Judiciary.[3] In addition, the office of Muftī, previously held by the President of the Judiciary, was divided into two separate offices, the Office of Religious Studies, the Issuing of Fatāwā and Religious Guidance, and the Board of the Grand 'Ulamā'.

B. APPLICABLE REGULATIONS

The Judicial Regulations of 1975[4] govern the organization of the sharī'ah court system. They are supplemented, *inter alia*, by those provisions of the Attributions of Sharī'ah Jurisprudence Responsibilities Regulations[5] ["Attributions Regulations"] that are not inconsistent therewith and with circulars and instructions issued by the President of the Judiciary during the period of existence of that office and by the Minister of Justice.[6]

C. MINISTRY OF JUSTICE

The Ministry of Justice is responsible for the administration of the courts and other judicial departments.[7] The Minister of Justice has assumed powers of the former President of the Judiciary not vested in other authorities.[8] In addition, the Judicial Regulations grant certain specific powers to the Minister.

The constitution of the lower courts and the delimitation of their jurisdiction are made by resolution of the Minister based on decisions of the Supreme Judicial Council.[9] The Minister also has the power to authorize the lower courts to change their seats in cases of necessity.[10] The Minister has general supervisory powers over the sharī'ah courts and

---

[3] *See* High Order No. A/126 (13/8/1390) (creating Ministry of Justice).

[4] Royal Decree No. M/64 (1975), *as amended by* Royal Decrees Nos. M/76 (14/10/1395), M/15 (3/4/1397) (repealing Royal Decree No. M/38 (8/5/1395)), M/4 (1/3/1401), & M/3 (1/4/1404).

[5] High Approval No. 109 (24/1/1372).

[6] Unlike many royal decrees, the Judicial Regulations contain no provision to the effect that they repeal prior or inconsistent law. Despite this silence, they repeal prior inconsistent rules of law under general principles of Saudi law. However, prior regulations not in conflict with the Judicial Regulations may still be applied. Even certain regulations or circulars which are no longer in effect retain utility with respect to the interpretation of Saudi law.

[7] Judicial Regs., art. 87.

[8] For powers of former President of the Judiciary, *see generally* Attributions Regs., arts. 2–13.

[9] Judicial Regs., arts. 22, 24.

[10] *Id.* art. 27.

judiciary.[11] He has the right to bring disciplinary actions against judges pursuant to a criminal or administrative investigation.[12] The Minister of Justice also possesses a limited judicial authority in that decisions of the General Commission of the court of appeals are not deemed final unless approved by the Minister or, if such approval is not granted, by the Supreme Judicial Council.[13] Additionally, the Minister's legal staff is responsible for assisting the courts in collecting and establishing general rules of law.[14]

However, the Minister's authority over the judiciary is checked by the Regulations' guarantee of judicial independence. Such independence is a basic principle of Islamic law;[15] however, none of the prior regulations expressly restated this principle.[16] In contrast, article 1 of the Regulations provides that "judges are independent and not subject to any authority in rendering judgment except as provided in the sharī'ah and applicable regulations. No person shall have the right to interfere in the judicial process." In addition, article 71 expressly subjects the Minister's supervisory powers over the judiciary to the principles of judicial neutrality and independence.

D. JUDGES

1. Appointment and qualifications

Judges are appointed by royal order executing decisions of the Supreme Judicial Council.[17] Appointments are for the judge's preretirement life.[18] Article 37 of the Regulations sets out six requirements with respect to members of the judiciary. Judges must be Saudi nationals of good conduct and having a degree from a Saudi Islamic law faculty or its equivalent. The minimum age is twenty-two years or, in the case of appellate judges, forty years. Persons convicted of a criminal offence or former public officials dismissed from office as a result of disciplinary proceedings may not serve

---

[11] *Id.* art. 71.

[12] *Id.* art. 74.

[13] *See id.* art. 20.

[14] *See id.* art. 89.

[15] *See generally* A. AL-ḤAMDĀWĪ, UṢUL AL-TASHRĪ' FĪ AL-MAMLAKAH AL-'ARABIYYAH AL-SU'ŪDIYYAH 131–32 (undated).

[16] *But see* Provinces Regs., Royal Decree No. 12, art. 10(a) (1383) (regional governors prohibited from interfering in judicial matters or attempting to influence judges); Trial of Ministers Regs., Royal Decree No. 88, art. 5(f) (1960) (penalizing personal interference in judicial affairs).

[17] Judicial Regs., art. 53.

[18] *See id.* arts. 2–3, 51, 85. The regulatory retirement age is 70 years.

as judges, even if the disabilities resulting from such proceedings are later removed.[19] Judges must also possess the Islamic law judicial qualifications.[20]

Judges remain under probation during their first year of service. They may be discharged during this period by means of a Supreme Judicial Council decision.[21] After the expiration of the probationary period, the Council issues a decision confirming the appointment.[22] As of this time, judges are considered fullfledged members of the judicial corps. Judges are promoted by means of royal order based on Supreme Judicial Council decisions. Promotions are made on the basis of absolute seniority, or, in case of equivalency of service, on the basis of performance. In case of equivalency of performance, promotions are to be made on the basis of seniority in age.[23] In addition, judges must have fulfilled certain regulatory terms of service and undergone a certain number of inspections in order to be eligible to hold higher offices in the judiciary.[24] For example, to be eligible to sit on a court of appeals, a judge must have held the rank of chief judge of degree (a) of a general court for a minimum of two years, or have performed equivalent judicial functions, or have taught Islamic law in a Saudi Islamic law faculty for a minimum of eighteen years.[25]

2. Rights and duties

Judges are a special class of public servants and are subject to the regulations generally applicable to civil servants except to the extent that the latter are inconsistent with the Judicial Regulations or other rules applicable to members of the judicial corps. Thus, salaries of judges are determined according to a scale applicable solely to members of the judiciary, and judges are exempted from disciplinary measures applicable to other civil servants.[26] Judges are not required to perform any duties imposed by regulations generally applicable to civil servants which would be inconsistent with the nature of the judicial office.[27] Judges are prohibited

---

[19] Exceptions to the degree requirement may be made in the case of persons of adequate knowledge: *id.* art. 37(d).

[20] These are subject to interpretation according to the legal schools: Islam, *i.e.* being a Muslim; good character; freedom; majority; mental capacity; maleness (although there are divergences of opinion on this point); possession of the sense faculties. *See, e.g.*, M. AL-BAHŪTĪ, SHARH MUNTAHĀ AL-IRĀDĀT 464–65 (Dār al-Fikr); H. ĀL AL-SHAIKH, AL-TANZĪM AL-QADĀ'Ī FĪ AL-MAMLAKAH AL-'ARABIYYAH AL-SU'ŪDIYYAH 61–64 (1983).

[21] Judicial Regs., art. 50.

[22] *Id.*

[23] *See id.* art. 53.

[24] *See generally id.* arts. 39–47, 53. Judges are subject to annual or semiannual inspections: *id.* art. 65.

[25] *Id.* art. 47.

[26] *See id.* arts. 52, 85(b). *Cf.* Disciplining of Officials Regs., Royal Decree No. M/7, art. 48 (1391) (excepting judiciary from scope of disciplinary regulations).

[27] Judicial Regs., art. 52.

from engaging in commercial activities and from performing any other work incompatible with the dignity of the judicial office and the principle of judicial independence.[28] The Regulations prohibit judges from discussing trial proceedings with third parties.[29]

3. Removal

In order to safeguard the independence of the judiciary, the Regulations secure judges against arbitrary removal and transfer.[30] They also provide that judges are only subject to legal action in accordance with the disciplinary rules applicable to the judiciary.[31]

Removal on regulatory grounds

Once members of the judiciary have completed their initial probation stage, their service does not end until the occurrence of certain stated events, namely, death, resignation, retirement,[32] or the reaching of seventy years of age.[33] They may not be otherwise removed except as provided in the Regulations.[34] Judges are removed from office by means of royal order executing a decision of the Supreme Judicial Council.[35] The specific regulatory grounds for removal are: illness continuing after an extended leave of absence, or medical reasons preventing performance of his judicial duties;[36] a judge's "loss . . . of the confidence and esteem required by his office;"[37] and a judge's receipt of the grade of "below average" in three successive administrative evaluations.[38] No pretermination hearing is provided; however, the judge is entitled to an administrative appeal of his grade.[39] The Regulations also provide that judges may not be transferred from their present posts unless they consent to the transfer, or the transfer is effected by means of promotion.[40] Judges may only be transferred to

[28] *Id.* art. 58.
[29] *Id.* art. 59.
[30] *See id.* arts. 2–3.
[31] *Id.* art. 4. This provision, which is not expressly limited to actions brought with respect to the exercise of judicial functions, must be read together with art. 79, which provides that disciplinary proceedings shall have no effect on a criminal or civil action arising out of the same incident. *See also id.* art. 84 (relating to criminal prosecution of judges).
[32] *Id.* art. 85(a)–(c).
[33] *Id.* arts. 51, 86.
[34] *Id.* arts. 51, 86.
[35] *Id.* arts. 51, 86.
[36] *Id.* arts. 57, 85(d).
[37] *Id.* arts. 51, 85(d).
[38] *Id.* arts. 69, 85(d).
[39] *Id.* art. 68.
[40] *Id.* art. 3. This rule is designed to protect judges, who are required to reside in the locality in which they sit: *id.* art. 60.

non-judicial posts by means of a royal order based upon a Supreme Judicial Council decision.[41]

Removal in disciplinary proceedings

Judges are subject to disciplinary proceedings before the Disciplinary Board[42] initiated by the Minister of Justice for breach of duty or failure to perform the functions of their office. Such proceedings may only be instigated pursuant to a formal administrative or criminal investigation.[43] The judge is entitled to notice of the charges and a hearing.[44] However, if the judge resigns, the proceedings are ended.[45] Disciplinary hearings are held in camera. The accused has a right to present both an oral and a written defense, and to be represented by another member of the judiciary.[46] Default judgments are permitted.[47] Decisions of the Disciplinary Board are final and nonappealable;[48] however, the sanction of removal must be enforced by royal decree.[49]

E. JURISDICTION AND CONSTITUTION OF COURTS

There are four adjudicative levels in the shari'ah court system, having subject-matter jurisdiction as provided in the Regulations.[50]

1. Summary courts

The summary courts have jurisdiction over

(a) Misdemeanors, offenses, the ḥadd (religious offense) of intoxication, and indemnifications for bodily injury whose amount does not exceed one fifth of the diyah.[51]

---

[41] *Id.* art. 55.
[42] The Disciplinary Board is a facet of the General Commission of the Supreme Judicial Council. *See id.* art. 73.
[43] *Id.* art. 74.
[44] *Id.* arts. 75, 77.
[45] *Id.* art. 79.
[46] *Id.* art. 80.
[47] *Id.*
[48] *Id.* art. 81.
[49] *Id.* art. 83.
[50] The territorial jurisdiction of the courts is determined by the competent regional governors as notified to the Ministry of Justice, which then effects the relevant attribution of jurisdiction. *See* Supreme Judicial Council Decision No. 37 (2/4/1397), *cited in* S. ĀL DURAIB, AL-TANẒĪM AL-QAḌĀ·Ī FĪ AL-MAMLAKAH AL-'ARABIYYAH AL-SUʿŪDIYYAH, 454–55 (1983).
[51] For diyah, *see generally* Chapter 6 *infra.*

(b) Civil claims of an amount not exceeding eight thousand riyals, with the exception of cases relating to matrimonial matters, maintenance, and real property.[52]

Decisions are made by one judge.[53]

2. General courts

The general courts have original jurisdiction over all civil and criminal cases. Decisions are made by one judge. However, sentences of death, stoning, or amputation must be rendered by a three-judge panel.[54] Persons charged with the crimes of assault and abduction are also tried before a three-judge panel.

3. Courts of appeal

The two appellate courts sit in Riyadh and Makkah.[55] The former has jurisdiction to hear appeals from lower courts sitting in the Central and Eastern Provinces, and the latter from the courts of the Western Province. The chairman of the court of appeal is selected on the basis of absolute seniority.[56] The courts are divided into three departments, having respectively responsibility for reviewing criminal cases, personal status cases, and cases not falling into either of the former categories.[57] Three-judge panels hear appeals. However, sentences of death, stoning, or amputation may only be imposed by a panel of five judges.[58] Decisions are by majority voice.[59] Decisions of the appellate courts are final, except sentences of death, stoning, or amputation.[60]

The appellate courts also sit *en banc* as General Commission, composed of all members of the court.[61] This body carries out administrative and disciplinary functions.[62] In addition, if an appellate panel desires to depart from a legal conclusion reached on the basis of independent reasoning

---

[52] Minister of Justice Resolution No. 14/12/t (20/1/1397), *approved by* High Letter No. 4/z/384 (6/1/1397), *reprinted in* H. ĀL AL-SHAIKH, *supra* note 20, at 55–56 (applicable although former terminology referring to first and second "expeditious courts" employed).

[53] Judicial Regs., art. 25.

[54] *Id.* art. 23, *as amended by* Royal Decree No. M/3 (1/4/1404).

[55] The Judicial Regulations contemplate a single appellate court, *see id.* art. 12, but in fact the division of appellate responsibility of prior law persists.

[56] *Id.* art. 49.

[57] *Id.* art. 10.

[58] *Id.* art. 13.

[59] Instructions for Reviewing Sharī'ah Judgments, High Approval No. 24836, art. 21 (29/10/1386).

[60] *See* Judicial Regs., art. 8(4); *cf.* Instructions for Reviewing Sharī'ah Judgments., art. 21 (appellate decision ends the case).

[61] Judicial Regs., art. 15.

[62] *Id.* art. 16.

(ijtihād) established by prior judgments, the General Commission is made the authority competent to authorize such a departure.[63] The decisions of the General Commission are deemed final upon approval by the Minister of Justice.[64]

4. The Supreme Judicial Council

This body is the highest adjudicative authority in the sharī'ah judicial system. It is composed of ten members and a chairman who holds the rank of minister.[65] Its functions are administrative, consultative, and judicial. The council functions in the form of two commissions.

Permanent Commission

This is composed of five fulltime members of the rank of chairman of an appellate court.[66] The Permanent Commission has jurisdiction to review all sentences of death, amputation, or stoning, to study issues referred by the King, and to express opinions on general legal principles and judicial matters on the request of the Minister of Justice.[67] All members must be present to review criminal sentences; otherwise, a quorum of three is sufficient. Decisions are by majority vote.[68] Finally, only the Permanent Commission may authorize the criminal investigation or prosecution of judges.[69] If a judge is preliminarily detained on suspicion of a criminal act, the Permanent Commission must be notified within twenty-four hours. It has the power to order his release, with or without bail, or his detention. In the latter case, the Permanent Commission may set the detention period and, if needed, extend it later.[70]

General Commission

This is composed of the chairman, the permanent members, and five part-time members. The latter are an appellate court chairman or his deputy, the Deputy Minister of Justice, and the three most senior chairmen of the general courts sitting in Makkah, Madinah, Riyadh, Jeddah, Dammam and Jizan.[71] The quorum for the General Commission is the totality of its membership. Decisions are by majority voice.[72]

---

[63] *Id.* art. 14.
[64] *Id.* art. 20.
[65] *Id.* arts. 6, *as amended by* Royal Decrees Nos. M/76 (14/10/1395) & M/4 (1/3/1401), 49.
[66] *Id.* art. 6(a).
[67] *Id.* arts. 8–9, *as amended by* Royal Decrees Nos. M/76 (14/10/1395) & M/4 (1/3/1401).
[68] *Id.* art. 9.
[69] *Id.* art. 84.
[70] *Id.*
[71] *Id.* art. 6(b).
[72] *Id.* art. 9.

The General Commission's judicial functions are limited. It has jurisdiction to review appellate decisions involving a precedential ijtihād or a departure from prior ijtihād.[73] The latter cases may reach the General Commission if the Minister of Justice refuses to approve the appellate court's ruling or if a two-thirds majority, required for departure, did not exist in the appellate court.[74] Finally, the General Commission has the authority to state general principles of Islamic law in response to legal questions referred to it by the Minister of Justice.[75]

The General Commission also has supervisory powers over the judiciary.[76] It is responsible for making recommendations to the Minister of Justice with respect to the seat and jurisdiction of the lower courts.[77] It is authorized to recommend the constitution of specialized courts.[78] Its decisions are the basis for appointment, transfer, and promotion of judges.[79] It has the power to prohibit judges from carrying on activities inconsistent with their duties.[80] Sitting as Disciplinary Board, the General Commission is the forum for disciplinary proceedings instigated against judges.[81] It has discretion to suspend judges from performing judicial activities pending such proceedings.[82] Decisions of the Disciplinary Board are final.[83] However, the sanction of removal can only be enforced by royal order, and the sanction of censure by decision of the Minister of Justice.[84] Lastly, the General Commission may hear appeals from judges whose grades of "below-average" received during routine inspections were affirmed by the administrative inspection committee. Such decisions of the General Commission are final.[85]

5. Conflicts of Jurisdiction Committee

The sharī‘ah courts are courts of general jurisdiction. In principle, all claims are cognizable by a sharī‘ah court. The Regulations, however, do contemplate divesting the courts of jurisdiction over certain types of

---

[73] Id. art. 14; cf. Rules Governing New Powers of Regional Governors, Minister of the Interior Resolution, Umm al-Qurā, 5/5/1395, para. 2(5)(c) (resolution unnumbered, undated) (appellate approval a prerequisite to enforcement in certain cases).

[74] See Judicial Regs., arts. 14, 20.

[75] Id. arts. 8(1), 9.

[76] Id. art. 7.

[77] Id. arts. 22, 24.

[78] Id. art. 26.

[79] Id. arts. 53, 55.

[80] Id. art. 58.

[81] Id. art. 73.

[82] Id. art. 78.

[83] Id. art. 81.

[84] Id. art. 83.

[85] Id. art. 68.

cases.[86] Additionally, the Regulations explicitly address the problem of concurrent jurisdiction in certain situations. Three types of situations are covered

(a) A sharīʿah court has taken jurisdiction of a case. The defendant raises a defense which must be decided by another judicial body. In this case, if the sharīʿah court finds that the final disposition of the defense is indispensable to the disposition of the case, the court is required to stay the proceedings pending such final disposition. The court is to give the party opposing the defense a time period within which to obtain a final judgment. If he is unable to do so within the time limit, the court has discretion to adjudicate the case. However, if the court initially determines that the disposition of the defense will not be dispositive of the case, it may disregard the defense entirely.[87]

(b) A case has been brought in sharīʿah court and in another entity with jurisdiction to resolve disputes. Both have taken jurisdiction of the case or, alternatively, have declined to do so.

(c) A sharīʿah court and another entity have both taken jurisdiction of a case and have given conflicting final judgments disposing of it. A problem has arisen with respect to the choice of the judgment to be enforced.

To resolve the latter two conflicts, the Regulations provide for the establishment of the Conflicts of Jurisdiction Committee.[88] This body is composed of three members, namely, two of the permanent members of the Supreme Judicial Council, and the chairman of the other adjudicating entity or his deputy.[89] Cases are to be brought to the Committee by means of a petition submitted to the Secretariat of the Supreme Judicial Council.[90]

When the Committee takes jurisdiction of a case, proceedings in the lower court are to be automatically stayed. If the petition concerns the enforcement of conflicting judgments, the chairman of the Committee has discretion to order a stay of execution of both judgments or either of them pending disposition of the conflict.[91] The Committee has the power to summon parties to its hearings.[92] Its decisions are not subject to appeal.[93]

---

[86] *See id.* art. 26.

[87] *Id.* art. 28.

[88] *Id.* art. 29. *Cf.* Regs. for the Organization of Administrative Functions in the sharīʿah Court System, High Approval No. 109, art. 92 (1952) (providing that once a case has been referred to a court or commission having jurisdiction, it may not be referred to another authority until a judgment has issued).

[89] Judicial Regs., art. 29.

[90] *Id.* art. 30.

[91] *Id.* art. 31.

[92] *Id.* art. 30.

[93] *Id.* art. 32.

F. PROCEDURE IN SHARĪ'AH COURT

The Regulations for the Organization of Administrative Functions in the Sharī'ah Court System ["OAF"][94] are presently applicable to procedure.

1. Venue

Civil claims may be brought directly to the sharī'ah courts.[95] With the exception of traffic incidents and offenses, venue is proper solely in the place of residence of the defendant, if he resides in Saudi Arabia.[96] If the defendant has more than one residence, venue is proper in the area of residence of the plaintiff.[97] If the defendant resides outside of Saudi Arabia, venue is proper in any sharī'ah court having subject-matter jurisdiction. If there are several defendants, the claim should be brought in the place where the majority are present.[98] The plaintiff, however, will bring his complaint to the local regional governor's office.[99] It will generally seek to persuade the parties to reach an amicable settlement. If no settlement is reached, it will refer the claim to the proper court *sua sponte* or upon a party's request.[100]

2. Pretrial

The complaint need not be in writing.[101] On the day the complaint is brought, the judge sets the hearing date.[102] If the defendant or his legal

---

[94] High Approval No. 109 (1952). These regulations are to be replaced by comprehensive civil procedure regulations.

[95] *See* Vice-President of the Judiciary Circular No. 8745/3 (22/12/1380) (based on Royal Approval No. 23512 (25/11/1380)) (civil claims not involving public right requiring investigation need not be brought to governor or police, but court must hear case).

[96] OAF, art. 5. In the case of traffic accidents, venue is proper either in the area of residence of the defendant or at the place of the accident, at the option of the plaintiff. This rule applies whether or not the defendant is released on bond. *See* Minister of Justice Circular No. 121/18/t (17/6/1396). This rule is also applicable in criminal cases brought by the public prosecutor. If the defendant is imprisoned, the case is heard in the location of his detention regardless of where the underlying accident arose. *See* President of the Judiciary Letter No. 36/3/t (30/3/1389) (based on High Letter No. 21046 (11/10/1388)); Minister of Justice Circular No. 46/3/t (14/3/1393) (affirming same), *cited* in S. AL DURAIB, *supra* note 50, at 455 n. 1. *See also* President of the Judiciary Circular No. 107 (2/4/1392) (relating to private rights in the context of case based on public right).

[97] *See* President of the Council of Ministers Letter No. 2714 (1/5/1382) *effected by* President of the Judiciary Circular No. 1707/3 (8/6/1382).

[98] *See* H. AL AL-SHAIKH, *supra* note 20, at 92.

[99] *See* Governors & Administrative Councils Regs., Royal Will No. 41/1/1, art. 9 (15/1/1359); Rules of Procedure to be followed by Civil Rights Departments in claims of Private Rights, Minister of the Interior Resolution No. 20, art. 1 (2/1/1406) [hereinafter cited as Civil Rights Rules].

[100] *See* Governors and Administrative Councils Regs., art. 5(a); Civil Rights Rules, art. 9; Rules Governing New Powers of Regional Governors, para. 2(1)–(2).

[101] OAF, art. 7.

[102] *Id.* art. 1.

representative is not found within the Kingdom, the judge, in setting the date, will take into account any additional time necessary for notification and travel of the defendant.[103] Flexibility in scheduling the hearing is available.[104] Thus, where both parties appear before the judge and request an immediate hearing, and the issue to be resolved is not complex, the judge may hear the case if his case load permits.[105] Similarly, if both parties appear at a time other than that scheduled for the hearing, the judge, if not actually engaged in hearing another case, may hear their case.[106]

3. Service of process

Courts may exercise both territorial and extraterritorial *in personam* jurisdiction.[107] Unless the defendant is present,[108] he is entitled to notice. Summons is made by means of personal service if the defendant is found within the Kingdom.[109] If he is not found in Saudi Arabia, service is made through diplomatic channels. If the defendant has an attorney, service may be made on him.[110] In all cases, the summoning papers must include a summary of the complaint.[111] Service is made when the defendant signs the summoning papers.[112]

4. Appearance of parties at trial

Both default judgments and the dismissal of the complaint for failure to prosecute[113] are contemplated by the procedural regulations. However, the

---

[103] *Id.* art. 4. *Cf.* President of the Judiciary Circular No. 5816/3 (5/1/1383) (affirming applicability of art. 4).

[104] Cases of persons imprisoned on penal charges are given priority. *See* OAF, art. 75; Vice-President of the Judiciary Circular No. 3451/t (5/11/1383).

[105] OAF, art. 10; President of the Judiciary Letter No. 1253/3 (2/3/1381) (generally setting forth trial procedure).

[106] OAF, art. 11.

[107] *See id.* art. 4.

[108] *See id.* art. 10.

[109] *See id.* arts. 3, 6, 9, *Cf.* Attributions Regs., art. 172 (process-server's statement that he could not find defendant proves lack of notice) (but suggesting that summoning papers could be left with another person if certain to reach defendant). Notice within Arab League States is normally given in accordance with the rules of the State where given. *See* Agreement among the Arab League States relating to Writs and Letters of Request, *opened for signature* Nov. 6, 1952, art. 2, 159 British & Foreign State Papers 612 (English translation).

[110] *See* OAF, art. 95.

[111] *Id.* arts. 4, 7.

[112] The defendant's signature is proof that service was made: *see id.* art. 8. Unless the defendant has signed the summons, he may retain the defense of lack of personal jurisdiction. Moreover, the defendant, even if found, may not be compelled to sign the summoning papers if in possession of a valid defense such as *res judicata*, prior suit pending, or the fact that the return date on the summons allows insufficient time for appearance or has elapsed. *See* Deputy Minister of Justice Circular No. 58/2/t (2/5/1390) (relating generally to notification of judicial matters). *See also* OAF, art. 6 (if defendant is illiterate, service provable by two witnesses).

[113] *See* OAF, art. 32.

judge has the power to compel, by means of the regional governor and police, the appearance of parties present within the jurisdiction.[114] Such compulsory appearance applies not only to defendants, but also to plaintiffs in certain cases. In two cases, the police are explicitly authorized to bring in parties by the use of force: first, where a party refuses to appear at a hearing at which he is scheduled to take the oath;[115] and second, in actions for an accounting against a guardian, endowment trustee, or other fiduciary.[116] If neither party appears and the plaintiff has no valid justification, the case will be dropped.[117]

5. Default judgments

If the defendant, without an acceptable excuse, does not appear at and cannot be brought to the initial hearing, the court is to fix a second hearing date not more than three days later.[118] The police are responsible for notifying the defendant of the second hearing.[119] If the defendant does not appear at the second hearing, the court may proceed to trial in his absence.[120] The defendant is entitled to a final notification of any third trial session and is not deemed legally in default until he has failed to appear twice in the same case.[121] Lastly, it should be noted that if a party's attorney resigns or is discharged and the party is not found within the jurisdiction, the court may proceed to trial and issue a default judgment in the case.[122] In all cases, if a defaulting party appears at any point before the court has given judgment, he has a right to present his defense and to offer proof.[123]

Default judgments are appealable and are required to be referred to the appellate court for review.[124] Interlocutory execution may be obtained after affirmation by the court of appeals.[125] The judgment may not be affirmed until the defaulting party receives notice thereof, in the form of two

---

[114] *See id.* arts. 24–26, 30–31.

[115] *Id.* art. 31.

[116] *Id.* art. 30.

[117] Dismissal does not have *res judicata* effect until two unexcused defaults by the plaintiff, after which the case may only be heard pursuant to executive order. *Id.* art. 32. A case dropped and rebrought, due to the default of either party, will be considered the same case, and proceedings will resume at the point where left off. Vice-President of the Judiciary Circular No. 1067/3 (12/4/1384).

[118] OAF, art. 26.

[119] *Id.*

[120] *Id.* arts. 26–27.

[121] *Id.* arts. 27, 29.

[122] *Id.* art. 95.

[123] *Id.* art. 39.

[124] *See* Instructions for Reviewing Shari'ah Judgments [hereinafter cited as Appellate Rules], High Approval No. 24836, art. 8 (29/10/1386).

[125] OAF, art. 37 (affirmation, however, does not bar defaulting party from entering plea on appearance).

conformed copies of the judgment.[126] Upon affirmation, a party may obtain interlocutory execution of the judgment if two conditions are fulfilled. First, the subject of the judgment must be present within the Kingdom. Second, the party seeking execution must post a bond from a Saudi guarantor in an amount sufficient to cover any judgment in favor of the opposing party, in case such party should later prove to be entitled to vacation of the default judgment.[127]

6. Trial

Right to counsel

Parties may represent themselves or be represented by an attorney.[128] Attorneys must be licensed Saudi nationals.[129] Parties who do not speak Arabic may be accompanied by interpreters.

Direction of proceedings

Civil cases are tried before individual judges. Trials are public. However, judges have discretion to close trials in the interest of morals, the inviolability of the family, or public policy.[130] In addition to closing the courtroom to the general public, the judge may exclude any person, including a party, who disrupts the proceedings, and may sanction such person for contempt of court.[131] The maximum sentence that may be imposed for contempt is twenty-four hours' imprisonment.[132] However, if any person actually commits an offense in the courtroom, the judge may pronounce summary judgment with respect thereto.[133] In this case, there is no regulatory limitation on the sentence that may be imposed.

The judge directs the proceedings.[134] Parties may present their claims and defenses, offer evidence, and question witnesses only with his permission. Likewise, the clerk of the court may receive supporting documents from a party only in the judge's presence and on his order.[135] If the judge so orders, a party may examine in court, but not obtain copies of, the documents submitted by the opposing party.[136] The plaintiff

---

[126] Minister of Justice Circular No. 220/1/k/t (3/12/1391) (relating to default judgments against members of Arab League States).

[127] OAF, arts. 38, 40.

[128] *Id.* art. 59.

[129] *See id.* art. 63 (listing conditions for obtaining shari̅'ah lawyer's license).

[130] Judicial Regs., art. 33; OAF, art. 70.

[131] OAF, art. 74.

[132] *Id.*

[133] *Id.* art. 73.

[134] *Id.* art. 74.

[135] *Id.* art. 16. Prior to trial a case file is prepared by the court clerk, and studied by the judge. *See id.* arts. 15, 41.

[136] *Id.* art. 72.

addresses the court first. He must establish the *prima facie* validity of his claim before the defendant is required to answer.[137] If he does so, the defendant is required to give a complete answer to the complaint at the hearing, unless it is difficult for him to do so on the basis of information in his possession at that time.[138]

Adjournment

The general rule is that a party who has the burden of going forward must respond promptly.[139] However, the court has discretion to adjourn the hearing on a party's request in case of "necessity."[140] Only one adjournment is available per response.[141] The regulations also deal with specific situations where parties may obtain a rescheduling of the trial.

Adjournment for production of evidence. If the defendant must consult his books and records or the like in order to rebut the plaintiff's claim, the judge will adjourn the hearing to another date but has discretion to decide the time period "sufficient" to enable the defendant to gather his evidence.[142] Either party may obtain an adjournment in order to produce missing evidence.[143] However, if the necessary evidence is found within the jurisdiction of another sharī'ah judge, the court will request such other judge in writing to receive the evidence. The trial judge will set a time period within which the party must adduce such evidence before such other judge.[144] Where the trial has been adjourned and rescheduled, and a party either does not produce his witnesses at the rescheduled hearing or produces unacceptable witnesses, he is entitled to a second adjournment. If, without a valid excuse, such as the absence of the witnesses, he again fails to produce his evidence at the following hearing, the judge will consider him in default and decide the case without receiving such party's evidence.[145]

Request by attorney. A party's attorney may request an adjournment to enable him to consult his client, not present at the hearing, with respect to a question asked of him in court.[146] However, if the court finds repeated requests of this nature to be dilatory tactics on the attorney's part, it has the power to summon the client in person.[147]

---

[137] *Id.* art. 18.
[138] *Id.* arts. 19–20.
[139] *See id.* arts. 19, 21.
[140] *Id.* art. 21.
[141] *Id.* art. ??
[142] *Id.* art. 19.
[143] *Id.* art. 34 (giving judge discretion to fix "sufficient" time period).
[144] *Id.*
[145] *Id.* art. 35.
[146] *Id.* art. 66.
[147] *Id.*

Examination of witnesses

The judge may examine parties and witnesses, and parties may question witnesses with the judge's permission. As a rule, parties may not question their own witnesses, since they would be apt to ask leading questions of them. The scope of cross-examination is not limited to the scope of direct examination. On cross-examination, the judge's questions are more frequently directed to the testing of the evidence, while parties are responsible for attacking the credibility and character of the opposing party's witnesses.

7. Evidence

Judicial notice

Courts will take judicial notice of the law of Saudi Arabia and of matters of common knowledge within the Kingdom.

Production of evidence

Saudi law adheres generally to the rule that the burden of proof is on the proponent of a statement. Thus, in civil proceedings, parties are responsible for producing evidence, whether in the form of testimony or documentary evidence, supporting their allegations. There are no pretrial discovery procedures. The general rule is that no compulsory process is available to assist parties in the production of witnesses, or documentary evidence in the possession of parties or witnesses, at trial. This rule is grounded on the Islamic legal principle that testimony may not be compelled. It is, however, offset by the religious and moral obligation of Muslims to testify in cases involving private rights.[148]

Testimony[149]

(a) *Ordinary witnesses.* According to Islamic law, the oral testimony of two competent male witnesses of good character is required to establish a fact at issue.

(i) **Competency.** In order to qualify as competent, a witness must be adult, sane, Muslim, and of good character.[150] In addition, the requirement of lack of bias may preclude parties from testifying in their own behalf. Conversely, persons may not testify against their enemies. Furthermore,

---

[148] *See, e.g.*, H. LAOUST, PRECIS DE DROIT D'IBN QUDĀMĀ 293 & citations n. 1 (1950).

[149] Witnesses are not sworn in in shari'ah court, nor required to make any formal representation that they intend to tell the truth. However, they must use the word "testify" with respect to their testimony.

[150] *See, e.g.*, 12 M. IBN QUDĀMĀ, AL-MUGHNĪ, SH. IBN QUDĀMĀ, AL-SHARH AL-KABĪR 'ALĀ MATN AL-MUQNI· 27 (1983). Reasonable memory and ability of speech may also be required.

testimony of parties' close relatives, partners, and the like is inadmissible under the rule against partiality. Parties are, however, competent to make admissions. Attacks on witnesses on the grounds of bias are made after the witness has testified.

(*ii*) **Good character.**[151] Good character is proved by showing that the witness habitually fulfills his religious obligations and behaves according to Islamic standards of morality and dignity. Character is attacked or established by means of two character witnesses after the testifying witness has completed his testimony. Should the opposing party decline or be unable to attack the witness's character, the proponent of the witness must then prove the good character of the testifying witness by means of two competent witnesses. However, in the absence of an attack on the character of the witness, his good character may be established by means of personal knowledge of the judge.

It should be noted that a party whose witness was disqualified on the grounds of bad character is not, as a rule, permitted to rehabilitate him, either by means of proving his good character or by attacking the character of the opponent's character witnesses. The rule is that the character of character witnesses need not be proved; nor may it be attacked. However, character witnesses as well as testifying witnesses are liable for giving false evidence.

(*iii*) **Out-of-court testimony.** Islamic rules of evidence, similar to the Anglo-Saxon common law, exclude hearsay evidence. Witnesses may only testify about matters within their personal knowledge. Furthermore, only testimony made in court is admissible. The combination of the requirement of in-court testimony and personal knowledge results in the exclusion of out-of-court statements made by a witness who refuses to testify to such statements before the court. However, out-of-court testimony is admissible in shari'ah courts if made before or attested to by another shari'ah authority. It is also admissible if made before another shari'ah court at the specific request of the trial judge in cases where a witness is not found within the jurisdiction of the latter.[152] Such testimony must be proved by a formal letter from the court having received the testimony and a transcript of the testimony as entered in the record.

(*b*) *Expert witnesses.*[153] Testimony of expert witnesses is admissible to prove issues involving technical and scientific data, *inter alia*, sanity or insanity, the genuineness or falsity of signatures or handwriting,[154] and the extent of damages in physical injury cases. The rules applicable to experts

---

[151] *See generally id.* at 29–38.

[152] *See* OAF, art. 34.

[153] *See generally* Judicial Regs., arts. 97–98 (relating to status of court experts).

[154] *Cf.* Commercial Court Regs., High Order No. 32, art. 501 (1931) (repealed in part) (three experts required to prove handwriting) (applicable in commercial tribunals).

differ from those applicable to ordinary witnesses in that experts may be excused from the rules of establishment of character and that their testimony may be admissible in writing.

Real evidence

Real evidence is classified as a presumption according to Islamic law. Although admissible, it must be proved by oral testimony or by admission.[155]

Documentary evidence

Documents are admissible provided that proof of execution is made. However, the weight afforded to depositions or affidavits may vary according to whether or not they were made before a shari‘ah authority.

(*a*) *Official documents.* Official documents must be executed in accordance with the procedural formalities of the issuing entity and signed by a competent official thereof. Official documents duly issued by a notary public or other shari‘ah authority in Saudi Arabia are conclusive proof of their contents, unless alleged to have been falsified or to be contrary to Islamic law.[156] Thus a Saudi may establish his identity by means of an identity card.

Foreign documents are admissible when certified by the Saudi Arabian embassy in the country of issuance and by the Saudi Ministry of Foreign Affairs, but are not conclusive proof of the facts stated therein.[157] Powers of attorney must, in addition, be certified by the Ministry of Justice.

(*b*) *Unofficial documents.* Execution may be proved by the admission of the relevant party, by attesting witnesses, or by ordinary or expert witnesses testifying as to the genuineness of the signature or the handwriting.[158]

(*c*) *Original required.* Shari‘ah courts apply a doctrine similar to the common law Best Evidence Rule. Thus, only the original document is admissible in evidence, unless the party is for a valid reason unable to produce the original, in which case the document may be proved by means of oral testimony or by the introduction of a copy. In the case of official documents, copies must be certified or themselves be official documents. Certified copies of judgments must be signed by the first clerk of the court and bear the seals of the trial judge and the court.

---

[155] *See, e.g.*, MAJALLAT AL-AHKĀM AL-‘ADLIYYAH, bk. 15, ch. 2. In some cases, location of evidence may require the judge to sit in the place of the dispute. *See* Judicial Regs., art. 27.

[156] *See* Judicial Regs., art. 96; *cf.* OAF, art. 93 (shari‘ah court may not invalidate document authenticated by notary public save on sole ground of illegality under shari‘ah); Attributions Regs., art. 182 (notary public prohibited from recording transactions contrary to Islamic law).

[157] If the document appears suspect on its face, the court is to return a copy for authentication to the issuing source. For procedures relating to authentication of certain foreign documents, *see generally* Appendix 33.

[158] *Cf.* Commercial Court Regs., arts. 500–501 (applicable in commercial tribunals).

8. Oath

The proponent of a statement has the burden of proof on that issue. However, in a civil case relating to money or property, a plaintiff who has no admissible evidence in support of his claim may demand that the defendant take the oath denying the validity of the plaintiff's claim. A nonMuslim plaintiff may demand the oath of a Muslim defendant. The value of the oath is procedural rather than evidentiary. It is not admissible to prove facts in dispute, but rather serves to rebut the plaintiff's claim. The plaintiff thus retains the burden of going forward to meet the defendant's denial. The defendant has the right to take the oath or to decline to do so.[159] The effect of his refusal is to establish the truth of the plaintiff's allegations. However, if the defendant does take the oath, he will prevail unless the plaintiff can prove his claim by evidentiary means. In this type of situation, if the plaintiff has no evidence to support his claim and does not demand that the defendant take the oath, the claim will be dropped. The plaintiff, however, is not precluded from raising the same claim later if he discovers relevant admissible evidence or if he decides to require the oath.

9. Judgment

After hearing the evidence and any attacks on the character of witnesses and attestations to their good character, the judge will issue his judgment.[160] The plaintiff may waive his claim at any time prior to judgment, if, for example, the parties reach a settlement. If so, the judge will drop the case. However, if the case involves both public and private rights, only the private right may be dropped. The public right survives.

The judgment must rest solely on evidence before the court; judges may not decide a case on the basis of personal knowledge. However, if the case presents a complex issue, the trial judge may seek the opinion of a higher judicial authority before he gives judgment.[161] The judgment will dispose of the rights of the parties and, if required, will establish damages under general rules of Islamic law. Judgment is pronounced in open court.[162] After deciding the case, the judge prepares a case record containing a summary of the pleadings and a verbatim transcript of the testimony of

---

[159] *See also* OAF, art. 31 (person refusing to attend when scheduled to take oath may be summoned by force; Pres. of the Judiciary Circular No. 269 (24/3/1381) (regarding circumstances where plaintiff is required to take the oath).

[160] *See* Pres. of the Judiciary Circular No. 1253/3 (2/3/1381); *cf.* Minister of Justice Circular No. 11/2/t (13/1/1391) (expression of opinion by judge is insufficient) (judgment required).

[161] OAF, art. 46.

[162] Judicial Regs., art. 33.

witnesses, and describing the trial proceedings and any oaths taken.[163] The record[164] and the judgment[165] must also state the legal grounds for the decision. The losing party must then be asked if he is satisfied with the judgment, and his signed statement of satisfaction or dissatisfaction must be entered in the record.[166] The document is then signed by the judge and registered.[167] The prevailing party may receive a copy of the judgment which also is registered.[168] However, a nonprevailing party having entered a statement of dissatisfaction in the record is entitled to a judgment in order to prepare an eventual appeal.[169] Judgments are handwritten on official paper, sealed with the seal of the court and the personal seal of the trial judge, and signed by him and by the head judge of the court if he was not the trial judge.[170]

G. APPELLATE PROCEDURE

1. Appealability

Provided that the nonprevailing party has not signed the record expressing his satisfaction with the judgment,[171] judgments of a value greater than 500 riyals and issued with respect to personal property are appealable. Judgments relating to real property are appealable regardless of value.[172] An appeal may also be made from the court's dismissal of a plaintiff's case on the grounds that no claim is stated, and of dismissal of a case prior to judgment. Interlocutory appeals are not permitted. Either party may appeal.[173]

2. Timeliness

The right to appeal may be lost if an objection to the judgment and an appeal are not timely made. If the party has timely stated lack of

[163] OAF, art. 42; *cf.* Attributions Regs., art. 68.

[164] OAF, arts. 42, 69.

[165] Judicial Regs., art. 35.

[166] Attributions Regs., art. 62; Appellate Rules, art. 5.

[167] OAF, art. 42; Attributions Regs., art. 62.

[168] *See also* OAF, art. 68 (settlements made during proceedings recorded and issued in shari'ah court document).

[169] Appellate Rules, art. 5.

[170] *See generally* Attributions Regs., art. 58 (authentication by court chairman and court seal required): A. HUQAIL, 'ILĀQĀT AL-MUWĀṬIN BI AL-DAWĀ'IR AL-SHAR'IYYAH 196 (1967) (reprinting President of the Judiciary circular requiring personal seal on judgments and authenticated documents).

[171] Appellate Rules, art. 3(b).

[172] *Id.* art. 3(e).

[173] However, art. 5 of the Appellate Rules expressly provides for appeals by the defendant only.

satisfaction, the trial judge has discretion to set the time-period within which an appeal must be made, provided that the period be not less than ten days nor more than fifteen days.[174] The court is required to inform the party that if he fails to perfect his appeal and to return the copy of the judgment within the prescribed period, he will lose his right to appeal.[175] In a proper case, however, the hearing of an untimely appeal made in good faith may not be precluded.[176]

3. Procedure for bringing appeals

Cases in which the defendant has made a statement of dissatisfaction are automatically reviewed.[177] The actual petition of appeal is submitted in the trial court. No particular form is required. The appeal need not be drafted by an attorney; nor need the appellant state the specific grounds on which he is appealing. However, an appellant should, if possible, submit with the appeal any evidence, either newly discovered or in the possession of such party prior to judgment, which was not introduced at the trial. The trial court will send the appeal, the case record, the file, and any supporting documents to the appellate court.[178] However, since the trial judge will send the case for review even if the appellant has failed to submit his petition, the main adverse consequence of the failure to do so is that review will be made on the basis of the record.

4. Stay of execution pending appeal

For purposes of enforcement, judgments are not final until affirmed. Thus, the lower judgment is automatically stayed pending appeal.[179]

5. Appellate review of judgments

Scope of review

The entire judgment may be reviewed, including those portions which were not appealed. Parties who did not join in the appeal may benefit from an appeal brought by other parties. The appellate court may vacate or affirm, in whole or in part, and, in case of vacation, will remand with

---

[174] *Id.* arts. 3(c), 5.

[175] *Id.* art. 5. *Cf.* Deputy Minister of Justice Circular No. 184/1/t (23/11/1392) (affirming that compliance with art. 5 required) (setting time period in view of inconsistency between arts. 3 and 5),

[176] *See* Appellate Rules, art. 4 (contemplating exceptional appeals).

[177] OAF, art. 44; Appellate Rules, art. 6.

[178] OAF, art. 44; Appellate Rules, art. 6; *cf.* A. HUQAIL, *supra* note 170, at 204–05, 207 (reprinting Presidency of the Judiciary circulars requiring submission of all supporting documents in order to expedite appeal).

[179] *See* OAF, art. 50 (judgments not final or enforceable until affirmed).

comments. Dissenting opinions are set forth in writing and kept by the court.[180] If the court sets aside the judgment, it may not enter its own decision but must remand it to the trial judge.[181] If the appellate court vacates or comments on the judgment in part only, on remand the pleadings and rehearing are limited to those portions vacated, unless the substance of the case is affected.[182]

Record and documents

Appellate review is, as a rule, limited to the study of the written documents submitted. The proceedings are not open to the public or, in general, to parties or their advocates.[183] However, parties may submit new relevant documentary evidence while the appeal is pending.[184] Moreover, the court may, if necessary, summon parties or witnesses for questioning.[185] The court may also ask the trial judge to clarify points made in his decision.[186]

Timing of appellate decisions

The court is supposed to rule on appeals within one month of their submission.[187] In practice, review may take longer. Furthermore, the court has discretion to postpone the reviewing of a judgment on the grounds that supplementary information or the conducting of an investigation is required before the case can be reviewed.[188]

Grounds for vacation of trial judgment

The appellate court will vacate any lower judgment in conflict with an express provision of the Qurān or sunnah or with any legal principle established by consensus.[189] Error of fact or a judgment rendered against the weight of the evidence may also be grounds for vacation. In contrast, technical errors on the face of the judgment or minor procedural defects are not grounds for vacation.[190] The court has discretion to reverse the dismissal of a *prima facie* claim which was not tried. Additionally, the court

---

[180] Appellate Rules, art. 22.
[181] *See* OAF, art. 49; Appellate Rules, art. 7.
[182] OAF, art. 49.
[183] Appellate Rules, arts. 25, 34; *cf.* Attributions Regs., art. 29 (applicable to review by former Presidency of the Judiciary).
[184] Appellate Rules, art. 7 (expressly applicable solely to nonprevailing party).
[185] *See id.* art. 25.
[186] *Id.* art. 11.
[187] *Id.* art. 27. *But see* OAF, art. 45 (20-day maximum limit).
[188] Appellate Rules, art. 28.
[189] *Id.* art. 13.
[190] *See id.* art. 18.

may in its discretion set aside final judgments on the grounds of lack of jurisdiction, procedural error resulting in actual prejudice to the appellant, newly discovered evidence, or insufficient or inadmissible evidence.

Precedent

An appellate department may not vacate a judgment supported by previous appellate conclusions of independent reasoning (ijtihād), whether issued by the same or another appellate department.[191] Any panel desiring in a pending case to depart from such an established principle is required to refer the case to the General Commission.[192] This body must make decisions authorizing departure from prior ijtihād by a two-thirds majority of its membership.[193] However, if the Minister of Justice does not agree with the result, he has the power to send the case back to the General Commission for reconsideration.[194] If the latter's decision on reconsideration remains unacceptable to the Minister, the case will then be brought before the Supreme Judicial Council, whose decision is final.[195] It may be noted that such referral to the General Commission may not be requested by a party, even if his theory on appeal is the invalidity of a legal principle previously established.

Remand

If the appellate court disagrees with the trial judge's decision, it will ask the latter to modify or reverse it. If the trial court agrees with the appellate court's comments, it will modify its judgment accordingly or reverse it *sua sponte* and reexamine the case. If it does not agree, it may send a memorandum defending its judgment to the appellate court.[196] If the latter is convinced by the trial judge's arguments, it will affirm the initial judgment. If not, it will vacate the judgment[197] and remand the case to another judge for a new trial.[198] The new judgment is also appealable.

[191] *See id.* art. 13 (not including differing legal conclusion as grounds for vacation).
[192] Judicial Regs., art. 14. *See also* S. AL DURAIB, *supra* note 50, at 445–46 (interpreting art. 14 to require a number of prior judgments containing such ijtihād to have issued) (one or two insufficient to justify referral).
[193] Judicial Regs., art. 14.
[194] *See Id.* art. 20.
[195] *Id.* art. 14. This result may also obtain where a two-thirds majority is not obtained in the General Commission.
[196] Appellate Rules, art. 14.
[197] *Id.* art. 15.
[198] *Id.* art. 17.

Affirmation

The vast majority of judgments are affirmed.[199] In this case, the appellate court sends a copy of its decision to the trial court, and, if no further review is available, the judgment is final.[200] This finality, however, does not preclude an appellate court from modifying or vacating its affirmation of the lower judgment on the basis of newly discovered evidence. It may do so on this ground even after it has informed the trial court of its decision.

6. Enforcement

Final judgments not subject to further appeal through normal judicial channels are enforceable. Judgments may acquire the quality of enforceability by means of affirmation by an appellate court in accordance with applicable rules of law, by virtue of the parties' statements of satisfaction, or by the running of the limitation period for appeal.[201] The party having obtained the judgment is entitled to have it enforced on presentation of the confirmed judgment and enforcement order to the appropriate regional governor's office.[202] The standard language of the enforcement order requires all competent government departments to enforce the judgment by all regulatory means, including the use of force by the police.[203] The rule is that no further procedural steps are required. However, prior to enforcement, the regional governor may be required to refer the judgment to the Ministry of the Interior if two final inconsistent sharīʿah judgments disposing of the same subject-matter have been issued;[204] if the instrument of judgment issued is in violation, procedurally or formally, of applicable rules of law; and, finally, if the legal substance of the judgment is an unprecedented ijtihād required, in the public interest, to be reviewed by the Supreme Judicial Council before enforcement.[205]

II. Specialized Commissions

The sharīʿah courts are courts of general jurisdiction over civil disputes (as well as criminal cases). However, the Judicial Regulations contemplate

---

[199] For example, in the year 1399, 5,581 cases were affirmed, 1,979 remanded with comments, and 62 reversed, al-Jazīrah, March, 31, 1981, at 7.

[200] OAF, art. 50.

[201] *See id.*; *cf.* Rules Governing New Powers of Regional Governors, para. 2(3).

[202] OAF, art. 50; Provinces Regs., art. 8(a); Civil Rights Rules, art. 8; Rules Governing New Powers of Regional Governors, para. 2(3).

[203] *See* Minister of Justice Circular No. 65/t (9/4/1394) (specifically relating to default judgments).

[204] *But see* Judicial Regs., art. 29 (Conflicts of Jurisdiction Committee has jurisdiction over conflicting final judgments of which one is issued by a sharīʿah court).

[205] Rules Governing New Powers of Regional Governors, para. 2(5).

the constitution of specialized courts.[206] Pending the constitution of specialized courts to handle commercial and labor cases and juvenile offenders,[207] specialized commissions adjudicate such cases by virtue of specific regulatory grant of jurisdiction delimiting their competence. In addition, enforcement and investigatory commissions are charged with the enforcement of certain regulations. The jurisdiction of the commissions is defined both in terms of subject-matter and of the parties to the action. The rule is that the commissions do not ordinarily have jurisdiction to adjudicate cases to which the Saudi Government or any of its agencies is a party.[208] However, the Government *qua* prosecutor may appear before the commissions in cases involving regulatory violations. This section discusses the principal specialized commissions.[209]

A. COMMISSION FOR THE SETTLEMENT OF COMMERCIAL DISPUTES

Established in 1967, the Commission is the forum for private commercial litigation in the Kingdom. It has general commercial jurisdiction without pecuniary limitation by virtue of various regulatory grants of jurisdiction and has generally assumed the jurisdiction of the former Commercial Court.[210] It applies the relevant provisions of applicable commercial law and those provisions, including the procedural provisions, of the Commercial Court Regulations that have not been superseded. The Commission is specifically granted jurisdiction over actions arising under the Companies Regulations[211] and the Regulations Governing the Relationship between the Foreign Contractor and its Saudi Agent ["Services Agents Regulations"].[212] In addition, the Commission has jurisdiction to hear disputes arising under the Commercial Agencies Regulations[213] and commercial land

---

[206] *See* Judicial Regs., art. 26.

[207] *See* Council of Ministers Resolution No. 167 (14/9/1401). For present commissions having jurisdiction over labor disputes, see generally pp. 316–19 *infra*. At present, there is a specialized juvenile court in Riyadh. Juvenile offenders are tried in other major cities before specialized sharī'ah judges, and in other cities before regular judges.

[208] For disputes to which the Government is a party, see generally pp. 231–43 *infra*.

[209] Other commissions may be constituted under various regulations, *see, e.g.*, Printed Matter and Publications Regs., Royal Decree No. M/17, art. 40 (1982) (providing for a three-member enforcement committee to be established by Ministry of Information).

[210] By virtue of Council of Ministers Resolution No. 186 of 5/2/1387, the commission established under art. 232 of the Companies Regs. was merged with the Commission for the Resolution of Commercial Disputes established under Council of Ministers Resolution No. 228 of November 11, 1960 and Minister of Commerce Resolution No. 262 of 26/11/1384.

[211] *See* Companies Regs., Royal Decree No. M/6, art. 232 (1965), *as amended by* Royal Decrees Nos. M/5 (12/3/1387), M/23 (28/6/1402) & M/46 (4/7/1405).

[212] Royal Decree No. M/2, art. 11 (1978).

[213] Royal Decree No. 11 (1962), *as amended by* Royal Decrees Nos. M/5 (8/24/1969), M/8 (1393), & M/32 (1980). No express grant of jurisdiction is provided in the Regulations.

and maritime cases, including vessel mortgage disputes, to which merchants, shippers, warehousemen, moneychangers, brokers, and their agents are parties.[214] The Commission is empowered to liquidate companies in a proper case,[215] and to impose penalties for violations of the Companies Regulations.[216] The Commission has no jurisdiction over criminal cases in the commercial context or, as a rule, over disputes relating to real property.[217] The Commission is also responsible for enforcing Council of Ministers Resolution No. 266.[218] The three branches of the Commission sit in Riyadh, Jeddah, and Dammam. Each is composed of three fulltime members, of whom two are trained in Islamic law and nominated by the Minister of Justice. The third is a legal consultant trained in regulatory law and nominated by the Minister of Commerce.

Complaints are first brought to the regional governor, who then refers the case to the Commission for settlement.[219] Venue is properly in the defendant's place of residence or, in case of a company, the main office of the defendant.[220] However, if the defendant has a local presence within the jurisdiction of one of the Commissions, venue may be proper there. Personal jurisdiction may be exercised over persons having no presence within the Kingdom, such as a foreign seller who has directly shipped goods to a Saudi customer.

Parties are entitled to be represented by counsel. The Commission applies Islamic rules of procedure and evidence.[221] The Commission also may compel the production of documentary evidence in the possession of government departments or private commercial entities.[222] Decisions may be by majority vote.[223] Default judgments are permitted upon the

However, the Commission hears commercial agency disputes by virtue of its general commercial jurisdiction. *See also* Ministry of Commerce Model Commercial Agency or Distribution Agreement, art. 16 (providing for disputes to be brought before Commission for the Settlement of Commercial Disputes) (translated in Appendix 2). In addition, there is a view that its jurisdiction, with respect to disputes between nonSaudi principals and Saudi agents, is grounded on art. 228 of the Companies Regs., providing that any "agencies" established by foreign companies are subject to the Companies Regs. and hence to the Commission's jurisdiction thereunder.

[214] *See* Commercial Court Regs., art. 443.

[215] Companies Regs., art. 15(7).

[216] *Id.* art. 232.

[217] *See* Commercial Court Regs., art. 3. *Cf.* al-Jazīrah, May 5, 1982, at 32, col. 3 (Ministry of Commerce notification to all its branches clarifies that jurisdiction over real property cases and the like is in sharīʿah courts).

[218] Resolution No. 266 (21/2/1398) (requiring use of Arabic language) (translated in Appendix 17).

[219] *See* Commercial Court Regs., art. 459; Civil Rights Rules, art. 9(b).

[220] *Cf.* OAF, art. 5.

[221] Commercial Court Regs., art. 506.

[222] *Id.* art. 498.

[223] *Id.* art. 509.

defendant's second failure to appear, but, if timely objection is made, the decision is vacated.[224]

The general rule is that the decisions of the Commission are final and enforceable.[225] However, if the prevailing party is seeking to enforce the judgment in the Kingdom, the Commission notifies the appropriate regional governor, in writing, that the judgment is final. The limitation period for appeals is thirty days as from the appellant's actual receipt of notice of the judgment.[226] In contrast, objections to default judgments are subject to a fifteen day limitation period beginning as from the date the defendant has actual notice of the decision.[227] The defendant must show some sign of interest in the decision within that period. Thus, objection may be made by telex or telegram. On receipt of the defendant's objection, the Commission will reopen the case. Appeals may be made through various channels, *inter alia* through the Minister of Commerce, the regional governor or the King, or directly to the Commission. Appeals are decided on the record and supporting papers and are deemed final on approval by the Minister of Commerce.

B. COMMITTEE FOR NEGOTIABLE INSTRUMENTS

1. Jurisdiction

Jurisdiction over actions arising under the Negotiable Instruments Regulations,[228] formerly in the Commission for the Settlement of Commercial Disputes, was vested in the Committees for Negotiable Instruments in 1968.[229] The Committees sit in Riyadh, al-Aḥsā, Jeddah, and Dammam. Each is composed of a chairman and two members appointed from among the legal experts in the Ministry of Commerce.

The Committees' jurisdiction over civil claims relating to negotiable instruments is exclusive. However, defenses to payment of the instrument based on the underlying facts are litigated before the Commission for the Settlement of Commercial Disputes. In addition, the Committees may punish violations arising under the Negotiable Instruments Regulations. However, their jurisdiction in this area is nonexclusive, to the extent that the Board of Grievances may punish the forgery or falsification of

---

[224] *Id.* art. 529.

[225] *See* High Letter No. 1018 (10/10/1390), *cited in* S. AL DURAIB, *supra* note 50, at 464.

[226] Commercial Court Regs., art. 543.

[227] *Id.* art. 531 (not counting time required for travel).

[228] Royal Decree No. 37 (11/10/1383).

[229] Ministry of Commerce & Indus. Resolutions Nos. 353 & 354 (11/5/1388) & 357 (16/5/1388). Certain procedures and formalities relating to the Committees have been recently updated. *Cf.* Civil Rights Rules, art. 9(c) (regarding jurisdiction).

negotiable instruments as provided in the antiforgery regulations.[230] The Committees also rule on offenses under the Boycott of Israel Regulations.[231]

2. Procedure

The Committees apply the provisions of the Commercial Court Regulations relating to the summoning of parties, trial procedure, rules of evidence, default judgments, objections to judgments, and provisional attachment.[232] The defendant will be deemed to have appeared if service of notice of the time of the hearing is made upon him personally or upon his authorized attorney, a person in his service, or a spouse or relative by kinship or marriage residing with him.[233] A company or sole proprietorship will be deemed to have appeared if notice is given at its place of business upon any of such enterprise's employees.[234] The defendant will also be deemed to have made an appearance if he appears at any session relating to the case or submits a memorandum in his defense, whether or not he fails to appear at subsequent sessions.[235] Pending the proceedings, the plaintiff is permitted to seek the provisional attachment of his debtor's funds, whether in the possession of such debtor or a third party, after submitting a bank guarantee or certified bank check, or guarantee from a solvent surety.[236]

Decisions of the Committees are enforceable without the posting of a bond by the prevailing party. An objection or appeal made by the nonprevailing party will not automatically stay execution. However, the Minister of Commerce or his authorized agent may order on petition of the party and after the posting of a bank guarantee or certified bank check, a temporary stay of execution pending a ruling on the appeal.[237] If the defendant has made an appearance, an appeal from a Committee's decision may be made to the Minister of Commerce within thirty days of a party's receipt of notification of the decision.[238] Supporting documents must be attached to the appellant's petition.[239] An objection to a default decision

[230] See generally pp. 241–42 infra.

[231] Royal Decree No M/8, para. 1(a) (26/5/1404) (amending art. 12 of Boycott of Israel Regs., Royal Decree No. 26 (25/6/1382)).

[232] See Minister of Commerce Resolution No. 859, art. 1 (13/3/1403) (repealing Minister of Commerce Resolution No. 2093 (18/6/1401)).

[233] Id. art. 2.

[234] Id.

[235] Id.

[236] Id. art. 5.

[237] Id. art. 3.

[238] Id. art. 6. Appeals are made to the Legal Committee in the Ministry of Commerce. See Minister of Commerce Resolution No. 918 (25/3/1403), cited in 1 Ministry of Commerce, collection of regulatory principles in matters of negotiable instruments 6 (1985) (also reporting appellate decisions).

[239] Resolution No. 859, art. 6.

may be made to the Committee issuing such decision within fifteen days from the defendant's receipt of a copy of the decision.[240] If the defendant fails to make its objection within such period, it may appeal the decision to the Minister of Commerce within thirty days from the date of expiration of the period for objection.[241]

C. COMMERCIAL AGENCY COMMISSION

The Commission sits in Riyadh. It is composed of three members, of whom at least one is required to be a legal consultant, appointed by the Minister of Commerce.[242] Its function is to enforce the Commercial Agencies Regulations.[243] It has no jurisdiction over civil claims. Violations of the Regulations and the implementing rules issued thereunder are established by an investigation team designated by the Ministry of Commerce. In the execution of their duties, the investigators have the status of "judicial" officers.[244] Thus, they have the right to enter offices and commercial premises, to inspect documents and records, to question parties, to carry out investigation procedures, and to prepare reports of violations discovered.[245] All penalties imposed by the Commission must be confirmed by the Minister of Commerce.[246] Parties have the right to appeal Commission decisions to the Minister within fifteen days from the date that the party or its representative actually received notice of the decision.[247] The Ministry of Commerce is required to notify the Minister of the Interior of all final penalties imposed upon nonSaudi offenders and of nonSaudi

---

[240] *Id.* art. 7.

[241] *Id.*

[242] *See* Commercial Agencies Regs. Implementing Rules, Minister of Commerce Resolution No. 1897, art. 21 (1981).

[243] Royal Decree No. M/5, para. 1(1) (8/24/1969). The Commission has discretion to impose fines of 5,000 to 50,000 riyals upon persons violating the Regulations or their implementing rules. If the violator is nonSaudi or a Saudi company with one or more foreign partners, dissolution of the business is prescribed. In cases involving nonSaudi nationals, the Commission may also bar the offender from engaging in commercial activities either permanently or during a period to be set at its discretion. *See* Royal Decree No. M/32, pt. 1 (amending Commercial Agencies Regs., art. 4). Furthermore, violators may also be subject to penalties for the same acts under the Commercial Register Regs., Royal Order No. 21/1/4470, arts. 14–18 (1955) and other applicable law. *See* Commercial Agencies Regs. Implementing Rules, art. 20.

[244] Commercial Agencies Regs. Implementing Rules, art. 19. *Cf.* Customs Regs. Implementing Rules, art. 255 (1953) (cognate term used of customs inspectors).

[245] Commercial Agencies Regs. Implementing Rules, art. 19.

[246] Royal Decree No. M/5, para. 1(2) (Aug. 24, 1969); Commercial Agencies Regs., Implementing Rules, art. 21.

[247] Royal Decree No. M/5, para. 1(2) (1969); Commercial Agencies Regs. Implementing Rules, art. 21. Even if a party does not appeal to the Minister, the latter has discretion to set aside the penalty.

partners in Saudi companies on which penalties were imposed.[248] The Minister of the Interior may, in his discretion, order the deportation of nonSaudi offenders.[249]

D. COMMITTEES FOR COMBATING COMMERCIAL FRAUD

Prior regulations

The three committees sat in Riyadh, Jeddah, and Dammam. Each was composed of a chairman and two members appointed by the Minister of Commerce. The functions of these bodies, supplemented by investigatory commissions of the same name, were to confiscate or destroy, *inter alia*, harmful or spoiled foodstuff, livestock, medical supplies and drugs, and to impose the penalties provided by the Regulations for Combating Commercial Fraud.[250] Decisions of the committees did not become final until approved by the Minister of Commerce. The Regulations provided for a fifteen day limitation period. If a party aggrieved by any such decision failed to complain to the Minister of Commerce within that period, the latter was to approve the committee's determination.[251]

Present regulations

The 1984 Regulations for Combating Commercial Fraud places the authority to impose regulatory punishments on offenders in committees formed by resolution of the Minister of Commerce, in such locations as he deems required.[252] Each committee is formed of three members, of whom two represent the Ministry of Commerce and the third represents the Ministry of Municipal and Rural Affairs. At least one of such members is required to be an expert in regulatory law.[253] Parties are entitled to one week's notice of the hearing. Notices are to be served personally or on parties' employees or legal representatives through the Ministry of Commerce or the regional governors. The committees are also empowered to undertake any investigations they deem necessary.[254] The committees' decisions are made by majority vote.[255] With the exception of decisions inflicting prison sentences, decisions of the Committees are final after

[248] Royal Decree No. M/32, pt. 1 (1980).
[249] *Id.*
[250] Royal Decree No. 45, arts. 9–11 (14/8/1381) (superseded 1404).
[251] *Id.* art. 11.
[252] Royal Decree No. M/11, art. 16 (29/5/1404) (March 1, 1984).
[253] *Id.*
[254] Regs. for Combating Commercial Fraud Implementing Rules, Minister of Commerce Resolution No. 1327/3/1, arts. 26–27, 31 (1/6/1405) (Feb. 20, 1985).
[255] *Id.* art. 29.

approval by the Minister of Commerce.[256] The Regulations provide for an appeal to the Board of Grievances from a decision imposing a prison sentence within thirty days of the date of notification to the defendant.[257] If an appeal is not made within the regulatory limitation period, such decision will become final after approval by the Minister of Commerce. If an appeal is duly made, the Ministry of Commerce will forward the relevant documents to the Board of Grievances together with the expression of its point of view. The decision of the Board of Grievances is final.[258]

E. COMMITTEE ON FRAUD AND DECEIT IN DEALINGS WITH THE GOVERNMENT

Established pursuant to the Rules Applicable to Persons Prohibited from Dealing with the Government,[259] the Committee's function is to study cases of fraud, deception, and dishonesty perpetrated upon government departments and agencies and to determine which parties, due to their fraudulent or dishonest acts, should be disqualified from future dealings with the Government.[260] Required to be composed exclusively of Saudi legal consultants from neutral government organs,[261] the five-member Committee includes legal consultants from the Bureau of Experts of the Council of Ministers, the General Audit Board, the Commission of Investigation and Discipline, and the Ministry of Finance and National Economy.[262]

Ministries, government departments, and government agencies having independent juristic personalities, are required to notify cases of fraud or deceit on the part of private contractors to the Ministry of Finance and National Economy.[263] Similarly, decisions of government authorities to

---

[256] Regs. for Combating Commercial Fraud, art. 17.

[257] *Id.* The decision must state the party's right to appeal within such limitation period. Regs. for Combating Commercial Fraud Implementing Rules, art. 30.

[258] Regs. for Combating Commercial Fraud, art. 17.

[259] Council of Ministers Resolution No. 11 (26/2/1400) [Rules], art. 3; Minister of Fin. & Nat'l Econ. Resolution No. 17/3623, art. 1 (2/8/1400).

[260] *See* Rules, arts. 1, 3. The Rules list seven categories of persons prohibited from making sales or submitting bids to the Government or performing public services or works. *See* Rules, art. 1. The Committee is authorized to decide which persons should be disqualified under article 1(f)–(g) of the Rules. However, the sanction of prohibition may also be imposed by other judicial bodies. *See id. Cf.* Regs. for Combating Bribery, Royal Decree No. 15, art. 12 (1962) (persons convicted of bribery crimes barred from executing public works, making sales, submitting bids to the Government) (translated in Appendix 6).

[261] Rules, art. 3. Committee members are barred from hearing cases relating to the government department or agency to which they belong. *See* Minister of Fin. & Nat'l Econ. Resolution No. 17/3623, art. 3.

[262] Minister of Fin. & Nat'l Econ. Resolution No. 17/3623, art. 1.

[263] Rules, art. 2. Cases must be reported whether discovered during the course of performance of the contract or after its execution.

withdraw work from contractors must be submitted to the Ministry.[264] The Committee studies such notifications and decisions[265] and may also take cognizance of grievances raised by contractors with respect to such administrative decisions.[266] In cases involving reported fraudulent acts, the private party is entitled to a hearing and to present its defense before the Committee. The government party involved may also argue in support of its prior determination at the hearing.[267] If any of the alleged violations reported is established at the hearing, the Committee is required to bar the offender from dealing with the Government, but has discretion to set the duration of such prohibition.[268] After reviewing administrative decisions to withdraw work, the Committee has discretion to decide whether the grounds on which such decisions were based are of a nature to justify barring the private party from dealing with the Government.[269] A private party objecting to the termination has the right to a hearing.[270] Decisions may be made by majority voice.[271] All decisions may be appealed to the Board of Grievances within sixty days of the party's receipt of notice.[272] They must be signed by at least three members and the chairman or his deputy, state the grounds on which the decision rests, and notify the party that it has a right to appeal the decision to the Board of Grievances within sixty days of receipt of notice of the decision.[273]

Names of persons banned, upon issuance of final decisions, are recorded in a special register and also circulated among government departments.[274] The period of prohibition may not be modified, nor the names of persons sanctioned removed from the register before the end of such period, except by means of a Council of Ministers resolution or high order.[275]

---

[264] *Id.*

[265] *Id.* arts. 4–5. Cases are referred to the Committee by its secretary, who is appointed by the Central Administrative Office for Government Purchases in the Ministry of Finance and National Economy Minister of Fin. & Nat'l Econ. Resolution No. 17/3623, art. 7.

[266] Rules, art. 3. *But see* pp. 240–41 *Infra.*

[267] *See* Rules, arts. 3–4.

[268] *Id.* art. 4. The regulatory guidelines for setting the prohibition period provide that the period should be "sufficient to deter". In its Decision No. 11 of 2/7/1402, in a case raised by the Ministry of Health, the Committee prohibited the company involved from dealing with the Government for a two-year period. This ruling was affirmed on appeal. *See* Board of Grievances Decision No. 3908/1 (30/8/1403) (in Institute of Public Administration library).

[269] Rules, art. 5.

[270] *See id.* art. 3.

[271] Minister of Fin. & Nat'l Econ. Resolution No. 17/3623, art.4.

[272] Rules, arts. 4–5. Notice is given by the Committee secretary, who is required to serve parties or their representatives with official notifications and a copy of the decision.

[273] Minister of Fin. & Nat'l Econ. Resolution No. 17/3623, arts. 3, 5.

[274] Rules, art. 6; Minister of Fin. & Nat'l Econ. Resolution No. 17/3623, arts. 6–7. The Central Administrative Office for Government Purchases performs these functions.

[275] Rules, art. 7.

F. CUSTOMS COMMITTEES

The Primary Customs Committees have original jurisdiction to investigate and punish all crimes of smuggling or attempted smuggling under the Customs Regulations.[276] The twelve Committees of first instance are each composed of four customs officials and one legal advisor.[277] They have the status of "administrative court[s]" and have the discretion to conduct full evidentiary hearings of smuggling cases.[278] Violations are prosecuted by customs officials.[279] The accused is entitled to notice of the hearing.[280] Notice may be made by publication in Umm al-Qurā.[281] Committee decisions may be made by a majority of members present.[282] The decision itself must be issued on official paper bearing the customs seal,[283] dated, signed by those Committee members who participated in the hearing,[284] and must contain a summary of the facts of

[276] Royal Decree No. 425, art. 52 (1953). The Regulations define "smuggling" as the importation or exportation of "goods, substances, or things of any kind" by unlawful means and without paying the prescribed customs duties on such articles. *Id.* art. 38. Furthermore, the fraudulent attempt to evade payment of all or part of applicable customs duties is deemed a smuggling offense. Customs Regs. Implementing Rules ["Customs Rules"], art. 241 (1953) (issued by the Minister of Finance). The term "smuggling" includes the attempt to import or export in violation of applicable regulatory law. Customs Regs., art. 38.

[277] *See* Customs Rules, arts. 256, 257, *as amended by* Minister of Fin. & Nat'l Econ. Resolutions Nos. 58 (24/3/1399); 3/1933 (26/4/1401) (amending Resolution No. 17/324 (21/1/1401)); 31/2221 (9/5/1401); 31/1043 (5/3/1400); 2060 (20/8/1395); 17/2721 (15/5/1398); 19/1/1 (4/7/1399) (appointing members and defining territorial jurisdiction of Primary Committees).

[278] Customs Regs., art. 52. The Committees also have independent investigatory powers in the area of smuggling. *Id.* art. 45.

[279] Customs officials performing their duties are deemed quasijudicial officers. Customs Rules, art. 244. As such, they may search dwellings and commercial premises outside the customs zone, if they have cause to believe they will find smuggled goods, in the presence of police or coast guard officials. *See* Customs Regs., art. 48; Customs Rules, art. 247. Customs officials may arrest persons pursuant to a lawful search which led to the discovery of smuggled items. *See, e.g.*, A. AL-ĀLIFĪ, AL-NIẒĀM AL-QAḌĀ'Ī BI AL-MAMLAKAH AL-'ARABIYYAH AL-SU'ŪDIYYAH 299 (1976). Persons who have no fixed residence in Saudi Arabia may not be released on bail except on the order of the relevant Customs Committee. However, the pretrial detention period, as determined at the preliminary hearing, may not exceed seven days. Customs Rules, art. 251. Other persons may be released without need for such an order, with the exception of persons accused of smuggling alcohol or narcotics or who were found guilty of a smuggling offense within the previous five years. The latter may not be released. *Id.*

[280] The right to interrogate the accused is given to the Committees. *See* Customs Regs., art. 45; *cf.* Customs Rules, art. 258 (requiring that the accused be summoned).

[281] Upon receiving an official communication from a Customs Committee, the regional governor is responsible for carrying out the notification. Customs Rules, art. 258.

[282] *Id.* arts. 257(3), *as amended by* Ministerial Resolution No. 2060 (20/8/1395), & 260. A quorum is found if a majority of the members are present.

[283] *Id.* art. 259.

[284] *Id.* art. 260. If the decision is not dated, is not signed, or is signed by Committee members who did not hear the case in lieu of members who did hear it, the Appellate Committee may rule that such decision is null and remand the case to the Primary Committee. *See* A. AL-ĀLIFĪ, *supra* note 279, at 301–02 (Jeddah Appellate Committee holding) (citation omitted).

the case, the grounds on which the decision rests, and describe with clarity the articles to be confiscated.[285] All decisions of the Primary Committees are subject to appeal.[286] The party has the right to notice of the decision.[287]

The two Appellate Customs Committees sit in Riyadh and Jeddah. They are composed of three members[288] and rule on all appeals from the lower committees within their territorial jurisdiction.[289] Both the convicted offender and the General Director of Customs may appeal primary decisions.[290] Appeals are timely only if made within fifteen days of the party's receipt of notification of the primary decision.[291] Otherwise, the decision becomes final and enforceable.[292] On appellate review, all findings of fact made by the Primary Committees enjoy a regulatory presumption of validity, in the absence of allegations of falsification.[293] The Appellate Committees may make their decisions by a majority vote of members present.[294] All decisions must be approved by the Minister of Finance and National Economy.[295]

III. Board of Grievances

The Board of Grievances ("Board") is the adjudicative body having subject-matter jurisdiction over cases to which the Saudi Government or

---

[285] Customs Rules, art. 261.

[286] *Id.* art. 264. Default judgments are also subject to attack, but objections are to be made before the Primary Committee which issued the judgment. If objection is timely made, the Committee is required to rehear the case. If the defendant again fails to appear, his appeal is deemed void. *Id.* art. 257(4), *as amended by* Ministerial Resolution No. 2060.

[287] *See, e.g.,* A. AL-ÀLIFĪ, *supra* note 279, at 302–03 (citing 1973 Appellate Customs Committee decision holding that lack of notice deprived defendant of his right of appeal and vacating primary judgment).

[288] Customs Rules, art. 257(2), *as amended by* Ministerial Resolutions Nos. 4/1902 (10/4/1395), 3/193 (16/1/1398), & 4/1240 (10/3/1397) (amending Resolution No. 4/1907 (30/7/1391)). The Riyadh Committee has a reserve member in addition.

[289] *Id., as amended by* Ministerial Resolutions Nos. 4/1907 (30/7/1391) & 3/193 (20/8/1395).

[290] *Id.*

[291] *Id.* art. 264. The 15-day rule also applies to default judgments. *Id.* art. 257(4), *as amended by* Ministerial Resolution No. 2060. Notice in all cases may be served by means of registered mail or by delivery to the office of the regional governor, who is then responsible for such notification. If the defendant has no known address, notification may be made by publication. Customs Regs., art. 45; Customs Rules, art. 263. In contrast, notice is not deemed properly made if delivered to the party's clearing agent. *See, e.g.,* A. AL-ÀLIFĪ, *supra* note 279, at 303 (relying on Jeddah Appellate Committee holding that clearing agent is not agent for service of process).

[292] Customs Regs., art. 45; Customs Rules, art. 264. Where service is not made by personal delivery, if the defendant does not appeal within 30 days of the date of publication or of the date of mailing of the notification, the decision is enforceable. Customs Regs., art. 45.

[293] Customs Regs., art. 52; Customs Rules, arts. 255, 261.

[294] Customs Rules, art. 257(3), *as amended by* Ministerial Resolution No. 2060. The subsection also states that in case of equality of votes, the side counting the chairman shall predominate.

[295] *Id.,* art. 257(2), *as amended by* Ministerial Resolutions Nos. 4/1907 & 3/193.

any of its agencies or instrumentalities is a party.[296] Its antecedents are in the historical jurisdiction outside the sharīʿah court system over "grievances" (maẓālim) against, *inter alia*, government officials.[297]

A. PRIOR TO 1982 RESTRUCTURING

The Board was first formally established in 1954 as a department of the Council of Ministers,[298] and was later reconstituted as an "independent Board" whose chairman was given the rank of minister.[299] However, its independence was made subject to the qualification that all Board decisions required the approval of the President of the Council of Ministers, and that the chairman of the Board was required to make detailed semiannual reports to the President of the Council of Ministers.[300]

The Board sat in Riyadh and had a branch in Jeddah,[301] forwarding complaints received to the chairman in Riyadh for instructions before taking action. Similarly, decisions of the Jeddah branch were forwarded to Riyadh for appropriate action, unless the chairman participated in the case in Jeddah.[302] The Board membership consisted of a chairman and vice-chairman appointed by royal decree;[303] a legal consultant trained in Islamic law, a legal consultant trained in regulatory law,[304] and investigators and administrative staff appointed by the chairman.[305]

---

[296] Prior to the 1982 Regulations the sharīʿah courts, by royal order, did not hear administrative cases. *See also* Royal Order No. 20941 (7/2/1388) (directing sharīʿah courts not to hear complaints by private parties against government authorities before referring case to King and receiving appropriate permission); Minister of Justice Circular No. 122/2/t (18/7/1391) (instructing courts to make such referral through the Ministry).

[297] *See generally* Explanatory Memorandum, Board of Grievances Regs., Royal Decree No. M/51 (1982); Tyan, *Judicial Organization*, in LAW IN THE MIDDLE EAST, 265–268 (M Khadduri & H. Liebesny eds. 1955).

[298] *See* Council of Ministers Regs., arts. 17–18 (1954) (issued by royal order) (superseded by 1958 Council of Ministers Regulations). However, the Board had informally existed since 1926 in the shape of a box in which complaints might be deposited and whose key was kept by King Abdul Aziz.

[299] Board of Grievances Regs. ["Board Regs."] Royal Decree No. 2/13/8759, art. 1 (1955) (repealed 1982).

[300] *Id.* arts. 2, 4. The Council of Ministers Regulations, Royal Decree No. 38, art. 46 (1958), transferred the executive supervisory authority over the Board from the King to the President of the Council of Ministers. *See generally* M. ṢĀDIQ, TAṬAWWUR AL-ḤUKM WA AL-IDĀRAH FĪ AL-MAMLAKAH AL-ʿARABIYYAH AL-SUʿŪDIYYAH 143–46 (1965). The Regulations, however, were not amended to reflect this modification in the law. One of the major changes under the present Regulations is the elimination of this requirement of approval.

[301] The Board was also authorized to establish additional branches if needed. Board of Grievances Internal Rules ["Internal Rules"], Chairman of Board of Grievances Resolution No. 3570, art. 1 (1/11/1379) (repealed 1982).

[302] *See also* Shamma, *Diwān al Maẓālim*, MAJALLAT AL-IDĀRAH AL-ʿAMMAH 14, 17 (Dec. 1966).

[303] Board Regs., arts. 1–2.

[304] The legal consultants also sat on other specialized commissions, such as the Commission on Bribery and Forgery, whose jurisdiction has since been vested in the Board.

[305] Board Regs., art. 3.

1. Jurisdiction

The Board was granted power to record all complaints submitted to it.[306] In practice, the Board had jurisdiction only over those cases to which the Government or one of its instrumentalities was a party[307] and was also competent to review administrative cases after a party had exhausted the remedies available in other administrative channels. Such cases were primarily of two types, namely, appeals from administrative decisions with respect to contracts between the Government and a private contractor, and appeals from administrative adjudications or administrative rulings.

Contract claims

The Board was the proper forum for litigation where the disputing parties were the Saudi Government, or one of its agencies or instrumentalities, and a private party claiming compensation under a supply, construction, services, or other contract between the parties.[308] Such a private party was permitted to bring complaints to the Board after a prior factual determination and administrative decision were made by the ministry, agency, or instrumentality concerned. Actions on contracts could, therefore, also be viewed as appeals from administrative actions.

Appeals from administrative actions

The Board had power to review unilateral administrative actions taken with respect to private parties if such parties alleged illegality, arbitrariness, injustice, corruption, fraud, and the like. Jurisdiction could either lie by virtue of specific regulatory grant or under the Board's general "grievances" jurisdiction.

(a) *Licenses and registrations.* The Board had express power to reverse the revocation of a foreign investor's foreign capital investment license by the Minister of Industry and Electricity.[309] Similarly, it could review any other penalties imposed upon such an investor.[310] The Board's rulings in such cases were final.[311] Although the Foreign Capital Investment Regulations do not address the question of whether a party may appeal to the Board from the denial, rather than the revocation, of a license, the Board did have the power to rule on the propriety of such denials.

---

[306] *Id.* art. 2.

[307] In the 1950's, however, the Board adjudicated complaints between private parties.

[308] This jurisdiction arose both under the Board's general jurisdiction and by specific regulatory grant. Council of Ministers Resolution No. 818 of 17/5/1396 vests exclusive final jurisdiction in the Board over claims for compensation arising under government contracts.

[309] Foreign Capital Investment Regs., Royal Decree No. M/4, art. 10 (1979).

[310] *Id.*

[311] *Id.* Such finality was qualified by the regulatory requirement of obtaining approval of the President of the Council of Ministers.

Similarly, it could review a Ministry of Commerce denial of registration to an agent or its deletion of an agent's registration. This power existed despite the fact that Minister of Commerce decisions on these issues are deemed final.[312]

(b) *Enforcement measures.* The Board had express power to review the decisions of the Commission on Fraud and Deceit in Dealings with the Government and the committee responsible for enforcing the Printed Matter and Publication Regulations.[313] It could also review penalties imposed by other enforcement commission decisions.

Appeals from judgments

The general rule was that the Board did not review either sharī'ah judgments or adjudicative decisions issued by the specialized commissions. However, despite the preclusion of a merits review of sharī'ah judgments, either with respect to questions of law or of fact, an extraordinary appeal could lie to the Board if a party alleged judical bias, gross or intentional error, or procedural defects of a magnitude sufficient to justify invalidating the judgment.[314] In such cases, the Board chairman had discretion to accept and investigate the complaint, or to reject it. In reaching his decisions, he would take into account the substance of the complaint, as well as the surrounding circumstances. However, if the complaint was referred to the Board by the King, the chairman was required to accept and investigate the complaint.[315] In any of the preceding cases, a collateral appeal to the Board would only in principle be available to a party who had exhausted the channels of appeal provided in the Judicial Regulations. Not only do these Regulations provide procedures for appeal of lower court judgments, but also article 4 thereof provides that actions against judges are to be brought in accordance with the disciplinary rules specific to the judiciary. Hence, complaints brought to the Board at an inappropriate stage might in practice be referred to the Minister of Justice as the competent authority.

Civil service appeals

Civil servants could appeal to the Board from administrative decisions relating to their promotion, salaries, pension, or retirement, and from any disciplinary penalties imposed on them.[316]

---

[312] Royal Decree No. M/5, para. 1(2) (1969); Commercial Agencies Regs. Implementing Rules, arts. 7, 18.

[313] Rules Applicable to Persons Prohibited from Dealing with the Government, arts. 4–5; Printed Matter and Publication Regs., arts. 21, 41.

[314] Internal Rules, art. 6. Under this article, the attack would be directed at the judge rather than made upon the judgment. In case of appeals on procedural grounds, the procedure challenged must have been "contrary to regulations." *Id.*

[315] *Id.*

[316] *See* Shamma, *supra* note 302, at 18–19.

Enforcement of judgments

In addition to its adjudicative jurisdiction, the Board was responsible for enforcing judgments rendered in states parties to the Arab League Agreement Regarding the Execution of Judgments.[317]

Labor jurisdiction

The Board also participated in the investigation and disciplining of labor officials.[318]

2. Procedure[319]

Structure

The Board membership was subdivided into the Chair, consisting of the chairman and vice-chairman, and the Judicial Division, composed of the remaining members. The latter division operated in the form of three committees: the Investigating Committee, the Reviewing Committee, and the Consultative Committee.

Investigation

Complaints could be brought directly to the Board. The Board chairman would refer complaints to the investigators, according to their special skills. However, if the defendant was a minister or department head, the chairman was required to submit the case to the President of the Council of Ministers for his order directing the appropriate action to be taken.[320] The Regulations granted plenary investigatory powers to the chairman, which he could delegate to Board officials.[321]

For the purpose of preparing their reports, the investigators were empowered, *inter alia*, to summon and question parties and witnesses, to call experts, to conduct investigations in government departments, to summon and question government officials, and, if necessary, to search

---

[317] Agreement on the Reciprocal Enforcement of Judgments, *opened for signature* Nov. 10, 1952, 159 British & Foreign State Papers 616 (English translation). *See generally* Shamma, *supra* note 302, at 19; M. MUHAMMAD, AL-TAṬAWWUR AL-TASHRĪ·Ī FĪ AL-MAMLAKAH AL-·ARABIYYAH AL-SU·ŪDIYYAH 165 (citing Council of Ministers Resolution No. 251 (28/12/1379)). The Board was in theory responsible for enforcing any foreign judgments rendered in States parties to international agreements for the enforcement of judgments to which Saudi Arabia is a party. In fact, the only such agreement to which the Kingdom was a party was the Arab League Agreement.

[318] Labor Regs., Royal Decree No. M/21, art. 12 (1969).

[319] The Council of Ministers will issue rules of procedure governing proceedings before the Board under the 1982 Regulations. Board of Grievances Regs., Royal Decree No. M/51, art. 49 (1982).

[320] Board Regs., art. 2(c).

[321] *Id.* art. 5.

them, their residences, or their places of work, and to inspect their books.[322] Government departments and private citizens were required to assist the Board.[323] Investigators could summon persons by means of a memorandum sent to them or "by any other means."[324] Following interrogation, the investigator was required to read his report to the person interrogated. Such person was required to sign or place his seal or stamp on every page of the report. Such due reading was required to be recited at the end of the report. The person interrogated could not write his own answer in the offical record but had the right to submit a memorandum in his defense. In this case, existence of the memorandum was required to be indicated in the record.[325] If any person committed an act of aggression upon an investigator, the latter was required to enter the incident in his report and obtain the signatures of eyewitnesses, if any. The Board chairman had authority to have the aggressor arrested, with the assistance of the police, and to have him brought before the appropriate judicial body for trial.[326]

Review

The Reviewing Committee was composed of a deputy of the Board chairman, the two legal consultants, and a number of investigators as required. It reviewed the reports prepared by investigators[327] and supporting documents from a legal standpoint. Parties were not allowed to be present or to present arguments. The Reviewing Committee submitted its report on the case to the Board chairman, who would approve any such investigators' determinations made in accordance with applicable law and principles of justice. If the investigators' conclusions appeared contrary to legal and/or equitable principles, the Reviewing Committee could present its own determinations implementing the applicable rules in its report.[328] The Reviewing Committee could require the investigator in the case to clarify any ambiguities in his report, and the Board chairman could also require him to make further factual findings in order to complete the report. Decisions of the Reviewing Committee could be made by majority voice. Any dissenters were required to state the grounds for their dissent at the end of the report.[329]

[322] Internal Rules, art. 7. However, the investigators' original powers were restricted to investigations executed inside the Board seat. All off-premise investigations required prior authorization by the Board chairman or his deputy. *Id.* art. 4(d).
[323] Board Regs., art. 5.
[324] Internal Rules, art. 7.
[325] *Id.* art. 8.
[326] *Id.* art. 9.
[327] *Id.* art. 4(w).
[328] *Id.*
[329] *Id.*

The Consultative Committee

This committee was composed of the Board's legal staff. Its function was to answer any legal questions raised by the Board chairman or vice-chairman and to assist the investigators in their areas of specialization.

Implementation of Board decisions

Under the Regulations, the Board's decisions were described as "suggestions" or "proposals."[330] In the early stages of the Board, this description was accurate, but the Board's decisions gained during later stages the force of definitive judgments.[331] Under the 1955 Regulations, however, they were not enforceable until signed by the President of the Council of Ministers. In addition, the Board's adjudicative power was subject to the limitation that it could not suggest to a minister or department head the imposition of a penalty or the taking of an action not provided in applicable regulations except on the order of the President of the Council of Ministers or the King.[332]

Board decisions based on applicable regulations were sent to the minister or department head concerned. Within two weeks, such authority was to notify the Board of its execution of the proposed action or, alternatively, of its objections. In the latter case, the minister or department head concerned was to state the ground for its objections. Where such authority did not voluntarily execute the Board decision, the Board would forward a report to that effect to the President of the Council of Ministers. The order of the latter was dispositive of the case and enforceable.[333] If the President of the Council of Ministers did not confirm a Board decision, due either to substantive legal or technical errors apparent on its face, he could refer it to the Council of Ministers' legal advisors or remand it to the Board for revision. If it disagreed with the comments of the President of the Council of Ministers, the Board was not required to amend its initial decision. In this case, the President of the Council of Ministers would not rule on the merits of the case, but would refer it to the Council of Ministers to make the appropriate final disposition. This final stage of review was made solely on the basis of the basis of the record. Parties were not entitled to an evidentiary hearing.

---

[330] *See* Board Regs., art. 2.
[331] *See, e.g.*, M. MUḤAMMAD, *supra* note 317, at 155.
[332] Board Regs., art. 2.
[333] *Id.*

B. BOARD OF GRIEVANCES REGULATIONS OF 1982 ["BGR"] [334]

The 1982 comprehensive regulations of fifty-one articles reconstituted the Board as the authority having general jurisdiction over administrative cases and resembling the French Conseil d'Etat. The major changes effected by the BGR were, first, to establish the Board as an independent judicial body whose decisions are final and whose members belong to the judicial corps and, second, to divest it of its investigatory functions. Thus, its adjudicative jurisdiction is extended to administrative disciplinary actions formerly heard by the Disciplinary Commission, while the Supervision and Investigation Commission, established as the latter's prosecutorial arm, now performs this function vis-à-vis the Board.[335] The result of the restructuring is, on the one hand, to integrate the Board more closely into the sharī'ah judicial framework, and, on the other hand, to vest jurisdiction over administrative law issues in a single authority.

1. Constitution

Under article 1 of the BGR, the Board is made an independent judicial commission for administrative cases linked directly to His Majesty the King. Its seat remains in Riyadh, but the Board chairman is authorized to establish branches according to need.[336]

The chairman, who is appointed by royal order, is directly responsible to the King and holds the rank of minister.[337] He exercises supervisory, disciplinary, and administrative powers over Board members similar to those exercised by the Minister of Justice over the sharī'ah judiciary.[338] He is required to make comprehensive annual reports to the King,[339] rather than to the President of the Council of Ministers, as was the case under the amended 1955 Regulations. The other Board members are one or more deputies of the chairman, members trained in sharī'ah and regulatory law, and technical and administrative staff.[340] The judicial members have the qualifications[341] and status of judges with respect, *inter alia*, to salary and other benefits, promotions, transfers, and retirement age.[342] They are

---

[334] Royal Decree No. M/51 (1982). The Regulations became effective as of one year of the date of their official publication. *Id.* art. 51. They repealed the 1955 Regulations and resolutions issued in implementation thereof. *Id.* art. 50.

[335] *Id.* arts. 2–4 (of royal decree approving BGR). BOR, arts. 8, 10.

[336] BGR, art. 1. Presently branches are sitting in Jeddah and Dammam.

[337] *Id.* arts. 2–3.

[338] *See, e.g., id.* arts. 19, 28, 31, 44.

[339] *Id.* art. 47.

[340] *Id.* art. 2.

[341] *See* Explanatory Memorandum, BGR.

[342] BGR, arts. 11, 15, 17–19.

afforded the same rights and guarantees as those given to the sharī'ah judiciary and are subject to the same duties.[343] The entire membership of the Board, together with the chairman, sits as the General Commission.[344] The Board operates in the form of departments, whose territorial and subject-matter jurisdiction is defined by resolution of the chairman.[345] Additionally, the Committee for Administrative Affairs of Board Members is designed to perform administrative functions similar to those of the Supreme Judicial Council in the sharī'ah court system.[346]

2. Jurisdiction

The Board is granted by the BGR jurisdiction over those disputes to which the Administration is a party, whether they arise from an administrative ruling, a government contract, or otherwise. The BGR do not distinguish between government acts in a commercial, as compared to an administrative, capacity.[347] However, they do distinguish "acts of sovereignty" from other government action. Article 9 denies the Board jurisdiction to rule on claims relating to acts of sovereignty. Furthermore, the Board may not entertain parties' challenges to sharī'ah court judgments or decisions of the adjudicative commissions with respect to cases within such bodies' jurisdiction.[348] Additionally, the Board is given penal jurisdiction over certain regulatory crimes and violations until such time as the necessary measures are taken to enable the courts to handle such cases in accordance with the Judicial Regulations.[349] Although not expressly so provided, the Board's jurisdiction is exclusive.

Article 8 of the Regulations sets forth the specific areas of the Board's jurisdiction, namely, civil service related claims, private party grievances, and criminal offenses.

Civil service claims

Subsection 1(a) makes the Board the proper forum for actions brought by officials and employees of the Government and its public agencies having independent juristic personalities, with respect to rights arising under the Civil Service Regulations and Retirement Regulations. Such

[343] *Id.* art. 16.
[344] *Id.* art. 7.
[345] *Id.* art. 6.
[346] *See, e.g., id.* arts. 17, 19.
[347] *See* Explanatory Memorandum, BGR.
[348] BGR, art. 9.
[349] *See* Explanatory Memorandum, BGR.

jurisdiction also extends to the heirs of such persons or parties claiming through them.[350]

Administrative decisions

The Board has jurisdiction over appeals made by parties in interest from administrative decisions.[351] Subsection 1(b) expressly permits appeals on the following grounds: lack of jurisdiction; formal defects; the ruling is contrary to regulations or rules; error in the interpretation or application of regulations or rules; or abuse of power. An administrative authority's refusal or failure to make a decision required of it by regulatory law, including the issuing of a license, is deemed a decision for purposes of this subsection. However, an exception to the Board's jurisdiction to hear appeals from administrative decisions exists in the case of those committees formed under a regulatory provision, a Council of Ministers resolution, or an order of the President of the Council of Ministers, if the regulatory act organizing any such committee provides that its decisions shall be final.[352]

Administrative actions

Under subsection 1(c), the Board has jurisdiction generally over private party claims for compensation against the Government or any of its independent agencies by reason of the administrative party's actions. Under this subsection, the Board is also the proper forum for grievances of users of public facilities and services, such as electricity or telephones.

Contract claims

Under subsection 1(d) the Board has jurisdiction over claims arising under contracts to which the Government or one of its independent agencies is a party.[353] This subsection incorporates the grant of jurisdiction

[350] Jurisdiction over cases brought by government workmen remains in the Labor Commissions. *See generally* pp. 316–19 *infra*.

[351] *See, e.g.*, Foreign Capital Investment Regs., art. 10 (revocation of license appealable to Board). The appeal must be made within 30 days of the party's receipt of notice of the Minister of Industry and Electricity's revocation decision. *Id.* Similarly, the Board may review penalties imposed on a foreign investor by the Minister or his refusal to grant an investment license.

[352] *See* Explanatory Memorandum, BGR. Consequently, tax rulings and decisions of the customs committees, *inter alia*, are at present nonappealable to the Board. *But see id.* (contemplating amendment of certain regulatory rules to provide for Board jurisdiction).

[353] *Cf.* Council of Ministers Resolution No. 487 (5/8/1398) (government supply contracts containing any provision contrary to provisions of Tender Regulations to be referred to Board). *But see, e.g.*, Agreement Relating to the Construction of Certain Military Facilities in Saudi Arabia, May 24–June 5, 1965, United States–Saudi Arabia, art. V, 16 U.S.T. 890, T.I.A.S. No. 5830 (appeals by nonSaudi contractors under contract "disputes" clauses to be heard and decided by U.S. Army Corps of Engineers' Board of Contract Appeals).

over contractors' claims for compensation provided in Council of Ministers Resolution No. 818.[354] The word "contract" is broad enough to include agreements concluded by the Government both in its administrative and commercial or quasi-private functions and includes both administrative and nonadministrative contracts. Thus, a claim against a municipality for failure to make rental payments with respect to a warehouse in which it stores office supplies would be as properly brought before the Board as a dispute arising under a contract to construct a dam. Similarly, disputes arising under a loan agreement between a Saudi public sector lender and a private borrower are brought to the Board. The Explanatory Memorandum to the Regulations notes that the word "contract" is interpreted to include all contracts, including employment agreements. However, employment disputes within the jurisdiction of the Labor Commissions are not cognizable by the Board since, in the case of government workmen, the administrative appointment decision or order stands in the stead of the employment contract.[355] Additionally, even though a company is a "contract",[356] the Commission for the Settlement of Commercial Disputes is generally the proper forum for disputes arising between the Government as equity-participant in, for example, a limited liability company and one of its private sector partners.[357]

Disciplinary and criminal cases

The Board rules on disciplinary cases brought against public officials.[358] Such cases are investigated and prosecuted before the Board by the Supervision and Investigation Commission.[359] The Board also has jurisdiction over criminal cases[360] formerly prosecuted before the Commission on Bribery and Forgery[361] arising under the Regulations for Combating

[354] Resolution No. 818 (17/5/1396). *See also* High Order No. 3/w/8900 (13/4/1402) (contractors' right to claim compensation limited to grounds of administrative fault as provided in Resolution No. 818) (issued prior to BGR).

[355] Labor Regs., art. 77.

[356] *See generally* pp. 82–84 *supra*.

[357] *See* Companies Regs., art. 232 (jurisdictional grant to Commission prevailing as more specific than BGR, art. 8(1)(d)). *But see id.* art. 2, *as amended by* Royal Decree No. M/23, para. 1(2)(b) (1982) (companies having government participation may be exempted from applicability of Companies Regulations).

[358] BGR, art. 8(1)(e); *cf.* Royal Decree No. M/51, art. 4 (vesting jurisdiction of Disciplinary Commission in Board). *See generally* Disciplining of Officials Regs., Royal Decree No. M/7, arts. 1–3, 5 (1391) (repealed in part 1982) (constituting independent commission authorized to investigate and prosecute public officials' financial and administrative violations). Such cases may arise under the disciplinary regulations or related Council of Ministers resolutions. *Id. See, e.g.*, Council of Ministers Resolution No. 677 (2/6/1395) (granting Disciplinary Commission jurisdiction to hear disciplinary actions on grounds of embezzlement).

[359] BGR, arts. 8(1)(e), 10.

[360] *Id.* art. 8(1)(f).

[361] *See* Council of Ministers Resolution No. 111 (17/1/1398); Council of Ministers Resolution No. 1230 (23/10/1393) (amending Council of Ministers Resolution No. 735 (9/9/1391)) (unifying Bribery and Forgery Commissions) (all three repealed 1982).

Bribery,[362] the Regulations for Combating Forgery,[363] and the Regulations of Officials Handling Public Funds,[364] and Royal Decree No. 43.[365]

Enforcement of foreign judgments

The Board remains the organ responsible for enforcing foreign judgments.[366]

Miscellaneous

The Board has general jurisdiction under article 8 to hear matters and cases referred to it by the Council of Ministers.[367] In addition, the Board has jurisdiction as provided in other applicable regulations.[368] For example, the Board is expressly granted jurisdiction to hear appeals from decisions

---

[362] Royal Decree No. 15 (1962) (repealed in part 1982) (translated in Appendix 6). Under the Regulations, public officials soliciting or accepting bribes, whether for themselves or third parties, and persons bribing or attempting to bribe public officials and accessories or accomplices of such persons are subject to maximum sentences of five years imprisonment or maximum fines of S.R. 100,000 or both. *Id.* arts. 1–3, 6, 8. A bribe may be either a "gift" or a "promise." *Id.* art. 1. These two terms apply to any material or nonmaterial "benefit" or "advantage" to the bribee, regardless of their nature or the name the actors have chosen to describe such benefit or advantage. *Id.* art. 11. Furthermore, acts of force or threats used to prevent public officials from performing their duties or to compel them to perform unlawful acts are treated as bribes by the Regulations. *Id.* art. 7. In theory, it is the act of bribery that is punishable. Thus, a person bribing an official to perform a lawful act which he would have performed in any event may be punished. *See id.* arts. 1, 6. An example of such an otherwise harmless act would be an official's use of his influence to expedite a party's obtaining a license under the Foreign Capital Investment Regulations. *See id.* arts. 5–6. Mistake of fact is no defense to a bribery charge. A person attempting to bribe an official who falsely misrepresented his authority to perform certain acts may thus be punished. *See id.* arts. 1, 6. Bribery crimes not punishable under the antibribery regulations may be prosecuted before the sharī'ah courts and penalized under general law.

[363] Royal Decree No. 114 (1961), *as amended by* Royal Decree No. 53 (April 30, 1963) (translated in Appendix 33). These Regulations are supplemented by the Penal Regulations on Forgery and Counterfeiting of Money, Royal Decree No. 12 (1960), *as amended by* Royal Decree No. 53. *See also* Council of Ministers Resolution Nos. 223 (14/8/1399) & 3 (3/1/1406) (extending applicability of articles 5–6 of antiforgery regulations). Convicted offenders are subject to maximum prison sentences of fifteen years hard labor if the offense involves legal tender, and maximum fines of S.R. 100,000. Royal Decree No. 53, art. 2; Royal Decree No. 12, art. 2. Forgery crimes involving private rights may also be referred to the sharī'ah courts.

[364] Royal Decree No. M/77, art. 9 (1395), *as amended by* Royal Decree No. M/5 (14/4/1400) (increasing maximum fine to S.R. 100,000) (applicable to officials covered by the Regulations and their accomplices, whether or not officials, convicted of crimes of embezzlement, misuse of public funds, stamps, property).

[365] Royal Decree No. 43 (29/11/1377). This decree sanctions *inter alia*, officials engaged in commerce or in liberal professions without permission and officials who accept gifts or bribes, embezzle public funds, or generally misuse their influence or position for their personal benefit. Maximum penalties provided thereunder are 10 years imprisonment and a fine of S.R. 20,000 in addition to civil liability for damages, also applicable to persons bribing officials and intermediaries. *Id.* arts. 2–3.

[366] BGR, art. 8(1)(g).

[367] *Id.* art. 8(2).

[368] *Id.* art. 8(1)(h).

of the Minister of Commerce or the Trademarks Committee by a party whose application for registration was denied or by a party whose objection to such registration was rejected.[369] The Board also has jurisdiction over cases relating to striking of trademarks and trademark licenses from the trademarks register.[370] Disputes between the Ministry of Communications and land transportation license-holders are to be brought before the Board.[371] The Board is also given jurisdiction to hear appeals from decisions relating to boycott crimes,[372] decisions of the Committee on Fraud and Deceit in Dealings with the Government,[373] penalties imposed with respect to violations of the Precious Minerals and Stones Regulations,[374] decisions imposing prison sentences with respect to commercial fraud violations,[375] to impose prison sentences provided in the Regulations for the Protection of Public Utilities[376] and to hear appeals from decisions requiring payment of compensation or fines thereunder.[377]

Private parties

Private party complaints may be brought directly to the Board. Its decisions are final, with no requirement of confirmation by any higher authority and nonappealable.

[369] Trademarks Regs., Royal Decree No. M/5, art. 19 (1984).

[370] Id. arts. 29, 42.

[371] Minister of Communications Resolutions Nos. 44, art. 15 (27/5/1400) & 45, art. 15 (27/5/1400).

[372] Royal Decree No. M/8, para. 1 (26/5/1404) (amending art. 12 of Boycott of Israel Regs.).

[373] Council of Ministers Resolution No. 11, arts. 4–5 (26/2/1400).

[374] Royal Decree No. M/42, art. 20 (10/7/1403).

[375] Regs. for Combating Commercial Fraud, art. 17 (1984).

[376] Royal Decree No. M/62, art. 13(a) (20/12/1405).

[366] Id. art. 13(b).

Chapter 5
LABOR

I. The Employment Contract

A. SCOPE OF REGULATIONS

The Labor and Workmen Regulations[1] are applicable to a contractual relationship existing between an employer and a workman subject to Saudi law,[2] whereby the latter personally renders services for the benefit and under the direction or control of the former in consideration of a wage.[3]

1. Workman

A workman is defined as "any person working for the account of an employer under the latter's direction or control, even though he may not be under the employer's direct supervision, in consideration of a wage."[4] A workman is a natural person of either sex[5] and of any nationality. The workman may also be a seaman or an apprentice.[6] Although "workmen", persons working in solely family-operated businesses, farmers, herdsmen,

---

[1] Royal Decree No. M/21 (1969), *as amended by* Royal Decree No. M/2 (7/2/1403). Article 1 of the Regulations provides that they are to be called the "Labor Regulations." Consequently, this title will be used throughout the chapter. It will also be noted that the English translation of the provisions of the Regulations used in this chapter is the Government Security Press translation.

[2] *See,* also High Order No. 7/161 (27/1/1404) (implying applicability of Labor Regulations to persons working in the Kingdom as part of cultural or other missions under bilateral international agreements).

[3] Labor Regs., art. 2.

[4] *Id.* art. 7(7).

[5] *But see* Royal Order No. 11575 (19/5/1401); Royal Order No. 1960/8 (23/12/1399); President of Council of Ministers Circular No. 11651 (16/5/1403) (all prohibiting intermingling of sexes at work).

[6] *See* Labor Regs., arts. 2(b), 99. *See also id.* art. 101 (term "seaman" also applicable to females).

and domestic servants are not subject to the Regulations.[7]

In the private sector, persons described above as "workmen" are subject to the Regulations.[8] In contrast, in the public sector, persons so described may be either workmen, civil servants, or servants. The Regulations do not apply to the civil servants or servants of the Government or its agencies and instrumentalities, whether or not these have a separate juristic personality.[9] However, the Regulations do apply to government "workmen."[10]

2. Employer

An employer is defined as "any natural or juristic person employing one workman or more in consideration of a wage."[11] An employer may be an administrative body.

3. Employment contract

Definition

Article 70 of the Regulations defines an employment contract as

a contract concluded between an employer and a workman, whereby the latter agrees to work under the direction or control of the employer for a specified or unspecified period in consideration of a

---

[7] *Id.* art. 3. *But see id.* art. 3(b)(1)–(2) (Regulations applicable to workmen in industrialized agriculture).

[8] The Regulations generally employ the term "workman." *But see id.* art. 93 (using "workman" and "employee" synonymously). This chapter will not distinguish between such terms. Hence the term "workman" as employed herein also applies to an "employee."

[9] Civil servants are subject to the Civil Service Regs., Royal Decree No. M/49 (1977). Government servants are generally subject to the Servants Rules, Civil Service Board Resolution No. 3 (20/9/1397).

[10] Labor Regs., arts. 2(c), 77; *cf.* Ministry of Labor & Social Affairs Circular No. 3625/6/M (1/5/1401), *published in* MAKTABAT AL-IDĀRAH (1401) (workmen of government and public agencies subject to Labor Regulations not subject to retirement age applicable to civil servants). "Government workmen" has been defined as workmen performing manual labor for government administrative departments, whether of technical professions, such as carpenters, electricians, mechanics, or others, such as porters, cleaning persons in municipalities, ditch-diggers, or transporters. The term does not apply to clerks. Council of Ministers Resolution No. 837 (28/10/1387), *cited in* N. AL-KAYALI, AL-WASIŢ FI SHARĤ NIẒAM AL-'AMAL AL-SUŢŪDĪ, at 54 n.1 (1973). Furthermore, the Labor Regulations are explicitly made applicable to workmen of the government employed in pastures and agriculture. Council of Ministers Resolution No. 209 (6/2/1398), *published in* 6 MAKTABAT AL-IDĀRAH (1398–1399).

[11] Labor Regs., art. 7(8).

wage, or for the performance of a specified job, and which contains the terms of employment agreed upon.[12]

In the case of government workmen, the administrative appointment stands *in loco* the employment contract.[13]

Formal aspects

The employment contract may be expressed in writing or be oral. However, only the workman is entitled by the Regulations to prove the existence of an oral employment contract. Article 77 provides

> [t]he employment contract must be in writing, drawn up in Arabic and in duplicate, one copy to be retained by each of the two parties. However, even though it is not written, a contract shall be considered existent, so that the workman alone may by all means of proof establish his rights, and either party may at any time demand that the contract be put in writing.[14]

Employment contracts are enforceable despite the absence of certain terms, most notably the wage term. Article 123(a) provides

> If neither the employment contract nor the Labor Regulations, nor the basic work rules stipulate the wage that the employer is obligated to pay, the wage determined for another work of the same kind, if it exists, shall be adopted; otherwise, the wage shall be determined in accordance with the generally accepted practice of the trade and of the area in which the work is performed. If no such practice exists, the appropriate Commission shall determine the wage according to the requirements of equity.

The nonessentiality of the wage term may be attributed to the presumption created by article 122, which provides that "service is presumed to be

---

[12] *Cf. id.* art. 56 defining "apprenticeship contract" as

. . . a contract whereby an employer agrees to employ a young workman in order to train him methodically in a certain trade or craft within a specified period during which the apprentice is bound to work under the employer's supervision.

Maritime employment contracts are subject to special rules and will not be discussed in this chapter. A "maritime employment contract" is defined as

[a]ny contract of employment made between the owner or financier of a Saudi Arabian ship of not less than 500 tons, or between the representative of either, and a seaman or master to perform work on board ship, or for a sea voyage.

Id. art. 99.

[13] *Id.* art. 77.

[14] *But see* M. ABŪ AL-'AINAIN, MABĀDI' AL-QĀNUN LI RIJAL AL-A'MAL FI AL-MAMLAKAH AL-'ARABIYYAH AL-SU'ŪDIYYAH 373 (1981) (employer may prove oral agreement by means of workman's admission or oath or written entry by workman in workman's file in employer's possession).

rendered for a wage if the service consists of work which is not customarily performed gratuitously or which is in the occupational line of the person who performed it."

However, in order to be enforceable, oral employment contracts must embody the parties' firm commitments. Manifestations made during the stage of mere negotiations will not support a cause of action. In one 1980 case turning on the existence of an employment contract, the plaintiff expatriate workman, who was already employed in the Kingdom, negotiated the terms of an oral agreement with a second employer in the Kingdom. The prospective employer then requested the workman's present employer to lend it the services of the workman for an unspecified period. The prospective employer was unwilling to take over the sponsorship of the workman at that time, while the present employer was unwilling to relinquish the services of the workman without a transfer of sponsorship. Thus, the second employer declined to employ the workman. The workman filed a claim for monetary damages alleging that the prospective employer had breached its obligations under the oral employment contract binding the parties. The sole defense of the employer was that no employment contract had ever existed. Dismissing the complaint, the Primary Commission for the Settlement of Labor Disputes ["Primary Commission"] held that the parties had not proceeded beyond the stage of negotiations and that the evidence introduced by the plaintiff was insufficient to prove the existence of an employment contract.[15]

Control–subordination relationship

The essential feature of the Saudi employment relationship distinguishing it from other contracts for the performance of services, such as agency or independent contractors' agreements, is the agreement of one of the contracting parties to serve the other party under the latter's direction, control, and supervision.

The legal subordination of the workman to the employer with respect to the employment contract is required by the Regulations.[16] It may be defined as the employer's authority to control the acts of the workman in a manner prejudicial to the workman's independence. The employer's right of control and supervision extends to all acts executed or to be executed by the workman in the performance of his work. This control and supervision may be exercised directly or indirectly.[17] However, in all cases, its exercise must be apparent during the entire period of the employment relationship.

[15] On appeal, the ruling was affirmed.
[16] See, e.g., Labor Regs., arts. 7(7), 70, 96(a).
[17] See id. art. 7(7).

Correspondingly, Saudi law imposes on the workman a duty to obey his employer's orders, to follow his directions, and to refrain from performing acts prohibited by him. However, this duty only extends to the execution of orders not contrary to the employment contract, the Regulations, and public morals and the like.[18] The workman's duty of obedience requires him to submit to the employer's control without argument. The workman's failure, whether intentional or inadvertent, to perform his work or comply with his employer's directions will entitle the latter to impose on him the penalties contemplated by the Regulations.[19]

The employer's right of direction and control and the workman's corresponding duty of obedience are the single most important element determinative of the existence of an employment contract. In the absence of a control–subordination relationship, an agreement between two parties will not be deemed an employment contract under Saudi law. Thus, company employees entitled under their employment contracts to receive shares in the company's profits will be deemed workmen, and not partners,[20] provided that they do not have the right to perform acts outside of the scope of control and supervision exercised by the company over other employees of their class.[21] In this case, profit shares will be deemed a portion of such employees' wages.

B. COMMENCEMENT OF SERVICE

The employment relationship arises at the time the workman's service commences. It is thus important to establish the date of commencement of service for the reason that his rights under the Regulations vest as of that date. Normally, the employment contract, whether oral or written, will determine the point of commencement of service. However, this is not always the case. While definitionally unsatisfactory, the date of commencement of service may best be described as that date on which the workman's wage is first payable or paid, but in no case later than the date

[18] *Id.* art. 96(a): *cf. id.* art. 83(2) (disobedience of unlawful orders not grounds for termination).

[19] *See generally id.* art. 125 (governing disciplinary rules); Model Rules Governing Penalties & Rewards & the Provisions for Imposing Such Penalties on or Granting Such Rewards to Workmen ["Model Disciplinary Rules"], Minister of Labor & Social Affairs Resolution No. 110 (12/4/1390), *as amended by* Minister of Labor & Social Affairs Resolution No. 15 (18/1/1397), (translated in Appendix 34).

[20] *See also* pp. 82–84, *supra.*

[21] In contrast, where a person performing services in exchange for determinable payments, even if called a "wage" by the parties, is not under the exclusive control of the other party to the agreement, an employment contract subject to the Regulations does not exist.

he actually begins to work with his employer's consent or subsequent ratification.[22]

1. Service distinguished from work

The date of commencement of service and the date of commencement of work will ordinarily be one and the same. Saudi labor law recognizes the general principle that wages are paid in compensation for work performed.[23] Thus, if the parties have not agreed otherwise, the workman's wage and any other benefits to which he is entitled under the Regulations accrue on the date he actually starts to work under the employer's direct or indirect direction or control. This date need not be the date provided in the employment contract. Thus, if the workman, with his employer's consent, begins to perform his contractual obligations, either before or after the date initially agreed upon by the parties, his wage will be payable and other rights will vest as of that date. Similarly, if prior to formally undertaking his work, the workman, on his future employer's instructions, executes a work assignment, related to the contracted-for work and whether inside or outside of the Kingdom, his service is deemed to commence on the date he undertook the assignment.

The parties, however, are free to agree that the employment relationship will commence prior to the date on which the workman actually begins to work. Therefore, a carelessly drafted employment contract may result in the workman's being entitled to receive all or part of his wage or other rights for a period of time prior to the date he actually begins to work. For example, in the case of an expatriate workman, the contract may provide for its effectiveness as of the date on which the workman obtains his work visa from the Saudi Arabian embassy in his home country or the country of execution of the agreement, or the date of his starting to travel or of signing the employment contract. In any of these cases, service will be deemed to commence as of the date provided in the contract. Therefore, counsel for the employer should, as a precautionary measure, include the following clause in employment contracts subject to the Labor Regulations

> Service of the workman shall commence and his wage and other rights shall accrue as of the date he actually and physically assumes and undertakes his work. The employer shall assign him his work when the workman personally and physically reports to the employer at his place of business and exhibits willingness to assume his work without any reservation or qualification and while in possession of a valid work visa and all other necessary documents and certificates.

---

[22] A workman may not lawfully begin to work either before or after the agreed-upon date, without the consent of his employer. A subsequent ratification by the employer, however, will cure any such defect.

[23] *But see* pp. 250–51 *infra*.

Nonetheless, if the employer in fact pays the workman his wage with respect to any period, such as the travelling period in the case of an expatriate workman, prior to the latter's actual commencement of work, the latter's service will be deemed to have commenced as of the beginning of the period with respect to which payments were made unless the employment agreement includes a provision such as the clause suggested *supra*.

2. Physical availability of the workman

Physical availability of the workman to the employer at the agreed time and place accompanied by the readiness to submit to his control and dominion entitles the workman to his wage. The legal principle that wages are paid in exchange for work actually performed must therefore be qualified. If the workman, at the agreed-upon time and place, whether inside or outside of the Kingdom, makes his services available to the employer, his service is considered to commence at that time, whether or not he has actually begun to work. The following examples illustrate the application of this rule.

(a) A nonSaudi workman, having entered outside Saudi Arabia into an employment contract, and having obtained a work visa permitting him to perform the contracted-for work, becomes incapable of travelling to the Kingdom for a bona fide reason, such as illness. Since he does not report to the employer at the time agreed upon for the purpose of undertaking his job, he is not entitled to receive his wage or other benefits for the period of delay, unless the parties agreed otherwise.

(b) The same workman actually did travel to Saudi Arabia and reported on time to the employer for the purpose of performing the agreed-upon work. Although willing to commence work, he becomes unable to do so for a certain period of time, for a bona fide reason, such as illness. He is entitled to his wage and other rights for this period.

(c) The same workman reports to the employer in the Kingdom at the time agreed upon, and is willing to begin work without reservation. However, he does not or cannot actually perform his work due to causes ascribable solely to the employer. Article 93 of the Regulations provides

> [i]f the workman or employee reports to work in the hours of the day stipulated in the labor contract or expresses his readiness to perform his work during these hours and is prevented from doing so only by a cause which is ascribed to the employer, the workman or employee shall be entitled to the wage of that day.

Thus, regardless of the nature of the reasons preventing the workman from performing his work, he is entitled to his wage and other rights as of the date he reported to the employer.

The preceding fact situations suggest the principle that, unless the parties have agreed otherwise even if the workman has not yet begun to work, he is entitled to his wage if he has put his services at the disposition of his employer at the agreed time and place. It is useful to observe the operation of the principle of good faith in the context of physical availability.

Example (b) indicates that mere physical availability does not create the right to the wage, where the workman is the defaulting party. Thus, the workman must establish a bona fide reason for his failure to begin to work in order to be entitled to his wage. If good faith is not established, the general rule that wages are paid for work is applicable.

In contrast, good faith alone will not save either party who fails to comply with the terms of the agreement. Thus, example (a) shows that good faith, in the absence of physical availability, will not support a workman's claim for wage payments. Likewise, where the employer is responsible for the workman's inability to perform his work, as in example (c), the employer's good faith is not a defense to a claim brought by a workman who is physically available and willing to work.

3. Training period

If the parties have agreed that the workman will undergo a training period prior to his beginning to work, the employment relationship is deemed to commence on the initial date of the training period and the workman is entitled to his wage during the training period. The rationale underlying wage payments in this context is that the workman has placed himself under the employer's dominion and control. Since such training period is required of the workman, it should be deemed to be performing work for the employer. Therefore, it is immaterial whether the training is performed by the employer itself or by another person designated by the employer, or whether the training takes place inside or outside Saudi Arabia. However, if the workman's undergoing of training is made a condition precedent to the validity of the employment agreement, the training period will have no effect on the commencement of service. Wages will first be due when the workman begins to work, unless otherwise agreed by the parties.

A practical problem exists where the employer requires the trainee to sign an undertaking to enter into an employment agreement after the completion of training, but the parties do not provide for the terms and conditions of future employment. Since, during the training period, the ultimate level of proficiency of the trainee cannot be foreseen, employers are naturally reluctant to specify the terms of the post-training employment. However, Saudi law will not enforce future agreements of uncertain terms.

Under these circumstances, the employer may protect itself by agreeing with the workman on minimum and maximum possible wage and other terms, all contingent upon the proficiency acquired during the training period. It should be noted that in no event, such as unsatisfactory performance of the workman in such training or his failure, may the cost of training be recovered from a trainee/workman if the employer has agreed to bear such costs.[24]

4. Practical application of doctrine

If the workman has neither begun to work nor physically submitted to the employer's control and dominion at the agreed time and place, and if no wages have been paid or are payable the workman's service will not be held to have commenced under Saudi law.

(a) In one case an employer and a nonSaudi workman entered into an employment contract outside of the Kingdom. The contract provided that it would become effective as of the date of the workman's arrival in Riyadh. The contract further provided that the employer would not be liable for any delay due to an unjustifiable or legally insufficient cause attributable to the workman. The understanding between the parties was that the workman would travel to Saudi Arabia within roughly three weeks of the date of signature of the contract. Believing that he had several visas available at the Saudi Arabian embassy in the workman's country, the employer gave a letter to the workman enabling him to obtain one of such work visas. However, the embassy rejected the workman's application for the reason that the duration of validity of the employer's visas had expired. Subsequently, the employer renewed the validity of the visas, and, having obtained one, the workman travelled to Saudi Arabia. He arrived in Riyadh approximately five months after the contract was signed. It is important to note that the employer did not allege that the workman was responsible for any part of the delay. On his arrival, the workman filed a claim against the employer on the grounds that, since the delay was not due to fault on his part, he was entitled to

(i) damages, because he had liquidated his business in preparation for and in anticipation of travelling to Saudi Arabia; and
(ii) salary payments for the period of delay.

The Primary Commission rejected both claims. First, the Commission held that the claimant was not entitled to damages for the loss of anticipated profits arising from the liquidation of his business because the

---

[24] *Cf.* Minister of Labor & Social Affairs Resolution No. 452 (25/11/1397) (employer to bear costs of training under Labor Regs., art. 44, whether inside or outside Saudi Arabia) (translated in Appendix 35).

plaintiff workman had agreed to travel to the Kingdom and did in fact so travel. The Commission did not give much weight to the faultlessness of the workman, nor to the fact that the delay in obtaining the visa was due to the employer's failure to use reasonable care in enabling the workman to obtain a visa. In rejecting the workman's claim for wage payments, the Primary Commission commented that the workman should have taken the necessary precautions to safeguard his own interest. Noting that salaries are customarily paid as of the assumption of work, it found that the plaintiff did not begin to work until he had arrived in the Kingdom and was therefore not entitled to payments for the delay period. It should also be observed that there was no evidence that the employer had in any way urged or caused the workman to liquidate his business. Consequently, the employer was not liable for any damages due to a business decision made freely by the workman.

The Commission's ruling is a proper illustration of the principle that wages are only payable for work performed, in the absence of the physical availability of the workman or a contractual provision to the contrary. The employer in this case had made no representations to the workman as to the time at which the latter would be able to obtain a visa and travel to Saudi Arabia. Instead, the contract expressly provided that it would become effective only upon the workman's arrival in the Kingdom. The Commission's interpretation of the delay provision in the employment agreement also exemplifies the Saudi rule of strict construction. The parties' agreement that the employer would not be liable for any delay caused by the workman was not construed to mean either that the employer would be liable for any other delay or that he would be liable for delays attributable to his acts or omissions. Rather, the plain language of the contract governed the parties' respective rights and duties.

C. PROBATION PERIOD

The Regulations do not require employment to begin with a probation period. However, the parties are permitted to agree on a probation period of a maximum of three months. If the parties agree to any such probation period, service is deemed to commence at the beginning of such period, despite any contractual provision to the contrary. Article 71 of the Regulations provides

> [a]n employer shall not be obliged to reemploy a workman under probation for a period exceeding three months in respect of workmen employed at a monthly wage, or exceeding one month in respect of other workmen.

A workman shall not be employed under probation more than once by one employer. The contract shall specifically and in writing provide that the workman is under probation, and the period shall be clearly defined, otherwise the workman shall be considered as a regular workman.

The first paragraph of article 71 expresses the rule of law that the maximum duration of the probation period is three months. Unless the parties have agreed to measure their relationship in terms of another calendar, the three months, or the month in the case of workmen not rated on a monthly basis, are deemed to be thirty days in length.[25] During the probation period, the employer has the right to discharge a workman.[26] In case of such a termination, the workman is not entitled to notice, or to severance pay or any other compensation unless so provided in the contract.[27] The employer is only obligated to pay the wages of the workman through the last day of actual work. In addition, the employer is required to give the workman a return ticket, or the value thereof, to the place where the employment contract was entered into or the place from which the workman travelled to the place of work.[28]

Due to the rule allowing the employer to terminate workmen during the probation period, Saudi law strictly adheres to the principle that only one probation period may occur between two parties. Article 71 is interpreted to mean that parties may not enter into more than one probation period, even if the total length of the various purported probation periods does not exceed three months.

In one case, after the workman's probation period had ended, the parties signed an employment contract which provided that it was to relate back to the date of the beginning of the probation period. Two to three weeks after the contract was signed, the employer discharged the workman because his performance was unsatisfactory. The employer asserted its right to terminate the contract on the grounds that the workman had not yet completed his second probation period, which commenced on the date the contract was signed. Rejecting this argument, the Primary Commission held that no second probation period could exist. Since service commences as of the beginning of the probation period as a matter of law, the parties could not by agreement exclude the probation period from the period of service. Thus, the employer could not subject the same workman to two probation periods. It may be noted that the same result would have

---

[25] Labor Regs., art. 20.
[26] *Id.* art. 83(6). Despite the introductory language of this article, no show-cause notice is required.
[27] *Id.* art. 83.
[28] *Id.* art. 85.

obtained even if the contract had provided that it would be effective as of the date of signature.

D. WORKMEN'S RIGHTS

The Regulations are extremely protective of workmen's rights. Furthermore, article 15 gives the workman's entitlements the status of "first class privileged debts" secured by a lien on all of the employer's property.[29] Article 6 of the Regulations invalidates any agreement by the workman to waive his regulatory rights.[30] It provides

> [i]t is illegal to violate the provisions of these Regulations or to prejudice any other rights acquired by workmen by virtue of any other regulations or concession agreements, or employment contracts, or any other agreements, or arbitration awards, or royal orders or in accordance with generally accepted practice or with what has been habitually granted by the employer to his workmen in a given area or areas.
>
> Any stipulation in a contract or agreement whereby the workman waives any right established in his favor by virtue of the provisions of these Regulations shall be null and void, even if such stipulation was made prior to the effective date hereof.

The workman's rights may be divided into the following categories

1. Legal rights

Legal rights are granted by any applicable law, regulations, and administrative orders or rules of Saudi Arabia.

2. Judicial rights

Judicial rights flow from the decisions of competent courts or administrative tribunals, arbitral awards, and settlement agreements

---

[29] Article 15 provides

[t]he amounts to which the workman or his dependents are entitled under the provisions shall be considered first-class privileged debts, and for the recovery thereof the workman or his heirs shall have a priority right over all the employer's property. In the event of the employer's bankruptcy or the liquidation of his establishment, such amounts shall be recorded as privileged debts, and the workman shall be paid immediately a portion equivalent to one month's pay before payment of any other costs, including judicial bankruptcy or liquidation costs.

Cf. Commercial Court Regs., High Order No. 32, art. 119 (1931) (wages of bankrupt's servants among debts having priority over all other debts).

[30] *But see* Royal Decree No. M/2 (7/2/1403) (creating exception to general rule of art. 6 with respect to commissions, sales percentages and other variable wage elements for purposes of calculating severance pay) (translated in Appendix 36).

registered with the Labor Commissions.[31]

3. Contractual rights

Contractual rights arise out of any agreement of the parties, whether or not an employment agreement and whether the agreement is oral or written, in whole or in part, provided that any such agreement is not contrary to Saudi law or public policy.

4. Customary rights

Customary rights are based on established customs, generally accepted practice, and usage. In addition, they include any rights that the employer habitually has granted to workmen in a given area.[32]

5. Acquired rights

Acquired rights may arise out of any rights or benefits which an employer, in the course of the employment relationship, gives to a particular workman in addition to the rights mentioned in the preceding four categories.

Acquired rights vesting by virtue of regularity

The vast majority of acquired rights vest if provided to a workman regularly and continuously during a reasonable period of time with the result that the workman comes to regard them as a part of his wage, as distinguished from an occasional gratuity or gift, or to consider that he is otherwise entitled to them.[33] The factors determinative of whether a certain benefit is an acquired right protected by article 6 are, first, its repetition or continuation over a reasonable period of time, and, second, the workman's subjective belief in his continuing right to such benefit. In this respect, the employer's subjective intention is irrelevant. However, if the workman's belief is not predicated on a reasonable time period, rights will not be deemed acquired. Acquired rights are distinguishable from customary rights in that the former are personal and specific to the workman. Hence, workman X may not claim rights acquired by workman Y despite the fact that both X and Y are employed under identical contracts and performing

---

[31] Although judicial rights are not mentioned in art. 6, Labor Commission decisions are protected as regulatory rights by virtue of art. 182 of the Regs. Settlement agreements are protected by art. 6 and, if registered, also by art. 182. Arbitral awards are protected by art. 6 and, on confirmation by a Labor Commission chairman, also by art. 184.

[32] See generally A. AL-HANFAWI, USUL AL-TASHRI FI AL-MAMLAKAH AL-ARABIYYAH AL-SUʿŪDIYYAH 72–73 (date unavailable) (defining "custom" as distinguished from habit) (custom must conform to Islamic express texts, regulations).

[33] See Labor Regs., art. 124(3).

identical tasks. The rationale underlying this doctrine is that Y may be more dynamic, efficient, obedient, or competent, or possess higher qualifications or other qualities than X. Thus, if any paid leave or "rest and recreation"[34] of a longer duration or of greater frequency than the leave required by law or originally agreed upon by the parties is given to a workman in succession over a reasonable period, it will become his acquired right. The same result will obtain if the workman receives any gratuities or gifts on religious or other days of significance. In brief, this principle applies to any benefits given to workmen, including, *inter alia*, medical care, travel allowances, excess baggage payments, food and lodging during travelling, and transportation expenses such as airplane tickets. An automobile provided for the private use of a workman for a reasonable period becomes his acquired right.

However, the doctrine of acquired rights is slightly different where the issue is in the form of food or housing. Assume that the workman has been provided food in kind and that, later, the employer offers him cash instead. The workman has every right to refuse this offer. However, if the employer is constrained to close down the feeding facility for a valid reason, such as a substantial reduction in the number of workmen he employs, the workman must accept the cash payments. The same logic applies in the opposite case where an employer, having given a food allowance to the workman, later desires to provide him with food in kind.[35] This modified

[34] The right to annual vacation accrues by virtue of art. 153, while the right to "rest and recreation" accrues solely by contract and is in addition to the annual vacation.

[35] Additionally, if the workman is employed in a remote area, he is obliged to accept food in kind approved by ministerial decision. *See id.* art. 143(b).
The following are designated as remote areas
   (a) The Empty Quarter.
   (b) The following regions except for the cities designated *infra* and places of work which are not more than thirty kilometers distant from the farthest developed area connected to these cities if the road is paved or asphalted or not more than fifteen kilometers distant if the road is not paved or asphalted. These regions and cities are
(1) The Western Province, except for the following cities: Makkah, Jeddah, Ta'if, Yanbu, Rabigh, al-Madinah, Amlaj, Zaba, al-Wajh, Haql, al-Quntudhah, and al-Laith,
(2) The Central Province, except for the following cities: Riyadh, al-Dir'iyyah, Lailā in the region of al-Aflāj, Shaqrā, 'Anaizah, Buraidah, al-Majma'ah, al-Rass, al-Duwadmi, 'Afif, Marat, al-Quwa'iyyah, Dhurmā, Hawta Bani Tamim, Hawta Sudair, al-Salil, al-Hariq, al-Zilfi, and Wadi Duwāsir.
(3) The Southern Province except for the following cities: Abha, Khamis Mishait, Najran, Bishah, Dhahran of the South, al-Namas, al-Bahah, Baljarshi, Subayya, and Abu 'Arish.
(4) The Eastern Province, except for the following cities: Dammām, al-Khobar, al-Qatif, Saihat, Rās Tānura, Abqaiq, al-Khafaji, Juabil, Hufuf and al-Mabraz in al-Ahsa, al-Thaqabah, Dhahran and Safwa.
(5) The Northern Province except for the following cities: Tobūk, 'Ar'ar, Sukākā, al-Jawf, Rafhah, Ha'il, al-Qurayyat, Turaif, and Hafir al-Batin.
Interview with Deputy Minister of Labor & Social Affairs, al-Jazirah, Jan. 28, 1982, at 5, col. 2 (quoting from Minister of Labor & Social Affairs Resolution No. 651 (1401) (defining remote areas with respect to workmen of companies, establishments, and factories)).

doctrine also applies in the case of housing in kind or housing allowances.

Exceptions

(*a*) *Overtime.* Whether provided in the contract or practised for a reasonable period of time, the performance of overtime work never becomes a right, either of the employer or the workman.

(*b*) *Rights deemed acquired once given.* Both salary increases and upward grade classifications become acquired rights of the workman the moment he receives them. Article 208 of the Regulations provides that "[t]he grade or the salary of a workman shall not be lowered except in the cases provided in the Regulations or in the resolutions issued thereunder." Article 79 provides

> [a] monthly-rated workman may not be reclassified as a daily-rated workman or as a weekly, hourly or a piecework-rated workman, unless he so agrees in writing and without prejudice to the rights he has acquired during the period he spent as a monthly-rated workman. The grade classification shall be considered an acquired right of the workman and he may not be reclassified in a lower grade.

In addition, certain other rights may be deemed acquired even if not repeated with regularity. In one 1976 case, the plaintiff, a nonSaudi workman, filed a claim, alleging, *inter alia*, his right to airplane tickets or their monetary equivalent, on the basis of contractual provisions. In 1972, the parties had initially entered into an employment contract for a period of one year, which provided that the workman would be entitled to three airplane tickets to his home country. The employment relationship was subsequently renewed on an annual basis. The plaintiff alleged that he was given only two tickets to his home country per year, except for the initial year of his service, when he was given three tickets, and maintained that he was entitled to three tickets for the succeeding years. The defendant employer explained that the contractual term providing for three tickets, rather than two tickets, in the first employment contract, was a mistake in the integration of the parties' agreement. Thus, according to the employer, the provision was amended in subsequent contracts to reflect the parties' true understanding. The Primary Commission found that the plaintiff was entitled to three airplane tickets with respect to all years of employment because they had become his acquired right by virtue of the provision in the initial employment contract.

Similarly, in one 1977 case, the initial employment contract, concluded in 1972 for a one-year specified period, provided that the company, in its discretion, would give the workman either housing in kind or a housing allowance of sixteen percent of his monthly base salary. During the four years following the expiration of this agreement, the parties annually signed employment contracts, each for a one-year period. However, none of the subsequent agreements contained a housing clause. The plaintiff workman later brought suit to recover the value of five years of housing allowance. The employer sought to defend against this claim on the grounds, *inter alia*, that each contract was for a one-year specified period. Therefore, it argued, if the Primary Commission were to award the workman any housing allowance, such award should only include the allowance for the first year and not for those years of employment covered by contracts devoid of housing clauses. The Primary Commission, rejecting this view, held that the plaintiff was entitled to five years of housing allowance. On appeal, the ruling was affirmed.

E. WAGE

1. Nature of the wage

Saudi law applies the term "wage", with respect to services, solely to consideration payable to workmen. Conversely, a person who receives consideration other than a wage in exchange for services performed does not come within the Labor Regulations' definition of "workman."[36] Section B *supra* discusses the legal principle that wages are paid for work. Article 122 of the Regulations expresses the corollary to that principle by creating a presumption that services are rendered in exchange for a wage if the service consists of work which is not customarily performed gratuitously or which is in the occupational line of the person who performed it. Since the wage is required to be paid in cash or in kind,[37] it is unlawful to employ a workman to perform services in consideration of acts or omissions, whether specific or nonspecific, of the employer, despite any material benefit which might accrue to the workman from such acts or omissions. For the same reason, expression of the wage solely in terms of future tangible benefits is not permitted. However, an employment contract will be enforceable and binding upon the parties despite the absence of a provision stating the workman's wage.[38]

2. Scope of the wage

The wage is the most important of the workman's rights protected by Saudi law.[39] The wage, in addition to contractual rights, may embrace both

---

[36] *See* Labor Regs., art. 7(7).

[37] *See id.* art. 7(6).

[38] *See id.* art. 123(a).

[39] *See, e.g., id.* art. 15 (wage among items deemed "first class privileged debts").

customary rights and acquired rights. It is important to be aware of the boundaries of the wage because it is the legal measure for certain payments and deductions.[40] Furthermore, the Labor Commissions in workmen's actions for wrongful discharge may award damages in an amount equal to the value of the plaintiff's wage for a certain period.[41]

Finally, for purposes of calculating the tax liability of nonSaudi employers or participants in a mixed participation company employer, the various components of the wages of workmen are deductible expenses, with the exception of contributions by the employer to nonSaudi social insurance systems and to thrift and savings plans.[42]

The "wage", as distinguished from the base salary, is defined by article 7(6), which provides

> [t]he "wage" is all that is given to the workman in consideration of his work under an employment contract, whether written or unwritten, regardless of the nature of the wage, whether it is in cash or in kind, and payable monthly, weekly, daily, or on a piecework basis or on the basis of the number of hours or the amount of production, regardless of whether all or any part of such wage consists of commissions or tips where the latter are paid in accordance with generally accepted practice and where there are rules permitting the accurate calculation thereof. In general, the wage shall include all increases and allowances of any kind, including the high cost of living allowance and the family allowance.[43]

[40] *See, e.g., id.* art. 73 (compensation for termination without notice measured in terms of wage); arts. 87–88 (same with respect to severance pay); art. 119 (deductions); Social Insurance Regs., art. 19 (1969) (social insurance contributions). *See also* Labor Regs., art. 80 (foreign workmen may not receive wages in excess of those paid to Saudis of equal qualifications and competence).

[41] *See also* Labor Regs., art. 74 (wage is factor to be considered in assessing damages).

[42] *See* Director-Gen'l of Dep't of Zakat & Income Tax ["DZIT"] Circular No. 4863/5181/3 (8/4/1395); Minister of Fin. & Nat'l Econ. Resolution No. 32/710 (Nov. 30, 1982) (disallowance of contributions to thrift and savings plans effective as from Feb. 15, 1972).

[43] Similarly, article 24 of the Social Insurance Regulations Implementing Rules, Minister of Labor & Social Affairs Resolution No. 2 (11/9/1392), *as amended by* Minister of Labor & Social Affairs Resolution No. 46 (17/6/1401), defines the wage to include the following elements

(1) The base salary, whether paid monthly, weekly, daily or by the piece, number of work hours, or amount of production.

(2) Commissions, that is, a percentage awarded to commercial representatives, insurance firms' representatives, agents and similar categories of workmen, whether the wage is limited to this percentage or includes a fixed sum in addition thereto.

(3) A percentage of the sales or revenues which are collected by the workman, whether this percentage is payable to the workman in addition to a fixed wage or comprises the only wage he receives.

(4) Tips which are customarily paid, where there are rules permitting the accurate calculation thereof as provided for in article 7(6) of the Labor and Workman Regulations.

(5) High cost of living allowance and family allowance provided for in article 7(6) of the

However, the regulatory language describing the wage as "all that is given to the workman in consideration of his work" is overembracing to the extent that certain items received by workmen are, in fact, excluded from the wage.[44] Furthermore, certain items received by the workman and normally includable in the computation of the wage may lawfully be excluded with respect to certain time periods. For example, the parties may agree that the workman will not be entitled to the high cost of living allowance for those periods in which he is on vacation outside of the Kingdom. However, unless the employer is able to establish such an agreement, whether by means of an express provision in the employment contract or otherwise, such items will be included in the computation of the wage.

For the most part, Saudi law will respect the parties' agreements on the amount of the wage where no conflict with a provision of law exists.[45] The terms of such agreements should in all cases be clearly drawn. Nonetheless, some items enter into the calculation of the wage by force of law. Article 124 provides

[t]he following amounts shall be considered an integral part of the wage and shall be taken into account in computing the amount that may be attached

(1) The commission given to peddlers, travelling salesmen, and commercial representatives.

(2) Percentages paid to employees of commercial establishments on the price of their sales, as well as the allowances paid to them on account of the high cost of living.

(3) Any grant made to the workman in addition to the salary, as well as any amount paid to him as a reward for his honesty, or for his increased family obligations and the like, if such amounts are stipulated in the employment contracts or in the basic work rules, or if such amounts are paid as a matter of generally accepted practice so that workmen have come to regard them as part of the wage, and not as a gratuity.

---

[44] See pp. 266–67 infra.
[45] See Labor Regs., art. 123.

Labor and Workmen Regulations.

(6) Overtime payments to workmen who have received such payments for at least eight months, whether consecutive or not, during the preceding year, because of the nature of their work.

(7) Expatriation allowance.

(8) Housing cash allowance according to the amount agreed upon between the employer and worker provided that the amount from which the contribution is to be deducted shall not exceed thirty-six thousand (36,000) riyals a year.

(9) With respect to housing in kind, the amount to be subject to the contribution deduction shall be equal to the base salary of two months but not exceeding thirty-six thousand (36,000) riyals a year.

However, article 124 is qualified by the 1982 amendment to article 87, providing

> [n]otwithstanding the provisions of article 6, an agreement may be made to exclude from the wage on the basis of which severance pay is calculated all or any of the amounts of commissions, percentages on sales prices, and similar elements of the wage which are paid to the workman and are subject by their nature to increase and decrease.[46]

If the parties so agree, the earnings of a workman may be entirely dependent upon the volume of sales that he generates without his having any base salary.

It is, of course, impossible to establish a firm rule as to which payments are deemed part of the wage. However, it should be noted that, in order to qualify as a component of the wage, a given form of payment must be fixed, and regular and periodical in nature, as distinguished from casual payments or payments made on a temporary basis.

In order to dissipate confusion relating to the treatment of specific items, this subsection will cover the various components of the wage.

(a) Base salary. Regardless of the place or manner of payment or the basis of computation, the base salary is part of the wage. It includes any and all increases in the salary. The employer should, in all cases, take the precaution of clearly specifying in the employment agreement the precise working period in exchange for which the salary is payable. Contractual provisions should thus state that the base salary includes payments due to the workman for nonworking days such as weekly rest days, official holidays, and vacations. In contrast, if the contract merely provides that the base salary is paid for forty-eight hours of work per week without mentioning the weekly rest day, and if the salary is paid on a weekly basis, the salary as provided may be regarded as not covering the minimum of eight hours per week, i.e. the weekly rest day, required to be compensated without actual work performed.

However, the risk of misinterpretation only arises in the case of weekly-rated workmen. No such risk is present if the workman is paid on a monthly basis. In one case, for example, a monthly-rated workman claimed additional compensation on the grounds that, because there were only twenty-six working days in the month and his salary as provided in the Agreement only related to the monthly working days, he was entitled to an extra four days of compensation. His complaint was dismissed. In the event that the employment contract provides the workman will work forty hours in certain weeks for a salary of, for example, 1,000 riyals and forty-eight hours in other weeks for a salary of 1,200 riyals, the salary will be

---

[46] Royal Decree No. M/2 (7/2/1403) (translated in Appendix 36).

aggregated for computation purposes.

(b) *Foreign service premium; remote area premium; or hardship allowance.* These premiums are part of the wage whether paid on a monthly, three-monthly, six-monthly, or annual basis.

(c) *Cost of living allowances.* These are part of the wage.

(d) *Pocket money/allowance for miscellaneous expenses.* This is part of the wage.

(e) *Extended work week bonus.* Some nonSaudi companies pay this bonus to their expatriate workmen transferred to Saudi Arabia from the company's foreign offices. It represents compensation for the Saudi work period in excess of that of the workman's home country. This bonus is part of both the base salary and the wage.

(f) *Housing.* Whether housing is part of the wage may depend on whether the housing is provided in cash or in kind. It is settled that housing allowances paid in cash are included in the wage. However, some confusion exists with respect to the treatment of housing in kind. Under one view, housing located outside city limits and provided by the employer in specific compliance with the Council of Ministers resolutions requiring certain employers to construct and provide housing[47] is not part of the wage. All other housing in kind would be considered a part of the wage, except the housing provided in remote areas in compliance with article 143 of the Regulations.[48]

The view that housing in kind may be excluded from the wage is supported by some relatively old Labor Commission decisions. In one 1979 wrongful discharge case, the Primary Commission, in computing the amount of severance pay, excluded housing from the wage on the grounds that the value of housing in kind was too difficult to assess accurately. However, the validity of the exclusion of housing in kind may be regarded as attenuated by Council of Ministers Resolution No. 210, which requires nonSaudi companies to rent housing for their workmen within city limits.[49] It should be noted that confusion still exists with respect to the inclusion of housing in kind in the wage and the method of evaluating such housing.

(g) *Food allowances* are part of the wage. If provided in kind, food shares with housing the same unclear legal status, with respect to inclusion in the wage.

[47] Resolution No. 448 (14/3/1396), *as amended by* Resolutions No. 1034 (17/6/1396), No. 1235 (12/10/1397) (translated in Appendix 37), & No. 210 (8/18/1981).

[48] Housing provided under article 143 may be excluded, first, on the grounds that its provision is a legal obligation of the employer rather than a right of the workman, and second, because its value is too uncertain to permit its translation into a monetary equivalent.

[49] Resolution No. 210, para. 2 (8/18/1981) (creating exception from in-city requirement for remote area housing specifically permitted by Minister of Interior). *See generally* note 35 *supra* (defining remote areas). *See also* Minister of Labor & Social Affairs Resolution No. 89 (10/3/1402) (giving specifications for remote area housing) (translated in Appendix 38).

(h) Increased family obligation allowances are part of the wage.

(i) Tuition fees paid for the schooling of the workman's children are part of the wage whether paid to the workman or directly to the educational institution.

(j) Insurance. If the employer pays the workman's share of mandatory contributions to the Social Insurance Fund without deducting such amounts from the workman's wage,[50] they become part of the wage.[51]

(k) Transportation. Cash allowances are part of the wage. Article 142 means of transportation in remote areas provided in kind are not part of the wage.[52]

Employers are not required under article 142 to provide their workmen with transportation, either in cash or in kind, for the purpose of going to or returning from the place of work, unless the workmen are employed in a remote area where no other transportation facilities are available.

(l) Taxes. The amount of any income tax owed by the workman and paid by the employer whether inside or outside Saudi Arabia, and whether to the workman or directly to the tax collection authorities is part of the wage.[53] In cases where the employer has paid such amounts, the doctrine of acquired rights may require the inclusion of such amounts in the wage even where the laws of the workman's home country or the country subjecting him to tax liability have subsequently relieved him of such liability or have increased the tax exemption or credit applicable to payments received by him.[54] However, the result in such case may differ if the employer previously paid such taxes directly to the tax collection agency.

[50] The workman's contribution is five percent of the total wage. Social Insurance Regs., art. 18(2). The employer is entitled, but not required, to deduct the workman's contributions from his wage. *See* Labor Regs., art. 119(b). However, the employer is solely liable for the actual payment of contributions owed by itself and the insured workman. Social Insurance Regs., art. 19(4). Social insurance payments of the workman's share of the contribution made by the employer are not deductible expenses of the employer for purposes of Saudi tax. *See also* Minister of Fin. & Nat'l Econ. Resolution No. 32/710 (Nov. 30, 1982) (translated in Appendix 39), Director-Gen'l of DZIT Circular No. 1170/2 (Dec. 4, 1982) (allowing deduction of social insurance contributions imposed by Social Insurance Regs.) (disallowing deductions of thrift and savings plans).

[51] This rule was specifically confirmed in one labor case. The Primary Commission for the Settlement of Labor Disputes held that, where the employer had been paying the workman's share of social insurance contributions, such contributions were to be considered part of his wage for the purpose of calculating his severance pay entitlements. On appeal this ruling was affirmed by the Supreme Commission for the Settlement of Labor Disputes.

[52] Article 142 of the Regulations provides

[e]very employer shall provide means of transportation to carry his workmen from their places of residence or from a given point of assembly to the places of work and to return them daily, if the places of work are not reached by ordinary, regular means of transportation.

[53] Saudi Arabia does not tax personal earned income. *See* Royal Decree No. M/37, para. 1 (4/5/1395).

[54] *See generally* pp. 255–59 *supra*.

(*m*) *Bonuses.* Contract completion bonuses or project completion bonuses, whether provided in the contract or otherwise agreed upon, become part of the wage upon "completion" unless specifically provided that such bonuses are paid in lieu of severance pay. They are also includable in the wage if the workman is prevented by the employer, without a legal excuse, from completing the contract or project. Although the amount of such bonuses will increase proportionately with the passage of time, they are not, as a rule, payable prior to the completion of the contract or the project, unless the parties so agree. Miscellaneous bonuses or awards provided in the contract, or otherwise agreed upon, and contingent on certain conditions, receive the same treatment as contract completion bonuses. A workman forfeits his right to such a bonus if he resigns without a valid reason or if he is discharged for a valid reason. If such a bonus is paid in pro rata monthly installments simultaneously with the workman's salary, the installments actually received are part of the wage. To the extent already paid, they can never be recovered by the employer even if the workman resigns without justification or is discharged for a valid reason. If the workman is wrongfully discharged by the employer, or the employer's breach of the employment contract discharges the workman's obligations thereunder, any such bonuses or awards are included in the wage, at least to the extent already paid or to the extent already accrued through the final day of employment. Such bonuses may or may not be paid for the remainder of the contract duration. Consequently, they may or may not become part of the wage, according to the facts of each case and such factors as the degree of arbitrariness of the termination and the like.

In one case, two workmen sought to recover damages for their alleged wrongful discharge. At issue were employment contracts entered into for a specified period of two years. The employer had terminated the workmen's services after about ten-and-one-half months. As provided in the agreement, the contract completion bonus had been paid regularly on a pro rata basis along with the monthly base salary. Therefore, the monthly amount of the contract completion bonus was permitted to be included in the monthly salary.

(*n*) *Commissions, percentages and tips.* These are part of the wage,[55] unless excluded by the parties' agreement.[56]

For the purpose of computing the wage of a workman whose work is seasonal and periodical, the commissions, percentages, and tips earned or

---

[55] Labor Regs., arts. 7(6), 124.
[56] Royal Decree No. M/2 (7/2/1403) (translated in Appendix 36).

receivable by the workman during the contract year should be averaged.[57] However, this averaging rule is a rule of convenience, based on equitable principles, and consequently the base period is not fixed. Depending upon the periodical or seasonal nature of the work and other piecemeal criteria, the length of time selected for averaging purposes should be such as to reflect a realistic figure of the workman's income.

3. Nonwage payments

In contrast, certain items are not part of the wage. The amount of severance pay due on termination of the employment contract and any damages award recovered by means of judicial decision are never part of the wage. In addition, the following items are excluded from the wage unless the employer by his actions causes them to be included.

(a) *Extra payments not required by law.* Occasional payments made by the employer on religious, historical, cultural, or any other days of significance which are not provided for in the employment contract or otherwise agreed upon, and are paid at the sole discretion of the employer are not part of the wage. However, if repeated with regularity, they may become acquired rights of the workman and, as such, includable in the wage.[58]

(b) *Overtime payments.* These are not normally part of the wage. Assume, however, that any employment contract provides that the workman will work forty-eight hours per week. His salary for forty hours of work is set at $200, and the other eight hours of work entitle him to receive an additional amount of $50 per week. On these facts, the additional $50 per week will be considered part of the wage. Alternatively, if no contract provision exists, but, as a matter of fact, overtime work is performed and compensated for a substantial period in one contract year, overtime payments will be includable in the wage because the workman will have begun to consider them to be part of the wage.[59] In this case, the monthly rate of the wage may be computed by averaging such overtime payments over a one-year period.

(c) *Travelling expenses.* These are not part of the wage. Such expenses include tickets from or to the workman's place of residence, or the monetary value thereof; food and lodging while travelling; payments made with respect to visas and passports in the case of expatriate workmen; inoculation expenses; payments for excess baggage transported and for the

---

[57] *Cf.* Social Insurance Regs. Implementing Rules, art. 24 (applicable to social insurance contributions).

[58] *See generally* pp. 256–57 *supra.*

[59] If the Labor Commissions analogize such period to that provided in art. 24(6) of the Social Insurance Regulations Implementing Rules, it will be established at eight months.

storage, warehousing, or insurance of baggage; or any other travel allowances. According to one view, the value of travel tickets is part of the wage, with the exception of the initial ticket(s) providing transportation for the workman and any family members, if he is entitled to family status, to the place of work, and the final ticket(s) for repatriating the workman and his family, if any. This view should be rejected on the grounds that Saudi law distinguishes between payments directly or indirectly made in consideration of the workman's service, and payments made in reimbursement of expenses that the workman has incurred by reason of his employment. The latter are not properly included in the wage because they are in the nature of compensation required either to put the workman in a position to perform his work or to restore the workman to his original position prior to his taking up work. Furthermore, this general rule may be deemed specifically applicable to the initial ticket(s) for the reason that the workman's right to his wage does not vest until he has physically made himself available to the employer at the appointed time and place.[60] Since Saudi law, unless the parties agree otherwise, excludes the pre-employment travelling period from the period of service, the initial ticket may not be deemed included in the compensation for services rendered. Second, since the workman's right to the final ticket does not vest until the employment relationship is terminated, it may be forfeited by the workman's wrongful action and it is not provided to the workman for services rendered, but is a legal obligation of the employer, it also should be excluded from the wage. Moreover, factual experience supports the exclusion of tickets from the wage.

The following is a representative example of how the Labor Commissions analyze the wage in their computation of severance pay and damage awards. In one 1978 case, the plaintiff workman claimed that, in calculation of his severance pay, his wage should include the following amounts

   (i)   Monthly base salary computed on the basis of the most recent rate;
   (ii) Housing allowance, which was provided in the contract as a percentage value of the base salary;
   (iii) Annual contract completion bonus as provided in the contract;
   (iv) The value of contributions paid by the employer to the Social Insurance Fund on his behalf and amounting to five percent of his wage;
   (v) The value of tickets for unused rest and recreation leaves.

The defendant employer first argued that calculations of severance pay under article 87 of the Regulations should take into account the base salary and not the wage. The employer then argued, alternatively, that, even if

---

[60] *See generally* pp. 250–51 *supra*.

severance pay were required to be computed on the basis of the total wage, the contract completion bonus should be excluded from the computation. It contended that its contracts provided for contract completion bonuses at the completion of each contract period in order to encourage its workmen to complete, rather than to terminate, employment. Thus, the employer and the workman had signed new contracts annually over the preceding years. The employer consequently maintained that if a workman does not totally complete the contract, even if he completed ninety percent of it, he is not entitled to the completion bonus. Since the workman's right to the bonus had not yet vested, it could not be considered as part of his wage. Finally, the employer pointed out that, since the bonus had not been paid at all, it had not been paid with the regularity required under article 124(3) to cause the workman to regard it as part of his wage. The employer based its argument for the exclusion of the social insurance contributions from the wage on the absence of any legal obligations on its part to make such payments. Since such contributions are properly deductible from the wage of the workman, the employer contended, it should not be penalized for having paid the workman's share of the contributions in order to encourage him to perform his duties with zeal.

Finally, the employer sought to exclude the value of the tickets for purposes of severance pay computation on the grounds that the provision of tickets to him had been a facilitation. Rejecting all but the defendant's final argument, the Primary Commission held that severance pay was computable on the basis of the workman's total wage, including, in addition to the base salary, other benefits such as his housing allowance, social insurance contributions in the amount of five percent of the wage, and the contract completion bonus. On appeal, the ruling was affirmed.

4. Payment of the wage

The employer's failure to pay or delay in payment of the wage as required by regulation subjects it to regulatory penalties.[61] Article 92 provides that "[w]ith due regard to the relevant regulations, the employer shall pay the workman his wages at the time and place specified in the contract or determined by accepted general practice." Article 116 provides

> [t]he workman's wages and any amount due to him must be paid in the official currency of the country. Wages must be paid during working hours and at the place of work in accordance with the following provisions
>   (a) Wages of daily-rated workmen shall be paid at least once a week.

[61] *See* Labor Regs., arts. 121, 199–200.

(b) Wages of monthly-rated workmen shall be paid once a month.

(c) If the work is performed by piece and it needs a period exceeding two weeks, a payment proportionate to the work completed by the workman must be made to him every week, and the full balance of his wages shall be paid within the week immediately following the delivery of the work.

(d) In cases other than those mentioned above, wages shall be paid to workmen at least once a week.[62]

However, the parties may lawfully agree that the wage, or portions thereof, are payable in the currency of a country other than Saudi Arabia. In addition, the timing of payments specified in article 116 need not be strictly observed with respect to all components of the wage, provided that the base salary and other essential obligations are paid in accordance with that article.

5. Deductions from the wage

Article 119 of the Regulations permits the employer to deduct certain amounts from the workman's wage. The categories of items properly deductible are specified in article 119, which provides

[n]o amount may be deducted from the workman's wages in satisfaction of private rights, except in respect of the following

(a) To recover the advances or any amounts paid to him in excess of his rights, provided that no deduction shall, in this case, be made from the workman's wages in excess of ten percent of such wages.[63]

---

[62] *Cf.* Ministry of Labor & Social Affairs, Principal Guidelines for the Rules for the Regulation of Work (requiring posting of time of payment of wage) (translated in Appendix 40).

[63] This 10 percent limit applies solely to deductions from the "wage" proper and not to nonwage payments, most notably severance pay. The employer may therefore make unlimited deductions from that item in satisfaction of loans it may have made to the workman. In all cases, it is advisable for employers not to lend, advance to, or otherwise become a creditor of their workmen with respect to amounts that may not be satisfied out of 10 percent of the wage plus the total severance pay due.

With respect to housing allowances, which in practice are generally paid in advance on an annual or semi-annual basis, it may be noted that, where the employment contract terminates in the middle of a rental period, although the employer is in principle entitled to recover the balance of any prepaid rent or housing allowance, its right to recover such amounts will vary on a case-by-case basis depending, in particular, on the terms of the lease agreement. If prepaid rent is refundable by the lessor, such amount is recoverable by the employer. If the lease is for a one-year term and the workman has received a full year's housing allowance but paid to the lessor only rental for a six-month period, at which point the employment contract terminates, the employer may recover from the workman the unpaid balance unless the lessor has the right to rental for the full term of the lease. Except in cases of unjustified termination of the employment contract by the workman, Saudi law will not require him to sustain the double burden of paying rent to the lessor and returning the same amount to his employer.

    (b) Social insurance premiums due from the workman.

    (c) The workman's contributions to the Savings Fund and the advances due to this Fund.

    (d) Installments pertaining to any plan for the construction of houses for the purpose of transferring ownership thereof to the workmen, or to any other benefits or services, if any, as decided by the Minister of Labor.

    (e) Fines that are imposed on the workman for offenses committed by him under the provisions of article 126, as well as any amount that is withheld from his pay in accordance with article 81,[64] for any damage he has caused.

    (f) Any debt to be recovered in execution of a judicial judgment, provided that the amount deducted in this respect shall not exceed one-fourth of the wages due to the workman and provided that an alimony debt and a debt for food, clothing, and lodging shall be satisfied in this order and before all other debts.

Deductions may as a rule be properly made by the employer without the need for judicial confirmation. However, in no case may the amount of deductions contemplated by article 119 exceed one-half of the workman's wage, in the absence of a Labor Commission order permitting a larger deduction.[65] Conversely, even if the amount deductible is less than the fifty percent limit, the Commission may, on a finding of hardship, require the employer to pay the workman up to seventy-five percent of his salary.[66] In addition, the maximum amount deductible with respect to any single disciplinary violation or in any single work month corresponds to the value of five days' wage.[67] The six regulatory categories of deductions found in

---

[64] Article 81 provides

> [i]f a workman causes the loss, damage or destruction of materials, machinery or products which belong to or are in the custody of the employer, where such loss, damage or destruction was the result of the workman's fault or contravention of the employer's instructions and not the result of a third party's fault or *force majeure*, the employer may withhold from the workman's wages the amount required for repairs or for restoring things to their original condition, provided that the amount so withheld shall not exceed five days' wages in each month. However, the employer may, if necessary, lodge a complaint to claim a higher amount if the workman has other property from which recovery can be made. The workman may also appeal the employer's assessment to the appropriate Commission, and if the latter rules that the employer had no claim against the workman for the amount he withheld from the workman's pay or if the employer is awarded a smaller amount, the employer shall refund to the workman, within seven days from the date of issuance of the ruling, the amount unduly withheld.

[65] *Id.* art. 120.

[66] *Id.*

[67] *Id.* art. 125; *cf.* Model Disciplinary Rules (translated in Appendix 34).

article 119 are exhaustive.[68] Additionally, article 91(c) denies the employer the right to make any deduction from wages with respect to time taken off from work by the workman in the exercise of his legal rights. Furthermore, deductions with respect to social insurance contributions under article 119(b) must be withheld at the time of payment of the wage. If omitted, their value may not be withheld from any subsequent wages to which the workman is entitled.[69]

The employer is liable for wrongful deductions from the workman's wage. Article 121 provides

> [i]f any amount is deducted from the workman's wages for reasons other than those specified herein, without the latter's consent, or if the employer delays, without justification, payment of the workman's wages when they fall due in accordance with the [Regulations], the workman, his representative, or the Head of the appropriate Labor Office may submit an application to the appropriate Commission so that it may order the employer to return to the workman any wrongfully-deducted amounts or to pay him his outstanding wages.
>
> If it is established to the said Commission that the employer has unjustifiably deducted the said amounts or delayed payment of the wages, the Commission may impose on the employer a fine that shall not exceed double the amount deducted from the workman's wages, or double the outstanding wages. All payments ordered by the Commission in this case shall be collected through administrative channels.

Finally, it should be noted that amounts actually deducted from the wage are not excluded from computations of the wage under the various provisions of the Regulations. Thus, penalties for misbehavior imposed by the employer on individual employees will not reduce their wages for the purpose of computing, for example, severance pay. The same rule applies in cases where the value of penalties is apportioned by the employer among its workmen.

F. WORKING HOURS

1. Work week

Under Saudi law, the work week consists of a maximum of six days of actual work. This rule applies whether the workman is employed on a

---

[68] Article 119's protection of the workman's wage, however, only extends to deductions in satisfaction of private rights. Thus, wages may be withheld in satisfaction of public rights pursuant to a judicial decision or administrative order. *See also id.* art. 120 (maximum percentage deductible is 50% in "all cases").

[69] Social Insurance Regs., art. 19(4).

monthly, weekly, or daily basis.[70] Article 149 of the Regulations provides

> Friday, which is the day observed as an official holiday, shall be a day of rest with full pay. The employer may [however] with the approval of the appropriate Labor Office, replace this day for some of his workmen by any other day of the week, provided that the number of working days per week shall not exceed six, and that the workmen shall in all cases be enabled to perform their religious duties.

Thus, the parties may select by agreement a day other than Friday as the weekly day of rest. However, unless the employer's work rules, as approved by the Ministry of Labor and Social Affairs, enunciate the employer's right to select a day of rest other than Friday,[71] or the employer otherwise obtains such permission from the Labor authorities, the workman has the right to insist on retaining Friday as his day of rest. Furthermore, even if the workman does consent to another rest day, official permission is required in all cases.

In addition, workmen are entitled to full pay with respect to official holidays.[72] At present, Saudi law recognizes eight holidays: three days at the end of Ramadan, four days for pilgrimage, and National Day.[73] In the case of weeks containing official holidays, workmen are entitled in addition to the weekly day of rest. If the holiday falls on a weekly rest day, the workman is not entitled to an extra day off in respect thereof.

The workman's right not to work on rest days and holidays is not absolute. However, any work performed on such days entitles workmen to receive their wages at overtime rates.[74] The Regulations do not differ in their treatment of weekly rest days and holidays, with respect to the employer's right to require the workman to work. However, the employer's right to require workmen to work on rest days is limited to certain exceptional circumstances.[75]

---

[70] In theory, it would also apply to workmen paid by the piece. However, the overwhelming majority of employment contracts in Saudi Arabia provide for employment on a monthly basis.

[71] *See generally* Labor Regs., art. 9(b) (applicable to employers of at least 20 workmen).

[72] *Id.* art. 155 (providing that the number of such holidays may not exceed 10 days).

[73] *See* Minister of Labor & Social Affairs Resolution No. 812, art. 1 (16/11/1394) (translated in Appendix 41). These are the minimum legal holidays, and the workman may be entitled to additional holidays. *See id.* art. 3. The legal holidays are applicable to Muslims and non-Muslims alike.

[74] Labor Regs., art. 151.

[75] *See generally id.* art. 150; p. 276 *infra*.

2. Work day

The general rule is that the maximum number of working hours in the work week is forty-eight hours of actual work. Article 147 of the Regulations provides

> [a] workman shall not be employed for more than eight actual working hours in any one day, or forty-eight hours a week, in all months of the year, with the exception of the month of Ramadan when actual working hours shall not exceed six hours a day or thirty-six hours a week, exclusive of the intervals reserved for prayer, rest and meals. The number of working hours may be raised to nine hours a day in respect of certain categories of workmen or in certain industries and operations where the workman does not work continuously, such as seasonal establishments, hotels, snack bars, restaurants and the like. The number of daily working hours may be reduced for certain categories of workmen or in certain industries or operations of a hazardous or harmful nature. The categories of workmen, industries and operations referred to in this article shall be determined by decision of the Minister of Labor.

The forty-eight hours[76] as provided in article 147 do not include preparation and winding up time, for which one half-hour daily is allotted.[77] In view of the plain language of article 147, if an employment contract provides that the workman is obliged to work for fifty-five hours a week in exchange for a given total wage, the Labor Commissions will regard the parties' agreement with respect to the number of hours as null. In this case, the wage as provided in the contract will be held to be in consideration of forty-eight hours of work. It may not be reduced pro rata to correspond to the lawful maximum number of hours. Rather, the workman will be entitled to overtime pay for any hours over the limit during which he was employed.

However, the permissible apportionments of the regulatory forty-eight hours over the maximum six-day work week is an issue disputed among Saudi labor lawyers. Case law is lacking on this point.

Despite the plain language of the first sentence of article 147, some practitioners are of the opinion that workmen may be required to work more than eight hours a day, provided that the forty-eight hour weekly total is not exceeded. Support, albeit slim, for the preceding proposition

---

[76] All arguments discussed with respect to the 48-hour week are applicable, proportionately scaled-down, to the month of Ramadan, when working hours are reduced to 36 per week.

[77] Labor Regs., art. 152(a); Minister of Labor & Social Affairs Resolution No. 16, art. 2 (18/1/1397) (maximum of 15 minutes for preparation and 15 minutes for winding up). *Cf. id.* art. 1(a) (defining preparation and transportation to include, *inter alia,* bringing and returning tools and materials, cleaning up, greasing machinery) (translated in Appendix 42).

is found in article 147. First, the initial sentence of the article provides that workmen may not be employed for "more than eight actual working hours *or* forty-eight hours a week." The use of the disjunctive conjunction "or" would, thus, permit an uneven distribution of working hours over a work week of six days or an even distribution over a work week of five days. Second, the phrase "may be raised" in the second sentence lends support to the permissibility of increasing the hours of work to a number greater than eight. In the absence of guidance from the Ministry of Labor and Social Affairs as to those situations in which working hours may be raised, commentators on article 147 derive additional support for the lawfulness of increasing the number of hours from the article's use of the conjunction "or" in the second sentence. Thus, increased hours would be permissible not only with respect to certain industries, but also with respect to "certain categories of workmen." According to another view, the maximum number of actual work hours in a nonexceptional work day is nine. Proponents of this view find support in the language of article 147 that provides that "working hours may be raised to nine hours a day." They interpret this regulatory authorization to embody a maximum limit on the number of hours. Moreover, they disregard article 147's explicit statement that the number of nine hours is applicable to "certain categories of workmen" or to "certain industries."

Under the third view, the maximum lawful number of hours of actual work in any given work day is nine and one-half. Proponents of this view look beyond article 147 for support. They rely chiefly on the language of article 148 prohibiting workmen from remaining in the place of work for longer than eleven hours in any given day. This prohibition would be meaningless unless work hours may be increased to nine and one-half. If maximum total working hours could not exceed eight, the result, unrealistically, would be a two and one-half-hour break in an eleven hour day spent in the place of work.

Another view holds that the maximum number of work hours in the day is ten, if so provided in the employment contract or otherwise agreed on by the parties. Support for a ten-hour work day would be found in article 150(d), which provides that in the exceptional situations overriding the limitations of article 147, the maximum number of actual working hours may not exceed ten. Not only is this the sole provision in the Regulations which directly addresses the issue of maximum actual working hours in any one day but also its language in no way restricts this ceiling to the situations covered by article 150.

To read article 147 as setting an eight-hour ceiling on actual work hours would be to deprive workmen of the possibility of having a two-day weekly rest period. This view would leave the workman free to choose between an eight-hour work day, and a six-day work week, or a ten-hour work day, and a five-day work week. Since the workman's freedom of choice would be unaffected, the Regulation's goal of protecting workmen's rights is achieved.[78] The strict view, which most closely adheres to the provisions of article 147, holds that the maximum number of actual work hours in a normal work day is eight, and any hours worked in excess of that number entitle the workman to overtime rates.

3. Work hours

Article 148 provides

> working hours shall be scheduled [so] that no workman shall work more than five consecutive hours without an interval of rest, prayer, and meals which shall not be less than half an hour each time, *or* one and one-half hours during the total working hours, and that the workman shall not remain in the place of work more than eleven hours in any one day.[79]

Article 148 is strictly enforced with respect to the continuous work period. This may not exceed five hours, even with the consent of both parties, and even though the workman receives overtime or additional discretionary payments. In contrast, there are two views relating to the permissible length of work breaks. One view interprets article 148 to bar reduction of "intervals" to less than one half-hour, even though it would permit increasing intervals above such a period. The other view holds that the employer has the right to reduce individual break periods to less than one half-hour. If he chooses to exercise this right, the total nonworking period is automatically increased to a one-and-one-half hour minimum. If, however, the breaks are at least one half-hour in length, no total nonworking period is set by law, provided that the workman does not remain at the place of work for longer than eleven hours in any one day. Thus, the maximum break to which workmen are entitled is one half-hour, even if rest, prayer, and meals must all occur during this period. However, if the break, at any time in a day, lasts for less than half an hour, the minimum total rest period is increased by fifty per cent. The employment contract may not provide for duration of work breaks in any manner inconsistent with the regulatory language. The timing and length of work breaks must be included in the employer's work rules.[80] The legal rules governing the timing of breaks differ according to the purpose of the break. The timing of rest and meal

---

[78] In addition, this view is based on allocation of rest intervals in art. 148.
[79] *Id.* (emphasis added).
[80] *Id.* art. 9(b) (applicable to employers of 20 workmen or more).

breaks is flexible, but the break for prayers must begin at the time of call for prayer. This is because Islam attaches a smaller reward to late prayers than to prayers performed on time. If a period of less than one half-hour is allocated to the break for prayers, its duration should nonetheless be reasonable.[81] For example, fifteen minutes might be sufficient for the performance of afternoon prayers, but not for evening prayers, which take longer. Furthermore, the travelling time from the place of work to the mosque must also be taken into consideration. Practically speaking, it is recommended in all cases to allow workmen breaks of a minimum of one half-hour. Shortening the breaks under this limit may result in a material risk of workmen's claiming that they are denied sufficient time for prayers or meals.

4. Exceptions

Articles 150 and 152 provide exceptions to the general rules regulating work weeks, days, and hours. Article 150 sets forth the extraordinary circumstances under which the workman may be required to work for a maximum of seven days a week and ten hours a day. It provides

> [t]he employer shall not be required to adhere to the provisions of articles 147, 148 and 149 of [these Regulations] in the following cases
>
>   (a) Annual stock-taking, preparation of the balance-sheet, liquidation, closing of accounts, preparation for sales at reduced prices and preparation for festive seasons, provided that the number of days during which the workman remains on the job in excess of the prescribed daily working period shall not exceed thirty days in any one year.
>
>   (b) Where the work is intended to prevent a dangerous accident, or to repair damage resulting from such accident, to avoid the certain loss of perishable materials.
>
>   (c) Where the work is designed to cope with unusual work pressure. In the last two cases, a report shall be made to the appropriate Labor Office within 24 hours, stating the emergency and the period required for completion of the work, and the Office's written confirmation of approval shall be obtained.
>
>   (d) Holidays, festive seasons and other occasions, and seasonal operations as may be determined by decision of the Minister of Labor. In all the foregoing cases, the number of actual working hours shall not exceed ten hours a day.

[81] *See, e.g.*, Deputy Minister of Labor & Social Affairs Circular No. 1187/6/1 (24/9/1396) (quoting Deputy President of Council of Ministers Letter No. 4/21075 (3/9/1396) (instructing employers to allow Muslim workmen sufficient time for prayer in congregation) (quoted in Director-Gen'l. of Central Province Head Labor Office Circular (9/10/1396) (unnumbered) (translated in Appendix 43).

Article 152, in contrast, is addressed to certain types of activities whose nature makes the ordinary rules inapplicable, rather than to unusual work pressure. Hence, unlike article 150, article 152 does not exempt the employer from the general rule of article 149, which guarantees a six-day work week to workmen. Article 152 provides

> [t]he provisions of articles 147 and 148 shall not apply to the following cases
> (a) Preparatory and supplementary operations which must be performed before the beginning or after the end of the work.
> (b) Work which is necessarily intermittent.
> (c) Workmen assigned to watch and janitorial duties.
> (d) Work in drilling or exploration for petroleum and minerals in remote areas.
> These operations referred to in paragraphs (a), (b) and (c) of this article and the maximum number of working hours in such operations shall be determined by decision of the Minister of Labor. In the operations referred to in paragraph (d), the total number of actual working hours shall not exceed 48 hours a week.

The term "work which is necessarily intermittent" of subsection (b) is defined as

> work which by its nature is not continuous and which includes periods during which workmen are inactive or not continuously concerned with their work or do not remain in their places [of employment] save to obey possible requests; or work which requires that workmen come to their places of employment during noncontinuous periods to perform their work.[82]

Examples of workmen employed intermittently are technicians and mechanics who are employed for the purpose of repairing or operating machinery; workmen employed in the transportation, or delivery, or loading, or unloading of merchandise or fuel, workmen employed in transportation, railroads, ports, airports, bus stations; and others engaged in similar activities.[83]

The total daily number of hours of actual work which may be performed in cases subject to article 152(b) is ten.[84] Furthermore, the workman, in all cases, is entitled, first, to a continuous period of rest

---

[82] Resolution No. 16, art. 1(b) (implementing art. 152).
[83] Id.
[84] Id. art. 3. In the month of Ramadan, the total number is reduced to eight.

which may not be reduced below ten hours in every twenty-four hour period, and second, to be permitted to perform his prayers at their proper times.[85]

Watchmen, under article 150(c), are defined as "workmen entrusted with guarding the employer's premises, or things, or materials, or tools, or property, whether at night or by day, without being assigned any other task during the hours of work that is not required by the nature of a watchman's work."[86] Cleaning men are workmen entrusted with ensuring the cleanliness of the place of work whether or not during working hours, provided that they do not actually work for a continuous period longer than six hours.[87] Watchmen and cleaning men may perform actual work for twelve hours in a day, provided that they are permitted to pray at the proper times.[88]

G. OVERTIME

1. Right to overtime

The rule of law that a workman may not be "employed" for more than forty-eight actual hours of work a week is settled. However, the Regulations do permit work to be performed in excess of that number, or on rest days and holidays, in exchange for compensation at a higher overtime rate. Article 151 provides

> [t]he employer shall pay the workman for additional work hours an additional wage equivalent to the workman's normal wage plus fifty percent (50%). Where the work is performed on the weekly day of rest or on feast days or official holidays, the employer shall pay the workman an additional wage for the regular or additional work hours.

The parties to the employment contract are powerless to alter the mandate of article 151 by agreement. The workman may not be required to work in excess of forty-eight hours a week unless he receives overtime payments at the rate provided in article 151.

---

[85] *Id.* The issue of work breaks is not otherwise addressed.

[86] *Id.* art. 1(c)(1)(1). Watchmen also include workmen guarding over and operating drinking water stations. *See id.* art. 1(c)(1)(2).

[87] *Id.* art. 1(c)(2).

[88] *Id.* art. 4. The maximum number of hours is reduced to nine during the month of Ramadan.

However, the workman's entitlement to an "additional wage" in exchange for "additional work hours" must be distinguished from any right or obligation, contractual or otherwise, to perform additional work. Contractual provisions containing the workman's firm commitment to work overtime are null and unenforceable, since in violation of the regulatory limit on weekly work hours. Conversely, just as Saudi labor law denies to the employer the right to require the workman to work overtime, it recognizes no right in the workman to perform additional work. Thus, in contrast to other rights, which may become acquired by virtue of regular recurrence, the right to work overtime may never become so acquired, despite any subjective belief in its acquisition on the workman's part.

One 1979 case illustrating the workman's right to refuse to work overtime involved an employment contract entered into for a specified period of two years. It contained a provision that the workman would work overtime from time to time whenever so required, according to a schedule set by the management of the employer company. The employer terminated the workman and argued that by refusing to perform overtime work, the workman had breached the employment contract. Thus, his discharge was lawful under article 83 of the Regulations.[89] Rejecting this argument, the Primary Commission stated that overtime work may not be continuously imposed except in cases involving danger or emergency situations or other exceptions provided in the Regulations. The Primary Commission thus clearly indicated that Saudi law will not tolerate that additional work be imposed on workmen continuously and regularly.

Nor may the parties succeed in circumventing article 151 by so structuring their agreement that the wage set for forty-eight hours' work is made contingent upon the condition that the workman perform work for five additional hours every week, although at overtime rates. In case the workman refuses, the employer may not reduce his wage, or deny or reduce any other benefits payable to the workman. In contrast, contractual agreements providing that no additional or overtime work will be performed are lawful and enforced by the Labor Commissions. Employers would therefore be well-advised to include in the employment contracts of workmen, such as managers, whom they do not desire to pay for overtime work, a clause to the effect that the workman will not be required to, and will not perform any overtime work, and will therefore not be entitled to any overtime payments. In this case, the

---

[89] Art. 83(2) provides that a workman may be discharged without notice or severance pay if he "fails to fulfil the essential obligations arising from the employment contract, or to obey legitimate orders."

contract should require the workman to use his best efforts or to execute his work with utmost diligence at whatever time is required to this end. Even the employment contracts of senior management personnel remunerated on a fixed salary-plus-bonuses or profit-sharing basis should provide that no overtime work will be required or compensated, in order to avoid any overtime claims. The contract may lawfully, and should, provide that such senior management personnel are not bound by the usual working or business hours. The preceding discussion is also applicable to employment contracts of salesmen, working on a fixed salary-plus-commission or on a straight commission basis.

2. Computation of overtime

Despite the plain language of article 151, overtime payments are computed on the basis of the workman's base salary and not his total wage. The Regulations do not define or elucidate the term "base salary." However, the base salary may roughly be described, under general principles of contract and labor law, as that amount which the parties have agreed will be the base salary, and which is paid regularly and continuously, and is not contingent upon the fulfillment or occurrence of certain conditions. Thus, those parts of the wage which may not be calculated with certainty, or any benefits, such as contract completion bonuses, the right to which vests in the future or is contingent, are excluded from the base salary for purposes of computing overtime payments. Regularity, rather than fixity, is determinative in most cases. Thus, a commission paid to a salesman regularly on the basis of sales made by him is a part of the base salary unless otherwise agreed. In contrast, any payment or bonus computed on the basis of the total sales of the employer commercial entity, even if paid with regularity, will be considered a part of the total wage but not the base salary.

The parties are free to agree upon the base salary in the employment contract. However, it will be fruitless for the employer to divide the total consideration payable into several categories in the attempt to reduce the base salary and consequently to reduce the basis for calculating the amount of overtime payments. Such paper attempts to frustrate the protective purpose of article 151 may be disregarded by the Labor Commissions. An amount entitled "extended work week bonus" by the parties, for example, was in 1977 held a part of the base salary for the purposes of computing overtime payments. However, the parties' freedom to agree upon the base salary is qualified in the case of employers employing twenty or more workmen. The work rules of such employers must be approved by the Ministry of Labor and Social

Affairs.[90] The Ministry has authority to determine those components of the wage which constitute the base salary for purposes of overtime computation, with respect to all workmen of such employers. In the vast majority of cases, the Ministry tends to be protective of workmen's rights.

Since overtime hours are hours in excess of normal hours of actual work, the workman may not assert any right to pay at overtime rates if the hours actually worked do not exceed the daily regulatory limit, unless the agreement provides for less hours, or if the hours worked in the week do not exceed forty-eight, unless the parties agreed on a weekly total of less than that number. During the hours considerec as hours worked, the workman need not have physically performed work in order to be entitled to overtime payments for additional hours as is the case, *inter alia*, with respect to sick leave. Rather, normal hours are the hours for which the workman has a legal right to receive his salary. Additional hours worked may not be carried forward or back to other days or weeks during which the hours worked were fewer than the regulatory or contractual limits, if the latter is lower. Thus, in the case previously discussed,[91] the employer also sought to defend against payment of overtime on the grounds that the workman had never performed more than ninety-six hours of actual work in any two-week period. This total, it argued, if divided in half would not violate the forty-eight hour weekly maximum provided by article 147. Under this theory, the workman did not perform any overtime work. The Primary Commission, however, rejected this line of reasoning.

In the computation of the hourly rate, assuming the maximum forty-eight hour work week, the week is deemed to include fifty-six hours, *i.e.* forty-eight hours of actual work and eight (paid) hours of weekly rest. Under article 151, overtime is calculated as follows: assume the workman's weekly salary including the weekly rest day is 700 and he works eight hours on his weekly day of rest: total salary plus overtime for the week = 850.

H. CONTINUOUS SERVICE

The concept of continuous service is important under Saudi labor law because rights based on the duration of service may be affected by interruptions in the continuity of service. However, only certain

---

[90] *Id.* art. 9.
[91] *See* p. 279 *supra*.

interruptions in the workman's service period are capable of cutting off certain regulatory rights such as annual vacation and severance pay, or certain contractual rights, or any rights he may have acquired in the course of the employment relationship.

Article 7(5) of the Regulations defines "continuous service" as

> [t]he uninterrupted service with the same employer or his legal successor from the date of commencement of service. Service shall be regarded as continuous in the following cases
> (a) Regular vacations or leaves authorized by the employer.
> (b) Where, for legitimate excuse, the workman absents himself from work for intermittent periods totalling not more than thirty days a year.[92]
> (c) Where the workman stops working for a reason imputable to or emanating from the employer, with which the workman had nothing to do.

Continuous service, therefore, describes the period from the legal commencement of service[93] to the termination of employment, whether employment is terminated by the parties or by force of law.

1. Same employer

Notably, continuity of service is primarily based on the employment relationship. Thus, any alteration in the terms of employment, the place of work, or the nature of the services rendered will not be deemed to interrupt the continuity. The fact that one or more agreements are entered into by the parties will not affect the continuity. Even if contracts of specified periods are entered into separately rather than renewed, the continuity of the workman's service will not be deemed interrupted. This concept applies not only to severance pay but also to other rights of the workman.

2. Legal successor

The word translated as "legal" in article 7(5) is "qānūnī," by statute. On its face, the term would thus not extend to any successors in interest under Islamic law, such as heirs or legatees, despite the rule that the

---

[92] These 30 days are, for the purpose of "continuous service" determinations, deemed in addition to the days of absence provided in arts. 82, 155–156, 159.

[93] *See generally* pp. 248–53 *supra*.

employment contract is not terminated by the death of the employer.[94] However, the workman's continuity of service is also safeguarded by article 89 of the Regulations, which provides

[a]ll obligations shall be discharged, notwithstanding the dissolution, liquidation, shutdown, bankruptcy, merger or subdivision of the establishment or its conveyance by inheritance, legacy, donation, sale, assignment or any other disposition. With the exception of liquidation, bankruptcy and authorized final shutdown, the labor contract shall be considered in force in all the above cases.

If the workman's service is continuous under the original employment contract, it will not be interrupted by a change in his actual employer or, in the case of an expatriate workman, by a change in his sponsorship to a legal successor of the original employer.[95] In this case, the continuity of service, with respect to any amounts payable by the new employer, will relate back to the commencement of service under the employment agreement executed by its predecessor in interest. Article 90 provides that "[t]he original and the new employer shall be held jointly and severally responsible for the discharge of the obligations arising from the contract which fell due prior to the transfer of ownership. As for obligations arising after such transfer, these shall be assumed by the new employer alone."

Continuity of service may survive several changes in employer. The same rule is applicable to subcontracts, since the original employment relationship remains unsevered. In this case, the original employer may not be relieved from liability for any benefits granted to the workman by the subcontractor during the period of the subcontract. Thus, article 8 provides

[i]f the employer entrusts to a natural or juristic person one of his original operations or any part thereof, the latter shall give his

[94] Art. 82 of the Regulations provides
[t]he employment contract shall not come to an end upon the employer's death unless his person was taken into consideration in concluding the contract. It shall, however, come to an end upon the death of the workman, his total disability to perform his work as established by a medical certificate, or his illness resulting in his absence from work for a period of not less than ninety consecutive days or for periods which in the aggregate do not exceed one hundred and twenty days within one year.

[95] For sponsorship, see generally pp. 6–8 *supra*. *See also* Director-Gen'l. of Central Province Head Labor Office Notification (2/6/1402) (unnumbered) (relating to borrowing of workmen) (translated in Appendix 44); Director-Gen'l. of Central Province Head Labor Office Circular No. 1176/2/16/2 (10/4/1400) (relating to loss of passports) (translated in Appendix 45); note 98 *infra*.

workman all the rights and privileges granted by the employer to his own workmen, and both shall be jointly and severally responsible for such rights and privileges.[96]

However, article 8 will not apply to services performed by the workman with respect to activities that are not among the original activities of the initial employer. The term "original operations" appearing in article 8 is defined, with respect to natural persons, as "the subject matter of their usual activities." With respect to companies, it means "those operations which the company was established to undertake and which were provided for in its articles of association."[97]

However, a clear severance of the employment relationship will interrupt the continuity of service. In one case, the plaintiff workman sued his present employer, Y Co., for certain amounts which he claimed should be computed on the basis of "continuous service". The plaintiff alleged that this employment contract had been automatically transferred to Y, when Y took over the execution of the project on which the plaintiff was employed from X Co., the plaintiff's original employer and sponsor. He added that the sponsorship of the X workmen had been transferred to Y en bloc but could neither form an opinion nor produce any evidence on the legal means by which the transfer of sponsorship had occurred. The plaintiff explained that he had continued to work on the project as usual, since he believed Y to be the new contractor for the same project, and also signed a contract with Y confirming the automatic transfer of his employment to it. The plaintiff submitted some documentary evidence probative of Y's legal status of successor in interest of X in order to invoke the applicability of articles 7(5), 8, and 90. Y rebutted this evidence by proving that it did not step into the shoes of X and that the project it was executing was substantially different from that of X. Y also proved that the plaintiff had received both proper termination notice and severance pay from X. Under the defendant's version of the facts, the plaintiff had applied to Y for employment and accepted the proposal offered by Y. If the plaintiff's employment had in fact been transferred, Y argued, there was no need for the plaintiff to apply for a new job and for Y to make him a new offer. The Primary Commission found that because the plaintiff had not met his burden of proof on the issue of Y's legal succession to X, his service was not continuous. Rather, his service with Y did not include any periods during which he was employed by X. On appeal, the lower decision was affirmed on this issue.

---

[96] *Cf.* Labor Regs., art. 138 (subcontracts of concession companies must contain express provisions to this effect).

[97] Council of Ministers Resolution No. 19 (26/2/1400) (available at the Institute of Public Administration library).

II. Termination[98]

A. CONTRACT OF SPECIFIED OR UNSPECIFIED PERIOD

Saudi law countenances both employment contracts for a specified period and for an unspecified period.[99] The classification of a given employment contract is not of any particular significance until either of the parties desires to terminate the relationship. Not only will the right to terminate vary according to the type of contract,[100] but also the amount of severance pay to which the workman is entitled may vary according to whether the contract is for a specified or an unspecified period.[101]

1. Distinction between contracts of specified and unspecified period

The Regulations employ the terms "contract of a specified period" and "contract of an unspecified period" to describe the two possible temporal

---

[98] It should be noted that termination of service is a concept distinct from transfer of sponsorship. This distinction is of significance in the case of a nonSaudi workman originally "imported" under his employer's sponsorship, as exhibited on his residence and work permits, and who, with his employer's consent (see generally Rules for Organization of the Labor Force Movement, Council of Ministers Resolution No. 826, arts. 3, 5 (1975) (translated in Appendix 46)), is to commence employment with another employer. In this case, the workman's sponsorship will be transferred to his new employer. However, while there can be no period during which the workman is not sponsored (see Residence Regs., Royal Assent No. 17/2/25/1337, art. 11 (1371)) there may be a transitional period between termination of his original service and commencement of his new service. With respect to this period, the original employer is not liable for any payments to the workman or provision of any of the benefits, such as housing, transportation, or other facilities, which it was providing for him prior to the end of his service, even if the workman is still under the sponsorship of the original employer. Conversely, until the workman commences his service with his new employer, the latter will not be liable for such payments or benefits. See generally pp. 281–84 supra. It may also be noted that the workman has no legal right to obtain his original employer's consent to the transfer of sponsorship. The latter has discretion to repatriate the workman to the country of origin, regardless of whether the employment contract was entered into in Saudi Arabia or another country. See Rules for the Organization of the Labor Force Movement, art. 5 (construed to permit employer to withhold consent). The Labor Commissions normally reject workmen's requests to compel their employers to consent to transfer of sponsorship, on the grounds that such claims arise under the Residence Regs. rather than the Labor Regs. Where the employer is willing to give its consent to transfer of sponsorship, such consent generally takes the form of the original employer's acceptance of the new employer's letter addressed to it stating that it is willing to take over the workman's sponsorship. Although, in theory, sponsorship and employment should be coextensive, in practice the labor authorities allow a reasonable period, during which the workman may have begun employment with his new employer while under his original sponsorship, for the transfer to take place. If the original employer wishes to repatriate the workman, it may nonetheless provide him with a "certificate of no objection". Otherwise, he may not ordinarily be "reimported" until one year from his date of exit. See Rules for the Organization of the Labor Force Movement, art. 5.

[99] See e.g., Labor Regs., art. 70.

[100] See id. art. 73.

[101] See id. art. 88.

employment relationships under Saudi law. Article 72 provides that "[a]n employment contract concluded for a specified period shall end upon the expiry of its term. If both parties continue to enforce the contract thereafter, it shall be considered renewed for an unspecified period."

No minimum duration is set for the contract of a specified period. However, because this type of contract is intended to expire automatically at the end of its term, no contract will be regarded as a contract of a specified period unless the date of expiry is known, or can be established with reasonable certainty, in advance.[102] This rule is designed to protect the parties against unfair surprise. However, the fact that the "period" specified in the contract is not measured in terms of any calendar, or in terms of a specific length of time, will not prevent the contract from being considered a contract of specified period, if the element of certainty is met. Thus, if the parties agree to limit their relationship to a given season of the year, they have entered into a contract of a specified period if the boundaries of the season are reasonably clear and known to the parties. Likewise, contracts concluded for the duration of a given project are contracts of a specified period, provided that the duration of the project is specified.[103] Moreover, while the general rule is that contracts measured by the piece are not contracts of a specified period, it has been maintained that they will be deemed of a specified period if the parties have agreed upon the number of pieces to be executed.[104]

In contrast, the contract of an unspecified period may be defined as a contract whose end point cannot be predicted. The method of payment or of computation of the wage is not determinative on the issue of whether or not the contract is for a specified period. In general, the parties' intent as expressed in their language will control, and contracts of an unspecified period are simply those contracts whose duration is not specified by the parties. However, if the parties enter into an agreement clearly specifying the duration of their relationship, but reserve the right to terminate it before that point without conditioning such right on furnishing a valid reason for termination, the contract may in certain cases be deemed of an unspecified period.[105] This rule may apply whether or not the right to terminate is contingent on giving notice.[106]

---

[102] See also N. AL-KAYALI, supra note 10, at 241 (agreement on termination point may be explicit or implicit).

[103] See Labor Regs., art. 70 (contract may be for "specified job").

[104] See M. ABU AL-'AINAIN, supra note 14, at 441.

[105] Provisions in employment contracts stating that the parties may terminate on the grounds provided in arts. 83–84 of the Regulations will not subject a contract for a specified period to the possibility of being deemed for an unspecified period. These articles are applicable by force of law to all employment contracts, whether or not explicitly provided therein, and despite any contractual language by which the parties may agree that arts. 83–84 will be inapplicable to their relationship.

[106] See, e.g., N. AL-KAYĀLĪ, supra note 10, at 230–231 & n.2 (citations omitted) (under prior regulations). Alternatively, the notice term may drop out.

The situation may be open to different interpretations where the parties specify the duration of their relationship but reserve the right to extend it beyond that point. Another related issue is whether the parties may in any way limit a contract of an unspecified period without thereby causing it to become a contract for a specified period. Assume, for example, a clause providing that the contract is for an unspecified period not to exceed two Gregorian calendar years. If the parties prolong the employment relationship beyond the two-year limit, the contract will be deemed to be of an unspecified period. However, if terminated no later than upon the expiry of two years, it might be found to be a contract of a specified period due to the maximum limit. In the opposite hypothetical situation, the contract provides that the employment agreement is for an unspecified period of a minimum of one year. In this case, the contract should be considered of a specified period of one year, and services performed thereafter be deemed performed under a contract for an unspecified period.

B. MODE OF TERMINATION

The employment relationship may end in one of three ways: pursuant to the agreement of the parties; by the unilateral act or omission of one of the parties; or by force majeure. Different consequences may result according to the nature of the contract and the mode of its termination.

1. Contract of a specified period

The contract of a specified period ordinarily ends automatically upon the expiration of such period, whether measured in terms of a length of time or by the duration of a specified objective. However, the parties may by mutual consent end their relationship at a point earlier than that contemplated by the employment agreement, provided that no regulatory right guaranteed to the workman is thereby lost or diminished in value.[107]

2. Valid reasons and notice

Contracts of an unspecified period may not be terminated except for a valid reason. The giving of due notice is also required. Article 73 provides that "if the contract is for an unspecified period, either party may cancel it for a valid reason, subject to giving the other party a thirty-day prior written notice in respect of workmen employed at a monthly rate, and a fifteen-day prior notice in respect of other workmen." However, contracts of a specified period may also be terminated for a valid reason. In this case, also, the parties are subject to the notice requirement of article 73,

---

[107] *See generally* p. 255 *supra.*

with the exception of termination pursuant to articles 83 and 84 of the Regulations.[108]

Any agreement purporting to give the employee the right to terminate the employment contract without notice or cause is void. However, if a provision to this effect is included in the employment contract, it will drop out but will not vitiate the force of the remaining valid provisions.

Notice period

The notice periods provided in article 73 are the minimum required by regulation. The parties are free to agree on a notice period exceeding the regulatory periods. The notice period does not begin to run until the party to be notified has actual knowledge of the notice.[109] Proof that such party has in fact received notification will in most cases be sufficient to prove actual knowledge. Notice must be given in writing.[110] However, this requirement may to a certain extent be regarded as serving evidentiary functions. Thus, it is said that notice is effective if proved by other means.[111] This would especially apply in a case where, for example, the workman was illiterate.

Notice must be given by a party in interest or its legal representative. To be effective, it must show a clear intention on the part of the serving party to terminate the employment relationship.[112] If the purported notice merely expresses an intention to dispense with the services of some workmen at a future time, it will not serve the legal function of giving notice.

Since the employment contract does not end until the expiry of the notice period, all rights of both parties survive until that point. The period consequently is included in the period of continuous service, for purposes of computing severance pay. Likewise, wage payments made to the workman during that period are included in the total wage. However, the employer does have the right to direct the workman not to perform any work during that period. Any such directions will not affect the workman's entitlement to his wage or other benefits. If, in contrast, the workman of his own volition ceases to work during the notice period, he thereby forfeits the right to receive wage payments with respect to that period.

[108] But see N. AL-KAYĀLĪ, supra note 10, at 237–38 nn.1–2; M. ABU AL-'AINAIN, supra note 14, at 444–45 & nn.1–2 (citations omitted) (suggesting that will of parties may prevail).

[109] Cf. Rules of Procedure & Conciliation & Arbitration Proceedings before the Primary Commissions & the Supreme Commission, Council of Ministers Resolution No. 1, art. 8 (1390) (applicable to notice periods provided in Regulations)

[110] Labor Regs., art. 73 (language "in writing" found in Arabic official text) (missing from Government Security Press translation (5th ed. 1983)).

[111] See, e.g., M. ABU AL-'AINAIN, supra note 14, at 447 (suggesting that notice may be proved by oath or admission). Whether notice may be proved by oral testimony or circumstantial evidence is a question not addressed here.

[112] See, e.g., id. at 446.

Damages for failure to give due notice

Article 73 provides

> [i]f the party who has cancelled the contract fails to observe the prescribed notice period, he shall pay the other party compensation equivalent to the workman's wage for the notice period or the remainder thereof. The workman's last wages shall be taken as a basis for determining the compensation in respect of workmen who receive their pay by the month, the week, the day or the hour.
> In the case of workmen whose wages are fixed on a piecework basis, compensation shall be determined on the basis of the average pay received by the workman for actual workdays during the last three months.

It is thus clear that, in cases where the employment contract is silent on the issue of notice or incorporates the regulatory notice period, either party may recover damages, for the entire notice period, where no notice is given, or any portion thereof, where the length of notice given is deficient. However, where the parties' agreement has extended the notice period beyond the regulatory minimum, the result, in the event of failure to give proper notice, is unclear. If the parties have expressly provided for damages to be measured on the basis of that extended period, such a clause is enforceable. If, in contrast, they have not covered this issue, the defaulting party may have a defense available based on the language of article 73, which only requires compensation with respect to the notice period "provided" in such article.

Valid reason

The reasons deemed legally sufficient to justify termination are not defined. The Regulations specify the extreme grounds which entitle the parties to terminate their relationship for cause under articles 83 and 84. However, they do not furnish any explicit guidance with respect to ordinary valid reasons for termination. However, valid reasons may generally be divided into the following categories

- (i) Valid reasons based on the Labor Regulations and other applicable law;
- (ii) Valid reasons based on contractual obligations;
- (iii) Valid reasons based on social, religious and customary rules;
- (iv) Valid reasons based on public policy;
- (v) Valid reasons based on impossibility or frustration of purpose;
- (vi) Valid reasons based on the employer's bylaws and work rules officially approved in accordance with articles 9 and 125 of the Regulations;

(vii) Valid reasons based on business considerations;[113]
(viii) Valid reasons based on equity and fairness.

In all cases, it should be noted that a terminating employer must demonstrate a bona fide reason under any of the above categories. The employer's act of termination may not be arbitrary, nor imputable to a discriminatory, retaliatory, or a general bad faith purpose. Discriminatory terminations may include those based on ideological or geographical considerations. Retaliatory terminations might arise, *inter alia*, out of the workman's reporting of regulatory violations committed by his employer to labor inspectors. Under normal circumstances, the burden of proof is placed upon the proponent of the statement. However, article 75 provides

> shall be regarded as having no valid reason if it is established that it followed the workman's demand for legitimate rights due to him by the employer and no other valid reason for termination is established. In such case, the employer shall be ordered to reinstate the workman, pay his wages from the date of his discharge to the date of his reinstatement, and to consider his services as continuous.
>
> The workman's discharge shall also be regarded as having no valid reason if such discharge was caused by the workman's refusal to comply with an order transferring him from his original place of work when such transfer is not based on an adequate, valid reason dictated by work requirements, or is such as to cause serious prejudice to the workman.

Thus, in the two instances explicitly regarded as arbitrary under article 75, namely termination where the workman has sought to implement his legal rights, and where he has refused to move to a different place of work, if such move was not itself supported by a valid reason, the burden of proof is shifted to the employer. Article 75 creates a presumption of invalidity with respect to these two termination situations which is, however, rebuttable if the employer disproves the truth of the underlying allegation,

---

[113] With respect to the employer, business considerations have been described as considerations relating to efficient management or to maximization of the utility of the elements of production and execution. Thus, technical advances requiring employment of skilled workmen or dispensing with the need for manpower may support termination. The unproductivity or inefficiency of the workman, if established by objective comparison with the level of performance of other workmen in his class may also be a valid reason. Repeated instances of negligence and unexcused absence also are valid reasons. Such terminations involving the workman's unsatifactory performance should be preceded by at least one warning but preferably several warnings or disciplinary measures, as provided in the employer's work rules. Finally, economic necessity, such as a general decline in the employer's business situation and its need to reduce expenses, may justify termination. Such termination for economic reasons is also supported by judicial decision (dictum). However, the sufficiency of the "valid reason" will depend on whether the contract is for a specified or unspecified period.

by establishing, for example, a valid reason for the transfer. Alternatively the employer may prove another independent valid reason supporting the termination. To the extent, then, that the rationale of article 75 extends to other bad faith terminations not expressly covered by the Regulations, the general rule governing validity is that, where the act of termination is supported by a legally sufficient reason apparently untainted by any improper purpose, the element of absence of bad faith need not be proved. In addition, it may be noted that the Regulations prohibit termination of a workman during a period of sick leave and workwoman during sick and pregnancy leave.[114] This prohibition also applies to contracts for a specified period.

Force majeure

This doctrine applies to employment contracts of either specified or unspecified periods. Thus, a contract ends upon the death or prolonged illness of the workman,[115] or the forced liquidation or bankruptcy, but not the death, unless the parties have agreed otherwise, of the employer.[116] It also ends when the workman is called to perform military service.[117] The doctrine of force majeure, it should be noted, is expressly made applicable to workmen with respect to their entitlements to severance pay.[118]

C. SEVERANCE PAY

1. Right to severance pay

Saudi law regards severance pay as a right of the workman and not as a punitive measure imposed on the employer. Thus, the employer may be liable for payment of severance pay even where it did not terminate the employment relationship. The general rule is that, where the employment relationship is ended without fault on the part of the workman, he is entitled to severance pay. For example, where a contract of a specified period is terminated before the end of its agreed term by a workman called to military service, he is nonetheless entitled to severance pay as provided in the Regulations. Indeed, the right to severance pay is so firmly established that it has been suggested that the workman can only be deprived thereof by means of judicial decision.[119]

---

[114] *See* Labor Regs., arts. 82, 167–168.
[115] *Id.* art. 82.
[116] *Id.* art. 89.
[117] *See id.* art. 87(a).
[118] *See id.* art. 87(c).
[119] *See* N. AL-KAYALI, *supra* note 10, at 372.

However, there are three major exceptions to the rule. First, a workman on probation is not entitled to severance pay if the employer decides not to employ him on a permanent basis at any point before the end of the probation period.[120] Second, where the employment contract is for an unspecified period and the workman terminates the relationship before he has completed two consecutive years of service, and third, if the workman is terminated for cause under article 83, he is not entitled to severance pay.[121]

2. Time of payment of severance pay

The right to severance pay does not vest until the end of the employment relationship, since the workman may either forfeit his right by improper behavior or resigning before completing the minimum two years of service required in the case of a contract of an unspecified period terminated by the workman. Therefore, severance pay is not payable before the end of the employment relationship.[122] Thus, where the parties have entered into a series of labor contracts of specified periods and the employer makes pro rata prepayments of severance pay at the end of each individual contract, the employer may be exposed to the risk of being held liable for the full amount when the relationship is permanently severed. One 1983 case involved an appeal by the employer from a Primary Commission decision awarding certain employees the regulatory severance pay despite the fact that they had received annual prepayments of severance pay pursuant to their employment contracts. The contracts provided that such "end of service" award was payable annually as an "incentive." Appellees maintained that such payments were incentive awards and not severance pay. The Supreme Commission reversed the decision. Finding that the appellees had not sustained their burden of showing that such payments were in fact incentive awards and were not severance pay, it held that, since the amounts prepaid pursuant to the contracts exceeded the regulatory amount of severance pay, the employees were not entitled to receive further severance pay payments. However, had the payments made pursuant to the contract been to the regulatory amount, the employer would remain liable for the difference upon actual termination of employment.

Nonetheless, in order to avoid ambiguity, employers may prefer not to make prepayments, annual or otherwise, with respect to severance pay. First, although severance pay is not normally an item included in the wage,

---

[120] *See* Labor Regs., art. 83(6).

[121] *See generally* pp. 294–95 *infra*.

[122] Furthermore, any amounts set aside in a future severance pay expense account are not expenses deductible by the employer under Saudi tax law until the year of actual termination of employment, provided that such amounts are actually paid to the workman. Director-Gen'l. of DZIT Circular No. 6902/2 (4/8/1398).

any prior severance pay payments may be held to be part of the wage for purposes of computing the ultimate severance pay receivable. Thus, the employer may risk not only being held twice liable but also being held liable at a higher rate with respect to the final payment. Second, such prepaid severance pay may not be recovered, even in those cases where the workman would otherwise not be entitled to severance pay.

3. Computation of severance pay

Regulatory measure

In the absence of any higher rate made applicable by the parties, the regulatory measure applies. The method of computation of severance pay differs according to whether the contract is of a specified or an unspecified period. Article 87 of the Regulations provides

> [w]here the term of an employment contract concluded for a specified period comes to an end or where the employer cancels a contract of unspecified period, the employer shall pay to the workman severance pay for the period of his service to be computed on the basis of half a month's wage for each of the first five years and one month's wage for each of the subsequent years. The last rate of the wage shall be taken as basis for the computation of severance pay. For fractions of a year, the workman shall be entitled to severance pay which is proportionate to his service period during that year. Furthermore, the workman shall be entitled to the severance pay provided for at the beginning of this article in the following cases
> (a) If he is called to military service.
> (b) If a workwoman resigns because of marriage or childbirth.
> (c) If the workman is leaving the work as a result of a force majeure beyond his control.

Additionally, article 82 entitles workmen whose employment is ended because of serious illness to full severance pay. Article 88, in contrast, provides

> [i]n contracts of unspecified term, if the workman resigns he shall be entitled to one-third of the severance pay provided for in the preceding article if his service period is not less than two consecutive years and not more than five years; he shall be entitled to two-thirds of the severance pay if his service period is more than five consecutive years and less than ten years; and to full severance pay if he resigns after ten years of service; provided that in all the said cases, he gives notice to the employer in writing of his intention to resign thirty days before he leaves work.

The regulatory language is straightforward, strictly enforced, and requires little comment. With respect to contracts of an unspecified period, the difference in the amount of severance pay based on the identity of the terminating party should not be viewed as a penalty to which the employer is subject on termination. Rather, the higher figure payable when the employer terminates is a paternalistic measure intended to protect the workman against the consequences of unexpected unemployment or hardship.[123]

Severance pay is computed for the entire period of service on the basis of the most recent monthly total wage.[124] This is interpreted to mean the wage that the workman actually received in the last month of service.[125] However, if the workman's monthly wage is subject to any variation, the amount of wages received over a prior reasonable period should be aggregated and averaged to reflect the true wage.

Service period

The period to which the monthly rate is applied in order to compute severance pay is the period of service. It may be defined as including all periods during which the workman was legally entitled to receive his wages. Thus, it includes all paid leaves, any probation period, and any applicable notice period. It also includes any period during which the workman did not work, as a result of his wrongful discharge, and prior to a reinstatement order.[126] In contrast, treatment of those periods during which the workman was officially detained or arrested prior to any conviction may vary according to the facts of each case. It is nonetheless clear that, if the workman is ultimately convicted, any detention periods are excluded from his service.[127]

D. TERMINATION BY EMPLOYER FOR CAUSE

Whether the employment contract is for a specified or an unspecified period, in certain limited cases the employer has the right to discharge the workman without notice and without liability for payment of severance

---

[123] See, e.g., N. AL-KAYĀLĪ, supra note 10, at 358–59, 362 & n.1 (citations omitted) (termination award deemed a sum tiding the workman over until new employment found, as defense against the dangers of need and hunger) (drafter's intent was to insure workman an amount sufficient to satisfy his needs while new work found) (under prior law)

[124] See generally pp. 259–66 supra and see Appendix 47.

[125] That month would be defined as the last 30 days unless the parties have agreed to apply another calendar to their relationship. See Labor Regs., arts. 17, 20.

[126] See id. art. 75.

[127] Cf. N. AL-KAYĀLĪ, supra note 10, at 367–68 (relating to situations where detention periods are included in workman's service).

pay. Article 83 of the Regulations lists those instances where the workman by law is deemed to have breached the employment contract. It provides

[t]he employer may not cancel the contract without severance pay, advance notice, or compensation except in the following cases, and provided that he gives the workman a chance to state his reasons for objecting to the cancellation

(1) If, during or by reason of the work, the workman has committed an assault against the employer or against any of his supervisors.

(2) If the workman fails to fulfill the essential obligations arising from the employment contract, or to obey legitimate orders,[128] or if, in spite of being warned in writing, he deliberately fails to observe the instructions posted by the employer in a conspicuous place for the safety of the work and workmen.

(3) If the workman is proved to have adopted a bad conduct or to have committed an act affecting honesty or honor.

(4) If the workman has deliberately committed any act or omission with intent to cause material loss to the employer, provided that the latter shall report the incident to the appropriate authorities within twenty-four hours from the time of its coming to his knowledge.

(5) If it is proved that the workman had resorted to forgery in order to obtain the job.

. . .

(7) If the workman absents himself without valid reason for more than twenty days in one year or for more than ten consecutive days, provided that discharge shall be preceded by a warning in writing by the employer to the workman after ten days' absence in the first case and five days' absence in the second.

(8) If it is proved that, without permission from the person supervising his treatment, the workman has left the hospital or any place provided for his treatment. This shall not prejudice his right to such compensation as he is entitled to under the provisions on injuries and compensation set forth in the Social Insurance Regulations.

(9) If it is proved that the workman has divulged the industrial and commercial secrets of the work in which he is engaged.

The preceding list of grounds justifying immediate termination is inclusive. Any termination not fitting into one of the categories will require the giving of notice and the payment of severance pay. Moreover, the employer bears the burden of proof with respect to showing that his termination of the employment contract was in fact covered by article 83. However,

---

[128] Legitimate orders may relate to general comportment of the workman. *See, e.g.,* Director-Gen'l of Central Province Head Labor Office Circulars No. 2/16/230 (18/1/1401) (prohibiting instamatic photography in public places) (translated in Appendix 48), No. 8882 (7/1/1398) (prohibiting wearing shorts in public places) (translated in Appendix 49).

unless exempted by the competent Labor Office, the employer remains liable for the cost of repatriation of the terminated workman. Article 85 provides

> [t]he employer shall bear the costs of returning the workman to the place where the contract was concluded or to the place from which the workman was brought, within the period to be specified by the appropriate Labor Office, after the date of the end of the work or the date of termination of the contract for one of the reasons set forth in articles 82, 83 and 84, provided that the workman shall not have engaged in another work at the place of the last job, or shall not have prematurely ceased to work for no valid reason, or shall have expressed in writing before the appropriate Labor Office his desire not to return to the place where the contract was concluded or to the place from which he had been brought. If the employer fails to fulfill this obligation, the appropriate administrative agencies shall, at the request of the director of the Labor Office, repatriate the workman immediately and recover the costs from the employer. The appropriate Labor Office may, in case the workman is discharged under Article 83, exempt the employer from this obligation if the employer so requests, with due regard to the circumstances surrounding the discharge of the workman.

Due to the severity of the consequences to the workman, the employer's burden of proof is particularly heavy. The validity of terminations for cause is contingent on satisfactory proof of two elements.

1. Substantive grounds

Act of aggression

Acts within the scope of subsection 1 must be directed against the employer, if a natural person, or one of the workman's supervisors. While this latter term is not defined, it is interpreted to include those persons having the right to supervise and control the employer's workmen, even if the superior is not the aggressor workman's direct supervisor. In contrast, the term excludes the workman's fellow servants. While severe acts of violence directed at another fellow workman may be considered a valid reason for termination,[129] they will not support termination under article 83. One 1982 case involved the termination without notice of a workman for fighting with a fellow workman. Finding that this was the first misconduct of the workman and that the defendant employer had failed to

---

[129] In this case, the employer must act with dispatch. *See, e.g.,* N. AL-KAYALI, *supra* note 10, at 335 & n.3 (citations omitted) (by delaying termination, employer could no longer support discharge on reason of aggression) (under prior regulations).

prove that the aggression had been initiated by the workman, even though it did not expressly distinguish between acts of aggression directed against an employer and against a fellow workman, the Primary Commission held that the termination was not within the ambit of article 83 and awarded the plaintiff workman the value of the notice period and his severance pay entitlements.

Article 83(1) acts of aggression need not be criminal offenses, nor technical batteries. However, they must involve more than mere offensive behavior. Furthermore, the act must either occur during working hours at the place of work or be somehow work-related. The rationale underlying this principle is that termination is justified by the need for the employer to maintain discipline and to deter other workmen from committing similar acts.[130] Where the workman was not the initial aggressor, he may have a valid defense against termination under article 83 if, under the circumstances, his behavior was reasonable, measured against the objective standard of the ordinary workman.[131]

Fundamental breach or disobedience

Subsection 2 is a catch-all provision, applicable to any breach going to the essence of the employment contract. It also applies to intentional violations of posted safety rules, provided the workman has been warned in writing.[132] Furthermore, in cases not covered by other subsections, the employer may be able to ground the termination on subsection 2. For example, where the employer has failed to fulfill the reporting requirement of subsection 4, it is barred from discharging a workman who intentionally caused material loss. However, if the employment contract imposed on the workman certain obligations which he intentionally did not carry out, his termination could be valid under subsection 2. In all cases, breaches must be material. Ordinary, trivial errors are punishable only by disciplinary measures.

Disobedience will justify termination only where the disobeyed order is lawful. Certain orders are specifically made unlawful by the Regulations, most notably the arbitrary transfer of the workman to a place of work requiring a change in his residence if serious prejudice could result by reason of such transfer. Article 78 provides

---

[130] *See, e.g., id.* at 332 n.1 (citations omitted) (purpose underlying regulations is the workman's duty to observe necessary respect toward employer) (under prior regulations).

[131] *See, e.g., id.* at 333–34 & n.1 (citations omitted) (provocation defense to termination where degree of violence would cause the ordinary person to behave as workman did) (under prior regulations).

[132] *Cf.* Model Disciplinary Rules, Schedule of Penalties & Rewards, pt. 2, arts. 12–13 providing for termination without severance pay for intentional misconduct at work resulting in actual and material injury to health and safety of fellow workmen or damage to equipment) (translated in Appendix 34).

> [t]he employer may not transfer the workman from his original place of work to another place necessitating a change in his place of residence, if such transfer is apt to cause a serious prejudice to the workman and is not justified by a valid reason dictated by the nature of the work.

Article 75, which applies to all "valid reasons" for termination, including article 83 grounds, provides that "discharge shall be regarded as having no valid reason if it is established that it followed the workman's demand for legitimate rights due to him by the employer and no other valid reason for termination is established."

Additionally, article 79 provides

> except in cases of necessity and as dictated by the nature of the work, a workman may not be called upon to perform a work which is essentially different from the work agreed upon, unless he so agrees in writing and provided that this is done on a temporary basis.[133]

Improper conduct

Misbehavior meriting termination must be gross and occur at the place of work. Typical examples include drunkeness or sex-related acts directed at other work persons. A final judgment of conviction of a crime such as fraud, forgery, theft, bribery, and the like, will support termination. However, mere allegations or preliminary detention will not justify discharging the workman under this subsection.

Causation of material loss

The language of subsection 4 makes the lawfulness of termination contingent on the workman's intent to cause material loss to the employer, whether or not the workman's act is a criminal offense.[134]

Unexcused absence

The "year" representing the basis for computing the period of absence permitting termination is the contract year, and not any given twelve-month period selected by the employer.[135] Where the workman seeks to excuse his absence on the grounds of sickness, a medical certificate is

---

[133] *Cf.* Labor Regs., art. 84(2) (allowing workman to terminate without notice and recover damages on these grounds).

[134] *Cf. id.* art. 81 (providing for deductions from workman's wages and for satisfaction of employer's claims out of other property of workman with respect to loss of or damage to employer's property caused by workman's error or failure to obey instructions).

[135] *See, e.g.,* N. AL-KAYĀLĪ, *supra* note 10, at 343 & n.5 (citations omitted).

required.[136] It should be noted that, where the absence due to sickness is prolonged for ninety consecutive days, the employment contract is terminated by force of law, whether or not a medical certificate is produced. However, if the workman does procure a medical certificate, he remains entitled to severance pay.[137] Lastly, as a matter of practice, the employer should refrain from terminating the contract under article 83(7), where the absence is allegedly due to sickness but is of less than ninety days in duration, until the workman returns to the job.[138]

2. Notice of objection

Termination under article 83 excuses the employer from giving article 73 notice. However, any termination under article 83 requires the employer to give the workman an opportunity to present his objections to the termination. The notice must be in writing, set forth the employer's reasons for termination, and give the workman a reasonable time to prepare and present his objections, if any. If the workman fails to respond within a reasonable time, it may be assumed that he has no valid objection to termination or that he is not interested in prolonging the employment relationship. However, the employer must ensure that the workman's time to respond was reasonable under all the circumstances. The time allotted should be generous enough to include any delays in response arising from valid reasons, such as sickness accompanied by valid proof thereof, emergencies, and the like since the standard used to measure the reasonableness of the time of the workman's response, or his failure to respond, takes into account the practicability of response. By failing to respond, the workman does not waive his right to challenge the termination in the Labor Offices and Labor Commissions at some future time.[139] However, allowing the workman adequate time to respond to the notice will be of practical importance to the employer in presenting an eventual defense.

E. TERMINATION BY WORKMAN WITHOUT NOTICE

Corresponding to the employer's right to terminate under article 83, article 84 gives the workman the right to sever the employment relationship, whether the contract is of a specified or unspecified period, in certain limited fact situations. It provides

---

[136] See, e.g., id. at 343 n.3 (citations omitted) (only certificate of accredited doctor probative of illness).

[137] Labor Regs., art. 82.

[138] See id. (prohibiting terminations during periods of sickness).

[139] However, he may not seek the remedy of a provisional stay order unless he brings his complaint within 15 days of receiving notice of termination. See id. art. 75.

[w]ithout prejudice to his right to severance pay for his period of service and compensation for any harm that he may have sustained, as if the cancellation has been initiated by the employer, the workman may, without advance notice, leave the work before the expiration of the contract in the following cases

(1) If the employer has not fulfilled his obligations towards the workman.

(2) If the employer calls upon the workman to perform a work which is essentially different from the nature of the work for which he has committed himself under the contract, or if the employer transfers the workman from his original place of work to another place, necessitating a change in his place of residence, which is apt to cause serious harm to the workman and has no valid reason dictated by the nature of the work.

(3) If the employer or whoever is acting on his behalf has committed an assault or an immoral act against the workman or against a member of his family.

(4) If there is a serious hazard which threatens the safety or health of the workman, provided that the employer has been aware of the existence of such hazard and has taken no steps to remove it.

(5) If at the time of concluding the contract, the employer or his representative has misled the workman with respect to the terms of employment.

(6) If the employer through his actions and particularly by his unfair treatment or by his breach of the terms of the contract, has caused the workman to appear as the party terminating the contract.

Although the general theory underlying both articles is identical, the treatment of the workman under article 84 is slightly more favorable than that accorded to the employer by article 83.

1. Substantive differences

(a) The workman is justified under subsection 1 if the employer has breached any of its obligations. These need not be "essential obligations", as required by article 83.

(b) Immoral acts as well as acts of aggression are valid reasons for termination under subsection 3. Moreover, such acts directed at members of the workman's family will discharge his obligations.

(c) Under subsection 5, the workman is entitled to terminate his employment on the grounds of fraud or misrepresentation, while the employer may only do so on the grounds of false or falsified writings.[140]

---

[140] *Compare id.* art. 84(5) *with id.* art. 83(5). Alternatively, this difference may be regarded as evidentiary. The workman is thus permitted to establish fraud by means of oral testimony, while the employer is limited to documentary fraud.

(d) Subsection 6 is a general safeguard irrelevant in the case of article 83 terminations. It protects a workman terminating an employment contract of an unspecified period where the workman's service period is of less than two consecutive years. If the workman leaves work in such case, he will not be entitled to severance pay. If, however, the workman can show that he left the job as the result of acts of harassment, humiliating treatment, or undeserved or excessive reproof in the presence of his fellow-servants, he will not be deemed the breaching party, and the employer will be liable for severance pay in accordance with article 87.[141] In view of this fact, employers should not give their workmen grounds for claiming that they were forced to leave work, despite the principle that the valid exercise of the workman's rights under article 84 contains an implied condition of good faith.

2. Formal and conceptual differences

The formal element of termination provided in article 83 is absent from article 84. Thus, the workman is not required to give the employer any opportunity to furnish an explanation or otherwise to satisfy the workman. Additionally, the language of the introductory paragraph of article 84 should be contrasted with that of article 83. Under the former, the workman's act of severing the employment relationship is not a "resignation," or unilateral termination of the employment contract by the workman. Rather, he is entitled to "leave work." Thus, the act of termination is deemed to be made by the employer. This semantic difference is of legal significance with respect to contracts for an unspecified period. The computation of severance pay in article 84 cases is governed by article 87 rather than by article 88. Since the workman has not "resigned," he does not fit within the language of the latter article and is entitled to the more liberal payments provided in article 87.

F. REMEDIES FOR WRONGFUL TERMINATION

1. Damages

The termination of the employment contract by one party may give the other party a cause of action to recover damages. Article 74 of the Regulations provides

> [i]f the contract is cancelled for no valid reason, the party who is harmed by such cancellation shall be entitled to compensation to be assessed by the competent Commission, provided that such assessment

---

[141] *Cf. id.* art. 91(a) (imposing duty on employers not to injure workman's dignity).

shall take into account actual and contingent material and moral damages suffered by such party. In the case of the workman, such assessment shall take into account the nature of the work, the period of service, the workman's age, the pay he was receiving, the family burdens he shoulders, the extent to which his income from his new job is lower than the income from his old job, the degree of arbitrariness of the discharge decision, the extent to which this decision affects the workman's reputation, and any other conditions and concomitant circumstances in accordance with the rules of equity and current generally accepted practice.[142]

The right to damages under article 74 is independent of and additional to the workman's right to receive severance pay. All claims for damages, however, must be based on the absence of a valid reason for the termination. Only damages for failure to give notice may be claimed under article 73. This is significant, since damages for lack of notice are calculated under the fixed regulatory measure. In contrast, the Labor Commissions have discretion under article 74 to award damages in an amount they deem appropriate.

Where no valid reason for termination exists, the workman's right to compensation is settled.[143] Article 74 permits the Labor Commissions, in making their assessment, to take into account a variety of factors, including the degree of arbitrariness of the termination. However, Saudi labor law does not award punitive damages. Article 74 applies whether or not the workman has already found new employment. In cases where the workman has not yet done so, the Labor Commissions are likely to base the award heavily on the actual and projected period of unemployment. It may be noted that in the case of a contract of a specified period, while the Labor Commissions are free to award the plaintiff damages equal to his salary due for the remainder of the contract period,[144] they are not limited by that amount. If the employer's breach has resulted in substantial harm to the workman's reputation and professional future, the Labor Commissions have discretion to award damages in excess of his salary for the remaining contract period. In practice, the Commissions generally measure damages with reference to the degree of arbitrariness of termination and the potential hardship which the workman may suffer. In most cases, damages are awarded in the amount of two or three months' salary of the workman.

---

[142] See also id. art. 75 (giving Commissions discretion to order reinstatement or award damages).

[143] See, e.g., N. AL-KAYĀLĪ, supra note 10, at 394 & n.2 (citations omitted) (if *the employer's* action was devoid of a legal cause, judgment for compensation required) (emphasis added) (under prior regulations).

[144] See, e.g., id. at 392 n.3 (citations omitted) (damages of remaining three months' wages awarded) (under prior regulations).

Incidental damages may also be awarded.[145] Damages may be awarded in monetary value or in kind.[146] However, the workman may not recover incidental damages by the mere fact of his discharge without a valid reason[147] but must also show that he suffered injury from the unjustified termination.[148] However, the employer may, at any stage in the proceedings prior to issuance of a final decision, avoid the risk of a damages award by reinstating the workman with back pay.[149]

The employer may also recover damages in a proper case. The Regulations give no guidance with respect to factors which the Labor Commissions may consider in assessing an award in favor of the employer. Such assessment, consequently, is left to their discretion.

2. Reinstatement

The remedy of reinstatement is, of course, available solely to workmen. Furthermore, Saudi law does not recognize any corresponding right of employers to compel specific performance of employment contracts by workmen.

The Labor Commissions have held that the workman, by accepting the termination award under article 74 and by renouncing all his other regulatory rights, is barred from seeking a reinstatement order.[150] Article 75 provides

> [a] workman who is discharged for no valid reason may apply for a stay of execution of such discharge . . .
>
> If the Commission finds that the workman's discharge was without a valid reason, it may order his reinstatement with payment of his wage arrears, or it may order payment of his statutory entitlements as well as any compensation due him for damages he has sustained. The burden of proof that the discharge was for a valid reason shall lie with the employer. The Commission's decision in this respect shall be considered a decision of first instance.

The Commissions have discretion to order the reinstatement of the workman in his former job where this relief was sought, to determine the propriety of this remedy,[151] and to grant it even in cases where the

---

[145] However, such awards are rare.

[146] *See, e.g.,* M. ABŪ AL-'AINAIN, *supra* note 14, at 473.

[147] The burden of proof is upon the employer to show the validity of the termination. Labor Regs., art. 75.

[148] *See, e.g.,* M. ABŪ AL-'AINAIN, *supra* note 14, at 473.

[149] *See, e.g., id.* at 472.

[150] *See, e.g.,* N. AL-KAYĀLĪ, *supra* note 10, at 386 n.3 (citations omitted) (under prior regulations).

[151] *Cf.* Council of Ministers Resolution No. 683 (25/9/1383) (where termination is arbitrary, either reinstatement or damages is proper), *cited in* M. ABŪ AL-'AINAIN, *supra* note 14, at 473.

workman did not seek a preliminary stay order.[152] Furthermore, in its disposition on the merits a Primary Commission is not bound by the granting or denial of a preliminary order staying the workman's termination, whether issued by the same or another Primary Commission.[153] However, in certain cases, the remedy of reinstatement is mandatory. The two mandatory grounds set forth in article 75 of the Regulations, which govern reinstatement, are: where the workman was terminated for the sole reason that he demanded his legal rights due from the employer; and where the workman was terminated for disobeying his employer's order unlawfully transferring him to another place of work where such transfer is not based upon a sufficient valid reason dictated by work requirements or is of a nature to cause serious prejudice to the workman.[154] Reinstatement is also said to be mandatory if the workman was terminated during a period of illness or, if a workwoman, during a period of illness or pregnancy, provided that the workwoman can furnish a medical certificate attesting to the genuineness of her illness or pregnancy and that the period of her absence did not exceed six months. This rule would also be applicable to terminations made during the six months following delivery, unless the termination is grounded on some other legal reason.[155] In cases where reinstatement is ordered, the commissions also award back-pay.[156] The reinstated workman's service is expressly required to be deemed uninterrupted only in the two circumstances of mandatory reinstatement provided in article 75.[157] However, in the case of any reinstatement, the workman's service should be considered continuous and uninterrupted.

In practice, the Commissions tend to give pecuniary rather than injunctive relief. This preference is particularly true of cases where the Commissions have reason to believe that the future employer-workman relationship is unlikely to be a harmonious one.[158] In contrast, the Commissions are more apt to issue a reinstatement order where the employer is a large company. In such a situation, the employment relationship is relatively impersonal, and the employer, due to its magnitude, would be unlikely to suffer the harm from the reinstatement that the workman, if, unreinstated, would suffer.[159]

[152] For procedural aspects, see pp. 321–22 *infra.*

[153] *See* Labor Regs., art. 75.

[154] *Id. Compare id.* art. 78 (prohibiting arbitrary transfers apt to cause serious harm) *with id.* art. 75 (either arbitrariness *or* harm requires reinstatement). All transfers are prima facie arbitrary unless the employer can make the required showing of necessity. *But see id.* art. 206 (penalizing workmen refusing to move where necessity present).

[155] *See* M. Abū al-'Ainain, *supra* note 14, at 472.

[156] Labor Regs., art. 75.

[157] *See id.*

[158] Labor Commission decisions have specifically made this point in dicta.

[159] *See, e.g.,* M. Abū -'Ainain, *supra* note 14, at 473.

G. TERMINATION CASES[160]

(1) The plaintiff workman, of Saudi nationality, sued for reinstatement under article 75 on the grounds of wrongful termination of his employment contract of a specified period. He alleged that he had worked for the defendant company as translator of technical lectures for a five-year period, under contracts renewed annually, during which he had received several good reports from his superiors. Therefore, he sought a stay order, back-pay, and recovery of amounts deducted from his paid vacation time for the year of termination. In addition, the plaintiff sought to recover housing and transportation allowances for his entire period of service under a claim pending before the same Primary Commission predating his termination. Although none of the plaintiff's employment contracts had provided for the payment of these allowances, the plaintiff asserted his right to them on the grounds that the Regulations entitled him to be treated on an equal basis with the defendant's other workmen, whose contracts provided for the payment of such allowances. He also supported this claim on the theory that the defendant had resorted to fraud in drafting the terms of his contract.

The employer countered with two defenses, substantive and formal. First, it maintained that termination was proper under article 83, and denied the plaintiff's allegation that his termination was arbitrary. It admitted that the plaintiff had efficiently performed his obligations as technical translator in Riyadh and had, upon his own request, been transferred to Ta'if. However, it stated, his service there became so unsatisfactory as to justify terminating him. Not only had the plaintiff absented himself from work without authorization or excuse, but he had also been the subject of complaints from various of his superiors, including an instructor who alleged that he had been forced to resign as a result of the plaintiff's uncooperative behavior. The defendant noted that the plaintiff's termination had been preceded by various warnings, which he had not heeded.

After hearing the defense, the Primary Commission addressed the following questions to the defendant

(i) Did the employer give a chance to the workman to explain and object to the termination as provided under article 83?

(ii) What did the defendant mean by saying that the plaintiff's behavior was not satisfactory?

(iii) How could the defendant show that the termination did not take

---

[160] The cases reported in this section are included for purposes of illustration. It should be noted that such cases, although representative of certain adjudicative attitudes, do not carry any force of precedent.

place because of the plaintiff's claim for house and transport allowances on an equal basis with the other workmen?

(iv) To prove the unauthorized absences.

(v) To submit the reports showing that the plaintiff's performance was not below the average level of performance.

(vi) Why did the defendant continue to keep him on the job while it was clear that he was not satisfactory?

(vii) To specify the nature of the plaintiff's work as a technical translator and the relationship of his job to the person alleged by the defendant to have resigned because of the plaintiff's attitude or behavior.

The defendant replied that the plaintiff had had the opportunity to object to his termination, as it addressed a memorandum to him to this effect, which he had answered. What was meant by the allegation that the plaintiff's behavior was not satisfactory was that his performance was not satisfactory. The defendant denied any relationship between the termination and the pending claim of the workman for housing and transportation allowance. The defendant said that it could prove the workman's absence from his job. On the issue of inefficient performance of work, the defendant said that it had already submitted all the relevant reports of the plaintiff's superiors. The employer stated that it had continued to employ the plaintiff because it had been satisfied with his work in the past, and his performance had only changed recently. The defendant explained that the plaintiff's work was to accompany the instructors to their classrooms and to translate their lectures and act as an interpreter. Therefore, his absences had caused delay in the delivering of the scheduled courses. Secondly, the employer defended on the grounds that the plaintiff had agreed to the termination and had signed a release stating that he had received his outstanding salary and two months' severance pay. The plaintiff admitted that he had signed the release but alleged that he was not bound by it, since he had signed it to preserve his pride.

The Primary Commission first noted that it had jurisdiction over the case under article 75. As a matter of fact, it then found that the signed release was an admission of the plaintiff proving that he had received his entitlements. Since this fact was established, the Commission held, as a matter of law, that the plaintiff was barred by his admission and his receipt of amounts due from obtaining a stay order. These acts established his acceptance of the termination decision, whether such acceptance was voluntary or due to motives of preserving his pride and dignity. The Commission did not explicitly address the claims for housing and transportation. These, however, appeared to be subsumed under the general release.

Finally, the Primary Commission held that its summary decision denying the stay order would also stand as a merits disposition of the underlying case. It based its holding on the fact that the plaintiff's signing of the release barred him not only from seeking a temporary stay order but also a reinstatement decision. Consequently, the decision was open to appeal without need for a rehearing. The case was decided in 1977, and the plaintiff appealed. Since the appellant failed to appear at the three scheduled hearings, the Supreme Commission for the Settlement of Labor Disputes ["Supreme Commission"] after reviewing the record and supporting documents, dismissed the appeal in 1978.

(2) In another 1977 case, the plaintiff sued under article 75 seeking reinstatement with back-pay, including recovery of his contract-completion bonus computed on a monthly basis. He also claimed the right to the value of a one-way airplane ticket from Los Angeles to Riyadh, which he would have used to return from his vacation, had he not been discharged, and a roundtrip ticket between those cities, to which he was entitled on completion of the contract at issue, according to its terms.

The defendant company had terminated the employment contract, of a specified period of one year, after five months of the plaintiff's service as an engineering technician on a project which the defendant was executing for the Saudi Government. Termination was effected pursuant to the instructions of the project owner and based on the latter's allegations that the plaintiff had been drunk.[161]

The plaintiff asserted that his discharge was unlawful because he had not been proved guilty of any offense. Nor had he been given the opportunity to present a defense. He argued that neither the Labor Regulations nor the defendant's work rules expressly provide for termination based on words ascribed to a workman.[162] The plaintiff admitted that he had signed a release stating that he had received all his regulatory entitlements until the date of his termination, but took the position that this release was applicable solely to his entitlements prior to that date and was not final.

In response to the plaintiff's allegation that he was denied the opportunity to present a pretermination defense, the defendant replied that the plaintiff had been orally informed of his alleged violations by his supervisor and had not denied them. The defendant added that it was not able to dispute any orders given it by the project-owner with respect to workmen. The plaintiff, however, responded that the Regulations require notifications of misconduct to be in writing. Finally, he argued that the defense of inability to dispute the project-owner's instructions was invalid, because the

---

[161] These allegations were not reported in detail but were contained in two letters ordering the plaintiff's discharge written by the project-owner and by its agent.
[162] The plaintiff's alleged words were not reported.

employment relationship was governed by the Labor Regulations, which, issued by royal decree, prevail over administrative orders.

The Primary Commission first held that the plaintiff was not entitled to a reinstatement order because he had committed an act in violation of Islamic rules of law.[163] Hence, his termination was lawful under article 83(3). Consequently, the Commission did not reach the issue of whether the plaintiff's signing of the release precluded him from seeking reinstatement. Nor did it address the issue of whether the plaintiff had been entitled to receive a notice of objection in writing.

Secondly, the Commission rejected the plaintiff's claims for post-termination wages and airplane tickets on the grounds that the employment relationship was severed as of the date of termination. However, while holding that the plaintiff had no contractual right to tickets, the Commission held that the defendant was required to repatriate him under article 85 of the Regulations.

(3) In a 1978 case, the nonSaudi plaintiff had been employed as the defendant's manager under an employment contract of a specified period. The contract provided that the defendant had the right to terminate the plaintiff's employment whenever his services were no longer required. After the plaintiff had successfully completed his probation period as provided in the contract, the defendant terminated him without advance notice on the grounds that it was dissatisfied with his performance and had been warned by other of its workmen that the defendant's project would never achieve completion if the plaintiff remained as its manager. The termination notice received by the plaintiff thus simply stated that the defendant was not satisfied with his work and that the project was not progressing.

The plaintiff brought suit before the Primary Commission claiming: his wages for the remainder of the contract period; severance pay; annual vacation pay; compensation for overtime hours during which he alleged that he had worked although the defendant had not asked him to do so; compensation for the defendant's failure to give him the three months' termination notice period provided in the employment contract; an airplane ticket to his home country; damages under article 74 of the Regulations in compensation for injury to his professional reputation and the loss of other career opportunities which he had foregone in his home country; and translation expenses and attorneys' fees.

The Primary Commission held that the termination was without valid reason because, according to the language of the termination notice, it was based on reasons other than the grounds for termination on which the

---

[163] The Commission stated that this factual finding was based on the documentary evidence introduced by the defendant.

parties had agreed in the employment contract. The Commission also held that the contract term providing that the defendant could terminate the plaintiff's employment at any time it no longer needed his services was insufficient to render the contract a contract for an unspecified period. The Commission thus awarded the plaintiff the following items: severance pay; one-third of his monthly salary for unused vacation leave; one month's wages in lieu of the termination notice period; and damages in the amount of two months' salary in compensation for wrongful termination. However, it declined to award him compensation for the full contract period and for injury to his reputation, or to award him legal and translation costs.

(4) In a 1979 appeal to the Supreme Commission, the appellant employer, the defendant below, attacked a 1979 decision of the Primary Commission. The respondent had been employed as an accountant for five years by the appellant money-changers, who had terminated his employment contract without giving him the two months' notice to which the contract entitled him. The Primary Commission had held that the termination was wrongful and awarded the respondent sixteen days' wages in completion of his final month of service, two months' wages as damages for wrongful termination, unused vacation pay, severance pay and airplane tickets to repatriate him and his wife.

The appellant maintained that the Primary Commission had erred in holding its termination of the respondent unjustified because it had lawfully discharged him in accordance with article 83(3) to (4) of the Regulations.[164] According to the appellant, the respondent's conduct with the appellant's cashier had been bad and he had used unseemly language during the performance of his work. More importantly, the employer alleged that, due to the respondent's negligence, it had suffered a loss estimated at slightly under 50,000 riyals representing deficient sums. It argued that the respondent was jointly responsible with the cashier for sums taken in and that the Primary Commission had improperly based its holding on the respondent's allegation that the cashier was solely responsible in this area and on the appellant's failure to object to this allegation. It explained that it had not responded to the respondent's allegation of nonresponsibility because the Primary Commission had not addressed it after the allegation was made.

The appellant thus not only asserted the respondent's nonentitlement to damages and severance pay, but also asserted its own right to recover the deficient amounts from him. It argued, in addition, that to hold his termination unjustified would encourage its other workmen to neglect their duties.

[164] For text of article 83, see p. 295 *supra*.

The Supreme Commission unanimously affirmed the Primary Commission's decision. It began its analysis by noting that the respondent was employed as an accountant and that he had responded at the lower hearing to the charge of his joint responsibility with the cashier by stating that the responsibility for sums present was that of the cashier and another of the appellant's workmen, that he was only responsible for checking the accounts. It then noted that the appellant had not denied the existence of another workman assisting the cashier, nor objected to the respondent's statement that he was solely responsible for accounting. Furthermore, the respondent's employment contract provided that his profession was that of an accountant,[165] and did not provide that he would perform the activities of a cashier. Hence, the Supreme Commission held that the appellant's allegation of his responsibility could not support its termination of the respondent.

It next held that, since the employment contract entitled either party to terminate it by giving the other party two months' notice, the appellant was liable for its failure to respect this obligation. It summarily dismissed the appellant's defense of the respondent's improper conduct, observing that the appellant should have given him warnings and imposed the appropriate disciplinary penalties, in case he repeated his improper acts, in accordance with the appellant's disciplinary rules. However, such acts could not justify his termination. Therefore the Supreme Commission, noting that the employment contract was the sharī'ah of the parties, affirmed the Primary Commission's award of two months' wages, in lieu of termination notice, to the respondent.

(5) Twin 1979 cases involving the same defendant turned on the issue of whether a transfer letter should be deemed a termination notice as a matter of law. In the first case, the plaintiff, a nonSaudi workwoman whose services related to computers but were not otherwise described, claimed that the defendant employer had wrongfully terminated her employment contract, which she alleged to be for a specified period of three years. Under her version of the facts, she had entered into an employment contract with the defendant in her home country and, roughly one month later, travelled to the Kingdom and began to work. After about eight months, the defendant notified her in writing that her services were unsatisfactory and would be deemed terminated eighteen days thence.

The plaintiff admitted knowledge of the defendant's argument that the notification letter purported to transfer her to her home country. However, she argued that the writing in reality was a termination denying her her legal rights. Noting that the alleged transfer would cause her material

---

[165] The Supreme Commission here observed that the nature of accounting is known, and thus appeared to take a sort of judicial notice of this fact.

harm, she sought to recover the following amounts: one month's wages corresponding to the regulatory termination notice period; severance pay computed on the basis of slightly over nine months of service; two months' unused vacation pay as provided in the employment contract; damages in the amount of her wages for the remainder of the contract period; wages for the two-week period ending on the date the alleged transfer letter scheduled her to recommence work in its home offices; a return ticket to her native country; cost of freighting her baggage; and attorneys' fees. Furthermore, the plaintiff maintained that amounts recoverable should be computed on the basis of her total wage, which she alleged to be more than five times her base salary. She claimed that it included, in addition to her salary: food allowance paid bimonthly; the rental value of her lodgings, which she received in kind and shared with her husband; medical insurance contributions paid by the defendant on her behalf in her home country; vacation bonuses; and, most importantly, the bonus of twenty percent of her salary, which the plaintiff's contract entitled her to receive on completion of her first year of service.

The employer's main defense was that it had sought to transfer, rather than to terminate, the plaintiff. It alleged that the notification letter at issue was a routine transfer letter. It noted that the plaintiff, having contracted in her home country, had originally agreed to her transfer to the Kingdom in a written instrument signed by her.[166] It stressed the inconsistency between the plaintiff's argument that the presently litigated transfer was in fact a termination with her argument that the period of her service should be deemed to include the month between the time of contracting and her arrival in the Kingdom. The defendant thus denied the plaintiff's right to severance pay, which accrues at the end of service, on the grounds that the plaintiff would continue in its employment after her transfer back to her home country. Furthermore, it noted that its letter of "transfer" had informed the plaintiff that her salary, which she now claimed for the period up to the filing of her claim, would be paid to her in its home offices, if she chose to continue in its employment. Alternatively, the defendant argued that, if the plaintiff's services in the Kingdom were deemed to have been rendered under a new contract, severance pay should be computed to exclude the period of service spent outside the Kingdom.[167]

The defendant next argued that the plaintiff was employed under a contract of an unspecified period. It noted that the only proof that the

---

[166] The defendant thus implied that she could lawfully be retransferred to her original place of work.

[167] The defendant supported this proposition on general territorial principles which would limit the reach of the Labor Regulations to the borders of the Kingdom. By this argument, the defendant impliedly admitted that the transfer could be deemed a termination.

plaintiff had introduced to show that the contract was of a specified three-year period was the contractual language providing for bonuses to be paid after the first, second, and third years of service.[168] Rather, the plaintiff's period of service was eight months, including the notice period, during which her work had been unsatisfactory. In support of the latter allegation, the defendant introduced a letter from the Ministry of Planning to that effect. It admitted that the Ministry was a stranger to the employment contract. However, it asserted that the Ministry's dissatisfaction was a legal ground for the plaintiff's transfer.[169]

The employer then contested the plaintiff's specific claims.[170] First, it denied her right to damages on the grounds that she was not terminated. Nor would she suffer material harm from her transfer, since her work could be performed anywhere in the world. It also disputed the plaintiff's method of computing her total wage. Initially, it claimed that her wage should exclude the annual bonus, the right to which, it claimed, had not accrued, since the plaintiff's service period had only been eight months. It then modified its position to assert that the plaintiff's wage only included her base salary and food allowance, totalling less than half of the initial figure that it had suggested. It sought to exclude the value of the plaintiff's lodgings on two grounds: that the housing had been provided in kind; and that the plaintiff's apartment had not been rented for her personally. Rather, the defendant had rented it for its workmen, without specifying their names, and had the right to assign its individual workmen to the lodgings of its choice, to which decision they were not entitled to object, provided that the lodgings were suitable.

The Primary Commission held that the defendant had wrongfully discharged the plaintiff. It found, first, that the notification letter which the defendant addressed to her stated that, if she refused to be transferred to her home country, the defendant would terminate her wage payments.

---

[168] In the companion case, *see* pp. 313–14 *infra*, the plaintiff also attempted to prove that the employment contract was for a three-year period by showing that the defendant's contract with the Ministry of Planning was for that duration. The defendant rebutted this argument by showing that the latter contract entitled the Ministry to terminate the defendant's services at any time.

[169] In the companion case, the defendant expanded this defense. It introduced a letter from the Ministry specifically requesting that the plaintiff be replaced at the earliest time possible in order to permit the execution of the project to progress and made reference to the plaintiff's low level of productivity and the negative consequences thereof. Furthermore, in support of the lawfulness of the plaintiff's retransfer home under art. 70, the defendant stressed that the Ministry of Planning had the right of direct supervision over the defendant's activities and the right to agree whether its workmen should continue their services, with respect to its project, or not.

[170] The parties agreed to settle on the defendant's payment of 12 days' wages in completion of the notice period, severance pay, 45 days of vacation pay from which 15 days paid after the termination letter would be deducted, excess baggage cost and airfare. This last item the defendant later refused to give except in kind.

Referring to the rule of law that a workman's place of work may not be changed unless he consents thereto in writing, the Primary Commission held that the plaintiff's transfer was without legal justification. Next, it noted that the employment contract provided that her services were to be performed in Saudi Arabia. It thus held that the defendant had breached an essential clause of the contract, which was required to be respected, unless the parties altered it by free and mutual agreement. Consequently, it held the defendant's act to be an unjustified termination of the plaintiff.[171]

The Primary Commission also found that the plaintiff's employment contract was of an unspecified period. Therefore, she was entitled to advance notice of termination and severance pay. Although it stated that the plaintiff began work on the date of executing the contract, it awarded severance pay on the basis of the period of her service within the Kingdom. In view of the brevity of her service period, it awarded damages in the amount of two months' wages. Since the plaintiff had not completed a full year of service, the right to the annual bonus was held not to have accrued.[172] It adopted the defendant's original estimate of the plaintiff's wage, which included the value of her housing.[173]

In contrast, the Primary Commission rejected the plaintiff's claim for post-notification period wages, which the defendant in its letter had promised to pay her if she agreed to the transfer to her home country. Since she neither agreed to it nor performed any work during that period, she was not entitled to recovery. The plaintiff was also denied attorneys' fees, because the parties' dispute had arisen out of a genuine difference in their views of the facts and because they had later reached a mutual agreement on the proper disposition of the majority of the plaintiff's claims.

The facts of the companion case, decided two weeks later, were more favorable to the defendant, but produced an identical legal result. The dates of the plaintiff workman's service period in the Kingdom were the same as in the prior case. However, the plaintiff had been employed in the defendant's home office for over one year before his initial transfer to the Kingdom. The alleged termination notice purported to reinstall him in his original post. The plaintiff, however, argued that the defendant's letter transferring the plaintiff to the Kingdom was an offer, subsequently accepted by the plaintiff, and hence a new contract was formed. Thus,

---

[171] Whether the defendant's act was deemed a transfer or termination is immaterial in terms of the legal result. *See* Labor Regs., art. 84(2).

[172] The commission noted that the bonuses provided in the contract were on the order of promises whose time of fulfillment had not yet occurred, and the right to which does not accrue until their appointed date.

[173] The commission observed that benefits in kind are difficult to estimate. However, it should be noted that the rent of the plaintiff's apartment was known.

Saudi Arabia was the plaintiff's original place of employment, from which he could not be transferred against his will.

Disregarding both parties' earnest arguments that the plaintiff's service had been continuous as of the date he first commenced work for the defendant,[174] the Primary Commission held that a new contract with respect to the plaintiff's services in the Kingdom had been formed and wrongfully terminated, and that severance pay should be calculated on the basis of that eight-month period. Despite the fact that the plaintiff alleged specific material injury and intangible harm resulting from his retransfer,[175] the Primary Commission awarded him damages in the amount of two months' wages.

(6) One 1978 termination case turned on the time of formation of the employment contract, which the parties had not reduced to writing until three-and-one-half months after the commencement of the plaintiff's services. Both parties were in agreement on the basic fact sequence underlying the dispute. The defendant employer had originally contacted the plaintiff, a nonSaudi living outside the Kingdom, through the intermediary of an employment agency located in his country of residence. It desired to employ him as its general project manager. On the first day of the year, the plaintiff began his travel to Saudi Arabia, where he arrived four days later, having stopped in Malta to pick up some of his personal possessions. After three weeks, the plaintiff returned to his residence country to carry on some of the defendant's business with the company designing the project with respect to which the parties had come into contact with one another. Six weeks later, he again returned to Saudi Arabia, where the parties on April 15 entered into a written employment agreement for a one-year period, which provided for a three-month probation period. Two weeks thereafter, the defendant terminated the plaintiff's services without notice.

The plaintiff alleged that a contract of a specified one-year period bound the parties as of the date of his initial voyage to the Kingdom[176] and that he had completed his probation period ninety days from the date he

---

[174] The plaintiff claimed that severance pay should be calculated on the basis of over two years' service. The defendant alleged that the continuum of the plaintiff's service had not yet been interrupted. On this issue, it introduced as proof copies of its internal records showing the format of the alleged transfer and retransfer between the defendant's branches. The Commission, however, was not impressed either by these records or by the defendant's testimony that it had continuously made medical insurance contributions on the plaintiff's behalf in his home country.

[175] He alleged, *inter alia,* that he had sold his furniture and automobile, and rented an apartment in reliance on the defendant's offer of three years of employment in the Kingdom, and that he would lose face before his acquaintances on returning home after such a brief absence. He also alleged that he would be unable to find new employment.

[176] The plaintiff was permitted to introduce a letter from the employment agency as proof on this issue.

actually commenced his service. The parties had then executed a written instrument which was deemed to relate back to the first day of the year. Alleging that his service had been continuous from that point on, and that the defendant had breached the contract, he claimed wage payments for the remainder of the contract period of eight months, severance pay of five days' wages; unused vacation leave; wages for the month of April; a return ticket; three months' wages in lieu of the termination notice provided in the contract; twenty percent of his wages, which the defendant had previously deducted; overtime payments for twelve additional weekly hours over a four month period;[177] damages for the loss both of reputation and employment opportunities in the value of eight months' wages.

The defendant, whose interpretation of the facts differed slightly from the plaintiff's, first alleged that the latter had originally come to the Kingdom on a visit, in order to appraise the defendant's activities and to allow the defendant to try him out. He had returned to his residence country to perform work for the defendant but had remained there one month longer than expected. About one month after his return to the Kingdom, the parties signed the employment agreement. The defendant thus alleged that the plaintiff's service could not be deemed continuous from the first of the year and that he had been lawfully terminated during his probation period.

In the alternative, the defendant argued that the employment contract was for an unspecified period, which it was entitled to terminate for a valid reason. It supported this contention with the provision of the employment contract which entitled the defendant to terminate the plaintiff's services if, in its own estimation, he was in excess of its needs. The grounds for termination, succinctly stated in the termination notice, were the defendant's general dissatisfaction with the plaintiff's performance and his lack of success during the probation period. On oral argument, the defendant stated that the plaintiff had not yet estimated the project budget, as he had been requested to do on his initial arrival in the Kingdom. He claimed that he could not do so until the project plans were completed, but was not able to estimate the budget despite his spending six weeks with the design company. The defendant also alleged that other reports and schedules made by the plaintiff were unrealistic and harmful to the interests of the project. Additionally, he had failed to discover a material error in the project plans, which the defendant alleged was the fault of the design company. Finally, the defendant's general manager had received reports from three of its workmen employed directly under the plaintiff that the project would fail if he remained as project manager. These reasons, the

---

[177] The plaintiff had apparently continued to work overtime despite his receipt of notice of his termination.

defendant noted, were in addition to its lack of need for the plaintiff's service.

The defendant conceded its willingness to pay one month's wages in lieu of termination notice, as well as vacation pay, severance pay, and a return ticket. It denied that the plaintiff had actually worked overtime, despite the clause in the employment contract providing for such work.[178] The plaintiff, in return, submitted additional claims, for translation costs, in connection with bringing suit, attorneys' fees, transportation of his baggage, and damages, in the amount of three months' wages, for the plaintiff's involuntary unemployment occasioned by the defendant's dilatory trial tactics.[179]

The Primary Commission held that the plaintiff's services commenced on the first of the year under an employment contract of a specified period. It specifically rejected the employer's defense that the contract was not reduced to writing until May 15 [sic]. Relying on the rule of law that the probation period, if any, must occur at the beginning of a workman's service period, it concluded that the defendant did not discharge the plaintiff during his probation period.[180] Next, the Primary Commission held that the termination was unjustified as a matter of law. It found that any error in the project plans was the fault of the draftsmen and not of the plaintiff. The latter's alleged failure to discover the error was ascribable to inadvertency, a human failing, and could not justify his termination. It rejected the defendant's argument that the plaintiff's services could be terminated if in excess of need, on the grounds that this proposition was inconsistent with the contract's being for a one-year specified period. The Commission thus awarded the plaintiff severance pay, unused vacation pay, a return ticket, one month's wages in lieu of notice, wages for the month of April, and damages for wrongful termination in the value of two months' wages. The Commission declined to award damages for the full contract duration and to award costs, on the grounds that the plaintiff had mixed invalid claims with his lawful claims and consequently should be required to bear some of the losses of litigation.

III. Labor Disputes

A. LABOR COMMISSIONS

The Labor Commissions have jurisdiction over labor cases.[181]

---

[178] In contrast, it admitted that the plaintiff had worked on Fridays. The parties reached a settlement on payments in this respect.

[179] The defendant had twice defaulted and requested one postponement of the hearing.

[180] Since the plaintiff was terminated more than three months after his services began, the Commission did not need to decide whether there had actually been a period of probation.

[181] A distinction may be drawn between labor disputes arising squarely out of the employer-workman contractual relationship and labor-related disputes. As to the first, the Labor Commissions' jurisdiction is exclusive. Labor Regs., art. 179 (giving Labor Commissions

1. Primary Commission for the Settlement of [Labor] Disputes

The three Primary Commissions sit in Riyadh, Jeddah, and Dammam. Each is composed of a three-member panel appointed by the Minister of Labor and Social Affairs. The chairman is required to have a degree in Islamic law, and at least one of the other two members is required to have a degree in law, either Islamic or decree law.[182]

Jurisdiction

The Primary Commissions have original jurisdiction over labor cases.[183] Their decisions with respect to relatively insignificant controversies are final. The Regulations set out three categories of disputes subject to such final disposition:[184] first, cases where the amount in dispute does not exceed 3,000 riyals, with the exception of compensation claims for labor injuries;[185]

---

exclusive right to look into disputes relating to labor contracts) (emphasis added). However, the Labor Commissions' jurisdiction is not exclusive with respect to certain labor disputes ancillary to rights guaranteed by the Labor Regs. For example, the sharīʿah courts hear claims for compensation brought by a workman's heirs for the wrongful death of their decedent in work-related circumstances. *Compare also* art. 179 *with* arts. 174, 176 (Labor Commissions' jurisdiction not expressly exclusive under latter articles in official text). The Commissions may also hear appeals from social insurance administrative rulings. Social Insurance Regs. Implementing Rules, art. 58.

[182] Labor Regs., art. 173.

[183] *Id.* art. 174. However, in work-related wrongful death suits, if the decedent workman's heirs have sued to recover the diyah in sharīʿah court and if a natural person was responsible for the decedent's death, the commissions are to refrain from hearing the case until the sharīʿah judgment is given. Council of Ministers Resolution No. 734 (5/5/1396) (catalogued in the Institute of Public Administration library).

[184] Labor Regs., art. 174.

[185] Art. 130 of the Regulations imposes on employers a duty to warn workmen of and to take precautions against activities exposing workmen to physical injury, poisoning, or disease, if the Minister of Labor [sic] determines such activities to be hazardous. *See generally* Minister of Labor & Social Affairs Resolution No. 435 (4/11/1404) (relating to lead poisoning and relevant precautionary measures) (translated in Appendix 50). However, the Regulations do not define the term "labor injury." An applicable definition may be taken from art. 27(1) of the Social Insurance Regulations, which provides

> [a]ny injury sustained by the insured (workman) by reason of the work or as a result of the performance thereof, regardless of the cause of such injury, shall be considered a labor injury. There shall also be considered a labor injury any injury sustained by the insured workman on his way from his dwelling to his place of work and back, or on his way from his place of work to the place where he usually has his meals and back, provided that he shall not have deviated from his route nor stopped on the way for a purpose dictated by his personal interest or by an interest not related to his work.
>
> Injuries sustained by the insured during the movements he makes on the instructions of the employer or during travel which is paid for by the employer, shall also be regarded as labor injuries.

Furthermore, diseases determined to be occupational diseases under Council of Ministers resolution are considered "labor injuries." *Id.* art. 27(2)–(3). *See also* Implementing Rules & Procedures of the Application of the Occupational Hazards Branch, Minister of Labor & Social Affairs Resolution No. 61/Insurance, art. 47 (6/4/1402) (relapses, worsening of condition

second, cases relating to disciplinary fines imposed by employers upon workmen pursuant to article 125 of the Regulations;[186] lastly, the Primary Commissions have injunctive power to issue nonappealable temporary stay orders to workmen seeking relief from termination decisions, provided that the workmen comply with the procedures set out in the Regulations.[187]

The Primary Commissions issue decisions of first instance in labor cases where the amount in dispute exceeds 3,000 riyals, and in all cases involving compensation for labor injuries or termination of employment, regardless of the amount involved.[188]

Venue

Venue is proper in the geographical area of the place of work.[189] However, the parties may change the venue by agreement. If so, the Primary Commission is to transfer the case to the designated forum.[190] If the venue is improper and the parties subsequently consent to such venue, the Primary Commission will hear the case.[191]

2. Supreme Commission for the Settlement of [Labor] Disputes

This body is the appellate commission for labor cases. It sits in Riyadh and is composed of four members and a chairman, of whom three represent the Ministry of Labor and Social Affairs, one represents the Ministry of Commerce, and one represents the Ministry of Petroleum and Mineral Resources. All are required to have a legal background.[192] The Supreme Commission also has three reserve members, of whom two represent the

---

also deemed labor injuries). *See also* Minister of Labor & Social Affairs Resolution No. 404 (17/6/1394) (relating to medical care at place of work) (translated in Appendix 51); Director-Gen'l. of Central Province Head Labor Office Circulars No. 3778/2/16/12 (14/11/1400) & No. 7776 (27/10/1397) (relating to medical care of workmen) (translated respectively in Appendices 52 and 53). The Labor Regs. also make employers responsible for injuries to licensees occurring on the premises, if the injuries were caused by failure to take the precautions required by the nature of the work. However, claims for damages brought by third persons are not within the jurisdiction of the Labor Commissions: Labor Regs., art. 132.

[186] The Primary Commissions are to rule on workmen's appeals from disciplinary penalties within one week from the date the objection was recorded. Labor Regs., art. 126.

[187] *Id.* arts. 75, 174.

[188] *Id.* art. 174. If a timely appeal is not made, such decisions of first instance become final and enforceable. *Id.* art. 182.

[189] *Id.* art. 180.

[190] Rules of Procedure & Conciliation & Arbitration Proceedings before the Primary Commissions & the Supreme Commission, Council of Ministers Resolution No. 1, art. 39 (March 11–17, 1970).

[191] In one 1977 case, after the defendant employer objected to the initial improper venue in Riyadh, the case was referred to the Jeddah Primary Commission, then returned to the Riyadh Primary Commission on the grounds that Riyadh was the seat of the defendant's main office and domicile of the plaintiff's representative. Both transfers were made upon agreement of the parties.

[192] Labor Regs., art. 175.

Ministry of Commerce. One of the Ministry of Labor representatives is required to have an Islamic law degree. The reserve members are authorized to sit by designation on the Primary Commissions if members of the latter are absent. In this case, such member is barred from reviewing the case on appeal.[193]

The Supreme Commission has no original adjudicative jurisdiction. It hears appeals from all nonfinal decisions of the Primary Commissions[194] and arbitral awards rendered in resolution of labor disputes.[195] Its rulings on appeal are final and may be enforced as soon as the parties receive notice of the decision.[196] In addition, the Supreme Commission has original enforcement jurisdiction to punish violations of the Labor Regulations and rules, decisions, and orders issued thereunder.[197] Unless other applicable regulations punish the same act more severely, the penalties provided in the Regulations apply.[198] In this latter case, the Supreme Commission has discretion to impose penalties within the prescribed range. Regulatory violations committed by employers are referred to the Supreme Commission by Labor Office directors, pursuant to factual reports made by labor inspectors.[199] However, the Supreme Commission's enforcement powers with respect to labor-related offenses are not exclusive. Administrative commissions also have limited jurisdiction to punish various regulatory violations.[200]

[193] Council of Ministers Resolution No. 1144 (25/12/1390); Minister of Labor Letter No. 2/81 (3/4/1392), *approved by* Council of Ministers (available at the Institute of Public Administration library).

[194] Labor Regs., art. 176.

[195] *Id.* art. 183.

[196] *Id.* arts. 176, 182. Parties refusing to execute a final decision of any Labor Commission or delaying in its execution may be punished by a doubling of the original penalty, by a fine of up to 1,000 riyals, by a maximum of three months' imprisonment, or by both of the latter. *Id.* art. 205.

[197] *Id.* art. 176; *cf. id.* art. 22 (generally penalizing acts constituting abuse of Regulations and rules). Chapter XII of the Regulations sets forth the penalties for violations. Article 191 prescribes the harshest punishment therein, namely a maximum sentence of six years' imprisonment, or a maximum fine of 10,000 riyals, or both, for the proscribed act of ceasing work with the purpose of protesting actions of public authorities or coercing public action.

[198] *Id.* art. 207 (harsher punishments applicable to employers).

[199] *See* Rules of Control & Regulation of Labor Inspection Activities, Council of Ministers Resolution No. 444, art. 27 (July 7, 1970) (translated in Appendix 54). *Cf.* Director-Gen'l. of Central Province Head Labor Bureau Circular (4/21/1397) (unnumbered) (requiring use of Arabic language in signs, printed material to facilitate inspection) (translated in Appendix 55).

[200] For example, the Commissions on Evasion of Workmen in the regional governors' offices are composed of delegates from Labor Offices, the police, and the regional governors' offices. They punish employers who fail to report the flight of workmen under their sponsorship within 15 days of their disappearance. The standard penalty imposed on such employers and any other person aiding fleeing workmen is a fine of 2,000–10,000 riyals, or imprisonment of two to six weeks, or both. Furthermore, wherever the fleeing workman is eventually arrested, he is sent to the commission of the region from which he originally fled. The only factual issue at the subsequent commission hearing is whether or not the workman

B. PROCEDURE

Procedure before the Labor Commissions is governed by the Rules of Procedure and Conciliation and Arbitration Proceedings before the Primary Commissions and the Supreme Commission ["Labor Rules"].[201]

1. Parties

Only parties in interest have standing to sue or to raise a defense before the Labor Commissions.[202] In the case of a deceased workman, his heirs are proper parties. Article 3 provides that "[o]ne of the heirs shall stand for the other heirs in his capacity as their representative in suits brought for or against the deceased."

Multiple party actions are permissible. Both parties have the right to implead third parties provided that such persons would have been proper parties at the time the original complaint was filed.[203]

The death or loss of capacity of a party stays the action except if all parties have presented all claims and have been heard. If so, the Commissions may decide the case on the merits. Article 42 of the Labor Rules provides

> [i]f any of the parties dies, loses his capacity to litigate or ceases to have the power by virtue of which he has been acting, proceedings shall be stayed automatically, unless the suit has become ready for a decision on the merits. The suit shall be considered ready for a decision on the merits, if the litigant parties had presented their final pleadings and claims before such death or loss of capacity or power.

However, even if the case is not ready for a merits disposition, a person with standing may serve a copy of the complaint upon the successor in interest of the former party. In this case, the proceedings will be deemed to have resumed at the stage they had reached at the time of the initial interruption.[204]

---

fled from his employment. If this is established, the workman is deported, after receiving any rights guaranteed by regulation. *See* TAHLAWI, *Workmen are Fleeing and Warning Notices are Continual,* al-Jazirah, Oct. 15, 1981, at 4, cols. 2, 5 (interviewing Labor Office director and Commission on Evasion of Workmen Challman of the Eastern Province).

[201] Council of Ministers Resolution No. 1 (March 11–12, 1970) (issued under art. 177 of Labor Regs.).

[202] *Id.* art. 2. In all cases, the Commission must determine the party's legal capacity to sue: *id.* art. 7.

[203] *Id.* art. 40.

[204] *Id.* art. 43.

2. Limitation periods

A twelve-month limitation period is applicable to labor actions. The point at which the limitation period starts to run depends upon the nature of the action. Article 13 of the Regulations provides

> [n]o complaint shall be heard by any commission in respect of violations of the provisions of this Law or of the rules, decisions or orders issued in accordance therewith, after the lapse of twelve months from the date of the occurrence of such violation. No case or claim relating to any of the rights provided for in this Law shall be heard after the lapse of twelve months from the date of termination of the contract.[205]

Even though article 13 provides that the period shall begin to run from the date of the end of the contract, the date of actual termination of service, rather than the date provided in the employment contract, begins the period.[206] Thus as long as the employment relationship continues uninterrupted, the date of ultimate termination applies, even with respect to rights acquired under prior contracts. Thus, where an employment contract is renewed annually, rights acquired under the initial contract may be enforced six years later, or within one year of termination of the fifth employment contract.[207] Where a contract of a specified period is converted into a contract of unspecified period the date of actual termination controls.

Stay orders

Workmen seeking orders temporarily staying their employers' termination decisions, on the grounds of wrongful termination, must file their demand within fifteen days of receiving actual notice of termination.[208] The date of receipt of notice starts the limitation period, regardless of the date of termination. In the computation of the regulatory fifteen days, major official holidays, such as "Id al-Adhā" or "Id al-Fitr," are excluded. The brevity of the period limiting this action for injunctive relief has been interpreted as signifying a regulatory intent to ascertain whether the workman in fact suffered from the allegedly unlawful termination. His

[205] It may be noted that the word "commission" found in art. 13 also means "committee" in Arabic and has been interpreted to include arbitration committees.

[206] In one 1977 case, the Riyadh Primary Commission held that since the plaintiff workman was lawfully terminated under art. 83 before the contract expiration date, the parties' relationship ended on the date of actual termination.

[207] Thus, 1977 appellate decisions awarded two workmen four years of retroactive housing allowance and airfare.

[208] The workman must be notified by personal delivery, by registered mail, or by other means proving receipt. Labor Regs., art. 75; Labor Rules, art. 58.

eagerness to keep his job would be probative of that issue.[209] A workman's failure to seek a stay order within that period will not bar him from seeking a permanent reinstatement order or damages for the period he spent unemployed.

Appeals

Appeals are timely if made within thirty days of the date the party has received a copy of the Primary Commission's decision.[210] Failure to file an appeal within the regulatory period will cause the lower decision to become final and enforceable.[211]

3. Notice

With respect to appeals and any other procedural steps predicated on the giving of notice, the limitation period begins to run on the date of actual notice.[212] The receipt signed by the person to whom the notification was delivered and returned to the Labor Office by the notice-server is prima facie evidence of the date of receipt but can be rebutted.

Notice is given by means of an order from the commission with jurisdiction.[213] Proper notice papers must be in Arabic[214] and include the following elements[215]

    (a) The day, month, year, and hour that notification was made;
    (b) The full name, occupation, and address of the plaintiff or his representative;
    (c) The name of the commissioner ordering the notification;
    (d) The name, occupation, and address of the party to be notified;[216]
    (e) The name and signature of the person to whom the notice was delivered;[217]
    (f) The signature of the notice-server on the original and the copy of the papers.

In addition, notification of the date of a second hearing given to a party who failed to appear at the initial hearing must inform such party that a judgment dispositive of his rights will issue at that hearing.[218]

---

[209] *See, e.g.,* M. Abū al-'Ainain, *supra* note 14, at 470.
[210] Labor Regs., art. 180.
[211] *Id.* art. 182.
[212] Labor Rules, art. 8.
[213] *See id.* arts. 12(c), 19
[214] *Id.* art. 11.
[215] *Id.* art. 12.
[216] If the party's present address is unknown, the last known address may be used: *id.* art. 12(d).
[217] The person to whom the notification is delivered signs the original and keeps the carbon.
[218] Labor Rules, art. 31.

4. Service

Service within a commission's territorial jurisdiction is made by means of delivery, by ordinary mail, unless the Regulations require otherwise,[219] or by refusal to take delivery.[220] Personal service must be made by Labor Office employees, post office employees or, if these are not available, by means of the police.[221]

Natural persons

If the person to be served is absent from his residence, service may be made by delivery of the papers to his agent, employee, or to a family member residing with him who appears to be at least eighteen years of age, provided that there is no conflict of interest between the named person and the person taking delivery.[222] If the party is represented by a lawyer, service may be made upon him.[223]

Commercial companies

Service is made at the central administrative office, upon the chairman of the board of directors, the general manager, or, in the case of a partnership, upon any partner. If the company has no central administrative office, one of the above persons may be personally served, or the notice may be delivered to his residence.[224]

Civil companies, associations, establishments, and all other juristic persons

Service is made at the main administrative office, upon the entity's representative.[225]

Long-arm service

a. Within the Kingdom. If service must be made outside of a Primary Commission's territorial jurisdiction, the chairman sends the papers to be served to the chairman of the Primary Commission of the area where the party resides or has its central office. The latter chairman then serves them.[226]

---

[219] *See, e.g.,* Labor Regs., art. 75 (requiring service by registered mail or means proving receipt).

[220] Labor Rules, art. 17. In the case where the person served refuses to take delivery, service may be proved by the testimony of two Muslim witnesses.

[221] *Id.* art. 13.

[222] *Id.* art. 14. Family members authorized to take delivery are the party's ascendants, descendants, spouse, brothers, or sisters.

[223] *See id.* art. 29.

[224] *Id.* art. 15(b).

[225] *Id.* art. 15(c).

[226] *Id.* art. 19.

b. Outside the Kingdom. Service may be made by means of registered mail or through official channels.[227]

5. Procedure; civil actions

Pretrial

All complaints must first be brought to the Labor Office in the geographical area of work. If the labor officials fail in their attempts to persuade the parties to reach an amicable settlement, they will send the complaint to the Primary Commission with jurisdiction.[228] The complaint must state

(a) The name, surname, occupation, nationality and domicile of both the plaintiff and the defendant.

(b) A statement of the matter in dispute and of the specific claims of the plaintiff.

(c) A statement of the information and evidence on which the plaintiff relies in support of his action.[229]

The chairman of the Commission sets the hearing date and summons the defendant.[230] The summons must be served at least three days before the hearing.[231]

If the plaintiff workman seeks the remedy of reinstatement, the Regulations provide time periods for the various procedural steps. The complaint is to be referred to the Primary Commission within one week of its receipt by the Labor Office. The hearing is to be scheduled within two weeks of the referral date; the stay order is to issue within two weeks of the initial hearing; a second hearing to dispose of the underlying claim must be scheduled within one week of the stay order.[232]

In all cases, parties and their representatives are given the right to see the case file at the Primary Commission office.[233]

---

[227] *Id.* art. 18.

[228] Only art. 75 of the Regs. governing stay orders, explicitly provides that complaints must initially be brought to the Labor Offices. However, as a matter of practice, this procedure is applicable to all claims, which may not be brought directly to the Labor Commissions

[229] Labor Rules, art. 23.

[230] *Id.* art. 24.

[231] *Id.* art. 25.

[232] *See* Labor Regs., art. 75; Labor Rules, art. 58. However, the commissions' failure to comply with the procedural time limits does not affect the validity of the stay order. *See, e.g.,* M. Abū al-ʻAinain, *supra* note 14, at 473.

[233] Labor Rules, art. 20.

Appearance

Parties may appear in person or be represented by an attorney.[234] If the defendant does not appear, the hearing will be rescheduled.[235] If the defendant does not appear at the rescheduled hearing and has no acceptable excuse for his nonappearance, the commission may give a default judgment in the plaintiff's favor.[236] However, either party may secure postponement of the hearing if he submits a legally valid reason for his contemplated nonappearance before the hearing date. If the commission accepts the excuse, the party will not be penalized and, if the defendant, will not be subject to a default judgment until the third scheduled hearing.[237]

Pleadings; hearing

Submission of briefs is permissible but not mandatory. However, all claims and defenses must be raised at the hearing.[238]

The plaintiff nonetheless has the right to amend his initial complaint to correct errors therein, to complete it, or to modify the claim to reflect changed conditions or facts discovered after the complaint was brought.[239] The plaintiff may also seek damages for claims resulting from the original claim or so closely connected with it that they cannot be tried separately. The legal theory underlying the claim may also be varied at the hearing.[240] The plaintiff has the right to present his case before the defendant is heard.[241]

The defendant has the right to counterclaim for set-off and to raise any other counterclaims whose effect would be to defeat the plaintiff's claim, in whole or in part.[242]

If the defendant has appeared, he is required to respond to the plaintiff's arguments. If he remains silent, the Commission has discretion to give judgment in favor of the plaintiff.[243]

The Primary Commission chairman is responsible for directing the proceedings. It is he who questions parties and witnesses; the other Commission members may also do so with his permission.[244] With respect

[234] The attorney must establish his right to represent his client by means of a notarized power of attorney. See id. arts. 7, 27.

[235] Id. art. 30.

[236] Id. art. 36.

[237] See id. arts. 33–34. Furthermore, a party who arrives at the hearing less than one hour late is considered to have appeared: id. art. 32.

[238] Id. art. 38.

[239] Id. art. 44.

[240] Id.

[241] Id. art. 35.

[242] Id. art. 45.

[243] Id. art. 36.

[244] Id. art. 37.

to parties, the burden of proof is on the proponent of the statement.[245] The Labor Commissions have the power, in addition, to summon witnesses for questioning and to compel the production of real or documentary evidence. Their investigatory powers also give them the right to enter and inspect any premises occupied by the (employer) companies.[246]

If an issue raised must be decided before the Primary Commission can give judgment on the merits, it has discretion to stay the proceedings pending the disposition of such issue.[247] The parties also may agree to stay the proceedings for a period not to exceed six months.[248]

Decisions

a. Formal aspects. Deliberations of the Commissions are closed.[249] Decisions may be made by majority voice.[250] The text of the decision must state whether it was reached unanimously or by majority and must be signed by all Commission members who participated in the proceedings.[251] The legal grounds on which the decision rests must be stated, and all defenses raised by the parties must be answered in the decision.[252]

Dissenters are required to record the grounds for their dissent in the case record; however, dissenting opinions are not included in the text of the decision.[253] Parties may obtain a clarification of any ambiguities in the decision.[254] If so, for all purposes, including appeal, the explanatory statement is deemed to complete the original decision.[255]

b. Costs. The Commissions have discretion to award costs, including attorneys' fees, in whole or in part, to the prevailing party.[256] The party must submit documentary proof of costs.[257]

6. Appeals

Nonfinal Primary Commission decisions may be appealed within the thirty-day period following a party's receipt of notification of the decision.[258]

---

[245] This procedural rule, expressed in art. 75 of the Regs., is not restricted to termination cases but is generally applicable.

[246] Labor Regs., art. 179 (also authorizing the commissions to "adopt any other measure [they] may deem fit").

[247] Labor Rules, art. 46.

[248] *Id.* art. 41.

[249] *Id.* art. 48.

[250] Labor Regs., art. 178; Labor Rules, art. 49.

[251] Labor Regs., art. 178; Labor Rules, arts. 49–50.

[252] Labor Regs., art. 178; Labor Rules, arts. 49, 51.

[253] Labor Rules, art. 50.

[254] *Id.* art. 55.

[255] *Id.* art. 56.

[256] *See* Labor Regs., art. 14; Labor Rules, art. 26.

[257] Acceptable proof would be, *inter alia,* an attorney's note of services or an itemized list of documents translated.

[258] Labor Regs., art. 180.

Parties may appeal directly to the Supreme Commission, or through the intermediary of the Primary Commission that made the decision appealed or a Labor Office.[259] The petition submitted to the Supreme Commission must set forth the decision and state the grounds on which it is appealed.[260] No new claims may be raised against parties to the lower decision; nor may new parties be joined.[261] However, either party may request an award of additional costs incurred with respect to the appeal. The appeal automatically stays the execution of the lower decision.[262]

Parties may appear in person at the Supreme Commission hearing or be represented by counsel.[263] If either party fails to appear, the hearing will be rescheduled. The defaulting party is entitled to notification of the rescheduled hearing. If he fails to appear a second time, the Supreme Commission may give judgment.[264] If both parties fail to appear, the appeal will be dismissed.[265]

The Supreme Commission generally rules on the basis of the parties' legal arguments and the record. However, it has the power to summon witnesses and require the production of evidence.[266] If it vacates the lower judgment in whole or in part, it is not required to remand the case but may enter judgment.[267] Appellate decisions are sent to the Minister of Labor and Social Affairs, who forwards them to the appropriate Labor Office. They are final and enforceable as of the date the parties receive notice thereof.[268]

7. Final decisions

The principle of res judicata is expressly made applicable to final Labor Commission decisions.[269] All final awards in favor of workmen, their dependents, and heirs have the status of first class privileged debts, giving such persons a priority right over all of the employer's property.[270]

---

[259] Labor Rules, art. 62.

[260] *Id.* art. 64. In addition to legal grounds, parties may attack a decision on the grounds that the Primary Commission abused its discretion to correct material errors on the face of the decision: *id.* art. 54. The Supreme Commission will not rule on issues not expressly raised. *See id.* art. 65.

[261] *Id.* arts. 66–67.

[262] *Id.* art. 70.

[263] However, appearance is mandatory. Thus, in one 1978 case, the Supreme Commission noted that under the Regulations both parties should be present for individual discussion in face of one another.

[264] Labor Rules, art. 68.

[265] *Id.* art. 69. In one 1978 case, the workman's appeal was dismissed on his third non-appearance when the respondent, who had previously appeared twice, also defaulted.

[266] Labor Regs., art. 179.

[267] Labor Rules, art. 73. Lower decisions facially in accordance with applicable law must be affirmed. *Id.* art. 72.

[268] Labor Regs., art. 182; Labor Rules, art. 75.

[269] Labor Regs., art. 186 (barring parties to the decision).

[270] *Id.* art. 15.

C. ARBITRATION

1. Procedure

Due, perhaps, to the Islamic tradition of arbitration as a means of resolving disagreements in personal relationships,[271] the area of labor disputes is one where regulations expressly provide for binding and automatically enforceable arbitration.[272]

Article 183 of the Regulations provides that in all cases the disputing parties may by mutual agreement settle their dispute by means of one or more arbitrators in lieu of bringing their claims before the Labor Commissions. A copy of the arbitration agreement must be deposited with the appropriate Labor Office. Where the parties have appointed arbitrators who fail to agree on the selection of an umpire, the chairman of the Primary Commission in the location of the place of work is required to select an umpire, unless the latter has been appointed in the arbitration agreement.

Article 183 also provides that the arbitration agreement "shall indicate the time-limits and rules of procedure to be followed." It would thus appear that the parties or the arbitrators have the right to determine the procedures to be followed in the arbitral proceedings.

2. Enforceability

Arbitral awards are of first instance, with a right of appeal before the Supreme Commission, and subject to the same procedural limitations applicable to a judgment of first instance issued by one of the Primary Commissions. However, if the arbitration agreement expressly provides that the arbitrators' award will be definitive, the rule is that it may not be appealed. The award must be registered with the office of the appropriate Primary Commission within one week of its having been rendered. It may be executed after registration and on issuance of an execution order by the chairman of the commission.[273]

3. Legal recognition

From the literal language of the Regulations and implementing rules, three general principles emerge. First, the institution of arbitration has

---

[271] *See, e.g.,* N. ANDERSON, LAW REFORM IN THE MUSLIM WORLD 112, 118, 200–01 (1976); *cf.* Egyptian Decree Law No. 25 of March 10, 1929, art. 9, *reprinted in* H. LIEBESNEY, THE LAW OF THE NEAR AND MIDDLE EAST 141 (1975).

[272] *See* Labor Regs., art. 183; Labor Rules, art. 76; *cf.* Labor Regs., art. 205 (penalizing employer or workman who refuses or delays the execution of an arbitral award or any *other* final decision issued by Labor Commissions) (emphasis added). Furthermore, the Regulations extend general protection to any rights acquired by workmen by virtue of arbitral awards. *Id.* art. 6 (employer's infringement of such rights deemed regulatory violation).

[273] Labor Regs., art. 184; Labor Rules, art. 77. *See also* Labor Regs., art. 182 (amicable settlements binding on registration).

received explicit legal recognition in the context of employment disputes. Not only do the parties possess an absolute right to settle their disputes by arbitration but they may also invoke an informal form of compulsory process by means of which the chairman of the appropriate Primary Commission is legally required to appoint an umpire in the case where the parties or their arbitrators have been unable to appoint one by mutual agreement. It would thus seem that, where the parties have agreed to proceed to arbitration and have duly registered their arbitration agreement in compliance with article 183, but have either been unable to appoint an umpire or have retreated from their intention to arbitrate, the Primary Commission will not hear the case but instead will direct the parties to proceed to arbitration or appoint an umpire to enable the arbitration to take place, should such appointment be required.

Secondly, the arbitral award is given the same legal weight as a judgment issued by one of the Primary Commissions and benefits from the safeguards applicable to such a judgment, namely, the thirty-day statute of limitations applicable to appeals. More importantly, any appeals taken from arbitral awards are to be made directly to the Supreme Commission.

The chief advantage to be derived from this provision is the saving of time. If awards carried a right of appeal to the Primary Commission, there would be small incentive to arbitrate, since the process of litigation would subsequently be required to be performed in its entirety. Finally, the parties may agree that the award shall be final and without the right to appeal. In this case, the Labor Commission would appear to be denied jurisdiction to look into the case on the merits or, indeed, even to examine the award on its face. This lack of power to review would, of course, be subject to the limitation that no enforceable award may conflict with either Islamic law or public policy, or be grossly inequitable.

Chapter 6
THE DIYAH

The general rule of Islamic law as applied in Saudi Arabia is that the heirs of a homicide victim are entitled to payment of the diyah, a term commonly translated as "blood-money."[1] This is a private right vested in the decedent's heirs and is independent both of their right to receive social insurance benefits and of the State's right to punish the homicidal act.[2]

1. Principle of unity/fixity of the diyah

The amount of the diyah is fixed by law. It is a uniform figure which does not vary according to the individual identity of the deceased.[3] Thus, in *Terry* v. *Transarabian Pipeline*,[4] a United States plaintiff attempted to sue a United States corporate defendant in a United States district court for the wrongful death of his decedent. Federal jurisdiction, however, was defeated since the amount in dispute, governed by Saudi law and limited thereunder to the diyah, fell short of the jurisdictional minimum.

---

[1] In the case of intentional homicide, the diyah is an alternative to retaliation. Islamic law does not permit the blood of a Muslim to be wrongfully shed unrequited. *See, e.g.*, Judicial Council Resolution No. 100 (6/11/1390) (catalogued in the Institute of Public Administration documentation center). In pre-Islamic times, it was believed that an owl sat crying for blood upon the grave of an unavenged decedent.

[2] Payment of diyah may also be the subject of international agreements. *See, e.g.*, Agreement for Friendship and Neighbourly Relations, April 20, 1942, Saudi Arabia-Kuwait, Schedule, para. 4 (except for cases of premeditated aggression and lawful self-defence, each Government to collect blood money payable by its nationals in respect of victims nationals of other Government to be calculated according to shariʿah).

[3] It will, however, vary on the basis of the sex and religion of the deceased. *See also* 4 IBN QAYYIM AL-JAWZIYYAH, AʿLĀM AL-MUWAQQAʿĪN ʿAN RABB AL-ʿĀLAMĪN 377 (Beirut) (diyah and one-third payable for killing in Holy Places). However the principle of fixity of the diyah is qualified by the fact that the court may issue a judgment for less than the total figure. *See, e.g.*, Pres. of the Judiciary Circular No. 177 (2/2/1381) (diyah reduced by amount of deceased's contribution to his death).

[4] U.S.D.C., S.D.N.Y., 66 Civ. 727 (1970). *Cf. Ahmed* v. *Boeing*, 720 F. 2d 224 (1st Cir. 1983) (relating to adequacy of diyah).

Originally, the diyah was set at one hundred camels, whose ages varied according to the circumstances of the act causing death. However, the payor retained the right to make payment in specie. Hence, periodic reassessments of the value of the diyah in kind have historically been required.

The original appraisal, made by the Caliph 'Umar, established the market value of the diyah at 1,000 gold dinars or 12,000 silver dirhams.[5] In Saudi Arabia, the diyah was set at 800 Maria Theresa dollars in the eighteenth century. In the twentieth century, it rose from 800 riyals to 4,000 riyals and in 1955 was set at 16,000 and 18,000 riyals according to the degree of fault involved.[6]

In 1970, the diyah rose to 24,000 and 27,000 riyals, figures reached by averaging the value of camels of different ages selected from different regions of the Kingdom, and then rose again to 40,000 and 45,000 riyals. As of the end of 1981, the diyah was set at 100,000 riyals for accidental homicide and 110,000 riyals for quasi-intentional homicide, which involves fault on the part of the defendant but not intent to kill, and is presently in the amount of 120,000 riyals.[7] However, the decedent's heirs may not be limited to this amount if they have another theory of recovery, such as, in the case of a workman, his employer's failure to take proper safety precautions.[8]

The Islamic jurists treat the subject of the civil consequences of homicide under the interchangeable headings of jināyāt (offenses), jirāḥ (wounds), and dimā' (blood).[9]

The first term appears to emphasize the fault of the defendant, the second the damage to the plaintiff, while the third term is best regarded as a mutual commodity whose referent may be either or both of the parties. The jurists divide the cost of blood into two major categories: the payment

---

[5] See, e.g., 7 M. IBN QUDĀMĀ, AL-MUGHNĪ, 759–60 (M. Rida ed. 1368). General propositions of Islamic law made in this chapter are derived for the most part from this work.

[6] See, e.g., Sheikh M. bn Ibrahīm, Payments of Diyah for a Muslim Person and Damages for his or her Various Wounds, Fractures of Bones and [Loss of] Teeth (fatwā of Mufti of Saudi Arabia) (1955) (available in Harvard Law School Library).

[7] High Order No. 2266 (29/9/1401) (implementing Supreme Judicial Council Decision No. 133 (3/9/1401) (based on rises in price of camels).

[8] See, e.g., Council of Ministers Resolution No. 734 (5/5/1396). See also Permanent Council of Legal Studies and Iftā' Fatwā No. 4218 (6/12/1401) (diyah and compensation are different, unrelated items). In practice, in the cases of workmen's work-related death or injury, the diyah and regulatory compensation are offset against one another. The regulatory amounts recoverable by workmen or persons claiming through them are provided in the prior Labor and Workmen Regs. of 1947. Art. 25 fixes the entitlements in the case of death or total disability at S.R. 27,000 in the case of a first class workman, S.R. 18,000 in the case of a second class workman. See generally Appendix 56 (giving compensation rates for permanent partial disabilities as provided in the 1947 Regulations).

[9] However, the term "jināyāt" differs from the others in that it also applies to damage to property.

to be made upon the death of a human and, derivatively, the payment to be made for damaging a human body. The expression of the base liability in terms of death contrasts with the theory of the Social Insurance Regulations, which calculate the cost of death on the basis of disability benefits,[10] and seem to follow the logic of the English common law, where the original action lay for loss of consortium and services, an action arising for injury to a man's wife, child, or servant. "In a civil court," Lord Ellenborough said in 1808, "the death of a human being could not be complained of as an injury; and in this case the damages as to the plaintiff's wife must stop with the period of her existence."[11] Islamic jurisprudence moves in the other direction. The whole precedes the sum of its parts. Since the root of liability is death, from which the diverse piecemeal damages are derived, analysis will follow that order. It should be noted, however, that the fact that liability arises from the homicidal act does not mean that the nature of the liability is either penal or tortious.[12] The discussion in the following sections is historical and theoretical and should not be considered to represent a restatement of current law.

2. When does the death of a human give rise to payment of the diyah?

Islamic law divides homicide into murder (qatl 'amd) and unintentional homicide (qatl khata'). In the interest of clarity, the analysis will follow the Mālikī doctrine and disregard the intermediate category of quasi-intent (shibh 'amd) recognized by the other schools and applied in Saudi Arabia.

The perpetration of murder gives rise to the right to retaliate (ḥaqq al-qiṣāṣ) in the next of kin of the decedent (awliyā' al-dam).[13] What they have a claim to thus is blood (dam). Should they desire to relinquish their right, they are free to do so. They may waive it gratuitously or relinquish it for valuable consideration. The law will not look into the terms of the bargain in which the next of kin of the decedent and the killer (defendant) have established the price payable.[14] The agreed consideration must be paid at once.

[10] See Royal Decree No. M/22, art. 35 (1969).

[11] Baker v. Bolton, 70 Eng. Rep. 1033 (K.B. 1808).

[12] See, e.g., 2 IBN QAYYIM, supra note 3, at 37 (rejecting penal nature of liability).

[13] This right must be exercised by unanimity. See, e.g., Pres. of the Judiciary Circular No. 10 (17/1/1393) (if some of kin waive right of retaliation, the convicted defendant will not be punished by death). For example, a 1983 beheading involved a murderer convicted in 1966 who was imprisoned until the victim's next of kin reached majority and requested the death penalty from the Ministry of the Interior. There are certain exceptions to the right of retaliation, e.g., a Muslim who has murdered an unbeliever is not subject to qiṣāṣ; nor is a father who has killed his son subject thereto. See, e.g., 4 IBN QAYYIM, supra note 3, at 362.

[14] In contrast, in the case of accidental homicide, it is not permissible to reach a settlement at a figure higher than the diyah. See, e.g., 4 IBN QUDĀMA, supra note 5, at 369 (Cairo 1968). The reason given is that the figure is fixed, i.e. a ceiling. More important, however, is that the defendant would not have capacity to bind his 'āqilah who are liable for payment in this case. See generally pp. 337–40 infra.

In contrast, the liability for unintentional homicide is strictly limited by law. Its Quranic source is sūrat al-Nisā', verse 92, which provides for, *inter alia* the delivery by the defendant of a diyah to the kin of the decedent, unless they forego it. If the decedent is from an enemy people, no diyah is due. Where it is due, the sunnah fixed it at one hundred camels, no more no less, for the killing of a Muslim male.[15] The defendant is free of liability to pay; this burden is born by his 'āqilah and may be paid in installments over a period of three years.

Islamic law thus contemplates two parallel systems of civil liability for homicide. Each purports to deal with a discrete problem. The one envisages the elimination of the defendant. The other entitles the relatives of the victim to receive one hundred camels, or the value thereof.

3. What is the liability for injury to the human body?

A defendant who has intentionally injured the plaintiff is, in theory, subject to retaliation upon his person on condition that the injury which he has inflicted is susceptible of being replicated in its exact terms. Such cases are the amputation of the various extremities and, unique among head wounds (which may be viewed as attempted amputations of the head), the "revealing" (mūḍihah), a wound of the sixth degree which cuts flush to the bone and stops. A legal issue may arise in cases where the defendant's head differs in size from the plaintiff's. The question is whether the wound should be reproduced literally or to scale. Again, the plaintiff is free to remit his claim or to settle.

What of liability for unintentional damage to the person? By applying the weapon of analogy to the concept of the diyah, legal thought found this rule: since the diyah payable to the decedent's heirs is established at one hundred camels, any injury stopping short of death, clearly the total injury, must necessarily entail payment of a lesser amount. The diyah thus comes to be seen as compensation for total destruction of the person, subsumed now under the conceptual if not legal heading of itlāf, which applies to damage to property. This misunderstanding of the nature of the diyah emerges from the following piece of logical reasoning

(A) The diyah is one hundred camels, payable on death.
(B) Loss of life is the greatest loss a body can sustain.
(C) A plaintiff who sustained lesser loss needs less to be made whole.
(D) The diyah is compensation in damages for death.

---

[15] The diyah of a Jew or Christian male is half that amount.

Due to the fact that the various losses and slices from the plaintiff are assessed against the fund of one hundred camels, the fund comes to be perceived as embodying the damaged individual, who is consequently assimilated to property. However, whether liability is founded on tort principles or absolute responsibility for damage to property is unclear. Al-Sanhūrī, for example, comments

> [d]ans le domaine des lésions corporelles (et autres délits sauf les atteintes à la propriété), dès qu'on applique une série de peines privées . . . et en dépit de l'intervention publique dans la poursuite du délit et dans l'éxécution de la peine, la confusion reste complète, dans le systeme islamique entre la responsabilité pénale et la responsabilité civile.[16]

The threshold of confusion, as al-Sanhūrī notes, is the legal threshold of tariffs, the floor above which payments are fixed by law. As demonstrated by the modern workmen's compensation schedules, payments can only be fixed where damage is clearly identifiable. This, we have seen, is also true of the Islamic system of retaliation. The precision of the standard applied has created a sort of mutual attraction between penalty and property. Let us consider the loss of an eye

(A) The intentional destruction of the eye of another shall cause the actor to lose one of his eyes, preferably the same one.

(B) The unintentional causing of the loss of another's eye shall result in the plaintiff's acquisition of fifty camels.

(C) An eye is worth fifty camels.
(Note that, according to the principle of strict equivalence, prerequisite to the application of qiṣāṣ, if the defendant is one-eyed, he is not liable to loss of his eye. This penalty would involve the loss of his eyesight and thus be unfair.)

Legal or fixed liability begins with the mūḍiḥah. It is with this wound that the schedule of payments commences. According to most jurists, qiṣāṣ cannot occur for less. The mūḍiḥah is "worth" five camels, as is a lost tooth. Consequently, any wounds less serious than the mūḍiḥah cannot give rise to liability for more than that amount. They do, however, call for some payment. Such compensatory "equitable awards" are made by the qāḍī through the exercise of his own judgment.[17] Three terms for blood

---

[16] Al-Sanhūrī, *La responsabilité civile et penale en droit musulman*, 15 REVUE AL-QĀNŪN W-AL-IQTIṢĀD 10 (1945).

[17] *See, e.g.*, al-Hakim, *Le dommage de source delictuelle en droit musulman*, 40 UNIVERSITÉ SAINT-JOSEPH, ANNALES DE LA FACULTÉ DE DROIT ET DES SCIENCES ECONOMIQUES 70 (1964).

money coexist under Islamic law. "Diyah" is properly used only with reference to payment made where extinction of life in a free man has occurred. It is not used of slaves, who had either a qīmah (value) or a fidā' (ransom or redemption value). "Arsh" refers to payments for injuries to the human body that do not cause death.[18] "Ghurrah," finally, is used exclusively of the payment to be made for causing the death of an unborn child. The payment is set at five camels, the threshold five percent of the legal diyah, where one hundred percent (one hundred camels) represents the human body in its integrity.

4. Who is liable for payment for nonmortal injuries to the human body?

The majority rule is that the defendant is personally liable for damage to property and damages to the person assessed at up to one-third of the diyah, which, it may be noted, is the legal maximum payable for a wound. The defendant's "'āqilah" is liable for all other payments.[19] The minority view of al-Thawrī and Abū Ḥanīfa is the more instructive. It maintains that the liability of the 'āqilah attaches at the point of "the tooth and the mūḍiḥah . . . because the Prophet made the 'āqilah liable for the ghurrah of the stillborn child and its value is one-twentieth of the diyah, and it is not liable for less than that because there is no fixed arsh."[20] The interconnection of the fixity of the sum of the diyah and third party liability discloses that the jurists are reluctant to make the 'āqilah liable for payment of equitable awards. The law stresses the legal nature of their duty to pay.

Equally clear from the various contexts is the fact that the liability of the 'āqilah arises out of the nonchattel nature of the victim. The legal floor represents the level where damage to property ends and the chattel, so to speak, becomes human. Thus, the majority rule, which holds the floor at

---

[18] Assessment of the extent of the injury is made in Saudi Arabia at the time of the accident, unless the victim's condition is too critical to permit delay, in which case evaluation by doctor's report is sufficient. *See* Minister of Justice Circular No. 121/1/t (17/7/1391) (reprinted in MINISTRY OF JUSTICE, REGULATIONS, RULES, CIRCULARS). The amount of the arsh is set by the judge after the recovery of the victim. *See* Pres. of Judiciary Circular No. 3041/3 (18/9/1382) (reprinted in same). If the victim maintains that his injury has not healed and the official doctor's report declares him recovered, the report is given effect for purposes of setting the time of calculation, unless the victim introduces proof of his nonrecovery. *See* Pres. of Judiciary Circular No. 2598/3 (11/8/1382) (reprinted in same). *See also* Pres. of the Judiciary Circular No. 119 (19/5/1391) (if death did not occur as a result of defendant's aggression but from another cause, only compensation for injury may be claimed). It may be noted that the diyah is payable in full for causing the victim to lose his reason, i.e. to become insane

[19] *But see* Pres. of the Judiciary Circular No. 540 (17/6/1381) (court's holding defendant personally liable for diyah where 'āquilah could not pay was valid); Pres. of the Judiciary Circular No. 777 (11/8/1380) ('āqilah only liable if they believe defendant).

[20] 7 IBN QUDĀMĀ, *supra* note 5, at 777.

one-third of the diyah, also holds that the diyah of a Muslim woman is one-half of a man's. With respect to injuries assessed up to one-third of the diyah, however, no fifty percent reduction occurs. This can only be because the liability of third parties, the 'āqilah, is not involved, or, alternatively the sex of a human is legally recognized to exist only from the floor up. Likewise, the neuterhood of the foetus. The same ghurrah is payable for both sexes. Some jurists permit the delivery of a mare (faras) as the ghurrah of the unborn child; indeed some thought the beast to be a superior form of payment. The symbolic gesture of tendering a living piece of property as ghurrah of the stillborn child is consistent with the doctrine of the four schools that such property is inherited by the child's heirs because it is the diyah of a human (diyah ādamī). Only Laith thought the mother should receive it because the foetus "is one of her members and resembles her hand."[21] This minority view shows a preference for property damage. There may be advantages to this view; in the absence of a ceiling, the award could exceed the legal limit.

The human-property conflict goes back to the time of the Prophet, farther surely, but not for the purposes of Islamic law. According to one tradition, the defendant's 'āqilah, endeavoring to disclaim liability for the stillborn child, complained that they should not be responsible for the diyah of something that neither ate nor drank nor spoke: "a nadī mā lā ta'ima wa lā shariba wa la ṣāḥa wa la-stahalla mithlu dhālika yuṭallu."[22] They speak not of ghurrah but of diyah; the root wdy is connected to life. Its primary meaning is sexual.[23]

No adequate explanation is tendered as to, first, why the 'āqilah should have to pay sometimes and, second, why they should have to pay at all. The jurists dismiss the issue in perfunctory fashion on the grounds that the 'āqilah has a duty to come to the aid of an overburdened member and that one-third or, under the minority view, one-twentieth of the diyah is too light a load to permit the defendant to shift the burden. This logic collapses when one recalls that the defendant may be destitute and, also, that he must personally pay for the property damage.

Although liability for payment can fall only upon one of two potential payors, there are two conceptual struggles
(a) Property: person.
    This regards both the nature of the damage and the nature of the payment;
(h) Civil liability: penal liability.

---

[21] *Id.* at 805. *Cf.* Egyptian Law of Inheritance of 1943 and Tunisian Law of Personal Status of 1956, *quoted in* N. ANDERSON, LAW REFORM IN THE MUSLIM WORLD 160 (1976) (mother receives compensation for damage to her body).

[22] 7 M. AL-SHAWKĀNĪ, NAIL AL-AWTĀR 73 (2nd ed. 1952).

[23] *See, e.g.,* IBN MANZŪR, LISĀN AL-'ARAB, at wdy.

The breakdown is thus into three groups and not two. The defendant is personally liable for the extremes of these two proportions and his 'āqilah for the means. If we attempt to put this in continuum form, it looks something like this

Bodily Injury	LIABILITY CONTINUUM Human Death-Civil Liability	Murder
Defendant is personally liable.	'Āqilah is liable.	Defendant is personally liable.
For wounds up to 1/3 (1/20) of diyah, slaves, equitable awards.	For diyah and scheduled ar<u>sh</u>.	To qiṣāṣ or for settlements.
Any blood shed is mahdūr (no qiṣāṣ can occur for it).	No qiṣāṣ.	If no settlement occurs, defendant's blood is mahdūr (as to wālī al-dam).
No kaffārah.	Kaffārah.	No kaffārah unless settlement.
Payment is immediate.	Payment is deferred.	Payment is immediate.

Islamic jurisprudence reconciled the duty of the 'āqilah with the Quranic principle enjoining the bearing of the burden of another.[24] This verse also specifies that what each soul has earned (using the root ksb), it is liable for; one of the meanings of jānī is kāsib. In order to determine why the 'āqilah should be liable for the jināyāt of its members which it has not personally earned, it may be of use to define the group.

5. What is the 'āqilah?

It is, as a rule, defined circularly as the group which must stand payment of the diyah when one of its members has unintentionally killed or damaged one-third or more of a member of another group. The identity of the 'āqilah varies according to time and place. The label has been attached to diverse bodies, all of which have a relational interest in the defendant arising out of

[24] Surat al-An'ām, verse 164.

(a) A relationship by blood possessed in common: the male agnates or 'aṣabah of the defendant. Disagreement exists as to whether the 'āqilah embraces all agnates or is restricted to collaterals. The specific choice of word "ikhwah"[25] (to the exclusion of 'umūmah) might well show a preference for the peer group of blood, i.e. battle brothers, of subsection (b) infra.

(b) A relationship by blood shed in common: the diwān, or combat unit, of the defendant. The Caliph 'Umar initiated this institution, subsequently disfavored by the jurists, which resembled a rudimentary system of social insurance. In his day, the troops were grouped by tribe, and it was a simple matter to withhold contributions from the wages—simpler than the recovery from the individual members of the actual amounts for which they were liable.

(c) A relationship by proximity in space and ties of profession: the maḥāll and the qurā.

(d) A relationship by former ownership: the mawālī.

(e) A relationship by paternalism: the public treasury. In the event that the defendant has no 'āqilah, the possibilities are two-fold. The plaintiff may bear the loss, as occurred in the rare case of the sā'ibah slave reported by Mālik.[26] The sā'ibah, Ibn Manẓūr tells us, is the slave who has no 'āqilah. More commonly, it is the public treasury who assumes the role of 'āqilah on one of two grounds

(i) The theory of the residual heirship of the public treasury, a theory valid only if duty to pay is defined as falling upon the 'aṣabah to the exclusion of the other competing groups. One could not, for example, make the argument that the public treasury stands in the position of all those engaged in carpentry in a particular neighborhood.[27]

(ii) The theory of the inviolability ('iṣmah) of Muslim blood.

6. What is the nature of the liability of the 'āqilah?

We have already seen that payment for causing death can be made with the person or with property. Among certain beduin tribes, the kin of the

---

[25] 7 IBN QUDĀMĀ, supra note 5, at 784.

[26] M. BN ANAS, AL-MUWAṬṬA', para. 1590 (Beirut 1971).

[27] However this theory is not completely convincing, as may be seen from the case of a married woman. If she has unintentionally killed another, her 'aṣabah is liable for the diyah. If she is killed, her husband and children inherit. See, e.g., 4 IBN QAYYIM, supra note 3, at 364. The Saudi Arabian public treasury continues to pay the diyah in qualifying cases. See generally Pres. of the Judiciary Circular No. 260 (6/9/1393) (stating applicable cases). However, where the defendant is nonSaudi, the diyah may not be paid from public funds unless the decedent was Saudi: Council of Ministers Resolution No. 205 (6/2/1398) (catalogued in the Institute of Public Administration documentation center). Furthermore, the State as employer may pay all or part of the diyah owed by one of its employees, if liability arises in the performance of his duties. This, however, is not the general rule: Council of Ministers Resolution No. 476 (13/4/1393) (catalogued in the Institute of Public Administration documentation center).

defendant has remained liable to qiṣāṣ within the k̲h̲amsah, the five degrees of agnatic kinship closest to the defendant. The agnates of the fourth and fifth degrees are permitted the privilege of paying the "camel of sleep" (baʿīr al-nawm), which entitles the payor to sleep in peace, *i.e.* exempts him from exposure to retaliation.[28] One might infer from this custom that the interest of the ʿāqilah is a personal interest. No altruism, no spirit of active solidarity or cooperation would be involved. Rather, according to the theory of Procksch, the duty to pay would result from the passive solidarity of the group, its vulnerability to revenge. The diyah, according to this theory, is no more than a bribe, a payment to the avengers to refrain from revenge. It is interesting that where the diyah is accepted, the victim and his descendants are entitled to receive a share of only one-third, his k̲h̲amsah receiving the remaining two-thirds.[29] Here we have the counterpart of the ʿāqilah's liability which attaches at the one-third base level. The parallel to the maximum bequest of one-third of an estate permitted under Islamic law also comes to mind.

It would appear that, as between two tribes, two vast undifferentiated corporate bodies, the right to receive and the duty to pay the diyah are invariable mirror-images of one another. The principle of equivalence applies, as if magnified. An injury to a member of the tribal body is sustained by the whole. It is for this reason that the injury must be material and capable of being established objectively in order to invoke the legal apparatus. An affront to the corporate dignity, an injury must be visible to be sustained by the group.

On what grounds can a group suffer an injury to one of its members? Is there not a way to detach oneself or the member causing annoyance and damage from the corporate group?

Islamic law made entry into the kinship group by means other than birth illegal. Adoption is barred. Entry into the blood had previously been permissible. This prohibition may not be circumvented by the expedient of concluding a mutʿah marriage in order to produce people. No marriage contract which contemplates its termination at the time of its making can be valid. However, the custom of the Sinai beduin was to include a girl in the diyah. She remained, so to speak, as hostage in the decedent's tribe until she bore a son who attained manhood. Then she could return to her kin.[30] This custom makes sense, since, where adoption is illegal, the loss of an agnate is irreparable. This is also the explanation of why the diyah of a woman is paid not to her kin, but to her husband and children. By the

---

[28] J. CHELHOD, LE DROIT DANS LA SOCIÉTÉ BEDOUINE 277 (1971).

[29] M. HARDY, BLOOD FEUDS AND THE PAYMENT OF BLOOD MONEY IN THE MIDDLE EAST 72 (1963).

[30] J. CHELHOD, *supra* note 28, at 317. The hostage was called "ghirrah," [sic] which is translated as "the white one".

loss of the victim's future children, which have belonged to the husband's kin, it is the latter, and not the kin of the victim, who sustained the loss.

Of the groups that have qualified over the centuries to be called the "'āqilah," only two do so on the basis of kinship, the 'aṣabah and the public treasury in the role of 'aṣabah. The liability of the other groups arises out of the community of their endeavor for gain, whether by arms or craft. The social insurance fund of the diwān established by 'Umar could be seen as akin to the social insurance of contemporary regulations where employees are under a duty to contribute, employers to compensate, by virtue of the contract of employment.

The liability of the 'āqilah is fundamentally contractual in nature.[31] This principle applies even where the 'āqilah is synonymous with the 'aṣabah, as is the majority view. The duty to pay diyah arises by virtue of the contract, and is an implicit obligation of the relationship, whether the bond be of kinship, fellowship at arms, or community of profession. This is probably why the early jurists debate so earnestly as to who was the 'āqilah of a woman. This argument may seem peculiar on the grounds that one cannot breach a kinship contract. Yet, Robertson Smith has shown that the pre-Islamic definition of "murder" is killing within the kinship unit. For this, there was no retaliation; the penalty was expulsion. Public announcements were made that the khalī' had been divested of his kinship membership; the blood of the outlaw became mahdūr, as is the blood of the murderer under Islamic law, with respect to the legal avengers. In one report, the Prophet was reluctant to allow a free Muslim to be killed in retaliation for killing his slave.[32] He sentenced him, therefore, to one year of banishment. Hardy found that, in 1961, a beduin sheikh still imposed the sanction of banishment upon one who murdered within his kin.[33] According to a fatwā reported by Tyan, a judge banished a murderer who had reached a monetary settlement with the parents of his victim.[34] Expulsion has survived as late as this century, now seen as sanction of ta'zīr.

The converse of the sanction of nonmembership as a penalty for breach of the common bond, whether it be the close tie of the ahl and ḥayy or the broad social contract of the ummah,[35] is the absolute liability of the group for the acts of its members in the absence of breach. Their relationship is that of

---

[31] This, it should be noted, is not an orthodox view. *See, e.g.*, 2 IBN QAYYIM, *supra* note 3, at 35–37 (Beirut) ('āqilah's liability resembles its duty to perform good works, such as to aid the poor and travellers)

[32] / M. AL-SHAWKĀNĪ, *supra* note 22, at 15.

[33] M. HARDY, *supra* note 29, at 92.

[34] E. TYAN, LE SYSTEME DE RESPONSABILITÉ DELICTUELLE EN DROIT MUSULMAN 112 (1926) (doctoral thesis Beirut).

[35] *See generally* O. PROCKSCH, UBER DIE BLUTRACHE BEI DEN VORISLAMISCHEN ARABERN UND MOHAMMEDS STELLUNG ZU IHR 65 (1899) (discussing Ibn Hishām).

participants in a mutual insurance fund. All property was commonly held (we speak here of camels, not of personal effects) in the pre-Islamic ḥayy.[36] The insurance idea is present in 'Umar's deductions from the combat payroll. Under Islamic law, booty taken in battle is jointly held until divided, but with one exception to the rule. The salab, or personal effects taken as spoils, is individually owned by the soldier who is willing to accept personal responsibility for the death as well as the personal benefit of his claim to the armor, clothes and weapons of the deceased.[37] The solemnity of the claim is shown by the need of a witness to establish legal ownership by the claimant of the spoils. The second witness is the decedent. In the absence of witnesses to the death, two rival claimants disputing the spoils of Abū Jahl stood before the Prophet. He examined their swords for blood in order to make judgment. The weapons bore witness to their acts.[38] It is clearly for this reason that the objective legal criterion for deciding whether a killing is "intentional," giving rise to qiṣāṣ, or not, is the defendant's choice of instrumentality and whether or not it habitually causes death. This particular report also shows the premeditated subjective standard of guilt: the two competitors for the salab had set out to kill Abū Jahl. They had requested that he be singled out for them as they did not know him, yet desired to kill him. Clearly, this was neither a case of accidental nor of quasi-intentional homicide; the killing was in cold blood.

The evidence of the instrumentality not only establishes a right to legal possession of the salab in the defendant, but contemporaneously gives rise to a right to qiṣāṣ in the heirs of the decedent and releases the 'āqilah of the defendant from liability, either to payment of diyah or to qiṣāṣ. The former bond is severed; the new blood unit is that of decedent and defendant. Their common blood is mahdūr in the absence of qiṣāṣ. When a killer acknowledges personal responsibility for having killed someone, he admits that the other's blood is with him ('indī).

As long as group membership is maintained, the blood of a member is maʿṣūm. Thus, in the final verse of the Lāmiyyat al-'Arab of al-Shanfāra, the khaliʿ par excellence, there is a play on words when he speaks of the peace and security attained by mountain goats with extremely long horns (swords) who, inviolate, have reached the high slopes at sunset, and associates the two roots 'ql and 'sm: "wa yarkudna bi-l-āṣālī ḥaulī ka'annanī min al-'uṣmi adfā yantaḥī l-kaiha a'qalu." As long as one has an 'āqilah, which will pay the 'aql, synonym of diyah, one may rest assured. The mutual insurance fund of the 'āqilah provides personal liability insurance without fault as long as the terms of the mutual contract are complied with. It is coverage with a legal floor and

---

[36] See, e.g., id. at 4.
[37] See 7 M. AL-SHAWKĀNĪ, supra note 22, at 276.
[38] See id. at 284.

ceiling strictly delimiting liability; the duty of the insurer to pay, where the act of the insured falls within the scope of the policy, is nondisclaimable. The obligation to pay is conditional upon the acts of the insured. Intentional acts are not covered. Even though the duty to pay the diyah arises contemporaneously with the act of the insured, the liability of the 'āqilah precedes it and, as insurer, the 'āqilah is bearing its own burden and not the burden of another. The duty to pay the diyah is a duty to defend, a duty to litigate, if one will, and not to hand over the insured. The right is in the insured to demand the payment of his insurance; the right is in the defendant to require that his 'āqilah pay the diyah and not in the heirs of the decedent.

The description of the diyah as "musallamah" in the Quran shows the symbolic substitution of delivery of the diyah for the handing over of the defendant. The poet Zuhair's use of the root slm is instructive. Praising the two heroes of his mu'allaqah, he says, "wa lā-l-jārimu l-jānî 'alaihim bi muslami."[39] They do not hand over one who has brought down liability upon them. When we recall that jānī can mean kāsib, that every soul is responsible for what it has earned (ksb) and that the jināyah in this verse is clearly against those who must pay the diyah and not against the victim of the wrongful act, it becomes obvious that mutual insurance of the corporate body against the surrender (amputation) of one of its members is involved. A peculiar prose passage in the Ḥamāsah of Abū Tammām makes this point. Before accepting the diyah, the heir of the decedent insists upon taking the defendant into his physical custody and promises then to release him.[40] This gesture of physical jurisdiction wipes out the affront to the tribal dignity.

Given that the 'āqilah is liable to pay one hundred camels when one of its members kills the member of an outside group and that one hundred camels represents an entire human life, it is manifest that the life in whose respect payment is made is the defendant's and not the life of the deceased. The decedent is not an object of sale; he was a free Muslim; now he is dead. It is for this that the 'āqilah was originally liable solely for a human life in its entirety. Under Islam, all human lives of the same class require payment of the same diyah. This follows the pre-Islamic system, where, after battle, the slain were counted on the field and the scores were evened.[41] Instances of inequality are referred to in terms of diyah. For example, the kin of one defendant offer seven diyāt in an effort to tempt the kin of the decedent not to seek qiṣāṣ. We learn that the diyah payable upon the death of the members of the Banū Quraizah was twice that due for the death of those of Naḍīr, as between the two tribes.[42] The diyah is whole. The importance of its unity appears in the numbers used: one hundred camels, one thousand dinars.

---

[39] ZUMAIR BN ABI SULMĀ, MU'ALLAQAH, verse 35.
[40] H. IBN 'AUF, AL-ḤAMĀSAH 25 (Freytag ed.).
[41] See O. PROCKSCH, supra note 35, at 61.
[42] Id. at 54.

In a desire, no doubt, for symmetry, the Ḥanafites reduced to 10,000 dirhams the figure of 12,000 used by the other schools.[43]

Before Islam, one hundred camels was the price of three things: a bride (mahr), the ransom of a prisoner (fidā') and the life of a killer (diyah). Five camels, the amount needed to redeem the ma'ūdah from death,[44] was to become the amount due as ghurrah of the stillborn child.

The payment is thus a "release," from death or from bondage. Ibn Qayyim, alone of the many scholars cited by 'Ukāz,[45] saw the analogy between the duty to pay diyah and the duty, on the part of the 'āqilah, to redeem the prisoner (fakāk al-'asīr).[46] No one seems to comment on the obvious analogy between the two rhyming roots, fdy and wdy. The word "fadā" can mean either of two things: to redeem a person with a person, *i.e.* to exchange prisoners, or to redeem him with property, to buy him back. An anonymous poet uses the word "fidyah" as a synonym of diyah: "fa-law anna ḥayyan yaqbalu l-māla fidyatan la-suqnā lahum sailan min al-māli muf'ama."[47] Thus, the word commonly used to express the heir's act of renunciation of his right to qiṣāṣ is "'afā" ("to forgive"). Alternatively he may accept the diyah: "yaftadī."[48] We now come to the mahr, third of the things formerly appraised at one hundred camels. Zuhrī, in a very minority view, was of the opinion that a man could not be killed in retaliation for murdering his wife because he owned her.[49] In the Ḥamāsah, laḥm (flesh) is used to describe both the slain foe and live women. Fidā', it may be noted, is a synonym for the khul' divorce. The wife buys her own freedom under this method. One may well wonder whether the khalī' was rejected by his kin, as historians generally maintain, or whether he was not the one who severed himself from the tribal body. When al-Shanfarā opens his Lāmiyyah, it is he who tells his kin to depart from him, he who desires to join another group: "aqīmū banī ummī ṣudūra maṭiyyikum fa-innī ilā qaumin siwākum la-amyalu."[50] It may also be

---

[43] *See* 7 IBN QUDĀMĀ, *supra* note 5, at 760.

[44] G. WILKENS, DAS MATRIARCHAT BEI DEN ALTEN ARABERN 54 (1884). The ma'ūdah was the female infant allegedly frequently killed in order to have a mouth less to feed.

[45] F. 'UKĀZ, FALSAFAT AL-QIṢĀṢ FĪ AL-FIQH AL-ISLĀMĪ 183 (1973).

[46] 2 IBN QAYYIM, *supra* note 3, at 36.

[47] H. IBN 'AUF, *supra* note 40, at 106. A rough translation would be: if the ḥayy would accept camels as a price for sparing [his] life, we would drive over a flood of camels to them.

[48] 7 M. AL-SHAWKĀNĪ, *supra* note 22, at 8.

[49] *See generally* W. ROBERTSON SMITH, KINSHIP AND MARRIAGE IN EARLY ARABIA 76 (1885) (discussing marriage by capture and by purchase). Robertson Smith defines mahr etymologically as "price," and also discusses the tradition in which women, particularly married women, are called "'awānī" (captives).

[50] A rough translation would be: "depart, sons of my mother, for I am going to another group." *Cf id.* at 59 (discussing formality of khalī' as prerequisite to entry into another tribal group by adoption). The fact that 'Urwah bn al-Ward, another khalī', uses identical language in beginning one of his most famous poems, "aqīmū banî ummi ṣudūra rikābikum," is more than an argument supporting the oral formulaic nature of pre-Islamic poetry. It presents the formula of reverse-adoption, or the formula of divestiture of kinship, pronounced by the

noted that the root ḥbs refers to imprisonment, its eighth form to the right to possession giving rise to the legal right to maintenance in the wife. Conversely, the root ṭlq refers both to divorce and to the releasing of a prisoner. The radical 'tq, whose main connotation is that of emancipation, is used by the Prophet to mean "ṭlq" in a variant of the same report using the latter form.[51] "'Atīq" also may mean a virgin, so called "because she has been freed from the service of her parents and no husband has as yet owned her" (lam yamlikhā zawjun ba'du).[52]

It is thus clear that one hundred camels is the price of redemption from servitude. There is an interesting tradition reported by Wā'il bn Hujr, where a defendant has confessed to his guilt but has only his clothes and his axe with which to redeem himself from death. This is not sufficient. The Prophet asked: "do you think your people might redeem you?" (fatarā qawmuka yashtarūnaka?).[53] The nature of the diyah paid by the 'āqilah appears here in its purest form. The diyah is in no way a compensation for physical damage to an injured person; one hundred camels is simply the extent to which members of a mutual insurance pool are covered. The price of a life was once one hundred camels; property damage has always been assessed at its market value. Thus, the diyah should realistically be perceived as the minimum level, rather than the sole level of liability/recovery required by law. Its governing principles of unity and fixity are not disturbed by this view, since any additional amounts recoverable would not relate to the diyah.

---

individual desiring to shed his tribal identity. The preceding proposition may be attacked on the grounds that the poet is rejecting his maternal kin, who are neither his aqilah nor 'aṣabah. On the other hand, the scant historical data available indicates that al-Shanfarā's agnatic ties were slim. However, the words "banī ummī" may themselves be the very formula of divestiture: you are no longer related to me by blood but only by al-arḥam (wombs).

[51] 7 M. AL-SHAWKĀNĪ, *supra* note 22, at 321.
[52] IBN MANZŪR, *supra* note 23, at 'tq.
[53] 7 M. AL-SHAWKĀNĪ, *supra* note 22, at 33.

APPENDIX 1

Council of Ministers Regulations

Royal Decree No. 38 of 22/10/1377 (11/5/1958), as amended
by *Royal Decree No. 14 of 14/7/1384 (18/11/1964)* and *Royal
Order No. 3/6/3121 of 26/12/1378 (2/7/1959)*

Having entrusted myself to Allah,

I, Saʿud bn ʿAbdul ʿAziz Al Saʿud, King of the Kingdom of Saudi Arabia,

In view of the fact that the interests of the country require that the Council of
Ministers Regulations be re-examined in accordance with the contents of my
Decree No. 37 of 2 Ramadan 1377, and in the desire to establish responsibilities
and to determine authorities and in due regard for the state of advancement and
development of the country,
And pursuant to Council of Ministers Resolution No. 120 of 1377,

And in accordance with the proposal presented to me by the President of the
Council of Ministers,

Decree as follows:

General Provisions
1. These Regulations shall be called the "Council of Ministers Regulations".
2. The seat of the Council of Ministers is in Riyadh; however, its sessions may be
held in another area of the Kingdom.
3. Only a Saudi national may be a member of the Council of Ministers. No
person of ill repute or who has been convicted of a crime or misdemeanour against
religion or honor may be a member.
4. After these Regulations are issued, the members of the Council shall undertake
their duties only when they have taken the following oath:

> "I swear by Allah that I will be true to my religion, my King and my country
> and will not reveal any state secrets and will preserve its interests and
> regulations and will perform my duties with integrity, faithfulness and sincerity."

5. Membership of the Council may not be combined with any other government
post unless the President of the Council of Ministers considers that this is necessary.

6. During the term of his membership, no member of the Council of Ministers may, directly or through an intermediary or at public auction, purchase or lease any government property.

He may not sell or lease any of his property to the Government and may not engage in any commercial or financial activity or accept membership on the board of directors of any company.

7. The Council of Ministers is a body constituted by regulation headed by His Majesty the King and whose meetings shall be convened under the presidency of His Majesty or the Deputy-President of the Council of Ministers. Its resolutions shall be published finally after they have been approved by His Majesty the King.

8. Members of the Council shall be appointed and dismissed from their posts and their resignations accepted by royal order. All members of the Council shall be responsible to His Majesty the King for their acts.

9. A minister shall be deemed to be the immediate head and the final authority for the affairs of his ministry and shall exercise his functions in accordance with the provisions of these Regulations and the internal rules of his ministry.

10. Only another minister may deputize for a minister and this shall be pursuant to a royal order issued on the proposal of the President of the Council of Ministers.

Constitution of the Council

11. The Council of Ministers shall be composed of:

(a) The President of the Council of Ministers.

(b) The first Vice-President of the President of the Council of Ministers and the deputies of the President of the Council of Ministers who shall be appointed by royal order on the proposal of the President of the Council of Ministers.

(c) Ministers with portfolio who shall be appointed by royal order on the proposal of the President of the Council of Ministers.

(d) Ministers of State who shall be appointed by royal order as members of the Council of Ministers on the proposal of the President of the Council of Ministers.

(e) Advisers to His Majesty the King who shall be appointed by royal order as members of the Council of Ministers on the proposal of the President of the Council of Ministers.

12. Attendance of the Council of Ministers' meetings is a right personal to its members only and to the Secretary-General of the Council of Ministers. At the request of the President or any of the members and after the approval of the Council of Ministers, an official or an expert may be granted permission to attend the Council's sessions to present information or explanatory material in his possession, provided that the right to vote belongs exclusively to the members.

13. A meeting of the Council shall not be deemed duly convened unless two-thirds of its members are present, nor shall its resolutions be valid unless made by a majority of those present. In the event of an equality in votes, the President shall have the casting vote. In exceptional cases, a meeting of the Council shall be valid if attended by one-half of its members, but in such event its resolutions shall not be

valid unless approved by two-thirds of the members present. The President of the Council of Ministers shall determine such exceptional cases.

14. Except in the case of necessity, the Council shall not adopt a resolution on any matter concerning the activities of any ministry unless the minister or his deputy is present.

15. The deliberations of the Council shall be secret, but its resolutions are public with the exception of resolutions deemed secret by means of a resolution of the Council.

16. Members of the Council of Ministers shall be tried for any offences committed by them in the course of their official duties in accordance with special regulations which shall include a list of offences and define the procedures for charging and trial or [sic] the manner of constituting the tribunal.

17. The Council of Ministers may form committees from among its members or third parties to study a matter included in its agenda in order to present a special report thereon.

The internal rules of the Council shall state the number of committees and the manner of conducting their activities.

Authority of the Council of Ministers

18. The Council of Ministers shall prescribe the State's policy on domestic and foreign affairs, finance, the economy, education, defence, and all public affairs and shall supervise the implementation thereof. It is invested with regulatory authority, executive authority and administrative authority, is the final authority with regard to financial affairs and all matters connected with the various ministries of the State and other government departments and shall determine the measures to be taken in respect thereof. Treaties and international agreements shall not be deemed in force until approved by the Council. The Council of Ministers' resolutions shall be final except for those requiring the issuance of a royal order or decree in accordance with the provisions of these Regulations.

Regulatory Affairs

19. Regulations, treaties and international agreements and concessions shall not be issued except by royal decree prepared after approval of the Council of Ministers.

20. Regulations, treaties and international agreements or concessions may not be amended except in accordance with regulations to be issued under Article 19 of these Regulations.

21. The Council shall decide on draft regulations submitted to it, article by article, and then vote on them as a whole in accordance with the procedures set forth in the internal rules of the Council of Ministers.

22. Any minister has the right to propose to the Council draft regulations coming within the scope of his ministry's activities for the purpose of the Council's determination thereon, and the Council may approve or reject them. If the Council rejects a proposal it may not be resubmitted to it except in the case of necessity. Any member of the Council of Ministers also has the right to raise a matter which he considers would be of benefit for the Council to study.

23. If His Majesty the King does not approve a decree or order submitted to him for signature, it shall be returned to the Council for study together with the reasons for such action. If the decree or order is not returned by the Royal Office to the Council of Ministers within thirty days from the date of its receipt, the President of the Council shall take whatever measures he considers necessary and inform the Council to this effect.

24. All decrees shall be published in the Official Journal and shall be effective from the date of publication unless a deferment period is provided therein.

Executive Affairs

25. The Council in its capacity as the direct executive authority has full control over executive affairs and has original authority to take all measures it considers to be in the interest of the country. The following matters lie within its executive competence:

1. Control over the implementation of resolutions and regulations.
2. Creation and organization of public departments and offices and the appointment, dismissal, promotion and pensioning of department directors and officials occupying Grade 3 (presently Grade 11) and above.
3. The Council of Ministers may decide to establish committees of investigation to investigate the activities of ministries and public departments generally or with respect to a specific case. The investigation committees shall submit the results of their investigations to the Council within the time period prescribed therefor and the Council shall decide on the results of the investigation in accordance with regulations.

Administrative Affairs

26. The Council of Ministers is the direct authority for the administration of the country and has full control over all administrative matters. The various provinces throughout the Kingdom shall be administered in accordance with regulations promulgated therefor.

27. Municipal affairs shall be administered in accordance with special regulations entitled "Regulations for Municipalities" which shall define the categories and duties of municipalities, the formation of municipal councils and other matters related to the activities of municipalities.

Financial Affairs

28. The Council of Ministers is the authority for the financial affairs of State.

29. No taxes or duties may be imposed except by regulation.

30. Duties and taxes shall be levied in accordance with the provisions of the regulations, and no exemption therefrom may be made except in accordance with the regulations.

31. No State property may be sold, leased or disposed of except in accordance with regulations.

32. No monopoly, concession or right of exploitation of any of the country's resources may be granted except in accordance with special regulations and with due regard for the public interest.

33. The Government may not contract any loan except after the approval of the Council of Ministers and the issuance of a royal decree permitting the same.

34. No undertaking by the Government that would result in the payment of funds from the Public Treasury may be made except in accordance with the provisions of a duly approved budget. In the event of such undertaking not being covered by the items of the budget, it shall be made in accordance with special regulations permitting it.

35. All State revenues shall be delivered to the consolidated Public Treasury and recorded and disbursed in accordance with the procedures established by regulation.

36. No salary may be allocated, nor compensation granted nor sum expended from State funds except in accordance with regulations or by a resolution from the Council of Ministers.

37. The Council of Ministers shall annually approve regulations for the State's budget which shall include estimates of revenues and expenditures for such year and shall be submitted to His Majesty the King for his approval. The budget shall be approved at least one month before the commencement of the fiscal year. If the fiscal year has begun and compelling reasons have prevented approval of the budget, the previous year's budget in a one-twelfth ratio shall be operative until issuance of the new budget.

38. No increase to the budget shall be made except in accordance with regulations or by a resolution from the Council of Ministers.

39. The procedures for approving the budget shall be carried out in accordance with the principles established for the promulgation of regulations, and the budget shall be voted on by individual section.

40. The financial regulations currently in effect shall continue to be complied with until regulations amending the same are issued.

41. The General Audit Board shall audit the Government's accounts to verify the accuracy of entries of revenues and expenditures in accordance with the provisions of the regulations for such department.

42. The Ministry of Finance shall submit to the Council of Ministers the final accounts of the financial administration of the preceding year for the purpose of its approval during the first three months of the new fiscal year.

43. The budget and final accounts of departments not attached to any ministry shall be subject to the same provisions as the budget and final accounts of the State.

Presidency of the Council of Ministers

44. The President [of the Council] of Ministers shall direct the public policy of the State. He shall ensure the direction of and coordination and cooperation between the various ministries, and shall ensure continuity and uniformity in the activities of the Council of Ministers. He shall receive high directives from His Majesty the King for implementation. He shall sign the Council's resolutions and order the notification thereof to the various authorities. He shall supervise the

Council of Ministers, the ministries and public departments and shall see to the implementation of the regulations and resolutions issued by the Council of Ministers.

Administrative Organization of the Council of Ministers

45. The administrative organization of the Council of Ministers shall include the following branches:
    First, the Office of the Presidency of the Council of Ministers.
    Second, the General Secretariat of the Council of Ministers.
    Third, the Bureau of Experts.
The internal rules of the Council of Ministers shall set forth the organization and competence of these branches and the manner of their undertaking their activities.

46. The Board of Grievances and the General Audit Board shall be under the authority of the President of the Council of Ministers in accordance with their respective regulations.

Final Provisions

47. The Council of Ministers shall approve these Regulations and submit them to His Majesty the King for high approval. They shall be issued after signature by His Majesty the King and the President [of the Council] of Ministers.

48. After these Regulations become effective, the Council of Ministers shall commence drawing up the following regulations:

1. Internal rules for the Council of Ministers.
2. Internal rules for each ministry.
3. Regulations for the administration of the provinces.
4. Regulations for municipalities.
5. Regulations for the trial of ministers.
6. Regulations for the sale and leasing of State property.

49. These Regulations shall become effective as of the issuance and publication thereof in the Official Journal.

50. These Regulations repeal the Council of Ministers Regulations issued on 12 Rajab 1373 (March 17, 1954) and all other regulations and resolutions inconsistent with the provisions thereof and any other provision inconsistent therewith.

APPENDIX 2

Ministry of Commerce Model Agency or Distribution Agreement

On this day .... 14 ...... H corresponding to .... 19 ...... in the city of .... this

agreement has been concluded between: (1) .... whose seat (or principal place of business) is at

....

Commercial Registration No. .... dated ....
city of ....
and represented herein by ....
(the First Party / Principal)

(2) ....
whose seat (or principal place of business) is at

....

Commercial Registration No. .... dated ....
city of ....
and represented herein by ....
(the Second Party / Agent)

Preamble

WHEREAS both Parties desire to establish a relationship to serve their common interests and to define the rights and obligations of each party towards the other, and

WHEREAS the Second Party (Saudi) desires that such relationship be in accordance with the requirements of the regulations relating to foreign commerce (import and export) and principally the Commercial Agencies Regulations and the amendments thereto in the Kingdom of Saudi Arabia, which require a direct relationship between the commercial agent or distributor and the producer company in its country, and nonSaudi nationals are prohibited from engaging in import and export activities and commercial agencies in the Kingdom of Saudi Arabia.

Now THEREFORE both parties hereby agree as follows:

General provisions

Article 1. The above preamble shall be deemed to be an integral part of this Agreement.

Article 2. The parties agree that the Second Party as Agent/Distributor for the First Party in the Kingdom of Saudi Arabia shall enter into contracts relating to the products or services subject of this Agreement in the name of .... and for the account of ....

Article 3. The subject of this Agency Agreement shall be the products and services provided by the First Party as set forth below:
....
....
....
The type of products covered by this Agency or Distribution Agreement is:...........
....

Article 4. The territory covered by this Agreement is ....
....
(specify whether it covers the whole of the Kingdom of Saudi Arabia or a specific region therein).

Article 5. The term of this Agreement shall be ....
commencing as of .... renewable automatically unless either party notifies the other in writing of its intention not to renew it at least three months prior to the end of the term.

Basic mutual obligations

Article 6. Whereas the Second Party (Saudi) is obliged by regulation towards the consumer to guarantee the quality of all the materials and products subject of this Agreement and to provide maintenance and spare parts at reasonable prices when requested by consumers, the First Party (Principal) shall also be bound vis-à-vis the Agent or Distributor by the same obligations in accordance with the quantities and dates as may be specified by the Agent or Distributor. The First Party (Principal) shall provide the Second Party (Saudi) with spare parts and necessary maintenance at reasonable prices throughout the term of the agency and for one year following the end date thereof or the date of appointment of another agent.

Article 7. Whereas the Second Party (Saudi) is responsible by regulation to the local consumer to ensure that products and materials which are the subject of this Agreement conform to approved standard specifications in the Kingdom of Saudi Arabia, the First Party (Principal) shall guarantee the quality of such products and materials and their conformity with the approved standard specifications in the Kingdom. The Agent or Distributor shall not be responsible for the acceptance or distribution of any quantity received from the First Party (Principal) which is contrary to the required standard specifications.

Article 8. The parties shall perform this Agreement in accordance with the provisions hereof and in conformity with the principles of commercial custom and good faith. Such obligation shall include that which is considered to be part of contractual requirements in accordance with commercial practice.

Particular obligations

Article 9. The Second Party (Saudi) shall be obligated as follows:

(a) to provide the premises in which it shall undertake agency activities in the Kingdom and to carry on its activity with its own staff, with the care of a prudent man. It shall have the right to make use of the services and technical expertise of the First Party when business conditions so require.

(b) to carry out all activities required to perform the Agreement locally for the introduction, promotion and marketing of the goods, furnish suitable storage facilities, open distribution centres as may be necessary and provide local services within the territory covered by the Agreement. It shall have the right to make use of the expertise and capabilities of the First Party. The Second Party shall in the performance of this Agreement have the right to use the First Party's trademark without any additions or modifications and shall endeavor to make the same known in the markets.

Article 10. The First Party shall be obligated as follows:

(a) to pay the Second Party a commission in the amount of .... of the value of the items sold within the Agreement territory even if the sale is made directly to a third party by the First Party. Payment schedules shall be as follows:

....

(b) on its part to perform the Agreement with the care of a prudent man whether with regard to maintaining the quality of the products and materials subject of the Agreement, ensuring safe delivery thereof in good condition to the Second Party, fulfilling the obligation to provide maintenance services and spare parts or fulfilling the obligation regarding quantities and dates specified in the Second Party's orders.

(c) to bear responsibility for its personal faults and the faults of its employees if the Second Party is injured as a result thereof.

Expiry and termination of the Agreement and compensation

Article 11. This Agreement shall end upon the impossibility of performance by, or the death, loss of capacity, or declaration of bankruptcy of either party. This Agreement may also be terminated by reason of a substantial failure in performance by the other party.

Article 12. The Commercial Agent or Distributor shall have the right to claim compensation for any damages that it has sustained as a result of the Principal's breach of its obligations under the Agreement or in accordance with commercial custom.

Article 13. If the Principal refuses to renew or continue to perform under the Agreement, the Commercial Agent or Distributor may claim appropriate compensation for any activity it has undertaken that in fact has resulted in evident success in the activities, promotion and generation and development of customers of the agency or distributorship if the same results in benefit to a new agent or distributor from the preceding activity.

Article 14. The principal may claim compensation from the Agent for any damages sustained by it in the event of the Agent's abandonment of its agency at an inappropriate time or its breach of the provisions of the Agency Agreement.

Article 15. If this Agreement ends or is terminated at an inappropriate time and as a result thereof either party sustains loss, the party having caused the damage shall be obliged to compensate the injured party for the loss sustained, taking into account the extent of effort expended and the material and nonmaterial resources provided to serve the Agency prior to the termination thereof.

Concluding provisions

Article 16. Disputes arising out of the performance of this Agreement shall be settled amicably between the parties. If this is not possible the matter shall be referred to the Commission for the Settlement of Commercial Disputes in the Kingdom of Saudi Arabia having jurisdiction or to a local arbitration committee in accordance with the Arbitration Regulations. In the event of a dispute between the Principal and the Agent, an Agency Agreement with a new agent may not be registered in the agency territory for the same products or services until a final decision or award has been issued by the authority hearing the dispute between the parties.

Article 17. This Agreement shall be governed by the provisions of the regulations in effect in the Kingdom of Saudi Arabia, in particular the Commercial Court Regulations, the Commercial Agencies Regulations and the amendments thereto and implementing rules thereof and the Arbitration Regulations and the implementing rules thereof.

Article 18. This Agreement is made in three counterparts of which each party retains one counterpart. The Second Party shall present an authenticated copy for the completion of the procedures for the Agreement in the Commercial Agencies and Distributors Register at the Ministry of Commerce in the Kingdom of Saudi Arabia.

First Party (Principal)

Name ....

Signature ....

Second Party (Agent)

Name ....

Signature ....

APPENDIX 3

Council of Ministers Resolution No. 124 of 29/5/1403 H

I. All nonSaudi contractors shall assign to Saudi contractors not less than 30 percent of the works of their contracts.

II. All contractors shall purchase the tools and equipment required to execute their contracts from Saudi agents for such machinery and equipment in the Kingdom. They may not directly import the same from abroad, except their own used machinery and equipment.

III. Contractors shall procure the following services from local Saudi enterprises:
1. Goods and persons transport services inside the Kingdom, unless the contractor provides such services directly with its own equipment and personnel;
2. Local insurance services;
3. Banking services;
4. Land and buildings leasing and purchase services;
5. Livelihood and foodstuffs supply services.

IV. The responsible government authorities shall ensure that the rules provided in paragraphs I, II, and III of this Resolution are applied in contracts signed with foreign contractors. They shall cooperate by all possible means to execute such rules, when entering into or performing a contract.

APPENDIX 4

Kingdom of Saudi Arabia
Ministry of Commerce

Commercial Registration Certificate (Company)

No. : ....

Date: ....

Company's business name: ....

Kind: .... Nationality: .... Duration of Company: ....

Head Office: ....

Post Office Box: .... Postal Code: .... Telephone: ....

Activity: ....
....
....

Capital—authorized: .... Paid-in: ....

Number of Shares or
Shares of Stock: ....

Value of a Share of Stock
or Share: ....

Managers.   1 ....   2 ....
           3 ....   4 ....
           5 ....   6 ....

Members of the Board of Directors:
           1 ....   2 ....
           3 ....   4 ....
           5 ....   6 ....

The Commercial Register Office in the city of .... witnesses that
the abovementioned company was registered in the Register of the city
of..........................

Seal   Director of the Commercial Register   Name: ....

                                                Signature: ....

APPENDIX 5

Labelling of Prepackaged Foods

Kingdom of Saudi Arabia
Saudi Arabian Standards Organization
P.O. Box 3437, Riyadh

This Saudi Mandatory Standard is issued in accordance with the Rules of the Royal Decree M/10 of 1392 H

SASO Board of Directors has agreed to amend this standard by adding items No. 3/7, and No. 4/1/5.

Date of SASO–Board of Directors' approval:	1393H (18/12/1973)
Date of Publication in the Official Gazette:	1394H (22/2/1974)
Date of enforcement of this standard:	1394H (19/8/1974)
Date of enforcement of item 4/8:	1396H (31/1/1976)
Date of enforcement of item 3/7:	1400H (14/1/1980)
Date of enforcement of item 4/1/5:	1399H (16/11/1979)

"The Arabic text is the official text having the legal force"

LABELLING OF PREPACKAGED FOODS

1—SCOPE

This standard is concerned with the labels of all prepackaged foods, imported or locally produced. Requirements of this standard shall be in addition to any other requirements related to labels or labelling which might be prescribed by Saudi Standards for specific foods.

2—DEFINITIONS

2/1 Label: Any statement, brand, mark, pictorial or other descriptive matter, photographed, written, printed, impressed on or attached to a container of food.

2/2 Labelling: Includes the label and any written, printed or graphic matter relating to and accompanying the food.

2/3 Container: Any form of packaging of food for sale as a single item, including the wrappers.

2/4 Prepackaged: Packaged in a container ready for retail sale.

2/5 Ingredient: Any substance, including food additives, used in the manufacture or preparation of a food and is present in the final product.

2/6 Component: Any substance which forms part of an "ingredient".

3—GENERAL PRINCIPLES

3/1 The information required to appear on the label of the prepackaged food shall be clear, prominent and readily legible by the consumer under normal conditions of purchase and use. It shall be presented in a color distinguishable from that of the background. The letters in the name of the food shall be of a size reasonably related to the most prominent printed matter on the label. No information shall be obscured by any other written, printed or graphic matter.

3/2 The labels shall provide the consumer with sufficient information about the contents of the container. Where the container is covered by a wrapper, the wrapper shall carry the necessary information, or the label on the container shall be readily legible through the outer wrapper and not obscured by it. In general, the items from 4/1 to 4/8 shall appear on the label normally intended to be presented to the consumer at the time of sale.

3/3 Prepackaged food shall not be described or presented on any label or in any labelling in a manner that is deceptive, misleading or false, or is likely to create an erroneous impression regarding its nature or character in any respect.

3/4 Prepackaged food shall not be described or presented on any label, or in labelling by words, or any manner that is suggestive, either directly or indirectly, of any other food product, or leads to confusion with any other food products.

When the product is artificial, the word "Artificial" shall be written in a clearly visible place on the container.

3/5 When the product contains any animal fats or meat or their products, the kind of animal from which it is taken shall be declared, or a statement such as (free from swine products) shall be printed, or a certificate stating that it is free from swine products should accompany it.

3/6 If another Saudi Standard calls for special requirement for certain foods, such requirement shall also be declared on the label.

3/7 The information on the container shall be indelibly written, illustrated, stuck or impressed so as not to be affected under normal conditions.

4—LABELLING REQUIREMENTS

The labels of all prepackaged foods shall bear the following information.

4/1 The name of the prepackaged food:

4/1/1 The name shall indicate the true nature of the food and preferably be specific and not generic.

4/1/2 Where a name or names for a locally produced food have been established in a Saudi Standard, at least one of these names shall be used. In case of imported foods, the name indicated in the International Standards shall be used. In other cases the common or usual name shall be used, if one exists.

4/1/3 Where no common name exists, an appropriate descriptive name may be used.

4/1/4 A "coined" or "fanciful" name, however, may be used provided it is not misleading and is accompanied by an appropriately descriptive term.

4/1/5 Names and phrases provocative to Islamic religious feelings such as "Made of pork flesh or its derivatives", "Alcoholic beverages" or any doctrinally forbidden symbols and marks in Islamic countries such as the sign of the Cross . . . etc., shall not be used.

4/2 List of Ingredients:

4/2/1 A complete list of ingredients shall be declared on the label in descending order of proportion (without any obligation to declare the proportions) except:

4/2/1/1 As otherwise provided in a Saudi Standard.

4/2/1/2 In the case of dehydrated foods which are intended to be reconstituted by the addition of water, the ingredients may be listed in descending order of proportion in the reconstituted product provided that the list of ingredients is headed by the words "Ingredients when reconstituted".

4/2/1/3 In the case of foods in respect of which the Saudi Legislation does not require a complete declaration of ingredients, provided that:
   a) Such exemptions have been granted because the food is of well known composition, and
   b) The absence of a declaration of ingredients is not prejudicial to the consumer, and
   c) The information provided on the label enables the consumer to understand the nature of the food.

4/2/2 Where an ingredient of a food has more than one component, the names of the components shall be included in the list of ingredients, except where such an ingredient is a food for which a Saudi Standard has been established and such standard does not require a complete list of ingredients.

4/2/3 Where water is added, it shall be declared in the list of ingredients if such a declaration would result in a better understanding of the product's composition. Exceptions to this obligation are when the water forms part of an ingredient such as brine, syrup, broth or any other ingredient used in a compound food.

4/2/4 If the food contains additives permitted for use according to Saudi or International Standards and Legislation such as preservatives, bleaching agents, flavoring agents, coloring matters, artificial sweeteners, maturing agents, stabilizers, thickening agents, antioxidants, antibiotics, anticaking agents, vegetable gums, spices, herbs or starches (except modified starches), titles of such additives shall be declared on the label.

4/3 Net Contents:

360

4/3/1 The net contents shall be declared in metric (SI) units in the following manner:

4/3/1/1 For liquid foods, by volume.

4/3/1/2 For solid foods, by mass except that when such foods are usually sold by number, a declaration by count shall be made.

4/3/1/3 For semi-solid or viscous foods, either by mass or volume.

4/3/2 Foods packed in a liquid medium normally discarded before consumption shall carry a declaration of the drained mass of the food.

4/4 Name, Address and Date:
The name and address of the manufacturer, packer or importer of the food as well as the date of production and its code number shall be declared.

4/5 Country of Origin:

4/5/1 The country of origin of the food shall be declared.

4/5/2 When a food undergoes processing in another country which changes its nature, the country in which the last stages of processing are performed shall be considered to be the country of origin for the purposes of labelling.

4/6 Additional Requirements for Specific Foods:
When foods are prepared to be used for special purposes such as certain diets, or are described as containing vitamins, minerals or any other materials, the necessary information indicating conformity with such descriptions shall be declared on the label.

Foods which have been treated with ionizing radiation shall be so designated, and the dose clearly stated.

4/7 Additional Labelling:
Any information or pictorial device may be displayed in labelling provided that it is not in conflict with what has been indicated in this Standard. The quality grade of the prepackaged food shall be declared (if any exists).

4/8 Language:
The Arabic language shall be one of the languages used for the declaration on any label or in any labelling of the foods as for the following items:

4/8/1 The name of the prepackaged food (accompanied with the declaration "artificial" if it is so).

4/8/2 Net contents.

4/8/3 List of ingredients.

REFERENCES

—Saudi Standards for foodstuffs issued by the Ministry of Health in accordance with the Ministerial Decree, dated 25/1/1385 H, (Page 56).

—Circular of the Ministry of Commerce and Industry (Standards and Metrology Department) concerning labels of prepackaged foods.

—ASMO final project on labels of prepackaged and canned foodstuffs.

—Preliminary project on labels of prepackaged foodstuffs prepared by the Joint Committee of the Research and Industrial Development Centre and the Ministry of Commerce and Industry.

—Recommended International General Standard for the Labelling of Prepackaged Foods, Codex Alimentarius Commission,
Joint FAO/WHO Food Standards Programme, CAC/RS 1-1969.
—Code of Federal Regulations, 1972.
Food and Drugs, 21 (Parts 1 to 119),
U.S. Government Printing Office, Washington, U.S.A.

APPENDIX 6

Regulations for Combating Bribery and Explanatory Memorandum

The Royal Will has been promulgated approving Council of Ministers Resolution No. 144 of 29/2/1382 H (1/8/1962) by Royal Decrees Nos. 15 and 16 of 7/3/1382 H (8/8/1962)

Royal Decree No. 15 of 7/3/1382 H, as amended by *Royal Decrees No. M/51 of 17/7/1402 H and No. M/35 of 13/10/1388 H*

With the help of God Almighty,

We, Saʿud bn ʿAbdul ʿAziz Al Saʿud,
King of the Kingdom of Saudi Arabia,

Having reviewed Articles 19 and 20 of the Council of Ministers Regulations issued by Royal Decrees No. 38 of 22/10/1377 H,
And pursuant to Council of Ministers Resolution No. 144 of 29/2/1382 H,
And pursuant to the proposal submitted to us by the President of the Council of Ministers,
Decree as follows:

First—We approve the Regulations for Combating Bribery in the attached form.

Second—These Regulations shall repeal all inconsistent prior regulations.

Third—The President of the Council of Ministers and the ministers, each within his own authority, shall implement this Decree of ours.

Royal Signature

Royal Decree No. 16 of 7/3/1382 H

With the help of God Almighty,

We, Sa'ud bn 'Abdul 'Aziz Al Sa'ud,
King of the Kingdom of Saudi Arabia,

Having reviewed Articles 19 and 20 of the Council of Ministers Regulations issued by Royal Decrees No. 38 of 22/10/1377 H,
And pursuant to Council of Ministers Resolution No. 144 of 29/2/1382 H,
And pursuant to the proposal submitted to us by the President of the Council of Ministers,
Decree as follows:

First—The President of the Council of Ministers shall, as required in the public interest make public officials accountable for the sources of their wealth, the wealth of their minor or major children who have no known income and the wealth of their wives. For the accountability of officials the Council shall form a three-member commission composed of the president of the General Audit Board as chairman and two investigators from the Board of Grievances as members. This commission may in performing its duties seek the help of any government accounting experts or other persons as desired.

Second—If a public official fails to prove a lawful source for his property or the property of the persons mentioned in the preceding article so as to give rise to doubt that the acquisition of such property was by means of bribery or gifts or the exploitation of national influence, the Council of Ministers shall—on the recommendation of the commission referred to in the preceding article—confiscate half of such property whose source is suspect and rule that he be dismissed from his government office.

Third—The provisions of these Regulations shall not bar criminal proceedings if the conditions therefor are present.

Fourth—The President of the Council of Ministers and our ministers—each within his own authority—shall execute this Decree of ours from the date of its publication.

Royal Signature

Council of Ministers Resolution No. 144 of 29/2/1382 H

The Council of Ministers,
Having reviewed the Draft Regulations for Combating Bribery and,
Having reviewed the Explanatory Memorandum to the Draft Regulations for Combating Bribery and,
Having reviewed the draft Royal Decree requiring that public officials be questioned and made to account for the source of their wealth, whose legality is suspect, and the wealth of their minor or major children, who have no known income, and the wealth of their wives, and on the recommendation of the Regulations Committee No. 34 of 17/2/1382 H resolves as follows:

1. To approve the Draft Regulations for Combating Bribery in the attached form.

2. A draft Royal Decree to this effect has been drawn up, a copy of which is attached.

3. To approve the Explanatory Memorandum to the Regulations for Combating Bribery in the attached form.

4. To approve the draft Royal Decree attached hereto requiring that public officials be questioned and made to account for their sources of wealth, whose legality is suspect, and the wealth of their minor or major children, who have no known income, and the wealth of their wives.

5. To establish an investigatory authority connected to the President of the Council of Ministers, with the basic function of investigating public officials and finding out the truth in respect of any suspicions surrounding them so that the State is able to prosecute them and impose on them the punishments provided for by the regulations.

6. To launch vigorous campaigns through the ministries and the various departments in order to warn against the effects and consequences of bribery, the religious judgment thereon and the damage resulting from it to individuals and society as a whole. Included in this activity shall be notices posted in government departments censuring those persons who offer or accept a bribe, stating that the public official is in the public service and making public the penalties that await those offering or accepting bribes.

7. A public official who is made to account for the source of his wealth and whose innocence is proved shall have such vindication made public.

Regulations for Combating Bribery

Article 1. Any public official who, for himself or third parties, seeks, accepts or receives a promise or gift to perform any act of his office or an act he claims is an act thereof, even if such act is lawful, shall be considered to accept a bribe and shall be punished with imprisonment for a term of one to five years and a fine of five thousand to one hundred thousand riyals or with either of such penalties. A public official's intention not to undertake the act which he promised to do shall have no effect on the commission of the crime.

Article 2. Any public official who, for himself or a third party, seeks, accepts or receives a promise or gift to fail to perform any act of his office or an act he claims is an act thereof, even if such failure to perform is lawful, shall be considered to accept a bribe and shall be liable for the penalties provided in Article 1 of these Regulations. The public official's intention not to undertake the act which he promised to do shall have no effect on the commission of the crime.

Article 3. Any public official who, for himself or a third party, seeks, accepts or receives a promise or gift to violate the duties of his office or in recompense for an act, even if without prior agreement, shall be considered to accept a bribe and shall be punished by the penalties provided in Article 1 of these Regulations.

Article 4. Any public official who violates the duties of his office by taking or failing to take any action of such office as a result of an expectation, recommendation or mediation shall likewise be considered to accept a bribe and shall be punished by imprisonment for a term not to exceed one year or (sic) a fine of not more than ten thousand riyals or by either of these penalties.

Article 5. Any public official who, for himself or a third party, seeks, accepts or receives a promise or gift to use actual or alleged influence to obtain or attempt to obtain from any public authority any acts, orders, decisions, obligations, licence or supply agreement or any office, service or advantage of any kind shall likewise be considered to accept a bribe and shall be punished by the fine provided in Article 1 of these Regulations.

Article 6. A briber, intermediary and any participant in any of the aforementioned crimes shall be punished by the penalty provided in the Article under which the crime is committed. Any person who agrees to, incites or aids in the commission of the crime with knowledge thereof at the time of commission of the crime pursuant to such agreement, inciting or aiding, shall be considered to be a participant in the crime.

Article 7. Any person who employs force, violence or threats against a public official to obtain his performance of an unlawful act or his failure to perform any act for which he is responsible by regulation shall be punished by the penalties set forth in Article 1 of these Regulations.

Article 8. Any person who offers a bribe which is not accepted or who employs force, violence or threats without attaining his purpose shall be punished by imprisonment for a term of six months to thirty months or (sic) a fine of two thousand five hundred riyals to fifty thousand riyals or with either of these two penalties.

Article 9. In applying the provisions of these Regulations, the following persons shall be deemed public officials:

(a) Servants or employees of the Government, government departments or public bodies, whether they be appointed permanently or temporarily;
(b) Arbitrators or experts appointed by the Government or a commission with judicial jurisdiction;
(c) Medical practitioners or midwives with regard to the certificates made out by them, even if they are not public officials;
(d) Any person entrusted with a task of a government committee or any other administrative authority;
(e) Officials of corporations or companies performing an obligation in public facilities.

Article 10. Any person designated by a person bribed or a briber to receive a gift or benefit who accepts it with knowledge thereof shall be punished by imprisonment for a term of one to six months and a fine of one thousand to five thousand riyals or with either of these penalties, provided that he has not acted as an intermediary in the bribe.

Article 11. In the application of these Regulations, any benefit or privilege which a bribed person may obtain, whatever the kind or designation of such privilege or benefit and whether it be material or nonmaterial, shall be deemed a promise or gift.

Article 12. A conviction of any crime provided in these Regulations shall definitively and by force of law result in dismissal from office and the barring of the convicted person from holding public office and from participating in public tenders or auctions, supplying or public works contracts made by the Government or local public authorities, even if this is by means of tender or direct agreement. The Council of Ministers may review the incidental punishment after five years have elapsed from the sentence of the principal punishment.

Article 13. In all cases, the property, privilege or benefit subject of the crime shall be confiscated where feasible.

Article 14. A briber or intermediary shall be exempt from punishment if he informs the authorities of the crime before the discovery thereof.

Article 15. Any person who provides information concerning any crime provided in these Regulations and whose information leads to the proof of the crime and who is not a briber, participant or intermediary, shall be granted a reward of not less than five thousand riyals and not more than half the property confiscated. If such property is less than the minimum reward, the Treasury shall bear the difference or the entire amount if there was no confiscation. The reward shall be estimated by the Commission which tries the crime in accordance with Article 17 (repealed).

Article 16. If the integrity of a public official and his resistance to the inducements of interested parties is proved by a material fact, the Council of Ministers shall encourage him by financial reward. The Council may exceptionally promote him to an office of a higher grade which he is competent to hold if the aforementioned material fact is repeated.

Explanatory Memorandum to the Regulations for Combating Bribery

The protection of the government administration from corruption requires the investigation of public officials who misuse their position or trade on its influence, whether such exploitation is a result of a promise or threat and whether such influence is real or alleged, in order to ensure the integrity of the government administration and to safeguard public departments under the control of public officials. The sharīʿah has combated the temptation of exploiting the influence of public office and deriving unlawful benefit therefrom and has forbidden the same and subjected its perpetrator(s) to the severest religious and earthly penalties. . . .*

All heavenly and positive legislation has likewise prohibited this crime and all the ways in which it can be committed have been pursued. Royal Decree No. 43 of 29 Dhu Al-Qa'da 1377 H has provided for the punishment of public officials who accept gifts and gratuities and the like from interested parties for the purpose of inducement. The said Decree has prohibited the acceptance of a bribe, the acceptance thereof on behalf of third parties, or the seeking thereof, but it has not defined what is deemed to be a bribe, nor has it pursued all the forms where practical experience shows a punishment is required. For this purpose, the State has issued the attached Regulations in order to confront the various forms of bribery and exploitation of influence and to combat this heinous crime in all its aspects, to facilitate its detection and to reward persons offering information about it. Article 1 of these Regulations provides for the punishment of a public official who seeks a gift whether for himself or a third party and prohibits the acceptance or receipt thereof or the acceptance of a promise thereof if it is to perform any act of public office or any duty which the public official claims to be within the competence of his office. The punishment of a public official in this Article extends to an advance bribe and the promise thereof, that is, even if the execution is deferred, whether the public official has performed or not performed the act, whether or not he intends to carry out the promised act, whether or not the act is a right and whether or not the briber is serious regarding his promise.

Article 2 provides for punishment in the various forms above if a bribe is sought or received or a promise is made to fail to perform any duty or alleged act of public office. Article 3 punishes the exploitation of a public office even if this is without prior agreement between the briber and the person bribed, that is, the subsequent acceptance of a bribe for the performance of, or failure to perform, an act or the general violation of the duties of public office. Article 4 includes punishment for violation of the duties of a public office if this is the result of an expectation, recommendation or mediation. It is clear that there can be no punishment in such a case unless there has been an actual violation of the duties of public office. Article 5 prohibits the use of real or alleged influence and any approach being made to public authorities to obtain benefits or to achieve purposes that do not lie within the scope of the duties of office or activity of the person making the approach.

The preceding Articles address the punishment of a person receiving a bribe. Article 6 provides for the punishment of a briber, intermediary or participant by the same penalty for any act in which any such persons are involved. The Article defines a person considered to be a participant. In view of the fact that the purpose of the briber resembles the purpose of the person who uses coercion or threats against a public official, Article 7 provides for the punishment of a person employing force, violence or threats to obtain from him the performance of, or to

---

* In order to avoid the risk of a translation of verses of the Qur'ān or traditions of the Prophet, inaccurately expressing the meaning thereof, it was decided to omit such translations from this work.

cause him to fail to perform, any act with which he is charged by regulation. Article 8 punishes a person who offers a bribe which is not accepted or a person who employs force, violence or threats but whose object is not attained.

Article 9 states which persons shall be considered public officials in the application of the provisions of these Regulations in the sense that, if they commit any of the acts which are forbidden thereunder, they shall be punished by the penalties provided. As further clarification, public facilities shall include departments having independent funds, and the like, and public bodies shall include Chambers of Commerce, the Saudi Arabian Monetary Agency, and the like. Because the person bribed may seek a bribe on behalf of a third party, such as, for example, his son or his wife, or the briber himself may select the beneficiary and the person designated by the person bribed, or the briber may accept that bribe, Article 10 provides for the punishment of such person when he has knowledge of the reason for which the briber has offered the gift or benefit. However, his punishment shall be lighter than that of the person bribed or the briber if the person designated by the person bribed or the briber was not an intermediary in the bribe. Such act on the part of the beneficiary shall be considered to be an independent punishable crime when committed by him in any of the three following forms:

First—if the public official bribed has designated him to receive the bribe.

Second—if he receives the gift or benefit without being designated by the person bribed but the latter knows this and agrees thereto.

Third—if he takes or receives the bribe and the public official who is the object of the bribe is ignorant of such fact or has knowledge thereof but does not consent thereto, as in the case when a briber offers a gift or present to the public official's son or wife without prior agreement with the public official, and the son or wife accepts the gift knowing the reason for which the gift was offered, and neither of them informs the public official, or he is informed and does not consent thereto.

Article 11 explains what may be considered to be a promise or gift. The form or name which the gift, promise or benefit may take is of no consequence, since the briber may seek to conceal the purpose of the bribe by offering the item in the form of a gift, or the two parties, in order to conceal the signs of the crime, may resort to depicting the bribe as a contract. Examples of this are when the briber sells the bribed person a house worth thirty thousand riyals for the sum of fifteen thousand riyals or the briber buys from the person bribed a house worth twenty thousand riyals for thirty thousand riyals or when the bribe is concealed in the form of a lease of a house. Article 12 provides that a conviction of any of the crimes provided in these Regulations shall definitively and by force of law result in the imposition of an incidental punishment on the offender even if it is not provided for in the judgment issued. Article 13 requires the judgment to provide for confiscation even though Article 12 has made no provision for this, so that the Commission which pronounces judgment shall be empowered to grant exemption from confiscation in accordance with the provisions of Article 14. Article 14 contains a provision exempting a briber or intermediary from punishment if he informs the authorities of the crime inasmuch as bribery crimes normally take place in secrecy and practical life does not provide satisfactory evidence that such crimes have been committed except in cases of *flagrante delicto,* and exemption from punishment in such a case helps to establish evidence of the crime. For this reason, the Regulations in relation to exemption treat in the same manner notification of the crime before it is discovered and the confession to it by the briber or intermediary, even if this occurs after it has been notified, because the discovery of the crime is a matter different from proving it, and the Regulations seek to establish evidence of the commission of the crime. For the same objective at which the Regulations aim in Article 14, Article 15 provides for the granting of a reward to anyone who provides information about any of the crimes set forth in the Regulations if such disclosure leads to proof of the crime. Article 16 imposes on the Council of Ministers the necessity of encouraging public officials if their integrity and resistance to inducement is proved. Article 17 sets out the authority which shall be entrusted with the investigation of the crimes committed in violation of the provisions of these Regulations and also the authority which shall be responsible for issuing judgment thereon.**

** Article 17 was repealed by Royal Decree No. M/51 (17/7/1402).

APPENDIX 7

Director-General of the
Department of Zakāt and Income Tax
Circular No. 788/1 of 5/2/1404 H

Re: Taxability of supply operations connected with delivery inside the Kingdom

Ref: 778/1

Kingdom of Saudi Arabia
Ministry of Finance and National Economy
Department of Zakāt and Income Tax

Circular to all Departments and Branches of the DZIT, Experts and Advisors

Enclosed is a copy of the letter of H.E. the Minister of Finance and National Economy No. 4/195 of 20/1/1404 H in reply to the Department's Letter No. 616/1 of 19/11/1403 H replying to H.E. the Minister's letter No. 4/2928 of 24/10/1401 H with respect to the tax treatment of contracts covering supply, delivery, training, maintenance and operation and providing for non-taxability of contracts for supply and delivery FOB or CIF loading port or port of arrival.

H.E. indicated that the operation of delivery connected with supply is considered in fact as carrying on commercial activity as long as delivery is made inside the cities of the Kingdom. Consequently, the operation of supply connected with delivery inside the cities of the Kingdom is subject to Saudi tax.

Kindly implement and comply with the preceding exactly.

APPENDIX 8
Final Tax Return No. 2 (For Foreign Companies only)

<table>
<tr><td>Kingdom of Saudi Arabia
Ministry of Finance and
  National Economy
Department of Zakāt &
  Income Tax
General Admininstration

File No.:</td><td colspan="2">In the Name of God

Income tax return
per Royal Decree
No. 3321 as amended</td><td>For the fiscal Period

Starting: ....

Ending: ....</td></tr>
</table>

NOTICE	1. All inquiries below are to be answered carefully. 2. All the spaces are to be completed in respect of the schedules & attachments with any important explanations enclosed.

Name:.. Nationality:...................................

Address:..................................... P.O. Box: ....

Legal status .... Type of activity: .... Tel: ....

Currency used:............................. Exchange rate:...................... per one SR:.......

Accounting method adopted: ....Cash ☐ Accrual ☐

Questions to be answered carefully and accurately.

1	Has the accounting method been changed from the previous year? (If yes, attach an explanation.)		Yes ☐ No ☐
2	Is inventory taken at the end of the period in the presence of a certified accountant?		Yes ☐ No ☐
3	Does the company record all transactions in respect of the following:		
	a	Revenues & sources thereof (analyses and explanations to be enclosed)	Yes ☐ No ☐
	b	Reserves	Yes ☐ No ☐
	c	General journal & sub-ledger books	Yes ☐ No ☐
	d	Year end adjustments	Yes ☐ No ☐
	e	Inventory	Yes ☐ No ☐
	f	Final trial balance	Yes ☐ No ☐
	g	General Ledger	Yes ☐ No ☐
4	Does the company keep the following books & records in the Kingdom of Saudi Arabia:		
	a	General journal	Yes ☐ No ☐
	b	Inventory book	Yes ☐ No ☐
	▮	General ledger & subsidiary books	Yes ☐ No ☐
	d	Cash payments journal	Yes ☐ No ☐
	e	Cash receipts journal	Yes ☐ No ☐
NOTE	If the company does not keep books & records in the Kingdom of Saudi Arabia, an explanation must be provided.		

Schedule No. (1): Income

A	Total Income			
Deduct	1. Opening inventory			
	2. Purchases from outside (the Kingdom)			
	3. Local purchases			
	4. Customs duties			
	5. Freight charges			
	6. Direct wages			
	7. Direct expenses (Attachment no.)			
	8. Sub-Contractors (Attachment no.)			
	9. Agent's commission			
	10. Other expenses (Attachment no.)			
	11. Total			
	12. Less closing inventory			
13.	Cost of sales			
14.	Gross Profit			
B	Deduct administrative and general expenses			
1.	Depreciation (Attachment no.)			
2.	Salaries and wages			
3.	Living expenses			
4.	Social insurance			
5.	Insurance (Attachment no.)			
6.	Travel expense			
7.	Repairs & maintenance			
8.	Bank charges (Attachment no.)			
9.	Head office expenses (Attachment no.)			
10.	Engineering consultancy (Attachment no.)			
11.	Termination indemnities			
12.	Professional fees			
13.	Equipment rental (Attachment no.)			
14.	Rent			
15.	Contributions & donations (Attachment no.)			
16.	Fuel			
17.	Post, telegram & telephone			
18.	Telex			
19.	Other (Attachment no.)			
20.	Total expenses			
21.	Net book profit			

Schedule No (2): Adjustments to book profit

1.	Net book profit			
2.	Add			
3.	Depreciation differences			
4.	Head office administrative expenses			
5.	Social insurance paid abroad			
6.	Employees' share of social insurance (5%)			
7.	Termination indemnity provision			
8.	Other provisions			
9.	Prior years' losses			
10.	Saudi income taxes			
11.	Disallowed agent's commission			
12.	Other			
13.	Total additions			
14.	Net profit subject to Saudi income tax			

Schedule No. (3): Calculation of income tax

1.	First Bracket – From SR 1 to SR 100,000	at 25%		
2.	Second Bracket – From SR 100,001 to SR 500,000	at 35%		
3.	Third Bracket – From SR 500,001 to SR 1,000,000	at 40%		
4.	Fourth Bracket – More than SR 1 million	at 45%		
5.	Total income tax due for the company			
Deduct	a	Paid as per Receipt #	on		
	b	Paid as per Receipt #	on		
	c	Paid as per Receipt #	on		
6.	Total payments			
7.	Difference to be paid or (reimbursed)	D		

Schedule No. (4): Other amounts payable

1.	Taxes on sub-contractors	(Attachment no.)		
2.	Taxes on non-resident parties	(Attachment no.)		
3.	Zakāt on other parties	(Attachment no.)		
4.	Other Amounts Payable			
	a	Paid as per Receipt #	on		
	b	Paid as per Receipt #	on		
	c	Paid as per Receipt #	on		
5.	Total payments			
6.	Difference to be paid or (reimbursed)	E		

Schedule No. (5): Totals

1.	Total Amount to be Paid or (Reimbursed) (D+E)	

Schedule No. (6): Assets and liabilities at:

Items	Beginning of period		End of period	
Assets	Riyals	H	Riyals	H
Cash in hand				
Cash in banks				
Accounts receivable & debit balances				
Inventory				
Accrued revenues				
Prepaid expenses & deferred charges				
Claims under collection				
Fixed assets, net				
Construction in progress				
Goods in transit				
Total assets				
Liabilities				
Credit balances				
Short-term loans				
Long-term loans				
Accounts payable (suppliers, sub-contractors)				
Accrued expenses				
Reserves (Attachment no.)				
Customer advances				
Other liabilities (Attachment no.)				
Head office account (Capital)				
Profit (loss) for the year				
Total liabilities				

Certificate of the preparer of this return

e:.. Title: ....

ess:.. P.O. Box .... Tel: ....

ereby certify that this return and the attachments hereto have been prepared in accordance with the ⬤any's books and records and that they reflect the financial position of the company for the fiscal period ⬤ich this return relates. I will bear complete responsibility if the information provided is proved to be ⬤rect.

ture: Date:

E   If you have any explanations, details of these are to be submitted and attached to this return.

APPENDIX 9

Minister of Industry and Electricity Resolution No. 952 of 4/11/1400 H

Regarding ventures considered development ventures in accordance with the Foreign Capital Investment Regulations

The Minister of Industry and Electricity,
Pursuant to his authority

Having reviewed Article 3 of the Foreign Capital Investment Regulations issued by Royal Decree No. M/4 dated 2/2/1399 H, and

Having reviewed Article 2 of the Foreign Capital Investment Regulations Implementing Rules, issued by Resolution No. 232/q/W/S dated 10/6/1399 H;

And pursuant to the recommendations of the Foreign Capital Investment Committee,

Decree as follows:

Article 1. The following ventures shall be considered development ventures for the purposes of the Foreign Capital Investment Regulations.

    A. Industrial production development ventures.
    B. Agricultural production development ventures.
    C. Health development ventures.
    D. Services.
    E. Contracting.

Article 2. Industrial production development ventures means the conversion of raw materials to manufactured or semi-manufactured materials or the conversion of semi-manufactured materials to fully manufactured materials or the preparation, filling and packaging of fully manufactured materials.

Article 3. Agricultural production development ventures means the development of:

    A. Agricultural wealth: such as the production of fruit, vegetables, grain, plantations, greenhouses, or active ingredients for crops, or green fodder.

B. Animal wealth: such as the breeding of cows, sheep, poultry, beehives, or milk and the derivatives thereof.

C. Fish wealth: such as fishing or the creation of artificial lakes for fish farms.

Article 4. Health development ventures means the establishment, administration, and operation of hospitals, clinics, laboratories, and the like.

Article 5. Services means, by way of example, banking or hotel and tourist services, training, maintenance and operation services, cleaning, environmental protection and antipollution services, transportation, loading and unloading services, advertisement, publication and publicity services, computer services, the construction of modern technical workshops, large warehouses, refrigerated depots for the service of third parties, shopping centers, commercial centers or quality restaurants.

Article 6. Contracting means the habitual undertaking of the execution of specified works for third parties for appropriate compensation including, by way of example, the following:

A. Civil construction contracting: such as buildings or the erection of prefabricated buildings, airports, roads, bridges, dams, harbors or water and sewage systems.

B. Electrical projects contracting: such as generating stations, transmission and distribution systems, or electronics.

C. Mechanical projects contracting: such as desalination units or plants.

Article 7. Other development ventures not provided herein may be accepted upon the recommendation of the Foreign Capital Investment Committee.

Article 8. The ventures provided herein may be amended upon the recommendation of the Foreign Capital Investment Committee.

Article 9. This Resolution shall be published in the Official Journal.

Minister of Industry and Electricity

APPENDIX 10

Minister of Commerce Resolution No. 1532 of 6/6/1395 H

Ministry of Commerce and Industry
Kingdom of Saudi Arabia

In the name of God, the Merciful, the Compassionate

The Minister of Commerce and Industry,

Having reviewed Article 228 of the Companies Regulations which provides:

> 'Foreign companies may not establish branches, agencies or offices to represent them, nor may they issue securities or offer them for subscription or sale within the Kingdom except with permission from the Minister of Commerce and Industry. These branches, agencies, or offices shall be subject to the regulations in force within the Kingdom applicable to the particular activity in which they engage. If such branch, agency, or office conducts business before fulfilling the requirements specified in these or other regulations, the persons who may have conducted such business shall be held personally and jointly responsible therefor',

And having reviewed the minutes of the committee formed by the Ministry for studying the subject of licensing certain foreign companies to open offices of their own in the Kingdom for the purpose of offering technical and scientific services,

And pursuant to his authority and the requirements of the public interest,

Decree as follows:

First: The following instructions in respect of foreign companies of opening offices of their own in the Kingdom for the purpose of offering technical and scientific services are hereby approved:

    A. The company shall submit an application to this effect to the Ministry of Commerce, indicating therein the technical and scientific services which it will offer to those dealing with it and attaching thereto the documents supporting its registration in the Commercial Register or the Companies

Register in its headquarters abroad as well as the authorization by such company granted to the person who will be in charge of its office in the Kingdom. The company shall also attach an Arabic translation of such documents. The documents and translation thereof shall be authenticated in accordance with the provisions of Ministerial Resolution No. 424 dated 26/2/1391 H relating to the authentication and translation of foreign documents.

B. The activities of such office shall be restricted to the offering of technical and scientific services to distributors of the company's products, agents and consumers of such products only. The office may carry out a market study in respect of its kind of activity and prepare reports of such study for the headquarters of the company which it represents. The office shall submit to the Ministry of Commerce and Industry an annual summary of its activity.

C. A resolution of the Minister of Commerce and Industry shall be issued determining the number of employees of the office in view of the company's requirements and the public interest. The number of said employees shall not be increased without the prior consent of the Ministry.

In the event that the Ministry's instructions require the obtaining of a special licence from any governmental authority by those licensed to deal in the company's products, the company shall be required to obtain an initial approval from the said authority for opening the company's own office in the Kingdom.

D. Offices authorized to operate in the Kingdom shall not conduct any commercial activity whether directly or indirectly and shall not receive any fees for the training of Saudi technicians.

Second: A register shall be kept in the Ministry of Commerce (General Companies Department) for the registration of offices authorized to operate in the Kingdom. In addition to the particulars of the company the register shall indicate the activity which the office is authorized to perform. A certificate based on such register shall be made for the company. Such certificate shall indicate the issuance of the same as well as the number of the resolution by which such licence was issued.

Third: In the event of the violation by the company of the provisions of this Resolution, the licence granted to the company for the opening of an office in the Kingdom shall be withdrawn by the Minister and the competent authorities shall be notified thereof.

Minister of Commerce and Industry

APPENDIX 11

Saudi Consulate, Washington D.C., Guidelines for Document Authentication

The Consulate of The Royal Embassy of Saudi Arabia

Please read the following details carefully and kindly comply with them

1. *All Commercial Documents*: Shipment of Goods Certificates, Certificates of Origin, Invoices, Vessels Navigation Certificates, Bills of Lading, Forwarding Bills, etc., must be first sealed and certified by the U.S. Arab Chamber of Commerce. It is important to note that the U.S. Arab Chamber of Commerce requests first the certification of the following offices:

   A. The American Board of Trade where the company has its credit; or by
   B. A local Chamber of Commerce in the respective State;
   C. U.S. Arab Chamber of Commerce,
      . . .

   After the U.S. Arab Chamber of Commerce completes the authentication and the sealing of the respective documents, then the Saudi Arabian Consulate General will legalize the respective documents free of charge.

2. *Other American Documents*: such as powers of attorney, commercial agreements, licences, marriage certificates, medical certificates, bills, authorizations by proxy, diplomas, academic transcripts of records, other agreements, and authorization by proxy certificates, all must be authenticated by the State Department Authentication Division which requests first that the above American documents must first be certified step-by-step by the following offices:

   A. By a notary public, who is available in any bank.
   B. By the county clerk of the respective county where the notary public is commissioned; the county clerk is usually stationed in the court of the specified county where the notary public is commissioned.
   C. They must be certified under the seal of the local state and by the Secretary of State of that particular state.
   D. Finally, after all the above offices have completed their certification, the respective documents must be sent to the Authentication Office of the Department of State in Washington, D.C.—

Tel. 202-632 0406

. . .

After the State Department Authentication Office completes the authentication of the documents, the Saudi Arabian Consulate will legalize them . . . the original and a xerox copy.

It is extremely important to note that the Saudi Arabian Consulate needs an authenticated copy—authenticated by the State Department for retention by the Saudi Arabian Consulate.

4. Of each set of documents we need an authenticated xerox copy, whether authenticated by the State Department or by the U.S. Arab Chamber of Commerce. Even if it were one sheet only, we need an authenticated copy.

5. The diplomas, the academic degrees, and the academic transcript of records must first be authenticated by the Department of Education in Washington, D.C. and their address is as follows, and then by the State Department Authentication Office, thirdly by the Saudi Arabian Consulate.

. . .

6. In the event that you choose to mail the documents for authentication first by the State Department and then for legalization by the Saudi Consulate, please enclose a self-addressed envelope with the appropriate stamps on it for the return of the documents after their authentication, together with an additional envelope and the appropriate stamps on it addressing it to the Consulate of the Royal Embassy of Saudi Arabia, 1520 18th Street, N.W., Washington, D.C. 20036—this is for transmittal by the State Department to the Consulate of Saudi Arabia; and then for transmittal to you.

. . .

8. Islamic marriage certificates and Islamic declaration certificates—*Al-Shahada* certificates—must first be authenticated by the Islamic Center of the respective county or state and then must be authenticated by the State Department Authentication Office at the previously mentioned address.

. . .

9. In the case of medical bills, hospital bills, or prescription bills, and when they consist of a large accumulation of bills—they all must be summarized, in one single statement indicating the total amount, and this summarized statement must be issued by either the hospital or the doctor or by the drug store; attaching all the accumulated collection of bills and making reference to them—as being attached to the summarized statement. Accordingly, the summarized statement must be signed either by the doctor of the hospital or by the pharmacist and must be notarized as well by the notary public in any local bank of the respective county, town or city and then must be authenticated by the State Department.

. . .

10. Company and personal checks are not accepted at all. Payment must be made in a money order to the Royal Embassy of Saudi Arabia.

Thank you for your cooperation.

APPENDIX 12

Part 1

Ministry of Finance and National Economy Letter No. 4633/402 of 23/8/1402 H (June 15, 1982)

Kingdom of Saudi Arabia
Ministry of Finance and National Economy
Legal Department

H.E. The Director-General of the Department of Zakāt and Income Tax

Greetings,

With reference to your letter No. 4133/2 of 21/5/1400 H stating that when the Department examined the accounts of certain foreign companies it was found: (1) that certain agreements between such foreign companies and their Saudi agents are entered into at a time subsequent to the submission of the tender or subsequent to the conclusion of the contract between the Government and the foreign company or that the written agreement is in confirmation of a prior oral agreement; (2) that certain foreign companies contracting with government authorities subcontract the contracted for work or part thereof and the foreign subcontractor then pays its Saudi agent his customary fee. You added that, in view of the fact that such transactions affect the level of net profits of foreign companies and consequently are reflected in the amount of tax, you considered it advisable to obtain the Ministry's views on the above, that is, the extent to which the Department of Zakāt and Income Tax may allow the amounts paid to the abovementioned agents shown in company accounts.

I advise you as follows:

First: With respect to agreements concluded between foreign companies contracting with the Government and their Saudi agent after the contract with the Government was made, the Ministry considers that such amounts should not be included in the foreign company's expenses which are deductible from its income when tax is imposed. The purpose of this is to cause foreign companies to comply with the provisions of the Regulations Governing the Relationship between the Foreign Contractor and the Saudi Agent [sic] on entering into a contract with the Government and because as a rule when the agreement is made with the agent at a date subsequent to the date of the conclusion of the government contract by the foreign contractor, the amount paid to the Saudi agent is fictitious, the contract being made solely for the purpose of tax evasion.

Second: With respect to amounts paid to its Saudi agent by a foreign subcontractor which has obtained a contract from a foreign contractor having entered into a contract with the Government or another party, the Ministry also considers that since such amounts are not paid in accordance with the Regulations and are not obligatory, and are paid subsequent to the conclusion of the contract between the Government and the foreign contractor, and since it has been decided not to allow the amounts which are paid to the Saudi agent if his contract is made subsequent to the foreign contractor's contract with the Government, then it is all the more reason for not allowing the amounts under discussion to be included as expenses deductible from income in assessing taxable income and indeed tax must be calculated thereon.

In view of the foregoing, I notify you of the preceding and trust that you will give instructions for compliance with these principles in assessing the income of foreign contractors.

Part 2

Director-General of the Department of Zakāt and Income Tax Circular No. 9721/2 of 15/10/1402 H (August 8, 1982)

Kingdom of Saudi Arabia
Ministry of Finance and National Economy
Department of Zakāt and Income Tax
Companies

Notification of H.E. the Minister's Letter No. 4633/402

To Departments, Divisions, Branches and Licensed Accountants

We attach a copy of Letter No. 4633/402 dated 23/8/1402 H of H.E. the Minister of Finance and National Economy concerning the principles to be complied with in the case of a foreign company contracting with the Government paying amounts to its Saudi agent, and when such amounts may be included in the expenses which may be deducted from the company's income when assessing the tax upon it.

The meaning of this is that in the application of H.E. the Minister's letter, the following shall be complied with:

1. Upon the receipt of a contract concluded between a government authority and a foreign company or the appearance of such a contract in the accounts submitted by a taxpayer, the examining accountant at the Department shall request the company to present a certificate from the government authority contracting with it, certifying that the foreign company had specified in its submitted tender the name of the Saudi agent and his commercial registration number allowing him to be its agent and stating the name and address of such agent.

Licensed accountants shall submit such a statement on submission of the company's annual accounts.

2. When the government authority certifies as to the existence of the Saudi agent in the tender submitted to it, the commissions paid to him by the foreign company, within the maximum limit of 5 percent in accordance with Royal Decree No. M/2 dated 21/1/1398 H shall alone be taken into account and allowed as a charge against profits and be deductible from the foreign company's income when tax is levied thereon.

3. However, if it is found that the appointment of the Saudi agent was made subsequent to the conclusion of the contract between the Government and the foreign company or that the written agreement to appoint him was in confirmation of a prior verbal agreement, the commissions paid to him shall not be taken into consideration and may not be allowed to be included as part of the deductible expenses from its income when tax is imposed thereon.

4. If the foreign company assigns all or part or parts of its contract concluded with the government authority to subcontractors, the commissions paid to Saudi agents by the subcontractors shall not be taken into consideration and consequently such commissions may not be deducted from the income of the subcontractors when tax is imposed thereon.

We trust that you will implement the above and comply therewith.

Director-General of the Department of Zakāt and Income Tax

APPENDIX 13

Contractor Classification Manual

Kingdom of Saudi Arabia
Agency for Classification of Contractors
Ministry of Public Works and Housing

I. General information

1. This Manual includes the forms to be filled out by Saudi and non-Saudi contractors seeking official classification by the Agency. Such classification action is mandatory for award of government contracts under the provisions of Council of Ministers' decrees regulating such matters.

2. Additional copies of the schedules may be obtained by contacting the Agency For Classification of Contractors, Ministry of Public Works and Housing, Riyadh, Kingdom of Saudi Arabia.

3. Applications submitted to the Agency For Classification of Contractors shall be in Arabic which will be the official version. Non-Saudi applicants are encouraged to complete the English version, which will be used for reference purposes only, and enclose it with the Arabic submission. Both Arabic and English versions should be typed. Name of projects, personnel and addresses not of Arabic origin may be written in English on the Arabic version.

4. A number of the schedules require supporting documentation which shall accompany the submission. Such documents should be photocopied on paper of the same size as the schedule. Such copies shall be certified as authentic by the Agency upon presentation of the corresponding original.

5. All information requested in the various schedules shall be completed in the format specified. Failure to complete the schedules as specified will result in rejection of the application.

6. Each page of the submission and supporting documentation shall be stamped on the reverse side with the company seal and signed by a designated company official attesting as to its accuracy and completeness.

7. The Agency For Classification of Contractors shall treat all information submitted as official, but reserves the right to conduct such enquiries as it deems necessary to verify the data. The applicant firm shall be solely responsible for the accuracy of the data, and shall be subject to whatever penalties may be imposed in accordance with

Saudi Law for any falsification or intentional inaccuracies. Such penalties include, but are not limited to, the cancellation or alteration of a firm's classification status.

8. The applicant firm is responsible for officially advising the Agency For Classification of Contractors of any material changes in its status which enhance or impair its technical, financial, manpower or management capabilities to carry out its work.

9. All financial information supplied in the schedules and in the supporting documentation shall be treated as highly confidential, and will only be used for classification purposes.

10. The applicant firm will be officially notified in writing of its classification status immediately following classification action by the Agency.

II. Guidelines for completing the schedules

This section of the Contractor Classification Manual provides specific guidance on the completion of each of the eleven schedules.

Schedule No. 1: General Information

Activities outside contracting. Maintenance work is considered a part of contracting and should not be entered here. Trading in building materials should be entered under 'Trading' only if this activity is significant in the total activity of the firm.

Schedule No. 2: General Information

Names of owners. Indicate in the first row whether a government, and in the second row whether a bank, holds shares of your firm.

Related firms. Relationships with other companies or individuals which are important for the company, *e.g.* subsidiary or parent firms or firms in which there are major investments. Important trading relationships such as business partners, key clients, sub-contractors or suppliers should be indicated.

Schedule No. 3: Financial Status

Fixed assets. The purpose of separating the fixed assets into land and buildings, contracting plant and equipment (net. dep.), and other fixed assets is to separate those assets which relate directly to contracting work and include them in item 1.2.

Other assets. Those assets which are neither fixed assets nor current assets should be entered under 3 (other assets), *e.g.* establishment expenses.

Net worth. 4.4. All partners (owners) accounts whether these accounts are debit or credit.

Other liabilities. Those liabilities which are neither long term nor current liabilities should be entered under 7 (other liabilities), *e.g.* provisions for pensions or other staff expenses.

Schedule No. 4: Financial Status

Total revenue. Total revenue is separated into contracting revenue (8.1) and trading and other revenue (8.2) in order to indicate the relative importance of contracting versus other activities. All contracting revenues should be entered under 8.1 and all trading and other revenues should be entered under item 8.2.

Total value of contracts in each of last 5 years. The value of contracts *awarded*, not work completed, is to be entered here.

Total cost of subcontractors. Enter the total cost of subcontractors in the year in which the revenue indicated in 8.1 is earned.

Increase (decrease) in capital, retained earnings, other reserves, owner (partners) accounts. These fields will be filled in by the Agency.

Value of work scheduled for completion. This item is required as an indication of future work load.

Schedule No. 5: Qualifications of Principal Executives

Data should be submitted for principals and senior executives only.

Schedule No. 6: Summary of Personnel Qualifications

Indicate total number of permanently employed personnel as of the date of the submission, broken down into the qualification categories indicated on the schedule. Firms already operating in Saudi Arabia should include employment contracts and residence permits for not more than five resident engineers.

Schedule No. 7: Activities of Firm

See following table for definition of activities.

The percentages for each of the major activity categories should add up to 100. The sub-categories within each major activity category should add up to the percentage shown for the major activity.

Include in this schedule projects completed during the last ten years. Cost item refers to the total cost of the project paid by the client to the firm.

Schedule No. 8: Details of Projects

Select and describe the most important and most appropriate projects which directly relate to classification categories sought.

Enter at least ten largest projects executed during last ten years and some other significant ones. A copy of the contract and of the hand-over document (if the project is finished) should be attached. A copy of the municipality permit for each non-government project undertaken in Saudi Arabia should also be attached. Mark the role of your firm on the project. Indicate the speciality and percentage of the project taken by the main contractor, joint venture partners and main subcontractors.

Project number, client code, activity code, contract and client data as well as the client and site inspection report will be filled in by the agency.

Do not include projects for less than 1 million SR.

This schedule also provides the applicant firm the opportunity to update their projects information.

For each new project over 1 million SR in Saudi Arabia awarded to your firm, fill in the schedule, attach both the contract and the permit copy and mail to the Agency.

Schedule No. 9: Machinery Equipment and Facilities

Indicate total number (pieces) of machinery and equipment in Saudi Arabia as well as their total capacity, their cost (new and net depreciation) and, within each general category, the piece with the highest capacity. Indicate the same information for computers and laboratories used in connection with your activities both inside and outside Saudi Arabia.

Schedule No. 10: Organization Chart

Provide a summary organization chart showing major operating and staff departments and assignments of the firm's principals. Describe the systems and procedures used by the applicant firm in scheduling project execution.

Schedule No. 11: Summary of Research and Development Activities

This optional schedule provides the applicant firm the opportunity to list useful information on their research and development activities.

III. Definition of terms

1. *Firm.* Includes all legal forms of business enterprise whether individual ownership or partnership, whether Saudi or non-Saudi.
2. *Contractor.* Any firm licensed to engage in construction and maintenance activities.
3. *Construction.* Activities of a civil, mechanical, electrical or architectural nature carried out in connection with the erection of plants, buildings and facilities, the building of roads, dams and tunnels, and other related activities.
4. *Maintenance.* Activities relating to repair and upkeep of equipment, plants, buildings, roads, etc. It includes responsibility for operation of equipment as well as cleaning, sanitation and related activities.

Buildings

Public buildings	Government and municipal offices, mosques, telecommunication buildings, prisons and correctional facilities. Judicial facilities, postal facilities. Military buildings.
Housing	Houses, villas, apartment buildings, compounds.
Commercial buildings	Office blocks, shops, banks, hotels, restaurants, car parks, warehouses, depots, exhibition centers, silos.
Educational facilities	Schools, colleges, universities, museums, libraries, auditoriums, theatres.
Recreational facilities	Swimming pools, sport stadiums, gymnasiums, parks, marinas, zoos, playgrounds.
Medical facilities	Hospitals, clinics, laboratories, medical research facilities.
Airport buildings	Terminal buildings, hangars, workshops, control towers, offices, warehouses.
Prefabricated buildings	—

Roads

Highways	Highways, feeder roads, rural roads.
Streets	Streets, sidewalks, parking areas, street and traffic lights, overpasses, street beautification.
Bridges	Concrete bridges, pre-cast concrete bridges, steel bridges, fly-overs.
Tunnels	Galleries, tunnels, caverns, shafts, lighting, ventilation.
Marine works	Harbors, jetties, piers, dikes, levees, canals, waterways, flood control, piling, caissons, dredging and land reclamation.
Railroads	Railroads, underground railways, tram-ways, rapid transit systems, mono-rail systems.
Airports	Runways, taxiways, parking facilities.
Dams	Earth and rock dams, concrete gravity dams, arch dams, water reservoirs.

Water and Sewage systems

Water networks	Pipe of asbestos cement, plastic, iron and concrete. Valves, fittings and fire hydrants. Setting up reservoirs, tanks, and pumping stations.
Sewage networks	Preparation of trench base and laying of pipes, manholes, and repaving.
Water treatment plants	Plants for various stages of treatment, disinfection and auxiliary work.
Sewage treatment plants	Plants for various stages of treatment, disinfection and auxiliary work.
Well drilling	—
Agricultural development	Irrigation systems, land improvement, farm development.

Electrical and Mechanical works

Power generation	Power plants and stations.
Power transmission and distribution	Overhead/underground lines, sub-stations, transformers, switching gear and related installations.
Communication systems	Telephone, telex, television, radio systems; other electrical contracting.
Air conditioning and refrigeration	Air conditioning in buildings, cold stores, freezing.
Pumping stations	Pumping stations of all types and related technical installations.
Other electrical and mechanical works	Other electrical contracting; specialized mechanical installations such as elevator installations.

Industrial works

Industrial plants	Plants of all types.
Refining and petrochemical works	Refineries, pipelines, reservoirs.
Desalination	Saline water conversion stations, pumping.
Other Industrial Works	—

Maintenance

Building maintenance	Cleaning, repairs and minor works.
Road maintenance	Cleaning, repairs (including the lighting) and minor works.
Water and sewage systems maintenance and operation	Operation, cleaning, periodical tests and services, repairs.
Electrical and mechanical installations maintenance and operation	Operation, cleaning, periodical tests and services, repairs.
City cleaning and waste disposal	—

Kingdom of Saudi Arabia Ministry of Public Works and Housing Agency for Classification of Contractors	Schedule No.	1	Contractors Manual	
	Form No.	AC1/2	General Information	
	Date	1/7/1401		

1020	Name of Firm		C1025	File No.

<table>
<tr><td colspan="5" align="center">Head Office</td></tr>
<tr><td colspan="2">Mailing Address</td><td></td><td colspan="2">Location</td></tr>
<tr><td>1420</td><td>P O Box</td><td>C1455</td><td colspan="2">Building</td></tr>
<tr><td>1425</td><td>City</td><td>C1460</td><td colspan="2">Room/Suite</td></tr>
<tr><td>1430</td><td>Postal Code</td><td>C1465</td><td colspan="2">Street</td></tr>
<tr><td>1435</td><td>Country</td><td>C1470</td><td colspan="2">City</td></tr>
<tr><td>1445</td><td>Telephone</td><td>C1475</td><td colspan="2">Country</td></tr>
<tr><td>1450</td><td>Telex</td><td></td><td colspan="2"></td></tr>
</table>

<table>
<tr><td colspan="5" align="center">For Foreign Firms</td></tr>
<tr><td colspan="2">Address in Saudi Arabia</td><td></td><td colspan="2">Address of Sponsor in S. A.</td></tr>
<tr><td>1920</td><td>P O Box</td><td>C1940</td><td colspan="2">Name</td></tr>
<tr><td>1925</td><td>City</td><td>C1945</td><td colspan="2">PO Box</td></tr>
<tr><td>1930</td><td>Telephone</td><td>C1950</td><td colspan="2">City</td></tr>
<tr><td>1935</td><td>Telex</td><td>C1955</td><td colspan="2">Telephone</td></tr>
<tr><td></td><td></td><td>C1960</td><td colspan="2">Telex</td></tr>
</table>

<table>
<tr><td colspan="6" align="center">Other Offices</td></tr>
<tr><td>1020</td><td>City</td><td>City</td><td>City</td><td>City</td><td>City</td></tr>
<tr><td>1085</td><td>Previous name of firm</td><td colspan="2">C1030</td><td colspan="2">Nationality</td></tr>
</table>

<table>
<tr><td colspan="6" align="center">Commercial Registration</td></tr>
<tr><td>1035</td><td>Number</td><td>C1045</td><td>Place</td><td>C1040</td><td>Date</td></tr>
<tr><td>1055</td><td colspan="2" align="center">Date of first contract award</td><td>day</td><td>mo</td><td>year</td></tr>
</table>

	Type of ownership			Activities outside of contr.
10601	Individual ownership	C10651		Trading
10602	Joint partnership company	C10652		Industry
10603	Limited liability company	C10653		Agriculture
10604	Stock company	C10654		Real estate
10605	Other (specify)	C10655		Cleaning
		C10656		Other (specify)

Kingdom of Saudi Arabia Ministry of Public Works and Housing Agency for Classification of Contractors	Schedule No.	2	Contractors Manual
	Form No.	AC1/1	General Information
	Date	1/7/1401	

C1020	Name of Firm		C1025	File No.

C2220	Names of owners, principal partners or major shareholders	C2225	Nationality	C2230	Share of capital %
	Government				
	Bank				
C1520	Names of related firms	C1525	Nature of relationship		

Legal Actions or Claims in Last Five Years

C10901	Failure to complete work on time	C10904	Termination of contract by client
C10902	Failure to complete work acc. to specifications	C10906	Other (specify)
C10903	Termination of contract by by contractor	C10905	Award to client (contractor)
	Explanation	☒	Check approriate box

Supporting Documents   C110
For Saudi firms: copy of commercial registration; articles of association
For non Saudi firms: copy of permit to undertake contracting work in Saudi Arabia, if obtained

<table>
<tr><td colspan="2">Kingdom of Saudi Arabia
Ministry of Public Works
and Housing
Agency for Classification
of Contractors</td><td>Schedule No.</td><td colspan="2">3</td><td colspan="5">Contractors Manual</td></tr>
</table>

Kingdom of Saudi Arabia Ministry of Public Works and Housing Agency for Classification of Contractors	Schedule No.	3	Contractors Manual				
	Form No.	AC1/2	Financial Status				
	Date	1/7/1401					

1020	Name of Firm		C1025	File No.			
	Finacial Statements Summary Over Last Five Years (SR '000)		Registered Capital (SR'000)				
			C2050				

		Fiscal year ending month of ...				
2320	Category	19 14	19 14	19 14	19 14	19 14
2330	1 Fixed Assets					
2335	1.1 Lands & buildings					
2340	1.2 Contracting plant & equipment (Net dep.)					
2345	1.3 Other fixed assets (Net. dep.)					
2350	2 Current Assets					
2355	2.1 Cash & receivables					
2360	2.2 Work in progress					
2365	2.3 Inventories					
2370	2.4 Other current assets					
2375	3 Other Assets					
2380	Total Assets (1+2+3)					
2385	4 Net Worth					
2390	4.1 Capital					
2395	4.2 Retained earnings					
2400	4.3 Other reserves					
2405	4.4 Owners (partners) accounts					
2410	5 Long Term Debts					
2415	5.1 Government loans					
2420	5.2 Non-government loans					
2425	6 Current Liabilities					
2430	6.1 Short term loans					
2435	6.2 Accounts payable					
2440	6.3 Other current liabilities					
2445	7 Other Liabilities					
2450	Total Liabilities (4+5+6+7)					

Kingdom of Saudi Arabia Ministry of Public Works and Housing Agency for Classification of Contractors	Schedule No.	4	Contractors Manual
	Form No.	AC1/2	Financial Status
	Date	1/7/1401	

C1020	Name of Firm		C1025	File No.

Finacial Statements Summary Over
Last Five Years   (SR '000)

		Fiscal year ending month of ...				
C2320	Category	19 14	19 14	19 14	19 14	19 14
C2455	8 Total Revenue (8.1+8.2)					
C2460	8.1 Contracting revenue					
C2465	8.2 Trading & other revenue					
C2470	Total value of contracts in each of last 5 yrs.					
C2475	Total fees to sub-contractors					
C2480	Net profit after tax/zakāt					
C2485	Total yearly depreciation					
C2490	Equipment in Saudi Arabia (Net dep.)					
C2495	Increase/decrease in capital					
C2500	Increase/decrease in retained earnings					
C2510	Increase/decrease in other reserves					
C2515	Increase/decrease in owners (partners) accounts					

	During the next -	0-6 months	6-12 months	12-18 months	18-24 months	more th 24 mon
	Value of work scheduled for completion					

Reference Banks

C2620	Name	C2625	City		C2635	Country
		C2630	Postal code		C2645	Telex
C2650	Name	C2655	City		C2665	Country
		C2660	Postal code		C2675	Telex

Auditor

C2820	Name	C2825	City		C2835	Country
		C2830	Postal code		C2840	Telex

Supporting Documents   C1105, C11
Copy of audited statement and of balance sheets for last two fiscal years ☐
Copy of statement of change in financial position for last two years, if available ☐

Kingdom of Saudi Arabia Ministry of Public Works and Housing Agency for Classification of Contractors	Schedule No.	5	Contractors Manual
	Form No.	AC1/3	Qualification Principal Executives
	Date	1/7/1401	

C1020	Name of Firm			C1025	File No.

C3020	Name (family-first-middle)				
C3035	Nationality			C3025	Date of birth
C3040	Current position			C3030	Years with firm
C3045	Educational degree	C3050	Field of study	C3055	Year received degree

Summary of experience in Saudi Arabia and outside

C3020	Name (family-first-middle)				
C3035	Nationality			C3025	Date of birth
C3040	Current position			C3030	Years with firm
C3045	Educational degree	C3050	Field of study	C3055	Year received degree

Summary of experience in Saudi Arabia and outside

C3020	Name (family-first-middle)				
C3035	Nationality			C3025	Date of birth
C3040	Current position			C3030	Years with firm
C3045	Educational degree	C3050	Field of study	C3055	Year received degree

Summary of experience in Saudi Arabia and outside

Kingdom of Saudi Arabia Ministry of Public Works and Housing Agency for Classification of Contractors	Schedule No.	6	Contractors Manual
	Form No.	AC1/4	Summary of Personnel Qualifications
	Date	1/7/1401	

C1020 Name of Firm		C1025	File No.

Insert number of employees in appropriate space. Do not include executives

	SPECIALIZATION	B.Sc. or above		Tech. diploma		No formal qualif.				Total	
						5 years exp.		Less than 5 years			
		S	O	S	O	S	O	S	O	S	O
C3215001	Architecture										
C3215002	Town and environmental planning										
C3215003	Road construction										
C3215004	Bridges										
C3215005	Tunnels										
C3215006	Concrete										
C3215007	Soil engineering										
C3215008	Steel structures										
C3215009	Water and sewage systems										
C3215010	Surveying										
C3215011	Other civil engineering										
C3215012	Agricultural engineering										
C3215013	Air-conditioning and plumbing										
C3215014	Other mechanical engineering										
C3215015	Power generation										
C3215016	Power distribution										
C3215017	Communications and electron. eng.										
C3215018	Other electrical engineering										
C3215019	Material engineering										
C3215020	Petrochemical engineering										
C3215021	Industrial engineering										
C3215022	Research and development										
C3215023	Quantity surv. and cost control										
C3215024	Project planning and control										
C3215025	Administration										
C3215026	Economics and accounting										
C3215027	Others										
	Total										

NOTE: S stands for "Saudi"
O stands for "non Saudi"

C3220 C3225 C3230 C3235 C3240 C3245 C3250 C3255 C3260 C3265

Kingdom of Saudi Arabia Ministry of Public Works and Housing Agency for Classification of Contractors	Schedule No.	7	Contractors Manual
	Form No.	AC1/5	Activities of Firm
	Date	1/7/1401	

C1020	Name of Firm			C1025	File No.	

	ACTIVITIES		% Total work in last ten years by value C2925	Number of projects in last ten years C2930	Average projects cost (SR millions) C2935
	Buildings				
C2915105	Public buildings				
C2915110	Housing				
C2915115	Commercial buildings				
C2915120	Educational facilities				
C2915125	Recreational facilities				
C2915130	Medical facilities				
C2915135	Airport buildings				
C2915140	Prefabricated buildings				
	Roads				
C2915205	Highways				
C2915210	Streets				
C2915215	Bridges				
C2915220	Tunnels				
C2915225	Marine works				
C2915230	Railroads				
C2915235	Airports				
C2915240	Dams				
C2915245	Earth moving				
	Water-sewage systems				
C2915305	Water networks				
C2915310	Sewage networks				
C2915315	Water treatment plants				
C2915320	Sewage treatment plants				
C2915325	Well drilling				
C2915330	Agricultural development				
	Electrical and mechanical works				
C2915405	Power generation				
C2915410	Power transmission and distribution				
C2915415	Lighting				
C2915420	Communication systems				
C2915425	Air-conditioning and refrigeration				
C2915430	Pumping stations & treatment plants				
C2915435	Other electrical and mechanical works				
	Industrial works				
C2915505	Industrial plants				
C2915510	Refining and petrochemical works				
C2915515	Desalination				
C2915520	Other industrial works				
	Maintenance				
C2915605	Building maintenance				
C2915610	Road maintenance				
C2915615	Water and sewage systems maintenance and operation				
C2915620	Electrical and mech. installations maintenance and operation				
C2915625	City cleaning and waste disposal				
C2915705	*Other contracting*				
		☒ Check activities for requested classification			

Kingdom of Saudi Arabia Ministry of Public Works and Housing Agency for Classification of Contractors	Schedule No.	8	Contractors Manual
	Form No.	AC1/6	Details of Projects
	Date	1/7/1401	

C1020	NAME OF FIRM				C1025		File No.	
P0035	Project No.			Client code		Activity code		
P0325	Client name							
P0330	PO Box			P0340	Postal code			
P0335	City			P0355	Telephone			
P0345	Country			P0360	Telex			
P0030	Project title							
P0045	Location			P0050	Role of firm*			

Related contractors   P043

P0425	Role*	P0420	Name		P0430	Specialty	% of p

Brief description of project

P1625	Consultant name

Project cost (SR '000)	Contractor		Contract		Client	
Project cost (SR '000)	P1630		P1650		P1670	
Starting date	P1635		P1655		P1675	
Completion date	P1640		P1660		P1680	
Execution period (months)	P1645		P1665		P1685	

Client and site inspection report

	Client		Site inspector	
Delay-at 50% completion	P1725		P1775	
Reasons	P1730		P1780	
Delay-at completion	P1735		P1785	
Reasons	P1740		P1790	

Performance

	Client		Site inspector	
Site organization	P1745		P1795	
Equipment supply	P1750		P1800	
Structural work	P1755		P1805	
Civil work	P1760		P1810	
Mechanical and electrical	P1765		P1815	
Finishing work	P1770		P1820	

P1825	Site inspector code

Supporting Documents   ☐ Contract   ☐ Handover   ☐ Municipality permit
                P0055   P0060   P0065

* Enter for Main contractor (M), for JV-partner (JV), for Subcontractor (S)

Kingdom of Saudi Arabia Ministry of Public Works and Housing Agency for Classification of Contractors	Schedule No.	9	Contractors Manual
	Form No.	AC1/7	Equipment and Facilities
	Date	1/7/1401	

| .020 | NAME OF FIRM | | File No. | |

Machinery and equipment in Saudi Arabia owned by firm

	General category	No. C3325	Capacity			Cost (SR '000)	
			Unit of measure	Total	Max. per piece	New	Net. dep.
320100	Crushing and separat. plants		m^3/h				
320110	Concrete batching plants		m^3/h				
320120	Concrete pumps		m^3/h				
320130	Truck-mixers		m^3				
320140	Tower cranes		tons				
320150	Mobile cranes		tons				
320160	Block-making machines		pc/h				
320170	Asphalt plants		tons/h				
320180	Asphalt finishers		tons				
320190	Concrete finishers		tons				
320200	Vibrating rollers		tons				
320210	Tire rollers		tons				
320220	Other rollers		tons				
320230	Excavators		kw				
320240	Bulldozers		kw				
320250	Loaders		kw				
320260	Scrapers		kw				
320270	Graders		kw				
320280	Trucks		tons				
320290	Dump trucks		tons				
320300	Trailers		tons				
320310	Tank lorries		litres				
320320	Driving plants		tons				
320330	Drilling plants		diamet.				
320340	Pumps		1/min.				
320350	Compressors		KN/m^2				
320360	Generators		KVA				
320370	Floating cranes		tons				
320380	Boats		kw				
320390	Dredgers		kW				
320400	Other plants and equipments						
					Total		
						C3530	C3535

Computers and laboratories both in Saudi Arabia and outside

320800	Computer systems		M byte				
320810	Concrete test labs		m^2				
320820	Soil investigation labs		m^2				
320830	Other test labs		m^2				
					Total		
						C3540	C3545

NOTE: The applicant firm should have proper receipts, rental agreements, customs releases and other supporting documents for above items, should they be requested

Kingdom of Saudi Arabia Ministry of Public Works and Housing Agency for Classification of Contractors	Schedule No.	10	Contractors Manual
	Form No.	AC1/8	Organization Chart
	Date	1/7/1401	

NAME OF FIRM		File No.

Provide on this page a simplified organization chart of the firm showing the titles, responsibilities and relationships of the principals. Indicate major technical and administrative departments.

Describe in this space the systems and procedures used by your firm in programming and controlling project execu e.g. PERT, CPM, other.

APPENDIX 14

President of the Council of Ministers Order No. 21909 of 15/9/1403 (June 26, 1983)

Kingdom of Saudi Arabia
Office of the President of the Council of Ministers

Subject: Reduction of the percentage which an administrative authority may add to the value of contracts made thereby from 20 percent to 10 percent

Crown Prince, Deputy President of the Council of Ministers and Head of the National Guard,

Greetings:

Whereas Article 25 of the Regulations for the Procurement of Government Purchases and Execution of its Projects and Works Implementing Rules authorizes an administrative authority to increase or decrease the obligations of the supplier or contractor up to 20 percent of the total value of the contract, and as the majority of agencies consider this right of increase to be normal practice to be effected in the majority of contracts, despite the fact that the Regulations state only that it is permissible, and as continuation of this principle has come to represent a financial burden which should be terminated, particularly as funds authorized for projects are within the limits of their necessary costs only, a situation giving rise to claims for additional credits or transfers from other projects, in addition to which such increase causes government agencies and consulting offices supervising execution to be less precise in stipulating when laying down conditions and specifications or during execution, due to their knowledge that it is possible to correct any errors or shortfall occurring by using their authority to add the 20 percent rate.

Therefore and in furtherance of the requirements of the public interest, we request you to reduce the said rate to 10 percent instead of 20 percent with respect to the increase of the supplier's or contractor's obligations. The rate of reduction shall remain at its present limit of 20 percent. You are to take the necessary action in accordance therewith. Copies of this Order have been circulated to the authorities concerned for compliance.

President of the Council of Ministers

APPENDIX 15

Minister of Commerce Resolution No. 680 of 9/11/1398 H (October 11, 1978)

The Minister of Commerce,
Pursuant to his authority,
And having reviewed the Companies Regulations issued by Royal Decree No. M/6 dated 22/3/1385 H;
And having reviewed paragraph 9 added to Article 229 of the Companies Regulations by Royal Decree No. M/5 dated 13/3/1387 H;
And in view of the requirements of the public interest,
Decree as follows:

First: Managers of foreign companies contracting with government agencies in the Kingdom pursuant to special contracts or entering into subcontracts with such companies with the approval of the competent government authorities shall within thirty days of the date of signature of the contract apply to the Ministry of Commerce to obtain the necessary licence to open an office in one of the cities of the Kingdom in order to undertake the execution of the works entrusted to them pursuant to such contracts. They shall submit all the particulars and documents necessary for issuance of the licence. Managers of foreign companies operating in the Kingdom which have not obtained the said licence shall file their applications within thirty days of the date of effectiveness of this Resolution.

Second: Branches and offices of foreign companies operating in the Kingdom shall be required to prepare for each fiscal year a statement on the financial position of the branch or office and a report on the activities of the branch or office in the Kingdom setting forth in particular all the works which it has undertaken during the year and the projects which it has executed or which are under execution.

The managers of such branches or offices shall send copies of such documents to the Companies Directorate within one month of the date of preparation of the said documents.

Third: The branches and offices referred to shall facilitate the task of the Ministry's representatives of inspecting their documents, books and records and shall furnish the particulars and information which they shall request.

Fourth: This Resolution shall be published in the Official Journal and shall be effective as of the date of publication.

Minister of Commerce

APPENDIX 16

Standard Application Form for Temporary License

KINGDOM OF SAUDI ARABIA

MINISTRY OF COMMERCE

DEPARTMENT OF INTERNAL COMMERCE

File No: ....
Foreign Companies: ....
Ref. No: ....
Date: ....

Application for
registration of foreign
companies contracting
with government
authorities and agencies

PARTICULARS OF THE FOREIGN COMPANY

Name of Company: ....
Type of Company: ....
Nationality: ....
Head Office Address Abroad: ....
Address of Company in the Kingdom: ....
City: .... Quarter: .... Telex No: ....
PB: .... Telephone: .... Street: ....
Name of Manager in Charge in the Kingdom: ....
Nationality: .... Passport No: .... Date of Issue: ....
Place of Issue: .... Residency: .... Telephone No. ....

PARTICULARS OF THE GOVERNMENT AUTHORITY OR AGENCY
CONTRACTING WITH IT

Name of the Authority with which the Company has Contracted: ....
Summary of the Work Pursuant to the Contract: ....
Place of Execution of the Work: ....
Term of the Contract: .... Commencing on: .... Terminating on: ....
Date of Final Acceptance: ....
Value of the Contract in Riyals: ....
Additional Particulars: ....

APPENDIX 16

PARTICULARS OF THE SAUDI AGENT

Name of Agent: .... Legal Form: ....
Address of Main Office: ....
City: .... Quarter: .... Street: ....
PB: .... Telephone: ....
Commercial Register: .... No: .... City: .... Date: ....
Name of the Manager in Charge of the Agent's Activities: ....
Nationality: ....
Identity Card No: .... Date: .... Place of Issue: ....
Passport No: .... Date: .... Place of Issue: ....
Amount of Commission: ....
Address of the Agent's Branches in the Kingdom (if any): ....

DECLARATION

It is hereby certified that the information contained in this application is correct and accurate and the manager of the foreign company shall bear full responsibility if it is proved otherwise.

It is understood that the Department of Internal Commerce at the Ministry of Commerce shall be notified of any changes that may occur in respect of such information.

Name: ....
Position: ....
Signature: ....
Company Seal: ....

CERTIFICATION BY THE CONTRACTING GOVERNMENT AUTHORITY OR AGENCY

We certify the validity of the particulars in this application.
Name: ....
Position: ....
Signature: ....
Official Seal: ....
Made On: ....

STATUS OF THE FOREIGN COMPANY IN THE RESOLUTIONS OF THE REGIONAL SAUDI BOYCOTT OF ISRAEL OFFICE*

Name of Company: ....
Nationality: ....
Head Office Address Abroad: ....

The above named company is/is not recorded currently on the black list at the present time.

Director General of the Regional Saudi
Boycott of Israel Office: ....
Signature: ....
Seal: ....

* The said particulars shall be given in writing by the company and certified by the Regional Saudi Boycott of Israel Office at the Ministry of Commerce before submission of the licence application to the Department of Internal Commerce.

APPENDIX 17

Council of Ministers Resolution No. 266 of 21/2/1398 H

The Council of Ministers,

Having reviewed the document attached to this Resolution including two letters addressed from H.E. The Minister of Commerce, No. 3/9/SH/7/9/487 dated 14/8/1394 H and No. 3/9/SH/7/9/5182 dated 24/5/1396 H wherein reference is made to Council of Ministers Resolution No. 1295 dated 26/10/1393 H relating to formation of a committee from the Ministry of Finance and the Ministry of Commerce to study the subject of foreign establishments and companies which are still using foreign languages in their records and correspondence in violation of Consultative Council Decision No. 48 of 1/6/1371 H, approved by Council of Ministers Resolution No. 233 of 17/12/1379 H in the light of circumstances prevailing at that time and which is in need of alteration.

H.E. has declared that the committee referred to above has been formed. The committee has prepared minutes and a draft of a resolution to discuss the subject. Therefore, H.E. hopes to take this into account and after reviewing Memorandum No. 181/8 dated 9/5/1396 H in this regard resolves the following:

1. Foreign companies and establishments, their branches and offices in the Kingdom of Saudi Arabia must use the Arabic language in their correspondence with government authorities.
2. Every violation of the preceding provision will be punished by a financial penalty not exceeding ten thousand Saudi riyals for each offence. The penalty will be doubled in case of repetition. In such event, a penalty consisting of not dealing with the violator for one year will be imposed in addition to the penalty. Any person repeating the violation within three years from the final approval of his previous punishment will be subject to this provision.
3. The Commission for the Settlement of Commercial Disputes shall hear any violation of the provisions hereof.
4. Every government authority shall inform the Ministry of Commerce of any violation of the provisions hereof. The Ministry through its public prosecutors shall bring the relevant claim before the Commission for the Settlement of Commercial Disputes.

Deputy Prime Minister

APPENDIX 18

Minister of Commerce Resolution No. 1502 of 8/3/1400 H

Relating to the Rules for Licensing Foreign Companies to Establish an Office in the Kingdom

The Minister of Commerce,

Having reviewed Article 228 of the Companies Regulations issued by Royal Decree No. M/6 dated 22/3/1385 H,

And in furtherance of the public interest,

And pursuant to his authority,

Decree as follows:

Article 1. By resolution of the Minister of Commerce foreign companies having contracted with government authorities may be licensed to establish a representative office to supervise their activities in the Kingdom and to facilitate communications with their head office in accordance with the conditions and rules set forth in this Resolution.

Article 2. The prerequisite for the issuance of the license is the submission of an application by the foreign company to the Companies Administration in the Ministry of Commerce to which shall be attached the following documents:

    a. A recommendation from a government department in the Kingdom, commission, public agency or company in which the State or public juristic persons participate having contracted with the company.

    b. Copies of the company's articles of association and its registration certificate in its home country.

    c. A copy of the resolution issued by the company to open a representative office in the Kingdom.

    d. A copy of the board of directors' resolution giving authority to the office manager.

Article 3. The ministerial resolution issuing the license shall specify the city of location of the office in the Kingdom and the number of employees therein in the light of the company's requirements and the public interest. The number of employees may not be increased without prior approval from the Ministry.

Article 4. The activity of the office is limited to undertaking services related to the supervision and follow-up of the company's activities in the Kingdom and the coordination of relations between it and the authorities having contracted with it.

Article 5. The office is prohibited from undertaking any direct or indirect commercial activity.

Article 6. A register for the registration of offices licensed to operate in the Kingdom shall be established in the Companies Administration in the Ministry of Commerce. The basic particulars pertaining to the company and its activities in the Kingdom shall be recorded in the register in addition to particulars relating to the office.

The office shall be granted a certificate indicating the issuance of the licence and the number and date of registration.

Article 7. In the case of violation by the office of the provisions of this Resolution or the resolution issuing the license, the license shall be withdrawn, the registration shall be cancelled, and the office and the concerned parties shall be notified to undertake its closing.

The license shall terminate automatically on the termination of the company's activities in the Kingdom.

The Minister of Commerce may at any time withdraw the license without stating the reasons therefor.

Article 8. The issuance of the license shall have no effect on the applicability of the provisions of the Regulations Governing the Relationship between the Foreign Contractor and its Saudi Agent issued by Royal Decree No. M/2 of 21/1/1398 H.

Article 9. This Resolution shall be published in the Official Journal and shall be effective from the date of its publication.

Minister of Commerce

APPENDIX 19

License Application Forms for Contracting and Industrial Ventures

Part 1

Ministry of Industry and Electricity
Industrial Affairs Agency

License Application Form for Industrial project‡ Establishment

H. E. The Minister of Industry and Electricity
Riyadh, Saudi Arabia

Greetings:

I hereby apply for a license for the establishment of an industrial project in the city of: ....

To produce: ....
....

in conformance with the Regulations in effect and I admit that the data, schedules and information inserted, attached hereto, are to the best of my knowledge, valid and [accurate].

....
(Applicant's Signature)

Date   /   /   13   A.H.

Remarks

(1) Applicant should sign all the pages of the application and the attachments therewith. Any cancellations, crosses and scratches should also be authenticated.

‡ Note that the term "project" should be understood as "venture".

(2) In case required raw material pre-supposes an official license from the concerned government department, the same should be attached.

(3) In case of foreign capital investment 3 copies of this application must be submitted. Also the documents showing the experience of the foreign partner in the field of relevant production and signed copy of the contract between Saudi and foreign partners should also be attached.

(4) If needed, separate sheets should be used and enclosed herewith.

License application for industrial project establishment

Applicant's name ....

Applicant's nationality ....

Identity card number (for Saudi nationals)/passport no. ....Date....................

Place of issue ....

Applicant's full address ....

....

A. Project legal form

1. Project proposed commercial title ....

2. Project proposed headquarters ....

B. Project statutory status (entity)

1. Individual.
3. Limited partnership.
5. Stock company.

2. Joint venture.
4. Limited liability [company].

N.B. The selected status shall be ticked with $\boxed{\sqrt{}}$

C. Type of investment (local/foreign/joint)...

D. Total investment (as per page 10 herein) and its resources

Resource	Value	Ratio resource/total investment	Interests %	Loan period
Paid-up capital	....	....	....	....
Long-term loans:				
1 -	....	....	....	....
2 -	....	....	....	....
3 -	....	....	....	....
Short-term loans.				
1 -	....	....	....	....
2 -	....	....	....	....
3 -	....	....	....	....
TOTAL				

Paid-up capital and partners' names and shares

Partner's name	Nationality	Address	Partner's share			
			Cash	Property	Total	%
....	....	....	....	....	....	....
....	....	....	....	....	....	....
		Total				

Statistical data

1. Imported quantities (during the last three years) of items to be produced

Item No.	Commodity	Year			Year			Year..............			Remarks
		Value	Qty.	Unit	Value	Qty.	Unit	Value	Qty.	Unit	
....	......										....
....	......										....

Source of above data: ....

2. Existing local factories (producing similar items or those to be produced)

Name of the factory	City	Maximum annual capacity	Markets	
			Zone	Percentage
....	....	....	....	....

Source of above data: ....

Capacity

3. Items to be produced and respective production

Items	Daily working hours	Annual working days	Daily productive capacity	Maximum annual productive capacity
....	....	....	....	....

411

Remarks:

Separate sheet attachments should include:

(a) Detailed description of production process for each item to be produced.

(b) Detailed layout, drawings and plans of production. Document showing technical know-how and technical assistance.

(c) Source and references on which designs and measurements are based shall be stated, and copy of each shall be attached.

4. Raw materials required for one year and prices CIF (including packages and packings)

Name and type of material	Unit	Qty	Unit price SR	Total SR	Place of origin
....	....	....	....	....	....
Total					

5. Manpower

CATEGORY	SAUDIS		nonSAUDIS		TOTAL		Remarks
	No.	Annual wages and salaries	No.	Annual wages and salaries	No.	Annual wages and salaries	
Non-technical labour							
Technical labour							
Engineer							
Administrator							
Total							

Remarks:

Please give details on separate sheets about the following:

1. Project's management: how it is run, managers' names and experience in production line etc.

2. Training programs and plans for training Saudis.

3. Rules and regulations adopted for the safety and protection of workers and employees.

4. Industrial safety devices and implements that should be rendered accessible and available in the factory.

I, ... the Applicant hereby undertake to adhere to and observe the clauses and terms of security and safety attached hereto and to cooperate with the Civil Defence Units in this respect.

Signature ....

6. Equipment, machinery and apparatus required for the project and value—CIF

Type and model of machine	Number	Unit price in foreign currency	Total price SR	Annual productive capacity	Remarks
....	....	....	....	....	....
Total					

Remarks:

1. Relevant catalogues of above should be attached.
2. Relevant offers (quotations) for such equipment should be attached.
3. For used items, if any, please mention years of use.
4. Place of origin wherefrom the equipment shall be imported is to be mentioned in remarks column.

7. Data about the factory/project

1 Total area of the factory: (sq. meters)   ....
   cost per sq. meter   ....

2 Total built-up area (sq. meters)   ....

   (A) Area of workshop: (sq. meters)   ....
       Height.........meters
       Type of building ....
       Cost per sq. meter ....

   (B) Area of storage: (sq. meters)   ....
       Type of building ....
       Cost per sq. meter ....

   (C) Area of administration building: (sq. meters) ....
       Type of building ....
       Cost per sq. meter ....

3 Project's requirements

   (A) Electrical power
       Installed power ....kW
       Peak load ....kW
       Annual energy consumption ....kWh
       Supply voltage .... volts
       Source of power supply ....

(B) Water
Source ....
Annual quantity of consumption (tons) ....
(C) Fuel
Diesel............................liters
Solar ....liters
Kerosene........................liters

8. Invested capital (total investment)

	SR
(A) FIXED CAPITAL:	
1. Land value (if owned by the factory)	....
2. Building costs (if owned by the factory)	....
3. Equipment and machinery value	....
4. Installation charges as percent of equipment and machinery and generators, if any	....
5. Vehicles and transport means value	....
6. Furniture value	....
7. Pre-production expenses, if any	....
Total	
(B) WORKING CAPITAL:	
1. Annual land rent (if not owned by factory)	....
2. Annual building rent (if not owned by factory)	....
3. Cost of raw materials required for three months	....
4. Quarterly wages, salaries and remunerations and bonuses	....
5. Quarterly power value	....
6. Quarterly fuel value	....
7. Quarterly water value	....
8. Quarterly maintenance value	....
9. Quarterly marketing costs	....
Total	
Grand Total fixed and working capital	

Note:

(1) Any variation on the aforementioned periods should be justified.
(2) Phases and stages proposed for execution of the project and periods pertaining to each (timetable attached).

9. Project feasibility study

To be submitted together with the application form. There should be a feasibility study covering production costs for every product separately (additional sheets may be used). Feasibility study, however, is based on annual production volume (quantity) proposed. The following offers some guidance:

1. Annual production fixed costs

(a) ANNUAL DEPRECIATIONS

SR

Buildings and constructions depreciation at 5% of prime value (or annual rent if not owned) ....

Equipment and machinery at 10% of prime value ....

Vehicles and transport means at 20% of prime value ....

Furniture at 10% of prime value ....

Pre-production expenses at 20% of prime value ....

Installation charges at 10% of prime value ....

Total _____

Note: Any variation on the aforesaid depreciation rates should be justified.

(b) MAINTENANCE

Mode of maintenance as well as amount appropriated and stipulated in contract for this purpose either a lump sum price contract or as percentages of equipment and machinery value ....

(c) STAFF

Salaries of employees, administrative engineers (such as managers, accountants, engineers, storage keepers and gatemen etc.) ....

End of service remuneration at 8% of annual total salaries and wages ....

Total _____

(d) ANY OTHER FIXED COSTS ....

Total fixed costs _____

2. Annual production variable costs

Direct raw materials ....

Labour wages (technical and non-technical) ....

Power ....

Fuel ....

Water ....

Marketing costs ....

Other variable costs ....

Total variable costs _____

Total fixed and variable costs _____

$$3. \ \textit{Unit production cost} = \frac{\text{Fixed Costs} + \text{Variable Costs}}{\text{Annual Units Produced}} = \underline{\hspace{3cm}}$$

10. Profitability of the project

Proposed selling price of the unit ....

Value of the annual sales (quantity × price) ....

Annual profit ....

Percentage of profit against invested capital % ....

Note:

Should plant produce more than one item, both fixed and variable costs should be duly channelled and properly distributed on all producible items, and detailed costs accounts and profitability worked out accordingly for each item produced.

11. Comparative price study

Comparing import prices with local production prices of similar commodities:

(a) Custom duties on similar items to be produced % ....

    Import cost port delivery (without customs) ....

    Import cost (with customs + transport + clearance) ....

    Wholesale price in local market ....

(b) Wholesale gross price of similar local products ....

(c) Wholesale proposed price of project's products ....

12. Detailed marketing zones and relevant production percentage to be absorbed by each

....

....

13. Methods of utilization or disposal of industrial production waste

14. Products quality control methods, and what equipment used for this purpose

15. Any further information applicant likes to add

(Please use separate sheets if required)

Civil defense department operation/safety section

Instructions for factories

1. A lot of factors should be taken into account such as factory size, kind of raw material processed and extent of risk and danger involved in case of fire. Also, harmful, unwholesome and disturbing conditions should equally be considered. By "factories" it is meant those which process and convert raw materials into processed, manufactured or semi-manufactured items. Included in factory designs should be

the safety devices explained hereinafter. But, for the already existing factories, only practically observable instructions are applicable.

2. Selection of location is one of the most significant preliminary steps in setting up a new factory. In this respect, direction of winds prevalent in the area and other climatic conditions, such as humidity and dryness, should be taken into consideration. Thus, soaring furnace smoke, foul smells and the like could be obviated.

3. In larger factories, inlets and outlets (entrances and exits) should be adequately wide. Corridors, passages and ways are to be of a one-way type and those used by pedestrians should lead directly to the outside of factory buildings, for easy and quick vacation in the event of fire or emergency.

4. There should be automatic fire extinguishing systems for putting out fire quickly after it has broken out; and the burning objects should be taken into account insofar as the said systems should be equipped and fed with proper anti-fire substances. For instance, plants producing dry products like wood, textiles, paper and cardboard should be equipped with systems using water or similar liquids for extinguishing fire, whereas in those plants producing inflammable liquids, their systems should be based on foams, carbon dioxide or dry chemical powders, since water is unsuitable here. Metals and gas manufacturing plants require fire extinguishing systems using dry chemical powders system piping, and will therefore be equipped with suitable extinguishing agents, such as certain chemicals or ordinary water. Under certain pressure and temperature, depending on thermostat efficiency, the automatic sprinklers should open and the agents start working. Automatic fire alarm systems should be installed, in addition to ordinary portable fire extinguishing devices, as required.

5. Power installations should combine both technicality and safety with relevant regulators to minimize discrepancies in voltage and frequency. All fuses must be automatic, wiring internal, and main breaker be mounted on a readily noticed and accessible place, to immediately break current wherever necessary.

6. Products and raw material stores and warehouses should be positioned away from the sources of energy (fuel, power etc.) and should be well ventilated. Products are to be properly stacked and stored with adequate passages in between, allowing free movement and easing the ventilation process.

7. In larger plants of more than one storey high there should be an emergency rescue stairway made of flameproof materials, separate from the main entrance and leading directly to the yard outside the plant.

8. Certain underground shelters should be built in large plants, well designed to accommodate all plant employees and workers. Such shelters must be multipurpose so as to be used, under ordinary circumstances, as parking areas, storing places for flameproof products and materials, etc. Shelters, should have emergency exits.

9. Special firemen teams should be formed from plant employees and workers and given sufficient training in combating fire. Plants should be equipped with first aid cabinets.

10. Plant owners should be notified to readily dispose of inflammable industrial waste and have it burnt in remote places designated for this purpose.

11. In plants releasing heavy smoke or giving off thick gases, suitable purifying-air-masks should be available.

12. Every plant owner should provide his employees and workers with protective wear, such as helmets, spectacles, footwear, gloves, etc.

13. Plants producing foam rubber and similar products, should be equipped with normal fire extinguishing devices with $2\frac{1}{2}$ inch main pipe connection. The auxilliary connection pipes inside the plant should be of $1\frac{1}{2}$ inch diameter, fitted with flexible hoses, of the same diameter, and of sufficient length to reach all the spots inside the plant. The main distributing connection should be installed outside the plant at a prominent place to be operated easily by the civil defence crew. A substantial supply of water should be ensured.

List of documents required for industrial projects

1. Application forms should be completed in triplicate.

2. The relevant feasibility study must be attached to the form; if in a language other than Arabic, an Arabic translation shall be enclosed.

3. A scheme for training Saudis, both managerially and technically, is required.

4. Permit to utilize product's industrial patent in the Kingdom, particularly for pre-fabricated housing projects and others.

5. The contract duly signed by the partners (in a new project) in accordance with the Saudi Companies Regulations.

6. The agreement for purchasing and procuring equipment and machinery or the commercial communications exchanged for procuring same; or the vendors' quotations and proposals relating to the said equipment and machinery. Whether or not the agreement would involve installation and operation must explicitly be stated therein.

7. Foreign participant's expertise shall, by documents, be evidenced (presentation of balance sheets shall be preferred but not be obligatory). Documents, however, shall be attested by the authorities concerned.

8. Foreign partner's address in his country of origin.

9. Approval of foreign partner's board of directors for entering into the new project in question.

10. Ministry of Health's approval, in the case of drugs manufacturing projects.

Part 2

Ministry of Industry and Electricity
Foreign Capital Investment Committee

License Application Form for Establishment of a Contracting Project‡ in Accordance with Foreign Capital Investment Regulations*

H. E. The Minister of Industry and Electricity, Riyadh

Greetings:

I submit to Your Excellency my license application form for establishing:

( ) A construction contracting project.
( ) A maintenance and services contracting project.
( ) An engineering contracting project.

This project will cover the following specialities:

—Civil (urban) projects (buildings; airports; roads; bridges; dams; ports; sewer systems; water systems; pre-fabricated buildings).
—Mechanical projects.
—Electrical projects (power generation stations; transmission and distribution networks).
—Sanitary works.
—Well drilling.
—Others.

In the city of ....

I am willing to execute the said project in the Kingdom of Saudi Arabia pursuant to the Regulations in effect. I admit the data and information contained in this form are correct, true and factual.

APPLICANT

Name: ....

Signature: ....

Dated   /   /   14   A.H.

Important Remarks:

(a) Each page of the application form should bear applicant's signature. Also every separate sheet added thereto, if any, should be signed. In case of any cancellation or scratch therein, the same should be authenticated.

‡ Note that the term "project" should be understood as "venture".
* This Form is to be used for the following: 1. Construction—Services—Maintenance; 2. Maintenance Undertakings.

(b) Each of the above activities to be conducted should be ticked with the mark ☑

1. Applicant's status

    (a) Name ....

    (b) Nationality ....

    (c) Number and date of identity card or passport ....

    (d) Permanent address .... Tel. no. ....
        ....

    (e) Applicant's role in or connection with the proposed project ....

    (f) Saudi partner's address ....

2. Project's status

    (a) Project's proposed commercial name ....

    (b) Project's proposed headquarters ....

    (c) Statutory entity: individual; joint venture; limited partnership; limited liability [company]; stock company ....

3. Distribution of proposed project's capital

Partner's Name	Nation-ality	Permanent Address	Partner's Capital Share			%
			Value (SR)			
			Cash	[Property]	Total	

4. Partners' names and addresses, and other activities in the Kingdom wherein partners hold capital shares

Partner's Name	Names of Firms he participates in	Activities of Firms	Addresses of Firms

5. Statement of the projects executed in the Kingdom by the foreign investor during the last three years

Project	Value SR (Million)	Commence-ment Date	Completion Date	Belonging To	Supporting Documents

6. Statement of the projects currently being executed by the foreign investor

Project	Value SR (Million)	Completion Date, per program	Belonging To	Remarks

7. Statement of machinery and equipment owned by the foreign partner outside the Kingdom

Machine Name	Model & Manufacture Year	Quantity	Value	Remarks

8. Statement of machinery and equipment owned by the foreign partner inside the Kingdom

Machine Name	Model & Manufacture Year	Quantity	Value	Remarks

9. Foreign partner's technical and administrative staff outside the Kingdom

....

....

10. Foreign partner's technical and administrative staff inside the Kingdom

....

....

11. Relation of [parent] company abroad to the proposed project should be explicitly explained. Also explain the facilities to be rendered to the said project

....

....

Documents required for

(a) Sea and land transportation companies;
(b) Hotels, restaurants and hospitals;
(c) Construction ventures;
(d) Maintenance and technical services;
(e) Specialized works.

1. Three application forms, showing the specific fields of activity, capital (cash or property) and shares.

2. The agreement signed by the Saudi and foreign partners.

3. An attested certificate whereby applicant is authorized in a specific manner (*e.g.*, to act for partners, etc.).

4. Certificates, duly certified by official authorities, indicating the most significant works the foreign partner carried out both inside and outside the Kingdom. His annual reports revealing the activities he performed are acceptable in this respect (revealing the value of the project completion date and the client).

5. Foreign partner's Board of Directors decision to invest in Saudi Arabia and set up the project under licensing.

6. A certified document indicating foreign partner's registration in Commercial Register of his country of origin.

7. Foreign partner's last three balance sheets and annual reports (if possible).

8. A document showing the facilities and support the foreign parent company is going to afford to the joint venture.

9. Quotations and catalogues for the equipment and machinery required for the proposed project.

10. Saudi partner's classification certificate in contractor's register, if any.

11. In case the project is intended for maintenance, a list of the equipment and machinery required for establishing a complete workshop in the Kingdom should be provided.

12. Foreign partner's address in the country of origin, Saudi partner's address in the Kingdom as well as the mailing addresses of both.

13. Copy of Saudi C.R. and identity card.

APPENDIX 20

Additional List of Required Documents to be Attached to License Application to Foreign Capital Investment Committee

Clarification and elaboration of the Official List of Required Documents

1. A copy of the draft articles of association of the proposed company in Saudi Arabia.

2. A copy of the duly certified power of attorney executed by the foreign investor to the person who shall sign the articles of association of the proposed company on its behalf.

3. A copy of the duly certified power of attorney issued by the foreign investor to a person applying on its behalf to take the necessary steps for obtaining the license to establish the company and for its commercial registration in Saudi Arabia.

4. A duly certified copy of the certificate of incorporation of the foreign investor in its country of origin.

5. The foreign investor's board of directors' resolution to invest in Saudi Arabia and to establish the proposed company.

6. A list of the most significant works carried out by the foreign investor outside Saudi Arabia in the field of activities which the proposed company proposes to carry on in Saudi Arabia, indicating the value and description of each project.

7. A list of machinery and equipment owned by the foreign investor outside Saudi Arabia, indicating the value of such machinery and equipment.

8. A document showing the support and facilities which the foreign investor will render to the proposed company in Saudi Arabia.

9. A statement indicating in categories and numbers the foreign investor's technical and administrative staff outside Saudi Arabia.

10. The foreign investor's annual reports and balance sheets for the last three years.

11. In case the objectives of the company include maintenance works, then a list of machinery, equipment, tools and other preparations necessary for setting up a

complete workshop in the Kingdom should be provided. The value of the equipment should be indicated.

Note

(a) Documents mentioned in items 2 to 7 above must be certified by the Saudi Consulate abroad.

(b) The remaining documents (except for 1 and 10) should be on the letterhead of the foreign investor and signed and stamped by a competent official of such foreign investor.

APPENDIX 21

Standard Foreign Capital Investment Licenses

Contracting Venture, Ministerial Resolution No. (   ) of
   /   /

The Minister of Industry and Electricity,
Pursuant to his authority,
Having reviewed the minutes of the meeting of the Foreign Capital Investment
Committee in Session No. (   ) of (   )H paragraph (   ) containing the
recommendation to approve the license of (   ) in (   ) and specifying
the objectives of the company,
And the letters of the owners of the venture received on   /   /H including
their agreement to be bound by the recommendation of the Foreign Capital
Investment Committee with respect to the objectives of the company,
And the minutes of the meeting of the Investment Committee No. (.) of
(/   /) H paragraph ( ) concerning the approval of the application of the
owners of the venture,
And in accordance with the provisions of Article 2 of the Foreign Capital
Investment Regulations issued by Royal Decree No. M/4 dated 2/2/1399 H,
Decrees as follows:

1. To approve the license for a limited liability company in the city of (   )
named (   ) to engage in the business of (   ) having a capital of
(   ) Saudi riyals allocated between the following partners:
   (1) (   )/Saudi/with a share of (   )% of the capital,
   (2) (   )/nonSaudi/with a share of (   )% of the capital.

2. The Ministry shall have the right to revoke this license if the owners of the
venture fail to initiate the measures necessary to implement it within six months of
the date hereof and also if they violate any of the conditions or instructions set
forth in this Resolution.

3. The owners of the company shall be bound to establish it in accordance with
the studies submitted to this Ministry, provided that they shall obtain the approval
of the Ministry regarding any change sought to be made to it relating to size and
activity.

4. The owners of the company shall register it at the Ministry of Commerce in
accordance with the requirements of the Commercial Register Regulations.

5. The owners of the company shall not sell it or sell or assign the license granted to them in whole or in part except after prior approval of the Ministry.

6. The owners of the company shall be obligated to provide the technical facilities necessary therefor and to prepare training programs for Saudis employed therein for the technical and specialized work engaged in by the company.

7. The owners of the company shall be obligated to use the products of national industry set forth in the list prepared by the Ministry of Industry and Electricity pursuant to Council of Ministers Resolution No. 377 dated 18/4/1398 H.

8. No partner named in paragraph 1 of this Resolution shall be entitled to a tax exemption with respect to contracts and work it has undertaken prior to this license, whether jointly or individually.

9. The owners of the company shall submit to the Ministry all particulars and information which the Ministry may require from them at the times specified therefor.

10. The owners of the company shall comply with the Accountants Regulations and submit their annual balance sheet to the Ministry.

11. The Deputy Minister for Industrial Affairs shall implement this Resolution and notify the competent authorities necessary for the implementation thereof.

Minister of Industry and Electricity

Industrial Venture
Ministerial Resolution No. (   ) of   /   / H

The Minister of Industry and Electricity,
Pursuant to his authority,
Having reviewed the minutes of the meeting of the Foreign Capital Investment Committee No. (   ) of (   )H paragraph (   ) containing the recommendation for a license to form (name of company) in the city of (   ),
And the venture assessment memorandum from the Industrial Licenses Department dated (   )H which recommended a license for the venture,
And in accordance with the provisions of Article 2 of the Foreign Capital Investment Regulations issued by Royal Decree No. M/4 dated 2/2/1399 H,
Decrees as follows:

1. To approve the license to form a limited liability company in the city of (   ) named (   ) having a capital of (   ) riyals, of which not less than 25% is paid up, allocated between the following partners:
   (1) (Name)/Saudi/with a share of (   )% of the capital,
   (2) (Name)/nonSaudi/with a share of (   )% of the capital.
For the purpose of (   ) having an estimated annual production capacity of (   ) and employing (   ) persons.

2. The Ministry shall have the right to revoke this license if the owners of the venture fail to initiate the measures necessary to establish it within six months of

the date hereof and also if they violate any of the conditions and instructions set forth in this Resolution.

3. The owners of the venture shall be bound to establish it in accordance with the studies submitted to this Ministry provided that they shall obtain the approval of the Ministry regarding any change desired to be made thereto.

4. The owners of the venture shall not sell it or sell or assign the license granted to them in whole or in part except after prior approval of the Ministry.

5. The owners of the venture shall comply with the standard specifications effective in the Kingdom. If such specifications are not available, the owners of the venture shall consult with the Saudi Arabian Standards Organization . . . to select the most suitable international specifications which fulfil the purpose until the issuance of Saudi specifications.

6. The owners of the venture shall submit all particulars and information which the Ministry may require from them at the times specified therefor.

7. The owners of the venture shall be obliged to provide the technical facilities necessary thereto and to prepare training programs for Saudis employed by the company for the technical works engaged in.

8. The owners of the venture shall comply with the Accountants Regulations and Depots Regulations and submit an annual balance sheet to the Ministry.

9. The products of the venture shall be subject to sale at the price which the Ministry shall determine on the basis of normal production costs plus a reasonable profit.

10. The Deputy Minister for Industrial Affairs shall implement this Resolution and notify the competent authorities necessary for the implementation thereof.

Minister of Industry and Electricity

APPENDIX 22

Minister of Commerce Resolution No. 151 of 17/8/1403 H (May 30, 1983) Relating to the Regulation of the Commercial Register

The Minister of Commerce,

Pursuant to the powers vested in him,

And pursuant to Council of Ministers Resolution No. 66 of 6/4/1374 H,

And having reviewed the report of the committee constituted to study the method of application of the Commercial Register and the possibility of developing registration procedures in conformity with the provisions of the Commercial Register Regulations,

And having reviewed Article 22 of the Commercial Register Regulations issued by High Order No. 21/1/4470 of 9/11/1375 H, and articles 1, 2, 3, 11 and 12 of the Regulations Implementing Rules,

And in accordance with the requirements of the interests of business,

Decrees as follows:

1. Without prejudice to Articles 2, 3 and 4 of the Commercial Register Regulations issued by High Order No. 21/1/4470 of 9/11/1375 H and Articles 2, 4 and 6 of the Regulations' Implementing Rules, a businessman or company may not have more than one main office. The competent officials in the Commercial Register Offices shall not enter acceptance of registration applications for main offices until having confirmed that the applicant has not previously registered a main office in any area of the Kingdom.

2. The Commercial Register Offices shall compile a list of the main offices of [businessmen] and companies registered in the Commercial Register and shall not register more than one sole proprietorship throughout the Kingdom for each businessman. If more than one place of business of a businessman is registered in the totality of Commercial Register Offices without a provision to the effect that the second place of business is a branch of the first place of business, whether the activity of each is different and whether such place of business is called a sole proprietorship, office, store, center or exhibition or any other designation, the competent official in the Commercial Register Office shall notify the businessman that he is required to change the names of his places of business to indicate that they are branches of the main office which he shall designate, provided that, in specifying the business name of any main office, it shall correspond to the name of

the businessman whenever possible and the procedures necessary for amendment shall be completed in accordance with the provisions of Article 6 of the Commerical Register Regulations.

3. Commercial Register Offices shall issue a registration certificate for businessmen's and companies' main offices whose particulars have been entered in the Commercial Register and which come within the jurisdiction of the Office in accordance with the two attached forms, provided that such certificate shall be numbered with the registration numbers of registration applications in the Commercial Register to which shall be added the sign of the location of the main office in accordance with the accompanying particulars. Registration certificates for branches of businessmen and companies whose particulars have been recorded in the Commercial Register and coming within the jurisdiction of the Office shall be issued in accordance with the two attached forms. Such certificate shall be numbered with the registration numbers of registration applications for branches in the Commercial Register without the addition of the location of their main offices. The preceding shall be effective as from 1/1/1404 H.

4. As of 1/1/1404 H the attached registration application forms for companies and businessmen and the forms for registering a change or deletion of registration shall replace the forms currently in use.

5. Every company or businessman whose activities require the opening of a branch in any locality of the Kingdom shall submit a registration application in the Commercial Register Office in which its main office is registered. The competent official in the Commercial Register Office shall study the application, fill in the facts relating thereto, prepare the registration certificate of the branch, record such information on the main office's page and register it in the Commercial Register if the location of the branch comes within the jurisdiction of the Office. If it is outside the Office's jurisdiction, the registration application for the branch shall, after fulfillment of the conditions, the recording of its acceptance and the filling out and signature of the registration certificate, be sent to the office within whose jurisdiction the branch is located for the registration of the particulars of the branch in the Commercial Register, the recording of the registration number of the branch on the registration certificate and delivery of the certificate to the businessman.

6. In registering the activities of places of business in the Commercial Register, the requirements of the international classification of commercial activities and the possibility of their conducting the specified activities shall be observed. The classification of registered activities shall be made in accordance with the attached list.

7. Commercial Register Offices shall compile a list of the registered places of business whose activities include noncommercial business, such as the professions and noncommercial services set forth in the Ministry's Circular No. 221/4968 of 29/12/1401 H, and shall notify the owners of such places of business that they shall apply for the deletion or amendment thereof. If the parties concerned fail to apply for deletion or amendment for more than one month from the date of their notification, the outcome shall be referred to us for the issuance of the necessary resolution.

8. The competent officials in the Commercial Register Offices shall not register unspecified commercial activities, such as general trade, miscellaneous trade, various commercial activities, trade in provisions, foodstuffs, consumer goods, luxury items and gifts, tenders, general contracting and commission agency. Commercial Register Offices shall compile a list of the places of business whose registered activities include general activities and notify the owners of such places of business that they shall apply for the deletion or amendment thereof. If the parties concerned fail to apply for deletion or amendment for more than one month from the date of their notification, the outcome shall be referred to us for the issuance of the necessary resolution.

9. If a businessman or company desires to open a place of business to engage in any kind of importing and exporting, or supply and contracting work, or the sale, purchase and leasing of real estate, or any other services related to commerce, he shall submit an application therefor to the Register Office in which his main office is registered, notifying such place of business as the services office therefor. The businessman shall adopt such office as his main office or a branch of his main office. The Commercial Register Offices shall compile a list of the places of business whose activities include any of the activities referred to and notify the owners thereof to amend their particulars accordingly. If the parties concerned fail to apply for deletion or amendment for more than one month from the date of their notification, the outcome shall be referred to us for the issuance of the necessary resolution.

10. This Resolution shall be published in the Official Journal and shall be implemented by the competent authorities.

Instructions for the Amendment of the Particulars of Companies and Sole Proprietorships

In implementation of H.E. the Minister of Commerce's Resolution No. 151 of 17/8/1403 H consolidating the main offices of companies and businessmen and introducing certain organizational measures for the Commercial Register, and due to the Ministry's wish to update the information recorded with it in the Commercial Register, two forms for such purpose have been prepared, one pertaining to companies and the other to businessmen registered in the Commercial Register. The Ministry requests every company or businessman to consult the nearest Chamber of Commerce and Industry or Commercial Register Office to obtain a copy of the form, complete it accurately and return it as soon as possible to the Register Office in which the company's or businessman's main office is registered, together with the completion of all the procedures required to amend the information in accordance with the Instructions, which may be obtained from the Chamber or the Office.

First Addresses of companies and sole proprietorships:

    (a) Documents required for amendment:

        (1) Submission of an application on the official letterhead of the company or sole proprietorship, together with an application form for the updating

of information to the Commercial Register Office in which the company's or sole proprietorship's main office is registered or the Commercial Register Office in which the place of business whose address is to be amended is registered.

(2) The original of the lease agreement or deed of title.

(3) The original of the commercial registration on which the address is to be amended.

(b) Procedures:

(1) Submission of the application to the competent Commercial Register Office or the main office.

(2) Payment of fees.

(3) Recording thereof in the Register.

Second Business name, activity, capital or allocations of shares:

(a) Documents required for amendment:

(1) Submission of an application on the official letterhead of the company or sole proprietorship, together with the form, to the Commercial Register Office in which the registration whose particulars are to be amended is registered or to the Commercial Register Office in which the main office of the sole proprietorship is registered.

And to the General Companies Administration, with respect to companies, provided that there shall be attached to the application with respect to companies the articles of association signed by the partners containing the provisions to be amended in the company's articles of association, together with the amendment resolution from the authority responsible for issuance thereof in accordance with the company's articles of association and the Companies Regulations and a copy of H.E. the Minister of Industry and Electricity's resolution amending the license, if the company is licensed under the [Foreign Capital] Investment Regulations.

(2) A copy of the approval of the other official authorities if the amendment relates to activities which in order to be registered require permissions with respect thereto.

(3) The original and a copy of the commercial registration whose particulars are to be amended.

(b) Procedures:

The same procedures shall apply as for the amendment of address, and in addition the articles, after being stamped by the General Companies Administration, shall be transmitted to the Notaries Public Department for notarization and compliance with the instructions concerning contracting work, real estate offices and licenses for general services.

Third New branches:

(a) Documents required for registration:

(1) Submission of an application on the official letterhead of the company or sole proprietorship, together with the form, to the Register Office in which the main office is registered or to the General Companies Administration with respect to companies, provided that the application

for registration of a company's branches shall be accompanied by the resolution authorizing the opening of the branch signed by the partners or persons duly authorized by the company's articles of association, a copy of the company's articles of association and bylaws and a copy of the resolution of the Minister of Industry and Electricity permitting the opening of the branch if the company is licensed under the [Foreign Capital] Investment Regulations.

(2) The original and a copy of the main registration.

(3) The lease agreement or deed of title of the branch's premises.

(4) A copy of the identity card of the person authorized to register the branch or his passport if he is a foreigner.

Fourth Managers of main offices and branches:

    (a) Documents required for registration:

(1) A copy of the identity card of the person to be authorized to manage the branch or his passport if he is a foreigner, provided that a foreigner shall be on the sponsorship of the company or sole proprietorship and shall have a valid residence and work permit.

(2) Submission of an application on the official letterhead of the company or sole proprietorship, together with the form to the Register Office in which the main office or branch that he is to manage is registered.

(3) A copy of the company's articles of association and bylaws and a copy of the resolution issued appointing him in accordance with the company's articles of association.

(4) The original and a copy of the commercial registration of the main office or branch in which the entry is to be made.

    (b) Procedures:

The same procedures shall be applied as for amendment of address.

APPENDIX 23

Saudi Industrial Development Fund
Loan Application, Standard Form Loan Application,
Loan Agreement, Note and Pledge Agreement*

Loan Application

1 Project Name: ....
Address ....
Telephone No. .... Telex (Cable) ....
Commercial Registration No. ....
City .... Date ....
Industrial Licence No. ....
Legal Form ....

2 Feasibility Study:

Applications can only be considered if a detailed Feasibility Study is provided, inclusive of:

(a) Market Analysis
(b) Management Structure Description
(c) Detailed, Project Cost Statement
(d) Detailed, Sources and Applications of Funds statement for the construction period
(e) Detailed Profit and Loss Projections
(f) Detailed Balance Sheet Projections
(g) Detailed Cash Flow Projections

Note: Profit and [Loss] Statements, Balance Sheets and Cash Flows should cover the full period of the projected life of the SIDF loan.

---

* This Appendix contains the English version of the documents, which differ in certain respects from the Arabic text thereof.

3 Project Representative: ....
Name ....
Address ....
Telephone No. .... Cable/Telex ....
Function ....
....
....

4 Technical Partner:

Name ....
Address ....
Telephone No. .... Cable/Telex ....
Activities ....
....
....

5 Nature of the project (including type of industry, product and market):
....
....

6 Purpose of the loan requested (check whatever is applicable):

Financing of:

☐ New Project ☐ Expansion ☐ Other (explain)
....

7 Expected date of Project implementation: ....

8 Project's financial requirements:

Current assets   SR ....
Fixed assets   SR ....
Total   SR ....

9 Sources of financing of the Project:

Debt   SR ....
Equity   SR ....
Total   SR ....

10 Percentage of equity owned by Saudis: ....

11 Amount of loan requested from SIDF: SR ....

Date of anticipated first borrowing: ....

---

12 Security offered (check whatever is applicable):

☐ Mortgage on plant   ☐ Investor guarantees

☐ Other security (explain) ....

....

---

13 Other Enclosures:

Documents:

☐ Company by-laws   ☐ Commercial registration

☐ Partnership agreement   ☐ Land title

☐ Industrial license   ☐ Decree

Agreements:

☐ Technical services   ☐ Management assistance

☐ Financing   ☐ Other

Contracts:

☐ Land   ☐ Lease

☐ Architect and civil engineering contractor   ☐ Sales

☐ Building contractor   ☐ Insurance

☐ Machinery and equipment   ☐ Other

Past financial statements (minimum 3 years):

☐ Investor(s)   ☐ Guarantor(s)

☐ Project entity   ☐ Technical Partner(s)

---

14 Date ....

Full name of applicant: (in print) ....

Signature of applicant ....

---

15 FOR S.I.D.F. USE ONLY

Application received on ....

By ....

Comments and action required: ....

....

....

Loan Agreement

........................14......H

(........................19......Gr.)

Borrower

Name ....

Address ....

....

Form of Entity

organized and existing under the Laws
and Regulations of the Kingdom of Saudi
Arabia and Registered in ....
under the Commercial Registration
No. ....
On ....

Loan No.

Maximum Loan:

SR ....   (..................)

(Saudi Riyals)

Drawdown Termination Date:

....13......H

(....19......Gr.)

Borrower's signature

Signature ....

Name of

Signatory ....

Position ....

Witnesses (1) ....

....

(2) ....

....

Fund's signature

Signature ....

Name of

Signatory ....

Position ....

Witnesses (1) ....

....

(2) ....

....

Repayment

Instalment No.	Date Gr.	Amount SR
....	....	....
....	....	....

Covenants

Maximum rental sum:

SR ....

Working capital ratio:

...............to........................... Period ....to ....

...............to........................... Period ....to ....

...............to........................... Period ....to ....

Liabilities to tangible net worth ratio:

...............to........................... Period ....to ....

436

..............to........................... Period ....to ....
..............to........................... Period ....to ....

Maximum dividend:
...................................percent.

Maximum capital expenditure:
SR ....

Operation date Gr. ....

Now it is hereby agreed as follows:

1. Definitions and interpretation

(1) In this Agreement:
    (a) "Business Day" means any day other than a Thursday, Friday or official holiday in Saudi Arabia;
    (b) "Drawdown Period" means the period commencing on the date hereof and ending on the drawdown termination date (stated on page 1) both dates inclusive;
    (c) "Loan" means the aggregate principal amount borrowed hereunder and for the time being outstanding;
    (d) "Mortgage Note" means the mortgage note in the form annexed hereto;
    (e) "Note" or "Notes" means the order note or notes executed and delivered pursuant to this Agreement in the form annexed hereto;
    (f) "Office of the Fund" means the office of the Fund in Riyadh, Saudi Arabia;
    (g) "Project" means the project described in Exhibit A hereto and "project description" means such description in the said Exhibit A.

(2) In this Agreement, unless the context otherwise dictates, words denoting the singular shall include the plural and vice versa, words denoting any gender shall include the other gender and the headings herein are for the purpose of reference only and shall not affect the construction hereof.

2. Agreement

Upon and subject to the terms and conditions of this Agreement, the Fund agrees to lend and the Borrower agrees to borrow an aggregate principal amount of up to but not exceeding the Maximum Loan stated on page 1.

3. Drawdown

(1) Whenever the Borrower desires to borrow hereunder it shall not later than five Business Days before the proposed date of such borrowing (which shall be a Business Day in the Drawdown Period) give to the Fund written or telex notice, effective upon receipt, specifying the date of the proposed borrowing and the amount thereof.

(2) Each drawing shall be paid by the Fund against the issue and delivery by the Borrower in favor of the Fund of a Note in an amount equal to the drawing concerned and with a maturity falling on the drawdown termination date stated on

page 1. Such Notes are hereinafter called "the Interim Notes". Upon the drawdown termination date each Interim Note shall be surrendered at the office of the Fund and cancelled against issue and delivery by the Borrower in favor of the Fund of a series of Notes ("the Final Notes") with aggregate face value equal to the aggregate face value of the surrendered Interim Notes and such series of Final Notes being in amounts and with maturities corresponding precisely to the repayment instalments on the Loan to become due under Clause 4 below.

4. Repayment

The Borrower will repay the aggregate principal amount of the Loan outstanding at the expiration of the Drawdown Period by instalments on the dates and in the amounts shown on page 2, each such payment being made against surrender of the then maturing Final Note provided that the amounts so shown shall be reduced *pro rata* in the event that the Maximum Loan (also so shown) is never drawn or the Loan outstanding is reduced by one or more prepayments during the Drawdown Period.

5. Prepayment

The Borrower may on any Business Day prepay the Loan in whole or in part without penalty. Amounts so prepaid may not be reborrowed hereunder. Such amounts prepaid during the Drawdown Period shall be applied *pro rata* against the repayment instalments referred to in Clause 4 above but such amounts prepaid after the Drawdown Period shall be applied against such instalments in inverse order of maturity. Each prepayment shall be made against surrender and cancellation of such of the Interim or Final Notes as may be appropriate and if the prepayment covers part only of any Note (whether Interim or Final) the Borrower shall at the same time as making the payment, issue and deliver to the Fund a substitute Note for the part not so covered.

6. Encouraging the private sector

The Borrower shall, during the construction phase of the Project and later during the production phase, observe and comply with the following:
(1) Purchase all building materials and equipment required for the project from Saudi manufacturers, in accordance with the offers presented, approved and mentioned in the project description sheet (Exhibit A of this Agreement);
(2) Award supervision of construction of the project and preparation of needed technical studies to Saudi consulting firms, if technical expertise is available at such firms;
(3) Engage only Saudi certified accountants to review and prepare financial statements.

7. Payments

All payments to be made by the Borrower hereunder shall be made in immediately available funds and in lawful money of Saudi Arabia without any deduction or withholding whatsoever either to the Office of the Fund or (if the

Fund shall from time-to-time so specify) to such bank account as may be so specified with direct telex/telegraphic advice to the Fund.

8. Conditions precedent

(1) The obligation of the Fund to make the Loan available hereunder is subject to the condition precedent that on or before the giving of the first notice of drawing under Clause 3(1) above the Fund shall have received all of the following in form and substance satisfactory to the Fund:

(*a*) Copies of the commercial registration and articles of association or other corporate documentation of the Borrower as requested and copies of the industrial license for the Project;

(*b*) Copy [of the] resolution of the Borrower to enter into this Agreement and the Mortgage Note;

(*c*) The original of the mortgage deed stated in the Mortgage Note duly executed by the Borrower together with evidence that the Mortgage Note has been notarized and recorded with a notary public and that the title deeds or documents to any land concerned with the Project have been deposited with the Fund or its nominee;

(*d*) Such other information and documents, including financial information concerning the Borrower and/or the Project as the Fund may request.

(2) At the time of giving of the notice of each drawing hereunder:

(*a*) The Borrower shall be deemed to represent, warrant and agree to and with the Fund that:

(1) The representations and warranties set out in Clause 9 below are true and accurate at that time as if made at that time; and

(2) No event of default as specified in Clause 11 below or event which with the giving of notice, lapse of time or other conditions would constitute such an event of default has occurred and is continuing or would result from the drawing then proposed to be made.

(*b*) The Borrower shall present the Fund with such evidence as the Fund deems satisfactory of project expenditures.

9. Representations, warranties and agreements

The Borrower hereby represents and warrants to and agrees with the Fund as follows:

(1) The Borrower is an entity and registered as shown on page 1 and the Borrower has the corporate power for, has taken all corporate action necessary and received all governmental authority necessary to authorize the undertaking and operation of the Project and entry into and performance of this Agreement, the Notes and the Mortgage Note and the same constitute legally valid and binding obligations of the Borrower enforceable against it in accordance with their terms;

(2) The Borrower will undertake and operate the project in accordance with the plans and specifications contained or referred to in the Project Description and the proceeds of the Loan shall be used exclusively for the Project;

(3) The execution, delivery and performance of this Agreement, the notes and the mortgage note by the Borrower will not violate any legal or contractual obligation of the Borrower;

(4) Save as otherwise disclosed to the Fund the Borrower is not in default under any contractual obligation and no event has occurred which with the giving of notice, lapse of time or other conditions would constitute such a default as aforesaid and no litigation, arbitration or administrative proceedings are presently current or pending or, to the knowledge of the Borrower threatened; and

(5) All information concerning the Borrower produced to the Fund is true and correct and the Borrower is not aware of any fact, matter or thing which ought to be disclosed to the Fund or which if disclosed to the Fund might materially affect the decision of the Fund to make the loan.

10. Covenants

So long as the Loan shall remain outstanding or any other amount shall remain payable hereunder the Borrower covenants and agrees that unless the Fund shall have first otherwise consented in writing:

(1) *Furnishing financial statements*

The Borrower shall furnish to the Fund: (a) as soon as possible but in no event later than 90 days after the end of its financial year a balance sheet of the Borrower as at the end of such year together with a profit and loss account of the Borrower covering such year and such balance sheet and profit and loss account shall be certified by independent auditors selected by the Borrower and satisfactory to the Fund; (b) within 30 days after the end of each period of three months from the date hereof interim financial statements including a statement of the application of all amounts disbursed by the Fund; (c) forthwith upon request from the Fund such further financial and other information and documents concerning the affairs and financial condition of the Borrower as the Fund may from time-to-time request.

(2) *Access to books and inspection*

The Borrower shall keep proper books of record and account and upon request of the Fund shall give any representative or agent of the Fund full and free access during such normal business hours to examine, audit and make copies of and take extracts from all or any of its books, records, contracts and other documents and to inspect the Project and its site and any other properties or assets of the Borrower.

(3) *Supplemental mortgages*

The Borrower shall execute further mortgages over the property comprised in the Mortgage Note from time-to-time as required by the Fund.

(4) *Maintenance of operations and compliance with laws*

The Borrower shall: (a) maintain and keep in force its commercial registration and the industrial license for the Project and shall obtain and maintain all authorizations, required in relation to the Project and/or in relation to the making and performance of this Agreement, the Notes and the Mortgage Note; (b) not carry on any business or activity save for the Project; (c) observe and comply with all laws, regulations, orders, decrees and directives of any governmental authority, agency or court having jurisdiction over the Borrower or its property or assets.

(5) *Litigation etc.*

The Borrower shall forthwith notify the Fund in writing and thereafter keep the Fund fully informed of any litigation, arbitration or administrative proceedings.

(6) *Taxes etc.*

The Borrower shall pay and discharge any and all tax assessments and governmental charges or levies imposed upon it or its property or assets, prior to the dates on which penalties would otherwise attach thereto.

(7) *Insurance*

The Borrower shall take out and maintain at its own expense with insurers acceptable to the Fund such insurances in such amounts against such risks and with only such restrictions and exclusions as may be satisfactory to the Fund. The policies relating to the said insurances shall contain or be endorsed with loss payee clauses in favour of the Fund if so requested by the Fund and such policies together with the premium receipts and any insurance certificates shall on demand be available for the Fund to inspect and take copies. In the event of any moneys being received under any insurance in respect of any of the property and assets of the Borrower such moneys shall be applied in replacing, restoring or reinstating the property or asset destroyed or damaged unless the Fund otherwise directs in writing.

(8) *Rentals*

The Borrower shall not incur obligations in respect of leases or rents requiring expenditures during any financial year of the Borrower aggregating more than the maximum rental sum stated on page 2.

(9) *Encumbrances*

The Borrower shall not (other than as provided in the Mortgage Note and unless otherwise consented to by the Fund) create incur or suffer to exist any mortgage, charge, lien, pledge or other encumbrance on any of its property, revenue or assets now owned or hereafter acquired.

(10) *Mergers etc.*

The Borrower shall not unless otherwise consented to by the Fund: (a) merge or consolidate with or into any person or entity; (b) sell, lease, transfer or otherwise dispose of (whether by a single transaction or by a number of transactions whether related or not) the whole or a substantial part of [the Project] or (except in the ordinary course of [business]), its assets, whether now owned or hereafter acquired; or (c) acquire all or substantially all of the assets and/or liabilities of any person or entity.

(11) *Substantial changes*

The Borrower shall not make any substantial change in the Project as described in the Project Description without the written consent of the Fund.

(12) *Working capital*

The Borrower shall at all times after the commencement of the commercial operation of the Project maintain a ratio of current assets of the Borrower to current liabilities of the Borrower of not less than the working capital ratio stated on page 2. For this purpose "Current Assets" and "Current Liabilities" shall be determined in accordance with generally accepted accounting principles and practices consistently applied and principal repayments on any indebtedness for borrowed moneys becoming due within 12 (twelve) months of the date when the calculation falls to be made (including repayments in respect of the loan) shall be included as current liabilities.

(13) *Total liabilities to tangible net worth ratio*

The Borrower shall at all times after the commencement of the commercial operation of the Project maintain a ratio of total liabilities of the Borrower to tangible net worth of the Borrower of no more than the liabilities to tangible net worth ratio stated on page 2. For this purpose "Total Liabilities" shall mean all liabilities of the Borrower which would, in accordance with generally accepted accounting principles consistently applied, be classified as liabilities but specifically including full provision for all contingent liabilities but excluding any indebtedness of the Borrower subordinated in a manner satisfactory to the Fund. Also for this purpose "tangible net worth" which shall be ascertained in accordance with generally accepted accounting principles consistently applied shall mean the amount for the time being of the paid up share capital of the Borrower plus any indebtedness of the Borrower subordinated in a manner satisfactory to the Fund plus or minus the amount for the time being standing to the credit/debit of the reserve accounts and profit and loss account of the Borrower minus any amount attributable to goodwill or other intangible assets or to the revaluation of assets.

(14) *Dividends etc.*

The Borrower shall not declare pay or make any dividend or other distribution of a similar nature to its shareholders:
  (a) except out of profits after deducting accumulated losses; or
  (b) if an event of default as specified in Clause 11 below or an event which with the giving of notice, lapse of time or other conditions would constitute such an event of default has occurred and is continuing; or
  (c) prior to the first maturity under Clause 4 above of a Final Note; or
  (d) if and to the extent that the aggregate amount of all such payments, dividends and distributions in relation to any financial year of the Borrower (the "Relevant Year") exceeds the aggregate of (1) the maximum dividend percentage (stated on page 2) of the paid up share capital of the Borrower at the end of its preceding financial year and (2) an amount equal to any prepayment made to the Fund in the relevant year under Clause 5 hereof.

(15) *Capital expenditure*

The capital expenditures by the Borrower in any financial year after the year in which commercial operation of the project commences shall not exceed the maximum capital expenditure stated on page 2.

(16) *Management*

The Borrower will at all times maintain management acceptable to the Fund.

(17) *Change of entity or proprietorship*

No change in the nature of the Borrower or the persons constituting the Borrower shall occur without the prior written consent of the Fund.

11. Events of default

If any of the following events (each an "event of default") shall occur, namely:

(1) default by the Borrower in the payment, when due, of any principal in respect of the Loan or the Notes or other amount payable hereunder;

(2) default by the Borrower in the performance or observance of any provisions contained herein or in the Notes (not being a default within paragraph (1) of this Clause) or in the Mortgage Note provided that in any such case in which the default is in the opinion of the Fund capable of prompt remedy the same shall not have been remedied within a period of 30 (thirty) days after notice to the Borrower requiring such remedy;

(3) any representation or warranty made by the Borrower herein or in the Notes or the Mortgage Note or in any statement or certificate furnished pursuant hereto or thereto shall prove to have been incorrect in any material respect;

(4) any indebtedness for money borrowed or for the deferred purchase price of property for which the Borrower is or may become liable, as principal obligor, guarantor or otherwise, becomes due and payable or is capable of being declared due and payable prior to its stated maturity or any such indebtedness is not paid on the stated maturity or at the expiration of any applicable grace period therefor;

(5) the Borrower shall: (a) apply for or consent to the appointment of a receiver, trustee or liquidator of itself, or of its property; (b) be unable, or admit in writing its inability to pay its debts as they mature; (c) make a general assignment for the benefit of creditors; (d) be adjudicated as bankrupt or insolvent; or (e) have a liquidator or other guardian of the Borrower appointed;

(6) the Project shall be abandoned at any time or commercial operation of the Project shall not commence prior to the operation date stated on page 2;

thereupon, and in any such event, the Fund may immediately terminate the obligations of the Fund hereunder, by written or telegraphic notice to the Borrower, immediately declaring the Loan hereunder and under the Notes and all other amounts payable by the Borrower hereunder or thereunder to be forthwith due and payable, whereupon the same shall be forthwith due and payable, without further demand, presentment, protest or other notice whatsoever, all of which are hereby waived by the Borrower.

12. Jurisdiction and applicable law

This Agreement, the Notes and the Mortgage Note are subject to, governed by, and shall be construed in accordance with both the substantive and procedural laws and regulations of the Kingdom of Saudi Arabia. The Saudi courts of justice shall be the only competent courts to deal with any question arising from this Agreement, the Notes or the Mortgage; except on occurrence of any events of default provided for in Clause 11 herein where the Fund shall collect the amount of the loan pursuant to the "Public Funds Collection Regulations" and preceding and subsequent amendments thereto or any other Regulations as elected by the Fund.

13. Miscellaneous

(1) No failure on the part of the Fund to exercise, and no delay in exercising or partial exercise of, any right hereunder or under the Notes or the Mortgage Note shall operate as a waiver thereof. The remedies provided herein and therein are cumulative and not exclusive of any remedies provided by law or regulation.

(2) Except as otherwise specified herein, all notices, requests and demands shall be deemed to have been sufficiently given to or made upon either party hereto when deposited in the mails, full postage prepaid, addressed to such party at its address set forth above or at such other address as it may have notified to the other party for the purpose in accordance with this paragraph.

(3) The Borrower hereby expressly consents and agrees that (in addition to the executed Notes for the time being outstanding) the books and records of the Fund shall at all times be conclusive evidence of the facts and matters stated therein with regard to the Loan.

(4) If any payment to be made by the Borrower shall become due on a day other than a Business Day, such payment shall be made on the next succeeding Business Day.

(5) This Agreement shall be binding upon and shall exist for the benefit of the parties hereto and their respective successors and assigns, provided that the Borrower may not assign any of its rights or obligations hereunder without the prior written consent of the Fund.

(6) The Borrower agrees to pay all costs and expenses in connection with the preparation, execution, delivery and enforcement of this Agreement, the Notes and the Mortgage Note including without limitation the performance of the Mortgage Note and the furnishing of such documents as the Fund may reasonably request.

(7) In the event of conflict between the Arabic and English versions of this Agreement, the Notes or the Mortgage Note the Arabic version shall in all cases prevail but the English version shall be used to assist in any interpretation.

(Project Description)

Order Note

The sum of   Saudi riyals only.

For value received, the undersigned, having authority to sign on behalf of established on   and registered in the Commercial Register in the city of   under Registration No.   undertakes to pay on   in accordance with this Note—without condition or reservation—to the Saudi Industrial Development Fund, or to the order of, in the city of Riyadh, the sum stated above of   Saudi riyals, being the official tender of the Kingdom of Saudi Arabia.

Recourse without charge

Signed in the city of Riyadh on this   day of   H, corresponding to the   day of   AD.

(Signature)

(Name)
(Title)
Witness
(Signature)

(Name)
(Address)

Pledge Agreement

I,   the undersigned and hereinafter referred to as "the Borrower" hereby declare and consent of my own free will and choice to pledge to the Saudi Industrial Development Fund hereinafter to be called "the Fund" all the undermentioned property or any other property, additions or rights that may be appended or attached thereto:
  Type of asset mortgaged
....
....
  The assets mortgaged above shall be referred to as "the property", the property having been mortgaged in implementation of the loan agreement signed by me and the Fund on the   day of   H corresponding to / / AD (and hereinafter called the Loan Agreement) and what was stated therein in respect of

my obligations and contractual undertakings and by virtue whereof I obtained a loan from the Fund in the value of   Saudi riyals payable in instalments specified in the Agreement.

I declare and affirm that this property is owned solely by me and is not encumbered with any personal or material right whatsoever and that I have on no previous occasion pledged it or any part thereof. I promise to preserve it and not to pledge it or offer it as a security other than to the Fund or to make any amendment to its tenure. At the same time, I declare and state my full agreement that in the event of any default on my part to pay any debt owed by me to the Fund or in the event of the non-fulfilment of my obligations or part thereof towards the Fund or the occurrence of any of the events of default stated in the Loan Agreement, the Fund shall have the right to sell the said mortgaged property in the way that it considers appropriate without need to inform me or to take any further procedures. Such sale shall be conducted on my account and at my liability, and the Fund shall receive payment from the proceeds of the sale for the sums owed to it and the remainder, if any, shall be returned to me. However, if the sale proceeds do not suffice to pay the said sums owed, the Fund shall receive payment for the outstanding amount from any of my funds and property whatsoever.

Implementation of this method shall not at the same time or any other time prevent the Fund from using against me all the rights which accrue thereto from the regulations in force.

If I discharge all my obligations and settle any sum or other entitlements owed to the Fund under the Loan Agreement, the Fund shall release me from any liabilities based on this mortgage and shall release the mortgage from the whole of the property.

I undertake to have this mortgage attested by the notary public or whoever is performing his function.

I hereby sign:

Borrower and mortgagor:

Signature:	Signature:
Name:	Name:
Proof of identity:	Proof of identity:

Witness:	*Witness:*
Signature:	Signature:
Name:	Name:
Identity Card No:	Identity Card No:

Date: Date:

Address: Address:

APPENDIX 24

Minister of Finance and National Economy Resolution No. 3/719 of 10/4/1405 H (Jan. 1, 1985)

Director-General of the Department of Zakāt and Income Tax Circular No. 2896/1 of 11/4/1405 H

Kingdom of Saudi Arabia
Ministry of Finance and National Economy
Department of Zakāt and Income Tax

Circular to All Branches of the Department of Zakāt and Income Tax, Directors of Divisions, Auditing Department and the Expert

I enclose to you herewith a copy of Ministerial Resolution No. 3/719 dated 10/4/1405 H providing for treatment of Gulf individuals, establishments and companies as Saudis with respect to Zakāt and assessment of income tax on non-Gulf participants in accordance with the second article of the said Resolution.

Kindly implement the above and settle the cases previously blocked in the Department and its branches, whether in Zakāt or tax, which have not yet been finally assessed in accordance with the Resolution.

Best regards,
Director-General of the Department of Zakāt and Income Tax

Minister of Finance and National Economy Resolution No. 3/719 of 10/4/1405 H (January 1, 1985)

Pursuant to the powers vested in him under the Income Tax Regulations issued by Royal Decree No. 3321 of 21/1/1370 H and the amendments thereto,

And pursuant to the Joint Economic Agreement among the States of the Gulf Co-operation Council, approved by Royal Decree No. M/13 of 21/3/1402 H, which provides that each member State shall apply to the citizens of the other member

States the same treatment as its own citizens without discrimination or distinction and adopt implementing rules for this in various areas including free exercise of economic activity and free transfer of capital,

And having reviewed the matters which the Ministry brought to the attention of His Majesty the King and President of the Council of Ministers by letter No. 6179/404 dated 29/11/1404 H and High Order No. 5/506 dated 19/3/1405 H,

Decree as follows:

First. Citizens of Gulf Cooperation Council States shall not be subject to the tax provided in the Income Tax Regulations issued by Royal Decree No. 3321 dated 21/1/1370 H and the amendments thereto. Only Zakāt shall be collected therefrom in accordance with the Regulations of Zakāt issued by Royal Decree No. 17/2/28/8634 dated 29/6/1370, and the amendments and orders relating thereto.

Second. Companies of which all the partners and shareholders are citizens of Gulf Cooperation Council States, shall not be subject to the tax provided in the Income Tax Regulations issued by Royal Decree No. 3321 dated 21/1/1370 H and the amendments thereto but shall be subject to Zakāt. As for companies formed of partners and shareholders citizens of Gulf Cooperation Council States and noncitizens, tax shall be assessed on the noncitizens' share of profits and Zakāt shall be assessed on the share of Gulf Cooperation Council citizens.

Third. Companies formed under the laws of any Gulf Cooperation Council State operating in the Kingdom shall, in order to benefit from the provisions of the preceding article, submit the following to the Department of Zakāt and Income Tax:

(a) An official document approved and certified by the Saudi Consulate in the State under whose laws the company is formed, showing its registration in the commercial register of such State and the allotment of the participants' shares and their nationalities and an official copy of the company's articles of association and any amendments thereto relating to ownership of capital and its allotment among the participants;

(b) Official copy of the license issued to the company or its branch to operate in the Kingdom.

Fourth. This Resolution shall repeal all prior provisions, resolutions and orders inconsistent therewith and shall be effective from 19/3/1405 H, the date of issurance of High Order No. 5/506/M. Its provisions shall apply to the settlement of all cases previously blocked in the Department of Zakāt and Income Tax or other cases which have not yet been finally assessed.

Minister of Finance and National Economy

APPENDIX 25

Notaries Public Regulations; Registration and Execution Fees Regulations; Amendments and Related Materials*

Notaries Public Regulations

High Order No. 11083 of 19/8/1364 H (July 28, 1945)

Part I

Notaries Public

1. These Regulations shall be called the Notaries Public Regulations and shall define their powers, duties and functions.

2. A notary public is the authority competent to issue, acknowledge and register the various deeds and documents relating to juristic matters and sharī'ah and regulatory transactions in an ordered system in accordance with these Regulations.

3. Notaries public shall be nominated and appointed by the Viceroy of His Majesty the King.

4. The notaries public department in Makkah, Madinah and Jeddah shall consist of a head, assistant, treasurer and clerks and messengers as necessary, and in al-Ahsā and Abhā of a head, clerks and a messenger.

5. In towns which have no designated notary public department, the judge, sharī'ah deputy or chief clerk shall act as notary public.

---

* Note that the materials in this Appendix are translated from the texts as originally published and do not reflect all subsequent developments, amendments and applicable circulars, instructions, orders and interpretations. Nonetheless, materials no longer current have been included for their historical value.

6. The following conditions shall be imposed for a notary public:
   (a) he shall be a national of the Kingdom of Saudi Arabia;
   (b) he shall be conversant with sharī'ah matters;
   (c) he shall be knowledgeable in drawing up documents in accordance with sharī'ahprinciples;
   (d) he shall have a reputation for integrity and rectitude;
   (e) he shall not have been convicted of any crime or misdemeanor offending against honor;
   (f) he shall not have been adjudged a bankrupt;
   (g) he shall be of age, sound mind, . . . of honorable record and conversant with sharī'ah matters and shall have fulfilled the remaining conditions required for a judge's clerk as stipulated in the law books of the [Hanbalī] school.

7. In the capital, a notary public shall be examined by the sharī'ah governor and the Commission of the Presidency of the Judiciary and in other locations by the sharī'ah governor and his deputy. If his competence is established, he shall take the following oath:

> "I swear by Allah that as long as I hold the office of notary public I shall not prepare or acknowledge any document before verifying the identity of the two parties and being satisfied of their full consent. I shall under no circumstances accept any legal instrument which appears to me to be forged or contains a legal stratagem or which is inconsistent with the interest of His Majesty's Government or the public interest. I shall look after the interests of parties and related persons with impartiality and complete probity and rectitude and shall refrain from any activity contrary to the provisions of the sublime sharī'ah in every matter relating to my office."

Part II

Functions, duties and powers of notaries public

8. Notaries public departments and the substitutes therefor in locations which have no notary public shall perform the following acts:
   (a) drawing up and acknowledgment of commercial documents;
   (b) drawing up and acknowledgment of the various types of financial instruments;
   (c) drawing up and acknowledgment of powers of attorney, executorships, revocations of powers of attorney and the like;
   (d) drawing up and acknowledgment of the various types of contracts;

(e) drawing up and acknowledgment of contracts of muqawalah, notices together with the notification thereof, and contracts of pledge;

(f) recording of abstracts of documents issued by the sharī'ah courts;

(g) registration of companies in accordance with the regulations therefor (provisionally);

. . . .

9. Notaries public and their assistants shall use in their departments five main registers (as listed below) of high quality paper with a margin around the edges, each bordered with a broad line. Each page shall be numbered and sealed with the seal of the sharī'ah court, and the number of the pages shall be certified by the judge holding office in the municipality. If the person performing the function of notary public is the judge, sharī'ah deputy or chief clerk, the registers shall be certified by the administrative council of the municipality in which he is located. The registers shall be strong and bound.

(a) The daily register in which shall be entered in consecutive order all types of daily transactions, the names of the contracting parties and the amount of the fee received. The register shall be closed each evening, and at the end of every week the receipts shall be delivered to the treasury of the [Ministry of] Finance by official voucher in accordance with applicable rules.

(b) The register of deposits, in which deposits delivered shall be recorded by serial number together with the type, number and description of the moveable or immoveable deposits and the full name, occupation and residence of the depositor, the date of receipt and the terms of the contracting parties in order to hold and deal with the same in accordance with the agreed terms, provided that deposits in excess of the guarantee of the treasurer shall be kept in a special deposit box sealed by the treasurer, the notary public and a financial inspector.

(c) The registration register, for the registration of all instruments and documents prepared by the notary public and those prepared outside the department and acknowledged by the notary public. Such register shall carry the running serial numbers of the daily register.

(d) The register of valuable paper, including stamps, in which shall be recorded the type and number of pages of valuable paper taken and used (for official expenditure).

(e) The register for registration of abstracts of documents issued by the sharī'ah courts.

10. Notaries public and their assistants shall also make use of registers necessary to order and facilitate transactions, such as a liability register, a general orders register, a correspondence register and a register for the entry of transactions before registration thereof.

11. Any paper whatsoever to be notified shall after notification thereof be kept with the original signed notified counterpart or the entry made by the authorized official. The manner of notification shall be recorded on another counterpart and certified and returned to the notifying party.

12. Contracts, instruments and all documents which are prepared or acknowledged by notaries public or their assistants or substitutes shall be in Arabic and expressed clearly and plainly on good quality paper. Words shall not be deleted or crossed

out, and there shall be no additions between lines. If a mistake is made and it is later found necessary to correct a sentence or to add another sentence, a line shall be drawn through the incorrect phrase, provided that it shall remain legible. The phrase which was added or corrected shall be written in the margin of the paper and shall be signed and acknowledged by the contracting parties and the notary public.

13. A person who is not proficient in Arabic and who has business with the notary public shall have his language translated by two interpreters in accordance with applicable rules in the presence of two identifying witnesses. The interpreters and identifying witnesses shall be of honorable record.

14. Documents and instruments drawn up and acknowledged by notaries public shall set forth clearly the full name, title, occupation and residence of the parties concerned, the witnesses, interpreters and every person required to sign official documents in his department.

15. Any person desiring the preparation and acknowledgment of contracts, documents and all types of powers of attorney, executorships, gifts, sales, pledges or notices shall prove his identity before notaries public by means of two identifying witnesses if he is not fully known to them.

16. Documents prepared by notaries public shall be read in the presence of the parties concerned and at least two witnesses. The manner of reading shall be entered and stated in the body of the document.

17. If the owners of a document or parties concerned request copies of any type whatsoever from the notary public's register, they shall be given to them. "Parties concerned" means the contracting parties and anyone connected with the contents of the document or part thereof or their legal representatives.

18. When the presence of a woman in seclusion or a sick or excused man is required and the person whose presence is excused is to take the oath, the notary public or his substitute shall go [to the place where such person is located] together with two witnesses of honorable record. If such place is distant, the transportation fare shall be borne by the person demanding the oath. If the purpose is to hear a declaration or testimony, hearsay evidence shall be sufficient as in al-Iqnā'.

19. Documents, financial instruments, powers of attorney, executorships, contracts and all deeds which are given and prepared by notaries public in the Kingdom shall be binding upon and effective throughout the sharī'ah courts. The contents thereof shall be given effect without supporting evidence, on condition that everything stated in and attached to all documents is in accordance with the legal precepts applied by the Hanbalī school.

20. Official guarantee receipts printed by the competent financial authorities shall be effective and relied upon after due acknowledgment thereof by notaries public.

21. The contracting parties and witnesses shall sign the entry registers. In the event of an erasure, crossing-out or notation on a document, the entry shall be consulted and it shall be corrected therefrom. If the case requires any of the foregoing, this shall be made on the entry and signed by the contracting parties and witnesses and shall then be added to the document and the register, both of which shall be signed by the notary public and the registrar.

Part III

Notaries public fees

22. A fixed fee shall be payable on the following transactions:

Saudi
qurush

50 – for a general power of attorney if given by one person to one or more agents as long as it is for one purpose. If more than one person gives a general power of attorney, the fee shall be multiplied by their number.

25 – for a special power of attorney whether given by one person to one agent or by more than one person to one or more agents as long as it is for one purpose.

30 – for each notice or notification not involving a specific amount.

20 – for each signature on a declaration or agreement not involving a specific amount such as executorships and the like.

10 – for each notification.

20 – for each revocation of a power or executorship whether there are one or more parties revoking or relinquishing.

23. A fee of two and a half percent shall be paid on the petition of co-owners of real estate pursuant to sharīʿah deeds for partition and division of shares. In such case, the real estate shall be appraised by two persons of honorable record selected by the notary public and a representative of the Ministry of Finance and a representative of the municipality. Such fee shall be collected from the partitioning parties in proportion to their shares, and each party concerned shall be given a deed.

24. A fee of two percent shall be paid on the following transactions:
   (a) final and rescindable contracts for the sale of immoveable property.
   (b) gifts.
   (c) pledges of moveable and immoveable property.
   (d) executorships if the entirety thereof involves a specific amount.

25. A fee of one percent shall be paid on the following transactions:
   (a) contracts for the sale of moveable property, debt instruments, guarantees, notices and leases if they involve an amount of one thousand to ten thousand qurush.
   (b) declarations involving a specific amount not exceeding ten thousand qurush, including acknowledgment of the receipt by one or more beneficiaries of their portion of the revenues of a religious endowment.

26. A fee of one-half percent shall be paid on the following transactions:
   (a) any document containing a declaration of release of a pledge.
   (b) any document containing a declaration of release with respect to a specific amount.
   (c) any document containing a declaration of satisfaction of a specific debt.
   (d) any document containing a declaration of rescission of a sale.
   (e) contracts for the sale of moveable property, debt instruments, guarantees, notices and leases if the amount of any type of such transactions exceeds

ten thousand qurush. Fractions exceeding ten thousand qurush, even if only one qirsh, shall be deemed one hundred qurush.

(f) declarations involving a specific amount if the amount exceeds ten thousand qurush.

27. One quarter of the original fee shall be paid for each copy of a document taken from the registers and given to the owners thereof.

28. A loan fee shall be collected from the borrower if the loan is valid and not subject to doubt, and a debt fee shall be collected from the creditor.

29. A pledge fee shall be collected from the pledgor if the pledge is a valid loan not subject to doubt.

30. A pledge fee shall be collected from the pledgee if the debt is other than the abovementioned loan.

31. The fee on the authorization of an executor or custodian to purchase real estate for a minor, lunatic or imbecile shall be collected from their funds.

32. In the case of the sale of a pledge, the pledgee shall pay the sale fee in full and shall not pay a pledge release fee.

33. If the fee of two percent on a specified amount is greater than the fee on an unspecified amount of twenty qurush for each signature of the contracting parties, the greater fee shall be collected.

34. The costs of notaries public document paper are the following:

Saudi
qurush

3 – for a power of attorney.

3 – for documents containing sales in which the price does not exceed five thousand to twenty thousand Saudi qurush.

3 – for executorships and declarations of any type whatsoever.

10 – for documents containing sales in which the price is from five thousand to twenty thousand Saudi qurush.

20 – for documents containing sales in which the price exceeds twenty thousand Saudi qurush.

Part IV

Exemptions from notaries public fees

35. The following shall be exempted from notaries public fees and stamp charges:

(a) registration of guarantees of treasurers and all officials who are assigned under the provisions of the Guarantees Regulations to tax and finance departments, municipalities, 'Ain Zubaidah, al-'Ain al-Zarqā, 'Ain al-Wazīrīyah, religious endowments and all official government departments and the release thereof.

(b) powers of attorney and executorships of members of the armed forces and police.

(c) stolen items to be restored to their owners by court order.

(d) any real estate purchased in exchange for the price of real estate in a religious endowment, on condition that the same terms and conditions apply thereto as are provided in the deed of the endowment real estate sold.

Part V

General provisions

36. The treasurer appointed to a notary public's department or his substitute in departments which have no appointed treasurer shall be guaranteed in accordance with the applicable part of the Guarantees Regulations.

37. Notaries public shall not divulge the secrets of the transactions before them.

38. A notary public shall have an official seal for sealing documents acknowledged by him in the form "Notary Public of the town of ——————————————".

39. Notaries public shall send an impression of their official seals and their signatures to all shari'ah courts, senior local government officials, municipal councils, official departments and administrative branches.

40. One or more policemen shall be assigned to the notary public to guard his department and all its contents.

41. A notary public shall not draw up or acknowledge documents related to his personal interest or his lineal kin. The town judge shall perform this function with respect to all the acts provided in article 8 of these Regulations. The transaction shall be effected in the records of the court and registered in its registers under the seal and signature of the judge, and at the same time the text of the contract shall be registered in the notary public's department in the registers maintained for the same which shall also be signed by the same judge as being a conformed copy of the original registered in the court registers. The notary public's fee only shall be paid thereon. In localities in which the shari'ah governor performs the function of notary public, the chief clerk of the court of such locality shall perform such act.

[42]. Notaries public and their assistants shall make notifications to persons present in the Kingdom through the notaries public of such locality or their substitutes. Outside the Kingdom, they shall be made through the general representative of His Majesty the King.

43. When a proven debt is due, the creditor may request the notary public to notify the debtor. Upon notification thereof, the creditor may request the shari'ah governor to order his debtor to pay the debt. If the debtor refuses although able to make payment, the judge shall order his imprisonment. If the debtor's situation is insufficient to satisfy the debt due, the judge shall detain him in order to question all or some of his creditors, and if he is insolvent he shall be granted a delay.

44. The costs of selling seized property in respect of transportation and auction fees and the like shall be deducted from the original price after the sale.

45. Notaries public shall not carry out any transaction which would result in the ownership, transfer or vacation of real estate until after verifying the identity of the transferee by means of an official document.

46. The provisions of the Regulations for the Ownership of Real Property by Foreigners shall apply to the ownership, transfer or vacation of real estate with respect to foreigners.

47. All notaries public, police departments and competent authorities, each within their jurisdiction, shall comply with the provisions of these Regulations as from the time of their receipt of high approval and promulgation.

48. These Regulations shall repeal all prior regulations, instructions, orders and resolutions inconsistent herewith.

Signed hereunder
Second Deputy   First Deputy   President of the
                                                                Consultative Council
                                                                By ....

Registration and Execution Fees Regulations

Part I

Definitions

1. These Regulations shall be called the Registration and Execution Fees Regulations.

2. Registration and execution fees are the same and were formerly termed "service and registration fees". The term "registration and execution fees" wherever occurring in these Regulations shall mean any fees received in consideration of the payment of amounts to their owners through the competent authorities, the registration of abstracts of documents and judgments issued by the shari'ah courts or the making of copies from the records.

3. The term "notification fee" appearing in the articles of these Regulations shall mean the fee payable in consideration of making a notification to a person dissatisfied with a judgment.

Part II

Obligatory basic procedures

4. The manner of obtaining documents from the notary public, the preparation thereof by the court, the payment of the value thereof and the price of stamps and the delivery thereof to persons entitled to receive them shall be as follows:

    (a) Quantities of document paper shall be delivered by notaries public to chief clerks of the courts in accordance with lists in which shall be set forth each category of valuable court document paper delivered. Chief clerks shall under their signatures send notaries public monthly lists of the paper expended and the categories thereof.

    (b) Upon conclusion of a transaction requiring document paper, every recording clerk shall make an official application to the chief clerk for document paper. The application memorandum shall be entered in the register for the judicial official's return of transactions to the secretariat and shall state the category of paper requested and the name of the party to the transaction. The chief clerk shall dispatch the document paper together with the clerk's letter, on which he shall state that he has dispatched the paper requested to him and the date of dispatch. He shall send it in the court's internal dispatch folder.

(c) Upon receipt of the document paper, the recording clerk shall prepare the document promptly within the period set forth in article 68 of the Procedure Regulations, with due regard for the fact that such stipulated period is not merely for the final preparation of the document, but is for the preparation and registration thereof and all procedures required for the processing of the document such that on expiry of this period all necessary court procedures shall have been executed with respect thereto.

(d) After preparation of the document, if the document is appealable, it shall be notified to the nonprevailing party for objection thereto and submitted to the Presidency [of the Judiciary]. After its return from the Presidency, the endorsement made on the document shall be entered in the margin of the record and entry thereof. If the endorsement is for reversal, there shall be a retrial in accordance with shari'ah principles. If it is for affirmation or the judgment was not appealable, the document shall be transmitted by the court to the notary public for payment of the paper fee and the price of the stamps required to be affixed to the document. He shall affix the stamps and submit the judgment to the Office of the Viceroy in the capital and to the administrative governors in the provinces for issuance of an order to the police department for the collection of the amount of the judgment and payment of the fee commensurate with the amount actually received of the amount of the judgment, with the exception of documents on which fees were paid voluntarily by the prevailing party in accordance with the provisions of article 8 of these Regulations.

5. If a prevailing party or a person whose claim has been set aside fails to pay the price of the paper and stamps, they shall be obliged to pay by means of the police and shall be debarred from benefitting from the judgment rendered in their favor until they pay the charge.

6. Upon receipt of a document by the directorate of public security or the police, the enforcement officer shall summon the two parties and require the nonprevailing party to pay the debt together with the fees. If he asks to pay in installments and the prevailing party consents thereto, the amount together with the fees shall be divided into installments. If he alleges insolvency, the prevailing party consents to such insolvency and such insolvency is actually established, the judgment shall be retained in the enforcement office, and the prevailing party shall be given a receipt therefor in order to reapply therewith for enforcement whenever he has knowledge of the nonprevailing party's ability to make payment. If the prevailing party does not consent and alleges his solvency, they shall be referred to the shari'ah court for legal adjudication of proof of solvency or insolvency within one month excluding

the periods of appeal and objection. If he is unable to prove insolvency within the abovementioned period, the debt shall become payable and he shall thereupon be required to pay the fee in full. If he fails to make payment thereof, the person failing to pay registration and execution fees shall for every twenty qurush be imprisoned for a period of twenty-four hours. On expiry of the term of imprisonment in such manner, the document shall be delivered to the person concerned by the notary public.

Part III

Parties required to pay fees

7. Registration and execution fees, including the notification fee, shall be received from the nonprevailing party except in the following cases in which they shall be paid by the prevailing party in proportion to the amount actually received:
   (a) in case of a default judgment (provided that the prevailing party may recover the amount from the nonprevailing party in this case only).
   (b) in case of a judgment on a legacy, minors or persons placed under interdiction by reasons of profligacy, insanity or imbecility.
   (c) in case a debt is proved otherwise than through the courts and is received directly by means of enforcement departments so that the debtor shall not bear any part thereof.

8. In case the nonprevailing party is liable for the fee in accordance with the preceding article and the prevailing party pays the fee voluntarily in order to obtain the document, the notary public shall receive the fee from him and deliver the document to him together with a statement certified by him of the fees paid by the prevailing party so that he may recover them therewith from the nonprevailing party. The enforcement departments shall collect such fees together with the amount of the judgment and deliver them to the prevailing party upon enforcement whether in installments or in full.

9. Amounts collected by the competent enforcement departments, whether in consideration of enforcement of judgments rendered by the courts or otherwise, shall be promptly dispatched by the enforcement departments to notaries public together with the relevant transaction papers for the necessary action to be taken thereon, payment of the fees determined thereon by the nonprevailing party and giving such party a receipt therefor. A receipt shall be obtained from the prevailing party for the amounts which he received, with the exception of documents on which the fee was previously paid.

10. Fees on documents of proof on which fees are payable, whether these comprise executorships, declarations or title documents, which were prepared in the courts shall be paid immediately together with the price of the paper and stamps and shall be delivered to their owners.

11. Fees on documents issued by the courts dismissing a claim and discharging the defendant shall be received from the applicant for the document, or, if such person is not found, by the person whose claim was dismissed.

12. Fees determined for the authorization of a guardian to purchase or sell real estate for a minor, person placed under interdiction or imbecile shall be paid from their funds.

Part IV

Specification of amounts of fees

13. Documents on which the fee payable is five percent are:
    (a) any document containing a judgment of sale at a specified known price.
    (b) any document containing a judgment for a specified amount, except as set forth in paragraph (b) of article 14.
    (c) any document containing a confirmation of title, on condition that the price of the property stated therein shall be appraised by the governor by the selection of two experts of honorable record, a representative from the Ministry of Finance and a representative of the municipality. The appraisal shall be entered in the document with a notation of the orders issued with respect thereto.
    (d) any document containing the assessment of the fee of a trustee, executor or custodian on the basis of the total annual fee determined for him, provided that payment of the fee shall be made once.
    (e) any document containing a judgment on chattels other than those of husband and wife. The provisions of article 29 of these Instructions shall be implemented in the appraisal of such chattels.
14. A fee of two-and-a-half percent shall be payable on the following:
    (a) any document containing a judgment of partition of real estate owned in common pursuant to sharīʿah deeds, provided that the real estate shall be appraised by the governor who shall appoint two reliable experts, a representative of the Ministry of Finance and a representative of the municipality. The fee shall be received from the partitioning parties in proportion to their interests, and each party concerned shall be given a deed.
    (b) any document containing a judgment on a debt, wages for service, real estate leases or a gift of a divided share.
15. Registration and execution fees shall be paid on the following documents in the amounts set forth below:
Saudi
qurush
50 – fifty Saudi qurush on every copy made from court records.
40 – forty Saudi qurush on the following documents:
    (a) any document not involving a sum of money or real estate, such as the appointment of executors, proof of a power and appointment of religious endowment trustees.
    (b) any document containing the appraisal of a building of a religious endowment or the property of an orphan.
    (c) any document containing a judgment on a right of preemption if the

property sold is registered or the sale is rescinded.

(d) any document proving an inheritance or executorship.

20 – twenty Saudi qurush on the following:

(a) any document containing a judgment barring an objection, whether with respect to a specific amount or otherwise.

(b) any document involving the handing over of children to their guardians after the completion of maternal custody.

(c) any document authorizing a trustee to lease.

(d) any document authorizing a trustee or executor to develop the real estate of a religious endowment or the real estate of an orphan or imbecile.

(e) any document containing a judgment of dismissal of a claim and discharge of the defendant.

10 – ten Saudi qurush on the following:

(a) any document authorizing an executor to sell or purchase the share of a minor, authorizing a religious endowment custodian to purchase premises for the endowment from endowment funds or authorizing the exchange of a religious endowment for another or the sale thereof.

(b) notification of documents issued by the sharī'ah courts.

Part V

Items exempted from fees and on which fees are again not payable

16. The following shall be exempt from registration and execution fees:

(a) transactions of all members of the armed forces, the police and the coast-guard relating to executorships, powers of attorney, proof of inheritance and division of legacies during their period of service and after their death while on service, including stamps and valuable paper.

(b) all marital matters, including dowry, divorce, maintenance of the wife and kin and property established as the wife's in her husband's legacy and the reverse.

(c) transactions of official departments, municipalities, departments of public endowments, 'Ain al-Wazīrīyah 'Ain Zubaidah and al-'Ain al-Zarqā'.

(d) documents issued by the sharī'ah courts on conversions to the Islamic faith.

(e) documents containing a judgment on an endowment . . . or a declaration thereof.

(f) documents of inheritance and executorship or both together if the total legacy or bequest is insignificant and not in excess of twice the total fee.

(g) items which are taken by theft and a judgment is made for their return to their owners.

(h) legacies whose sale or appraised value is less than two hundred riyals.

(i) powers of a judge to give a woman without a guardian in marriage when her poverty is established before him and likewise the fee on her power to represent her in seeking marriage.

(j) documents proving and establishing a religious endowment of any type whatsoever, whether of moveable or immoveable property, except for livestock.

(k) custodians and executors whom the judge appoints for pauper imbeciles, lunatics and minors.

17. Transactions exempted from registration and execution under article 16 above shall also be exempt from stamp charges. The exemption shall not cover the price of the document paper except as provided in paragraph (a) of the abovementioned article.

18. No fees shall be payable a second time on documents having acquired finality by the expiration of the period for appeal where the nonprevailing party was unable to object thereto for compelling reasons and likewise in the case of default judgments and similar situations which require a retrial.

19. If proceedings are necessary with respect to documents issued by a notary public, no fee shall be received thereon after the judgment unless the judgment document contains something which was not recorded in such documents, in which case a fee shall be received thereon.

20. Any document on which the competent authorities have received payment of the stipulated fee shall not be subject to another fee on enforcement.

21. Any amount which a creditor receives directly from a debtor without the intervention of any government department shall not be subject to a registration and execution fee.

Part VI

General provisions on fees

22. Registration and execution fees shall not be paid until the judgment becomes final in one of three ways:

(a) by the nonprevailing party's satisfaction with the judgment.

(b) or the judgment is affirmed by the competent authority.

(c) or the specified period for appeal has expired and no party made an objection thereto during the same.

23. With respect to documents issued by the courts for payment by installment, the fee for each installment shall be paid when it is due.

24. Registration and execution fees shall not be payable on amounts collected by enforcement departments without a judgment except for amounts actually collected whether in installments or in full.

25. One fee shall be paid on any document containing the appointment of several executors where each executor is appointed with respect to separate property or the proof of their executorships.

26. If one document covers several transactions, whether the fee thereon is fixed or percentage or both, the greatest fee only shall be paid. The same shall also apply to stamp charges.

27. Fees shall be paid on amounts awarded even if the original claim was greater than the amount awarded.

28. Debts and all private juristic transactions occurring solely between members of the armed forces and between members of the armed forces and other persons

shall not be covered by the exemption from registration and execution fees and the price of paper and stamps.

29. The value of personal property subject of a judgment when brought before the sharī'ah governor shall be appraised by experts nominated by the sharī'ah governor.

30. The same fee shall be paid on conciliation documents and proof thereof which are prepared by the courts as would be received thereon had they been prepared by notaries public in accordance with the Notaries Public Regulations without being covered by the registration and execution fee.

31. An owner upon making any disposition with respect to his property shall not be required to take out a deed for any increase in his property but may use the original deed.

32. The application of any person to make a copy from the court records or the notary public or to register a transaction directly with the notary public shall not be accepted until after payment of the paper and stamp charges and the fees required by regulation.

33. Notaries public and judges of the courts in provincial areas where there are no notaries public shall be responsible for the registration of abstracts of documents and receipt of the fees specified therefor.

34. All notaries public and courts which substitute therefor in areas in which there are no notaries public shall affix stamps on all documents and legal instruments of the types enumerated in these Regulations in the amount of the fees stipulated thereon and which are paid to them by the persons concerned.

35. Notaries public and the competent authorities shall receive fees promptly without delay.

36. The articles of these Regulations shall replace the Service and Registration Fees Instructions issued under No. 3524/942 of 3/5/1352 H, any approved orders and resolutions issued thereafter and anything therein inconsistent with these articles, and the provisions of these Regulations shall be applied.

37. All notaries public, police departments and the competent authorities shall comply with the provisions of these Regulations each within their jurisdiction as from the date of approval thereof and notification thereto.

Signed hereunder
Chief Clerk of the Office of the Viceroy of H.M. the King
Chief Clerk of the Office of the Presidency of the Judiciary

Consultative Council Resolution No. 59 of 11/4/1364 H (March 25, 1945)

The Council has reviewed the accompanying transaction returned by His Highness to the Council under No. 4463 of 4/4/1364 H to the effect that in view of the fact that the royal order issued in the letter of the Royal Office under No. 2025/344 of 22/2/1364 H requires approval of the amendments made by Shaikh 'Abdullah bin

Zahim on the two Regulations in question and acceptance of the comments of the Council of Deputies, it is necessary to confirm the said amendments as they stand with respect to everything covered by the articles of the two abovementioned Regulations without any change or substitution in execution of the requirements of the royal order and to cast them in their final mold after compliance therewith and to submit them for notification to the competent authorities in timely fashion. On reexamining what was decided previously under No. 39 of 16/3/1364 H it was found that the Consultative Council had not deviated from the substance of the amendments which were referred to in the Royal Will and His Highness drew attention in his abovementioned decision to the measures considered appropriate by the Council in relation to the applicable rules in drawing up regulations particularly to quoting the sources referred to. In short he must be of legal age, sane, free and male and shall fulfill all the conditions and specifications acknowledged by the sharī'ah, *i.e.* that he shall be of legal age, sane, free, just and conversant with sharī'ah matters, as well as all the other conditions stipulated for a judge's clerk provided in the books of the [Hanbali] school. In addition, the last provision contains a repetition of certain paragraphs previously made in this respect in the same draft. Nevertheless, in implementation of the high order the two regulations have been amended on the basis of the abovementioned Royal Will and the Council is honored to submit them to His Highness whilst retaining the contents of Articles 2, 4 and 5 set forth in its accompanying Resolution No. 39 of 11/3/1364 H, the text of which is as follows.

2. In the amendment made to Article 21 of the Notaries Public Regulations the conditions which must be fulfilled for the entry registers of notaries public and the method of effecting deletions therefrom and amendments were omitted. The Council considers it necessary to stipulate such conditions in this Resolution as follows:

"The entry registers of notaries public shall be firmly bound with their pages made of strong, glossy paper and numbered consecutively. The handwriting therein shall be clear without any erasures or obliterations made to entries or writing between the lines. If any such action is necessary, the entry shall be crossed out in a manner such that the striken text remains legible. The phrase added or corrected shall be written in the margin of the page and signed and certified by the contracting parties, witnesses and the notary public, as is the case with the records of the courts."

4. With regard to the accumulation of legal instruments with the notary public, this is an independent question which the Council has dealt with and issued its accompanying resolution on the subject. Therefore the Council has not included it in the body of the Regulations for the abovementioned reason and because it is a temporary measure for a limited period which ends with the termination of delayed notices. Although the Council cites the opinion of Shaikh bin Zahim on the subject in question from the point of view of compelling the persons concerned to receive them (that is delayed notices), it nevertheless considers that the conditions which the Council laid down in its abovementioned prior resolution should be applied in this matter, namely that such instruments should be sent out with just the signatures of the persons concerned in the entries without need for signatures of the

contracting parties and witnesses on the instruments and in the records, on condition that the Presidency of the Judiciary shall send the inspector of the shari'ah courts and another competent and knowledgeable member of the shari'ah judiciary to compare such instruments with the originals thereof and to confirm that they are correct and true copies containing no item subject to doubt prejudicing the value of such instruments. If it appears that some entries contain obliterations, erasures or addenda not signed by the parties to the transaction which give rise to doubt, the items in doubt shall be referred to the Presidency of the Judiciary for guidance on the necessary action.

5. If this Resolution is approved, it shall be circulated to all notaries public and persons concerned together with the two accompanying drafts, since they are not inconsistent with the abovementioned Royal Will and there is no provision in the Regulations thereon.

Signed hereunder

Second Deputy	First Deputy	President of the Consultative Council
		By

Consultative Council Resolution No. 223 of 25/10/1364 H (November 22, 1945)

The Consultative Council has reviewed the accompanying High Order No. 12773 of 24/9/1364 H issued on the subject of accumulated legal instruments which may be summarized to the effect that upon notification to the notary public of Makkah of the Notaries Public Regulations and Service and Registration Fees Regulations, he submitted the attached letter No. 2155 of 12–13/9/1364 H containing his request for the resolution made on the subject No. 82 of 25/5/1360 H. His Highness considers that the explanatory notes made at the end of Consultative Council Resolution No. 59 of 11/4/1364 H on commenting on the opinion of Shaikh bin Zahim on the matter referred to is sufficient indication of the applicability of the requested resolution in this respect. Therefore, His Highness requests that the Council express its opinion thereon after reference to the two resolutions in question and in compliance with the high order. The matter was studied and a unanimous decision was reached in fulfillment of the royal wish and in response to the request of the notary public of Makkah that the following shall be circulated to all notaries public on the subject of accumulated legal instruments:

1. Owners of delayed legal instruments shall be compelled to accept them by the competent authorities each of which shall hand over those items within his jurisdiction after carrying out the required procedures in accordance with applicable rules.

2. On handing over delayed accumulated legal instruments, the signatures of the owners thereof shall be entered without need for the signatures of the contracting parties or witnesses on documents or in the records, on condition that the Presidency of the Judiciary shall delegate the inspector of the courts and another

competent and knowledgeable member of the sharīʿah judiciary to compare the instruments with the originals thereof in the entry register and to confirm that they are correct and true copies.

3. If it appears that some entries contain obliterations, erasures, additions or addenda and so forth not signed by the parties to the transaction giving rise to doubt and prejudicing the value of the instruments, the items subject to doubt shall be referred to the Presidency of the Judiciary for guidance on the necessary action.

Signed hereunder

Second Deputy	First Deputy	President of the Judiciary
		By

Fee payable on Notices of Confirmation of Ownership

To the Minister of Finance,

We refer to your correspondence submitted under cover of No. 35065/1988/4 dated 27/10/1364 H concerning the subject of the fee to be paid on notices of confirmation of ownership and we enclose herewith a copy of Consultative Council Resolution No. 242 of 25/11/1364 H on the subject and No. 673 of 25/11/1364 H respectively. We inform you that when the matter was referred to His Majesty, the Royal Will was issued in High Office letter No. 17/2/93 dated 14/1/1365 H approving it and action is to be taken in accordance therewith.

President of the Council of Deputies

Consultative Council Resolution No. 242 of 25/11/1364 H (October 31, 1945)

The Consultative Council has reviewed the attached Ministry of Finance letter No. 35065/1988/4 dated 27/10/1364 H received from His Highness under No. 14262 dated 7/11/1364 H stating that the fee payable on any notice of confirmation of ownership is five percent in accordance with Article 21(f) of the Service and Registration Fees Regulations. This article was amended reducing the fee to two and one-half percent for a period of five years by High Order No. 9793 of 1/9/1360 H. The Ministry of Finance received from His Highness under No. 11083 of 19/8/1364 H a copy of Consultative Council Resolution No. 59 of 11/4/1364 H and attached to the Notaries Public and Registration Fees Regulations [sic] currently being drawn up. On perusal, it was noted that the fee for confirmation of ownership had been set at five percent. Inasmuch as the stipulated period of five years has not yet expired and as the increase of such fee has resulted in a falling off in the number of confirmation of ownership writs being issued and a decrease in the Treasury's revenues, the Ministry of Finance considers that the payment of this fee at the rate of two percent should be continued for a further five-year period from the expiry date of the initial period. After thorough study of the matter and deliberation, the Council has unanimously resolved the following.

First: The original rate determined for the abovementioned fee was five percent, and the reduction was made in the requirements of the [public] interest. Therefore, the rules in such a case require that the original amount of the fee be kept and that an exception be made as required in the [public] interest and approved by High Order. In compliance therewith the Council has set out the original amount of the fee in the Regulations.

Second: In respect of the Ministry of Finance's opinion, in its accompanying letter referenced above, to the effect that the reduction should be continued for a further five years from the date of expiry of the initial period, the Council considers that this should be approved in view of the significant benefit therefrom, provided that a notice shall be published on several occasions in the newspaper Umm al-Qurā to inform the public and all competent authorities shall be notified thereof.

Signed hereunder

Second Deputy · · · · · First Deputy · · · · · President of the Consultative Council

By

Consultative Council Resolution No. 258 of 2/11/1364 H (October 8, 1945)

The Consultative Council has reviewed Memorandum No. 2493 of 18/11/1364 H submitted to His Highness by the notary public of Makkah containing his comments on Article 26 of Part VI of the Registration and Execution Regulations [sic] No. 11083 of 19/8/1364 H notified to him by His Highness providing that if one legal instrument contains several transactions whether the fee is fixed or percentage or both, the greatest fee only shall be paid, the same being applicable to stamp charges. Reference was also made to Article 26(c) of Part III of the last Notaries Public Regulations notified to him by His Highness and covering the half percent fee payable on any legal instrument containing a declaration of payment of a specific debt and the omission of the foregoing paragraph (c) from the Registration and Execution Fees Regulations. He mentions that according to his understanding of Article 48 of the Notaries Public Regulations, if anything is not covered by one of the Regulations, effect shall be given to the other, and he requests guidance as to what is to be applied in the matter.

When the subject was referred to the Council's Regulations Committee, it was decided by agreement with the notary public of Makkah, Shaikh 'Arabi Sajini, that it would be just for the two Regulations to cover the first request concerning payment of the greater of the fees where there are several fees, namely that this method should be applied to transactions relating to the Notaries Public Regulations and the Registration and Execution Fees Regulations but that this does not relate to the matter of one-half percent or two-and-one-half percent, since a provision exists for each and so action should continue as determined in the Regulations. The matter was put forward for discussion in the Council during a general session and it was unanimously agreed to approve the determination of the abovementioned committee in the presence and with the agreement of the notary public of Makkah as stated above.

Signed hereunder

Second Deputy   First Deputy   President of the Consultative Council
By

Consultative Council Resolution No. 266 of 21/11/1364 H (October 27, 1945)

The Consultative Council has reviewed the attached matter received from His Highness under No. 14881 of 22/11/1364 H which may be summarized as a request for clarification by the notary public of Makkah in his attached letter No. 2154 of 12–13/9/1364 H as to the meaning of the honorable record of the two interpreters and identifying witnesses provided in Article 13 of the Notaries Public Regulations and of the testimony of a woman in seclusion and sick man and swearing them on oath. The President of the Judiciary replied to him by the attached letter No. 4513 of 7/11/1364 H confirming the interpretation of the notary public that "honorable record" means the reputation therefor as has been effective since olden times and not the attestation of third parties as appears from the tenor of the abovementioned article. He considers that the article should be interpreted in such manner as it is not within the jurisdiction of notaries public to hear testimony on honorable record. With respect to Article 18, he considers that it should be repealed as what is stated therein comes only within the jurisdiction of the sharīʿah courts and not notaries public. After study and discussion of the above and consideration of the determination of the Regulations Committee made in the presence and with the approval of the notary public of Makkah, it was found that the current practice of the notary public relating to the two interpreters and identifying witnesses is to look to their reputation for honorable conduct and not to third party attestations. His practice with respect to the subject of Article 18 is to comply with the request of a woman in seclusion and a sick man for their declarations to be taken at home within the jurisdiction of the notary public. On review of the origins of the Notaries Public Regulations, it was found that Article 18 as originally approved by the Council provides the following:

> If necessary, the notary public or his substitute shall go (without payment) to the location of a woman in seclusion or excused from attendance or a sick or excused man to determine the action necessary to carry out the subject transaction. If the excused man or woman resides on the outskirts of a town or a remote area in the town, they shall be required to provide some means of transport for the notary public or his substitute.

One of the comments of Shaikh bin Zahim on the Regulations approved by His Highness is that the article in question should be amended to read: when it is necessary for a woman in seclusion or a person who is sick or excused to attend, if the person who is unable to attend is to take the oath, the notary public or his substitute shall go [to their location] accompanied by two witnesses of honorable record and the transportation fare, if the location is distant, shall be paid by the person demanding the oath. If the purpose is to hear a declaration or testimony, hearsay evidence shall be sufficient as in al-Iqnā'. In view of the aforementioned and in order to eliminate any ambiguity, the Consultative Council resolves unanimously as follows:

First: The article included in the Regulations shall be deleted on the basis of the opinion of Shaikh bin Zahim. Notaries public shall act in accordance with past usage as provided in the article approved by the Council.

Second: With regard to the honorable record of interpreters and identifying witnesses appearing in Article 13 of the Regulations, this means the reputation of an honorable record and not the attestation of third parties thereto as clarified by the Presidency of the Judiciary in its abovementioned letter.

Third: In the event of high approval of this Resolution, it shall be circulated to all notaries public in the Kingdom to give effect thereto.

Signed hereunder

Second Deputy	First Deputy	President of the Consultative Council
		By

Consultative Council Resolution No. 246 of 28/11/1364 H (November 4, 1945)

The Consultative Council has reviewed the transaction papers forwarded by His Highness under No. 12736 of 22/9/1364 H concerning the request of the notary public of Medinah in his attached letter No. 1377 of 8–9/9/1364 H that a high order be issued on the principles to be applied in the matter of exemption of the Bedouin from fees on ewes and camels in view of the fact that he has received a high order to this effect whereas the Registration and Execution Regulations [sic] thereafter provided in Article 36 that fees are payable.

After study and discussion of the above, review of the determination of the Regulations Committee made in the presence and with the approval of the Ministry of Finance's representative, Shaikh Khalil 'Abdul Jabbar and deliberation on the subject, the Council has resolved unanimously to give approval thereto, including the finding that the matter queried by the notary public of Medinah did not adequately explain the treatment of a Bedouin party and that a paragraph should be added to the Registration and Execution Regulations in the exemptions part providing for the exemption from fees of any ewe or camel belonging to the Bedouin in accordance with the text of the high royal order.

On the basis thereof, the Council resolves that the following paragraph (1) shall be added to the paragraphs of Article 16 of the Regulations:

(1) The fees on ewes and camels in transactions of the Bedouin whether the judgment concerns the chattel or value thereof.

In the event of high approval of the aforementioned, the said Resolution shall be circulated to all competent authorities. With regard to the statement made by the notary public of Medinah in his letter under reference to the effect that the amount of fees payable on the value of camels has not been clearly specified, this is omitted because the fee is a fee on registration and execution and such is covered by the special conditions and provisions in the Regulations.

Signed hereunder
Second Deputy   First Deputy   President of the Consulta-
                                                             tive Council
                                                             By

Consultative Council Resolution No. 229 of 24/8/1366 H (July 7, 1947)

The Consultative Council has reviewed the notary public of Makkah's letter No. 506 of 3/6/1366 H received from His Highness under No. 6441 of 18/6/1366 H stating that royal donations made to charitable agencies are not covered by a paragraph with regard to fees. A high order was issued for the registration of the land donated to Sidqi Ka'Ki to build a hospital thereon, and a high order was also issued for the registration of the land donated to 'Abbas Qattan to found a school for the instruction of children in the Quran. A representative from the department in the capital came and assessed the latter donation in accordance with its conditions and requested that it be registered and that he be given a deed to such effect. Sidqi Ka'Ki also applied for a document of his donation. This administration examined the question of fees and found that the Notaries Public Regulations contained no article imposing or exempting from fees except Article 35 which provides for the exemption of treasurers' guarantees in official government departments and Article 16(c) of Part V of the Registration and Execution Fees Regulations which provides for the exemption of transactions of official departments, municipalities, the department of public religious endowments and the like.

This was not an applicable provision to be complied with in the matter. After study and discussion of the above and review of the determination of the Regulations Committee made in the presence of the representative of the Ministry of Finance, Mr. Hasan Faqi, and recourse to the Registration and Execution Fees Regulations referred to above, the Council has resolved the following:

First: As the principle applicable to religious endowments and charitable societies is exemption from government fees as is provided in the majority of existing regulations, as well as for the department concerned therewith, and as the matter at hand has no general rule laid down for it in the exemptions provided in the Registration and Execution Fees Regulations, the Council resolves to add a paragraph to follow Article 16(l) of the Registration and Execution Fees Regulations as follows:

(m) Sharī'ah documents and instruments relating to charitable matters including the registration of land donated for charitable works, documents attesting to ownership of land and buildings and other items relating to religious endowments and charitable societies, such as hospices, mosques, schools and hospitals and the donations made thereto and any public project having a public philanthropic purpose.

Second: In the event of high approval of the foregoing, the abovementioned paragraph shall be added to the Regulations in question and shall be circulated by resolution to all competent authorities for application thereof.

Signed hereunder

Second Deputy	First Deputy	President of the Consultative Council By

Amendment to Paragraphs (b) and (c) of Article 24 of the Notaries Public Regulations of 21/3/1368 H (January 21, 1949)

To the Ministry of Finance,

We enclose herewith a copy of Consultative Council Resolution No. 14 of 6/2/1368 H concerning the amendment of paragraphs (b) and (c) of Article 24 of the Notaries Public Regulations. Whereas royal approval was granted in High Office letter No. 25/2/720 dated 6/2/1368 H, it shall be effective and notified to all notaries public and competent authorities for compliance.

President of the Council of
Deputies

Consultative Council Resolution No. 14 of 6/2/1368 H (December 10, 1948)

The Consultative Council has reviewed the opinion of the notary public of Ta'if expressed in his letter No. 133 of 18/1/1368 H received from His Highness under No. 480 of 15/1/1368 H which includes the following.

Many applicants do not set forth their testamentary dispositions, gifts and pledges and fail to state their intentions and wishes in matters concerning executorship, gifts and pledges in order to avoid paying the percentage fee prescribed for the abovementioned matters under Article 24(b), (c) and (d) of the Notaries Public Regulations requiring the payment of a fee on known items at the rate of two percent. Whereas the failure of people to set forth such matters and the failure of some to carry out the obligatory registration thereof can create future problems and disputes between people and heirs and whereas the reliance of many people on ordinary documents does not safeguard against the occurrence of disagreements and disputes in respect thereof, it is believed that if royal approval is granted, the said paragraph should be repealed and added to Articles 25 and 26 of the Regulations in question to provide that the fee payable on executorships, gifts and pledges not exceeding ten thousand qurush shall be one percent and if in excess of ten thousand qurush shall be one-half percent. This will enable people to register and preseve their rights and clear them of any ambiguity on the one hand, and on the other hand revenue from these types of transactions will be increased. To implement the high order requiring that the aforementioned matter be studied in the presence of the notary public of Makkah and a representative of the Ministry of Finance, the Council referred the said matter to the Regulations Committee which resolved in their presence and with their agreement the following:

1. In view of the fact that the reduction of fees would incontestably increase revenues in proportion to the increase in applicants and in order to protect rights and urge holders of interests to register the same in notaries public departments, it is resolved to retain the fee at its present rate of two percent and to reduce the rate [on amounts] in excess of ten thousand from two to one percent.

2. In the event of royal approval of this Resolution, paragraphs (b) and (c) of Article 24 of the Notaries Public Regulations shall be amended in the agreed manner.

When the aforementioned was put before a general session of the Council, it was decided to approve the abovementioned resolution of the Regulations Committee made in the presence and with the agreement of the notary public of Makkah, Shaikh 'Arabi Sajini, and the representative of the Ministry of Finance, Mr. Hasan Faqi.

Signed hereunder

Second Deputy   First Deputy   President of the Consultative Council
By

Amendments to the Registration and Execution Regulations Fees No. 6033 Date 3/8/1368 H

To the Ministry of Finance,

Enclosed herewith is Consultative Council Resolution No. 111 of 11/6/1368 H dated 11/6/1368 H submitted under cover of letter No. 358 dated 11/6/1368 H passed with regard to the amendment of certain articles of the Registration and Execution Regulations Fees. We have approved it and authorize that its provisions be implemented and notified by you to notaries public or their representatives in the provinces for compliance therewith.

Deputy of H.M. the King

Consultative Council Resolution No. 111 of 11/6/1368 H (August 26, 1949)

The Consultative Council has reviewed the transaction papers received from the public prosecutor's office No. 8116 of 4/12/1367 H concerning the Registration and Execution Regulations [sic] on which the Council previously adopted Resolution No. 200 of 26/8/1367 H and submitted under No. 598 of 27/8/1367 H together with the comments of His Highness thereon, the text of which is:

1. Article 1 of the Council's Resolution provides that Article 13(d) clearly applies to contested real estate if the owner possesses a deed, claims against a person who has taken illegal possession and such illegal possession is proved. Since the paragraph referred to provides for the payment of five percent of the value, which is equivalent to the registration fee, what is the purpose of making an additional fee payable on real estate on which the fee has already been paid and which has been registered on the one hand? On the other hand, there is no exception for payment except on a specific amount and after appraisal by experts, and in this case only for documents attesting to ownership in accordance with Article 13.

2. Article 2 provides that the provisions of Article 15(a) apply to contested real estate if the illegal possession thereof is not proved and the person in possession is a purchaser or transferee by inheritance, gift or donation. As the said paragraph provides for the payment of a fee of twenty qurush and the abovementioned article in your resolution contains no provision relating to the prior registration of such real estate, it is therefore understood that a fee of twenty qurush is payable on unregistered contested real estate. On comparing the meanings of the first and second articles, it will be clear to you that what has been decided does not conform with the required principle of determining fees according to registration or non-registration.

Regarding the matter of not paying double fees on transactions that should not carry such fees, the essence of the above is that a fee of five percent is payable on registered real estate whereas a fee of twenty Saudi qurush is payable on unregistered real estate, this being the difference in the method to be followed. It appears from the above that the method adopted by the notary public is in conformity with the provisions of the Registration and Execution Regulations. Therefore, we were of the opinion that a decision should be made to reconsider the matter in the presence of the representative of the Ministry of Finance and the notary public and that the decision on the subject be submitted to us. On referring the matter to the Regulations Committee of the Council for study in the light of the comments of His Highness the following was decided:

1. The comment on Article 1, which provides that Article 13(d) clearly applies to contested real estate if the owner possesses a deed, claims against a person who has taken illegal possession and such illegal possession is proved, does not involve a repetition of payment of the fee on his property since the fee is collected from the nonprevailing party in accordance with Article 7 of the Registration Regulations and the nonprevailing party in such case is the person who has taken illegal

possession, therefore the collection of a fee from him is a punishment for his illegal possession.

2. The comment on Article 2, which provides that the provisions of Article 15(a) apply to contested real estate if the illegal possession thereof is not proved and the person taking possession is a purchaser or transferee by inheritance, gift or donation, is valid. The three articles were amended in the presence of and with the agreement of the notary public of Makkah, Shaikh 'Arabi Sajini, and the representative of the Ministry of Finance, Mr. Hasan Faqi, to read as follows:

1. Contested real estate if the claimant possesses a registered deed and the person in possession has taken illegal possession thereof is subject to Article 13(d) in that the judgment fee shall be borne by the nonprevailing party in proportion to the value of the real estate stated in the deed.

2. Contested real estate if the claimant possesses a registered deed and the defendant is not in illegal possession by the fact that the property was transferred to him by inheritance, gift or donation is subject to Article 15(a), namely the fee for dismissal of the complaint.

3. With regard to contested real estate if the claimant does not possess a registered deed and he proves his ownership thereof vis-à-vis the person in possession, the fee on attestation proving ownership of the real estate shall be paid by the person who has established his right and no fee shall be payable in this case by the nonprevailing party.

When the aforementioned was submitted for study by the Council, approval was granted regarding the decision of the Regulations Committee set out above and which was made in the presence of and with the agreement of the notary public of Makkah and the representative of the Ministry of Finance.

Signed hereunder
President of the Council   First Deputy   Second Deputy

High Order No. 9142 of 22/6/1372 H

No. 5868 Date 6/7/1372 H
To the Ministry of Finance,

We refer to telegram No. 2703 of 13/4/1372 H sent to us by the Ministry of the Interior on the subject of the exemption from the fees on sharī'ah documents and we likewise refer to your letter in reply on the subject sent to us under No. 43422/4 of 9/5/1372 H and inform you that when we referred the subject for the opinion of H.H. the Crown Prince, His Highness issued High Order No. 9142 of 22/6/1372 H, the text of which is:

"Concerning the exemption of sharī'ah documents from fees. We have cognizance of the matters mentioned by you. The scope of the exemption is as notified by the Ministry of Finance to notaries public as follows:

1. All paragraphs of Article 15 of the Registration and Execution Regulations [sic], namely copies from the records, documents concerning the appointment of executors, proof of powers, appointment of religious endowments trustees, documents concerning the valuation of a building of a religious endowment or the property of an orphan, documents containing a judgment on a right of preemption, proof of inheritance and executorship, barring an objection, handing over children to their guardians after the completion of maternal custody, authorization of a trustee to lease or develop a religious endowment or the real estate of an orphan or imbecile, judgments dismissing a complaint and discharging the defendant, authorizations of an executor to sell or buy the share of a minor, permission for a religious endowment custodian to purchase premises for the religious endowment from endowment funds or authorization of the exchange or sale of a religious endowment, with the exception of paragraph (b) concerning the notification of documents issued by the sharī'ah courts.

2. Fees for general and special powers of attorney and fees for each signature on a declaration or agreement under Article 22 of the Notaries Public Regulations and paragraphs (a), (b), (c) and (d) of Article 26 of the Notaries Public Regulations relating to documents of release of pledges and debts, satisfaction of debts and rescission of sales.

3. All documents of the abovementioned transactions shall be given free of charge. Stamps shall be affixed thereto in view of their nominal cost and in order that such documents shall acquire official character. Please inform all competent authorities to give effect thereto."

We trust that you will take cognizance of the provisions of the High Order and give effect thereto and notify the necessary parties.

Viceroy of H.M. the King

APPENDIX 26

Standard Form Undertaking of Public Sector Contractors and Consultants*

Part 1

Ministry of Commerce Standard Form Undertaking of Consultants

The form of the written undertaking has been prepared in Arabic and English which the representative of a contracting company or consultant is required to sign and in which he acknowledges on behalf of his company that he has read and understood the provisions of Royal Decree No. 14 dated 7/4/1397 H, Council of Ministers Resolutions No. 1977 dated 17/11/1396 H, No. 377 dated 18/4/1398 H and No. 124 dated 29/5/1403 H and High Order No. 24851 dated 5/10/1397 H which all relate to the obligation of companies contracting with the Government to purchase national products and not to have recourse to importation and to give Saudi contractors the right to execute not less than 30 percent of a government project and to the restriction of the execution of certain work to the Saudi contractor. The text is as follows:

1 The contractor/consultant shall be obliged to contract out to a 100 percent Saudi contractor according to the Commercial Register and certificate of classification the execution of not less than 30 percent of the value of the project, such percentage not including supply and installation work.

2. The contractor/consultant acknowledges that the instructions do not allow him any right whatsoever to import from abroad and that he is not entitled to establish factories for the service of the project or the company's requirements until after authorization of the Ministry of Industry.

3. The contractor/consultant shall be required to give priority in procuring the requirements of the project to products of national factories licensed by the Ministry of Industry after checking and consulting the lists which the Ministry shall

* Prepared by Special Committee Constituted in October 1984 to Supervise Compliance with Certain Regulations and Resolutions (Published in Al-Riyadh (Daily), November 6, 1984 at 11, cols. 3–5).

issue. In case of the nonavailability of a similar or substitute item from national industry for any goods required, they shall be procured from the local market through the authorized agent.

4. The contractor/consultant shall be required to keep a special file with the company manager and the project manager containing the orders and instructions regulating the relationship between it and the official and civil authorities and which shall be available to its new managers successively and also to obtain authorization from the Ministry of Commerce for any new projects or additions.

5. The contractor/consultant shall be required to obtain the following services from local Saudi firms:

   (a) services for the transportation of goods and persons within the Kingdom unless the contractor performs the same itself and with its own equipment and employees;
   (b) local insurance services;
   (c) life-support and food supply services;
   (d) banking services;
   (e) services for the leasing and purchase of land and buildings.

6. The contractor/consultant shall be required to provide the Council of Saudi Chambers [of Commerce and Industry] with a copy of any contracts which it has obtained to execute government or civil projects, together with adequate up-to-date information on the company's address within the Kingdom and abroad and the names of the managers of the company and the project and submission to the Council of a quarterly report on the products supplied by national industry and the work executed by the Saudi contractor of the 30 percent specified for him.

7. The contractor/consultant agrees to be bound by the above instructions and to act in accordance therewith. Any violation thereof shall give the Ministry the right to withdraw its license to carry on its activities, and the authorities concerned shall be notified thereof to apply any penalties to which it may be subject under the regulations.

8. The contractor/consultant shall be required not to ask Saudi factories and Saudi contractors to submit applications for qualification at the company and to be satisfied with the license of the Ministry of Industry and Electricity with respect to factories and to the classification certificates with respect to Saudi contractors in assigning work or tasks.

9. Any enquiries concerning the above shall be referred to the Ministries of Commerce and Industry and their branches or the Council of Chambers of Commerce in the region in order to achieve mutual understanding and to cooperate to overcome any difficulties that may impede its application.

A copy of this Resolution shall be accepted and kept in the company's records and complied with.

Part 2

Ministry of Commerce Standard Form Undertaking of Consultants

Kingdom of Saudi Arabia
Ministry of Commerce

No. ....

Date ....

Undertaking

I,   representing the Consulting
Company   located at
acknowledge that I have read and understood Council of Ministers Resolution No.
1977 dated 17/11/1396 H, which provides that the technical departments in ministries'
public agencies and consulting companies working with the State shall, in preparing
the specifications of government projects, give priority to the products of national
industry set forth in the attached list provided that they satisfy the purpose.

I have also read and understood High Order No. 18301 issued by His Royal
Highness, the Crown Prince, dated 27/7/1397 H, which provides for strict observance
of the aforementioned Council of Ministers Resolution and Council of Ministers
Resolution No. 377, dated 18/4/1398 H which obliges companies contracting with
the State to purchase national products. They may not import from abroad products
similar to those included on the attached list.

I undertake to be bound by the provisions of the said Resolution and High Order
and to control the observance and compliance of the executing company under my
supervision with such provisions. I shall keep a copy of this Undertaking in the
company's records to give effect thereto, whether on my part or the part of other
company's, officials. Any violation thereof, whether on my part or on the company
at any time shall subject us to liability and the taking of the prescribed measures
against us.

Made on   /1401 H

Name   Title   Signature   Company Seal

List

Construction Supplies

Adhesives
Aggregates and Sand
Airconditioners
Air Ducts
Aluminium Extrusions
Asbestos Sheets
Asphalt
Bathroom Fitments
Blocks
Bricks
Cement
Concrete Curing Compounds
Curbstones
Decorative Building Materials
Desert Coolers
Doors, Windows and Partitions
Electrical Equipment
Explosives
Insulation
Lighting for Street

Manhole Covers
Nuts and Bolts
Paints and Protective Coatings
Pipes
Plastic Hoses
Prefabricated Buildings
Reinforced Steel
Ready-Mix Concrete
Steel Structure
Stone
Tanks
Tiles
Timber
Tools and Equipment
Water Filters
Water Heaters
Welding Electrodes
Windows-Insulated
Wire Mesh

Consumer Products

Bakery Products
Ball Point Pens
Batteries
Biscuits
Bleach
Brushes & Brooms
Carpets
Confectionery
Cosmetics
Dairy Products
Desert Coolers
Detergents
Disinfectants
Eyeglasses
Fruit Drinks
Furniture
Gas
Ice
Insecticides

Lamps
Matches
Meat
Napkins
Paper-Towels
Plastic Containers & Housewares
Plastic Hoses
Pots, Pans & Utensils
Ropes
Salt
Sandwiches/Snack Foods
Soaps
Soft Drinks
Textiles
Tissues
Water-Bottled
Water-Coolers
Water-Portable
Water-Softening Equipment

478

Commercial Supplies

Furniture-School
Paper Bags
Plastic Bags

Printing
Stationery

Industrial Products

Adhesives
Aluminium Extrusions
Batteries
Bottle Caps
Brushes & Brooms
Cans
Cables
Chemicals
Disinfectants
Farm Equipment-Poultry
Feeds-Animal

Gas Insecticides
Packaging
Plastic Bags-Industrial
Polyester Resins
Polystyrene Containers
Pressure Vessels
Salt
Silos
Timber-Chipboard
Water-Softening Equipment

Transport & Automotive Products

Buses
Batteries
L.P. Gas Distribution
Motor Coil Rewinding
Radiators

Roll-on, Roll-off Transport
Spare Parts
Tire Retreading
Trucks
Truck Body Fabrication

APPENDIX 27

Minister of Finance and National Economy Circulars No. 5767/404 of 9/11/1404 H (August 6, 1984) and No. 3/1743 of 12/3/1406 H (November 24, 1985)

Kingdom of Saudi Arabia
Ministry of Finance and National Economy
Office of The Minister

Subject: Rules for Application of Council of Ministers Resolution No. 124 of 29/5/1403 H (March 14, 1984)

Greetings:

The Ministry has received a number of queries from various government departments, companies and sole proprietorships concerning the rules of Council of Ministers Resolution No. 124 dated 29/5/1403 H relating to the encouragement of local contractors. In order to reply to such queries, the Ministry appointed a committee consisting of the Deputy Ministers of the Ministries of Planning, Commerce, Communications, Industry and Electricity and Finance and National Economy and the General Audit Board, on the basis of which appropriate rules were adopted by the Committee and approved by the authorities referred to as follows:

First: Scope of application of the Resolution

(1) The Resolution is applicable without limitation to contracts for public works which require executory works, such as construction contracts generally and contracts for maintenance and operation.

(2) "Saudi contractors" as stated in paragraph (I) of the Resolution, by means of whom a minimum of 30 percent of the foreign contractor's work is required to be executed, are defined as individual contractors or Saudi wholly-owned companies registered in the Kingdom of Saudi Arabia by virtue of commercial registrations and the classification register.

(3) The percentage set in paragraph (I) of the Resolution may be in the form of executory works or the form of the supply and installation of materials included in

the execution of the project if this represents a percentage of not less than 30 percent of the value of the contract.

(4) This percentage may be divided among a number of Saudi contractors.

Second: Contractors to whom the Resolution applies

a. Contractors who are obliged to contract out a proportion of 30 percent of the contract value to Saudi contractors are defined as:
(1) Individuals or companies having a foreign character.
(2) Mixed companies existing in the Kingdom pursuant to licenses under the Foreign Capital Investment Regulations.
(3) Joint ventures formed by Saudi and foreign companies for the purpose of executing specific projects.

b. Contractors subject to the obligations provided in paragraphs (II) and (III) of the Resolution which require the purchase of equipment and tools for the execution of the contract from Saudi agents and likewise the obtention of services of transportation, insurance, leasing and purchase of land and livelihood and banking services from local Saudi firms are all defined as contractors, whether Saudis or nonSaudis.

Third: Procedures in support of the application of the Resolution

(1) The general conditions set out for tender documents which are prepared by the technical department in government agencies or by the consultant with whom a contract is entered into for the purpose of preparing conditions and plans shall clearly and specifically make full reference to the Resolution and the provisions contained therein.

(2) The authority contracting with the foreign contractor shall make it conditional that in application of paragraph (I) of the Resolution relating to the execution of not less than 30 percent of the contract value, he shall submit with his tender or when entering into the contract with the Saudi contractor all regulatory documents concerning the Saudi contractor such as the commercial register number, Zakāt and income tax certificate, Chamber of Commerce and Industry membership certificate, classification certificate and so forth.

(3) No advance payment or initial payment for work executed shall be made until the foreign contractor submits proof of his compliance with paragraph (I) of the Resolution by entering into a contract with a Saudi contractor or a number of Saudi contractors to execute not less than 30 percent of his contract value. This may be effected partially in that he may contract in stages with Saudi contractors to execute such percentage in part. If he wishes to delay this until the final phases of the project, the authority which is responsible for payment shall not pay more than 50 percent to the contractor under normal circumstances until he has shown compliance with this obligation.

(4) Contracts concluded with consultants to supervise the execution of projects shall include a similar provision obliging them to confirm that the contractor is complying with and applying the provisions of the Resolution.

(5) Agencies supervising the execution of projects shall follow up the work performed by Saudi contractors to check that the work assigned to them is in fact

performed by them and by a body under their control. This shall be indicated in the reports submitted by them to the government authority in that they shall include the reports of supervision of the work undertaken by the contractor and the correspondence and documents of the supervising party verifying the accuracy thereof. If the government authority employs specific forms for supervisors' reports, such forms shall be modified to include columns therefor.

It is therefore requested that all your authorities and departments concerned, including the tender committees, projects departments, engineering, contractors and consultants departments and consultants contracting therewith (currently or in the future) be furnished with a copy of this circular to ensure that they give effect to the rules and arrangements contained therein in preparing the conditions and specifications of government projects and in following up their execution so that the desired objectives of the Resolution shall be realized.

Minister of Finance and National Economy

Minister of Finance and National Economy Circular No. 3/1743 of 12/3/1406 H (November 24, 1985)

Subject: Supplementary Rules for Council of Ministers Resolution No. 124 of 29/5/1403 H

Greetings:

With reference to the queries that the Ministry has received regarding the application of Council of Ministers Resolution No. 124 dated 29/5/1403 H and the previous rules laid down by the Ministry as No. 5767/404 dated 9/11/1404 H, a copy of which is attached,
The Ministry has studied such queries and has decided upon the following clarifications which shall be considered answers to the queries previously received, whether oral or in writing, from government authorities. Such clarifications are as follows:

First: Saudi companies established under the Foreign Capital Investment Regulations in which foreign individuals or companies participate shall not be obliged to assign 30 percent of the value of their contracts with administrative authorities to Saudi contractors if the contracting administrative authority ascertains the fulfillment of the following conditions with respect to such company. The purpose of such conditions is to ensure that the company has actual activity in the Kingdom.

(a) the proportion of the capital of the Saudi partner or partners is not less than 51 percent of the capital of the company contracting with the administrative authority.

(b) the employees and workmen working on the project contracted for with the administrative authority belong to the company itself and were recruited from abroad under its sponsorship.

(c) the company has a classification in the area of works subject of the contract.

If the conditions referred to are fulfilled and the administrative authority establishes the correctness of all information submitted on the company and that the participation is actual and not fictitious, such a company is not required to assign 30 percent of the value of the contract to a Saudi contractor because in such case it is considered a Saudi company.

Second: The contractors who shall benefit from the performance of the 30 percent are those Saudi individuals or companies whose capital is wholly-owned by Saudis in accordance with the particulars of the Commercial Register and the Classification Register.

Third: Procedures aiding the proper application of the Resolution:

To guarantee that foreign contractors abide by the Resolution and consequently to achieve the goals thereof, the Ministry recommends considering the following procedures, which will aid the administrative authorities concerned to realize the objective:

(a) the general conditions of the tender documents shall refer clearly to the provisions and rules of the Resolution in their entirety.

(b) the general conditions shall state that the foreign contractor shall, upon submission of the Saudi subcontractor's bid, attach the legal documents relating to the Saudi contractor, such as the commercial registration and zakāt/income tax payment certificate.

(c) the advance or initial payment for the works performed shall not be made unless the foreign contractor has submitted documents proving its application of paragraph I of the Resolution, that is, by contracting with one or more Saudi contractors to perform a proportion not less than 30 percent of the value of its contract. This may be done partially, such that contracting with Saudi contractors to perform such proportion is done progressively and in part. In case it desires to postpone this to the final stages of the project, the authority making payment shall be entitled not to make payments to the contractor in excess of 50 percent under ordinary circumstances until it proves its compliance with such obligation.

(d) the contracts concluded with consultants for the supervision of the performance of projects shall include a similar provision obligating the supervising consultant to assure the contractor's compliance with and application of the provisions of the Resolution.

(e) the authority supervising the performance of projects shall undertake the following up of the works performed by Saudi contractors to assure that the works assigned to them are actually performed by them by their own workforce and shall refer thereto in its reports which it submits to the government authority, such that supervision reports shall include the works rendered by the contractor and the means and documents examined by the supervisor to ensure the correctness thereof. If the government authority uses special forms for consultant's reports, such forms shall be modified to include spaces therefor.

Fourth: In order to facilitate procedures, it shall not be necessary to require the foreign contractor to submit bids from several Saudi subcontractors, as it is preferable to leave it the choice of its Saudi contractor. The submission of the bid which it prefers shall suffice, together with items proving that he is a Saudi contractor to whom the Resolution applies. A foreign contractor may not include in its contract with the Saudi contractor provisions in conflict with the provisions of the Regulations for the Procurement of Government Purchases, such as requiring bank guarantees or imposing delay penalties in excess of those provided in the Regulations, and may not prequalify the Saudi contractor if he is classified. The Saudi subcontractor may not assign the performance of the work he contracted for to another contractor but shall perform it himself.

Fifth: This Circular is supplementary to the rules provided in Circular No. 5767/404 dated 9/11/1404 H of this Ministry.

Accordingly, we kindly request you to notify your competent authorities, including tender committees, project departments, engineering departments, and legal advisors and consultants contracting or to contract therewith, of the rules contained in the two Circulars to achieve the desired goals.

Best regards,
Minister of Finance and National Economy

APPENDIX 28

Ministry of Commerce Model Articles of Association of a Limited Liability Company

With God's help this Agreement is made on the   day of /   /14   H corresponding to /   /   /19   AD between:

1. Mr/ .... of Saudi nationality on the basis of Identity Card No. .... dated .... issued by .... whose occupation is .... resident of the city of .... street .... First party

2. Mr/ .... of Saudi nationality on the basis of Identity Card No. .... dated .... issued by .... whose occupation is .... resident of the city of .... street .... Second party

3. Company/   which is a company .... formed pursuant to .... represented in this contract by Mr .... of .... nationality and holder of passport no. .... dated .... issued by .... Third party

The abovementioned parties have agreed to form a limited liability company in accordance with the Companies Regulations issued by Royal Decree No. M/6 dated 22/3/1385 H and the following terms:

One—Name of the Company .... ,,,,,,,,,,,,...
Two—Objectives of the Company .... ,,,, ,,,,,,,,,,,,,,,,,,
Three—Main office of the Company ....

The main office of the Company shall be in the city of .... and the Company shall have the right to open branches inside and outside the Kingdom whenever the Company's interests so requires by the agreement of all the partners.

Four—Term of the Company

The Company has been established for a term of .... year/years commencing from the date of its registration in the Commercial Register and renewable for similar periods unless at least six months before the expiry of the original term specified one of the partners notifies the others of his desire by registered letter to their addresses not to continue.

Five—Capital

The capital of the Company has been fixed at .... Saudi riyals (to be written in letters and figures) divided into .... (cash/in kind) shares of equal value. The value of each share shall be .... riyals. They have been allotted among the partners as follows:

	Number of Shares		Value of each Share	Total
	cash	*in kind*	*riyals*	*riyals*
1. Mr/	....	....	....	....
2. Mr/	....	....	....	....
3. Mr/	....	....	....	....
	....	....	....	....

The partners declare that the shares have been allotted among them and that their value has been paid in full and deposited in the .... bank .... branch in accordance with the certificate issued by the said bank in this regard.

The partners acknowledge that they shall be jointly and personally liable to third parties for the correct valuation of the shares in kind as set forth herein.

Six—Increase or reduction of capital

The Company's capital may be increased with the approval of all the partners either by issuing new shares or by increasing the value of the original shares. If new shares are issued, the partners shall have preemptive rights thereon in proportion to the percentage which each partner owns of the original shares. The Company's capital may be reduced by resolution of the partners' general meeting, provided that it shall not be less than the minimum provided in Article 158 of the Companies Regulations.

Seven—Shares

Shares shall be transferable among the partners and their legal heirs. No partner may assign one or more of his shares to third parties, whether or not for valuable consideration, except with the approval of the remaining partners. Notwithstanding this, the remaining partners shall have the right to recover the share or shares which any of the partners wishes to assign in accordance with Article 165 of the Companies Regulations.

Eight—Share register

The Company shall prepare a special register of shares in which shall be entered the names of the partners, the number of shares owned by each partner and all dispositions made with respect to such shares. No transfer of ownership of such shares shall be effective vis-à-vis the Company or third parties unless the reason for the transfer of ownership is entered in the said register.

The register must contain all the particulars provided in Minister of Commerce Resolution No. 1214 of 29/1/1400 H.

Nine—Direction of the Company

The partners have agreed that Mr. .... shall undertake the direction of the Company and for such purpose shall have all the authority and powers necessary therefor. He shall represent the Company in law in its relations with third parties and before the courts and shall be entitled to appoint third parties as representatives with respect to legal proceedings and defense on behalf of the Company.

Ten—Auditors

The company shall have an auditor to be selected by the partners annually by resolution adopted by them at the partners general meeting. He shall be an accountant licensed to practise in the Kingdom in accordance with the provisions of the Accountants Regulations. The auditor shall ensure that the Company's articles of association and the Companies Regulations are complied with, and shall audit the inventory lists and the annual final accounts, examine the balance sheet and present an annual report thereon to the partners. For this purpose, he shall be entitled to inspect all the Company's books, documents and contracts concluded with third parties and shall have the right to request any clarifications and information that he considers necessary to obtain. The partners shall by resolution fix his annual fees.

Eleven—Partners' general meeting

The partners' general meeting shall be convoked at the request of the general manager (or board of directors) or the auditors to consider any matter required to be brought before the meeting within the three months following the end of the financial year, . . . to consider the general manager's report on the Company's activities and financial position and the auditors' report, to approve the Company's balance sheet and final accounts and to decide on the distribution of profits and the appointment of another auditor or the reappointment of the same one and the determination of his fees.

Twelve—Partners' resolutions

The partners' resolutions shall be adopted by unanimity in respect of a change in the nationality of the Company or an increase in the financial liabilities of the partners. With this exception, the Company's articles may be amended by the approval of a majority of the partners representing at least three-quarters of the capital. Resolutions on matters not relating to an amendment of the Company's articles shall be adopted by a majority representing at least one-half of the capital. A partner may appoint by written proxy any person as his representative to attend a partners' meeting and to vote on his behalf. The Company shall prepare special books in which shall be recorded the minutes and resolutions of the partners' general meeting, and the partners present shall sign the minutes and resolutions adopted.

Thirteen—Fiscal year

(a) The fiscal year of the Company shall commence on .... until the end of .... of each year with the exception of the Company's first fiscal year which shall commence from the date of its registration in the Commercial Register until the end of .... of the following year.

(b) The Company's manager shall, within two months from the end of the Company's fiscal year, prepare a general balance sheet, profit and loss statement, a report on the Company's activities and financial position and his proposals concerning the distribution of profits. He shall send a counterpart of such documents to each partner and to the Companies Directorate at the Ministry of Commerce, together with a copy of the auditor's report within fifteen days of preparation thereof.

Fourteen—Profits and losses

The Company's net annual profits after deduction of general expenses and costs shall be allocated in the following manner:

(a) Ten percent of net profits shall be set aside to form the regulatory reserve provided in Article 176 of the Companies Regulations. The Company may discontinue setting aside such reserve when it amounts to one-half of the capital.

(b) The remainder shall be allocated among the partners in proportion to their respective shares in the capital unless the partners resolve to create other reserves or to carry over the balance of profits in whole or in part to the following year.

(c) In the event of realization of losses, the partners shall bear them in proportion to the shares they respectively own in the capital or they shall be carried over to the following financial year. Profits shall not be distributed until after such losses have been made good. If the Company's losses amount to three-quarters of the capital the manager/board of directors shall call a partners' meeting to consider whether the Company should continue or be dissolved before the term specified in its articles.

Fifteen—Dissolution and liquidation of the Company

The Company shall be dissolved upon any of the reasons for dissolution appearing in Article 15 of the Companies Regulations. Upon dissolution, it shall enter the stage of liquidation in accordance with the provisions of Chapter Eleven of the Companies Regulations.

Sixteen—Notices

All notices among the partners or among them and the company shall be sent by registered letter to their addresses stated in the Share Register at the Company referred to in Article 8 of these Articles.

Seventeen—General provisions

1. The Company shall be subject to all regulations in effect in the Kingdom.
2. In every matter where the provisions of these Articles are silent, the Companies Regulations shall be applied.

Eighteen—Counterparts of the articles

These Articles are made in .... counterparts, of which each partner has received a counterpart to act in accordance therewith, and the other counterparts

[   ] for submission to the competent authorities for registration in the Commercial Register and the Companies Register. The partners have authorized Mr. .... to complete the regulatory procedures necessary to form the Company, to take follow-up action with the competent authorities and to sign on their behalf in matters relating thereto.

Made on: /   /14 H corresponding to   /   /19   AD

First Partner   *Second Partner*   *Third Partner*

....

APPENDIX 29

Ministry of Commerce Powers and Duties of Liquidators

The company's articles of association or the decision appointing the liquidator shall define the powers granted to him. If they are not defined, he shall be entitled to undertake all acts required in accordance with the provisions of Chapter 11 of the Companies Regulations (Articles 216 to 226), of which the most important acts are the following:

1—That the liquidator shall publish the decision appointing him—and the restrictions imposed on his powers—in the manner of publication specified for the amendment of the company's articles of association or bylaws (in Umm al-Qurā with respect to limited liability companies and in a daily newspaper with respect to general or limited partnerships) in accordance with the model attached hereto.

2—The liquidator shall establish the financial position of the company on commencement of liquidation within three months of undertaking his activities. After preparation of a complete and inclusive inventory of the company's property, assets and liabilities and approval of the financial position by the partners, he shall send a copy thereof to the General Companies Directorate in the Ministry of Commerce—together with a brief report of his estimations of the operation of liquidation including the period anticipated for the completion of the operation of liquidation.

3—At the close of every financial year of the company, the liquidator shall prepare for the company under liquidation a balance sheet, profit and loss statement and report on the liquidation operations and shall send a copy of such documents to the General Companies Directorate (after approval thereof by the partners or the general meeting) within the period set forth in Article 175 of the Companies Regulations.

4—The liquidator shall add the phrase "company under liquidation" beside the company's name on all of its correspondence and documents issued by it. Otherwise, the liquidator shall be liable for damages resulting therefrom to third parties in accordance with Article 12 of the Companies Regulations.

5—The realization of the company's assets including the sale of its personal and real property by negotiation or auction unless the appointment decision provides for the sale to be carried out by a specific method.

6—The liquidator may not sell the property of the company in one lot or contribute such property as another [sic] share in another company unless so authorized by the authority that appointed him.

7—Satisfaction of the company's rights vis-à-vis third parties or the partners.

8—The liquidator shall deposit the amounts he receives in a bank [   ] for the account of the company under liquidation within twenty-four hours of the time of receipt.

9—The liquidator shall keep a book for the recording of acts connected with the liquidation. The Commercial Court Regulations shall be complied with in keeping such book.

10—The liquidator may not commence new operations on behalf of the company except if they are necessary for the completion of previous operations such as the company's obligation to supply or deliver certain products. However, the liquidator may continue to perform the contract and fulfill the company's obligations in order to avoid a judgment in damages.

11—To pay the company's current debts, such as workmen's and employees' entitlements, judicial costs, liquidation costs and the like, and to reserve amounts required to pay future or contested debts.

12—The liquidator, after payment of the company's debts, shall return to the partners or shareholders the value of their shares in the capital and shall distribute the surplus or the losses among them in accordance with the rates fixed for the distribution of losses.

13—Upon completion of liquidation, the liquidator shall prepare a final account of the liquidation, have the same approved by the partners or the general meeting and send a copy thereof to the General Companies Directorate, together with the submission of a final report on the liquidation operations—including the date of completion of liquidation—and the period of liquidation and the difficulties encountered in the operation of liquidation.

14—The liquidator shall publish [a notice of] the completion of liquidation—in the manner of publication specified for the amendment of the company's articles of association or bylaws in accordance with the model attached hereto.

15—If there are more than one liquidator, they shall act jointly unless the authority having appointed them authorizes them to act individually.

16—The liquidator shall submit to the partners or shareholders any information or particulars to the extent that the interests of the company will not be injured thereby nor delay in the operations of liquidation resulting therefrom.

17—The liquidator shall represent the company before the judicial authorities and make settlements during the period of liquidation—inasmuch as he is considered the legal representative of the company.

18—The liquidator shall not distribute the liquidation proceeds gradually, since the results of liquidation are a total operation whose distribution is to be carried out after the completion of such operation, and shall determine the net proceeds with the exception of privileged debts.

19—If it appears to the liquidator that the company's assets are insufficient to pay its debts during the period of liquidation, he shall:

    a—Demand that the general partners in general and limited partnerships pay the debts due from the company from their personal property.

    b—Notify the partners and creditors of limited liability companies of the exhaustion of all of the company's property by its debts, the insufficiency of its assets to satisfy its obligations and the necessity of the partners' payment of the company's debts and obligations from their personal property; or demand the declaration of bankruptcy thereof by the partners, creditors or interested parties in accordance with Article 108 of the Commercial Court Regulations.

Ministry of Commerce Model Liquidation Resolution

Kingdom of Saudi Arabia   Ref. No. ....

Ministry of Commerce   Date ....

Riyadh 11162   Enclosures ....

(1) Limited Liability Company

Partners' Resolution

To liquidate the company .... a limited liability company registered in the Commercial Register No. .... in the city of .... On the day of   /   /140— corresponding to   /   /198   a meeting of the partners in the company was held, present:

    (1) Mr. ....

    (2) Mr. ....

    (3) Company .... represented in this meeting by

         ....

    And they resolved the following:

(1) The voluntary dissolution and liquidation of the company for the following reasons:

    (1)   (2)

    (3)   (4)

    and in accordance with the provisions of the articles of association of the company and in accordance with the liquidation provisions of Chapter 11 of the Companies Regulations.

(2) The appointment of Mr./Messrs. ....,,,,,, no liquidator/ liquidators of the company ,,,,,,... and the granting to him of all authorities and powers necessary to execute his duties.

Signatures of the Partners

    (1) Mr./Partner .... Signature

    (2) Partner .... Signature

    (3) Partner .... Signature

(4) Company .... represented by
Mr. .... Signature
Remarks:

(1) In case there are restrictions imposed on the powers of the liquidator, they must be stated.
(2) The liquidator shall publish this resolution in accordance with Article 221 of the Companies Regulations—and notify interested parties of his appointment as a liquidator and the manner of communicating with him for the settlement of their rights.

Kingdom of Saudi Arabia	Ref. No. ....
Ministry of Commerce	Date ....
Riyadh 11162	Enclosures ....

Announcement of Completion of Liquidation (Limited Liability Company)

Company .... a limited liability company

In accordance with Article 223 of the Companies Regulations, the liquidator of Company .... announces the completion of its liquidation, and after the meeting of the partners of the company on the date   / /
and their approval of the final liquidation account and the report of the liquidator.

The liquidator declares that all debts and liabilities of the Company have been settled and there are no debts due to others.

This is for the fulfilment of the regulatory procedures for striking the Commercial Registration of the Company No. .... in the city of
....

Signature of the Liquidator

Ministry of Commerce Model Final Liquidation Account

Realization of the Company's Assets	Riyal	h	Riyal	h
Sale Price of Fixed Assets				
Land	xxxx	—		
Buildings and constructions	xxxx	—		
Machinery and equipment	xxxx	—		

Realization of the Company's Assets	Riyal	h	Riyal	h
Furniture and fixtures	xxxx	—		
Tools and instruments	xxxx	—		
Total sale of fixed assets			xxxx	—
Sale price of goods in stock	xxxx	—		
Sale price of raw material in stock	xxxx	—		
Proceeds of company's claims against customers	xxxx	—		
Proceeds of company's claims against various debtors	xxxx	—		
Proceeds of company's claims against partners	xxxx	—		
Receipts of receivables	xxxx	—		
Sale price of securities	xxxx	—		
Receipts on value of investments in affiliated companies	xxxx	—		
Cash in treasury	xxxx	—		
Cash in banks, current accounts	xxxx	—		
Total sale and receipts on current assets			xxxx	—
Total cash realized on company's assets			xxxx	—
Payment of Company's Debts	Riyal	h	Riyal	h
a—Payment of Privileged Debts Workmen's entitlements	xxxx	—		
Judicial costs	xxxx	—		
Liquidation costs	xxxx	—		
Value of legal Zakāt	xxxx	—		
Value of income tax	xxxx	—		
Value of secured debts	xxxx	—		
b—Payment of company's creditors	xxxx	—		
c—Payment of short-term loans	xxxx	—		
d—Payment of long-term loans	xxxx	—		
e—Payment of bank overdrafts	xxxx	—		
Total payment of company's debts			xxxx	—

494

Realization of the Company's Assets	Riyal	h	Riyal	h
Payments to partners or shareholders after payment of debts				
Payment of partners' loans	xxxx	—		
Payment of partners' capital	xxxx	—		
Payment of shareholders' capital	xxxx	—		
Total payments to partners or shareholders			xxxx	—
Distribution of liquidation surplus (profit or loss) among the partners or shareholders	xxxx	—	xxxx	—

APPENDIX 30

Director-General of the Department of Zakāt and Income Tax Circular No. 3 of 14/10/89 H (December 23, 1969), as amended by Acting Minister of Finance and National Economy Letter No. 902/4/92 of 13/3/1392 H

Disallowance of the deduction of indirect expenses

In accordance with sound accounting principles requiring that books of account should accurately reflect income and expenses and use the correct professional description and term for each entry,

And in accordance with taxation principles settled by tax legislation and judicial decision in most countries of the world requiring that the expenses the deduction of which is allowed from the gross income of a firm in calculating net profit shall fulfill the following conditions:

First: that they should represent real expenses actually incurred.

Expenses include cash expenditures, rights foregone, amounts or rights lost by the firm, debts incurred during the fiscal year if they are not satisfied within such period and any depreciation in the value of fixed assets or in the value of goods established by comparing values established at the end of the fiscal year with book value at the beginning of such year.

Second: that they should not have been offset by an appreciation in the value of fixed assets or the value of goods or a reduction in liabilities at the end of the fiscal year (as in the case of expenses paid in consideration of the redemption of part of the capital or payment of a debt shown as a liability).

Third: that the expense should have been incurred in generating or preserving profit.

Fourth: that such profit should be subject to tax, the basis of which is to be determined (No expenses shall be deducted if associated with profit not subject to tax or associated with profit subject to tax in a prior or subsequent fiscal year.)

And in view of the fact that it has been observed that many persons engaged in an activity generating profit from a local source in the Kingdom, which is consequently subject to income tax on companies or individuals, have been including in their expenses large amounts which do not fulfill the abovementioned conditions, in particular amounts deducted under the heading "indirect expenses" as representing the share of the activities in the Kingdom of the expenses of the main firm having its head office abroad, thus resulting in the reduction of the amount of tax due to the Treasury in accordance with sound taxation principles.

Therefore, we have resolved the following:

1. (a) To repeal Circular No. 10 of 1376 H issued by the Department of Zakāt and Income Tax on 12/7/1376 H (February 22, 1957) concerning the accounting of the branches or agencies of foreign companies present in the Kingdom having their head offices abroad relating to the inclusion of the share of the local branch in the general expenses of the company.

(b) To repeal Circular No. 7 of 1381 H issued by the Department of Zakāt and Income Tax on 25/8/1381 H (January 31, 1962) concerning the accounting of branches or agencies of airlines and shipping companies and firms conducting business activities in the Kingdom having their head offices abroad, including the arbitrary assessment in such Circular of the net profits of such branches or agencies.

2. Every foreign taxpayer conducting an activity generating profit from a local source in the Kingdom, whether such profit is subject to company or individual income tax, and operating in the Kingdom as a branch, agent, representative or affiliate of any kind of a firm, establishment, or individual having its head office abroad, shall be required to submit concerning its activity in the Kingdom an account specifying its profits independently of the profits of its head office abroad to the Department of Zakāt and Income Tax at the times fixed in the Regulations. Likewise, any firm, establishment or individual having its head office abroad and not represented in the Kingdom receiving income from a local source in the Kingdom, whether yielded by capital investment or leasing of moveable or immoveable property, arising from commissions, profits on shares, suretyships and guarantees (insurance operations) or arising from any other source mentioned in articles III as amended and XIII of the Income Tax Law shall be required to submit an account of its profits arising from a local source in the Kingdom separate from the accounts of its general activities abroad.

In all cases the taxpayer shall be entitled to deduct from its general income solely the expenses relating to its activity in the Kingdom of the specific types set forth in article XIV of Royal Decree No. 3321 of 1370 H and elaborated in article XIII of the Implementing Rules issued by Ministerial Resolution No. 340 dated 1/7/1370 H, provided that they shall be directly related to its profits in the Kingdom as having satisfied all of the general tax conditions referred to in the preamble of this Circular.

3. In application of the preceding articles:

(a) No taxpayer may deduct any amount from the income of its activity in the Kingdom as "indirect expenses" representing the share of its activity in the Kingdom of the general overhead expenses expended by its head office abroad, since its profits arising from a local source in the Kingdom should be affected only by expenses directly related to such profits.

(b) Technical expenses incurred abroad by the head office or otherwise in consideration of technical services directly contributing to the generation of profit in the Kingdom may be deducted, provided that a detailed and accurate statement thereof is submitted describing the nature of the work or service, the actual execution thereof, the recipients of payment and receipts confirming the expenditure.

(c) General overhead expenses mentioned in paragraph (a) of this article shall be deemed to include all expenditures of banks, financial institutions engaged in banking operations and money changing and their branches, insurance companies, reinsurance companies and their branches or agencies and all firms and enterprises whose activities are limited to the sale and purchase of goods and the operations of importing, exporting or acting as intermediaries therein. Administrative acts and services with respect to which amounts may not be deducted include in the aforementioned cases the head office's carrying out promotion, control, supervision, direction and guidance of the branch, agent, or representative operating in the Kingdom.

(d) "Technical expenses" appearing in paragraph (b) of this article means expenses related to the execution of engineering works of any kind or chemical, geological or industrial works and research.

4. Shipping and air transport firms and agencies shall be exempted from the provisions of paragraphs (a) and (b) of article 3 above. The amount of expenses which may be deducted from the income arising from a local source in the Kingdom shall be determined by a method appropriate to the nature and circumstances of each case independently, without prejudice to agreements concluded between the Kingdom of Saudi Arabia and other nations on reciprocal exemption from income tax.

5. The provisions of this Circular shall apply to all fiscal years ending after 14/10/1389 H (23/12/1969 AD).

14/10/1389 H
Director-General of the Department of Zakāt and Income Tax

APPENDIX 31

Arbitration Regulations Implementing Rules

Council of Ministers Resolution No. 7/2021/M of 8/9/1405 H (May 27, 1985)

CHAPTER I

Arbitration, Arbitrators, and Parties

Article 1. Arbitration is not permitted in matters in which conciliation is not permitted, such as the hudud [crimes for which the Quran provides punishments], accusation of adultery between spouses and all matters relating to public order.

Article 2. An agreement to arbitrate shall not be valid unless made by a person having full capacity of disposition. The guardian of a minor, appointed guardian or endowment trustee may not resort to arbitration unless so authorized by a court having jurisdiction.

Article 3. An arbitrator shall be a Saudi national or Muslim foreigner of the liberal professions or otherwise. He may be a public official upon approval of the department to which such official belongs. If there is more than one arbitrator, the chairman shall be knowledgeable in sharī'ah rules and the commercial regulations, custom and traditions in effect in the Kingdom.

Article 4. A person having an interest in the dispute, having been convicted of a hadd [Quranic crime] or penalty for a crime of dishonor, having been dismissed from public office by disciplinary decision or adjudged bankrupt, unless relieved thereof, may not be an arbitrator.

Article 5. Subject to the provisions of articles 2 and 3, a list of names of arbitrators shall be prepared by agreement among the Minister of Justice, the Minister of Commerce and the Chairman of the Board of Grievances. The courts, judicial commissions and Chambers of Commerce and Industry shall be notified thereof. Parties may select arbitrators from such lists or otherwise.

Article 6. The arbitrator or arbitrators shall be appointed by agreement of the parties in an arbitration document which shall adequately define the subject of the dispute and the names of the arbitrators. An agreement to arbitrate may also be made by a contractual clause relating to disputes arising out of the execution of such contract.

Article 7. The authority originally having jurisdiction over the dispute shall issue a decision approving the arbitration document within fifteen days and shall notify the arbitral tribunal thereof.

Article 8. In disputes to which a government authority is a party with third parties and desires to resort to arbitration, such authority shall prepare a memorandum concerning arbitration in such dispute stating therein the subject thereof, the justifications for arbitration and the names of the parties for submission to the President of the Council of Ministers to consider approval of the arbitration. A government body may by prior consent of the President of the Council of Ministers be permitted in a specific contract to resolve disputes arising therefrom by means of arbitration. In all cases, the Council of Ministers shall be notified of the awards rendered therein.

Article 9. The clerk of the authority originally having jurisdiction over the dispute shall act as secretary for the arbitral tribunal, establish the records necessary for the registration of requests for arbitration and submit them to the competent authority for approval of the arbitration document, and shall also be responsible for the notifications and communications provided in the Arbitration Regulations and any other responsibilities determined by the competent minister. The competent authorities shall make the necessary arrangements therefor.

Article 10. The arbitral tribunal shall fix the date for hearing the dispute within a period not exceeding five days from the date of its notification of the decision approving the arbitration document and shall notify the parties thereof through the clerk of the authority originally having jurisdiction over the dispute.

CHAPTER II

Notification of Parties, Appearance and Default, and Representation in the Arbitration

Article 11. Every communication or notification relating to the dispute under arbitration made by the clerk of the authority originally having jurisdiction over the dispute shall be effected by server or through the official authorities, whether carried out at the request of the parties or initiated by the arbitrators. The police posts and local officials shall assist the competent authority in the performance of [its] duties within their sphere of competence.

Article 12. A notification or communication shall be drawn up in Arabic in two or more copies according to the number of parties and shall include the following particulars:

(a) The day, month, year and hour in which the communication or notification was made.

(b) The name, surname, profession or office, and residence of the person requesting the notification or communication and the name, surname, profession or office and residence of his legal representative if he is acting for another person.

(c) The name of the server who effected the communication or notification, the department in which he works and his signature on the original and the copy.

(d) The name, surname, profession or office and residence of the person to be notified or communicated to or, if he has no known residence at the time of notification, his last preceding residence.

(e) The title of the person to whom the copy of the notification was delivered, his signature on the original acknowledging receipt or a notation of his refusal to do so on the original upon its return to the competent authority.

(f) The name and seat of the arbitral tribunal, the subject of the proceedings and the date fixed therefor.

Article 13. The papers to be notified shall be delivered to the person himself or to his residence and may be delivered to a selected residence designated by the parties. In case the person to be notified is absent from his residence, the notification papers shall be delivered to a person declaring himself to be his agent, responsible for the conduct of his affairs or his employee or a spouse, agnate or servant residing with him.

Article 14. If the server does not find a person to whom delivery of the papers may be validly made in accordance with the preceding article or the persons referred to therein refuse to accept delivery, he shall state the same on the original and shall deliver it on the same day to the chief of police, local official or substitute for either if the residence of the person to be notified is located within his jurisdiction according to circumstances. He shall also, within twenty-four hours, send to the person to be notified at his original or designated residence a registered letter informing him that the copy was delivered to the administrative authority and state the same in its entirety at such time on the original notification and the copy thereof. The communication or notification shall be deemed valid and effective from the time of delivery of the copy in the preceding manner.

Article 15. Except as provided in special regulations, the copy of the notification or communication shall be delivered as follows:

(a) In matters relating to the State, it shall be delivered to ministers, regional governors and heads of government authorities or to their substitutes according to competence.

(b) In matters relating to public persons, to the representative thereof authorized by regulations or his substitute.

(c) In matters relating to companies, associations and private establishments, it shall be delivered to the main offices thereof as set forth in the Commercial Register to the chairman of the board of directors or general manager or to an employee substituting for such person and, with respect to foreign companies having a branch or agent in the Kingdom, it shall be delivered to such branch or agent.

Article 16. The responsible official shall transmit the arbitration file to the authority originally having jurisdiction over the dispute for approval of the arbitration document. The clerk of such authority shall notify the parties and the arbitrators of the decision issued approving the arbitration document within one week from the date of issuance thereof.

Article 17. On the day fixed for hearing the arbitration, the parties shall appear in person or through a representative pursuant to a power-of-attorney issued by a notary public or any official authority or certified by a Chamber of Commerce and Industry. A copy of the power-of-attorney shall be deposited in the case file after review of the original by the arbitrator, without prejudice to the right of the arbitrator or arbitrators to require the personal appearance of a party if the circumstances so require.

Article 18. If one of the parties fails to appear at the first hearing and the arbitral tribunal is satisfied that he was served personally, it may decide the dispute if the parties have deposited [in] the arbitration file memorials of their claims, defense, answers and documents. The award in such case shall be deemed made as if all parties were present. If he was not duly summoned, the tribunal shall adjourn to a subsequent hearing to be notified to the defaulting party. If there is more than one defendant party, some of whom were duly summoned and the other was not duly summoned and they all fail to appear or the party who was not duly summoned fails to appear, the tribunal shall—except in urgent cases—adjourn hearing the matter to a subsequent hearing to be notified to the nonappearing parties who were not duly summoned. The award in the matter shall be deemed made as if all parties failing to appear at the subsequent hearing were present.

An award shall be deemed made as if a party were present if the party or his representative makes an appearance at any hearing or submits a defense memorial in the case or document related thereto. If a defaulting party makes an appearance before the end of the hearing, any award made therein shall be deemed null and void.

Article 19. If, on the nonappearance of a party, it appears to the arbitral tribunal that his summons by publication was invalid, it shall adjourn hearing the claim to a subsequent hearing to be validly renotified to such party.

CHAPTER III

Hearings, Procedure and Recording of the Case

Article 20. The case shall be publicly heard before the arbitral tribunal unless the tribunal on its own initiative decides to hold the hearing in camera or one of the parties requests the same for reasons to be evaluated by the tribunal.

Article 21. Hearing of the case may not without a satisfactory excuse be adjourned more than once for the same reason attributable to one of the parties.

Article 22. The arbitral tribunal shall enable each party to present his comments, defense and answers orally or in writing to an appropriate extent on the dates which it shall fix.

The defendant shall be the final speaker, and the arbitral tribunal shall complete the case and prepare it for decision.

Article 23. The chairman shall be in charge of controlling and directing the hearing and shall direct questions to the parties or witnesses. He shall have the right to order that anyone disturbing the hearing be expelled from the room, provided that, if a violation is committed by anyone present, he shall prepare a report of the incident and transmit it to the competent authority. Each arbitrator shall have the right to direct questions to and cross-examine parties or witnesses through the chairman of the tribunal.

Article 24. The parties shall have the right to request the arbitral tribunal at any stage of the case to record their agreement as to an admission, settlement, waiver or otherwise in the record of the hearing, and the tribunal shall make an award thereof.

Article 25. Arabic is the official language which shall be used before the arbitral tribunal whether in oral discussions or in writing. The tribunal, the parties and other persons may speak solely in Arabic. A foreigner who does not speak Arabic shall be accompanied by an accredited interpreter who shall sign with him the record of the hearing as to the oral statements which he translated.

Article 26. Any party may request an adjournment of the hearing for an appropriate period to be determined by the arbitral tribunal in order to present documents, papers or comments material or relevant to the case. The tribunal may take a further adjournment for another period if there is justification therefor.

Article 27. The arbitral tribunal shall record the facts and proceedings of the hearing in a record prepared by the secretary of the tribunal under its supervision. The date and place of the hearing and the names of the tribunal [sic], the secretary and the parties shall be recorded in the record, which shall include the oral statements of the parties. The chairman of the tribunal, the arbitrators and the secretary shall sign the record.

Article 28. The arbitral tribunal may on its own initiative or at the request of one of the parties require the opposing party to produce any document in his possession material to the case in the following cases:

   (a) If it is a joint document between two such parties. In particular, a document shall be deemed joint if such document is for the benefit of both parties or establishes their mutual obligations and rights.
   (b) If the opposing party relies thereon at any time of the case.
   (c) If regulations authorize the request for production or delivery thereof. Such request shall set forth:
      (1) the description of the particular document.
      (2) the contents of the document in as much detail as possible.
      (3) the fact to be proved thereby.
      (4) evidence and circumstances showing that it is in the possession of the opposing party.
      (5) the obligatory nature of production thereof.

Article 29. The arbitral tribunal may order investigation measures having a material effect on the case if the facts sought to be established are relevant and material to the dispute and are admissible.

Article 30. The arbitral tribunal may depart from the evidentiary procedures it has ordered on condition that it set forth the reasons therefor in the record of the hearing. The tribunal may disregard the result of the procedure and shall state the reasons therefor in the award.

Article 31. A party requesting that oral statements of witnesses be heard shall state the facts sought to be proved in writing or orally at the hearing and shall accompany the witnesses, the hearing of whose oral statements is requested, before the tribunal in accordance with sharīʿah principles. The other party shall have the right to disprove the facts in such manner.

Article 32. The arbitral tribunal may interrogate the parties at the request of a party or on its own initiative.

Article 33. The arbitratal tribunal may if necessary seek the assistance of one or more experts to present a report concerning technical and material matters or facts affecting the case and shall furnish in the text of its award a precise statement of the mission of the expert and the urgent measures he is authorized to adopt. The arbitral tribunal shall determine the expert's fees, the party who is to bear the same and the deposit to be made for the account of the expert's costs. In case the party liable therefor or any other party fails to make such deposit, the expert shall not be obligated to perform the mission and in such case the right to adhere to the decision appointing the expert shall be forfeited if the tribunal finds the excuses advanced therefor to be unsatisfactory. The expert in the performance of the mission may hear the oral statements of the parties or other persons and shall submit a report on his acts and his opinion on the specified date. The tribunal may examine the expert at the hearing as to the findings of the report. If there is more than one expert, the tribunal shall specify the manner of their action if individual or collective.

Article 34. The arbitral tribunal may require the expert to submit a supplementary report to rectify any omission or deficiency in his previous report. The parties shall have the right to submit advisory reports to the tribunal. In all cases the tribunal shall not be bound by the opinion of the experts.

Article 35. The arbitral tribunal may on its own initiative or at the request of one of the parties decide to relocate to inspect disputed facts or matters affecting the case. The tribunal shall prepare a record of the inspection procedures.

Article 36. The arbitral tribunal shall comply with litigation principles including confrontation in the proceedings, affording each party knowledge of the proceedings of the case, examination of the material papers and documents therein at appropriate times and granting him a sufficient opportunity to submit his evidence, answers and arguments in writing or orally at the hearing and shall record the same in the record.

Article 37. If in the course of the arbitration a preliminary issue outside the jurisdiction of the arbitral tribunal arises, a document is contested on the grounds of forgery or criminal proceedings are instigated with respect to the forgery thereof or another criminal case, the tribunal shall stay its action and suspend the date fixed for the award until a final judgment is rendered by the authority having jurisdiction to decide such issue.

CHAPTER IV

Making of Awards, Objection and Enforcement Order

Article 38. When the case is ready for decision, the arbitral tribunal shall declare the proceedings closed and bring the case under review and deliberation. The deliberations shall be held in camera and may be attended solely by the arbitral tribunal which collectively heard the proceedings. Subject to the provisions of articles 9, 13, 14 and 15 of the Arbitration Regulations, the tribunal on closing the proceedings or at another hearing shall fix a date for making the award.

Article 39. The arbitrators shall make their awards without being bound by regulatory procedures except as provided in the Arbitration Regulations and their Implementing Rules. Their awards shall be made in accordance with the provisions of the Islamic sharīʿah and regulations in effect.

Article 40. The arbitral tribunal may not during review of the case and deliberation hear explanations of one of the parties or his representative except in the presence of the other party nor may it receive memorials or documents unless the other party examines the same. If it considers them to be material, it may extend the date for pronouncing the award and reopen the proceedings by an award in which shall be recorded the reasons and justifications and shall notify the parties of the date fixed for hearing the case.

Article 41. Subject to articles 16 and 17 of the Arbitration Regulations, awards shall be made by majority voice. The chairman of the arbitral tribunal shall pronounce the award at the hearing fixed therefor. The award shall contain the names of the members of the tribunal which made it, the date and place of the making thereof, the subject thereof, the names, surnames and capacities of the parties and the residence of each, their appearance and default, a summary of the facts of the case, then their claims, a brief résumé of their answers and their basic defense, then the grounds and text of the award. The arbitrators and the clerk shall sign the original award containing the preceding items, which shall be placed in the case file within seven days of deposit of the draft.

Article 42. Without prejudice to the provisions of articles 18 and 19 of the Arbitration Regulations, the arbitral tribunal shall be in charge of correcting any mere technical typographical or arithmetical errors in its award by an award which it shall make on its own motion or at the request of one of the parties without proceedings. Such correction shall be made on the original award and shall be signed by the arbitrators. If the tribunal exceeds therein its right as provided in this article, the award making the correction may be appealed against in the manner permitted for appeal of the award subject of the correction. An award made refusing correction may not be appealed against independently.

Article 43. The parties may request the tribunal which made the award to explain any ambiguity or unclarity in the text thereof. An explanatory award shall be deemed complementary in all respects to the original award and shall be subject to the rules relating to the manner of appeal applicable thereto.

Article 44. Upon issuance of the order for enforcement of the arbitral award, it shall become an enforceable instrument. The clerk of the authority originally having jurisdiction over the dispute shall deliver to the prevailing party the enforcement copy of the arbitral award on which shall be set forth the enforcement order ending with the following legend:

> "All competent government departments and authorities shall take action to enforce this award by all applicable regulatory means even to the extent of the use of force by the police."

Article 45. If each party has not prevailed on some claims, a judgment may be made apportioning the fees between them according to the determination of the authority originally having jurisdiction over the dispute or allocating the entirety thereof to one of them.

Article 46. Any party may object to an order assessing the arbitrators' fees to the authority which issued such order within eight days from the date of his notification of such order. Its decision on the objection shall be final.

Article 47. The competent authorities shall implement these Rules.

Article 48. These Rules shall be published in the Official Journal and shall be effective from the date of publication thereof.

APPENDIX 32

Deputy Minister of Commerce Circular
No. 3/9/sh/331/9/2903 of 13/3/1399 H

Kingdom of Saudi Arabia
Ministry of Commerce
Companies Department

In the name of God, the Merciful, the Beneficent

Re: That companies' articles of association shall not contain a provision permitting arbitration concerning disputes to be held outside the Kingdom.

Notification to all branches of the Ministry and the Commercial Register Office in Riyadh.

Mr. .... Manager of ....

This Ministry has received several queries concerning the extent to which the articles of association of companies may contain an arbitration clause providing for referring a dispute arising between partners for settlement by an arbitration commission outside the Kingdom.

The Legal Department at the Ministry, having studied the said subject, issued Memorandum No. 174/K dated 22/2/1399 H approved by His Excellency the Minister on 23/2/1399 H, which states that a clause providing for arbitration (outside the Kingdom) included in the articles of association of Saudi companies shall be considered absolutely void.

Therefore, we hope that no articles of association will be approved or registered if the same contain a provision which refers disputes and differences arising between partners or between the partners and the company for settlement by an arbitration commission or arbitrators outside the Kingdom. Rather, arbitration shall be performed inside the Kingdom in accordance with effective regulations and instructions.

Deputy Minister of Commerce

APPENDIX 33

Regulations for Combating Forgery; Penal Regulations on Forgery and Counterfeiting of Money

Royal Decree No. 53 of 5/11/1382 H (March 30, 1962)

With the help of God Almighty—in the name of H.M. the King We, Faisal bn 'Abdul 'Aziz Al Sa'ud, Deputy of H.M. the King of the Kingdom of Saudi Arabia, Having reviewed Royal Order No. 42 of 9/10/1381 H,

And having reviewed Articles 19 and 20 of the Council of Ministers Regulations issued by Decree No. 38 of 22/10/1377 H,

And having reviewed Decree No. 114 of 26/11/1380 H approving the Regulations for Combating Forgery and Decree No. 12 of 20/7/1379 H issuing the Penal Regulations on Forgery and Counterfeiting of Money,

And pursuant to Council of Ministers Resolution No. 550 of 3/11/1382 H,

And pursuant to the proposal submitted to us by the President of the Council of Minister,

Decree as follows:

Article 1. The text of Article 4 of the Regulations for Combating Forgery issued by Decree No. 114 of 26/11/1380 H shall be replaced by the following:

> Any person who counterfeits or falsifies bank notes or company bonds, whether the banks or companies are Saudi or foreign, or who counterfeits or falsifies Saudi postage or government stamps, treasury bills or receipts of public treasuries or Ministry of Finance departments, or who manufactures or possesses equipment for the forgery of such instruments and stamps with the intent to use the same for himself or third parties shall be punished by imprisonment from three to ten years and a fine from three thousand to ten thousand riyals. A principal or accessory shall, in addition to the preceding penalties, be fined in the amount of all resulting losses to the Treasury, companies, banks or individuals. A person who informs of the crimes provided in this article before the completion thereof shall be exempt from punishment. The punishment of a person who provides information about the principals or accessories thereto after the commencement of regular legal prosecution shall be reduced to one third of the minimum penalty, or the minimum fine only

may be imposed. In order to benefit from such reduction, such person shall be required to return all funds he has received as a result of the forgery.

Article 2. The counterfeiting of currency and all crimes connected therewith shall be punished in accordance with the provisions of the Penal Regulations on Forgery and Counterfeiting of Money issued by Decree No. 12 of 20/7/1379 H.

Article 3. The text of Article 11 of Decree 12 of 20/7/1379 H shall be replaced by the following:

All counterfeit and forged money and all equipment and materials used in the crime or arising therefrom shall be seized and confiscated and shall be turned over to the Saudi Arabian Monetary Agency. Under no circumstances whatsoever shall any compensation be paid therefor.

Article 4. The President of the Council of Ministers, the Minister of Finance and National Economy and the Minister of the Interior shall, each within his jurisdiction, implement these Regulations and give effect thereto from the date of their publication in the Official Journal.

Royal Decree No. 114 of 26/11/1380 H (May 10, 1960)

With the help of God Almighty,

We, Sa'ud bn 'Abdul 'Aziz Al Sa'ud, King of the Kingdom of Saudi Arabia,

Having reviewed Article 19 of the Council of Ministers Regulations issued by Decree No. 38 of 22/10/1377 H,

And pursuant to Council of Ministers Resolution No. 653 of 25/11/1380 H,

And pursuant to the proposal submitted to us by the President of the Council of Ministers,

Decree as follows:

First. We approve the Regulations for Combating Forgery in the form attached hereto.

Second. The President of the Council of Ministers and the Ministers shall implement this Decree of ours from the date of its publication.

Draft Regulations for Combating Forgery

Article 1. Any person who with the intent to commit forgery imitates royal seals and signatures or seals of the Kingdom of Saudi Arabia or the seal or signature of the President of the Council of Ministers, and any person who uses or facilitates the use of such seals and signatures, with the knowledge that they are forged, shall be punished by imprisonment from five to ten years and a fine of five thousand to fifteen thousand riyals.

Article 2. Any person who falsifies or forges a seal, stamp or mark belonging to any public department in the Kingdom of Saudi Arabia or to Saudi representatives in foreign countries, or belonging to a foreign State or the public departments thereof, or who uses or facilitates the use of such signatures, marks or seals shall be punished by imprisonment from three to five years and a fine of three thousand to ten thousand riyals.

Article 3. If the person who commits the acts provided in Articles 1 and 2 of these Regulations or the accessory thereto is a public official or a person receiving a salary from the state Public Treasury he shall be sentenced to the maximum punishment.

If the principal or accessory destroys the forged items referred to in the two preceding articles before the use thereof or provides information thereof prior to the instigation of legal proceedings, he shall be exempt from the punishment and fine.

Article 4. Any person who counterfeits gold, silver or metal currency or imitates bank notes, whether of the Kingdom of Saudi Arabia or foreign states, or who circulates them within the Kingdom or abroad, or who imitates or falsifies bank notes or company bonds, whether the banks or companies are Saudi or foreign, or who imitates or falsifies Saudi postage and government stamps, treasury bills and receipts of public treasuries and Ministry of Finance departments, or who manufactures or possesses equipment for the counterfeiting of currency, notes and stamps with the intent to use the same for himself or any other person shall be punished by imprisonment from three to ten years and a fine of three thousand to ten thousand riyals.

A principal or accessory who circulates the counterfeit items shall, in addition to the preceding penalties, be fined in the amount of all resulting losses to the Treasury, companies, banks or individuals.

Any person who provides information about the crimes provided in this article before the completion thereof shall be exempt from punishment. The punishment of any person who provides information about the principals or accessories thereto after the commencement of regular legal prosecution shall be reduced to one third of the minimum penalty, or the minimum fine only may be imposed. For such reduction to be applied such person shall be required to return all funds he has received as a result of such forgery or counterfeiting.

Article 5. Any public official who in the course of his duty commits forgery by intentionally fabricating a legal instrument or manuscript or altering a copy of an original or by using a forged signature, seal or fingerprint or who destroys in whole or in part an official instrument or documents having the force of proof, or who falsifies an academic certificate or a certificate of government or civil service or who wrongfully signs a blank [document] entrusted to him or who sets forth false facts and oral statements as being true and accepted or who records information and oral statements other than those provided by the persons concerned or who intentionally changes or alters the wording of official papers, records and documents by defacement, deletion, the addition, suppression or intentional omission of words, or who changes names entered in official documents or records and enters false or fictional names in place thereof or who changes figures in official documents and records by addition, deletion or alteration shall be punished by imprisonment from one to five years [1]

---

[1] The provisions of Article 5 apply to official and unofficial documents. Council of Ministers Resolution No. 223 (14/8/1399). Removing, destroying, tampering with or substituting photographs affixed to official or unofficial papers or documents is also a crime subject to Article 5. Council of Ministers Resolution No. 3 (3/1/1406).

Article 6. Ordinary persons who commit crimes provided in the preceding article or who use forged documents and records and the documents provided in the preceding article with the knowledge of the facts shall be punished by the penalties provided in the said article and a fine of one thousand to ten thousand riyals.[2]

Article 7. Notes made out to bearer or to the order of another person or financial instruments or stock which may be issued in the Kingdom of Saudi Arabia or which have been issued in foreign countries and are not prohibited from being circulated in the Kingdom, and in general all financial instruments, whether made out to bearer or transferable by endorsement, shall be deemed official documents and notes with respect to all the acts provided in Article 5 of these Regulations.

Article 8. Any official or person in the public service or medical or health profession who provides another person with an incorrect document, certificate or statement resulting in an unlawful benefit or damage to any individual shall be punished by imprisonment from fifteen days to one year.

Article 9. Any person who assumes the name or signature of any of the persons referred to in the preceding article to forge an authenticated document or who alters or falsifies an official document, identity card, passport or residence permit or any official visa document in order to enter, traverse, reside in or exit from the Kingdom of Saudi Arabia shall be punished by imprisonment from six months to two years and a fine of one hundred to one thousand riyals.

Article 10. Any person who imitates or forges a signature or seal of another person or who alters an instrument or private document by obliteration, deletion or modification, shall be punished by imprisonment from one to three years.

Article 11. Persons provided in Articles 8 and 9 shall be exempt from punishment if they confess to the crimes before use of the forged document and before commencement of prosecution.

Royal Decree No. 12 of 20/7/1379 H

We, Saud bn 'Abdul 'Aziz Al Sa'ud, King of the Kingdom of Saudi Arabia,
In order to ensure the circulation of currency within the Kingdom of Saudi Arabia solely by means of sound money and to protect the interests of the public appropriately and to protect currency within and outside the Kingdom,
And having reviewed Articles 19 and 20 of the Council of Ministers Regulations,
And pursuant to Council of Ministers Resolution No. 104 of 7/7/1379 H,
And pursuant to the proposal submitted to us by the President of the Council of Ministers,
Decree as follows:

---

[2] The provisions of Article 6 apply to the use of forged notes or documents whether official or unofficial and whether or not the user is a public official. *Id.*

Article 1. The term "money" as used in these Regulations means all types of coinage, whatever metal the coins are minted in, and paper currency in lawful circulation within or outside the Kingdom of Saudi Arabia.

Article 2. Any person who counterfeits or imitates money in lawful circulation within or outside the Kingdom of Saudi Arabia or who imports, issues, transacts with or circulates counterfeit or forged money by any means or manner whatsoever or who in bad faith and without justification manufactures, acquires or owns any machines, tools, materials and means of counterfeiting shall be punished by imprisonment at hard labor for a period of five to fifteen years and a fine of not less than three thousand riyals and not more than one hundred thousand riyals.

Article 3. Any person who with evil intent alters the features of money in lawful circulation within the Kingdom of Saudi Arabia or who mutilates, tears or washes it with chemicals or who reduces its weight or size or destroys it in whole or in part shall be punished by imprisonment for a period of three to five years and a fine of not less than three thousand riyals and not more than ten thousand riyals or either of such penalties.

Article 4. Any person who with the intention of sale for cultural, industrial or commercial purposes manufactures or possesses pieces of metal or notes similar in appearance to legal tender in the Kingdom of Saudi Arabia such that such resemblance could mislead the public shall be punished by imprisonment not exceeding one year and a fine not exceeding two thousand riyals or either of such penalties.

Article 5. Any person who for the purposes stated in Article 4 of these Regulations prints, diffuses or uses copies representing a side or part thereof of paper currency in lawful circulation in the Kingdom of Saudi Arabia without obtaining authorization from the competent authorities and acting in accordance with the conditions imposed in such authorization shall be punished by imprisonment for a period not exceeding one year and a fine not exceeding one thousand riyals or either of such penalties.

Article 6. Any person who in good faith accepts forged or counterfeit money and thereafter transacts therewith with the knowledge that it is defective shall be punished by imprisonment for a period not exceeding one year and a fine not exceeding two thousand riyals or either of such penalties.

Article 7. Any person who participates in the commission of any crime provided in these Regulations, whether by incitement, participation or aiding, shall be punished by the same penalties prescribed for the crime.

Article 8. An attempt to commit any crime provided in these Regulations shall be punished by half the punishment prescribed for the completed crime.

Article 9. The crimes provided in these Regulations shall be punished whether they are committed within or outside the Kingdom of Saudi Arabia.

Article 10. Persons who commit any crimes provided in these Regulations shall, by royal decree pursuant to the proposal of the President of the Council of Ministers, be exempt from punishment if they inform the competent authorities of such acts before the completion thereof and facilitate the arrest of their other accessories.

Article 11. All counterfeit or forged money shall be seized and confiscated and shall be turned over to the Saudi Arabian Monetary Agency. Under no circumstances whatsoever shall any compensation be paid therefor.

Article 12. The Government shall be entitled to collect a fine by forced execution against the immoveable or moveable property of a convicted defendant or forcibly to detain the convicted defendant for a period of one day for every five Saudi riyals, provided that the period of detention shall not exceed six months.

Article 13. The Government or any person who has suffered damage by reason of the crimes provided in these Regulations may claim compensation from a convicted defendant for any material or nonmaterial damage sustained.

Article 14. The President of the Council of Ministers, the Minister of Finance and National Economy and the Minister of the Interior shall each within his jurisdiction implement these Regulations.

Article 15. These Regulations shall be effective from the date of their publication in the Official Journal.

APPENDIX 34

Model Disciplinary Rules

Minister of Labor and Social Affairs
Resolution No. 119 of 12/4/1390 H, as amended by Resolution
No. 15 of 18/1/1397 H

The Minister of Labor and Social Affairs,

Pursuant to the provisions of Articles 9 and 125 of the Labor Regulations approved by Royal Decree No. M/21 of 6/9/1389 H,

Decrees as follows:

Article 1. The attached model rules governing penalties and rewards and the provisions for imposing such penalties or granting such rewards to workmen are approved.

Article 2. Any employer employing twenty workmen or more shall be guided by the attached model rules in preparing its rules of penalties and rewards.

Article 3. This resolution shall be published and notified to those concerned for implementation of the provisions thereof.

Model Rules Governing Penalties and Rewards and the
Provisions for Imposing such Penalties or Granting such
Rewards in Implementation of the Provisions of Articles 9 and
125 of the Labor Regulations

Article 1. These Rules shall be considered model rules and are intended to guide employers who employ twenty or more workmen in preparing their rules of penalties and rewards and to prompt such employers to expedite the submission [of their rules] to the Ministry for discussion and approval thereof.

Article 2. Employers concerned may add any other violations not covered by these Model Rules to their draft rules of penalties and rewards if the nature and the type of work in their establishments so require.

Article 3. Employers concerned shall, however, submit the draft rules of penalties and rewards prepared by them to the Ministry for approval. Such rules as well as any amendment thereto shall not be considered effective with respect to workmen unless such rules are approved by the Ministry in accordance with the legal rules set forth in Articles 9 and 125 of the Labor Regulations.

Part One: Penalties

Article 4. By virtue of the provisions of these Rules, the following matters shall be considered violations:
(a) Any refusal or negligence on the part of the workman in the performance of his work;
(b) Any failure or delay on the part of the workman in performing his work;
(c) Any absence from work without permission or valid reason;
(d) Leaving work without complying with legal rules or instructions.

Article 5. The following matters shall be considered violations against work discipline in the place of work:
(a) Repeated lateness for work;
(b) Frequent leaving of the place of work without permission or authorization;
(c) Disobeying orders duly transmitted by the employer or by the workman's direct superiors;
(d) Quarrelling, handfighting or cursing during work;
(e) The workman's adoption of bad conduct in a public and apparent manner.

Article 6. The penalties that may be imposed on workmen are classified into two types:

TYPE 1, LIGHT PENALTIES:
(a) Notice: this is an oral or written communication addressed to the workman by his direct superior, and referring to the violation committed by the workman. He shall be requested to comply with the Regulations and to perform his duty properly;
(b) Written warning: this is in writing addressed to the workman in the event of a violation on his part directing his attention expressly in the writing to the possibility of imposing a more severe penalty upon him in the event of continuation or repetition of the violation;
(c) Deduction of a percentage of wages within the limits of a part of a day.

TYPE 2: SEVERE PENALTIES:
(a) Deduction of a portion of the workman's wages: this portion ranges from the wages of one day to five days a month and it may not exceed this limit;

515

(b) Suspension without wages: this is the barring of a workman from performing his work for a period of time without any wages or compensation. This penalty may be imposed from one to five days. Such suspension shall not exceed this limit in a month;

(c) Cancellation or delaying of promotion: this is the depriving of any increase of wages prescribed for the workman under the provisions of these rules or in accordance with the bylaws of the establishment or firm in which he works or in implementation of any provision [of law] or other agreement;

(d) Termination with severance pay: this is the termination or dismissal of the workman for a valid reason because of his admission of a violation and giving him the severance pay due for his period of service;

(e) Termination without severance pay: this is the termination of the workman's contract without severance pay if he has committed an act to which the provisions of Article 83 of the Labor Regulations apply.

Article 7. The penalties provided for in these rules shall be imposed by the employer or his representative. The penalty imposed on the workman shall be in proportion to the type and extent of the violation on his part.

Article 8. Violations deserving light or severe penalties shall be determined according to the schedule attached to these Rules. However, other violations may be added thereto according to the nature and the type of work of the establishment after approval by the Ministry in accordance with the provisions of Articles 9 and 125 of the Labor Regulations.

Article 9. A violation shall not be subject to more than one penalty. In addition, no other penalty shall be combined with that of deductions from wages.

Article 10. No penalty shall be imposed upon a workman except after his being notified in writing of what he has been charged with and investigation into such [charges], hearing his statements and defense, and the recording of the same in his file.

Article 11. A workman shall be notified in writing of the penalties imposed upon him, the kind and amount of such penalties as well as the penalty which he will be subject to in the event of repetition of the violation. In the event of refusal on the part of the workman to take delivery of the notification, it shall be sent to him by registered mail at his address stated in his own file. In all cases, the workman shall have the right to object before the competent commission in accordance with the provisions of Article 126 of the Labor Regulations.

Article 12. Without prejudice to the provisions of Article 83 of the Labor Regulations, no penalty shall be imposed on the workman for an act committed by him outside the place of work unless such an act is directly connected to [his] work, the employer or the responsible director.

Article 13. Every workman shall have a sheet of penalties in which shall be recorded the type of violation which he has committed, the date of its commission, and the penalty which was imposed on him for such [violation]. Such sheet shall be kept in the workman's file.

Article 14. The penalties imposed upon workmen shall be registered in a special register in accordance with the provisions of Article 127 of the Labor Regulations. The result of such penalties shall be annually submitted to the Ministry to determine the manner of action to be taken for providing the social, health, and educational services to the establishment's workmen.

Part Two: Rewards

Article 15. The rules of penalties and rewards of the establishment shall contain procedures and rules for the granting of rewards to hardworking and loyal workmen in conformity with the nature of work in the establishment for the purpose of encouraging such workmen to pursue their activity and as an incentive for the qualitative and quantitative improvement of production and, consequently, increasing the workmen's income.

Article 16. Rewards are classified into two types:

TYPE 1: MORAL REWARDS:
These consist of a letter of praise or appreciation or promise of a material reward or exceptional promotion if the workman perseveres in hard work and activity.

TYPE 2: MATERIAL INCENTIVE REWARDS:
  (a) Allowance or promotion;
  (b) Production rewards, bonuses;
  (c) Invention rewards and the improvement of methods of production;
  (d) Annual rewards, bonuses.

Article 17. These two kinds of rewards shall be granted by the employer or his representative. Such rewards shall be based on periodic reports prepared by the workman's superiors who are responsible for his work. Such reports shall refer in particular to the workman's experience, his perseverance, his creativity, his personality, behavior, and ability to perform work.

Schedule of Penalties and Rewards

TYPE OF VIOLATION	DEGREE OF PENALTY FROM DAILY WAGE			
Violations Relating to Work Time	First Time	Second Time	Third Time	Fourth Time
1. Lateness in being present for work for up to fifteen minutes without acceptable excuse or permission "if such lateness does not result in the inactivity of other workmen."	Written notice	5%	10%	20%

TYPE OF VIOLATION	DEGREE OF PENALTY FROM DAILY WAGE			
Violations Relating to Work Time	First Time	Second Time	Third Time	Fourth Time
2. Lateness in being present for work for up to fifteen minutes without permission or acceptable excuse "if such lateness results in the inactivity of other workmen."	Written notice	15%	25%	50%
3. Lateness in being present for work for more than fifteen minutes up to thirty minutes without permission or acceptable excuse "if such lateness does not result in the inactivity of other workmen."	10%	15%	25%	50%
4. Lateness in being present for work for more than fifteen minutes up to thirty minutes without permission or acceptable excuse "if such lateness results in the inactivity of other workmen."	25%	50%	75%	Whole day
5. Lateness in being present for work for more than thirty minutes up to sixty minutes without permission or acceptable excuse "if such lateness does not result in the inactivity of other workmen."	25%	50%	75%	Whole day
6. Lateness in being present for work for more than thirty minutes up to sixty minutes without permission or acceptable excuse "if such lateness results in the inactivity of other workmen."	30%	50%	Whole day	Two days
7. Lateness in being present for work for more than an hour without permission or acceptable excuse "whether or not such lateness results in the inactivity of other workmen."	Written notice	Whole day	Two days	Two days
	This penalty is in addition to the deduction of the wages for the hours of delay.			
8. Stopping work or leaving before the fixed time without permission or acceptable excuse for not more than a quarter of an hour.	Written notice	10%	A quarter of a day	One day

TYPE OF VIOLATION	DEGREE OF PENALTY FROM DAILY WAGE			
Violations Relating to Work Time	First Time	Second Time	Third Time	Fourth Time
9. Stopping work or leaving before the fixed time without permission or acceptable excuse for more than a quarter of an hour.	Written notice	10%	25%	Whole day
	This is in addition to the deduction of the wages for the period during which work was stopped.			
10. Remaining in the establishment or returning to it after work has ended.	Written notice	10%	25%	Whole day
Violations Relating to Organization of Work	First Time	Second Time	Third Time	Fourth Time
1. Going out from other than the usual exit.	Written notice	10%	15%	25%
2. Receiving visitors other than the workmen of the establishment in the place of work without the permission of the management.	Written notice	10%	15%	25%
3. Eating at a place other than the prepared place for eating or at a time other than the fixed time.	Written notice	10%	15%	25%
4. Sleeping during work[times].	Written notice	10%	25%	50%
5. Sleeping in cases when continuous wakefulness is required.	Half a day	One day	Two days	Three days
6. Lingering or presence of workmen in other than their places [of work] during work hours.	10%	25%	50%	One day
7. Use of telephone for personal purposes without permission.	Written notice	10%	25%	50%
8. Cheating in proving attendance.	25%	50%	One day	Two days

TYPE OF VIOLATION	DEGREE OF PENALTY FROM DAILY WAGE			
Violations Relating to Organization of Work	First Time	Second Time	Third Time	Fourth Time
9. Disobeying ordinary orders pertaining to work.	25%	50%	One day	Two days
10. Not carrying out the instructions relating to work on condition that these instructions are posted in a noticeable place at the place of work.	25%	50%	One day	Two days
11. Instigating the violation of orders and written instructions relating to work.	Two days	Three days	Five days	Termination with severance pay
12. Negligence or carelessness at work resulting in injury to the health or safety of workmen or to materials and tools.	Two days	Three days	Five days	Termination with severance pay
13. Smoking in prohibited places in view of preserving the safety of the workmen and the place [of work].	Two days	Three days	Five days	Termination with severance pay

Termination without severance pay is permitted in cases 12 and 13 if the violation results in material harm and is coupled with intent.

Violations Relating to the Conduct of Workmen	First Time	Second Time	Third Time	Fourth Time
1. Quarrelling with fellow workmen or creating a disturbance at the place of work.	One day	Two days	Three days	Five days
2. Pretending to be sick.	One day	Two days	Three days	Five days
3. Failing to undergo a physical examination at the request of the establishment's doctor.	One day	Two days	Three days	Five days
4. Refusing to be inspected when leaving.	25%	50%	One day	Two days
5. Violating the health instructions posted in the places of work.	50%	One day	Two days	Five days

TYPE OF VIOLATION	DEGREE OF PENALTY FROM DAILY WAGE			
Violations Relating to Conduct of Workmen	First Time	Second Time	Third Time	Fourth Time
6. Failure to deliver money collected for the account of the establishment at the fixed times without acceptable justification.	Two days	Three days	Five days	Termination with severance pay
7. Collecting subscriptions or money without permission.	Written notice	10%	25%	50%
8. Writing on walls or affixing posters.	Written notice	10%	25%	50%
9. Making false statements to superiors or fellow workmen which may result in interrupting work.	25%	50%	One day	Two days
10. Excessive consumption of raw materials without acceptable excuse.	Written notice	50%	One day	Two days
11. Use of tools, machinery, or raw materials for personal purposes.	Written notice	Two days	Three days	Five days

NOTE:
1. Any violation shall, after the lapse of six months, be considered the first of its kind and shall be subject to the successive penalties in this schedule.
2. The employer may, with respect to any violation made for the first time, substitute a written warning for the penalty prescribed.

APPENDIX 35

Minister of Labor and Social Affairs Resolution No. 452 of 25/11/1397 H (November 7, 1977)

Kingdom of Saudi Arabia
Ministry of Labor and Social Affairs
Office of the Deputy Minister for Labor Affairs
Vocational Training Department

The Minister of Labor and Social Affairs,

Having reviewed Article 44 of the Labor and Workmen Regulations approved by Royal Decree No. M/21 of 1389 H,

And in accordance with the proposal submitted by the Deputy Minister for Labor Affairs,

Decrees as follows:

Article 1. Technical work in Article 44 of the Labor Regulations means: occupations, professions, activities and crafts whose exercise requires technical training of the workman.

Article 2. The training of workmen in the country or abroad shall be carried out at the expense of the employer.

Article 3. The General Training Department shall draw up a training program for workmen in companies and enterprises. Such program shall in particular include the following:
   (a) theoretical and practical study programs as required by each occupation or craft.
   (b) trainees to be provided with every aid relating to the aplicie of their work, whether from the scientific aspect or practical applications which will help to develop their potential.
   (c) minimum and maximum training periods based on the requirements of each occupation or craft.

Article 4. The General Training Department shall take follow-up action on training programs during their implementation in accordance with the guidelines laid down for each program, and shall by an appropriate method make a full assessment of such programs.

Article 5. All enterprises and establishments subject to the provisions of this Resolution shall appoint a training officer.

Article 6. A trainee trained within the Kingdom shall take a written and practical examination after the end of the training period. The General Training Department shall lay down the rules and conditions for such examination.

Article 7. An employer shall provide every workman who has completed his training with a certificate indicating completion of training including the type of occupation in which he was trained and the grade or level which he attained in the examination. The General Training Branch may specify the form of such certificate and may request that any other particulars be added.

Article 8. A workman who has been trained by the company or establishment by which he is employed shall be obliged to remain in the service thereof for the period which it shall specify, not to exceed the period of local or foreign training.

In the case of breach of such obligation, the company or enterprise shall be entitled to recover all the expenditures which it incurred in his local or foreign training.

Article 9. Employers shall prepare a register to record the names of workmen who have been trained. Such register shall include the full name of the workman, his identity card number and the date and place of issuance thereof, his date of birth, the type of occupation in which he was trained, the period of theoretical and practical training and the grade or level attained by him.

Article 10. The provisions of this Resolution shall be without prejudice to the provisions relating to training and secondment for training of the Rules for the Regulation of Labor approved by the Ministry.

Article 11. The Deputy Minister for Labor Affairs at the Ministry of Labor and Social Affairs shall notify this Resolution to the persons required to implement it and it shall become effective from the date on which it is published in the Official Journal.

Minister of Labor and Social Affairs

APPENDIX 36

Royal Decree No. M/2 of 7/2/1403 H

With the help of God the Almighty,

In the name of His Majesty the King,
We Abdullah bn 'Abdul 'Aziz Al Sa'ud, Viceroy of the Kingdom of Saudi Arabia,
Having reviewed Royal Order No. A/45 dated 6/2/1403 H,
And having reviewed Article 20 of the Council of Minister Regulations issued by Royal Decree No. 38 dated 22/10/1377 H,
And having reviewed Article 6 and Article 87 of the Labor and Workmen Regulations issued by Royal Decree No. M/21 dated 6/9/1389 H,
And having reviewed Council of Ministers Resolution No. 4 dated 1/1/1403 H,
Decree as follows:

First: The following paragraph shall be added to the end of Article 87 of the Labor and Workmen Regulations, issued by Royal Decree No. M/21 dated 6/9/1389 H.

Notwithstanding the provisions of Article 6 of these Regulations an agreement may be made to exclude from the wage on the basis of which severance pay is computed, all or some of the amounts of commissions and percentages of sale prices and similar components of the wage paid to the workmen which are subject by their nature to increase and decrease.

Second: This Decree shall be published in the Official Journal and shall be effective as from the date of publication thereof.

Third: The Deputy President of the Council of Ministers and the ministers, each within his jurisdiction, shall implement this Decree of ours.

APPENDIX 37

Council of Ministers Resolution No. 1235 of 12/10/1397 H (September 26, 1977)

Kingdom of Saudi Arabia
General Presidency of the Council of Ministers

The Council of Ministers,

Pursuant to the resolution adopted in its session held on 13/11/1395 H to form a ministerial committee composed of their Excellencies the Minister of Industry and Electricity, the Minister of Communications, the Minister of Finance and National Economy, the Minister of Commerce, the Minister of Planning and the Minister of Labor and Social Affairs to study the problems of increases in prices and workmen's wages and the situation which the country is presently facing as a result thereof and to find appropriate solutions therefor,

And whereas the said committee presented a report thereon containing proposals which it considered should be adopted to deal with the aforementioned conditions and drew up a draft resolution accordingly,

And whereas the Council, having reviewed such report in its session of 17–18/11/1396 H, resolved to form a committee of H.E. the Minister of the Interior, H.E. the Minister of Labor and Social Affairs and H.E. the Minister of Commerce to study the report of the above committee and to consider the manner of halting the increase in prices. The said committee presented its report No. 39 of 25/11/1396 H, and the Council, having considered it, resolved to form a third committee under the chairmanship of H.E. the Minister of the Interior and membership of H.E. the Minister of Commerce, H.E. the Minister of Planning, H.E. the Minister of Commerce and H.E. the Minister of Labor and Social Affairs to undertake the following:

(a) Regulation of the status of daily workmen who are not bound currently by employment contracts, in view of the fact that workmen are not permitted to remain and work in the Kingdom unless on contract, and to lay down a maximum and minimum wage for such category of unskilled workmen.

(b) Study of the feasibility of determining wages for skilled or semi-skilled workmen and to deal with the impediments to such determination of wages and thereafter to submit the result to the Council of Ministers.

And having considered H.E. the Minister of the Interior's Letter No. 3/18230 of 3/7/1397 H attached to the report of the said committee,

Decree as follows:

First. Rules for regulating the status of workmen exempted from the rules of recruitment procedures

1. Individuals exempted from the rules of recruitment procedures who are given special treatment, working or coming to work in the Kingdom without a recruitment application, shall obtain a work permit (on which the word "workman" shall be recorded) without their being required to have employment sponsors, unless both employment parties desire an employment sponsorship commitment and the same is required.

A permit may not be granted to a skilled workman unless he produces certificates of attestation or passes a vocational examination at a vocational training center in the Kingdom or authorities approved by the Ministry of Labor and Social Affairs.

2. The said workmen shall be permitted to work for a wage, including employment in commercial establishments owned by Saudi nationals on the basis of commercial registrations or which are licensed in accordance with the Foreign Capital Investment Regulations.

3. The provision of paragraph 1 shall apply to professionals who work for their own account, subject to the continuation at this stage of their basic status as workmen on issuance of work permits to them and recording of their occupations thereon.

4. Any of the said workmen shall be required to complete an application form for the permit which shall contain general information about the workman, his occupation, his field of work and his working life in the Kingdom.

5. The Passport and Civil Affairs Departments may not grant or renew residence permits of the aforementioned workmen unless they have obtained valid work permits. Except for this, the Passport Departments shall continue to apply existing instructions with respect to such workmen.

6. The Ministry of Labor and Social Affairs shall regulate the manner of issuing work permits for the aforementioned workmen within six months. It may for such purpose divide workmen into categories and fix one or more periods for their obtaining of permits, provided that priority shall be given in this respect to newly arrived workmen and to those whose residence permits have expired.

7. Establishments, regardless of their designation and activities, may not employ workmen exempted from the rules of recruitment procedures except by written contract. Such workmen shall promptly enter into contracts with their employers. With regard to workmen who are not engaged in continuous employment in the same establishment or with the same employer but who work on a transitory basis to meet the daily and temporary needs of their family and others, such persons and their employers shall be required to conclude written contracts if performance of the work which the workman undertakes will take a period in excess of one week. If the period is less, either party shall be entitled to request that a written contract be drawn up, and in such case the other party shall not be entitled to refuse.

8. A workman may not leave his employment before the end of his contract period.

9. Every employer will hold the passport of any workman in his employ and shall not return it to him except upon the termination of the employment relationship between the two parties or in the event of the expiry of the passport and the desire of the workman to renew it, or in any other case satisfactory to the employer. Reference to the number, date and place of issuance of the passport and to the residence permit shall be made in the employment contract.

10. Every employer shall notify the governor's office of the town in whose area of jurisdiction his place of work is located of any of the aforementioned workmen having violated these Rules.

11. Any person who contravenes any of the provisions of these Rules shall be punished by a fine of not less than two thousand riyals and not more than ten thousand riyals for each workman or by imprisonment from two to six weeks, or both. If the offender is a workman, he shall only be deported from the Kingdom and not be allowed to return for employment until three years have elapsed from the date of his deportation.

12. A committee shall be formed in each governor's office composed of a representative from such governor's office, the Labor Office and the Passport and Public Security Departments with jurisdiction to consider any violations of the aforementioned Rules and to propose the appropriate punishment from the punishments prescribed in the preceding paragraph. The committee will hold its meetings at the governor's office. In areas which have neither a Labor Office nor Passport Department, the representatives of the other aforementioned authorities will suffice for the function.

13. The punishments laid down in these Rules shall be imposed by the governor of the province or his delegate.

14. The governor's office shall provide the Passport Department with a copy of the decision for the deportation of a workman having violated these Rules for the follow-up of his deportation. Such department shall take the necessary measures to notify the Ministry of Foreign Affairs not to allow such workman to enter the Kingdom for employment until the expiry of the period referred to in paragraph 12 [sic]

15. The fines imposed in implementation of the provisions of these Rules will revert to the Social Insurance Fund provided in article 207/2 of the Labor Regulations.

16. Governors' offices will publish the decisions issued on penalties in the press.

17. The Ministry of Information shall publicize these Rules in the various information media. The Ministry of Labor and Social Affairs shall alert both workmen and employers as necessary to ensure compliance with these Rules.

18. These Rules shall be published in the Official Journal and shall become effective from the date of publication.

Second. The Ministry of Labor and Social Affairs shall within a period of two years prepare vocational classifications and specifications for the occupations and professions in the private sector.

Third. The Ministry of Agriculture shall import foreign agricultural workmen in order to reduce the pressure on the local market, and workmen engaged in agriculture will be reassigned to their other original occupations.

Fourth. Paragraph 1 of Clause 2—"Manpower Section"—of Council of Ministers Resolution No. 448 of 14/3/1396 H shall be amended to read as follows:

(a) Without prejudice to the priority of providing employment for Saudi nationals, all companies contracting with ministries, government departments, public agencies and concession companies for the execution of industrial, housing and other projects whose value is not less than fifty million riyals shall import all their unskilled and skilled workmen or complete their requirements in this respect from abroad and shall provide them with the necessary accommodation without inflicting pressure on the local market.

[All of the aforementioned authorities shall provide for such obligation in the contracts for their projects.]

(b) A subcontractor assigned the performance of any work entrusted to the prime company or part thereof shall be bound by the same obligation as the prime company. Such obligation shall be provided in the subcontract, and the prime company shall be jointly liable with subcontractors in this respect. The prime company shall notify the project owner of the name or names of the subcontractors and the project owner shall notify the Ministry of Labor of the names of the companies contracting with it and any subcontractors thereof upon signing the contract.

(c) The responsible government authority shall gather the necessary information about the extent of compliance on the part of contractors with the conditions relating to workmen and shall cooperate with the Ministry of Labor to ensure the follow-up of implementation in this area.

(d) Any person who contravenes the abovementioned Rules shall be punished by a fine from fifty thousand to one hundred thousand riyals and shall be obliged to cure the violation; the amount of fines imposed will be commensurate with the number of violations.

The Ministry of Labor and Social Affairs shall have jurisdiction to apply this penalty, and such fines shall revert to the Workmen's Social Insurance Fund provided in Article 207 of the Labor and Workmen Regulations. In case of continuation or repetition of a violation, the Minister of Labor may propose to His Royal Highness that the project be withdrawn from the company in breach.

(e) Ministries, public agencies, and government departments which perform their own works shall be bound by the obligation provided in paragraph (a) if the workmen whom they require to perform such works number two hundred or more.

Fifth. Paragraph 2 of Clause 2—"Manpower Section"—of Council of Ministers Resolution No. 448 of 14/3/1396 H shall be amended as follows:

Preference shall be given to tenders offered to the various government agencies to execute their projects which provide for the use of mechanized equipment and require less workmen. The competent government authorities shall, where possible, endeavor to use machinery in the specifications of their projects.

Sixth. Approval is given for the establishment of Saudi offices for the importation of foreign workmen. Licenses for such offices shall be restricted to Saudis, and nonSaudis may not be licensed to open the same, in accordance with rules to be agreed upon between the Ministries of the Interior, Labor and Commerce.

Second Deputy President of the Council of Ministers

APPENDIX 38

Minister of Labor and Social Affairs Resolution No. 89 of 10/3/1402 H (January 6, 1982)

Kingdom of Saudi Arabia
Ministry of Labor and Social Affairs
Office of the Deputy Minister for Labor Affairs
Central Province Head Labor Office
Inspection Department

Determination of the Conditions and Specifications of Workmen's Housing in Remote Areas and the Consideration for the Use thereof

The Minister of Labor and Social Affairs,

Having reviewed Article 143(a) of the Labor and Workmen Regulations issued by Royal Decree No. M/21 of 1389 H,

And Ministerial Resolution No. 651 of 1401 H designating remote areas,

And pursuant to the proposal submitted by the Deputy Minister for Labor Affairs at the Ministry of Labor and Social Affairs,

Decrees as follows:

Article 1. Any employer who employs workmen in the remote areas designated in Ministerial Resolution No. 651 of 1401 H referred to and in particular in mines, quarries and oil drilling sites shall, with regard to the housing required to be provided for such workmen and without prejudice to the regulations and rules in effect, comply with the following conditions and specifications.

Article 2. A housing area shall be located at a distance of not less than one kilometer from industrial installations and work places which generate matter polluting the air, gases, dust, smoke, liquid or solid waste or anything disruptive or harmful to the health. Where possible, the area shall be sited away from the prevailing winds blowing from the aforementioned installations and places of work.

Article 3. The land of the site shall be well drained and located at a distance of not less than sixty meters from swamps, pools or puddles of stagnant water.

In coastal areas, the site shall be as high as possible above sea level.

Article 4. Housing shall be built in the form of housing compounds of two types, one for married personnel and the other for single personnel. Each compound shall be completely separate from the other.

Article 5. In respect of adjacent housing compounds, a dividing space shall be left between each compound with a width measuring not less than the highest building facing onto it and a minimum width of ten meters.

Article 6. The main front face of the houses shall face north. The houses shall be open from the south, and the buildings in each compound shall adjoin on the east and west in order to avoid sunlight and to ensure adequate ventilation.

Article 7. Designated living space shall not be less than the following dimensions:
(a) Single quarters shall have an individual living space of not less than twelve square meters including bathroom and kitchen such that each workman is allocated a separate bedroom measuring a minimum of nine square meters or a bedroom for two workmen measuring a minimum of sixteen square meters.

The bathroom measuring four square meters and the kitchen measuring eight square metres shall serve four workmen at the most.

If an employer allocates a communal dining hall, the area of the kitchen shall be reduced to four square meters.

(b) With regard to housing for married persons, each family made up of husband and wife shall be provided with a bedroom measuring a minimum of fourteen square meters, a sitting and dining room measuring sixteen square meters, a kitchen measuring six square meters, and a separate bathroom measuring four square meters.

(c) If the members of the family number more than husband and wife, a room similar to the bedroom shall be added for each three legal dependents at the most, but children below the age of three shall not be counted.

Article 8. In all housing, the interior height of rooms from floor to ceiling shall measure not less than three meters except for bathrooms, which may measure two and a half meters in height.

Article 9. Housing shall be constructed for natural ventilation and lighting such that each room or appurtenance in the building shall have openings for ventilation and light (windows and so forth) overlooking the outer space or facing onto a vent or skylight which meets the conditions set forth in the following article. North-facing apertures shall be wide and low, and south-facing apertures shall be high and narrow, such that the area of such apertures shall not be less than ten percent of the ground area of the room or appurtenance and a minimum of half a square meter for bathrooms and kitchens. Rooms shall also be fitted with suitable artificial ventilation during the summer.

Article 10. Skylights and vents for ventilation and lighting of bedrooms and dining and sitting rooms shall measure not less than two-fifths of the highest facing wall and a minimum of ten meters with the shortest side measuring a minimum of two and a half meters. Skylights and vents for the ventilation and lighting of the other appurtenances of the building, such as bathrooms, toilets and kitchens, shall have no dimension less than two and a half meters and shall have a surface area of seven and a half square meters.

Article 11. In the construction of buildings, building materials shall be used which are available and customary in the area where the housing is constructed, whether such buildings are made of breeze blocks and concrete, stone or baked or sun-dried bricks or whether they are prefabricated. However, in oil drilling areas and areas subject to water seepage or sea water, types of anti-saline and anti-sulphate cement shall be used.

Article 12. Ceilings, floors and walls shall give adequate protection to residents from the effects of weather and shall meet safety and health standards. The floor of the ground level shall be treated with an anti-damp course, and the floors of all rooms and appurtenances shall be made of a hard material which is washable, water-resistant and nonerodable.

Article 13. The level of the ground floor of housing shall not be below adjacent ground level. If this is not feasible, horizontal and vertical insulating strips shall be placed in the walls and floors to prevent dampness and leakage. Floor levels shall permit the drainage of toilet water.

Article 14. Walls and ceilings shall be coated with a substance suitable to the materials used for the construction of the building, provided that kitchen and toilet walls shall be painted with oil paint and covered with glazed tiles up to a height of one and a half meters from the floor.

Article 15. Housing shall be provided with adequate drinking water from a source approved by the competent authorities.

If it is necessary to use water from an unapproved source (unapproved wells and springs), such water shall be treated chemically, such chemical treatment shall be carried out in accordance with the results of the analysis of samples of such water in a government laboratory.

If the water contains sediments, they shall be removed by means of appropriate filters before use.

Article 16. Tanks installed to store water shall be made of galvanized zinc or any other rust-proof metal whose elements do not interact with water or the salt content thereof, the same principle being applicable to water supply pipes. Constructed storage tanks shall be well built so as not to allow any water leakage in or out of the tanks, and their inner and outer walls and floor shall be covered with insulating material so as to be nonporous, thus preventing the growth of fungi, and to be easily washable. Tanks shall be required to have a well-fitting cover to keep out dust, dirt or insects and every precaution shall be taken to prevent tanks from being exposed to direct sunlight.

Article 17. Washing, cleansing and purification of drinking water tanks shall be carried out at least once every three months.

Article 18. Bachelor housing shall be provided with a toilet, shower and sink for every four persons. Each housing unit for married persons shall be provided with a toilet, shower and sink.

Article 19. Water closets shall not open directly to the west but shall be reached via a passageway.

Article 20. The toilet area shall measure not less than 80 by 30 centimeters from the interior, and where the shower is installed inside the toilet, the toilet area shall not be less than 120 by 150 centimeters. Each toilet shall be supplied with a tank with a minimum capacity of two gallons.

Article 21. Toilet sewage shall be disposed of by means of main sewers, if any. In the absence of main sewers, disposal shall be effected by way of a cesspit, which shall not affect the buildings or drinking water and provided that such sewage first passes through a sedimentation hole connected with the cesspit.

Article 22. The necessary means shall be provided for the sanitary disposal of refuse and garbage by the supply of dustbins and the collection thereof in a designated area at a suitable distance from the housing and away from the prevailing direction of winds in the area.

Article 23. All electricity supplies shall be conveyed in insulated conduit, or use shall be made of cables made of insulated plastic, in compliance with national and international specifications and standards for electricity supplies. All switches, wires and other electrical appliances shall be appropriate for the voltage in use without risk of danger.

Article 24. Bachelor and married housing shall be provided with the necessary furniture of a standard form for each category of workmen according to their domestic status.

Article 25. The following facilities shall be added to housing compounds:
A mosque or place for prayer;
A resthouse for persons on temporary and short assignments and a place of recreation, subject to nonmingling between the sexes;
A health center comprising an outpatient clinic, a consultation area and small pharmacy together with at least one ambulance to transport serious and urgent cases to the nearest hospital;
A center to provide workmen's requirements in food, fabrics, clothes and other necessaries;
Fire-extinguishing equipment.

Article 26. In cases where work in remote areas is temporary or mobile, the Ministry may allow the construction of such temporary housing as it deems appropriate, such as mobile housing units or residential trailers and so forth, made from approved materials.

Article 27. Employers shall provide housing with continuous maintenance so that they remain suitable for use.

Workmen shall not misuse their living accommodation and shall be liable for the costs of repairing any damage as a result of misuse.

Article 28. The consideration for the workman's use of housing shall be determined in the light of the conditions and specifications of his accommodation, provided that it does not exceed ten percent of the wage of a single workman and twenty percent of the wage of a married workman, and provided that this shall not prejudice any related rights acquired by the workman.

Article 29. Prior to the commencement of building, employers shall submit the engineering, architectural and construction drawings and plans to the Office of the Deputy Minister for Labor Affairs and shall specify the building materials to be used and the site on which the housing is to be constructed. Employers may not commence implementation before approval of the plans submitted, the building materials and the site is given by the Office of the Deputy Minister.

Article 30. The Deputy Minister for Labor Affairs at the Ministry of Labor and Social Affairs shall supervise the implementation of the provisions of this Resolution, and for such purpose he may:

    (a) Approve the designation of housing sites with respect to industrial installations;

    (b) Approve the materials from which buildings are to be constructed;

    (c) Approve engineering, architectural, construction, health and electricity plans submitted by employers;

    (d) Dispense with one or more conditions required for workmen's housing.

Article 31. Workmen's housing constructed before the effectiveness of the provisions of this Resolution shall be referred to the Deputy Minister for Labor Affairs at the Ministry of Labor and Social Affairs for an independent determination on each case.

Article 32. This Resolution shall be published in the Official Journal and shall be effective from the date of publication.

Minister of Labor and Social Affairs

APPENDIX 39

Minister of Finance and National Economy Resolution No. 32/710 of 15/2/1403 H (November 30, 1982)

Kingdom of Saudi Arabia
Ministry of Finance and National Economy

The Minister of Finance and National Economy,

Pursuant to the contents of Letter No. 8/2 dated 28/1/1403 H (November 14, 1982 from the Director-General of the Department of Zakāt and Income Tax, in which he requested the repeal of Department Circular No. 1 for 1381 H, issued 25/1/1381 H (July 8, 1961) which allowed companies to deduct amounts from their profits for what are called thrift or savings plans on certain conditions,

And having reviewed the Social Insurance Regulations issued by Royal Decree No. 22 dated 6/9/1389 H (November 15, 1969) which gave workmen rights protecting them from need, such as pensions, severance pay and the like,

And whereas the Department of Zakāt and Income Tax is required to accept deduction of all amounts imposed by the said Regulations upon employers and not to accept any other amounts,

And pursuant to Article 19 of the Income Tax Decree No. 17/28/3321 issued on 21/1/1370 H (November 2, 1950) which grants the Minister of Finance and National Economy sufficient powers to take all measures required for the application of these Regulations,

Decrees as follows:

First: The repeal of Department Circular No. 1 for the year 1381 H issued on 25/1/1381 H.

Second: The effectiveness of such repeal as from 1/1/1392 H (commencement of effectiveness of the Social Insurance Regulations in the Kingdom) for companies whose final assessments have not yet been completed.

Minister of Finance and National Economy

APPENDIX 40

Principal Guidelines for the Rules Regulating Work

Kingdom of Saudi Arabia
Ministry of Labor and Social Affairs
Deputy Ministry for Labor Affairs
Central Department of Work Inspection

On classification and appointment, including

—Classification of workmen according to their occupational categories;
—Appointment and related conditions and the manner of occupying the post.

On the organization of training, including in particular

—Training for new workmen before they begin work;
—Periodic training for workmen;
—Technical training for raising the level of competence of workmen;
—Occupational training and related conditions and rules;
—Training for apprentices and the determination of related rules and statuses;
—Scholarship including educational and training missions and scholarships and the determination of the conditions and procedures of each.

On wages, allowances, compensations, promotions, and bonuses, including

—Determination of the days of payment of wages;
—Determination of the manner of confirming the payment of wages;
—Determination of the kinds of various allowances and the bases and rules governing them;
—Determination of the kinds of compensations relating to family costs;
—Other privileges;
—Determination of the regulation of the rules for promotion and the granting of bonuses

On work schedules and leaves, including

—Presence and departure times;
—Determination of work days and work hours per week;

—Determination of periods of work hours;
—Determination of the weekly rest day;
—Determination of work shift and preparing schedules organizing them;
—Mandatory directions for primary first aid;
—Stipulation of the ways of control and notification of work accidents and occupational diseases;
—Stipulation of educational and cultural services and elimination of illiteracy;
—Other social services.

On termination of service, including

—Definition of the various reasons for ending and terminating service;
—Determination of procedures for and form of submitting resignation;
—Stipulation of entitlements and aids due to the workmen in case of death during his service: financial aid . . . funeral expenses . . . the salary of the month in which he died . . . ;
—Statement of procedures for granting the workmen a certificate of termination and delivery to him of his documents deposited with the enterprise.

General rules, including

—Definition of circumstances of grievances and handling complaints within the enterprise;
—Stipulation of effectiveness of the rules from the date of their approval by resolution of His Excellency the Minister of Labor and Social Affairs No. dated   /   /;
—Statement of the rules related to delay and absence and the manner of entering and leaving places of work and inspection;
—Preparing rules relating to leaves and the conditions of entitlement thereto and the procedures for obtaining and postponing such leaves including the following:
   annual leave
   fully paid leaves during feasts
   sick leave
   special or exceptional leave
   marriage leave
   delivery leave
   death leave
   other leaves with full or partial pay or without pay.

On seconding and transportation costs, including

—Procedures for seconding and related conditions and statuses;
—Determination of special categories for the seconding allowance and travel expenses;
—Determination of categories of transportation costs and others.

On medical care, precautions, and social services, including in particular

—Determination of the regulations for medical check-up and treatment, provided that the nature, and conditions of work and the prescribed additional privileges be observed;
—Duties of workmen related to safety, health, and vocation;
—Stipulation of the provision of the various precautionary and safety measures at work.

Remarks

1 Every enterprise employing twenty or more workmen is required to prepare rules regulating work in implementation of Article 9 of the Labor Regulations.

2 The purpose of the rules regulating work is the achievement of cooperation and human relations between the workmen and the enterprise, which creates tranquillity and benefits both parties and production. It is therefore obligatory that the rules include all procedures settling work problems.

3 The abovementioned principal guidelines are not considered exhaustive. The enterprise may adopt items consistent with its circumstances and conditions including its financial, labor, and internal situation and its work modalities.

4 The enterprise shall submit through its main headquarters to the competent Labor Office eight copies of model rules to enable the Ministry to implement them and make a decision on them.

5 The enterprise shall submit at the same time draft rules of penalties and rewards in implementation of Article 125 of the Labor Regulations in the same manner set forth in the preceding paragraph.

APPENDIX 41

Minister of Labor and Social Affairs Resolution No. 812 of 16/11/1394 H (1974) Definition of [Official] Holidays

The Minister of Labor and Social Affairs,

Having reviewed Article 155 of the Labor Regulations issued by Royal Decree No. M/21 of 6/9/1389 H;

And having reviewed Ministerial Resolution No. 357 of 24/11/1389 H issued to specify holiday leaves; and for the public welfare,

Decrees as follows:

Article 1.
    (a) The holiday of Id-Al-Fitr (Lesser Bairam) is three days beginning on the day following the 29th day of Ramadan in accordance with Umm al-Qurā;
    (b) The holiday of Id-al-Adha (Corban Bairam) is four days beginning the day of halting on Arafat;
    (c) The national day of the Kingdom is on the 1st of Al-Mizan (Libra).

Article 2. If the employer wishes to increase holidays over the periods specified in article 1, he may determine such increase before or after the time specified in that article or distribute it before or after that time in a manner furthering the interests of work.

Article 3. This Resolution will not affect more favorable terms acquired by workmen by virtue of any regulations, agreement, contract, rules, custom, traditional practice, or the like.

Article 4. This Resolution shall be notified to the required parties for implementation.

Minister of Labor and Social Affairs

APPENDIX 42

Minister of Labor and Social Affairs Resolution No. 16 of 18/1/1397 H (January 9, 1977)

Kingdom of Saudi Arabia
Ministry of Labor and Social Affairs
Office of the Deputy Minister for Labor Affairs

The Minister of Labor and Social Affairs,

Having reviewed Article 152 of the Labor and Workmen Regulations issued by Royal Decree No. M/21 of 6/9/1389 H,

And pursuant to the proposal submitted by the Deputy Minister for Labor Affairs at the Ministry of Labor and Social Affairs,

Decrees as follows:

Article 1.
(a) The term "preparatory and supplementary operations" which must be performed before the beginning or after the end of work means operations that the workman performs as a preliminary to the commencement of work, such as preparing materials and tools which he uses in his work, fetching them from storage or collecting them from the person assigned by the employer to hold and store them; and also operations performed by the workman at the end of the work period to return materials and tools used by him to storage or to the person assigned to hold them, the cleaning, lubrication and oiling of machinery, and also operations in which a workman hands over his task to his successor in cases where work is performed in shifts and other similar types of activity.
(b) The term "work which is necessarily intermittent" means work which by its nature is not continuous and which includes periods during which workmen are inactive or not continuously concerned with their work or do not remain in their places [of work] except to carry out possible requests, or work which requires that workmen come to their places of work during noncontinuous periods to perform their duties, such as technicians and mechanics who are employed for the purpose of repairing or operating machinery, workmen employed in the transportation, delivery, loading or unloading of merchandise, or workmen employed in the sale of fuel, garage attendants and workmen employed in transportation, railroads, ports, airports, and bus stations and others engaged in similar activities.

(c) Workmen assigned as watchmen and cleaners:

First. The term "workmen assigned as watchmen" means:

    1. Workmen entrusted with guarding the employer's premises, things, materials, tools or property, whether at night or by day, without being assigned any other task during work hours that is not required by the nature of a watchman's work;

    2. Workmen entrusted with guarding and operating drinking water machines.

Second. The term "workmen assigned as cleaners" means:

    Workmen entrusted with ensuring the cleanliness of places of work or installations during or after work hours, provided that they do not actually work for a continuous period of more than six hours.

Article 2. The total time allotted to a workman for performing preparatory and supplementary operations shall not exceed thirty minutes added to the work hours such that a maximum of fifteen minutes therefrom shall be allocated to preparatory operations and a maximum of fifteen minutes to supplementary operations.

Article 3. Actual work hours for work which is necessarily intermittent shall be fixed at ten hours a day reduced to eight hours during the month of Ramadan, provided that a workman shall be given a rest period of not less than ten consecutive hours during every twenty-four-hour period and the employer shall allow workmen to pray at prayer times.

Article 4. Actual work hours for workmen assigned as watchmen and cleaners shall be fixed at twelve hours a day reduced to nine hours during the month of Ramadan, provided that the employer allows workmen to pray at prayer times.

Article 5. The application of this Resolution shall not prejudice any more advantageous acquired rights of workmen covered by the provisions of this Resolution which are established by any other regulations, work rules, employment contracts, judgment, resolution or prior agreement or which are accepted practice.

Article 6. This Resolution shall be published in the Official Journal and shall be effective from the date of publication.

Minister of Labor and Social Affairs

APPENDIX 43

Director-General of the Central Province Head Labor Office Circular of 9/10/1396 H

Kingdom of Saudi Arabia
Ministry of Labor and Social Affairs
Central Province Head Labor Office

Circular to all Companies and Enterprises in Riyadh

Dear Sir:

We are in receipt of Circular Letter No. 1187/6/1 of 24/9/1396 H of H.E. the Deputy Minister for Labor Affairs which reads as follows:

"We have received Letter No. 5/3/8/521 dated 6/9/1396 H of H.E. the Minister and the enclosed copy therewith of the letter of H.E. the Deputy President of the Council of Ministers No. 4/21075 dated 3/9/1396 H addressed to this Ministry concerning the circular requiring all companies operating in the Kingdom to give sufficient time to their workmen and personnel to perform prayer in congregation. Following is the text of the letter of H.E.:

> We have been informed that the personnel employed by national and foreign companies in the Kingdom do not perform prayer in congregation but some of them fail to perform prayer due to ignorance of their religion. In consideration of our desire to take care of their religious interests and guide them to their religious duties you should notify all companies of the necessity of alerting all their Muslim personnel to perform this pillar of Islam in congregation and of giving them sufficient time for this purpose during work and of providing a suitable place for the performance of prayer.

Therefore we wish that you execute the order of H.E. and notify its contents to all companies and sole proprietorships attached to your office and impress upon them the necessity of compliance therewith."

We therefore wish that you alert all your Muslim personnel to the necessity of performing prayer in congregation and grant them sufficient time for this purpose during work hours and provide a suitable place for the performance of this duty and be bound by and desirous of the same in accordance with the High Order.

Director-General of the Central Province Head Labor Office

APPENDIX 44

Director-General of the Central Province Head Labor Office Notice of 2/6/1402 H (March 28, 1982)

Kingdom of Saudi Arabia
Ministry of Labor and Social Affairs
Central Province Head Labor Office
Labor Inspection Department

Items to be Submitted for the Consideration of Applications for Lending [Personnel]

As a facilitation for lending applicants and to save the time and effort of applicants and Office officials, and so that applications submitted to the Office shall fulfill the required conditions, the following shall be observed:

1. Workmen lent in the building and construction field shall be skilled or unskilled, such as smelters, plasterers, tilers, carpenters, iron workers, builders, painters and electricians.

2. Foreign workmen may not be lent until six months have expired from the date on which they began work with their sponsor.

3. Lending shall be for a limited period not to exceed three months or the term of the work permit, whichever is less, but may be renewed for a similar period.

4. Lending shall be effected to cover work for the borrowing employer of the same nature as the workman's occupation.

5. Lending shall be within the limits of a specific percentage of the number of foreign workmen imported under the sponsorship of the lending employer, not to exceed 30 percent of the number of workmen.

6. Lending shall be pursuant to a written agreement signed by the lending and borrowing employers and the workman on loan. The agreement shall include all the terms necessary to define the rights and obligations of each party and in particular the following:

(a) The continuation of the employment contract between the lending employer and the workman during the lending period and the continuation of the former's sponsorship of the latter;

(b) The computation of the lending period within the term of service of the workman with the lending employer;

(c) Nonimpairment of any of the workman's rights agreed upon in his employment contract by reason of the loan;

(d) Joint liability of the lending and borrowing employers for all rights due to the workman or any other party with respect to the lending period.

7. Submission of copies of the commercial registration of the lender and borrower.

8. Submission of the passport and copy thereof, the residence and work permits and employment contract of the workman to be lent.

9. Completion of the form for lending foreign workmen at the Inspection Department to be signed and sealed by the lender, the borrower and the workman to be lent.

Note that the submission and follow-up of transactions is restricted to Saudi nationals and the person following up shall be required to produce a power from the company or enterprise which he represents.

We trust that the above will be complied with by all applicants and that no application will be made to the Office until fulfillment of the aforementioned.

Director-General of the Central Province Head Labor Office

APPENDIX 45

Director-General of the Central Province Head Labor Office Circular No. 1176/2/16/2 of 10/4/1400 H (February 27, 1980)

Kingdom of Saudi Arabia
Ministry of Labor and Social Affairs
Central Province Head Labor Office
Inspection Department

Circular to Companies and Public Establishments in the Riyadh Area

Director,
Dear Sir,

We have received the circular of the Deputy Minister for Labor Affairs at the Ministry of Labor and Social Affairs No. 1780/6/2 dated 17/3/1400 H which reads:

"We have received H.E. the Minister's letter No. 52/S dated 12/3/1400 H with the attached copy of H.R.H. the Minister of the Interior's Circular No. 1237 SAT of 8/3/1400 H which reads:

We trust that you will advise your authorities responsible for foreign contract-holders of the necessity of notifying the Passport Offices upon knowledge of the loss of any foreign contract-holder's passport. The Ministry of Commerce and the Ministry of Labor and Social Affairs shall notify companies and enterprises in the Kingdom to such effect."

You are requested to act accordingly and notify all companies and enterprises in the area under your authority that they are to inform the Passport Office of the loss of any foreign contract-holder's passport.

We emphasize the necessity of complying with the aforementioned.

Director-General of the Central Province Head Labor Office

APPENDIX 46

Rules for the Regulation of the Labor Force Movement Council of Ministers Resolution No. 826 of 1975

1. All companies and enterprises, including concessionary companies undertaking the execution of public and private sector projects, shall import from abroad the required number of competent workmen in all areas of specialization to perform the work entrusted to them.

2. All companies and enterprises, when entering into agreements with the workmen imported by them, shall specify the duration of the agreement. No workman may leave his work before the expiry of this term.

3. No company, enterprise or individual may enter into an agreement with a workman who has been imported for another employer including house servants and workmen of similar nature, unless his sponsor (employer) has agreed to transfer the workman's sponsorship or unless his contract has been terminated and the employer does not wish to renew it.

4. A workman who breaches his obligation with respect to the agreement period and leaves his work before its termination, shall be repatriated to the country from which he was brought at the employer's expense and the expense deducted from the amounts due to such workman. No one may conclude a contract with him until the expiry of two years from the date of his repatriation.

5. A workman whose contract period has come to an end and refuses to renew it despite the employer's wish to this effect may not be employed by another employer except with the former's consent. If the former employer withholds such consent, he shall be obligated to repatriate him to his country. He may not be brought back until after the lapse of one year from the date of his departure.

6. If the workman whose contract period has come to an end is engaged in a profession related to the trade secrets of his employer, he may not enter into an agreement with another employer nor shall he be allowed to work for his own account until after the expiry of three years from the date of termination of his former employment, unless the employer agrees to his work, . . . a physician working for a private dispensary or clinic, an accountant or consultant who works for an employer in the area of his specialization.

7. A company or enterprise, when applying for the importation of one or more workmen, shall undertake in its application in writing not to import any workmen whose importation is prohibited according to the above rules.

8. Any violation of the above rules shall be subject to a fine not exceeding ten thousand riyals and not less than two thousand riyals. The fine shall be multiplied by the number of workmen in respect of whom the violation was committed. The penalty shall be imposed by the Labor Commissions specified in Chapter XI of the Labor and Workmen Regulations. The workmen shall be deported from the country by the application of paragraph 4.

9. Fines imposed under the previous paragraph shall be deposited in the Workmen's Social Insurance Fund provided in Article 207 of the Labor and Workmen Regulations.

10. In the case of workmen exempted from importation rules, such as Yemenis, Hadramis, etc., the employers by whom they are employed shall be notified to regulate the work for each of them by contract. If the workman breaches the provisions of the contract, he shall be deported from the country and shall not be permitted to return until after the expiry of one year.

11. The Immigration Department shall be furnished with statements including the nature of violations and the names of offenders in order to apply the provisions of these Rules to them.

12. These Rules shall come into effect as from the date of publication.

APPENDIX 47

Director-General of the Department of Zakāt and Income Tax Circular No. 1933/1 of 5/3/1405 H (November 29, 1984)

Kingdom of Saudi Arabia
Ministry of Finance and National Economy
Directorate of Zakāt and Income Tax

Circular to all Certified Accountants and Sections and Branches of the General Administration

Further to paragraph 3 of the Department's Circular No. 2/8414 dated 8/8/1392 H concerning payments to workmen and employees and to paragraph 3 of the Department's Circular No. 60902/2 dated 4/8/1398 H concerning the termination of service award. Whereas the Department has noticed that certain companies and enterprises operating in the Kingdom fail to enclose explanatory statements setting out the method of calculating severance pay and vacations in their accounts and in order to facilitate the procedures of assessing tax and zakāt on taxpayers, the Department requests that all taxpayers when submitting their accounts to the General Administration or its branches comply with the following:

(1) Submit a detailed statement setting forth the name of the workman, his base salary, the date of his commencement of service, the date of termination of service and the amount of severance pay due.

(2) Submit a detailed statement setting forth the name of the workman or employee, his base salary, the period of service for which the vacation is due and the amount paid to him with respect thereto.

(3) Comply when calculating severance pay and vacations with the provisions of the Labor and Workmen Regulations issued by Royal Decree No. 21 [sic] of 6/9/1389 H.

(4) The Department will not approve any amount entered under these two items in excess of the amounts provided in the abovementioned Labor and Workmen Regulations.

Director-General of the Department of Zakāt and Income Tax

APPENDIX 48

Director-General of the Central Province Head Labor Office Circular No. 2/16/230 of 18/1/1401 H (November 26, 1980)

Kingdom of Saudi Arabia
Ministry of Labor and Social Affairs
Central Province Head Labor Office
Inspection Department

Circular to Companies and Enterprises Operating in the Riyadh Area

Director,
Dear Sir,
   We have received the Circular of the acting Deputy Minister for Labor Affairs No. 17/6/1 dated 3/1/1401 H which states that the Ministry has received a copy of the letter of H.E. the Deputy Minister of the Interior originally sent to H.E. the Deputy Minister of Foreign Affairs under No. 16S/4668 dated 28/11/1400 H in confirmation of the prior instructions issued by the Ministry of the Interior under No. 16S/2053 dated 8/9/1398 H prohibiting foreigners from engaging in instant photography in streets, public gardens and parks. We have been requested to take whatever action we consider appropriate in this respect.
   We notify you accordingly and trust that you will notify all your foreign representatives to refrain from the practice of instant photography.

Director-General of the Central Province Head Labor Office

APPENDIX 49

Director-General of the Central Province Head Labor Office Circular No. 8882 of 7/1/1398 H (December 18, 1977)

Kingdom of Saudi Arabia
Ministry of Labor and Social Affairs
Central Province Head Labor Office
Inspection Department

Circular to Companies and Private Enterprises

Director,
Dear Sir,

We have received Circular Letter No. 987/6/3 of 12/10/1397 H of the Central Department for Labor Inspection which states that the responsible authorities have observed a reprehensible phenomenon that is almost prevalent in certain of the Kingdom's cities where nonMuslim foreigners work or visit. The phenomenon in question is that such individuals wear only shorts, leaving the rest of their bodies bare and frequent and mix with people in the markets and in areas where women gather. This practice is considered reprehensible and unaccepted by the sharīʿah and is not in keeping with our Islamic values. Therefore, appropriate action must be taken to prevent such phenomenon and to advise foreigners of their obligation to respect the traditions of this country and frequent the markets dressed modestly. Such measures should be applied in a polite, civil and nonviolent manner, and all companies are to be notified to this effect.

Therefore, we trust that you will act accordingly and advise your foreign personnel of the contents of this order in a proper and polite manner so that they understand the same and comply therewith. You are requested to comment and take follow-up action.

We thank you for your kind cooperation in view of the public interest and the preservation of the ideals and values of this country.

Director-General of the Central Province Head Labor Office

APPENDIX 50

Minister of Labor and Social Affairs Resolution No. 435 of 4/11/1404 H (August 1, 1984)

Kingdom of Saudi Arabia
Ministry of Labor and Social Affairs
Office of the Deputy Minister for Labor Affairs
Labor Inspection Department

Designating the Activities and Occupations which Expose Workmen to Lead Poisoning and the Measures to be Taken by Employers to Protect their Workmen

The Minister of Labor and Social Affairs,

Having reviewed Article 130 of the Labor and Workmen Regulations approved by Royal Decree No. M/21 of 6/9/1389 H,

And having reviewed the letter of the Ministry of Health No. 45/2/22 of 13/1/1404 H,

And pursuant to the proposal submitted by the Deputy Minister for Labor Affairs at the Ministry of Labor and Social Affairs,

Decrees as follows:

Article 1. The types of work which might expose workmen to lead poisoning are designated as follows:
    (1) Work in lead mines.
    (2) Extraction, grinding, smelting, refining and moulding of lead.
    (3) Typesetting in printing.
    (4) Production of various pigments, dyes, inks and paints or working enamel, lacquer or bi-metal inlaying which contain lead or using or removing such items.
    (5) Manufacture and repair of batteries.
    (6) Welding by the use of lead.
    (7) Manufacture of zinc derivatives, galvanization and tinning processes in which lead or its compounds are used.

(8) Adding certain organic lead compounds such as tetra-ethyl of lead or tetra-methyl of lead to petroleum products.

(9) Manufacture of rubber in which lead compounds are used.

(10) Manufacture of glass in which lead compounds are used.

(11) Production and use of certain insecticides containing lead compounds.

(12) Extraction, grinding, smelting, moulding, refining and polishing of metals containing lead.

(13) Other work requiring the use or handling of lead or its compounds or materials containing lead.

Article 2. Upon employing a workman in any of the aforementioned types of work, the employer shall inform him by written declaration, to be retained by the employer in the workman's file, of the risk of exposure to lead poisoning and the safety measures for his protection.

Article 3. Employers shall comply with all or some of the following measures, according to the nature of the work, to ensure the protection of their workmen from exposure to lead poisoning.

First. Technical measures:

(a) Use of completely sealed machinery, separation of which allows no escape of fumes or dust from lead or its compounds.

(b) Elimination of fumes or dust containing lead or its compounds at the source of generation by the use of on-site extractors and vaporizing equipment and providing adequate ventilation by natural or artificial means so that the lead concentration in the air of the work area is not in excess of .15 milligrams per cubic meter of air.

(c) Selection of automated machinery and equipment which does not require direct control by the workman, but can be operated by him at a safe distance.

(d) Replacement of manual handling operations with motorized or mechanical methods where possible.

(e) Isolation of operations and projects which generate large quantities of fumes or dust from lead or its compounds.

Second. General measures:

(a) No person under the age of eighteen may be employed in the activities referred to in Article 1.

(b) Juveniles and minors may not be permitted to enter work premises.

(c) Personal protective equipment shall be supplied to workmen, such as protective masks for lead and lead compound fumes and dust, protective gloves, aprons and boots which prevent the workman's body from coming into direct contact with lead or its compounds and the like.

(d) Items for personal hygiene shall be provided, such as soap, hand scrubbers and towels.

(e) Proper facilities shall be provided to clean work premises in such manner as not to create dust, such as sweeping after laying the dust with water or using vacuum cleaners.

(f) Certain places away from the work area shall be designated for eating and others for changing clothes, provided workmen change their working clothes before leaving work.

Article 4. Employers shall comply with the following:

(a) Initial medical examination: to be performed on employment of the workman. It shall establish that the circulatory, digestive, urinary, nervous system and the liver are in good order.

(b) Periodic medical examination: this must be performed at least once every six months for workmen exposed to lead fumes and annually for workmen exposed to the risk of lead or lead-compound poisoning in operations not involving exposure to lead fumes. Such examination shall show the following:

    (1) the condition of the digestive system and the liver;

    (2) the condition of the blood;

    (3) the condition of the urinary system;

    (4) the condition of the nervous system.

(c) The results of the initial and periodic medical examinations shall be kept in the medical file of the workman. Information manifested in such examinations may not be divulged or circulated to any person other than a treating physician, representatives of the employer or responsible officials from the competent authorities.

(d) Notification of the labor office with jurisdiction immediately upon the discovery of any case of lead or lead-compound poisoning, and taking of measures for the medical treatment of the workman and appropriate measures to prevent the recurrence of occupational poisoning.

Article 5. This Resolution shall be published in the Official Journal and shall become effective from the date of publication.

Minister of Labor and Social Affairs

APPENDIX 51

Minister of Labor and Social Affairs Resolution No. 404 of 17/6/1394 H (July 8, 1974)

Kingdom of Saudi Arabia
Ministry of Labor and Social Affairs
Office of the Deputy Minister for Labor Affairs

Medical Care Measures at Places of Work

The Minister of Labor and Social Affairs,

Having reviewed Article 134 of the Labor [and Workmen] Regulations issued by Royal Decree No. M/21 of 6/9/1389 H, the approval by H.E. the Minister of Health in Letter No. 50000/1/17/829 dated 12/5/1394 H and the approval by H.E. the Deputy Minister for Labor Affairs at the Ministry of Labor and Social Affairs,

Decrees as follows:

Article 1. Any employer who employs less than fifty workmen shall provide a first aid chest at the place of work containing the following bandages, medicine and antiseptics:

(1) A sufficient quantity of not less than twelve sterile dressings of small size for fingers;

(2) A sufficient quantity of not less than six sterile dressings of medium-size for hands;

(3) A sufficient quantity of not less than six sterile dressings of large size;

(4) A sufficient quantity of medical cotton of not less than two hundred grams in small rolls of twenty-five grams and two cotton rolls of five hundred grams each for dressing and tying splints;

(5) A sufficient quantity of gauze bandages not less than twelve by seven centimeters wide;

(6) A sufficient quantity of gauze bandages not less than twelve by eleven centimeters wide;

(7) Rolls of adhesive tape of not less than four yards in length by one centimeter wide;

(8) A quantity of water mercurochrome solution of not less than one hundred grams;

(9) Sterilized sulphur powder in two containers of ten grams each with a perforated lid for spraying on wounds;

(10) Solution of ammonia spirit in a ten gram bottle with glass stopper;

(11) Thomas medium-size thigh splint, wooden leg splint, wooden angular arm splint, wooden forearm splint, wooden hand splint and other kinds of splints ready for use;

(12) A minimum of six triangular bandages;

(13) A minimum of twelve safety pins;

(14) Antiseptic and soothing ointment for burns;

(15) At least ten pieces of white cloth measuring seventy by seventy (centimeters) for burns.

If work is being carried out in separate areas with a distance of more than three hundred meters between each group, one chest shall be allocated to each group with more than ten workmen.

Article 2. The employer shall assign one or more responsible individuals to render first aid to injured persons at all times of work. The individual responsible shall be a workman of the establishment trained in first aid in accordance with a program agreed upon with the Saudi Red Crescent Society or holding a certificate from a hospital to the effect that he has practised first aid and is capable of performing the same.

Article 3. An employer who employs fifty or more workmen shall provide at the place of work a first aid room meeting the following requirements:

(a) It shall satisfy health requirements;

(b) Such room shall be in an appropriate place to which injured persons may go or be transported easily and quickly;

(c) Such room shall be not more than three hundred meters distant from the farthest place of work unless there is a means of speedy transportation available for injured persons;

(d) A sufficient number of stretchers shall be provided for carrying injured persons to the first aid room;

(e) The contents of such room, such as equipment and first aid materials, shall not be less than the quantities specified in article 1 and shall be proportionate to the number of workmen;

(f) A registered nurse shall be available for care at all times of work under the supervision of a doctor.

Article 4. Any deficiencies in first aid chests or first aid rooms shall be made up if the quantity of any items fall below the minimum laid down in this Resolution.

Article 5. The first aid chest shall be made of strong wood or iron 85 centimeters long by 45 centimeters wide by 30 centimeters deep, painted in white and with one or more locks. It shall have the sign of the Red Crescent drawn on it in red with the words "First Aid Chest". First aid chests shall be placed in convenient and hygienic places and raised off the floor, and shall be ready for use at all times and easily accessible. Notices shall be clearly posted in various places of work indicating the location of the first aid chest and the name of the person responsible therefor.

Article 6. Any employer employing less than fifty workmen shall designate an appropriate number of his workmen to be trained in first aid in implementation of the provisions of article 2.

Article 7. The Director-General of the Central Department for Labor Inspection shall be authorized to implement the provisions of this Resolution. He may increase the contents of first aid chests or rooms for certain industries or occupations as is necessary, or require specific first aid methods in the case of the application of the preceding articles. He may also decide that a first aid box be provided for any group numbering less than ten workmen if he considers it necessary and specify the number of stretchers and the appropriate number of workmen to be designated for training.

Article 8. This Resolution shall be published in the Official Journal and shall be effective from the date of publication.

Minister of Labor and Social Affairs

APPENDIX 52

Director-General of the Central Province Head Labor Office Circular No. 3778/2/16/12 of 14/11/1400 H (September 24, 1980)

Kingdom of Saudi Arabia
Ministry of Labor and Social Affairs
Central Province Head Labor Office
Inspection Department

Circular to all Enterprises Employing More than Fifty Workmen

Director,
Dear Sir,
   In accordance with the requirements of Articles 134 and 135 of the Labor and Workmen Regulations, which provide the following:
   1. The obligation of enterprises and companies employing more than fifty workmen to engage a doctor for the medical care and treatment of workmen and to employ a licensed nurse for nursing and first aid duties in accordance with Minister of Labor and Social Affairs Resolution No. 404 of 1394 H, a copy of which is attached.
   2. Any person who employs more than one hundred workmen shall, in addition to the aforementioned, provide the workmen with all other means of medical treatment requiring specialist care or surgical operations. Workmen of such enterprises shall not use government hospitals, as the employer is responsible for their comprehensive medical treatment.
   3. The abovementioned companies shall notify the labor office of the names of the physicians, specialists and hospitals contracted with for the treatment of workmen according to the number of their workmen.
   4. Pursuant to letter No. 1103/6/1 dated 18/9/1400 H of the acting Deputy Minister for Labor Affairs based on letter No. AS 568 dated 27/8/1400 H of H.E. the Minister of the Interior, companies and enterprises shall prior to contracting with a workman confirm the availability of medical certificates attesting to his good health and his ability to work.
   You are asked to act accordingly and provide us urgently with the requirement.

Director-General of the Central Province Head Labor Office

APPENDIX 53

Director-General of the Central Province Head Labor Office Circular No. 7776 of 27/10/1397 H (October 11, 1977)

Kingdom of Saudi Arabia
Ministry of Labor and Social Affairs
Central Province Head Labor Office
Inspection Department

Circular to Companies and Private Enterprises

Director,
Dear Sir,

Pursuant to Letter No. 6561/3796/57 dated 1/8/1397 H of H.E. the Deputy Minister of Health, received by Deputy Minister for Labor Affairs, stating that certain complaints have been made to them from the owners of private hospitals to the effect that some companies are not observing the agreements concluded with them in respect of the medical treatment of their workmen and that some companies have their workmen treated in government hospitals, we are sending you this letter trusting that you will comply with the provisions of Articles 134 and 135 of the Labor Regulations relating to the medical care of workmen. We stress to you the necessity of providing such care and of posting clearly in the place of work a notice of the name and address of the doctor, the hospital designated for the treatment of the workmen and visiting hours so that workmen will be fully aware thereof. You are requested to notify us accordingly in compliance with Article 135 of the Labor Regulations.

We await your early reply that the requisite action has been taken and thank you for your cooperation as it relates to the public interest.

Director-General of the Central Province Head Labor Office

APPENDIX 54

Rules for the Control and Regulation of Labor Inspection Activities, Council of Ministers Resolution No. 444 of 3/5/1390 H (July 7, 1970)

The Council of Ministers,

Having reviewed the enclosed file which was received from the Bureau of the Presidency of the Council of Ministers under No. 21772, dated 17 Dhu al-Qa'dah 1389 (January 24, 1970), and which had been submitted under cover of H.E. The Minister of Labor and Social Affairs' letter No. 667, dated 10 Dhu al-Qa'dah 1389 (January 17, 1970), in which it was stated that, in execution of the provisions of Article 28 of the Labor and Workmen Regulations which stipulate that the Ministry of Labor shall prepare appropriate implementing rules for the control and regulation of inspection activities, which rules shall be issued by a decision of the Council of Ministers, H.E. submits the attached draft Implementing Rules for the Control and Regulation of Labor Inspection Activities which have been prepared in accordance with the powers granted for labor inspection under the provisions of the Labor Regulations in force; and

Having reviewed the Regulations Committee's recommendation No. 17, dated 20 Rabi' I, 1390 (May 26, 1970),

Decrees as follows:

To approve the draft Implementing Rules for the Control and Regulation of Labor Inspection Activities in the form attached hereto,

Wherefore this has been written.

Implementing Rules

Chapter I: General Organization of the Labor Inspection Apparatus

Article 1. Labor inspection is the inspection carried out by labor inspectors who are designated by a resolution of the Minister of Labor for the purpose of ensuring the application of the provisions of the Labor and Workmen Regulations and the rules and decisions issued for the execution thereof, and of guiding both parties of production, *i.e.* the workmen and the employers alike, to the best methods which should be followed for improving the circumstances and conditions of work, particularly those which relate to health and safety at the place of work.

Article 2. The labor inspection apparatus shall consist of a central section at the Labor Affairs Agency and subsections at the Labor Offices existing in the areas.

Article 3. The terms of appointment, number, and grades of the labor inspection personnel shall be defined in the regulations related to State employees. They shall, however, be qualified, unbiased, and completely impartial, shall have no direct interest in the establishments which they inspect, and shall pass a special professional examination following a training period of not less than three months.

In all cases, these inspectors, once appointed, may not be replaced or required to perform additional duties save within the following conditions:

(a) That the replacement be made by a decision of the Minister of Labor and for reasons connected with the public interest;

(b) That the additional duties not be in conflict with the inspectors' main duties;

(c) That the requisites of competence and impartiality which the inspectors should possess in accordance with the regulations not be affected in any way.

Article 4. The labor inspectors and their supervisors shall, on their appointment and before proceeding to carry out the duties of labor inspection, take the following oath before the Minister of Labor and Social Affairs:

"I swear by God to discharge the duties of my office honestly and faithfully, and not to disclose the secret of any trade or industrial invention or any other secret which may come to my knowledge by reason of my office, even after I cease to have any connection with this office."

After taking the said oath, a report shall be prepared of which a copy shall be referred to the Chief of Labor Inspection in the Ministry for keeping in the inspector's file. A second copy shall be referred to the Labor Office to which the inspector belongs.

Article 5. The labor inspectors shall carry their identification cards when performing labor inspection duties. These shall bear their photographs and be signed by the Minister of Labor and stamped with the official seal. The inspector shall return the card on quitting his inspection work, or when he ceases to have this status for any reason.

Article 6. The central section for labor inspection shall assume the following duties:

(a) Supervising the work of the inspectors in the Labor Offices, guiding them, controlling the inspection activities, and following up on inspection plans and programs;

(b) Looking after the health and safety of the workmen, protecting them against the hazards of machinery, occupational diseases and work injuries, and promoting hygiene and preventive awareness by all means possible;

(c) Drafting decisions, regulations, and instructions relating to labor inspection;

(d) Preparing an annual general report on the achievements of labor inspection in the Kingdom as required under Article 35 of the Labor and Workmen Regulations;

(e) Preparing samples for the reports, statements, forms and registers relating to labor inspection, and supplying these to the labor inspection departments at the (Labor) Offices;

(f) Studying the monthly reports prepared by the labor inspection departments, auditing them, and noting down their observations on them;

(g) Organizing training courses for the labor inspectors in order to qualify them for performing their duties and acquaint them with the latest scientific and practical developments in the field of labor inspection, in accordance with a training program to be prepared for this purpose and made to include theoretical and applied curricula relating to the training courses;

(h) Making guidance tours to inspect the work progress in the labor inspection departments at the (Labor) Offices and ensure their carrying out the duties entrusted to them under these Rules and the Labor and Workmen Regulations;

(i) Performing such other duties as may fall within the scope of labor inspection.

Article 7. Labor inspectors at the Labor Offices shall perform the following duties:

(a) Supervising the application of the provisions of the Labor and Workmen Regulations and the rules and decisions issued thereunder in the factories, establishments, and occupations which are subject to labor inspection, by making sure, through inspector visits, that the statutory precautions and conditions which are the subject of the inspection are carried out, and by subsequently taking the necessary measures in the event they are not;

(b) Assisting both the workmen and the employers and guiding them as to the best methods to be followed for applying the provisions of the law, implementation rules and decisions, and technical instructions concerning the work;

(c) Studying the circumstances, terms, and conditions related to work, and submitting reports thereon to the Ministry, particularly with regard to any shortcomings observed which the provisions of the existing pertinent regulations have failed to remedy or deal with;

(d) Preparing a monthly report about the labor inspection activity in the area, the establishments in which labor inspection has been carried out, the number and types of violations observed, and the problems that have stood in the way of implementation and suggestions for overcoming such problems;

(e) Preparing an annual report about the labor inspection activity in the area and its results and effects, giving comments and suggestions as necessary in this regard;

(The Ministry shall issue special instructions about the method of preparing these two reports and the form which should be used in this regard.)

(f) Performing such other duties as may fall within the jurisdiction of labor inspection in these offices.

Chapter II: Duties of Labor Inspector

Article 8.　The labor inspectors shall supervise the application of the statutory provisions, particularly those which relate to the terms of work, health, and safety at the places of work, in order to be sure that they are complied with.

They shall visit the places of work which are subject to their supervision, in accordance with the instructions of their supervisors, in order to carry out labor inspection there and submit comprehensive reports about all their observations and findings concerning the application of the statutory provisions.

Article 9.　The labor inspector shall notify the employer or his representative upon his entry into his establishment to perform labor inspection there, unless he feels that such notification may prejudice his duties. Under no circumstances, however, may prior notification of the inspection visit be made for any reason whatsoever. In ordinary cases, the inspector shall introduce himself to the employer, produce his (identification) card on request, and proceed to explain to him his assignment and the purpose of his visit with enough courtesy and tact to win his appreciation and confidence in respect of the inspection assignment for which he has been commissioned.

Article 10.　The labor inspectors and their supervisors shall supply the employers and workmen with technical information and practical directions for the proper implementation of the statutory provisions. They shall also advise and direct them in the application of the best standards of hygiene and safety, in addition to encouraging cooperation between them for intensifying the technical and hygienic precautions and upholding the methods of safety in the places of work.

Article 11.　The labor inspectors and their supervisors shall cooperate to the utmost extent possible with both parties of production, *i.e.*, the workmen and the employers alike, in order to help in improving human relations and productive efficiency, and consequently in creating an atmosphere of stability in labor relations in which mutual understanding and fruitful cooperation between the parties concerned shall prevail.

Article 12.　The labor inspectors shall devote all their time and attention to the inspection duties assigned to them. They shall deal with the problems submitted to them from their various aspects, and shall endeavor to solve them with the parties concerned with efficiency and tact and in a spirit of fairness and equity. They shall have no direct or indirect interest in the establishments and factories which are under their supervision. They shall avoid accepting gifts, shall refuse any offer or service of any private nature, even if it be of low cost, and whether it be from the employers or the workmen, under penalty of applying the punishments provided for in the regulations in force.

Chapter III: Powers of Labor Inspector

Article 13. The labor inspectors shall, in the course of performing the labor inspection duties assigned to them, exercise the following powers:

(a) Enter, without prior notice, all places of work during work hours, at daytime or at night, for the purpose of carrying out labor inspection there and investigating matters in connection with the inspections, provided that this shall be done in accordance with instructions communicated to them by their supervisors;

(b) Examine the registers, papers, books, files or any other documents relating to workform, for the purpose of ascertaining their conformity to the requirements provided for in the Labor and Workmen Regulations and in the decisions issued for the application thereof. The inspector may request the employer or his representative to put all the said documents at his disposal, and he may draw his attention to the necessity of posting the statements and notices provided for in the regulations;

(c) Obtain samples of the materials used and handled in the establishment for the purpose of analyzing them, and examine the various machines and fixtures to ascertain the presence of adequate and effective means for protecting the safety and health of the workmen. The inspector may issue the necessary orders for carrying out urgent changes required for providing the necessary elements of protecting the safety and health of the workmen and machinery;

(d) Question the employer, or his representative, and the workmen, either privately or in the presence of witnesses, about any matter relating to the application of the statutory provisions in order that it is possible, in the light thereof, to infer whether, and to what extent, the requirements provided for in the Labor and Workmen Regulations and the decisions issued for the execution thereof are duly complied with;

(e) Discuss with employers and the workmen, separately or jointly, the best methods of facilitating the application of the statutory provisions relating to work, and of overcoming the difficulties that stand in the way of such application, especially as regards ignorance of the provisions of the regulations.

Article 14 In the course of their labor inspection in any establishment or industrial or commercial concern in execution of the provisions of the Labor and Workmen Regulations and the decisions issued for the application thereof, the labor inspectors may take the following measures, as applicable, in respect of those who violate the statutory provisions:

(a) Offering counsel and guidance to the employer, and considering that sufficient in the event of his acceptance and favorable response, provided that this be accompanied by an official letter through the Labor Office containing the observations resulting from the visit to his establishment and the directions and guiding instructions for the avoidance of violations;

(b) Addressing an oral reminder which shall be recorded by the inspector in the inspection report which he prepares about his visits to the establishment, provided that it shall be signed by the employer or his representative who shall undertake to remedy the violations observed in his establishment within a reasonable period as agreed with the labor inspector;

(c) Addressing a written warning to the offending employer through the Labor Office in which it shall be stated that failure to remedy the violations within a period to be fixed by the inspector at his discretion would make the violator liable to the penalties provided for in the Labor and Workmen Regulations;

(d) Drawing a report in the place of work in which the violations witnessed by the inspector shall be recorded.

Article 15. The labor inspectors shall have complete freedom to address warnings or give advice to the employer in lieu of drawing a report of the violations observed, depending on the graveness of the violation committed and other circumstances to be evaluated by the inspector.

Chapter IV: Regulation of Day and Night Inspection Visits

Article 16. The head of labor inspection in each (Labor) Office shall regulate the inspection visits that take place during official work hours in accordance with weekly programs put in advance and approved by the responsible director of the office, which programs shall be prepared on the following basis:

(a) The occupations and establishments which are subject to inspection shall be distributed so that each inspector shall be responsible for certain occupations and establishments. In making the distribution, consideration shall be given to the number, nature, and size of the establishments which are subject to inspection and which lie within the area of jurisdiction of (a certain Labor) Office, as well as to the number and categories of the workmen employed there, the diversity of the statutory provisions whose application is to be ensured, and the physical means of enforcement at the disposal of the inspectors.

Distribution shall be made in accordance with administrative orders to be approved by the responsible director of the Office and communicated to the inspectors.

These may be superseded (by other orders) according to the circumstances and exigencies of the work, provided that a copy thereof shall be transmitted to the Deputy Minister's Office as soon as they are issued.

(b) A program shall be prepared in advance, in agreement with the labor inspectors, for the visits which should be carried out during the week, such program to show the following:

—The name of the labor inspector assigned to make the visit;

—The occupations and establishments in which each inspector is required to carry out labor inspection on each day of the week;

—The date and time of the visit;

—The type of visit, so as to distinguish between visits carried out for purposes of general inspection, in which an examination of the circumstances and conditions of work in the establishment from all aspects is made, and special visits, such as re-inspection and visits for investigating complaints, accidents, and occupational diseases.

(c) In fixing inspection visits care shall be taken for the proper choice of time, so that the visits to the establishments shall be made while their activities are in full swing and with due regard to the distribution of work hours in the establishment. The labor inspector shall dedicate part of his work hours for carrying out administrative and clerical work at the Labor Office, provided that this shall not affect the time required for the performance of his basic work of inspection.

Article 17. Labor inspection at night or outside the official work hours shall be carried out in accordance with the written instructions and orders of the authorities which are given to the labor inspectors by their supervisors. Such orders shall include the names of the establishments to be inspected, the times of inspection, and the names of the inspectors assigned for it.

Article 18. Inspectors who have been assigned labor inspection at night or outside the official work hours shall submit their reports on the results of the inspection to their supervisors on the day following the carrying out of the inspection.

Article 19. Remuneration for inspection at night or outside official work hours shall be fixed by a decision of the Minister of Labor within the limits of the allocations appropriated for this purpose in the budget of the Ministry.

Chapter V: Inspection Rules and Procedures

Article 20. Places of work shall be inspected as frequently as possible with such thoroughness as may be needed for the actual enforcement of the statutory provisions. Periodical visits devoted to the purposes of general inspection shall include at least one visit a year to each establishment, with special emphasis on visiting the big establishments, or those whose management is unsatisfactory from the point of view of safety and health protection for the workmen, or in which dangerous or unhygienic operations are conducted. In the event of discovery of a serious violation of the conditions which should be observed in the places of work, the inspector shall make an early return visit to such places to ensure that the said violation has been remedied.

Article 21. In periodical visits devoted for the purposes of general inspection, the inspection should cover all the work conditions, terms, and circumstances in the establishment inspected, and it may not be confined to a special aspect. In this type of visit, the inspector shall visit the whole establishment where work is performed, and shall examine the methods that are applied for the implementation of the statutory requirements for the protection of workmen.

Article 22. Only one labor inspector shall carry out inspection in each establishment or occupation, unless the director of the Labor Office sees fit to assign two or more inspectors to make a joint inspection in one establishment or conduct any investigation therein, subject to the following:

(a) In case there are health and safety specialists in the Labor Office, these shall join the labor inspectors in the inspection activities each according to his speciality;

(b) In case there are no specialists in the fields referred to, the labor inspectors shall observe the aspects relating to health and safety in the places of work. They may seek the assistance of specialists in the other ministries or their branches in the areas, as well as request necessary guidance from the Ministry of Labor.

Article 23.   The labor inspector shall prepare a report on each inspection he carries out in each establishment or concern he visits, which should be submitted to his immediate supervisor for study and action. Such report shall include the following information:

(a) Administrative data relating to the inspector's visit, *viz.* the labor inspector's name, the date and time of the visit, and the names of the persons he has met;

(b) Identification of the establishment which he has visited, including its name and address, the names of its owner and responsible manager, the nature of its work, and the date of its foundation;

(c) The number of workmen who work in it, together with their nationalities, sex and ages;

(d) A summary of the study carried out by the inspector, covering the rules, notices, and schedules provided for in the regulations, the work and rest hours, vacations, registers, workmen's permits, wages, the bringing of foreign workmen, the health and safety measures, the violations observed, the result of the visit, the statements of the workmen and of the employer, the measures and steps taken, and all other information which would give a complete picture of the work conditions and terms applied in the establishment pursuant to the provisions of the Labor and Workmen Regulations and the rules and decisions issued thereunder.

Article 24.   The labor inspectors shall be cautious and honest in (choosing) the information and statements they include in their reports concerning the establishments and occupations in which they have carried out labor inspections. In particular, they shall base their observations on what they themselves see or witness. They shall also refrain completely from making any comments on matters with which they are not adequately acquainted, in order to maintain the employer's and workmen's confidence in them.

Article 25.   The labor inspectors shall follow up those employers who are found to have violated the Labor and Workmen Regulations and the decisions issued for the application thereof by means of consecutive visits after granting them sufficient and reasonable respite to remedy the violations.

Article 26.   In the case of resort to drawing up a report of the violations, such report should be drawn up in the place of work, unless this cannot be done for any exceptional reason. The labor inspector shall ask the employer about the reasons for committing each of the violations he has witnessed, and he shall record in the report a summary by the inspector and the employer or his representative of his reply. The report shall be signed by the employer or his representative. In the event of refusal to sign, a reference shall be made to this effect in the report. The inspector shall bear in mind that his fundamental duty consists in offering guidance and direction and in cooperation with the employers to the utmost extent possible, with a view to putting the provisions of the regulations into effect, which would be considered proof of the inspector's success in performing his task in the proper manner.

Article 27. The reports of violations that are drawn up by the labor inspectors in respect of those who violate the statutory provisions shall be submitted to the Director of the Labor Office through proper channels. The director concerned shall refer these to the responsible committee.

Article 28. The Ministry shall lay down forms for the reports on violations, inspection registers, notices and warnings, and other forms relating to the enforcement of the provisions of these Rules and the provisions of the Labor and Workmen Regulations which relate to labor inspection, giving the necessary instructions on how to use, keep and circulate them, and it shall circulate these instructions to the Labor Offices in the various areas, which Offices may not use any forms other than those approved by the Ministry.

APPENDIX 55

Director-General of the Central Province Head Labor Office Circular of 4/2/1397 H (January 25, 1977)

Kingdom of Saudi Arabia
Ministry of Labor and Social Affairs
Central Province Head Labor Office
Inspection Department

Circular to all Companies, Enterprises and Employers in Riyadh

Director,
Dear Sir,

We refer to Circular Letter No. 89/6/1 dated 22/1/1397 H of the Deputy Minister for Labor Affairs at the Ministry of Labor and Social Affairs which reads:

"The Western Province Head Labor Office has noticed that some national and foreign companies use languages other than Arabic in their printed material and advertisements and on notice boards both within their buildings and premises and outside on street corners, in the entrances to their establishments and on their vehicles, thus making it difficult for labor inspectors or government officials to identify the establishment. Whereas Article 16 of the Labor and Workmen Regulations of 1389 H requires employers to use the Arabic language in:

—drawing up resolutions, records, registers, files, statements, and the like provided by the Labor Regulations, including notices and bulletins which the Regulations require to be hung, documents which should be maintained, and also the information that employers are required to notify to the Labor Office, such as the name, type, head office and mailing address of the establishment.

—issuing any resolution or order pursuant to the provisions of the Labor Regulations and also Instructions and circulars issued by employers to their workmen.

It is clear that the purpose underlying such provision is to aid and facilitate knowledge of companies and their Rules both by labor inspectors and government officials and the workmen themselves.

Therefore, the use by establishments of languages other than Arabic in their printed matter, signs and so forth is in contravention of Article 16 of the Labor Regulations. We are of the opinion that you should notify establishments that they are required to use the Arabic language as set forth above."

We trust that you will comply and act in accordance with the abovementioned letter of the Deputy Minister for Labor Affairs and comply with Article 16 of the Labor Regulations.

Director-General of the Central Province Head Labor Office

APPENDIX 56

Compensation Rates for Permanent Partial Disabilities (Schedule Implementing Article 24 of the Labor and Workmen Regulations of October 10, 1947) *

Amendment No. 1

Due to the dispute over the meaning of the phrase "loss of the part below the nose or loss of the sense of smell" which occurs in the compensation table, and is considered a permanent partial disablement, Royal Order No. 1984 dated 10/5/1371 H to the Ministry of Finance, approves Resolution No. 24 of 1/5/1371 H adopted by the Consultative Council in respect of amending the said phrase, which reads as amended:

"Loss of the tip of the nose or loss of the sense of smell."

Amendment No. 2

High Order No. 7218 dated 1/11/1367 H has declared the following statement of the Consultative Council No. 212 dated 20/9/1367 H as a supplement to the Labor and Workmen Regulations.

The phrase "during work" which occurs in the Labor and Workmen Regulations published in Umm al-Qurā No. 1212 dated 20th Rajab, 1367, means from the judicial point of view the right of a workman performing a work assigned to him to all the privileges granted by the Labor and Workmen Regulations for the work he is performing, whether that be at his official place of work or on his way to such place, or while he is performing the work assigned to him by the company outside his official place of work. Any injury suffered by an employee during the same and within the lands and structures covered by the company's concession shall be compensated according to the compensation rule, including the times of transportation from place to place, *e.g.* when the workman is exposed on his way

---

* Note that the compensation rates as established under prior regulations may be subject to amendment in the near future.

to work to demolition or shipwreck; all this gives the employee the right to compensation throughout the period of his employment by contract with the company. Therefore, and in view of the foregoing, the meaning of the phrase "during work" shall be a general expression of all the cases where the employee or workman is entitled to compensation for any injury suffered by him according to compensation rules during the period of his employment.

Amendment No. 3

Whereas the Consultative Council adopted Resolution No. 131 of 13/8/1368 H that the eye-tooth is from the point of view of function of a medium status in comparison with the molar and ordinary teeth and that the compensation for its loss shall be as follows:

1st class	*2nd class*	*3rd class*

Royal Decree No. 6851 of 25/8/1368 H affirms the Resolution and orders attaching the same to the schedule of compensation for workmen's injuries which are considered permanent partial disablement in accordance with the Labor and Workmen Regulations.

Amendment No. 4

(Published in Umm al-Qurā, October 1, 1948)

The following has been advised to us by the Ministry of Finance

High Order No. 7218 was issued on 1/11/1367 H in order to approve the following definition made by the Legislative Council No. 212 dated 29/8/1367 H as a lawful act within the Labor and Workmen Regulations.

The phrase "during work" which appears in the Labor and Workmen Regulations published in Umm al-Qurā No. 1212 of Rajab 20, 1367, means from the judicial point that an employee who is performing any work incumbent on him is entitled to all the rights granted by the Labor and Workmen Regulations for the duties he is performing, whether in his official place of work or on his way to his official work or during his performance of any work assigned to him by the company outside the official place of work.

Any injury which may be sustained by any workman during his work and on any land and structures from which the company receives benefit should be indemnified in accordance with the Compensation Regulations including the period of travelling from one place to another in case he is exposed to any accident, drowning or demolition on his way. This will give the workman the right of compensation as long as he is employed on the company's work and, in accordance with the above, the phrase "during work" will include generally all the situations in which the employee or the workman will be entitled to compensation for any injury sustained by him in accordance with the Compensation Regulations during his period of employment.

Schedule of Injuries which shall be Considered Permanent Partial Disabilities

INJURIES	1st class SR	2nd class SR	3rd class SR
Loss of entire sight or loss of both eyes together	18,000	12,000	8,000
Loss of one eye or loss of the sight thereof . .	8,100	5,400	3,600
Loss of the sight of one eye	3,100	5,400	3,600
Loss of general hearing permanently . . .	12,000	8,000	3,330
Loss of the hearing in one ear permanently .	5,400	3,600	2,400
Loss of nose or portion thereof and loss of sense of smell	12,000	8,000	5,330
Loss of the tongue or the causing of permanent muteness	12,000	8,000	5,330
Loss of teeth: for each tooth	300	200	130
Loss of molars: for each molar	600	400	260
Loss of both arms together, complete, from the shoulder joints	30,000	20,000	13,000
Loss of both arms together, from the elbows or above them.	24,000	16,000	10,660
Loss of both arms together, from below the elbows	21,000	14,000	9,330
Loss of the right arm, complete, from the shoulder joint or above the elbow . . .	13,000	12,000	8,000
Loss of the left arm, complete, from the shoulder joint or above the elbow	16,200	10,800	7,200
Loss of the right forearm, from the elbow and below it	16,200	10,800	7,200
Loss of the left forearm, from the elbow and below it	13,500	9,000	6,000
Loss of the right hand from the wrist . . .	10,120	6,740	4,000
Loss of the left hand from the wrist . . .	8,800	5,860	3,900
Loss of all fingers of the left hand, including thumb.	7,700	5,100	3,420
Loss of the thumb from the right hand . .	3,000	2,000	1,330
Loss of the thumb from the left hand . .	2,500	1,660	1,100
Loss of the index finger of the right hand .	2,000	1,330	880
Loss of the index finger of the left hand .	1,500	1,000	660
Loss of the middle finger of the right hand .	1,500	1,000	650
Loss of the middle finger of the left hand .	1,300	960	570
Loss of the ring finger of the right hand .	1,300	860	570
Loss of the ring finger of the left hand .	1,000	660	440
Loss of the little finger of the right hand .	1,000	660	440
Loss of the little finger of the left hand .	850	560	370
Loss of the end phalanx of the thumb of the right hand	2,000	1,330	890
Loss of the second phalanx of the thumb of the right hand	1,000	660	440
Loss of the end phalanx of the thumb of the left hand	1,600	1,060	700

INJURIES	1st class SR	2nd class SR	3rd class SR
Loss of the second phalanx of the thumb of the left hand	900	600	400
Loss of the second phalanx of the index finger of the right hand	700	460	300
Loss of the second phalanx of the index finger of the left hand	500	280	220
Loss of the end phalanx of the index finger of the right hand	1,000	660	440
Loss of the end phalanx of the index finger of the left hand	750	500	330
Loss of the end phalanx of the middle finger of the right hand	660	430	290
Loss of the end phalanx of the middle finger of the left hand	560	330	220
Loss of the second phalanx of the middle finger of the right hand.	500	330	220
Loss of the second phalanx of the middle finger of the left hand	450	300	200
Loss of the end phalanx of the ring finger of the right hand	560	430	290
Loss of the second phalanx of the ring finger of the right hand	450	300	200
Loss of the end phalanx of the ring finger of the left hand	500	330	220
Loss of the second phalanx of the ring finger of the left hand	350	230	150
Loss of the end phalanx of the little finger of the right hand	500	330	220
Loss of the second phalanx of the little finger of the right hand	350	230	150
Loss of the end phalanx of the little finger of the left hand	420	280	180
Loss of the second phalanx of the little finger of the left hand	320	200	140
Loss of complete legs together from the two hips	24,000	16,000	10,660
Loss of one of the two legs from the hip . .	10,000	6,660	4,440
Loss of both legs together, from the knees or above	18,000	12,000	8,000
Loss of one of the two legs from the knee or above	8,500	5,660	3,770
Loss of both legs together from below the two knees	16,200	10,800	7,200
Loss of one of the two legs from below the knee	3,000	5,330	3,550
Loss of both feet together from the two heels or forward therefrom	12,000	8,000	5,330
Loss of one foot, from heel or forward therefrom	5,000	3,330	2,220
Loss of all the toes of one foot, including large toe	4,000	2,660	1,770
Loss of all the toes of one foot except the large toe	2,000	1,330	830
Loss of the large toe of the foot	2,000	1,330	380
Loss of one of the toes of the foot except large toe	800	530	350
Loss of the genital organs	12,000	8,000	5,330

Articles appended to Schedule of Compensation

1. Permanent total paralysis or a brain injury resulting in incurable mental derangement or madness shall for compensation purposes be equal to total disablement.

2. The compensation for losing the use of a limb or part of the body shall be the same as that for the total loss of such limb or part of the body.

3. If the injured person is left-handed the compensation for injuries to his left arm shall be calculated on the same rates as those for injuries to the right hand of another and vice versa.

4. Loss of part of the phalanx shall be regarded as its total loss. The loss of three phalanges (7 distalphalanx) of a finger is compensated for by the difference between the compensation for the loss of two phalanges and that for the whole finger.

5. Injuries that are not mentioned in the schedule of compensation, whether a maiming, derangement or change of normal position of any limb or part of the body or any of the senses if related to a limb mentioned in the schedule, shall be compensated by estimating the percentage of such injuries as compared to injuries entailing full compensation and paying accordingly. If such injuries are not related to any limb mentioned in the schedule, the compensation shall be estimated by a doctor nominated by the Government, another doctor nominated by the company, and the representative of the Ministry of Finance. In case of disagreement between the two doctors, the Public Health Department of the Kingdom of Saudi Arabia shall decide.

6. Permanent total disablement and similar matters shall be ascertained by the committee referred to in Article 5 above.

SUBJECT INDEX